Footprint Handbook
Vietnam, Cambodia & Laos

DAVID W LLOYD WITH ANDREW SPOONER

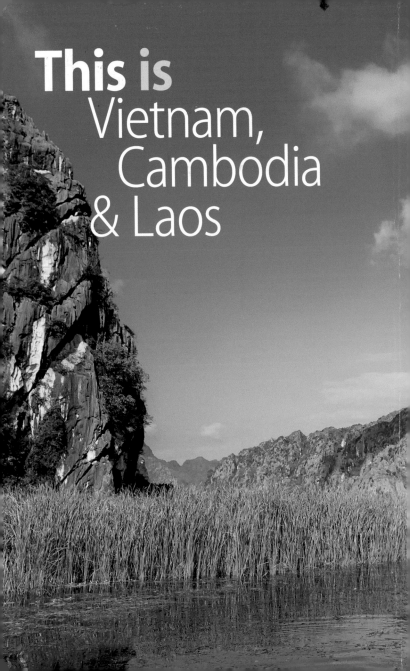

This is
Vietnam,
Cambodia
& Laos

Vietnam, Cambodia and Laos offer unrivalled attractions in the form of ruins, colonial remnants, stunning scenery, ethnic diversity and exotic food. Their shared history as part of Indochina is still evident in the fading French architecture, the cuisine and the ubiquitous reminders of bloody wars, but it is their distinct differences that render the area such a fantastic travel experience.

In Vietnam, vivid rice paddies climb up mountainsides or sit alongside beautiful coastal scenery while feverish Ho Chi Minh City plays more modern and moneyed brother to the enchanting, romantic capital, Hanoi.

Cambodia is home to the magnificent Angkor Wat, the zenith of Southeast Asian architecture, and a multitude of other awe-inspiring monuments. Phnom Penh, the fascinating modern-day capital, offers the glistening Royal Palace, eclectic markets and poignant relics of a turbulent past.

Laid-back Laos, rousing after years of isolation, is home to wonderfully remote mountainous national parks, the picturesque gilded temples of the former royal capital, Luang Prabang and the chilled-out Mekong islands of Siphandon.

David W Lloyd

Best of
Vietnam, Cambodia & Laos

top things to do and see

❶ Hanoi

Vietnam's capital city is one of a kind. Chaotic it may be, but its charms far outweigh the traffic, with peaceful lakes, crumbling colonial buildings, narrow streets of the Old Quarter and one of the best street food scenes in the world. There are also plenty of great day trips to be made from your base here. Page 28.

❷ Ha Giang Province

Bordering China, Ha Giang Province serves up the most dramatic road-trip scenery in Vietnam with magnificent, rugged peaks and deep, sheer-sided gorges. Add to this a host of local minority villages and markets bustling with life and you have a rewarding destination to travel off the beaten path. Page 80.

❸ Halong Bay

A UNESCO-listed site, Halong Bay is a true wonder of nature. Thousands of limestone islands and islets punch abruptly skyward out of a pan-flat, deep-green sea. Enjoy an overnight cruise on a traditional junk boat, explore caves and hike to the top of an island for captivating vistas. Page 82.

❹ Phong Nha

From tourist backwater to adventure hotspot, Phong Nha is the most exciting new destination in Vietnam. With some of the world's largest and most spectacular caves to explore as well as rich cultural diversity, Phong Nha is the highlight of the Central Coast for many visitors. Page 93.

❺ Hoi An

Hoi An is an exquisitely pretty little riverside town and a former Chinese trading port. It has been remarkably well preserved and, while it is now unashamedly aimed at tourists, it manages to retain much of its charm and character. The nearby beaches are also fantastic and the ancient Cham ruins of My Son are within striking distance. Page 121.

❼ Phnom Penh

Cambodia's capital retains the sort of landscape most travellers dream of: a skyline punctuated by spires, turrets and pinnacles of royal and religious origin rather than by office blocks. The Royal Palace and Silver Pagoda are highlights of the city's concoction of temples, summerhouses and palaces. Page 222.

❽ Angkor Wat

Cambodia's top tourist attraction is the most magnificent and largest of all the Angkor temples. Built by one of the world's greatest civilizations in the early 12th century, it remains one of the finest monuments in the world. Page 252.

❻ Ho Chi Minh City

Ho Chi Minh City is an enthralling and captivating place with an infectious buzz. There is a palpable sense of dynamism here and life is fast-paced, particular compared to Hanoi. The city's face is rapidly changing, with new urban zones taking shape and shiny new skyscrapers altering the skyline. This is a fantastic place to eat, catch a band, view art, shop and party. Page 156.

⑨ Kratie

A port town on the Mekong, Kratie is delightful with a relaxed atmosphere and good examples of shophouse architecture. It makes an excellent base to spot the endangered Irrawaddy dolphins. Page 285.

⑩ Luang Prabang

One of Asia's most captivating and classically stylish cities. Protected by its UNESCO status, the town is a pure joy to wander around, with dozens of temples, lovely cafés and riverside bars. Local life here still plays out to the sound of chanting monks and the rhythmic boom of temple drums. Page 353.

⑪ Champasak and Wat Phou

The atmospheric 12th-century ruins of Wat Phou are an enchanting place to wander at sunrise or in the late afternoon light. Nearby Champasak is a charming town on the banks of the river. Pages 440 and 443.

⑫ Four Thousand Islands

At the far south of the country in the broad sweep of the mighty Mekong, the pace of life on these river islands is super relaxed, even by Lao standards, and there's little else to do but sink in and enjoy it. Page 454.

East Sea
(South China Sea)

Route planner
Vietnam, Cambodia & Laos

putting it all together

If time is limited, a good option is to get an open-jaw flight where you fly into one city and out of another. Both Vietnam Airlines and Laos Airlines have excellent domestic networks (see pages 543 and 548). Distances are huge and in Cambodia and Laos, especially, roads are not always sealed, making overland journey times lengthy and sometimes tortuous, especially in the wet season. Note that there are strict visa regulations that need to be taken into account when planning your trip (see page 565).

Two weeks

imperial cities, hilltribes, beaches and temples

A short trip will require careful planning and prioritizing. Either take internal flights or limit yourself to just one area. In Vietnam, start in energetic Ho Chi Minh City to visit the war relic of the Cu Chi Tunnels and the fantastical Cao Dai Temple. From here, fly to Danang and enjoy Hoi An's ancient town and perhaps a day trip to the imperial city of Hué. Next head to historic Hanoi. Magical Halong Bay can be seen in a day/night trip from

Below: Hué
Left: Danang
Opposite page: Cao Dai Temple

Hanoi but in order to visit Sapa, known for its stunning scenery and hilltribes, you'll need to set aside three days.

Alternatively, the Mekong Delta can be visited in a day trip from Ho Chi Minh City, or make your way through the delta (visiting the floating markets at Can Tho) to Phnom Penh and Choeung Ek, with a day either at the laid-back beaches of Sihanoukville or in colonial-inspired Kampot. From Phnom Penh travel by boat to Siem Reap where up to four days could be spent around the exceptional ruins of Angkor, visiting some of the outlying ruins such as Koh Ker and Beng Melea and the brilliant cliff-top temple of Preah Vihear. You could then fly from Siem Reap to Pakse for Wat Phou, the sublime Tad Lo and Tad Fan falls and Siphandon, or to Vientiane to access northern Laos.

For Laos, fly to Vientiane before heading north to wonderfully preserved Luang Prabang via Vang Vieng. Or fly from Vientiane to Luang Namtha to the interesting trekking region in the north before overlanding back to Luang Prabang. Alternatively, after visiting Luang Prabang, fly to Pakse for a trip to the tranquil, laid-back Siphandon (4000 islands) in the south.

Top: Sihanoukville
Middle: Flower Hmong woman, Bac Ha
Bottom: Koh Ker ruins

if you have more time you can afford to take things more slowly and explore places in greater depth. Having visited Sapa, Dien Bien Phu and the area around Mai Chau in northwest Vietnam, take an overnight train from Hanoi down to Dong Hoi for the caves of Phong Nha or head further on to Hué. From here, you could either travel west into central Laos or take the splendid train journey from Hué to Danang and visit nearby Hoi An. Next, travel to coastal Mui Ne and on to Ho Chi Minh City. Those with the budget for an extra flight could take a side trip to Con Dao island.

From Ho Chi Minh City, either take a flight to Phnom Penh or Siem Reap or travel by bus and boat through the Mekong Delta. Visit Angkor and then, from Phnom Penh, go south to Sihanoukville and explore the beaches and islands. A day or two can be spent at Kampot and the seaside town of Kep, as well as exploring the eerie Bokor Mountain National Park.

With one month it is better to start at the extreme north or south of Laos to cover as much territory as possible. From Phnom Penh you could travel overland to Siphandon in southern Laos via Stung Treng. Before heading north in Laos, take a side trip to the interesting Bolaven Plateau with its stunning coffee plantations and waterfalls. Overland it to Thakhek past charming Savannakhet, and do the motorcycle loop around the limestone scenery of central Laos, visiting the Kong Lor River Cave en route. Alternatively, fly direct to Vientiane from Pakse and catch a flight to Phonsavanh and explore the mysterious Plain of Jars, then overland it to Xam Neua to see the Pathet Lao caves at Vieng Xai. A long but interesting overland route will take you west from

here via increasingly popular Nong Khiaw to Luang Prabang, from where you can head north to the trekking areas of Luang Namtha, Muang Sing and Phongsali, or catch a boat up the Mekong towards the Thai border.

Top: Mui Ne
Middle: Hoi Chi Min City
Bottom: Tad Wuang waterfall, Bolaven Plateu

The
Mekong

The Mekong River is the heart and soul of mainland Southeast Asia, a sinuous thread that binds Vietnam, Cambodia and Laos geographically, historically, culturally and economically. Indeed, the Mekong – or the Mae Nam Khong (the Mother of Waters) – is the most important geographical feature of mainland Southeast Asia.

The Mekong's origins in eastern Tibet have only been pin-pointed in the last 20 years. From here the giant river plies 4500 km through six countries, cutting through almost the entire length of Laos, dissecting Cambodia, and plunging into Vietnam's Mekong Delta before emptying into the South China Sea. The river is the 12th longest river in the world and is the world's 10th largest by volume of water dispersed into the ocean – 475 km^3.

French explorer Francis Garnier once commented: "without doubt, no other river, over such a length, has a more singular or remarkable character". The Mekong has indeed woven itself into the cultural fabric, shaping the region's history. The river is the one constant from the ancient Funan settlement in the Mekong Delta, through to the Khmer Empire who established its capital at Angkor, relying on the river for transport and agricultural production. After several European expeditions, the French took an interest in the river and the region in the mid-19th century,

developing grandiose plans to transform the Mekong into a river highway from China (the plans were thwarted upon discovering that the Mekong could not be traversed).

The river later played an integral role in shaping history during the Vietnam War when it became an important conduit for the running of Viet Cong supplies and was the scene of heavy fighting.

The river has been a major purveyor of culture, ushering in various religions, arts, customs and folklore. The enormous, colourful, boat-racing festivals of Vietnam, Cambodia and Laos are staged on the water. Similarly, the annual water festivals in Cambodia and Laos come from deep-rooted traditions stemming from the Mekong and its importance to agricultural production. The river is not free from superstition or strange

phenomena. In Laos thousands of people gather each year to witness naga fireballs rising from the river's surface. Major arts have also developed from these waters including Vietnam's water puppetry. It also provided inspiration in the Apocalypse Now mission down the fictional Nung River, said to represent the Mekong.

Today, the Mekong is instrumental in the region's survival, with more than 60 million people in Southeast Asia dependent on the river and its tributaries for their survival.

Traditional lamps in old town Hoi An

When
to go

Overall the best time to visit the region is between November and April when it should be dry and not too hot. In the south it is warm with lovely cool evenings. However, in Cambodia wind-blown dust invades everything at this time of year. In the north of Vietnam and Laos the highlands will be a bit chilly but they should be dry with clear blue skies. Upland areas like the Plain of Jars, the Bolaven Plateau and some towns in the north of Laos can be cold with temperatures dropping as low as 8°C.

From late March to April the region heats up and temperatures can exceed 40°C. In northern Laos, the months from March through to the first rains in May or June can be very hazy as smoke from burning off the secondary forest hangs in the air. On the worst days this can cause itchiness of the eyes. It also means that views are restricted and sometimes flights are cancelled. Travel on the region's mud and laterite roads is difficult and sometimes impossible by June and July; transport will be slower and may cease altogether in some parts. It is also difficult to do any outdoor activities in June and July because of the rain. However, the area is at its most lush and beautiful during these months. Travel in the south and Mekong Delta can be limited at the height of the monsoon (particularly during September, October and November). The central regions and north of Vietnam sometimes suffer tropical storms from May to November. Hué is at its wettest wet from September to January.

Tet, the Vietnamese New Year, is not really a good time to visit. This movable feast falls between late January and March and lasts for about a fortnight. It is the only holiday most Vietnamese get so popular destinations are packed, roads are jammed, flights fully booked and, for a couple of days, restaurants are shut; many hotels increase their room rates and the cost of car hire rises by 50% or more. Problems also occur during **Khmer New Year** in Cambodia and **Pi Mai** in Laos (both usually mid-April), when public transport is full and and hotels booked out in popular places. For Festivals and public holidays, see page 552.

What to do

activities from trekking to traditional massage

Vietnam and Laos are well known for their wonderful trekking opportunities amid stunning mountainous landscape. Other activities, such as rafting, kayaking, rock climbing and cycling, are slowly emerging and are not as developed as they are in Thailand. Safety is always an issue when participating in adventurous sports. Make sure you are fully covered by your travel insurance, check the credentials of operators offering adventure activities, and make sure that vehicles and safety equipment are in a good condition. Note that medical care in Cambodia and Laos is very limited, see page 554.

Caving

Laos has some of the most extensive and largest caves in the region. Some of the best can be found around Vang Vieng, where caving tourism has been developed. Contact **Green Discovery,** www.greendiscoverylaos.com. Another highlight is the amazing Kong Lor River Cave in the centre of the country. There are hundreds of caves around Vieng Xai (www.visit-viengxay.com) but only a few open to tourists; for those interested in history these caves should be a first stop. The caves around Phong Nha in Central Vietnam are some of the world's most spectacular and there are options from a self-guided half-day tour to a week-long adventure on offer.

Cycling and mountain biking

In Vietnam cycling is a popular activity, although the traffic on the roads can be hazardous. It's therefore recommended that any tour is planned off-road or on minor roads. In Cambodia and Laos, cycling is offered by several tour agencies; Luang Namtha is a popular place to start, and **Green Discovery**, www.green discoverylaos.com, runs excellent cycling tours. New cycling opportunities have opened up in Udomxai and in Xieng Khouang Province, the latter with the expertise of German NGO **GIZ**, www.giz. de. Other operators include: **Discover Adventure**, www.discoveradventure.com; **Symbiosis**, www.symbiosis-travel.com; **Spice Roads**, www.spiceroads.com; and **Tien Bicycles**, www.tienbicycles.com. Many cyclists prefer to bring their own all-terrain or racing bikes but it's also possible to rent them from tour organizers. Other good cycling destinations include Hué, Dalat and the Mekong Delta.

ON THE ROAD
Visiting ethnic minorities: house rules

Scores of different ethnic minority groups inhabit northern Vietnam, the Central Highlands of Vietnam and northern Laos. Their distinctive styles of dress and age-old rituals may be of special interest to Western travellers. If you choose to visit or stay in a minority village, please remember that it is not a human zoo. Etiquette and customs vary between the minorities, but the following are general rules of good behaviour that should be adhered to whenever possible.

→ Organize your visit through a local villager or a travel agency that supports the village.
→ Inform yourself of local trekking rules and guidance.
→ Dress modestly and avoid undressing/changing in public.
→ Ask permission before entering a house.
→ Ask permission before photographing anyone (old people and pregnant women often object to having their photograph taken).

Be aware that villagers are unlikely to pose out of the kindness of their hearts so don't begrudge them the money; for many, tourism is their livelihood.
→ Buy handicrafts that support local industry.
→ Avoid sitting or stepping on door sills.
→ Avoid excessive displays of wealth and do not hand out gifts.
→ Avoid introducing Western medicines.
→ Do not touch or photograph village shrines.

Diving and snorkelling

Underwater adventures are limited in the seas around Vietnam. In those places where snorkelling and diving is good (Nha Trang, Phu Quoc and Whale Island) it is possible almost year round and is not necessarily dictated by the dry and wet seasons. Contact **Rainbow Divers**, www.divevietnam.com. The dive industry in Cambodia is in its infant years, but the coast boasts lots of pristine coral reefs and unexplored areas. There are several dive operators in Sihanoukville, including the nation's first PADI 5-star dive centre: **Scuba Nation Diving Centre**, T012-604680, www.divecambodia.com. Koh Kong town is now also emerging as a dive destination.

Kayaking

Kayaking in Vietnam is centred around Halong Bay. This World Heritage Site, crammed with islands and grottoes, is a fantastic place to explore by kayak. There are also kayaking options around Dalat. In Laos, head to the Nam Song River at Vang Vieng for kayaking, rafting and tubing; there is also excellent kayaking around the Bolaven Plateau.

Operators in Vietnam include: **Buffalo Tours**, www.buffalotours.com; and **Exotissimo**, www.exotissimo.com. In Laos: **Green Discovery**, www.green discoverylaos.com; and **Riverside Tours**, www.riversidetourslaos.com.

Kitesurfing and windsurfing

Kitesurfing and windsurfing are found largely in Mui Ne (Vietnam), which offers just about perfect conditions. Equipment can be rented at many places, including **Jibe's Beach Club**, www.windsurf-vietnam.com. Windsurfing is also popular in Nha Trang where dive schools offer this and other watersports.

Motorbiking tours

Touring northern Ha Giang province in Vietnam on a motorbike is one of the most exciting things you can do in the country. A permit and a great sense of adventure is required. Several operators now offer cross-country and cross-border tours throughout Indochina, including **Cuong's Motorbike Adventure**, www.cuongs-motorbike-adventure.com. The Loop in Central Laos is a popular 3- to 5-day motorcycle tour, which runs through beautiful karst landscape, taking in some impressive caves along the way.

Rock climbing

Laos has stunning karst rock formations, caves and cliffs. Vang Vieng is the hot spot for this activity; contact **Green Discovery**, www.greendiscoverylaos.com. Climbing is also popular in Vietnam, particularly in Halong Bay and Cat Ba Island. Contact **Asia Outdoors,** www.asiaoutdoors.com.vn.

Spas

Hotels offering massage, treatments and therapies can be found across the region and offer good value for money. Devoted spa resorts in Vietnam are on the increase, especially in new developments along the Danang beaches and in and around Mui Ne. Original developments include the **Six Senses**, www.sixsenses.com, in Ninh Van Bay, and the **Six Senses Evason Ana Mandara** in Nha Trang. Other good hotels, such as the **Life Wellness Resorts**, www.life-resorts.com, and the **Victoria Hotels**, www.victoriahotels.asia, also offer spa facilities. There are also some wonderful spas in Luang Prabang; for extreme indulgence try The Spa at **La Résidence Phou Vao** (see page 368).

Trekking

The main focus for trekking in Vietnam is Sapa, but more recently oportunities have opened up around Dalat, Ha Giang and the Mai Chau area. Some treks are straightforward and can be done independently, whereas others require accommodation and there may be a legal requirement to take a licensed guide. Homestays in ethnic minority villages must be organized through a tour operator. For a different perspective on the landscape, elephant trekking is possible in Yok Don National Park (see page 144).

Laos offers stunning scenery inhabited by a diverse range of ethnicities. The most popular areas for trekking include Luang Namtha, Muang Sing, Nong Khiaw, Muang Ngoi Neua, Phongsali and around Savannakhet. There are also treks from Luang Prabang and Vang Vieng.

Where to stay

from colonial villas and ecolodges to homestays

Vietnam

Accommodation ranges from luxury suites in international five-star hotels and spa resorts to small, family hotels (mini hotels) and homestays. During peak seasons – December to March and during busy holidays such as Tet, Christmas, New Year's Eve and Easter – booking is essential. Staff in top hotels will almost certainly speak English, but do not expect it in cheaper hotels or in more remote places.

Private, mini hotels are worth seeking out as, being family-run, guests can expect good service. Mid-range and tourist hotels may provide a decent breakfast which is often included in the price. Some luxury and first-class hotels charge extra for breakfast and, on top of this, also charge VAT and service charge. There are world-class beach resorts in Phu Quoc, Nha Trang, Mui Ne, Hoi An and Danang. In the northern uplands, in places like Sapa, Ha Giang province and Mai Chau, it is possible to stay in an ethnic minority house. Bathrooms are basic and will consist of a cold or warm shower and an alfresco or Western toilet. To arrange a homestay you can book through a tour operator or local tourist office. Homestays are also possible on farms and in orchards in the Mekong Delta. Here, guests sleep on camp beds and share a Western bathroom with hot and cold water. National parks offer everything from air-conditioned bungalows to shared dormitory rooms to campsites where, sometimes, it is possible to hire tents. Visitors may spend a

Price codes

Where to stay	Restaurants
$$$$ over US$100	$$$ over US$12
$$$ US$46-100	$$ US$6-12
$$ US$20-45	$ under US$6
$ under US$20	

Price codes refer to the cost of two people sharing a double room in the high season.

Price codes refer to the cost of a two-course meal for one person excluding drinks or service charge.

romantic night on a boat in Halong Bay or on the Mekong Delta. Boats range from the fairly luxurious to the basic. Most people book through tour operators.

You will have to leave your passport at hotel reception desks for the duration of your stay. Credit cards are widely accepted but there is often a 2-4% fee. Tipping is not expected in hotels in Vietnam.

Cambodia

Accommodation standards in Cambodia have greatly improved over the last few years. Phnom Penh now has a good network of boutique hotels – arguably they are overpriced and management can be a bit Fawlty Towers but the bar has certainly been raised. Siem Reap, without doubt, has become a destination for the upmarket international traveller. The range, depth and quality of accommodation here is excellent. Even if you travel to some of the smaller, less visited towns, family-run hotels should now provide hot water, air-conditioning and cable TV even if they can't provide first-class service.

Laos

Rooms in Laos are rarely luxurious and standards vary enormously. Prices can be double what you would pay in Bangkok for similar facilities and service. However, the hotel industry is expanding rapidly and standards are rising. First-class and boutique hotels exist in Vientiane and Luang Prabang with more luxurious offerings now appearing in Vang Vieng and Pakse. Vientiane, however, still lacks sufficient budget choices. The majority of guesthouses and hotels have fans and attached bathrooms, although more and more are providing air-conditioning where there is a stable electricity supply, while others are installing their own generators to cater for the needs of the growing tourist trade. Smaller provincial towns, having previously had only a handful of hotels and guesthouses (some of them quaint French colonial villas) are now home to a growing number of rival concerns as tourism takes off. In rural villages, local homes are enthusiastically transformed into bed and breakfasts on demand. Many towns in the north, such as Vang Vieng, Muang Ngoi Neua, Muang Sing and Luang Namtha, have a large choice of very cheap, and in some cases, very good accommodation, including dorm beds. In the southern provinces, upmarket and boutique accommodation has popped up in Champasak Province. There are several excellent ecolodges in the country, most notably the **Boat Landing** at Luang Namtha and the **Kingfisher Ecolodge** at Ban Kiet Ngong in the south. Many tour companies offer homestay in ethnic minority villages and camping as part of a package tour. At higher end hotels, rates are subject to 10% government tax and 10% service charge.

Food
& drink

sticky rice, aromatic spices and French cuisine

Vietnam

Vietnam offers outstanding Vietnamese, French and international cuisine in restaurants ranging from first class to humble foodstalls. The quality of food at all levels will be, in the main, exceptional. The accent is on local, seasonal and fresh produce with rich pickings from the sea, both along Vietnam's 2000-km coastline and inland. Many restaurants offer a variety of local cuisine and some specialize in certain types of food. For example, Hué cuisine is known for its robust yet delicate flavours, such as *bun bo Hué* (round white noodles in soup, with slices of beef laced with chilli oil). *Pho* (pronounced *fer*), noodle soup, is Vietnam's best known dish and is utterly delicious.

All Vietnamese food is dipped, whether in fish sauce, soya sauce, chilli sauce, peanut sauce or pungent *mam tom* before eating. Follow the guidance of your waiter or Vietnamese friends to get the right dip with the right dish.

FOOD
Bird's nest soup

The tiny nests of the brown-rumped swift (*Collocalia esculenta*), also known as the edible-nest swiftlet or sea swallow, are collected for bird's nest soup, a Chinese delicacy, throughout Southeast Asia.

The semi-oval nests are made of silk-like strands of saliva secreted by the birds which, when cooked in broth, softens and becomes a little like noodles. Like so many Chinese delicacies, the nests are believed to have aphrodisiac qualities and the soup has even been suggested as a cure for HIV. The red nests are the most highly valued, and the Vietnamese Emperor Minh Mang (1820-1840) is said to have owed his extraordinary vitality to his inordinate consumption of bird's nest soup. This may explain why restaurants serving it are sometimes associated with massage parlours.

Collecting the nests is a precarious but profitable business and in some areas mafias of concessionaires vigorously guard and protect their assets. The men who collect the nests on a piecework basis risk serious injury climbing rickety ladders to cave roofs in sometimes almost total darkness, save for a candle strapped to their heads.

Locally produced fresh beer is called *bia hoi*; this is a weak brew that is ideal on steaming hot days. Many major cities in Vietnam produce their own bottled beer, most of which are light and refreshing. Rice and fruit wines are produced and consumed in large quantities in upland areas, particularly in the north of Vietnam. The Chinese believe that snake wines increase their virility and as such are normally found in areas of high Chinese concentration. Soft drinks and bottled still and sparkling mineral water are widely available. Tea and coffee is widely available. Coffee is often served ices and with condensed, not fresh milk.

Cambodia

For a country that has suffered and starved in the way Cambodia has, eating for fun as opposed to eating for survival, has only recently begun to catch on. There are some good restaurants and the quality of food is improving but don't expect Cambodia to live up to the standards of Thailand, Vietnam or even Laos. Cambodian food does, however, show clear links with the cuisines of its neighbours. The influence of the French colonial period is also in evidence, most clearly in the availability of good French bread. Chinese food is also available owing to strong business ties between Cambodia and China. True Khmer food is difficult to find and much that the Khmers would like to claim as indigenous food is actually of Thai, French or Vietnamese origin. Curries, soups, rice and noodle-based dishes, salads, fried vegetables and sliced meats all feature in Khmer cooking.

Phnom Penh and Siem Reap have the best restaurants with French, Japanese, Italian and Indian food available. Those who want to sample a range of dishes and get a feel for Khmer cuisine should head for the nearest market where dishes will be cooked on order in a wok – known locally as a *chhnang khteak*.

International soft drink brands are widely available in Cambodia. Tea is drunk without sugar or milk. Coffee is also served black, or *'crème'* with sweetened condensed milk. Bottled water is easy to find, as is local mineral water. Fruit smoothies – known locally as *tikalok* – are ubiquitous. Local and imported beers are also available everywhere.

Laos

Lao food is similar to that of Thailand, although the Chinese influence is slightly less noticeable. Lao dishes are distinguished by the use of aromatic herbs and spices such as lemongrass, chillies, ginger and tamarind. The best place to try Lao food is often from roadside stalls or in the markets. The staple Lao foods are *kao niao* (glutinous sticky rice), which is eaten with your hands and fermented fish or *pa dek* (distinguishable by its distinctive smell), often laced with liberal spoons of *nam pa*, fish sauce. Being a landlocked country, most of the fish is fresh from the Mekong. One of the delicacies that shouldn't be missed is *mok pa* (steamed fish in banana leaf). Most of the dishes are variations on two themes: fish and bird. *Laap*, also meaning 'luck' in Lao, is a traditional ceremonial dish made from (traditionally) raw fish or meat crushed into a paste, marinated in lemon juice and mixed with chopped mint. It is called *laap sin* if it has a meat base and *laap paa* if it's fish based. Beware of *laap* in cheap street restaurants. It is sometimes concocted from raw offal and served cold and should be consumed with great caution. Overall though *laap* is cooked well for the *falang* palate.

Restaurant food is, on the whole, hygienically prepared, and as long as street stall snacks have been well cooked, they are usually fine and a good place to sample local specialities. Really classy restaurants are only to be found in Vientiane and Luang Prabang. Good French cuisine is available in both cities. Salads, steaks, pizzas and more are all on offer but, in terms of value for money, the Lao restaurants are a better bet.

Lower-end Lao restaurants are prevalent in every town. Right at the bottom end – in terms of price if not necessarily in terms of quality – are stalls that charge a US$1-2 for filled baguettes or simple single-dish meals.

Soft drinks are expensive as they are imported from Thailand. Bottled water is widely available and produced locally, so it is cheap (about 5000 kip a litre). *Nam saa*, weak Chinese tea, is free. Imported beer can be found in hotels, restaurants and bars but is not particularly cheap. *Beerlao* produce a hugely popular lager, a stronger dark beer and two lesser seen varieties – *Beerlao Gold* and *Beerlao Light*. The chief local brew is *lao-lao*, a rice wine which varies in taste and strength from region to region; drunk in shots, it is usually poured from a recycled plastic bottle. Less common, but great fun, is *lao hai* – often weaker than standard *lao-lao*, this is drunk communally from a clay pot using long straws.

FOOD
Nam pa

No meal would be complete without a small dish of *nam pa* to spoon onto almost any savoury dish. Like *nam plaa* in Thailand, *nuoc mam* in Vietnam and *ngan-pyaye* in Myanmar (Burma), *nam pa* is an essential element of Laotian gastronomic life. To make the sauce, freshwater fish is packed into containers and steeped in brine. (Elsewhere in the region, it is made from saltwater fish, but because Laos is landlocked, freshwater fish is used instead.) The resulting brown liquid – essentially the by-products of slowly putrifying fish – is drained off and bottled. A variation is *pa dek*, *nam pa* with small chunks of fermented fish added, often with rice husks too. This variation tends to be used in cooking and is kept in an earthenware pot – often outside as the aroma is so strong.

This is
Vietnam

Vietnam has overcome Chinese, French and American occupation to emerge strong and fiercely proud. And there is much to be proud of, from the many UNESCO-listed sites to a cuisine that is now making its mark on the world stage thanks to its emphasis on fresh ingredients and mountains of herbs. The national dish, *pho*, with its perfectly balanced blend of flavours with hints of star anise is just the tip of the iceberg. Every lunchtime the capital's streets are filled the irresistible scent of barbecuing *bun cha*, while all along the coast seafront restaurants serve up the very freshest of seafood. Meanwhile, in the former royal capital of Hué, a whole other world of food awaits with delicately prepared dishes originally created for bygone emperors now served up to us mere mortals.

While it remains a Communist state, the economic reforms of 'doi moi' in 1986 provided a springboard towards Vietnam's blistering growth. In recent years scores of gleaming high-rises have risen from paddy fields and whole new districts have grown from swampy wastelands. Among this development stand the pagodas and temples of old, the scent of incense wafting onto streets still padded by conical hat wearing fruit sellers and pedalled by cyclos, albeit against the heavy tide of motorbikes and rising number of SUVs.

And then there are the country's utterly beautiful and diverse landscapes. The dramatic mountains of the far north are dotted with minority ethnic villages and criss-crossed by a network of roads which serve up mountain passes that road trip dreams are made of. East of Hanoi the islands of Halong Bay compete for attention with a coastline bursting with peaceful, pristine beaches.

Elsewhere, adventure beckons in Central Vietnam with the world's largest caves now open for exploration, while further south the seas of Mui Ne are renowned for world-class kitesurfing, just minutes away from Sahara-like dunes.

Hanoi

Hanoi is a city of broad, tree-lined boulevards, lakes, parks, weathered colonial buildings, elegant squares and some of the newest office blocks and hotels in Southeast Asia. It is the capital of the world's 14th most populous country, but, in an age of urban sprawl, the city remains small and compact, historic and charming.

Much of the charm of Hanoi lies not so much in the big 'sights' but in the unofficial and informal: small shops, sidewalk coffee, an evening visit to Hoan Kiem, watching the older inhabitants exercise and practice t'ai chi around one of the city's many lakes.

Another appeal lies in the novelty of exploring a city that, until recently, has opted for a firmly socialist road to development and has been insulated from the West. Today, you'll find it enlivened by an entrepreneurial spirit manifest in new shops, bars and building developments, and an ever more cosmopolitan air reflected in the opening of new galleries and a fantastic contemporary art scene.

Best for
Architecture ▪ Coffee shops ▪ History ▪ Lakeside walks

Footprint picks

★ **Hoan Kiem Lake,** page 31
A walk around the lake in the early
morning or at dusk is a must.

★ **Old Quarter**, page 33
Hectic and intoxicating – if you feel overwhelmed, jump in a cyclo.

★ **Ambassadors' Pagoda**, page 42
Not one of the conventional sights, but easily one of the most
atmospheric – arrive early or late to watch badminton.

★ **Temple of Literature**, page 44
Vietnam's first university and now its most famous temple.

★ **The Citadel**, page 46
One of the most recently opened of the official sights, the Citadel
grounds are a peaceful retreat and offer plenty of history.

★ **Tay Ho Pagoda**, page 46
The waterfront setting of this pagoda is hard to beat.

★ **Museum of Ethnology**, page 47
The country's best place to learn about the 54 ethnic groups which
inhabit it.

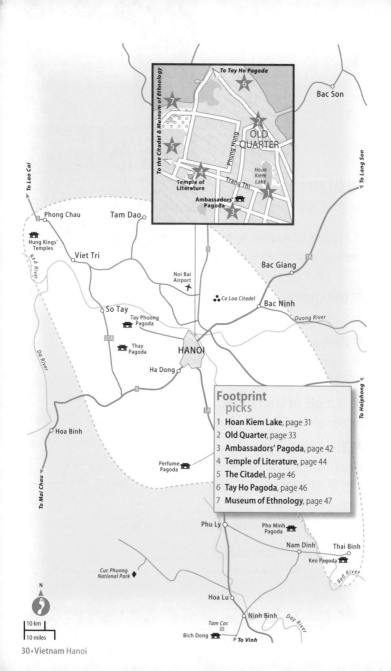

To Tay Ho Pagoda

Bac Son

OLD QUARTER

To the Citadel & Museum of Ethnology

Phung Hung

Hoan Kiem Lake

Trang Thi

Temple of Literature

Ambassadors' Pagoda

To Lang Son

To Lao Cai

Phong Chau

Tam Dao

Red River

Hung Kings' Temples

Viet Tri

Bac Giang

Noi Bai Airport

Co Loa Citadel

Bac Ninh

Duong River

So Tay

Tay Phuong Pagoda

Thay Pagoda

HANOI

Ha Dong

To Haiphong

Hoa Binh

Perfume Pagoda

To Mai Chau

Do River

Da River

Footprint picks

1 **Hoan Kiem Lake**, page 31
2 **Old Quarter**, page 33
3 **Ambassadors' Pagoda**, page 42
4 **Temple of Literature**, page 44
5 **The Citadel**, page 46
6 **Tay Ho Pagoda**, page 46
7 **Museum of Ethnology**, page 47

Phu Ly

Pho Minh Pagoda

Nam Dinh

Thai Binh

Keo Pagoda

Cuc Phuong National Park

Red River

Hoa Lu

Tam Coc

Ninh Binh

Day River

Bich Dong

To Vinh

N

10 km
10 miles

Sights
Hanoi

boulevards, baguettes and bars

Hanoi has some worthy historical sights lying as it does at the heart of a region rich in history. It also has stylish shops and plentiful market stalls, and plenty of places to stop for coffee. *Colour map 2, B4.*

Hoan Kiem Lake and Central Hanoi

heart of the capital

★Hoan Kiem Lake

Hoan Kiem Lake, or Ho Guom (the Lake of the Restored Sword) as it is more commonly referred to in Hanoi, is named after an incident that occurred during the 15th century. Emperor Le Thai To (1428-1433), following a momentous victory against an army of invading Ming Chinese, was sailing on the lake when a golden turtle appeared from the depths to take back the charmed sword which had secured the victory and restore it to the lake whence it came. Like the sword in the stone of British Arthurian legend, Le Thai To's sword assures Vietnamese of divine intervention in time of national crisis and the story is graphically portrayed in water puppet theatres across the country. There is a modest and rather dilapidated tower (the **Tortoise Tower**) commemorating the event on an islet in the southern part of the lake. In fact, the lake does contain a turtle and one captured in 1968 was reputed to have weighed 250 kg. The Ho Guom tortoise has now been named *Rafetus leloii*. The wide pavement that surrounds the lake is used by the residents of the city every morning for jogging and t'ai chi. The light around the lake has a filmic quality, especially in the early morning.

Ngoc Son Temple and bridge
10,000d.

The temple was built in the early 19th century on a small island on the foundations of the old Khanh Thuy Palace. The island is linked to the shore by the Huc (Sunbeam) Bridge, constructed in 1875. The temple is dedicated to Van Xuong, the God of Literature, although the 13th-century hero Tran Hung Dao, the martial arts genius Quan Vu and the physician La To are also worshipped here. Shrouded by trees and surrounded by water, the pagoda's position is its strongest attribute. To the side of the temple is a room containing a preserved turtle and photographs of the creatures in the lake.

Essential Hanoi

Finding your feet

At the heart of the city is Hoan Kiem Lake. The majority of visitors make straight for the Old Quarter (aka 36 Streets) area north of the lake. The French Quarter is south of the lake. Here you'll find the Opera House, grand hotels, shops and offices. A large block of the city west of Hoan Kiem Lake (Ba Dinh District) represents the heart of government. To the north is West Lake, Tay Ho District, fringed with the suburban homes of the new middle class and the expat quarter with bars and restaurants. Away to the southern and eastern edges are the industrial and residential zones.

Best bars

Barbetta, page 54
CAMA ATK, page 54
Madake, page 54
Tadioto, page 55

Getting around

Hanoi is getting more frenetic by the minute, and pavements are often used for parking making walking a challenge, but walking can still be pleasurable. If you like the idea of being pedalled, then a cyclo is the answer – but be prepared for some concentrated haggling. There are also *xe om* and self-drive motorbikes for hire as well as a fleet of metered taxis. Local buses are rammed and the network is not well designed for the uninitiated.

Best museum and galleries

Vietnamese Women's Museum, page 46
Museum of Ethnology, page 47
Nha San, page 56

When to go

Hanoi benefits from glorious European-like springs and autumns when temperatures are warm and crisp. From May until September Hanoi is often fearfully hot and steamy and you cannot take a step without breaking into a sweat. From December to February it can be chilly and Hanoians wrap themselves up. Most museums are closed on Mondays.

Time required

Most sights can be seen in a weekend, but lazing in Hanoi cafés and by lakes is worth more of your time.

Weather Hanoi

Month	High	Low	Rainfall
January	20°C	14°C	26mm
February	21°C	15°C	26mm
March	23°C	18°C	47mm
April	28°C	22°C	93mm
May	32°C	24°C	155mm
June	34°C	26°C	182mm
July	33°C	26°C	221mm
August	33°C	26°C	234mm
September	32°C	25°C	137mm
October	30°C	32°C	96mm
November	26°C	18°C	59mm
December	23°C	15°C	22mm

★Old Quarter and 36 Streets

Stretching north from the lake is the Old Quarter (aka Pho Co or 36 Streets). Previously, it lay to the east of the citadel, where the emperor had his residence, and was squalid, dark, cramped and disease-ridden. This part of Hanoi has survived surprisingly intact, and today is one of the most beautiful areas of the city, although the old fronts of most of the buildings are now covered with unsightly advertising hordings. Narrow streets, each named after the produce that it sells or used to sell (**Basket Street**, **Paper Street**, **Silk Street**, etc), create an intricate web of activity and colour.

By the 15th century there were 36 short lanes here, each specializing in a particular trade and representing one of the 36 guilds. Among them, for example, were the **Phuong Hang Dao (Dyers' Guild Street)** and the **Phuong Hang Bac (Silversmiths' Street)**. In fact, Hang Bac (*hang* means merchandise) is the oldest street in Hanoi, dating from the 13th century. The 36 streets have interested European visitors since they first started coming to Hanoi. For example, in 1685 Samuel Bacon noted how "all the diverse objects sold in this town have a specially assigned street", remarking how different this was from "companies and corporations in European cities". The streets in question not only sold different products, but were usually also populated by people from different areas of the country – even from single villages. They would live, work and worship together because each of the occupational guilds had its own temple and its own community support networks.

Some of this past is still in evidence: at the south end of Hang Dau Street, for example, is a mass of stalls selling nothing but shoes and Hang Bac is still a place for gold to be bought and sold. Generally, however, the crafts and trades of the past have given way to new activities, but it is remarkable the extent to which the streets still specialize in the production and sale of just one type of merchandise.

The dwellings in this area are known as *nha ong* (**tube houses**). The majority were built at the end of the 19th century and the beginning of the 20th; they are narrow, with shop fronts sometimes only 3 m wide, but can be up to 50 m long (such as the one at 51 Hang Dao). In the countryside the dimensions of houses were calculated on the basis of the owner's own physical dimensions; in urban areas the tube houses evolved so that each house owner could have an, albeit very small, area of shop frontage facing onto the main street; the width was determined by the social class of the owner. The houses tend to be interspersed with courtyards or 'wells' to permit light into the house and allow some space for outside activities such as washing and gardening. As geographers Brian Shaw and R Jones note in a paper on heritage conservation in Hanoi, the houses also had a natural air-conditioning system: the difference in ambient temperature between the inner courtyards and the outside street created air flow, and the longer the house the greater the velocity of the flow.

A common wall can sometimes still be seen between tube houses. Built in a step-like pattern, it not only marked land boundaries but also acted as a firebreak. The position of the house frontages were not fixed until the early 20th century and consequently some streets have a delightfully irregular appearance. The structures were built of bricks 'cemented' together with sugar-cane juice.

The older houses tend to be lower; commoners were not permitted to build higher than the Emperor's own residence. Other regulations prohibited attic windows looking down on the street; this was to prevent assassination and to stop people from looking down on a passing king. As far as colour and decoration were concerned, purple and gold were strictly for royal use only, as was the decorative use of the dragon. By the early 20th century inhabitants were replacing their traditional tube houses with buildings inspired by French

1 Hanoi

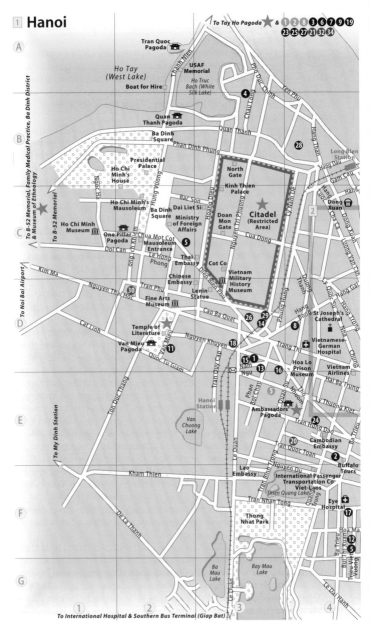

To Tay Ho Pagoda ★ & 1 2 3 8 3 6 7 9 19
23 25 27 21 32 34

Tran Quoc Pagoda

Ho Tay (West Lake)

USAF Memorial

Ho Truc Bach (White Silk Lake)

Boat for Hire

Quan Thanh Pagoda

Ba Dinh Square

Phan Dinh Phung

North Gate

Presidential Palace

Ho Chi Minh's House

Kinh Thien Palace

To B-52 Memorial, Family Medical Practice, Ba Dinh District & Museum of Ethnology

To B-52 Memorial

Ho Chi Minh's Mausoleum

Ba Dinh Square

Bac Son

Doan Mon Gate

★ Citadel (Restricted Area)

Ho Chi Minh Museum

Ministry of Foreign Affairs

One Pillar Pagoda

Mausoleum Entrance

Cua Dong

Doi Can

Le Hong Phong

Thai Embassy

Cot Co

Chinese Embassy

Vietnam Military History Museum

Lenin Statue

Long Bien Station

Hang Than

Dong Xuan

St Joseph's Cathedral

To Noi Bai Airport

Kim Ma

Nguyen Thai Hoc

Tran Phu

Fine Arts Museum

Cao Ba Quat

Vietnamese-German Hospital

Cat Linh

Temple of Literature

Nguyen Khuyen

Trang Thi

Hoa Lo Prison Museum

Vietnam Airlines

Van Mieu Pagoda

Chua Tu Giam

Nam Ngu

Hai Ba Trung

To My Dinh Station

Ton Duc Thang

Hanoi Station

Phan Boi Chau

Ambassadors' Pagoda

Tran Hung Dao

Cambodian Embassy

Van Chuong Lake

Lao Embassy

Tran Quoc Toan

Nguyen Du

Buffalo Tours

Kham Thien

International Passenger Transportation Co Viet-Laos

Thien Quang Lake

Tran Nhan Tong

Eye Hospital

De La Thanh

Thong Nhat Park

Hoa Ma

Ba Mau Lake

Bay Mau Lake

Le Dai Hanh

To International Hospital & Southern Bus Terminal (Giap Bat)

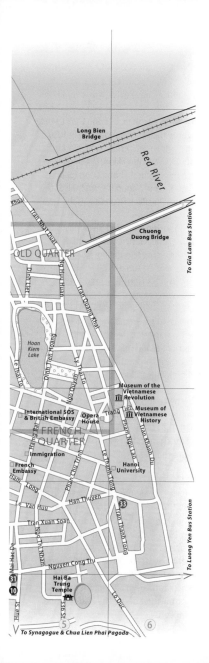

Long Bien Bridge

Red River

Chuong Duong Bridge

To Gia Lam Bus Station

OLD QUARTER

Hoan Kiem Lake

Museum of the Vietnamese Revolution

International SOS & British Embassy

Opera House

Museum of Vietnamese History

FRENCH QUARTER

Immigration

French Embassy

Hanoi University

To Luong Yen Bus Station

Han Thuyen

Tran Xuan Soan

Nguyen Cong Tru

Hai Ba Trung Temple

To Duc

To Synagogue & Chua Lien Phai Pagoda

➡ **Hanoi maps**
1 Hanoi, page 34
2 Hoan Kiem, page 37

N

400 metres

400 yards

Where to stay 🛏
InterContinental Hanoi
  Westlake **8** *A3*
Movenpick **5** *E3*
Sheraton **1** *A3*
Sofitel **2** *A3*

Restaurants & cafés 🍴
Café 129 **10** *D3*
Café Puku **14** *D3*
Chiem Beo **23** *A3*
Chim Sáo **12** *F4*
Com Chay Nang Tam **24** *E4*
Cong Café **5** *F4 and C2*
Cousins **3** *A3*
Da Paulo **6** *A3*
El Gaucho **7** *A3*
Foodshop 45 **25** *A3*
Hanoi Cooking Centre **4** *B3*
Hanoi Social Club **8** *D4*
The Kafe **26** *D3*
KOTO **11** *D2*
La Badiane **1** *D3*
La Bicicleta **9** *A3*
Luna d'Autonno **15** *D3*
Maison de Tet **27** *A3*
Manzi **28** *B4*
Namaste **16** *D3*
Net Hue **29** *D3*
Pots n Pans **17** *F4*
Quan An Ngon **13** *D3*
Ray Quan **18** *F4*
Republic **19** *A3*
Verticale **2** *E4*

Bars & clubs 🍸
84 Bar **20** *E4*
Barbetta **30** *D2*
Cama ATK **31** *G5*
Hanoi Rock City **32** *A3*
Hoan Vien **33** *F6*
Madake **34** *A3*
Summit Lounge **21** *A3*

BACKGROUND
Hanoi's history

The original village on the site of the present city was located in a district with the local name of Long Do. The community seems to have existed as a small settlement as early as the third century AD.

The origins of Hanoi as a great city lie with a temple orphan, Ly Cong Uan. Ly rose through the ranks of the palace guards to become their commander and in 1010, four years after the death of the previous King Le Hoan, was enthroned, marking the beginning of the 200-year-long Ly Dynasty. On becoming king, Ly Cong Uan moved his capital from Hoa Lu to Dai La, which he renamed **Thang Long** (Soaring Dragon). Thang Long is present-day **Hanoi**. A number of pagodas were built at this time – most have since disappeared, although the One Pillar Pagoda and the Tran Vu Temple both date from this period

During the period of French expansion into Indochina, the Red River was proposed as an alternative trade route to the Mekong. Francis Garnier, a French naval officer, was dispatched to the area in 1873 to ascertain the possibilities of establishing such a route. Despite having only a modest force of men under arms, when negotiations with Emperor Tu Duc failed in 1882, Garnier attacked and captured the citadel of Hanoi under the dubious pretext that the Vietnamese were about to attack him. Tu Duc acceded to French demands, and from 1882 onwards, Hanoi, along with the port city of Haiphong, became the focus of French activity in the north. Hanoi was made the capital of the new colony of Annam, and the French laid out a 2-sq-km residential and business district, constructing mansions, villas and public buildings incorporating both French and Asian architectural styles. Many of these buildings still stand to the south and east of the Old City and Hoan Kiem Lake.

In the 1920s and 1930s, with conditions in the countryside deteriorating, there was an influx of landless and dispossessed labourers into the city. Before long, a poor underclass, living in squalid, pathetic conditions, had formed. At the end of the Second World War, with the French battling to keep Ho Chi Minh and his forces at bay, Hanoi became little more than a service centre of some 40,000 inhabitants.

After the French withdrew in 1954, Ho Chi Minh concentrated on building up Vietnam and in particular Hanoi's industrial base. At that time the capital had only eight small, privately owned factories. By 1965, more than 1000 enterprises had been added to this figure. However, as the US bombing of the north intensified with Operation Rolling Thunder in 1965, so the authorities began to evacuate non-essential civilians from Hanoi and to disperse industry into smaller, less vulnerable units of operation. Between 500,000 and 750,000 people were evacuated between 1965 and 1973, representing 75% of the inner-city population. Nevertheless, the cessation of hostilities led to a spontaneous migration back into the capital. By 1984 the population of the city had reached 2.7 million, and today it is in excess of three million.

architecture. Many fine buildings from this era remain, however, and are best appreciated by standing back and looking upwards. Shutters, cornices, columns and wrought-iron balconies and balustrades are common decorative features. An ornate façade sometimes conceals the pitched roof behind.

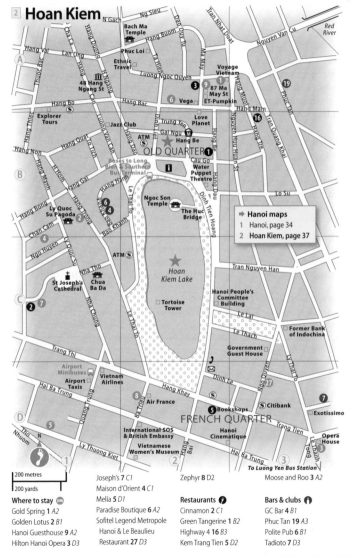

2 Hoan Kiem

➡ **Hanoi maps**
1 Hanoi, page 34
2 Hoan Kiem, page 37

BACKGROUND
Urban renewal

Although Ho Chi Minh City has attracted the lion's share of Vietnam's foreign inward investment, Hanoi, as the capital, also receives a large amount. But whereas Ho Chi Minh City's investment tends to be in industry, Hanoi has received a great deal of attention from property developers, notably in the hotel and office sectors. Much of the development has been in prestigious and historical central Hanoi and has included the construction of a huge office complex on the site of the notorious 'Hanoi Hilton' prison, much to the mortification of Vietnamese war veterans, see page 41. Some commentators applauded the authorities for this attempt at putting the past behind them.

Although some architecturally insensitive schemes have dominated the cityscape, numerous old colonial villas have been tastefully restored as bars, restaurants and homes with a very positive effect on Hanoi's architectural heritage. Pollution levels in Hanoi have soared as a result of the construction boom: dust from demolition, piling, bricks and tiles and sand blown from the back of trucks add an estimated 150 cubic metres of pollutants to the urban atmosphere every day. But while asthmatics may wheeze, Hanoi's army of builders grows daily ever stronger.

48 Hang Ngang Street ⓘ *At the north end of Hang Dao St, before it becomes Hang Duong St, 0800-1130, 1330-1630, 10,000d.* This is the spot where Ho Chi Minh drew up the Vietnamese Declaration of Independence in 1945, ironically modelled on the US Declaration of Independence. It now houses a museum with black and white photographs of Uncle Ho.

87 Ma May Street ⓘ *Daily 0800-1200, 1300-1700, 10,000d, guide included.* This is a wonderfully preserved example of an original shophouse, now open to the public. The house was built in the late 1800s as a home for a single family. The importance of the miniature interior courtyards providing light, fresh air and gardens can be appreciated. The wooden upstairs and pitched fish-scale-tiled roofs are typical of how most houses would have looked. From 1954 to 1999 five families shared the building as the urban population rose and living conditions declined.

The Bach Ma (White Horse) Temple ⓘ *76 Hang Buom St.* Dating from the ninth century, this temple honours Long Do and is the oldest religious building in the Old Quarter. In 1010, King Ly Thai To honoured Long Do with the title of the capital. It is said that a horse revealed to King Ly Thai To where to build the walls of the citadel.

Cua Quan Chuong Venturing further north is the last remaining of Hanoi's 16 gates. In the 18th century a system of ramparts and walls was built around Hanoi. Quan Chuong Gate was built in 1749 and rebuilt in 1817.

Dong Xuan Market Further north still, on Dong Xuan Street, is this large covered **market**. It was destroyed in a disastrous fire in 1994 and stallholders lost an estimated US$4.5 million worth of stock. They complained bitterly at the inadequacy of the fire services; one fire engine arrived with no water. The market has been rebuilt and it specializes mainly in clothes and household goods.

The streets around the market are full of street traders selling all manner of foods and spices making this a wonderful area to wander with a camera.

West of Hoan Kiem Lake
religious buildings worth a peek

To the west of Hoan Kiem Lake in a little square stands the rather sombre, twin-towered neo-Gothic **Saint Joseph's Cathedral** ⓘ *open 0500-1130, 1400-1930 through a door at the back; Mass Mon-Fri 0530, 0815, Sat 0530, 1800, Sun 0500, 0700, 0900, 1100, 1600, 1800.* Built in 1886, the cathedral is important as one of the very first colonial-era buildings in Hanoi finished, as it was, soon after the Treaty of Tientsin, which gave France control over the whole of Vietnam (see page 472). It was located at the centre of the Catholic Mission. Some fine stained-glass windows remain. The area around the cathedral is hugely popular by day and night with Hanoi's youth who gather in huge numbers to drink ice lemon tea and eat sunflower seeds.

About 100 m in front of the cathedral on Nha Tho Street is a much older religious foundation, the **Stone Lady Pagoda (Chua Ba Da)**, down a narrow alley. It consists of an old pagoda and a Buddhist school. On either side of the pagoda are low buildings where the monks live. Although few of the standing buildings are of any antiquity it is an ancient site and a tranquil and timeless atmosphere prevails. Originally built in 1056 as Sung Khanh Pagoda, by the late 15th century it needed rebuilding. A stone statue of a woman was found in the foundations and was worshipped in the pagoda. By 1767 the walls needed rebuilding. Each time they were built they collapsed. The foundations were dug deeper and the stone statue was found again. Since then the walls have held fast. Although now a pagoda for the worship of Buddha it is clear that the site has had a mixed spiritual history.

North of the cathedral on Ly Quoc Su Street is the **Ly Quoc Su Pagoda**, once home to Minh Khong, a physician and the chief adviser to Ly Than Tong, the Ly dynasty emperor. He became famous in the 12th century after curing the emperor of a disease that other doctors had failed to treat. It was restored in 2010.

South of Hoan Kiem Lake
tree-lined boulevards and coffee shops

Opera House
www.hanoioperahouse.org.vn. Not open to the public except during public performances. See the billboards outside or visit the box office for details.

To the south and east of Hoan Kiem Lake is the proud-looking French-era Opera House. It was built between 1901-1911 by François Lagisquet and is one of the finest French colonial buildings in Hanoi. Some 35,000 bamboo piles were sunk into the mud of the Red River to provide foundations for the lofty edifice. The exterior is a delightful mass of shutters, wrought-iron work, little balconies and a tiled frieze. The top balustrade is nicely capped with griffins. Inside, there are dozens of little boxes and fine decoration evocative of the French era. Having suffered years of neglect the Opera House was eventually lavishly restored, opening in time for the Francophone Summit held in 1997. Original drawings in Hanoi and Paris were consulted and teams of foreign experts were brought in to supervise local craftsmen. Slate was carried from Sin Ho to re-tile the roof, Italians oversaw the relaying of the mosaic floor in the lobby and French artists repainted the fine ornamental details of the auditorium. The restoration cost US$14 million, a colossal sum to spend on the reappointment of a colonial edifice. A Hanoi planning department architect explained that although the Opera House was French in style it was built by Vietnamese hands and represented an indelible part of Vietnamese history.

Sofitel Metropole
15 Ngo Quyen St.

The Metropole, built in French-colonial style in 1901, is an icon of elegance in the French quarter of the city. It quickly became the focal point of colonial life for 50 years. In 1916, it screened the first movie shown in Indochina. In 1944, Japanese POWS were temporarily housed here. In the 1950s the Vietnamese government appropriated it, named it the **Thong Nhat Hotel**, and used it as a hotel for VIPs; during the Vietnam War years the press and diplomats used it as their headquarters. Many famous celebrities and diplomats have stayed here including Graham Greene (writing *The Quiet American*), Somerset Maugham, Noel Coward, Stephen Hawking, Oliver Stone, Charlie Chaplin, Sir Roger Moore, Jane Fonda, Mick Jagger, Catherine Deneuve, George Bush Senior, Fidel Castro, Robert McNamara, Jacques Chirac and Boutros Boutros Ghali.

Museum of the Vietnamese Revolution
216 Tran Quang Khai St, T4-3825 4151, Tue-Sun 0800-1145, 1330-1615, 20,000d.

The Museum of the Vietnamese Revolution (Bao Tang Cach Mang Vietnam), housed in an old French villa, traces the struggle of the Vietnamese people to establish their independence. Following the displays, it becomes clear that the American involvement in Vietnam has been just one episode in a centuries-long struggle against foreign aggressors. The 3000 exhibits are dryly presented across 29 rooms and in chronological order. They start with the cover the struggle for independence (1858-1945); the final rooms show the peace and prosperity of reunification: bountiful harvests, the opening of large civil engineering projects, and smiling peasants.

Museum of Vietnamese History (Bao Tang Lich Su)
1 Trang Tien St, T4-325 3518, Tue-Sun 0800-1130, 1330-1630, 15,000d.

A short distance south of the Museum of the Vietnamese Revolution is the History Museum. It is housed in a splendid building, completed in 1931. It was built as the home of the École Française d'Extrême-Orient, a distinguished archaeological, historical and ethnological research institute, by Ernest Hébrard. Hébrard was responsible for many fine colonial-era buildings in Vietnam. Here he employed a distinctly Indochinese style appropriate to its original and, indeed, its current function.

The museum remains a centre of cultural and historical research. The École Française d'Extrême-Orient played an important role in the preservation and restoration of ancient Vietnamese structures and temples, many of which were destroyed or came under threat of demolition by the French to enable the growth of their colonial city.

The museum remains a centre of cultural and historical research. The collection spans Vietnamese history from the Neolithic to the 20th century of Ho Chi Minh and is arranged in chronological order. Galleries lead from the Neolithic (Bac Son) represented by stone tools and jewellery; the Bronze Age (Dong Son) with some fine bronze drums; Funan and the port of Oc-Eo; Champa is represented by some fine stone carvings of *apsaras*, mythical dancing girls. There are relics such as bronze temple bells and urns of successive royal dynasties from Le to Nguyen. An impressive giant turtle, symbol of longevity, supports a huge stela praising the achievements of Le Loi, founder of the Le Dynasty, who harnessed nationalist sentiment and forced the Chinese out of Vietnam. Unfortunately some of the pieces (including a number of the stelae) are reproductions.

Other French Quarter buildings

Other buildings of the 'French Concession' include the impressive former residence of the French Resident Superior of Tonkin opposite the Metropole.

The enormous **Post Office** ⓘ *6 Dinh Le St*, facing Hoan Kiem lake, was designed by Henri Cerruti in 1942. Next door is the **Post and Telegraphic Office** ⓘ *75 Dinh Tien Hoang St*, designed by Auguste-Henri Vildieu and completed in 1896. Further up Dinh Tieng Hoang is the **Hanoi People's Committee** building, formerly the town hall and built by Vildieu between 1897 and 1906. The main section at the front dates from the late 1980s and early 1990s demonstrating brutalist communist architecture. Vildieu also designed the **Supreme Court** ⓘ *48 Ly Thuong Kiet*, between 1900 and 1906. It's a fine symmetrical building with a grey-tiled roof, two staircases and balustrades.

Ernest Hébrard, who worked at the Central Services of Urban Planning and Architecture, designed the **Indochina University**, now **Hanoi University** ⓘ *19 Le Thanh Tong St*, which was completed in 1926. It bears a remarkable resemblance to the history museum, which he also designed. Furthermore, Hébrard designed the **Ministry of Foreign Affairs** (then the **Bureau des Finances**) ⓘ *Dien Bien Phu St*, in 1931.

Around 1000 colonial villas are still scattered around Hanoi, especially west of the Old Quarter. Many of them have been superbly restored and are used by embassies.

Hoa Lo Prison

1 Hoa Lo, T4-3824 6358, Tue-Sun 0800-1130, 1330-1630, 20,000d.

Hoa Lo Prison (Maison Centrale), better known as the **Hanoi Hilton**, is the prison where US POWs were incarcerated, some for six years, during the Vietnamese War. The final prisoners were not released until 1973, some having been held in the north since 1964.

At the end of 1992 a US mission was shown around the prison where 2000 inmates were housed in cramped and squalid conditions. Despite pleas from war veterans and party members, the site was sold to a Singapore-Vietnamese joint venture and is now a hotel and shopping complex, **Hanoi Towers**. As part of the deal the developers had to leave a portion of the prison for use as a museum, a lasting memorial to the horrors of war.

'Maison Centrale' reads the legend over the prison's main gate, which leads in to the museum. There are recreations of conditions under colonial rule when the barbarous French incarcerated patriotic Vietnamese from 1896: by 1953 they were holding 2000 prisoners in a space designed for 500. Many well-known Vietnamese were incarcerated here: Phan Boi Chau (founder of the Reformation Party; 1867-1940), Luong Van Can (Reformation Party leader and school founder; 1854-1927), Nguyen Quyen (founder along with Luong Van Can of the School for the Just Cause; 1870-1942) and five men who were later to become general secretaries of the Communist Party: Le Duan (served as general secretary 1976-1986), Nguyen Van Cu (served 1938-1940), Truong Chinh (served 1941-1956 and July-December 1986), Nguyen Van Linh (served 1986-1991) and Do Muoi (served 1991-1997). Less prominence is given to the role of the prison for holding American pilots, but Douglas 'Pete' Peterson, the first post-war American Ambassador to Vietnam (1997-2001), who was one such occupant (imprisoned 1966-1973) has his mug-shot on the wall, as does John McCain (imprisoned 1967-1973).

★Ambassadors' Pagoda
73 Quan Su St.

In the 15th century there was a guesthouse on the site of the Ambassadors' Pagoda (Quan Su Pagoda) for visiting Buddhist ambassadors. The current structure was built between 1936 and 1942. Chinese in appearance from the exterior, the temple contains some fine stone sculptures of the past, present and future Buddhas. It is very popular and crowded with scholars, pilgrims, beggars and incense sellers. The pagoda is one of the centres of Buddhist learning in Vietnam (it is the headquarters of the Vietnam Central Buddhist Congregation): at the back is a schoolroom that is in regular use; students often spill-over into the surrounding corridors to listen.

Nearby, on Le Duan Street just south of the railway station, stalls sell a remarkable array of US, Soviet and Vietnamese army-surplus kit.

Ho Chi Minh's Mausoleum complex and around
resting place of Vietnam's greatest hero

Ho Chi Minh's Mausoleum
Summer Tue-Thu, Sat and Sun 0730-1100. Winter Tue-Thu, Sat and Sun 0800-1100, closed 6 weeks from Sep for conservation. Before entering the mausoleum, visitors must leave cameras and possessions at the office (Ban To Chuc) on Huong Vuong, just south of and a few mins' walk from the mausoleum. Visitors must be respectful: dress neatly, walk solemnly, do not talk and do not take anything in that could be construed as a weapon, for example, a penknife.

The Vietnamese have made Ho Chi Minh's body a holy place of pilgrimage and visitors march in file to see Ho's embalmed corpse inside the mausoleum (Lang Chu Tich Ho Chi Minh).

The mausoleum, built between 1973 and 1975, is a massive square forbidding structure and must be among the best constructed, maintained and air-conditioned buildings in Vietnam. Opened in 1975, it is a fine example of the mausoleum genre and is modelled closely on Lenin's Mausoleum in Moscow. Ho Chi Minh lies in state with a guard at each corner of his bier. The embalming of his body was undertaken by the chief Soviet embalmer Dr Sergei Debrov, who also worked on such communist luminaries as Klement Gottwald (President of Czechoslovakia), Georgi Dimitrov (Prime Minister of Bulgaria) and Forbes Burnham (President of Guyana). Debrov was flown to Hanoi from Moscow as Ho Chi Minh lay dying, bringing with him two transport planes packed with air conditioners and other equipment. To escape US bombing, the team moved Uncle Ho to a cave, taking a full year to complete the embalming process. The embalming and eternal display of Ho Chi Minh's body was however contrary to his own wishes: he wanted to be cremated and his ashes placed in three urns to be positioned atop three unmarked hills in the north, centre and south of the country.

Ba Dinh Square
In front of Ho Chi Minh's Mausoleum is Ba Dinh Square where he read out the Vietnamese Declaration of Independence on 2 September 1945. Following Ho Chi Minh's declaration, 2 September became Vietnam's National Day. Coincidentally 2 September was also the date on which he died in 1969, although his death was not officially announced until 3 September. In front of the mausoleum on Bac Son Street is the **Dai Liet Si**, a memorial to the heroes and martyrs who died fighting for their country's independence. It appears to be modelled as a secular form of stupa and inside is a large bronze urn. The new parliament building, completed in 2014, now also stands proud directly across from the mausoleum.

Ho Chi Minh's house and the Presidential Palace

Ho Chi Minh's house, 1 Bach Thao St, T4-3804 4529; Summer Tue-Thu, Sat and Sun, 0730-1100, 1400-1600, Fri 0730-1100; winter Tue-Thu, Sat and Sun 0800-1100, 1330-1600, Fri 0800-1100, 20,000d; the Presidential Palace is not open to the public.

From the mausoleum, visitors are directed to Ho Chi Minh's house built in the compound of the former Presidential Palace. The palace, now a Party guesthouse, was the residence of the Governors-General of French Indochina and was built between 1900 and 1908 by Auguste-Henri Vildieu. In 1954, when North Vietnam's struggle for independence was finally achieved, Ho Chi Minh declined to live in the palace, saying that it belonged to the people. Instead, he stayed in what is said to have been an electrician's house in the same compound. Here he lived from 1954 to 1958, before moving to a new stilt house built on the other side of the small lake (Ho Chi Minh's 'Fish Farm', swarming with massive and well-fed carp). The house was designed by Ho Chi Minh and an architect, Nguyen Van Ninh. This modest house made of rare hardwoods is airy and personal and immaculately kept. Ho Chi Minh conducted meetings under the house, which is raised up on wooden pillars, and slept and worked above (his books, slippers and telephones are still here) from May 1958 to August 1969. Built by the army, the house mirrors the one he lived in while fighting the French from his haven near the Chinese border. Behind the house is his bomb shelter, and behind that, the hut where he actually died in 1969.

One Pillar Pagoda

Close by is the One Pillar Pagoda (Chua Mot Cot), one of the few structures remaining from the original foundation of the city. It was built in 1049 by Emperor Ly Thai Tong, although the shrine has since been rebuilt on several occasions, most recently in 1955 after the French destroyed it before withdrawing from the country. The emperor built the pagoda in a fit of religious passion after he dreamt that he saw the goddess Quan Am (Vietnam's equivalent of the Chinese goddess Kuan-yin) sitting on a lotus and holding a young boy, whom she handed to the emperor. On the advice of counsellors who interpreted the dream, the Emperor built this little lotus-shaped temple in the centre of a water-lily pond and shortly afterwards his queen gave birth to a son. As the name suggests, it is supported on a single (concrete) pillar with a brick and stone staircase running up one side. The pagoda symbolizes the 'pure' lotus sprouting from the sea of sorrow. Original in design, with dragons running along the apex of the elegantly curved tiled roof, the temple is one of the most revered monuments in Vietnam. But the ungainly concrete pillar and the pond of green slime in which it is embedded detract considerably from the enchantment of the little pagoda.

Ho Chi Minh Museum

19 Ngoc Ha St, T4-3846 3752, Tue-Thu and Sat 0800-1130, 1400-1600, Fri 0800-1130, 20,000d.

Overshadowing the One Pillar Pagoda is the Ho Chi Minh Museum – opened in 1990 in celebration of the centenary of Ho Chi Minh's birth. Contained in a large and impressive modern building, likened to a white lotus, its displays trace Ho's life and work from his early wanderings around the world to his death and final victory over the south.

★ Temple of Literature

The entrance on Quoc Tu Giam St, T4-3845 2917, open daily summer 0730-1730, winter daily 0730-1700, 20,000d, 45-min tour in French or English 100,000d, 8000d for brochure.

The Temple of Literature (Van Mieu Pagoda) is the largest, and probably the most important, temple complex in Hanoi. It was founded in 1070 by Emperor Ly Thanh Tong, dedicated to Confucius who had a substantial following in Vietnam, and modelled, so it is said, on a temple in Shantung, China, the birthplace of the sage. Some researchers, while acknowledging the date of foundation, challenge the view that it was built as a Confucian institution pointing to the ascendancy of Buddhism during the Ly Dynasty. Confucian principles and teaching rapidly replaced Buddhism, however, and Van Mieu subsequently became the intellectual and spiritual centre of the kingdom as a cult of literature and education spread among the court, the mandarins and then among the common people. At one time there were said to be 20,000 schools teaching the Confucian classics in northern Vietnam alone.

The temple and its compound are arranged north–south, and visitors enter at the southern end from Quoc Tu Giam Street. On the pavement two pavilions house stelae bearing the inscription *ha ma* (climb down from your horse), a nice reminder that even the most elevated dignitaries had to proceed on foot. The main **Van Mieu Gate** (Cong Van Mieu Mon) is adorned with 15th-century dragons. Traditionally, the large central gate was opened only on ceremonial occasions. The path leads through the Cong Dai Trung to a second courtyard and the **Van Khue Gac Pavilion**, which was built in 1805 and dedicated to the Constellation of Literature. The roof is tiled according to the yin-yang principle.

Beyond lies the **Courtyard of the Stelae** at the centre of which is the rectangular pond or Cieng Thien Quang (Well of Heavenly Clarity). More important are the stelae themselves, 82 in all, on which are recorded the names of 1306 successful examination scholars (*tien si*). Of the 82 that survive (30 are missing) the oldest dates back to 1442 and the most recent to 1779. Each stela is carried on the back of a tortoise, symbol of strength and longevity but they are arranged in no order; three chronological categories, however, can be identified. Fourteen date from the 15th and 16th centuries; they are the smallest and are embellished with floral motifs and yin-yang symbols but not dragons (a royal emblem). Twenty-five stelae are from the 17th century and are ornamented with dragons (by then permitted), pairs of phoenix and other creatures mythical or real. The remaining 43 stelae are of 18th-century origin; they are the largest and are decorated with two stylized dragons, some merging with flame clouds.

Passing the examination was not easy: in 1733, out of some 3000 entrants, only eight passed the doctoral examination (*Thai Hoc Sinh*) and became Mandarins – a task that took 35 days. This tradition was begun in 1484 on the instruction of Emperor Le Thanh Tong, and continued through to 1878, during which time 116 examinations were held. The Temple of Literature was not used only for examinations, however: food was also distributed to the poor and infirm, 500 g of rice at a time. In 1880, the French Consul Monsieur de Kergaradec recorded that 22,000 impoverished people came to receive this meagre handout.

Continuing north, the **Dai Thanh Mon** (Great Success Gate) leads on to a courtyard flanked by two buildings which date from 1954, the originals having been destroyed in 1947. These buildings were reserved for 72 disciples of Confucius. Facing is the **Dai Bai Duong** (Great House of Ceremonies), which was built in the 19th century but in the earlier style of the Le Dynasty. The carved wooden friezes with their dragons, phoenix, lotus flowers, fruits, clouds and yin-yang discs are all symbolically charged, depicting the order of the universe and by implication reflecting the god-given hierarchical nature of human society, each in his place. It is not surprising that the communist government has hitherto had reservations about preserving a temple extolling such heretical doctrine. Inside is an altar on which sit statues of Confucius and his closest disciples. Adjoining is the **Dai Thanh Sanctuary** (Great Success Sanctuary), which also contains a statue of Confucius.

To the north once stood the first university in Vietnam, Quoc Tu Giam, which from the 11th to 18th centuries educated first the heir to the throne and later sons of mandarins. It was replaced with a temple dedicated to Confucius' parents and followers, which was itself destroyed in 1947.

Fine Arts Museum
66 Nguyen Thai Hoc St, T4-3733 2131, Tue-Sun 0830-1700, Wed and Sat 0800-2100. Free tours in English or French, register in advance, no photography. Restaurant in museum grounds.

Not far from the northern walls of the Van Mieu Pagoda is the Fine Arts Museum (Bao Tang My Thuat), contained in a large colonial building. The oriental roof was added later when the building was converted to a museum. The ground-floor galleries display pre-20th-century art – from Dongsonian bronze drums to Nguyen Dynasty paintings and sculpture, although many works of this later period are on display in the Museum of Royal Fine Arts in Hué. There are some particularly fine stone Buddhas. The first floor is given over to folk art. There are some lovely works from the Central Highlands and engaging Dong Ho woodblock prints – one block for each colour – and Hang Trong woodblock prints, a single black ink print that is coloured in by hand. There are also some fine lacquer paintings. The top floor contains 20th-century work including some excellent watercolours and oil paintings. Contemporary Vietnamese artists are building a significant reputation for their work. There is a large collection of overtly political work, posters and propaganda (of great interest to historians and specialist collectors), and a collection of ethnic minority clothes is exhibited in the annex.

Vietnam Military History Museum and Citadel
28 Dien Bien Phu St, T4-3733 6453, www.btlsqsvn.org.vn, Tue-Thu, Sat and Sun 0800-1130, 1300-1630, 20,000d, camera use, 5000d, ATM and Highlands Coffee Café on site.

A five-minute walk east from the Fine Arts Museum is the Military History Museum (Bao Tang Quan Doi). Tanks, planes and artillery fill the courtyard. Symbolically, an untouched Mig-21 stands at the museum entrance while wreckage of B-52s, F1-11s and Q2Cs is piled up at the back. The museum illustrates battles and episodes in Vietnam's fight for independence from the struggles with China (there is a good display of the Battle of Bach Dang River of AD 938) through to the resistance to the French and the Battle of Dien Bien Phu (illustrated by a good model). Inevitably, of course, there are lots of photographs and exhibits of the American War and although much is self-evident, unfortunately a lot of the explanations are in Vietnamese only.

In the precincts of the museum is the Cot Co, a flag tower, raised up on three platforms. Built in 1812, it is the only substantial part of the original citadel still standing. There are good views over Hanoi from the top. The walls of the **citadel** were destroyed by the French in 1894 to 1897, presumably as they symbolized the power of the Vietnamese emperors. The French were highly conscious of the projection of might, power and authority through large structures, which helps explain their own remarkable architectural legacy. Across the road from the museum's front entrance is a **statue of Lenin**.

★ The Citadel

The UNESCO listed Citadel complex received protected status in 2010 honouring the site's importance as a military base for centuries. Work began in the 11th century on the Thang Long citadel complex by Emperor Ly Thai To. The site is home to more modern additions too, including the concrete bunker in which general Giap and his fellow officers planned their campaigns against the US invaders in the South. An exhibition space features old artefacts found when construction of the new Assembly building and also some interesting old pictures of the area. Apart from the history, this is one of the capital's most peaceful enclaves and the grounds are a lovely place to wander and enjoy some (relative) quiet. Long closed to the public, this is a relatively new tourist site in the capital and a great addition, especially for history buffs.

Vietnamese Women's Museum

36 Ly Thuong Kiet St, T4-3825 9936, www.baotangphunu.org.vn, daily 0900-1630, closed Mon, 30,000d.

A well-curated, fascinating museum containing 25,000 objects and documents that give visitors an excellent insight in to women's roles in Vietnam, past and present. Information on many of the country's 54 ethnic groups is displayed. It holds regular exhibitions and is highly recommended.

Outer Hanoi

lakes, temples and museums worth exploring

★ North of the Old City

North of the Old City is **Ho Truc Bach** (**White Silk Lake**). Truc Bach Lake was created in the 17th century by building a causeway across the southeast corner of Ho Tay. At the southwest corner of the lake, on the intersection of Hung Vuong, Quan Thanh and Thanh Nien streets is the **Quan Thanh Pagoda** was originally built in the early 11th century in honour of Huyen Thien Tran Vo (a genie) but since has been much remodelled. Despite renovation, it is still very beautiful. The large bronze bell was cast in 1677.

The much larger **Ho Tay** (**West Lake**) was originally a meander in the Red River. The **Tran Quoc Pagoda**, an attractive brick-red building, can be found on an islet linked to the causeway by a walkway. It was originally built on the banks of the Red River before being transferred to its present site by way of an intermediate location. The pagoda contains a stela dated 1639 recounting its unsettled history. It is a popular place of worship and sees massive crowds around Tet (New Year). Just south, pedaloes called 'dap vit' are available for hire. Opposite, facing Truc Bach Lake, is a monument recording the shooting down of USAF's John (now US Senator) McCain on 26 October 1967. It reveals the pilot falling out of the sky, knees bent.

A few kilometres north, on the tip of a promontory, stands **Tay Ho Pagoda**, notable chiefly for its setting. It is reached along a narrow lane lined with stalls selling fruit, roses and paper votives and a dozen restaurants serving giant snails with bun oc (noodles) and fried shrimp cakes. Dominating it is an enormous bronze bell held by a giant dragon hook supported by concrete dragons and two elephants; notice the realistic glass eyes of the elephants.

★Museum of Ethnology and B-52 memorials

Some distance west of the city centre in Cau Giay District (Nguyen Van Huyen Rd), T4-3756 2193, www.vme.org.vn, Tue-Sun 0830-1730, 25,000d, photography 50,000d, tour guide, 50,000d. Catch No 14 minibus from Dinh Tien Hoang St, north of Hoan Kiem Lake, to the Nghia Tan stop; turn right and walk down Hoang Quoc Viet St for 1 block, before turning right at the Petrolimex station down Nguyen Van Huyen; the museum is down this street, on the left. Alternatively take a taxi. Branch of Baguette & Chocolat bakery on site.

The museum opened in November 1997 in a modern, purpose-built structure. The collection here of some 25,000 artefacts, 15,000 photographs and documentaries of practices and rituals is excellent and, more to the point, is attractively and informatively presented with labels in Vietnamese, English and French. It displays the material culture (textiles, musical instruments, jewellery, tools, baskets and the like) of the majority Kinh people as well as Vietnam's 53 other designated minority peoples. The highlight is wandering the gardens at the rear where ethnic minority homes have been moved from their original homes and painstakingly re-built. There is a very good shop attached to the museum.

On the routes out to the Ethnology Museum are two B-52 memorials. The remains of downed B-52s have been hawked around Hanoi over many years but seem to have found a final resting place at the **Bao Tang Chien Tang B-52 (B-52 Museum)** ⓘ *157 Doi Can St, free.* This curious place is not really a museum but a military hardware graveyard, but this doesn't matter because what everyone wants to do is walk over the wings and tail of a shattered B-52, and the B-52 in question lies scattered around the yard. The size and strength of the B-52 is simply incredible and needs to be seen to be believed.

On Hoang Hoa Tham Street, between Nos 55 and 57, a sign points 100 m down an alley to the wreckage of a B-52 bomber sticking up out of the pond-like Huu Tiep Lake. There's a plaque on the wall stating that at 2305 on 27 December 1972, Battalion 72 of Regiment 285 shot down the plane. At the time Huu Tiep was a flower village and the lake a lot bigger.

Perfume Pagoda

50,000d entrance plus 40,000d/person for the boat (maximum 6 people). Taking a tour is the best way to get here.

The Perfume Pagoda (Chua Huong or Chua Huong Tich) is 60 km southwest of Hanoi. A sampan takes visitors along the Yen River, a diverting 4-km ride through a flooded landscape to the Mountain of the Perfume Traces. From here it is a 3-km hike up the mountain to the cool, dark cave wherein lies the Perfume Pagoda. Dedicated to Quan Am, it is one of a number of shrines and towers built among limestone caves, and it is regarded as one of the most beautiful spots in Vietnam. The stone statue of Quan Am in the principal pagoda was carved in 1793 after Tay Son rebels had stolen and melted down its bronze predecessor to make cannon balls. Emperor Le Thanh Tong (1460-1497) described it as "Nam Thien de nhat dong" (foremost cave under the Vietnamese sky). It is a popular pilgrimage spot, particularly during the festival months of March and April.

Tourist information

Tourist Information Center
7 Dinh Tien Hoang St, at the northern end of the lake, T4-3926 3366, www.ticvietnam.com. Daily 0800-2200.
Provides information and maps and will book hotels and transport tickets at no extra cost; also currency exchange and ATM. Good tourist information is available from the multitude of tour operators in the city, see also page 58.

Where to stay

There has been a spate of hotel building and renovation in recent years and Hanoi is now home to an excellent variety of high-quality accommodation for every budget. Cheaper hotels tend to be found in the Old Quarter.

Hoan Kiem Lake and Central Hanoi

$$$$ Sofitel Legend Metropole Hanoi
15 Ngo Quyen St, T4-3826 6919, www.sofitel.com.
The French-colonial-style cream building with green shutters is beautifully and lusciously furnished and exudes style. It boasts a diversity of bars and restaurants including the Italian **Angelina** restaurant. **Le Beaulieu** is one of the finest restaurants in Hanoi; a pianist plays nightly at **Le Club** bar. The **Le Spa du Metropole** is seriously chic. There's also a business centre, cluster of luxury shops and smart deli, and a small pool with attractive poolside **Bamboo Bar**. The hotel has retained most of its business despite competition from newer business hotels away from the city centre and remains a hub of activity and the classiest hotel address in the country. The Graham Greene suite is sumptuous Indochine chic.

$$$ Cinnamon Hotel
26 Au Trieu St, T4-3993 8430, www.cinnamonhotel.net.

This is a stylish boutique hotel with lovely, comfortable rooms. Part of a small chain with other hotels elsewhere in Hanoi and down in Saigon. The regular bong of the cathedral bell may be disturbing so you may wish to avoid the cute balconied rooms overlooking the cathedral square and opt for a back room with a lesser view.

$$$ Golden Lotus Hotel
39 Hang Trong St, T4-3928 8583, www.goldenlotushotel.com.vn.
The **Golden Lotus** has a series of smart, attractive rooms from standard single to deluxe. Dark woods, smart white linens and black and white photography create a smart space.

$$ Joseph's Hotel
5 Au Trieu St, T4-3938 1048, www.josephshotel.com.
Right near St Joseph's Cathedral, on Au Trieu St – a cosy street filled with good cafés, salons and souvenir shops – **Joseph's Hotel** is small, with just 10 smart, very clean rooms. Some rooms have a great view over the cathedral at the rear and others have tiny balconies facing the street. Recommended.

$$ Paradise Boutique Hotel
62A Hang Bac St, T4-3935 1556, www.paradiseboutiquehotel.com.
Right in the heart of the Old Quarter, this small hotel offers a range of clean rooms, each with a desk and a computer, bright white linens and good en suite bathroom. Some rooms have little balconies giving great views over the buzzing street below. Despite the central location, the rooms remain very quiet thanks to some serious double glazing. Extremely friendly staff who make a point of remembering guests' names. Highly recommended at this price.

$ Gold Spring Hotel
22 Nguyen Huu Huan St, T4-3926 3057, www.goldspringhotel.com.vn.

On the edge of the Old Quarter. 22 fine rooms that are simply decorated. Breakfast and free internet included. Good value.

$ Maison d'Orient
26 Ngo Huyen (off Hang Trong), T4-3938 2539, www.maison-orient.com.
This is a real find in the budget range. Designed by an award-winning architect, it's a unique place with one-off furniture, propaganda prints and lots of pretty touches such as red lacquer lamps and colonial-era easy chairs. There is also a beautiful breakfast room and the location is excellent. Highly recommended.

South of Hoan Kiem Lake

$$$$ Hilton Hanoi Opera
1 Le Thanh Tong St, T4-3933 0500, www1.hilton.com.
Opened in 1999 and built adjacent to, and architecturally sympathetically with, the Opera House. It is a splendid building and provides the highest levels of service and hospitality.

$$$$ Meliá Hanoi
44B Ly Thuong Kiet St, T4-3934 3343, www.meliahanoi.com.
A huge tower block in Central Hanoi. Well-appointed rooms. Popular venue for international conferences. Excellent buffets and brunches.

$$$$ Movenpick
83A Ly Thuong Kiet St, T4-3822 2800, www.movenpick-hotels.com.
Formerly the **Guoman** this Swiss-run hotel chain is housed in an attractive building on Ly Thuong Kiet Street, in the middle of Hanoi's business district. Rooms are smart and stylish.

$$$ Zephyr
4 Ba Trieu St, T4-3934 1256, www.zephyrhotel.com.vn.
A little business-like, but nonetheless very popular hotel, largely due to its excellent location within sight of Hoan Kiem Lake

and solid service. Serves a good breakfast, including *pho* and international options.

Outer Hanoi
Hanoi's relatively small central district means that some new office complexes and hotels have tended to open a short distance out of the centre.

$$$$ InterContinental Hanoi Westlake
1A Nghi Tam, Tay Ho District, T4-6270 8888, www.ichotelsgroup.com/intercontinental.
This is a brilliant hotel and one of Vietnam's finest with its fantastic over-water rooms and great views of the lake. Rooms are large and decorated using traditional Vietnamese elements. Fantastic buffet breakfast and impeccable service. The **Sunset Bar** here is a great place for a sundowner. Wonderful pool area too. Highly recommended.

$$$$ Sheraton Hotel
K5 Nghi Tam, 11 Xuan Dieu, Tay Ho District, T4-3719 9000, wwwsheraton.com/hanoi.
Opened in early 2004, the **Sheraton** has a scenic spot overlooking West Lake. It offers luxurious rooms and the swimming pool backs onto a lawn that leads down to the lakeshore.

$$$$ Sofitel Plaza Hanoi
1 Thanh Nien St, T4-3823 8888, www.Sofitel.com.
The 2nd Sofitel in town, it lacks the cache of the **Metropole** but is in an equally good location, by Truc Bach Lake. The rooftop bar, Summit Lounge, has the best views in town and is a must-visit for sunset cocktails.

$$$ La Maison Hai Ly
No 8, 437 Ngoc Thuy, Long Bien, T4-3976 6246.
On the far side of Long Bien Bridge, this is an extraordinarily beautiful replica of an 18th-century Hoi An house standing in a private flower garden. The property includes polished wood floors and a huge glass front with views on to a garden from a grand living area. Very elegant and very highly recommended for those seeking something truly unique.

Restaurants

Hanoi has one of the best street food cultures in the world and a growing band of great Western-style restaurants offering everything from excellent steaks to tapas and wood-fired pizzas. Korean and Japanese food is abundant and well priced.

Hoan Kiem Lake and Central Hanoi

$$$ Le Beaulieu
15 Ngo Quyen St (in the Metropole Hotel), T4-3826 6919.
A place to treat yourself in the wonderful surrounds of the classic Metropole, this is a good French and international restaurant open for breakfast, lunch and dinner. Its Sun brunch buffet is regarded as one of the best. A great selection of French seafood, oysters, prawns, cold and roast meats and cheese.

$$$ Pots n Pans
57 Bui Thi Xuan, T4-3944 0204, www.potsnpans.vn. Daily 1130-late.
An offshoot of the **KOTO** training school restaurant, this minimalist upmarket fusion restaurant serves some of the capital's most innovative cuisine. Also offers an excellent wine list and well-mixed cocktails. Best to dine on a weekend when it is busier – be sure to book ahead.

$$$ Verticale
19 Ngo Van So St, T4-3944 6317, verticale@ didiercorlou.com. Open 0900-1400, 1700-2400.
Didier Corlou, former chef at the **Sofitel Metropole**, runs this restaurant. The tall multi-storey building includes a shop, restaurant, private rooms and a terrace bar. The food and presentation are an adventurous culinary journey of gustatory delight; this is certainly one of the best dining experiences in the city for those who like high-end dining.

$$$-$$ La Badiane
10 Nam Ngu St, T4-3942 4509.
Run by a couple of Hanoi old hands, **La Badiane's** French aesthetic stops

at the food. Fusion is what this restaurant is about and while its intricately decorated plates of seasonal meals won't appeal to everyone there are many who swear this is the best restaurant in town. Service is good, if over-attentive at times. The converted colonial villa is delightful. The set lunch menu is a very good deal indeed.

$$$-$ Green Tangerine
48 Hang Be St, T4-3825 1286, greentangerine@vnn.vn.
This is a fanciful and rather touristy restaurant that is worth a visit for the courtyard seating or the indoor dining area with its lovely spiral staircase, wafting fans, tasselled curtains and abundant glassware. It's a Hanoi stalwart in a lovely 1928 house in the centre of the Old Quarter serving slightly fruit-heavy fusion and Vietnamese food. Best to come for the good value set lunch as the evening à la carte menu is a little overpriced for the quality.

$$ Luna d'Autonno
Nam Ngu St, T4-3823 7338.
Regarded as one of the city's best Italian restaurants, **Luna** has a large menu and the pizzas – particularly the *diavola* – are excellent.

$$ Moose and Roo
42 Ma May, T4-3200 1289. Daily 1000-late.
Opened in 2014, this Aussie-run joint has quickly established itself as a firm favourite with expats. The pork hash is delectable, the burgers are first-rate and the Sunday roasts are the finest in town. Also runs the **Smoke House** at the American Club on Hai Ba Trung where massive ribs and hunks of barbecued beef are drawing accolades.

$$ Namaste
49 Tho Nhuom, T4-3935 2400, www. namastehanoi.com. Daily 1100-late.
Run by Mr Gopi this is a runner for best Indian in town. It lacks the views of **Foodshop 45**, but it serves a range of excellent curries including a great balti, and the lemon rice

is second to none. Good service, but the ambience can be rather lacking.

$$-$ Chim Sáo
65 Ngo Hue St, T4-3976 0633, www.chimsao.com.

Set in an atmospheric old colonial villa, **Chim Sáo** is famous for its Northern Vietnamese food. highlights include the grilled buffalo, ethnic minority sausage, sautéed duck and the pork in a clay pot. Serves good rice wine too – try the apple variety for a milder version. Seating upstairs is on floor cushions, so book a downstairs table if needs be.

$$-$ Highway 4
3 Hang Tre St, T4-3926 4200, www.highway4.com. Open 0900-0200.

With funky decor and a variety of different cosy dining rooms, Highway 4 specializes in ethnic minority dishes from North Vietnam and also serves dishes from around the country. The popularity of the Highway 4 concept has seen it spread across Hanoi and as far afield as Hoi An. Also serves a great range of local rice wines from Son Tinh.

$$-$ Quan An Ngon
18 Phan Boi Chau St, T4-3942 8162, www. ngonhanoi.com.vn. Daily 0700-2130.

This place is insanely popular at lunch and dinner time with locals as well as tourists. In a massive and very pretty open-air courtyard setting with enormous umbrellas shading wooden tables. Diners can wander around looking at all the street food style stalls each making just 1 or 2 of the dishes from the vast menu. This is a great place for an introduction to food from all over Vietnam. There are now sister branches around town – check the website for addresses.

$$-$ Ray Quan
8A Nguyen Khuyen, T9-1357 8588. Daily 1100-late.

It is reached by literally walking along the train tracks from Hai Ba Trung St). This quirky place offers the option to dine feet away from the trains as they thunder past. Serves a fantastic array of Vietnamese dishes from the mainstream to some very curious options. Also has one of the best rice wine menus in town including a very good cinnamon version… you've been warned!

$ Café 129
129 Mai Hac De St.

A real oddity, this is a hole-in-the-wall place run by Vietnamese ladies serving huge US, Canadian and English breakfasts alongside filling Mexican meals. Chiefly popular with the English teacher set.

$ Com Chay Nang Tam
79A Tran Hung Dao St, T4-3942 4140. Open 1100-1400, 1700-2200.

A hit with veggies, this is hidden down an alley off Tran Hung Dao St and serves excellent and inexpensive dishes in a small, family-style dining room.

$ Net Hue
36C Mai Hac De, T4-3944 9769, www.nethue.com.vn. Daily 1030-2200.

Excellent classic Hué dishes including *bun bo nam no* and a superb *bun thit nuong*. Order a few dishes to share. Rather raucous at lunch times with crowds of office workers. There are a number of **Net Hue** restaurants – see the website.

Cafés

Hanoi probably has more cafés per square foot than anywhere in the world. Almost every street has at least one simple café with tiny plastic stools on which Hanoians enjoy a *ca phd da* (iced coffee) in warmer months or a *ca phe nong* (hot) in winter. Until a few years ago there was very little other than these old school coffee houses, but recently the caffeine scene has exploded with modern local and foreign run cafés completing the more traditional options. Alongside this, the likes of **Coffee Bean** and **Tea Leaf** and **Starbucks** are attempting to muscle into the market, but the Hanoian's love of Vietnamese coffee and quirky one-off coffee shops means the individuality of the coffee culture looks set to remain strong. For a local café experience, it is best to simply wander the streets of the Old Quarter, take a stroll along Trieu Viet Vuong or check out the road lining Truc Bach Lake – there are hundreds of places to choose from.

Café Puku

16/18 Tong Duy Tan St, T4-3928 5244.
An old favourite, **Puku** was one of the first modern, Western-style cafés to open. Alongside coffee it serves a good range of comfort food. It is also now open 24 hrs and there is a sports bar upstairs at the rear.

Cong Café

152D Trieu Viet Vuong St.
This is the original **Cong Café** but there now upwards of 12 scattered around town and as far afield as Danang. Hugely popular thanks to the great retro/military design as well as excellent coffee and smoothies. Other good Congs can be found on Dien Bien Phu, Quan Su, opposite St Joseph's Cathedral and at Truc Bach.

Hanoi Social Club

6 Hoi Vu, T4-9382117, facebook.com/ TheHanoiSocialClub.
On one of Hanoi's quieter little lanes, this Aussie-Viet partnership is a major hit. Set over 3 floors in an old town house with beautiful caustic tiled floors and comfy, funky furniture with art, music posters, and great tunes. Serves a small menu of quality international dishes and first-rate coffee. Also sells books, courtesy of **The Bookworm** store. Great roof terrace. Regular live music.

The Kafe

18 Dien Bien Phu, T4-3747 6245, www.thekafe.vn. Daily 0800-late.
Popular with Hanoi's younger crowd and hipster set, **The Kafe** has a bright, airy indoor space with whitewashed walls and light wooden tables plus a small outdoor terrace area. Alongside the drinks is a food menu that resembles a Jamie Oliver cookbook with

a range of tapas style dishes, plus burgers, fried chicken and some great salads. The freshly made fruit juices and shakes are excellent – try the carrot and apple. Also now has a sister branch, the **Kafe Village**, over at 4 Ha Hoi.

Manzi

14 Phan Huy Ich, T4-3716 3397. Daily 0900-late.
Housed in a beautiful old colonial villa, **Manzi** is part café, part gallery and part art shop. Owned by artists and run for the artistic community, it hosts shows and talks. The coffee is good, the staff are friendly and the space is gorgeous, with whitewashed walls allowing the artwork to shine.

Ice cream

Fanny Ice Cream

Ly Thuong Khiet St, T4-3828 5656, www.fanny.com.vn.
A huge range of ice creams and sorbet with an ice cream buffet on weekends.

Kem Trang Tien

35 Trang Tien St.
This is probably the most popular ice cream parlour in the city and it's a drive-in and park your moto affair. It's also a flirt joint for Hanoian young things. Flavours are cheap and change as to what's available.

Ho Chi Minh's Mausoleum complex and around

$$-$ KOTO

59 Van Mieu St, T4-3747 0337, www.koto. com.au. Mon 0730-1800, Tue-Sun 0730-2230.
A training restaurant for underprivileged young people. Next to the **Temple of Literature** so an ideal place to pop in for a good lunch after a morning's sightseeing. The food is international, filling and delicious. Upstairs is the **Temple Bar** serving good cocktails. Recommended.

Outer Hanoi

The following places are located north of the old city.

$$$ El Gaucho
99 Xuan Dieu, T4-3718 6991,
www.elgaucho.asia.
Perhaps the best steak in town – all the cuts negate the need for any of the sauces on offer and certainly merit the journey from the city centre. The chicken dishes are less inspiring, however – stick to the beef. Cool, bare-brick surroundings. Superb cocktails and a good cellar.

$$$-$$ Cousins
Quang Ba on Quang An, T12-3867 0098.
Daily 0900-late.
Tucked away at the north of West Lake, is a French-run bistro offering an interesting range of European dishes and daily specials. Slightly hipster and arty vibe, but welcoming with a lovely outdoor courtyard space. Good wine list and a decent house red. A recommended stop on your Tay Ho excursion.

$$$-$$ Republic
7A Quang An, T4-6687 1773,
www.republic.vn.
Part bar, part restaurant, **Republic** is another of the new places to take advantage of the lake front location along Quang An. Highlights of the menu include the pies with superbly light crusts and the fish and chips. The only real downside is the starters are bizarrely expensive. Gets very busy on weekends when DJs play later on.

$$ Da Paulo
18 Lane 50 Dang Thai Mai St, T4-3718 6317.
Daily 1100-late.
The location of this Italian restaurant is unrivalled looking out across the West Lake. Serves great food across the board from pizzas to pastas. On a fine day it is nicer to sit at a nearby café right on the lake and order the excellent wood fired pizzas takeaway and enjoy them with a cool lemon *sinh to* (shake) with the breeze blowing off the water. Inside, the upstairs area is cosier than downstairs.

$$ Hanoi Cooking Centre
44 Chau Long St, T4-3715 0088,
www.hanoicookingcentre.com.
Lunch and breakfast only. A restaurant, café and cooking centre housed in a restored colonial villa near Truc Bach Lake. Some good Vietnamese options and also an excellent fish and chips and a solid falafel. Serves some of the best coffee in town too with a particularly good latte. Great staff. The upper floor can also be hired for functions.

$$ La Bicicleta
44 Alley 31 Xuan Dieu St, T4-3718 8246.
Open 1130-late, closed Mon.
This restaurant started life as a bike shop, with the Catalan owner, Guim, converting it when his cravings for authentic Barcelona tapas became too strong. Also serves hot chocolate with churros and massive gins and tonics. Not the easiest place to find deep down an alleyway, but it is now signposted off Quang An and Xuan Dieu streets.

$$ Maison Tet Decor
36 Duong Ven Ho, T9-6661 1383, www.tet-lifestyle-collection.com. Open 0700-2300.
Bursting with character, this is a popular Tay Ho neighbourhood spot thanks to its excellent coffee, wonderful decor, home-made cakes and quiches and a solid wine list. Most of the produce is sourced from a dedicated organic farm not far from the capital.

$$ Pho Yen
66 Cua Bac St, T4-3715 0269.
This down-at-heel tables and chair joint does tasty *pho cuon*. Popular with locals.

$$-$ Chien Beo
192 Nghi Tam St, T4-3716 1461.
A Vietnamese steakhouse named after the rather portly owner who clearly enjoys his product. Serves huge platters of beef and other meats. Best to come in a group as the portions are gargantuan. Can get quite rowdy.

$ Foodshop 45
59 Truc Bach St.

A Vietnamese-run Indian restaurant with a very pretty location on Truc Bach Lake. Consistently good food for years and very welcoming, swift service. Don't miss the chicken kalmi kebab.

Bars and clubs

Hanoi's main bar street is Ta Hien, heading towards Hang Buom after it has cut across the famous Bia Hoi Corner (at Luong Ngoc Quyen). The bar scene here has exploded in recent years and now there are too many to count and the atmosphere almost every night is buzzing.

+84
23 Ngo Van So, T3-943 4540. Daily 0900-late.

Run by some of the people behind Barbetta, this bar wouldn't look out of place in East London with its bare brick walls, dark red paint and well-stocked bar. Has live music 3 or 4 nights a week and a good vibe.

Barbetta
34C Cao Ba Quat, T4-3734 9134.

Barbetta is one of a kind. Inside it's chock full of retro knick knacks, from TV sets to type writers, while the rooftop terrace is a great spot for a well-mixed cocktail (if Cuong is behind the bar at least).

CAMA ATK
Mai Hac De. Wed-Sat 1800-2400.
Happy hour 1800-2000.

Run by the boys behind Hanoi's music promotion collective – CAMA – this is a very welcome addition. Superb cocktails, regular DJ sets and film nights. No smoking.

GC
5A Bao Khanh St, T4-3825 0499.

A popular 'gay friendly' bar a few doors away from **Polite Pub**, the GC (orginally the **Golden Cock**) has been around a long time and is still crowded years on.

Hanoi Rock City
27 To Ngoc Van, T9-1351 5356,
www.hanoirockcity.com.

Around the corner from Madake in the heart of expat-ville, 'HRC' is run by a Vietnamese-British partnership with a focus on live music, DJ nights and art shows. Has a great courtyard with an open fire. Depending on the night the atmosphere can be buzzing or chilled out. A great venue.

Hoa Vien
1 Tang Bat Ho St, T4-3972 5088.

Possibly the biggest and best-known of Hanoi's European-style beer halls, **Hoa Vien** is a multi-level behemoth serving beer in glasses ranging from standard to 1 litre steins. Pilsner and dark beer are both on offer as well as heart-clogging wonders such as Russian salad and pork cutlets.

Madake
81 Xuan Dieu, T4-6276 6665. Daily 0930-late.

A very welcome addition to the DJ and live music scene in the capital, **Madake** is a venue of 3 parts. The upstairs bar has a minimalist vibe, the leafy outdoor courtyard backs onto a small lake and the main music room is a brilliantly intimate space for live music with a quality sound system.

Phuc Tan Bar
Phuc Tan St, T915-9077 8551.

An out and out dive bar club. Come the weekend there are precious few places open very late at night where you can both drink and dance. Out the back **Phuc Tan** has a gorgeous view over the Red River, large outdoor seating area and a barbecue. This is where the expats end up when **Madake** and **Rock City** have kicked out and there are plenty of locals on the dance floor too.

Polite Pub
5 Bao Khanh St, T4-3825 0959.

Recently renovated, **Polite** now stocks an excellent range of single malt whisky and a good choice of bourbons. The old policy of cranking bad music has been ditched and a

Tet is the traditional New Year. The biggest celebration of the year, the word Tet is the shortened version of *tet nguyen dan* (first morning of the new period). Tet is the time to forgive and forget and to pay off debts. It is also everyone's birthday – the Vietnamese tend not to celebrate their birthdays; instead everyone adds a year to their age at Tet. Enormous quantities of food are consumed (this is not the time to worry about money), new clothes are bought, houses painted and repaired and firecrackers lit to welcome in the New Year – at least they were until the government ban imposed in 1995. Cumquat trees are also bought and displayed. They are said to resemble coins and are a symbol of wealth and luck for the coming year. As a Vietnamese saying has it: 'Hungry all year but Tet three days full.' It is believed that before Tet, the spirit of the hearth, Ong Tao, leaves on a journey to visit the palace of the Jade Emperor where he must report on family affairs. To ensure that Ong Tao sets off in good cheer, a ceremony is held before Tet, Le Tao Quan, and during his absence a shrine is constructed (Cay Neu) to keep evil spirits at bay until his return. On the afternoon before Tet, Tat Nien, a sacrifice is offered at the family altar to dead relatives who are invited back to join in the festivities. Great attention is paid to the preparations for Tet, because it is believed that the first week of the New Year dictates the fortunes for the rest of the year. The first visitor to the house on New Year's morning should be an influential, lucky and happy person, so families take care to arrange a suitable caller.

good cigar menu added. The most pub-like of Hanoi's drinking dens.

Summit Lounge
*Sofitel Plaza, 1 Thanh Nien, T4-3823 8888.
Open 1600-2400.*
On the top floor of the **Sofitel Plaza**, **Summit** has the best views in town towering between Truc Bach Lake and West Lake. Aim to enjoy a cocktail here at around 1730. Definitely warrants the price tag.

Tadioto
*24 Tong Dan St, T4-2218 7200,
www.tadioto.com.*
Run by one of the key figures on Hanoi's creative scene, Nguyen Qui Duc, this is a sophisticated yet relaxed bar full of interesting furniture, art and people. Plays good tunes, stocks good whisky and hosts readings and talks on occasion. This is now

Tadioto's 4th incarnation and probably the best yet. Highly recommended.

Cinema
CGV, *Vincom City Towers, 191 Ba Trieu St, T4-3974 3333, www.cgv.vn.* Western films with Vietnamese subtitles in this modern multiplex.
Hanoi Cinematique, *22A Hai Ba Trung St, T4-3936 2648, info2@hanoicinema.org.* This is a wonderfully atmospheric cinema-cum-film club. Membership can be bought on the spot. Film festivals, local documentaries and a nice courtyard to enjoy a drink in.

Dance and theatre
Opera House, *www.hanoioperahouse.org.vn.* Staging a variety of Vietnamese and Western concerts, operas and plays. Check *Vietnam News* or at the box office.

Water Puppet Theatre, *57b Dinh Tien Hoang St, at the northeast corner of Hoan Kiem Lake, T4-3936 4335, www.thanglongwaterpuppet. org*. This traditional Vietnamese art form is not to be missed. Very popular so advanced booking is required at the box office.

Music

The best places for live music are all bars – **Madake**, **Hanoi Rock City** and **CAMA ATK** – see the bars section for details and check the *Hanoi Grapevine* for listings.

Festivals

Jan/Feb **Dong Da Hill festival** (5th day of Tet). Celebrates the battle of Dong Da in which Nguyen Hue routed 200,000 Chinese troops. Processions of dancers carry a flaming dragon of straw.
Perfume Pagoda Festival, 6th day of the 1st lunar month-end of the 3rd lunar month. This focuses on the worship of Quan Am. There are dragon dances and a royal barge sails on the river.
Hai Ba Trung Festival, 3rd-6th day of the 2nd lunar month. The festival commemorates the Trung sisters. On the 3rd day the temple is opened; on the 4th, a funeral ceremony begins; on the 5th the sisters' statues are bathed in a ceremony; on the 6th day a ritual ceremony is held.
Hung Kings' festival, 10th day of the 3rd lunar month. A 2-week celebration when the temple site comes alive as visitors from all over Vietnam descend on the area, as Ho Chi Minh encouraged them to. The place seethes with vendors, food stalls and fairground activities spring up. There are racing swan boats on one of the lakes.
2 Sep **National Day**, featuring parades in Ba Dinh Sq and boat races on Hoan Kiem Lake.

Shopping

The city is a shopper's paradise with cheap silk and good tailors, handicrafts and antiques and some good designer shops.

Hang Gai St is well geared to souvenir hunters and stocks an excellent range of clothes, fabrics and lacquerware. It's rather like the small-time Silk Road of Hanoi. Hats of all descriptions abound. You will not be disappointed.

Antiques

Along **Hang Khay** and **Trang Tien** streets, south edge of Hoan Kiem Lake. Shops sell silver ornaments, porcelain, jewellery and carvings – much is not antique, not all is silver; bargain hard.

Art galleries

Hanoi has always been known as the 'artistic' city compared to Ho Chi Minh's powerhouse economy. Although many galleries do the typical conical hat and buffalo paintings, more galleries stocking the work of serious artists are popping up. Galleries abound near Hoan Kiem Lake, especially **Trang Tien St** and on **Dinh Tien Hoang St** at northeast corner.
Art Vietnam Gallery, *LACA, off Ly Quoc Su, www.artvietnamgallery.com*. Art Director Suzanne Lecht has found a new Old Quarter space here in the **Ly Quoc Su Art and Cafe Area**. It is a fine place to hang her excellently curated exhibits. Lecht represents a number of the country's top artists and has an encyclopaedic knowledge of Vietnam's contemporary art scene.
Hanoi Gallery, *17 Nha Chung St, T4-3928 7943, propaganda_175@yahoo.com*. Sells propaganda posters.
Manzi, *see Cafés*. This space show-cases the work of local and international artists.
Nha San, *LACA, off Ly Quoc Su St, www. nhasanstudio.org*. Run by a group of young artists in this new small cultural quarter. Shows contemporary art and holds talks. Recommended.
Propaganda Art, *8 Nha Chung St, T4-3928 6588*. More propaganda posters and other propaganda items such as mugs and key rings.

Bicycles

Hanoi's bicycle scene has boomed in recent years and now there are scores of good quality bike shops in town. Check out THBC or **Thang Long Cycling** in Tay Ho or **Nam Anh Bikes** at 1A Tran Thanh Tong. For something cheaper, there are plenty of shops along the southern end of Ba Trieu St.

Books and maps

Private booksellers operate on Trang Tien St and have pavement stalls in the evening. On Sun book stalls appear on Dinh Le St, parallel with Trang Tien St. Many travel cafés operate book exchanges.

The Bookworm, *44 Chau Long, T4-3715 3711, www.bookwormhanoi.com*. Excellent collection of books on Vietnam and Southeast Asia, alongside the city's biggest selection of English-language novels.

Foreign Language Bookshop, *61 Trang Tien St*. A reasonable range of English-language books with plenty about Vietnam.

Camera shops

Available all around Hoan Kiem Lake. Several shops have download and printing services for digital cameras. Vu Nhat at 22 Trang Thi is a good shop for cleaning, repair and also sales.

Clothes, fashions, silk and accessories

The greatest concentration is in the Hoan Kiem Lake area particularly on Nha Tho, Nha Chung, Hang Trong and Hang Gai.

Bo Sua, *beside skate shop Boo, 24D Ta Hien St, T4-6657 8086*. Owned by the same people as **Boo**, **Bo Sua** is revolutionary for a Hanoian label. Day-to-day objects, such as coal briquettes, plastic sandals or foamy glasses of *bia hoi* have been turned into stylish T-shirt icons.

Chula, *Nhat Chieu, T4-3710 1102, www.chulafashion.com*. Run by long-term Spanish expat Diego, Chula has striking distinctive designs with a focus on dresses.

Co, *18 Nha Tho St, T4-3928 9925, conhatho@yahoo.com*. Clothes shop with a very narrow entrance. Some unusual prints, the craftsmanship is recommended.

Ginkgo, *44 Hang Be, T4-3936 4769, www.gingko-vietnam.com*. A great place to pick up a Hanoi or Vietnam themed T-shirt. Quality fabrics and great designs.

Ha Truong Studio, *75b Alley 56, Yen Phu, Tay Ho, T4-3715 4345, www.hatruong.com*. Stunning range of contemporary clothing from a Ha Truong, one of the leading lights on the Vietnam fashion scene.

Ipa Nima, *73 Trang Thi St, T4-3933 4000, www.ipa-nima.com*. Shiny shoes, bags, clothes and jewellery boxes. Hong Kong designer Christina Yu is the creative force behind the label.

Mosaique, *6 Ly Quoc Su St, T4-6270 0430*. Embroidered table runners, lamps and stands, silk flowers, silk curtains, metal ball lamps, and lotus flower-shaped lamps.

Things of Substance, *5 Nha Tho St, T4-3828 6965, contrabanddesign@hn.vnn.vn*. Selling swimwear, silk jewellery bags and attractive jewellery, this small shop, with excellent service in the shadow of the cathedral, offers something a bit different. An Australian designer is in charge and everything is made with the motto 'Western sizes at Asian prices' in mind.

Handicrafts and homeware

There has been a great upsurge in handicrafts on sale as the tourist industry develops. Many are also made for export. A wide range of interesting pieces is on sale all around the popular cathedral shopping cluster of Nha Tho, Ly Quoc Su and Nha Chung streets. Further shops can be found on Hang Khay St, on the southern shores of Hoan Kiem Lake, and Hai Gai St. A range of hand-woven fabrics and ethnographia from the hill tribes is also available.

Aloo Store, *37 Hang Manh St, T4-3928 9131*. An abundance of well-priced ethnic goods from the north.

Chi Vang, *63 Hang Gai St, T4-3936 0601, chivang@fpt.vn*. Sells exquisite hand-embroidered goods: baby's bed linen and clothing, cushion covers, table cloths and unusual-shaped cushions artfully arranged. **Craft Link**, *43 Van Mieu St, T4-3843 7710, www.craftlink-vietnam.com*. Traditional handicrafts from a not-for-profit organization. Many are made by ethnic minorities. **Mosaique**, *22 Nha Tho St, T4-3928 6181, mosaique@fpt.vn. Open 0830-2000*. An Aladdin's cave of embroidered table runners, lamps and stands, silk flowers for accessorizing, silk curtains, silk cushions, ball lamps, pillow cushions and lotus flower-shaped lamps.

Shoes
Walking boots, trainers, flip flops and sandals, many in Western sizes, are sold in the shops around the northeast corner of Hoan Kiem Lake. They are remarkably inexpensive, but bargaining is expected.

Supermarkets
Fivimart, *27a Ly Thai To St*. Large-ish supermarket stocking all the necessities.

What to do

Cookery classes
Hanoi Cooking Centre, *44 Chau Long St, T4-3715 0088, www.hanoicookingcentre.com*. Run by cook book author Tracey Lister, this cooking school is the pick of the bunch in Hanoi. A large kitchen in a spacious building with a great courtyard café. Lunch is eaten in the peaceful restaurant space above the kitchen. This is also a great location as it is just a short walk to one of the very best markets in town, Chau Long, where cooking students are taken to learn about the local produce before whipping up a feast. Classes for children also. Highly recommended.
Highway 4, *see Restaurants, page 51*. This popular restaurant chain also offers fun cooking classes including a cycle trip to a local market.

Health clubs
All the big hotels provide fitness facilities, pool and gyms. Open usually free of charge to residents and to non-residents for a fee or subscription. There are now also scores of gyms all over town, but most require long-term memberships. One exception to this rule is **Olympia** at 4 Tran Hung Dao, which is extremely cheap and offers 2 rooms with a massive choice of weights and cardio.

Therapies
Le Spa du Metropole, *Sofitel Metropole, 15 Ngo Quyen St*. A truly luscious and deliciously designed spa in the grounds of the hotel. Themed rooms provide the ambience for the ultimate spa rituals. Expensive but worth it.

Tour operators
The most popular option for many is the budget cafés that offer reasonably priced tours and an opportunity to meet fellow travellers. While an excellent way to make friends, these tours do tend to isolate visitors from local people. Operators match their rivals' prices and itineraries closely.

Make sure to use only recommended tour operators. Also keep in mind that you get what you pay for and if something is too cheap to be true, it probably is.
Asia Pacific Travel, *87 Hoang Quoc Viet St, Cau Giay District, T4-3756 8868, www.asiapacifictravel.vn*. Arranges tours throughout Vietnam, Cambodia and Laos. Branch office in Danang.
Asian Trails, *24 Hang Than St, Ba Dinh District, T4-3716 2736, www.asiantrails.travel*. Offers various package tours across Asia.
Buffalo Tours, *L10, Vietbank Building, 70-72 Ba Trieu, Hoan Kiem District, T4-3828 0702, www.buffalotours.com*. Well-established and well-regarded organization. It has its own boat for Halong Bay trips and offers tours around the north as well as day trips around Hanoi. Cross-country and cross-border tours and tailor-made trips too. Staff are friendly and the guides are informative and knowledgeable.
Cuong's Motorbike Adventures, *46 Gia Ngu St, T09-1876 3515, www.cuongs-motorbike-adventure.com*. Tours all over Vietnam

on motorbike or in military style jeeps. Specializes in trips to the northern highlands including Ha Giang which Cuong and his team know like the back of their hands.

David W Lloyd Photography Tours, *T+84-1228-403 308, www.davidwlloyd photography.com*. Professional photographer and guidebook author David Lloyd offers photography tours ranging from half-day city walks to week-long adventures into the mountains of the north or the caves of Quang Binh.

Ethnic Travel, *35 Hang Giay St, T4-3926 1951, www.ethnictravel.com.vn*. Owner, Mr Khanh, runs individual tours to Bai Tu Long Bay – next to Halong Bay – and to Ninh Binh, the Red River Delta and trekking in the Black River area around Mai Chau. Always offers homestays and always, in a non-gimicky way, tries to ensure that travellers see the 'real' Vietnam. Book exchange inside.

Exotissimo, *26 Tran Nhat Duat St, T4-3828 2150, www.exotissimo.com*. Specializes in more upmarket tours, good nationwide service.

Footprint Travel, *30 Alley 12A, Ly Nam De St, T4-3933 2844, www.footprint.vn*. This company arranges good value, custom-made cycling tours and off-the-beaten-track treks throughout Vietnam, and also in Cambodia and Laos.

Haivenu Tours, *12 Nguyen Trung Truc St, Ba Dinh District, T4-3927 2917, www.haivenu-vietnam.com*. Arranges a large variety of customized trips throughout Vietnam, Cambodia and Laos.

Handspan Adventure Travel, *80 Ma May St, T4-3926 2828, www.handspan.com*. A reputable and well-organized business with very friendly staff. Specializes in adventure tours, trekking in the north and kayaking in Halong Bay. It has its own junk in Halong Bay and kayaks. Booking office in Sapa also.

Hanoi Street Eats, *www.sreetfoodtourshanoi. blogspot.com*. Run by long-term expat Mark (author of the excellent Sticky Rice blog) and Tu who hails from Nha Trang, these street eats tours can be tailored to guest's tastes and allow people to see the Hanoi that these two foodies love most. Tours range from a 1-hr market visit to a full-on all day eat-a-thon. Fun and highly recommended.

Luxury Travel, *5 Nguyen Truong To St, Ba Dinh Dist, T4-3927 4120, www.luxurytravelvietnam. com*. This outfit is an Asian specialist in luxury privately guided and fully bespoke holidays in Vietnam, Laos, Cambodia, Myanmar and Thailand. They also have a new joint venture with a junk specialist in Halong Bay, **Emperor Cruises**, www.emperorcruises.com, offering 5-star cruises in Nha Trang Bay.

Topas Travel, *52 To Ngoc Van St, Tay Ho, T4-3715 1005, www.topasvietnam.com*. Excellent, well-run tour operator offering cross-country tours as well as those in the north. Also has an office in Sapa using local guides. It organizes treks to Pu Luong Nature Reserve. A major draw card is its ecolodge in Sapa, with gorgeous villas offering peace and quiet. See page 79.

Transport

The traffic in Hanoi is becoming more frantic as each month goes by. Bicycles, cyclos, mopeds, cars, lorries and buses fight for space, but somehow it continues to function. The addition of more and more cars everyday, however, makes many wonder how much longer the city's infrastructure will be able to cope before Bangkok-style gridlock becomes a reality here.

Air
Airport information
There are an increasing number of direct international air connections with Hanoi's **Noi Bai Airport**, north of the city. The new international terminal opened in Dec 2014. Facilities include cafés, shops, restaurants, ATMs, mobile phone shops and tour desks.

It is 35 km from the city, about a 1-hr drive. The best way to get to town, other than with your own hotel's bus, is a meter taxi. These line up outside and while there is more order than in the past, it is still a slight hassle getting a taxi. The best bet is to go for a yellow **Noi Bai taxi** – there are people with clipboards standing by the taxi rank. Look for someone in yellow and point to the fee written on the taxi board and the side of the cab. This is a fixed fare. Some taxis will offer you a meter rate, but it is best to go with one that simply states the flat fee as written on the boards. While Ho Chi Minh City has worked wonders with its taxi rank in the last year, Hanoi's has not caught up with this standard – hopefully this is something that will be addressed with the opening of the new international terminal.

Bicycle
Once the most common form of transport in town, it is no longer popular. However, cycling around the West Lake area is a pleasure. Bikes can be hired all over town, but good quality bikes are available at **Paradise Boutique Hotel**, see Where to stay, page 48, and at **La Bicicleta**, see Restaurants, page 53.

Bus
Local
The Hanoi city bus service is comprehensive but not easily navigable for tourists. With *xe om* and taxis so cheap and widely available, only the most fervent bus fans will hop on the crammed local variety.

Long distance
Hanoi has a number of bus stations. The **Southern bus terminal** (Giap Bat, T4-3864 1467) is out of town, but linking buses run from the northern shore of Hoan Kiem Lake. The terminal serves destinations south of Hanoi: **HCMC, Buon Ma Thuot, Vinh, Danang, Thanh Hoa, Nha Trang, Dalat, Qui Nhon, Ninh Binh, Nam Dinh** and **Nho Quan** for **Cuc Phuong National Park**. Express buses usually leave at 0500; advance booking is recommended.

Luong Yen bus station, 1 Nguyen Khoai St. The **Hoang Long** bus company, T4-3928 2828, https://hoanglongasia.com, runs deluxe buses to **HCMC** with comfortable beds, 36 hrs, 12 a day 0500-2300. **Hoang Long** also leaves for **Haiphong** from here; 7 daily from 0415-1645 and on to **Cat Ba Island** by ferry. From **Ha Dong bus station**, Tran Phu Rd, Ha Tay Province, T4-3825 209, buses leave for **Mai Chau, Hoa Binh, Son La** and **Dien Bien Phu**. Take a local bus or *xe om* to the bus station.

From **My Dinh station**, T4-3768 5549, there are buses to **Halong**, every 20 mins, 3 hrs 15 mins. Other destinations in the north are also served from here such as **Thai Nguyen, Tuyen Quang** and **Ha Giang**.

International
International buses to **Laos** are best booked via agents in the Old Quarter – many post times on notice boards in their shops.

Cyclo

Hanoi's cyclo drivers expect foreigners to pay more than locals, but have taken this to extremes; prices quoted are often radically inflated. Drivers also may forget the agreed fare and ask for more: be firm and perhaps write the price down to be clear. A good way to go about getting a hassle-free cyclo is to book via the reception at your hotel. All this said, many of the drivers are superb and friendly and this is a great way to get about town.

Motorbike

Hiring a motorbike is a good way of getting to some of the more remote places. Tourist cafés and hotels rent a variety of machines. **Cuong's Motorbike Adventures**, 46 Gia Ngu St, T9-1876 3515, www.cuongs-motorbike-adventure.com. This is the place to head to rent a larger bike with lots of choice and some high quality 250cc off road machines. Also runs excellent tours around the country – see Tour operators, page 58. **Rentabike Hanoi**, 27, Alley 52, To Ngoc Van St, T09-1302 6878, www.rentabikevn.com. Run by Danny and Thu, **Rentabike** has a wide range of machines on offer from automatic to 125cc rides. Everything is available for short- or long-term rents. Also sells second-hand machines. Easy to deal with and full of local advice and information on touring.

Taxi and private car

Hanoi has hundreds of good taxi drivers, but rogue cabs remain, especially around tourist sites and at the train station in the early morning. Luckily these are easily avoided by ignoring taxi drivers who approach you and simply going for one of the reputable companies. These include **Mai Linh** and ABC. All restaurants and bars will also be happy to call you a cab.

Private cars can be chartered from most hotels and from many tour operators, see page 58.

Train

The **central station (Ga Hanoi)**, 120 Le Duan St, at the end of Tran Hung Dao St, T4-3747 0666, is a 10-min taxi ride from the centre of town. There's an information desk at the entrance, (T4-3942 3697, open 0700-2300) but minimal English is spoken, and luggage lockers at the end of the ticket hall. The **Thong Nhat** (north–south train) booking office is on the left; northern trains office, on the right. Train times and prices can be found at www.vr.com.vn and online bookings are set to become a reality soon. The train station remains old-fashioned but fast-food joints – such as the Korean-owned **Lotteria** – have opened up near the premises if you need a last minute snack before boarding. The easiest way to book a ticket is to pay a small commission to a travel agent.

5 daily connections with **HCMC**. There are also daily trains to **Haiphong** and 3 trains daily to **Ninh Binh**. **Long Bien Station** is at the western end of Long Bien Bridge near the Red River. It is very rarely necessary to use this station, but if you are dropped there you can reach town by taxi or *xe om*.

A variety of trains ply the route to **Lao Cai (Sapa)** offering varying levels of comfort. **ET-Pumpkin**, www.et-pumpkin.com and **Ratraco**, www.ratraco.com.vn, run standard comfortable a/c 4-berth cabins in its carriages with complimentary water, bedside lights and space for luggage. For luxury, the **Victoria Hotel** carriages (www.victoriahotels-asia.com) rare the best choice. Places are only available to **Victoria Sapa** hotel guests.

The train is the romantic way to travel, but a new highway linking Hanoi and Lao Cai means many tour companies are now gearing up to sell high-speed bus tickets and also use the buses for their itineraries to the northwest.

Northern Vietnam

culturally interesting, breathtakingly beautiful

To many the Northwest and Far North represents the finest Vietnam has to offer. In terms of scenery, colour, human interest and the thrill of discovering the unknown, it is unrivalled. It is, in short, that myth of travellers' folklore: unspoilt Vietnam.

There are good reasons for this. The distance, rugged environment and infrastructure have all contributed to placing the area at the edge of Vietnamese space. Pockets have been discovered – Sapa for example – but for those who wish to avoid the backpacker trail and are prepared to put up with a little discomfort, the rewards are great. The region has wider significance too: the course of world history was altered at Dien Bien Phu in 1954.

No less remote are the beautiful, rugged, lime green hills that roll across the Northeast. Hilltribe minorities are much in evidence. Despite its sparse population, Northeast Vietnam features prominently in the annals of nationalist and revolutionary history.

To the east of Hanoi is Halong Bay with its thousands of jagged islands rearing dramatically from the sea. South of the city is Ninh Binh and the UNESCO-listed Trang An Landscape Complex where rivers weave among paddy fields and jungle-clad limestone peaks.

Best for
Pagodas ▪ Road trips ▪ Trekking

Footprint
picks

★ **Moc Chau**, page 69

The tea plantations of Moc Chau attract photographers by the bus full.

★ **Sapa**, page 73

Trekking, minority villages and fantastic mountain lodges.

★ **Mount Fan Si Pan**, page 78

The highest mountain in Indochina, adventurous tourists can summit this peak in one day or two.

★ **Dong Van**, page 80

Remote, high mountain town with stunning surrounds.

★ **Ma Pi Leng Pass**, page 81

One of the most epic roads in the country.

★ **Halong Bay**, page 82

One of Vietnam's most visited attractions, it lives up to the hype.

★ **Tam Coc**, page 88

Here rivers cut through dramatic limestone karst scenery.

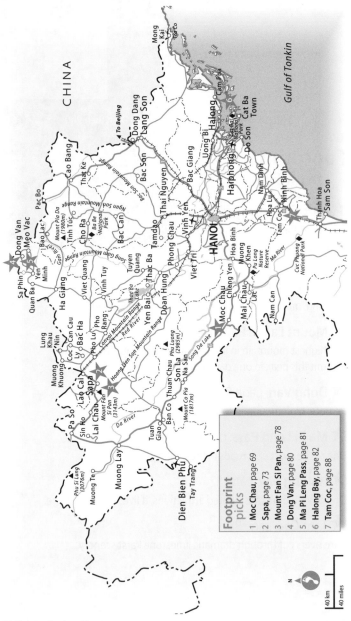

CHINA

Gulf of Tonkin

To Beijing

HANOI

Haiphong

Footprint picks

1 Moc Chau, page 69
2 Sapa, page 73
3 Mount Fan Si Pan, page 78
4 Dong Van, page 80
5 Ma Pi Leng Pass, page 81
6 Halong Bay, page 82
7 Tam Coc, page 88

N

40 km
40 miles

The Northwest

one of the most evocative landscapes in Vietnam

This is a mountainous region punctuated by limestone peaks and luscious valleys of terraced paddy fields, tea plantations, stilt houses and water hyacinth-quilted rivers. Large cone-shaped peaks rise dramatically, their steep sides striped with the greens and yellows of the rice crop.

Sapa is a former French hill station, home of the Hmong and set at the head of a stunning valley. Scattered around are market towns and villages populated by Vietnam's ethnic minorities. To the east, the far less visited Ha Giang Province borders China to the north, its endless mountain scenery offering up other-wordly vistas of rocky plateaus. This is extremely rewarding road trip territory with the Ma Pi Leng Pass winding vertiginously around a sheer sided gorge. The region isn't without wider significance; the course of world history was altered at Dien Bien Phu in May 1954 when the Vietnamese defeated the French. Closer to Hanoi is Hoa Binh where villages of the Muong and Dao can be seen and the beautiful Mai Chau Valley, home to the Black and White Thai whose attractive houses stand amid the verdant paddies and surrounding hills.

Essential Northwest Vietnam

Finding your feet

There are three points of entry for the Northwest circuit: the south around Hoa Binh (reached by road); the north around Lao Cai/Sapa (reached by road or by train) and in the middle Dien Bien Phu reached by plane or road. Which option you pick will depend upon how much time you have available and how much flexibility you require. Most people arrive by train or by luxury bus, the cheapest option, to Sapa.

Getting around

An option, for those so inclined, is to do the whole thing by motorbike. The rugged terrain and relatively quiet roads make this quite a popular choice for many people. It has the particular advantage of enabling you to to make countless side trips and get to

Best motorbike journeys
Moc Chau to Son La, page 69
Dien Bien Phu to Sapa, page 70
Ha Giang to Meo Vac, page 80

remote and untouched tribal areas. Doing the whole thing by local public transport is possible, but it would require lots of time and plenty of patience.

Best mountain lodges
Topas Ecolodge, page 79
Nam Cang Riverside Lodge, page 79

When to go

The wettest season is from May to September, but the rice terraces look very beautiful from August to September. Owing to the altitude of much of the area winter can be quite cool, especially around Sapa, so make sure you go well prepared.

Time required

To see Sapa and around, two or three days is the minimum amount of time required, but to branch out further and include a tour of Ha Giang, five days to a week is needed.

Temperature Sapa

January	20°C / 13°C / 22mm	**February**	22°C / 14°C / 33mm
March	26°C / 17°C / 49mm	**April**	30°C / 20°C / 105mm
May	32°C / 24°C / 182mm	**June**	32°C / 25°C / 242mm
July	32°C / 24°C / 242mm	**August**	32°C / 24°C / 322mm
September	31°C / 23°C / 216mm	**October**	28°C / 21°C / 110mm
November	24°C / 17°C / 53mm	**December**	22°C / 14°C / 25mm

an epic road trip on winding mountain roads

The road from Hanoi to Dien Bien Phu offers some of the most spectacular scenery anywhere in Vietnam. It winds its way for 420 km into the Annamite Mountains that mark the frontier with the Lao People's Democratic Republic; the round trip from Hanoi and back via Dien Bien Phu and Sapa is about 1200 km. There are, of course, opportunities to meet some of Vietnam's ethnic minorities and learn something about their lives and customs.

Hanoi to Hoa Binh

Highway 6 leads southwest out of Hanoi to Hoa Binh. Setting off in the early morning, the important arterial function of this road is evident. Ducks, chickens, pigs, bamboo and charcoal (the energy and building materials of the capital) all pour in to Hanoi. Beyond the city limit the fields are highly productive, with bounteous market gardens and intensive rice production.

Hoa Binh → *Colour map 2, B4.*

Hoa Binh, on the banks of the Da (Black) River, marks the southern limit of the interior highlands. It is 75 km from Hanoi, a journey of about 2½ hours. Major excavation sites of the **Hoabinhian prehistoric civilization** (10,000 BC) were found in the province, which is its main claim to international fame. In 1979, with Russian technical and financial assistance, work began on the **Hoa Binh Dam** and hydroelectric power station; it was complete 15 years later. The reservoir has a volume of nine billion cubic metres: it provides two functions, to prevent flooding on the lower reaches of the Red River (that is Hanoi) and to generate power. Architecture buffs may want to swing by to see the Russian-influenced industrial architecture, but most people will drive straight past en route to more attractive destinations.

The road to Mai Chau

After leaving Hoa Binh, Highway 6 heads in a south-southwest direction as far as the Chu River. Thereafter it climbs through some spectacular mountain scenery before descending into the beautiful Mai Chau Valley. During the first half of this journey, the turtle-shaped roofs of the Muong houses predominate, but after passing **Man Duc** the road enters the territory of the Thai, northwest Vietnam's most prolific minority group, heralding a subtle change in the style of stilted-house architecture. While members of the Thai will be encountered frequently on this circuit, it is their Black Thai sub-ethnic group, which will be seen most often. What makes the Mai Chau area interesting is that it is one of the few places en route where travellers can encounter their White Thai cousins.

Mai Chau → *Colour map 2, B4.*

An isolated farming community until 1993, Mai Chau has undergone significant change in just a few short years. Its tranquil valley setting, engaging White Thai inhabitants and superb rice wine make Mai Chau a very worthwhile stop and it is now extremely touristy, with large groups of Vietnamese tourists packing out the homestays every weekend and a good number of Hanoi's expats also using it as a weekend getaway. The growing number of foreign and domestic tourists visiting the area in recent years has had a significant impact on the economy of Mai Chau and the lifestyles of its inhabitants.

People of the north

Ethnic groups belonging to the Sino-Tibetan language family such as the Hmong and Dao, or the Ha Nhi and Phula of the Tibeto-Burman language group are relatively recent arrivals. Migrating south from China only within the past 250-300 years, these people have lived almost exclusively on the upper mountain slopes, practising slash-and-burn agriculture and posing little threat to their more numerous lowland-dwelling neighbours, notably the Thai.

Thus was established the pattern of human and political settlement that would persist in North Vietnam right up until the colonial period – a centralized Viet state based in the Red River Delta area, with powerful Thai vassal lordships dominating the Northwest. Occupying lands located in some cases almost equidistant from Hanoi, Luang Prabang and Kunming, the Thai, Lao, Lu and Tay lords were obliged during the pre-colonial period to pay tribute to the royal courts of Nam Viet, Lang Xang (Laos) and China, though in times of upheaval they could – and frequently did – play one power off against the other for their own political gain. Considerable effort was thus required by successive Viet kings in Thang Long (Hanoi) and later in Hué to ensure that their writ and their writ alone ruled in the far north. To this end there was ultimately no substitute for the occasional display of military force, but the enormous cost of mounting a campaign into the northern mountains obliged most Viet kings simply to endorse the prevailing balance of power there by investing the most powerful local lords as their local government mandarins, resorting to arms only when separatist tendencies became too strong. Such was the political situation inherited by the French colonial government following its conquest of Indochina in the latter half of the 19th century. Its subsequent policy towards the ethnic minority chieftains of North Vietnam was to mirror that of the Vietnamese monarchy whose authority it assumed; throughout the colonial period responsibility for colonial administration at both local and provincial level was placed in the hands of seigneurial families of the dominant local ethnicity, a policy which culminated during the 1940s in the establishment of a series of ethnic minority 'autonomous zones' ruled over by the most powerful seigneurial families.

Lac, see below, is the main tourist village. You can stay overnight there, or alternatively, there are two up-market options in Mai Chau, with a new ecolodge offering wonderful accommodation and a swimming pool with views across the valley.

A number of interesting and picturesque **walks** and **treks** can be made in the countryside surrounding Mai Chau. These cover a wide range of itineraries and durations, from short circular walks around Mai Chau, to longer treks to minority villages in the mountains beyond. One such challenging trek covers the 20 km to the village of Xa Linh, just off Highway 6. This usually takes between two and three days, with accommodation provided in small villages along the way. Ask at the People's Committee Guesthouse or at any homestay in Lac.

Lac (White Thai village) → *Colour map 2, B3.*
Easily accessible from the main road. From the direction of Hoa Binh take the track to the right, immediately before the ostentatious, red-roofed People's Committee Guesthouse. This leads directly into the village.

This village is very popular and turning into the village one's heart may sink: minibuses are drawn up and stilt houses are full of groups gearing up for an evening karoeke session. But before you turn and flee take a stroll around the village and find a house tucked further away with a view of the paddy fields and ask if you can stay the night. Rent a bicycle from your hosts and wobble across narrow bunds to the neighbouring hamlets, enjoying the views over the rice fields as you go.

★ Moc Chau and Chieng Yen → *Colour map 2, B3.*
North of Mai Chau, on the road to Son La, is Chieng Yen. Home to 14 villages of Thai, Dao, Muong and Kinh, there are new homestay options with trekking and biking opportunities as well as tea farm visits at Moc Chau. These tea farms are every inch as beautiful as the rice terraces that Vietnam is more famous for, and they are starting to attract lots of visitors from Hanoi who come to photograph the stunning scenery here. Another highlight is the weekly Tuesday market.

Listings Hanoi to Dien Bien Phu

Where to stay

Mai Chau

$$$$-$$$ Mai Chau Ecolodge
Signposted from the main road, T090-326 3968, www.maichau.ecolodge.asia.
This is a fantastic addition to the valley, with beautiful thatched roof bungalows, each with glorious views from balances complete with fine wooden furniture. A number of different rooms are on offer, many of which have tasteful tiled flooring. There is also a pool with superb views and a restaurant with a small outdoor balcony. Recommended.

$$$$-$$$ Mai Chau Lodge
A short walking distance southwest of Lac village, T18-386 8959, www.maichaulodge.com.
Owned and operated by **Buffalo Tours** and staffed by locals, there are 16 warmly furnished rooms with modern facilities. The attractive lodge has 2 restaurants, a bar, swimming pool, sauna and jacuzzi. Bicycling, kayaking and trekking tours are

offered. Room prices include round-trip transfer from Hanoi.

Lac (White Thai village)

$ Ethnic Houses
Visitors can spend the night in a White Thai house on stilts. Mat, pillow, duvet, mosquito net, communal washing facilities (some hot showers) and sometimes fan provided. This is particularly recommended as the hospitality and easy manner of the people is a highlight of many visitors' stay in Vietnam. Food and local rice wine provided. Avoid the large houses in the centre if possible. **Mr Binh's place**, Number 9 (T021-8386 7380) is a good option. In the adjoining, quieter, village of Ban Pom Coong, **House 3** (aka **Hung Tu**) is run by an absolutely lovely family and has good views – contact Nga at **Wide Eyed Tours** (T4-2213 2951) to request it.

Moc Chau and Chieng Yen
Homestays
Homestays, with meals are possible in 2 villages. Contact Son La Province well-

respected tour operator **Handspan** (www.handspan.com) in Hanoi. There are also a number of very basic guesthouses (*nha nghi*), all of which offer simple rooms.

Restaurants

Hoa Binh

$ Thanh Toi
22a Cu Chinh Lan St, T18-385 3951.
Local specialities, wild boar and stir-fried aubergine.

Mai Chau

Most people will eat with their hosts. Mai Chau town itself has a couple of simple *com pho* places near the market. The Mai Chau Lodge, see Where to stay, has 2 restaurants and the Mai Chau Ecolodge offers lunch and dinner to non-guests.

Entertainment

Mai Chau

Mai Chau Ethnic Minority Dance Troupe, this troupe performs most nights in Lac moving from house to house.

Shopping

Mai Chau

Villagers offer a range of woven goods and fabrics on which they are becoming dependent for a living. There are also local paintings and well-made wicker baskets, pots, traps and pouches.

What to do

Hoa Binh

Hoa Binh Tourism, *next to the Hoa Binh 1 hotel, T18-385 4374, www.hoabinhtourism. com. Daily 0730-1100, 1330-1700.* Can arrange boat hire as well as visits to minority villages, trekking and transport.

Mai Chau

Hanoi tour operators, see page 58, run overnight tours to the area.

Transport

Hoa Binh

Bus station on Tran Hung Dao St. Morning departures to **Hanoi**, 2 hrs. Buses also to **Mai Chau** and onward to **Son La**.

Mai Chau

Bus connections with **Hoa Binh**, 2 hrs, **Hanoi**, 4 hrs, and onward buses northwest to **Son La**. While it is easy and cheap to get here by bus most people visit on an organized tour.

Dien Bien Phu → *Colour map 2, B2.*

visited either for its historical significance or to cross into Laos

Deep in the highlands of Northwest Vietnam, close to the border with Laos and 420 km from Hanoi (although it feels much further), Dien Bien Phu is situated in a region where even today ethnic Vietnamese still represent less than one-third of the total population. The town lies in the Muong Thanh Valley, a heart-shaped basin 19 km long and 13 km wide, crossed by the Nam Yum River.

For such a remote and apparently insignificant little town to have earned itself such an important place in the history books is a considerable achievement. And yet the Battle of Dien Bien Phu in 1954 was a turning point in colonial history. It marked the end of French involvement in Indochina and heralded the collapse of its North African empire. Had the Americans, who shunned French appeals for help, taken more careful note of what happened at Dien Bien Phu they might have avoided their own calamitous involvement just a decade later.

Sights

The town of Dien Bien Phu with its neat streets is quite easy to negotiate on foot. The battlefield sites, most of which lie to the west of the Nam Yum River, are, however, a bit spread out and best visited by car or by motorbike.

On the sight of the battlefield **General de Castries' bunker** ⓘ *daily 0700-1100, 1330-1700, 5000d*, has been rebuilt and eight of the 10 French tanks (known as bisons) are scattered over the valley, along with numerous US-made artillery pieces.

On **Hill A1** (known as Eliane 2 to the French) ⓘ *daily 0700-1800*, scene of the fiercest fighting, is a bunker, a war memorial dedicated to the Vietnamese who died on the hill and around at the back is the entrance to a tunnel dug by coal miners from Hon Gai. Their tunnel ran several hundred metres to beneath French positions and was filled with 1000 kg of high explosives. It was detonated at 2300 on 6 May 1954 as a signal for the final assault. The huge crater is still there. The hill is a peaceful spot and a good place from which to watch the sun setting on the historic valley. After dark there are fireflies. Hill A1 and other sites in the area were improved in readiness for Dien Bien Phu's 60th anniversary of the French defeat in 2014.

The **Dien Bien Phu Museum** ⓘ *daily 0700-1100, 1330-1800, 10,000d*, has a good collection of assorted Chinese, American and French weapons and artillery in its grounds. It has been renovated and there are photographs and other memorabilia together with a large illuminated model of the valley illustrating the course of the campaign and an accompanying video. The **Revolutionary Heroes' Cemetery** ⓘ *opposite the Exhibition Museum adjacent to Hill A1, 0700-1100, 1330-1800*, contains the graves of some 15,000 Vietnamese soldiers killed during the course of the Dien Bien Phu campaign.

Located close to the sight of de Castries' command bunker is the French War Memorial (Nghia Trang Phap). It consists of a white obelisk surrounded by a grey concrete wall and black iron gates sitting on a bluff overlooking the Nam Yum River.

Dien Bien Phu's newest sight towers over the town. Erected on Hill D1 at a cost of US$2.27 million, the **Victory Monument (Tuong Dai Chien Dien Bien Phu)** ⓘ *entrance next to the TV station on 6 Pho Muong Thanh (look for the tower and large, gated pond)*, is an enormous, 120-tonne bronze sculpture. It was sculpted by former soldier Nguyen Hai and depicts three Vietnamese soldiers standing on top of de Castries' bunker. Engraved on the flag is the motto *Quyet Chien, Quyet Thang* (Determined to Fight, Determined to Win). One of the soldiers is carrying a Thai child. It was commissioned to mark the 50th anniversary of the Vietnamese defeat over the French in 1954.

Listings Dien Bien Phu

Where to stay

Dien Bien Phu is still sorely lacking in quality accommodation, particularly at the budget end. Many of the guesthouses (*nha nghi*) go by the hour, as well as the night.

$$ Muong Thanh Hotel
25 Him Lam-TP, T0230-381 0043.
The most upmarket option, this dated but comfortable hotel has spacious, retro rooms with TV. Breakfast included with the more expensive rooms. 62 standard rooms with TV, a/c, minibar and fan. Wi-Fi,

swimming pool complete with bizarre statues (10,000d for non-guests), karaoke, Thai massage and free airport transfer. Tacky souvenir shop. Very overpriced motorbike rentals – hire elsewhere.

$$-$ Nha Khach VP
7/5 Muong Thanh (behind the lake), T023-283 0338, thanhhoa.dph@gmail.com.
Hotel right in the middle of town. Absolutely massive suites complete with 70s style living areas. Doubles are clean and spacious with ac. Considering the alternatives, a very good option.

$ Hung Ha
Number 83, opposite the bus station, T023-0650 4187.
Strictly for those on a tight budget, this is the best of a bad lot, but is handy for the station. The balcony rooms aren't so bad, but interior rooms are drab and corridor-facing.

Restaurants

The main street, Nguyen Chi Thanh, has plenty of simple noodle and rice joints, but they are not places to linger. A few *bia hoi* also serve *lau* (hotpots) – Phuong Thuy at number 60 is busy in the evenings.

$$-$ Muong Thanh Hotel Restaurant
25 Him Lam-TP, T230-381 0043.
Daily 0600-2200.
Popular with tour groups. Menu includes plenty of Vietnamese choices, from familiar pork and chicken dishes to more offbeat options.

$ Lien Tuoi
6427 Street 22, behind the cemetery, Muong Thanh 8 St, next to the Vietnamese cemetery and Hill A1, T0230-382 4919. Daily 0700-2200.

Simple delicious local fare, including good fried spring rolls and grilled chicken in a family-run restaurant.

Transport

Air
The **airport** (T230-382 4416) is 2 km north of town, off Highway 12; there are daily flights to **Hanoi**.
   Airline offices Vietnam Airlines, Nguyen Huu Tho Rd, T230-382 4948.

Bus
Buses snake their way up from Hanoi via Hoa Binh and Son La. Expect overland journeys to be slow and sometimes arduous in this mountainous region but the discomfort is compensated for by the sheer majesty of the landscapes.
   The bus station is close to the centre of town, on Highway 12. It's an easy walk to the hotels. There are daily direct bus connections with **Hanoi**, 13 hrs; daily connections to **Son La**, 5½ hrs; to **Muong Lay**, 3 hrs and some buses to **Sapa**. It is also possible to reach **Mai Chau** via Thai Binh and to Hoa Binh en route to Hanoi. There's a bus to the Laos border crossing at **Tay Trang** to Muang Khua (Laos) every day. A Laos visa is available at the border; Vietnamese visas are not available at land borders.

Car
The main roads in the Northwest have been improved in the last few years, but a 4WD is still recommended for those going off the main routes. The price of hiring a jeep has come down, and many tour operators in Hanoi (see page 58) rent them out for the 5- or 6-day round trip (1200 km via Sapa).

★Sapa retains great charm despite the countless thousands of tourists who have poured in every year for the past decade. Its beauty derives from the impressive natural setting high on a valley side with Vietnam's tallest mountain, either clearly visible or brooding in the mist.

The huge scale of the Fan Si Pan range gives Sapa an Alpine feel and this impression is reinforced by *haute savoie* vernacular architecture with steep-pitched roofs, window shutters and chimneys. But, with an alluring blend of European and Vietnamese vegetation, the gardeners of Sapa cultivate their foxgloves and apricot trees alongside thickets of bamboo and delicate orchids, just yards above the paddy fields. In addition to trekking (see page 77), the markets of the region are popular one-day or overnight trips.

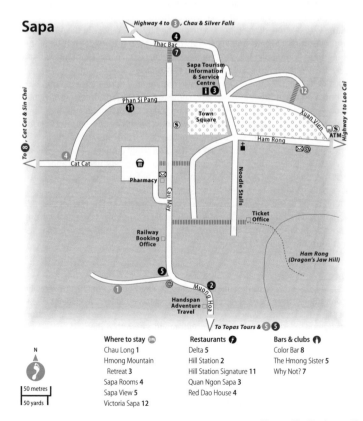

Sapa

Where to stay
Chau Long **1**
Hmong Mountain
  Retreat **3**
Sapa Rooms **4**
Sapa View **5**
Victoria Sapa **12**

Restaurants
Delta **5**
Hill Station **2**
Hill Station Signature **11**
Quan Ngon Sapa **3**
Red Dao House **4**

Bars & clubs
Color Bar **8**
The Hmong Sister **5**
Why Not? **7**

BACKGROUND

Sapa

Originally a Black Hmong settlement, Sapa was first discovered by Europeans when a Jesuit missionary visited the area in 1918. By 1932 news of the quasi-European climate and beautiful scenery of the Tonkinese Alps had spread throughout French Indochina. Like Dalat in the south it served as a retreat for French administrators when the heat of the plains became unbearable. By the 1940s an estimated 300 French buildings, including a sizeable prison and the summer residence of the Governor of French Indochina, had sprung up. Until 1947 there were more French than Vietnamese in the town, which became renowned for its many parks and flower gardens. However, as the security situation began to worsen during the latter days of French rule, the expatriate community steadily dwindled, and by 1953 virtually all had gone. Immediately following the French defeat at Dien Bien Phu in 1954, victorious Vietnamese forces razed a large number of Sapa's French buildings to the ground.

Sapa was also one of the places to be invaded by the Chinese in the 1979 border skirmish. Chinese soldiers found and destroyed the holiday retreat of the Vietnamese Communist Party Secretary-General, Le Duan, no doubt infuriated by such uncomradely display of bourgeois tendencies.

Distinctly oriental but un-Vietnamese in manner and appearance are the Hmong, Dao and other minorities who come to Sapa to trade. Interestingly, the Hmong have been the first to seize the commercial opportunities presented by tourism; they are engaging but very persistent vendors of hand-loomed indigo shirts, trousers and skull caps and other handicrafts. The Dao women, their hands stained purple by the dye, sell clothing on street corners, stitching while they wait for a customer. The girls roam in groups, bracelets, earrings and necklaces jingling as they walk. Saturday night is always a big occasion for Black Hmong and Red Dao teenagers in the Sapa area, as youngsters from miles around come to the so-called Love Market to find a partner. The market proved so popular with tourists that the teenagers now arrange their trysts and liaisons in private. The regular market is at its busiest and best on Sunday morning when most tourists scoot off to Bac Ha.

Sights

The beauty of the town is a little compromised by the new hotels sprouting up everywhere. Certainly none of the new ones can compare with the lovely old French buildings. Sapa is a great place to relax and unwind but being comparatively new it has no important historical sights though several French buildings in and around are worth visiting.

The small **church**, built in 1930, dominates the centre of Sapa. Recently rebuilt, the church was wrecked in 1952 by French artillerymen shelling the adjacent building in which Viet Minh troops were billeted. In the churchyard are the tombs of two former priests, including that of Father Jean Thinh, who was brutally murdered. In the autumn of 1948, Father Thinh confronted a monk named Giao Linh who had been discovered having an affair with a nun at the Ta Phin seminary. Giao Linh obviously took great exception to the priest's interference, for shortly after this, when Father Thinh's congregation arrived at Sapa church for mass one foggy November morning, they discovered his decapitated body lying next to the altar.

Ham Rong (Dragon's Jaw Hill) ① *0600-1800, 30,000d, free for children under 5*, on which the district's TV transmitter is stuck, is located immediately above Sapa town centre. Apart from offering excellent views of the town, the path winds its way through a number of interesting limestone outcrops and miniature grottoes as it nears the summit.

Market villages

In the region it's possible to visit **Can Cau** (Saturday market), **Muong Hum** (Sunday market), **Muong Khuong** (Sunday market), **Coc Ly** (Tuesday market), **Lung Khau Nhin** (Thursday market), **Tam Duong** (Thursday market).

Listings Sapa *map p73*

Tourist information

Sapa Tourist Information Center
2 Phan Si Pang St, T20-387 1975, www.sapa-tourism.com. Daily 0800-1130, 1330-1730.
Free tourist information.

Where to stay

Prices tend to rise Jun-Oct to coincide with northern hemisphere university holidays and at weekends. Hoteliers are accustomed to bargaining; healthy competition ensures fair rates.

$$$$ Victoria Sapa
T020-387 1522, www.victoriahotels.asia.com.
With 77 rooms, this hotel is the best in town. Comfy, with well-appointed rooms, it is a lovely place in which to relax. In winter there are very welcome open fires in the bar and dining rooms. The food is very good and the set buffets are excellent value. The **Health Centre** offers everything from the traditional massage to reflexology. The centre, pool, tennis courts and sauna are open to non-guests. Packages available.

$$$ Sapa Rooms
18 Phan Xi Pang St, T020-650 5228, www.saparooms.com.
While the lobby and café is decorated to a very high standard, the rooms offer more of a boutique hostel experience. The owners

have also opened the **Hmong Mountain Retreat**, www.hmongmountainretreat.com, outside Sapa, where guests can stay in wooden stilt houses among paddy fields with very special views. Treks can be combined with a stay here.

$$$-$$ Chau Long Hotel
T020-387 1245, www.chaulonghotel.com.
All rooms here have fantastic views down the valley and private balconies. Cosy decor. Serves an excellent buffet breakfast in the restaurant with a panoramic vista. Rates drop in low season.

$$$-$$ Sapa View Hotel
41 Muong Hoa, T020-3872388, info@sapaview-hotel.com.
With a Swiss alpine feel, many rooms have jaw-dropping views through large windows and from private balconies. Each room has its own log fire for the colder months. Good restaurant with open kitchen. Very hospitable management.

Restaurants

There are rice and noodle stalls in the market and along the path by the church.

$$$ Ta Van
In Victoria Sapa, see Where to stay, T20-387 1522.
The food served in this large restaurant is 1st class and the service is exceptional.

Choose from à la carte or buffet dinners; the latter are excellent value. You'll want to eat here at least twice to savour the full range of haute cuisine. The large dining room is dominated by an open fire that is hugely warming during those chilly days and nights.

$$$-$$ The Hill Station
7 Muong Hoa St, T020-388 7111, www. thehillstation.com. Open 0800-2300.
A very sleek blend of Nordic and Hmong design from friendly Norwegian owners. Cold cuts, cheese boards, gourmet baguettes and good wine. Great Hmong staff. Recommended.

$$ Delta
Cay Mau St, T20-387 1799. Open 0730-2200.
Sapa's Italian restaurant serves good portions of pasta and pizzas as well as tasty seafood. It's great for people-watching from its big windows as it's on the main bend on the main road. There's a good wine list too.

$$ The Hill Station Signature
www.thehillstation.com.
From the same team behind the Hill Station, this restaurant has massive windows giving breath-taking views down the valley. The dishes here are inspired by the local area, with highlights including the Ta Van pork, the recipe for which comes straight out of a nearby village. Interesting prints hang on the walls and there is a choice of floor cushion on tabled dining. A cracking spot – delicous and highly recommended.

$$ Quan Ngon Sapa
2 Phan Xi Pan, T09-34430838.
It's wrong to visit Sapa and not try the local speciality – salmon hot pot (*lau ca hoi*). It's served well here, alongside other Vietnamese dishes, in basic, sometimes raucous, surroundings.

$$ Sapa Rooms
See Where to stay, T020-387 2130, www.saparooms.com.
Aussie owner Pete and a Hanoian artist have done a great job decorating this funky establishment with hilltribe-inspired works. The **KOTO**-trained chefs (see page 52) whip up delicious meals. Fantastic cakes and good coffees. Try the home-made cookie and ice-cream dessert and the Sapa Rooms smoothie.

$$-$ Red Dao House
4B Thac Bac St, T020-3872927. Open 0900-2400.
Homely and warm chalet-style restaurant with very friendly waiting staff. Large range of reasonable Vietnamese food. Gets busy – reserve a table by the front windows.

Bars and clubs

Color Bar
56 Phan Si Pan, T09-7928 3398. Open 1600-2300.
A shack of a bar decorated with tens of paintings by the enthusiastic owner. Free games. Bob Marley and the like on the stereo.

The Hmong Sisters
7 Hmong Hoa St, homngsistersbar@ yahoo.com.
Atmospheric, low-ceilinged bar with ethnic fabrics covering walls and seats and funky paintings. Free American pool, tasty finger foods and quality tunes. Daily happy hours from 4–7 on drinks, including lethal daiquiris. The best bar in town.

Entertainment

Ethnic minority dancing, *Dragon's Jaw Hill. Daily at 0930 and 1500.* Also at the **Victoria Sapa**.

Shopping

The central square plays host to tens of friendly minority women selling fabrics every day, many of whom also follow tourists down the street attempting sales – if you buy from one expect more to latch on. The local authorities are trying in vain to manage this process and bring it under control. There are plenty of shops selling walking shoes, rucksacks, coats, jackets and mountaineering equipment.

May Gallery, *32 Cau May St, T020-873789*. The best place to purchase original art in town. Prices from US$10-1500. Most works are by the lovely manager's husband who exhibits internationally. Oil, lacquer and sculptures.
Wild Orchid, *29 Cau May St, T0912-135868*. A good place to pick up souvenirs and ethnic fabrics.

What to do

Therapies
Victoria Sapa, *see Where to stay, above*. Massage and other treatments are available. The hotel also has an indoor swimming pool.

Tour operators
Handspan, *Cau May St, T20-387 1214, www.handspan.com*. Tours in the vicinity of Sapa, including treks, mountain bike excursions, homestays and jeep expeditions. This is a booking office for the **Handspan Adventure Travel** group with offices in Hanoi.
Topas, *24 Muong Hoa St, T20-387 1331, www.topastravel.vn*. A combined Danish and Vietnamese operator offering numerous treks varying from fairly leisurely 1-day walks to an arduous 4-day assault on Mount Fan Si Pan. It also organizes bicycling tours and family tours. Well-run operation employing hundreds of local people and providing equipment where necessary. It has an office in Hanoi.

Transport

You get to Sapa either by road as part of the Northwest loop, via Lao Cai on the newly built highway linking it with Hanoi, or by overnight train from Hanoi via Lao Cai. A fleet of minibuses ferries passengers from Lao Cai railway station to Sapa.

Bus
Frequent connections from the main square run to **Lao Cai** (access point) with a small extra charge payable for larger luggage. It is also possible to arrange tickets to **Hanoi** in town.

Train
Overnight trains from and to **Hanoi**, via Lao Cai. There are numerous classes of seat or berth on the trains and some hotels have their own private carriages. It is quite easy to make the travel arrangements, but booking with an operator removes the hassle. A railway office in Sapa also sells tickets for the journey back to Hanoi.

Treks around Sapa
treks through terraced rice fields to ethnic minority villages

From half-day downhill ambles with van transfers back to town to multi-day trek and the overnight climb of Indochina's highest peak, Sapa has a trek for every taste and ability. You should never just turn up in a village for homestay opportunities; book with a tour operator.

Ta Phin
The derelict French seminary is near the village of Ta Phin. The names of the bishop who consecrated it and the presiding Governor of Indochina can be seen engraved on stones at the west end. Built in 1942 under the ecclesiastical jurisdiction of the Parish of Sapa, the building was destroyed 10 years later by militant Vietnamese hostile to the intentions of the order.

To get there from Sapa, take the road 8 km east towards Lao Cai then follow a track left up towards Ta Phin; it's 3 km to the monastery and a further 4 km to Ta Phin. Beyond the seminary, the path descends into a valley of beautifully sculpted rice terraces and past Black Hmong settlements to Ta Phin.

★ Mount Fan Si Pan

At a height of 3143 m, Vietnam's highest mountain is a two- or three-day trek from Sapa. The climb involves some steep scrambles, which are quite tough in wet conditions. Only the fit will make it to the summit. A good tour operator, either in Sapa or Hanoi, will provide camping equipment and porters.

Lau Chai (Black Hmong) village and Ta Van (Giáy) village

This is a round trip of 20 km taking in minority villages and beautiful scenery. A leisurely stroll through these villages is a chance to observe rural life led in reasonable prosperity. Wet rice forms the staple income; weaving for the tourist market puts a bit of meat on the table. Here nature is kind, there is rich soil and no shortage of water. Again it's possible to see how the landscape has been engineered to suit human needs. The terracing is on an awesome scale (in places more than 100 steps), the result of centuries of labour to convert steep slopes into level fields, which can be flooded to grow rice. Technologically, and in no sense pejoratively, the villages might be described as belonging to a bamboo age. Bamboo trunks carry water huge distances from spring to village; water flows across barriers and tracks in bamboo aqueducts; mechanical rice huskers made of bamboo are driven by water requiring no human effort; houses are held up with bamboo; bottoms are parked on bamboo chairs; and tobacco and other substances are inhaled through bamboo pipes. Any path chosen will lead to some hamlet or other; the Hmong in villages further from Sapa tend to be more reserved and suspicious; their fields and houses are often securely fenced off.

Heading southeast out of Sapa (see map, opposite), **Lao Chai** is 6 km away on the far valley side. Follow the track leading from the right-hand side of the road down to the valley floor, cross the river by the footbridge (*cau may*) and then walk up through the rice fields into Lao Chai village. You will find **Ta Van** 2 km further on.

Cross back to the north side of the river by the suspension bridge. A dip in the deep pools of the **Muong Hoa River** is refreshingly invigorating. Engraved stones are a further 2 km southeast (away from Sapa, that is) by the side of road; it is believed they are inscribed in ancient Hmong. The return walk to Sapa from the inscribed stones is a steady 10-km uphill climb. It's exhausting work but, stimulated by the views and the air and fuelled by hard-boiled eggs and warm Lao Cai beer from roadside shacks, and the prospect of cold beer at home, it is a pleasure, not an ordeal. In the late afternoon sun the rice glows with more shades of green than you would have thought possible and the lengthening shadows cast the entire landscape into vivid three-dimensional relief.

Cat Cat and Sin Chai villages
20,000d fee for taking the track.

The track heading west from Sapa through the market area offers either a short 5-km round-trip walk to Cat Cat Black Hmong village or a longer 10-km round-trip walk to Sin Chai Black Hmong village; both options take in some beautiful scenery. The path to Cat Cat leads off to the left of the Sin Chai track after about 1 km, following the line of pylons down through the rice paddies to Cat Cat village; beyond the village over the river bridge you can visit the Cascade Waterfall (from which the village takes its name) and an old French hydroelectric power station that still produces electricity. Sin Chai village is 4 km northwest of here.

The **Silver Falls** are 12 km west of Sapa on the Muong Lay road and are spectacular following rain. They are hardly worth a special visit but if passing it's quite nice to stop for a paddle in the cold pools.

Listings Treks around Sapa

Where to stay

It is possible to spend the night in one of the ethnic houses in the Sapa district. However, homestays must be organized through reputable tour operators. Villages include Ta Van (Day), Ban Ho (Tay), Nam Sai (Tay), Sin Chai (Red Dao) and Ta Phin (Red Dao).

$$$$ Topas Ecolodge
20 km southeast of Sapa, www.
topasecolodge.com (Sapa office:
24 Muong Hoa St, T020-387 1331).
25 bungalows with balconies built from white granite crown a hill overlooking stunning valleys. The walk from reception to the bungalows cuts right through the area's trademark rice terraces. Bungalows are simply furnished and powered by solar energy. The food is good – evening buffets are a particular treat. Treks and mountain bike rides lead to less touristed Red Dao areas. For nature, views, peace and an eco-philosophy, the lodge is unique in Vietnam. Highly recommended.

$$$ Hmong Mountain Retreat
6 km along the Ban Ho road, T020-650 5228,
www.hmongmountainretreat.com.
5 bungalows and a large, 2-bedroom Hmong House which is perfect for groups. Set on an isolated rice terrace, complete with a good restaurant. A stay can be combined with a trek to the Retreat.

$$$ Nam Cang Riverside Lodge
www.namcangriversidelodge.com.
Located deep in a remote Sapa Valley, this newcomer sits right on the bank of a fast flowing river backed by forest and next to a local minority village. The property is owned by a Red Dao minority family (headed by Mr Phu and Mrs Nhan) and operated in partnership with Topas Travel. A very special place in a very remote area, this is a great option for those looking for a true escape. Rooms are tastefully furnished and good food is served.

$ Homestays in Nam Sai and Nam Cam. Contact Sapa-based operators for homestays in this newly opened up area.

The Far North

The steep slopes of this mountainous region, which skirts the Chinese border, have been carved into curved rice terracing with paddies shimmering. Further north, where the steepness increases, patches of corn take over from rice cultivation, clinging to the rocky soil. The sparse populations that live here are predominantly indigenous groups and life goes on as it has for years. As one of the least-visited areas of the country, it offers the chance to see traditional Vietnamese life in some of the country's most spectacular scenery.

Ha Giang and around → *Colour map 2, A3.*

Ha Giang
The provincial capital of Ha Giang lies on the banks of the Lo River just south of its confluence with the River Mien, perched picturesquely between the beautiful Cam and Mo Neo mountains. Like Cao Bang and Lang Son, Ha Giang was badly damaged during the border war with China in 1979 and has since undergone extensive reconstruction. The best thing to do in Ha Giang is go motorbike touring.

Dong Van-Meo Vac Region → *Colour map 2, A4.*

high mountain scenery like nowhere else in Vietnam

This is the northernmost tip of Vietnam, close to the Chinese border. The road between Don Van and Meo Vac, including the Ma Pi Leng Pass, is one of the most spectacular roads in all of Vietnam.

★Dong Van
This remote market town is a great place to spend a night set in an attractive valley populated mainly by Tay people. It has a street of ancient houses that is very attractive, one of which has been converted into a wondeful litte café. Dong Van has a Sunday market, but is very quiet at other times of the week.

Essential Far North

Getting around

Unlike Northwest Vietnam, which has so conveniently aligned its attractions along one road circuit, the far north is somewhat fragmented although through road links have improved.

When to go

There are four distinct seasons in the north (spring, summer, autumn and winter). The best times to visit are autumn and spring. From January to March the weather can be very cool, but Ha Giang remains a popular place to visit with Vietnamese due to the flowers that bloom. From August to September the rice paddies are at their most beautiful.

Time required

The loop from Ha Giang to Meo Vac and back can be done in three days on a motorbike, see Transport.

★Ma Pi Leng Pass to Meo Vac

Passing over the Ma Pi Leng Pass around 1500 m above the Nho Que River, the scenery is simply awesome. Like Dong Van, Meo Vac is a restricted border area and foreigners need to register with police for a permit to stay here. Mountainous peaks and chasms abound. A small **market** is held every day in the town square, frequented mainly by White Hmong, Tay and Lolo people. Meo Vac is also the site of the famous **Khau Vai 'Love Market'** held once every year on the 27th day of the third month of the lunar calendar, which sees young people from all of the main ethnic groups of the region descending on the town to look for a partner. The Lolo people, with their highly colourful clothes, make up a large proportion of the town's population. A Lolo village is nearby, up the hill from the town centre.

East & south
of Hanoi

where dramatic limestone crags rear from the ground

Off the coast to the east of Hanoi lies Halong Bay with its thousands of limestone islands rearing out of the sea. Cruising these waters is now firmly established as one of Vietnam's top tourist draws.

To the south is Ninh Binh and an area know as 'Halong Bay on Land' where rivers weave among rice paddies surrounded by dramatic limestone karst formations.

Halong Bay and around → *Colour map 2, B5.*

on almost every tourist's itinerary and with good reason

★Halong means 'descending dragon', and an enormous beast is said to have careered into the sea at this point, cutting the fantastic bay from the rocks as it thrashed its way into the depths. Vietnamese poets (including the 'Poet King' Le Thanh Tong) have traditionally extolled the beauty of this romantic area with its rugged islands that protrude from a sea dotted with sailing junks. The bay is now a UNESCO World Heritage Site and one of Vietnam's key tourist draws with thousands sailing on overnight cruises here every year.

Most people book their tour in Hanoi, but boat tours of the bay can be booked at the Bai Chay Tourist Wharf in Halong City and Cat Ba Town. To see the bay properly allow four to five hours but an overnight trip is enjoyable and preferable. Grotto of Wonders, Customs House Cave and Surprise Grotto are generally included in tour and the entrance fee will be included in your package price.

Geologically the tower-karst scenery of Halong Bay is the product of millions of years of chemical action and river erosion working on the limestone to produce a pitted landscape. At the end of the last ice age, when glaciers melted, the sea level rose and inundated the area turning hills into islands. The islands of the bay are divided by a broad channel: to the east are the smaller outcrops of Bai Tu Long, while to the west are the larger islands with caves and secluded beaches.

Among the more spectacular caves are **Hang Hanh**, which extends for 2 km. Tour guides will point out fantastic stalagmites and stalactites that, with imagination, become heroes, demons and animals. **Hang Dau Go** is the cave wherein Tran Hung Dao stored his wooden stakes prior to studding them in the bed of the Bach Dang River in 1288 to destroy

Essential East and south of Hanoi

Finding your feet

Haiphong is well connected, with regular flights, trains and buses. Haiphong is the departure point for Cat Ba Island; it takes an hour by hydrofoil. There are two bases from which to explore Halong Bay: Halong City or Cat Ba. Traditionally, visitors to Halong Bay went direct to Halong City from Hanoi and took a boat from there. This is still a valid option, but Cat Ba Island is becoming increasingly popular as a springboard to Halong Bay, largely because Cat Ba itself is interesting.

Getting around

Tour operators are a popular way to visit Haiphong and the Halong Bay area, especially if short of time, but equally there are plenty of frequent public transport options to this area.

When to go

It can be stormy in June, July and August; it is no fun in the bay area in the rain or fog, so get a weather forecast if you can. On Cat Ba, the busiest and most expensive time is during school summer holidays from May to September. Winters are generally cool and dry.

> **Best** boating
> **Halong Bay**, page 82
> **Tam Coc**, page 88

the boats of invading Mongol hordes. **Hang Thien Cung (Heavenly Palace)** is a hanging cave, a short 50-m haul above sea level, with dripping stalactites, stumpy stalagmites and solid rock pillars. A truly enormous cave and one of those most visited is **Sung Sot Cave (Surprise Cave).**

Listings Halong Bay and around

Tourist information

Quang Ninh Tourism Information Promotion Centre
C29 Royal Park Area opposite the Halong 1 Hotel and near the Novotel, T33-362 8862, www.halongtourism. com.vn. Mon-Fri 0730-1630.
Provide advice about boats and hotels.

Where to stay

The past few years have seen an explosion in the number of hotels and guesthouses in Bai Chay and Hon Gai. Many of the newer hotels are badly built and, apart from the fact that some of the taller ones look structurally unsound, are quite frequently damp and musty; check the room first.

There are few hotels in Hon Gai but they tend to be more competitively priced than those in Bai Chay. In Bai Chay there are 2 main groups of hotels, 2 km apart. Most are to be found at the west end on the way in to town, set back a little from the seafront, and include Vuon Dao St composed entirely of 5- to 8-room mini hotels. A couple of kilometres further on, nearer the bridge, is a smaller group, some of which have good views.

$$$$-$$$ Halong Plaza
8 Halong Rd, Bai Chay, T33-384 5810, www.halongplaza.com.
200 rooms and suites and fantastic views over the sea, especially from upper floors. Pool, restaurants and friendly staff – a lovely seafront hotel.

$$ Viethouse Lodge
Tuan Chau Island, T33-384 2233,
www.viethouselodge.com.

With rooms scattered around a hillside this can be a more pleasant alternative to staying in the city. There's a restaurant, bar, games and transport to hire. The island is now connected to the mainland by a bridge.

Restaurants

Seafood is fresh and abundant and fairly priced. Le Qui Don St in Hon Gai has good seafood restaurants. Other than the hotels (see Halong Plaza especially), Halong Rd, near the junction with Vuon Dao St, Bai Chay, is lined for several hundred metres with restaurants – the best policy here is simply to pick a busy place.

$$ Emeraude Café
Co/Royal Park, T33-384 9266.
Open 0900-2100.

An oasis of comfort food close to the main hotels and restaurants. Free Wi-Fi.

What to do

Boat tours
Boat tours can be booked from hotels in Halong and in Hanoi, see below.
Buffalo Tours, *Ba Trieu St, Hanoi, T4-3828 0702, www.buffalotours.com.* A top-class operator and a recommended agent with which to book. They can also arrange scenic flights to the bay from Hanoi with **Hai Vu Aviation**.

Emeraude Classic Cruises, *46 Le Thai To St, Hanoi, T4-3935 1888, www.emeraude-cruises. com.* The best way to see Halong Bay in style is on the reconstructed French paddle steamer, the *Emeraude*. There are 39 cabins with extremely comfortable beds and nice touches (gift-wrapped biscuits) and old-style fans although the bathrooms are on the tiny side. There's a sumptuous buffet lunch and more delicious food than you can eat for dinner. Entertainment includes a Vietnamese spring roll demo, swimming off the boat, squid fishing, t'ai chi exercise on the sun deck at dawn and a massage service. There is also a bar.

Transport

Boat
To Cat Ba Jump on a tourist boat for a 1-way (4-hr) ride from the Bai Chay Tourist Wharf (Halong Rd, T33-384 6592).
From Hon Gai (Halong City) boat station (98 Ben Tau Rd near Long Tien pagoda) to **Quan Lan Island** and **Mong Cai**, daily.

Bus
Halong City bus station is now 5 km west of Halong city, near Halong train station. There is a bus stop right outside the Bai Chay Tourist Wharf. There are regular connections from Bai Chay bus station to **Hanoi** from 0700, taking 4-5 hrs. Buses are slow, crowded, uncomfortable and full of pickpockets. Regular connections with Haiphong's Lac Long bus station. There are also buses to **Mong Cai** and to **Bai Dai** (for ferries to Quan Lan).

Home to rare langur monkeys in the forested interior, Cat Ba Island is many Hanoians' number one weekend getaway. The island occupies a stunning setting in the south of Halong Bay. Much of the island and the seas around are designated a national park.

Cat Ba's remoteness has been steadily eroded (it only plugged into mains electricity in 1999), but despite the growth in numbers of karaoke-loving weekenders, it remains an attractive place (minus a few of the uglier buildings). Best of all it is a great springboard into the surrounding waters of Halong Bay and an increasingly popular alternative to Halong City as there is a lot to see including the stunning scenery of the interior.

Exploring the island

Cat Ba is the largest island in a coastal archipelago that includes more than 350 limestone outcrops. It is adjacent to and geologically similar to the islands and peaks of Halong Bay but separated by a broad channel as the map illustrates. The islands around Cat Ba are larger than the outcrops of Halong Bay and generally more dramatic. Cat Ba is the ideal place from which to explore the whole coastal area: besides the quality of its scenery it is a more agreeable town in which to stay, although the countless new hotels springing up are slowly eroding the difference. The island is rugged and sparsely inhabited. Outside Cat Ba town there are only a few small villages. Perhaps the greatest pleasure is to hire a motorbike and explore, a simple enough process given the island's limited road network.

Cat Ba National Park → *Colour map 2, B5.*

Park office, T31-388 8741, open 0700-1700. Town to park gate, 15 km, is 30 mins on a motorbike.

The national park (Vuon Quoc Gia Cat Ba), established in 1986, covers roughly half the island and is some 252 km sq. Of this area, a third consists of coast and inland waters. Home to 109 bird and animal species, and of particular importance is the world's last remaining troupe of white-headed langur (around 59 animals). Their numbers dropped from around 2500 in the 1960s to 53 in 2000; the primate is critically endangered and on the World Conservation Union Red List (www.catbalangur.org). These elusive creatures (*Trachypithecus poliocephalus poliocephalus*) are rarely spotted as they inhabit wild and remote cliff habitats. There are also several types of rare macaque (rhesus, pig-tailed and red-faced) and moose deer. Vegetation ranges from mangrove swamps in sheltered bays and densely wooded hollows, to high, rugged limestone crags sprouting caps of hardy willows. The marine section of the park is no less bounteous: perhaps less fortunate is the high economic value of its fish and crustacea populations, which keeps the local fishing fleet hard at work and prosperous. In common with other coastal areas in the region the potential for snorkelling here is zero.

Visitors are free to roam through the forest but advised not to wander too far from the path. Many hotels arrange treks from the park gate through the forest to Ao Ech (Frog Lake) on to the village of Viet Hai for a light lunch then down to the coast for a boat ride home. This takes the best part of a day (six to 10 hours). It is a good way to see the park but those preferring solitude can go their own way or go with a park guide. A short trek leads to the Ngu Lam Peak behind the park headquarters. July to October is the wet season when leeches are a problem and mosquitoes are at their worst. Bring leech socks if you have them and plenty of insect repellent. Collar, long sleeves and long trousers advisable.

Tourist information

The Cat Hai District People's Committee Tourism Information Centre
Along the seafront, T31-368 8215, www.catba.com.vn.
Offers free travel information as well as tours. Most of the hotels also offer information and tours.

Where to stay

While in summer prices may be slightly higher than those listed, as far as possible the price ranges below give a fair indication of seasonal variations. It may still be possible to negotiate discounts in quieter periods. There are no addresses, and to confuse matters further, many hotels claim the same name.

$$$$ Cat Ba Island Resort & Spa
Cat Co 1, T31-368 8686, www.catbaislandresort-spa.com.
There are 109 pleasant rooms decorated with white rattan furniture across 3 buildings facing the bay with a lovely outlook and fronting right on to the beach. The obtrusive water slides cannot be seen from the 2nd and 3rd building. 3 restaurants provide Western and Asian food and there are 2 pools, water slides, jacuzzi, massage, billiards and a tennis court. Trekking and Halong Bay tours are offered.

$$$$ Sunrise Resort
Cat Co 3, T31-388 7360, www.catbasunriseresort.com.
Lowkey resort on a beach linked by road to the town and by footpath to Cat Co 1. It has beach loungers and thatched umbrellas, a pool, jacuzzi, massage, 3 restaurants and travel services.

$$-$ Cat Ba Homestay
10 mins' drive from the town, T091-664 5858, www.catba-homestay.com.

A restored century-old house in pretty grounds offers both dorm and private accommodation. With its yellow walls, wooden pillars and tiled roof, this is a quaint spot with traditional architecture. Popular with groups.

$ Cat Ba Sea View
220 Harbourfront, T031-388 8210.
The pick of the budget options along the seafront, about half of the rooms have good views in this clean and friendly hotel. Also has a decent inexpensive restaurant on the ground floor.

Cat Ba National Park

$ Park guesthouse
Viet Hai Village, Viet Hai Community Based Tourism Association, T31-388 8836.
Homestays have beds with mosquito nets. A mattress and bed sheets can also be provided.

Restaurants

After dark the front fills up with Vietnamese tourists on bicycles and tandem bikes and those out for an evening stroll. Cat Ba is not a great place for those seeking a culinary experience, but some good seafood can be found. There are tens of seafood restaurants on the island all serving the same menu of grilled and steamed varieties along with the hugely popular *lau* (hotpot), which often comes with packet instant noodles which swiftly kills the flavour of any seafood you add to the broth. None of the restaurants are particularly inspiring, so it is best to wander along and choose one with the atmosphere that suits; being a tourist town with a high turnover, a seafood restaurant can be family friendly one night and full of rowdy, beer swilling weekenders the next. There are also plenty of fried rice and *pho* places along the main road selling both beef and prawn noodle soups.

$$ Green Mango
T31-388 7151.
If the local seafood spots aren't for you, this is the island's best Western-style restaurant. It serves a variety of reasonable burgers and pastas and also offers fresh fish.

$ Oasis Bar
Near the main pier, T098-270 4659.
During the day and in the early evening this is an okay choice for a quick, budget meal, while later in the night it becomes one of the town's most popular bars.

What to do

Boat tours
Halong Bay is the most famous excursion from Cat Ba. Almost all hotels in Cat Ba offer tours as do the touts along the seafront. It is better to use a service provided by a reputable hotel (as listed in Where to stay, above).

Kayaking
Kayaking in Halong Bay and Lan Ha Bay are now regular features, especially in the summer months. It is best to go via one of the established tour operators in Hanoi, such as **Handspan** and **Buffalo Tours** or to book with **Asia Outdoors**.

Rock climbing
Climbing the rock karst limestone faces and towers on Cat Ba and Halong Bay is now possible with experienced, licensed and enthusiastic climbers, see Tour operators below. They offer roped climbs on dry land in the extremely beautiful Buffalo Valley as well as deep water solo climbing on the bay itself for which no ropes are needed – you simply jump straight into the ocean when you finish (or fall…).

Tour operators
Asia Outdoors, *222 1/4 St, Group 19, Ward 4, T31-368 8450, www.asiaoutdoors.com.vn.*
Rock climbing, kayaking, trekking, boat cruises, islands stays and other adventures. Works directly with the local community on Cat Ba Island, employs both domestic and international staff and promotes the efforts to protect the endangered langur and the park's other conservation efforts. A highly recommended outfit.

Transport

There are direct hydrofoils from Haiphong or via the Dinh Vu ferry from Haiphong. Boats also leave Bai Chay and Tuan Chau 'Island' in Halong City for **Gia Luan** in the north of Cat Ba Island where a bus transports you to Cat Ba Town in the south. It is also possible to get a one-way ride with a tour leaving from the tourist wharf at Bai Chay (Halong City) direct to **Cat Ba Town** where tourist boats dock. Alternatively, organize a tour from Hanoi. The easiest way to reach Cat Ba from Hanoi is by the combined bus and ferry service (see page 60).

To get around the island go by *xe om*, hire a motorbike or get on a tour organized by a local hotel or tour operator in Hanoi.

Boat
From Haiphong, **Transtour Co** runs the Cat Ba–**Haiphong** ferry twice daily, T31-388 8314, office on the seafront. Express boats also run in the morning and afternoon. Tourist boats use the new Cat Ba pier in the middle of town.

Bus
There is a bus service between Cat Ba town and **Phu Long** where the Haiphong ferry docks along the new road and to **Gia Luan** where the Bai Chay and Tuan Chau 'Island' boats dock.

Ninh Binh city is capital of the densely populated province of Ninh Binh. It marks the most southerly point of the northern region. The town itself has little to commend to the tourist but it is a useful and accessible hub from which to visit some of the most interesting and attractive sights in the north.

Travellers can get to the places around Ninh Binh as a day trip from Hanoi through tour agencies or by taking tours or hiring transport from the hotels in Ninh Binh. With your own transport, Hoa Lu, Tam Coc and Phat Diem can all be comfortably covered in a day.

Hoa Lu → *Colour map 2, B4.*

Hoa Lu lies about 13 km from Ninh Binh near the village of Truong Yen. It was the capital of Vietnam from AD 968 to AD 1010, during the Dinh and Early Le dynasties. Prior to the establishment of Hoa Lu as the centre of the new kingdom, there was nothing here. But the location was a good one in the valley of the Hong River – on the 'dragon's belly', as the Vietnamese say. The passes leading to the citadel could be defended with a small force, and defenders could keep watch over the plains to the north and guard against the Chinese. The kings of Hoa Lu were, in essence, rustics. This is reflected in the art and architecture of the temples of the ancient city: primitive in form, massive in conception. Animals were the dominant motifs, carved in stone.

A large part of this former capital, which covered over 200 ha, has been destroyed, although archaeological excavations have revealed much of historical and artistic interest. The two principal temples are those of Dinh Bo Linh, who assumed the title King Dinh Tien Hoang on ascending the throne (reigned AD968-980), and Le Hoan, who assumed the title King Le Dai Hanh on ascending the throne (reigned AD 980-1009).

★Tam Coc → *Colour map 2, B4.*
Boats depart daily from 0700-1700.

Tam Coc means literally 'three caves'. The highlight of this excursion is an enchanting boat ride up the little Ngo Dong River through the eponymous three caves. Those who have seen the film *Indochine*, some of which was shot here, will be familiar with the nature of the beehive-type scenery created by limestone towers, similar to those of Halong Bay. The exact form varies from wet to dry season; when flooded the channel disappears and one or two of the caves may be under water. In the dry season the shallow river meanders between fields of golden rice. You can spot mountain goat precariously clinging to the rocks and locals collecting snails in the water. Women row – with both their hands and feet – through the caves at a leisurely pace. On a busy day the boats are nose to tail – to enjoy Tam Coc at its best make it your first port of call in the morning.

Phat Diem Cathedral → *Colour map 2, B5.*
24 km southeast of Ninh Binh in the village of Kim Son, daily 0800-1700, services daily. The journey takes in a number of more conventional churches, waterways and paddy fields. Take a motorbike from Ninh Binh or hire a car from Hanoi.

Phat Diem Cathedral is the most spectacular of the church buildings in the area, partly for its scale but also for its remarkable Oriental style with European stylistic influences. Completed in 1899, it boasts a bell tower in the form of a pagoda behind which stretches for 74 m the nave of the cathedral held up by 52 ironwood pillars. The cathedral was built under the leadership of parish priest Father Tran Luc between 1875 and 1899. He is buried in a tomb between the bell tower and the cathedral proper. Surrounding the cathedral are several chapels: St Joseph's, St Peter's, the Immaculate Heart's, the Sacred Heart's and St Roch's.

Listings Ninh Binh and around

Tourist information

Ninh Binh Tourism
www.ninhbinhtourism.com.vn.
The hotels all have good information.

Where to stay

Ninh Binh

$ Hoang Hai Hotel
36 Truong Han Sieu St, T30-3871 5177,
www.ninhbinhhotel.com.vn.
The 11 rooms are divided into 3 types;
the bigger rooms are more expensive.
Runs a good tour desk and is a good
source of information.

$ Thanh Thuy's Guesthouse
128 Le Hong Phong St, T30-387 1811,
www.hotelthanhthuy.com.
A clean budget choice with a variety
of room options, most have bathtubs.

$ Thuy Anh
55A Truong Han Sieu St, T30-387 1602,
www.thuyanhhotel.com.
37 rooms in this spotless hotel in the town
centre; the deluxe rooms come with a view.
Breakfast included. Will arrange tours.
Rooftop garden.

Tam Coc

$$$$ Tam Coc Garden Bungalows
Near the Tam Coc boat station,
www.tamcocgarden.com.
An absolute gem of a resort in extremely
pretty surrounds. 16 wonderful bare-
stone bungalows with very tasteful
furnishing are set in a garden with
unbeatable views of the karsts and
paddy fields. Highly recommended.

Restaurants

Ninh Binh

$ Hoang Hai Hotel
36 Truong Han Sieu St, T30-3871 5177.
Open 0800-2200.
This centrally located restaurant has
zero atmosphere but service is prompt.
Breakfast, lunch and dinner served.

$ Thanh Thuy's Guesthouse
See Where to stay, above.
The portions are plentiful.

$ Thuy Anh
See Where to stay, above.
A choice of Vietnamese fare.

Transport

Ninh Binh
Bus
From Ninh Binh's bus station at 207 Le Dai
Hanh St to Hanoi's southern terminal, **Giap
Bat**, hourly, 3 hrs and also to **Haiphong**,
4 a day; minibuses to **Hanoi**, 2 hrs. To **Phat
Diem**, 1 hr; to **Kenh Ga** 30 mins. Take the
same bus for **Van Long** and take a moto
at the turn-off to the reserve. Some **Open
Tour Buses** stop here on their way to Hanoi
and Hué.

Car, motorbike and bicycle
Hoang Hai Hotel (see Where to stay, above)
rents cars, motorbikes and bicycles. **Thanh
Thuy's Guesthouse** also rents bikes and
motorbikes. To get to Cuc Phuong National
Park independently of a tour, take a *xe om*
or hire a car for the day.

Central Vietnam

endless beaches, gigantic caves and ancient ruins

The Central Region includes the mountains of the Annamite chain which form a natural frontier with Laos to the west and in places extend almost all the way to the sea in the east. Many of Vietnam's ethnic minorities are concentrated in these mountains.

The narrow, coastal strip, sometimes only a few kilometres wide, supported the former artistically accomplished Kingdom of Champa.

The region is traversed by Highway 1, which runs all the way from Hanoi to Ho Chi Minh City. Along much of its route, the road runs close to the coast. The northern provinces are among the poorest in the country but their inhabitants are among the friendliest.

The middle part of the Central Region is home to World Heritage Sites of the Phong Nha-Ke Bang National Park with its amazing caves; the old Imperial City at Hué, a former capital of Vietnam; My Son, one-time capital of the Cham Kingdom; and Hoi An, an old mercantile port town which retains traditional architecture. This region is richly rewarding and would easily fill a two-week holiday in its own right.

The southern part of this diverse region has stunning coast and beaches, many of which are now home to high-class resorts, while many others remain blissfully untouched.

Best for
Adventure ▪ Beaches ▪ History

Footprint picks

★ **Phong Nha**, page 93

Peaceful riverside town
surrounded by caving adventures, jungle treks and more.

★ **Hué**, page 98

The former Imperial capital is filled with history and
magnificent mausoleums.

★ **Bach Ma National Park**, page 113

A former French Hill station with crumbling buildings, cascading falls
and jungle treks.

★ **Danang**, page 115

Fast developing, beach-side city with superb cuisine, the Son Tra
Peninsula and the Hai Van Pass.

★ **Hoi An**, page 121

An enchanting 17th-century mercantile town with stunning
nearby beaches.

★ **My Son**, page 131

Vietnam's answer to Angkor Wat.

CHINA

East Sea

LAOS

THAILAND

Footprint
picks

1 **Phong Nha**, page 93
2 **Hué**, page 98
3 **Bach Ma National Park**, page 113
4 **Danang**, page 115
5 **Hoi An**, page 121
6 **My Son**, page 131

CAMBODIA

PHNOM PENH □

Thanh Hoa   Sam Son

Truong Son Mountain Range   Ca River

Cua Lo
Vinh   Ong Mountain
(1587m)
Cau Treo   Ha Tinh

Phong Nha-Ke Bang   Dong Hoi
National Park   Da Mao Mountain
(665m)
Len Mu Mountain   Con Cao
(918m)   Island
Dong Ha
Voi Mep
Mountain (1701m)   Quang Tri
Lao Bao   Khe Sanh   Hué
(Huong Hoa)   Cau Hai Lagoon
Bach Ma National Park   Lang Co
Danang
Bana   Hoi An
My Son
Tam Ky
Chu Lai
Ngoc Linh
(2598m)   Quang Ngai
Dak Glei
Dak Nay
Bo-Y   Dak To
Kontum   Hoai Nhon
Plateau   Kontum   Kien   Bo Mountain
Bien Ho   My   (892m)
Lake   Dekop   Cha Ban
Play Ku   Quy Nhon
Le Thanh   Song Cau
Central   Ba River   Tuy Hoa
Highlands
Da Rang
River
Ban Don   Dac Lac Plateau   Dam Mon
Buon Ma Thuot
Lak Lake   Ninh Hoa
Nha Trang
Ta Dung
(1971m)   Dalat
Nam Cat Tien
National Park   Cam Ranh
Bao   Khanh Hai
Phan Rang
Dau   Tri An   Ca Na
Tieng   Lake   Phan   Bac Binh
Tay Ninh   Lake   Thiet   Ham Thuan Bac
Cu Chi   Hoa   Mui Ne
Chau Doc   Cao   Xuan
Lanh   Tan An   Loc
Long Xuyen   My Tho   Ho Coc
Duong   Ha Tien   Sa Dec   Ben Tre
Dong   Hon   Rach   Can Tho   Vinh Long   Vung Tau
Phu Quoc   Chong   Gia   Tra Vinh
Island   Rach Soi
Soc Trang   Mekong Delta
Ca Mau   Bac Lieu

HO CHI
MINH CITY

N

50 km
50 miles

▼ To Con Dao Archipelago

Thanh Hoa
to Hué

recently discovered caves have put this area on the tourist map

In the past, visitors would largely ignore this swathe of Vietnam, but the discovery of one of the world's largest caves, Hang Son Doong, has catapulted the area to fame.

Today, Phong Nha – the small town that functions as a base for exploring the caves – is one of the country's most up-and-coming spots. Alongside the caves, the ethnic minority cultures of the area are fascinating. Not far from here in Dong Ha is the former Demilitarized Zone (DMZ), which was the scene of heavy fighting in the American War.

Dong Hoi and around → Colour map 3, B4.
Vietnam's hottest adventure playground with the world's most spectacular caves

Until a few years ago there was little to entice the tourist to this area, but the opening of the area's mind-blowing caves, including Hang En and Son Doong, has put province of Quang Binh firmly on the tourism map.

Dong Hoi
The town can be used as a stopping-off point on the way north or south and it is from here that Phong Nha, the caving base, is accessed. Dong Hoi itself was virtually annihilated during the war as it lies just north of the **17th parallel**, marking the border between North and South Vietnam. Just south of the town is the **Hien Luong Bridge,** which spans the Ben Hai River – the river forming the border between the two halves of former North and South Vietnam.

★Phong Nha
Phong Nha is a small riverside town that, until just a few years ago, saw almost zero tourism and remained very poor, with the population getting by on farming, fishing and hunting. Today, however, tourism is booming thanks to the caving opportunities opened up since 1990 by British Caving Association teams and now Oxalis Adventure Tours.

The star attraction is Hang Son Doong, one of the world's largest caves. Tours of this cave are limited in number and very costly (US$3000), but tours of other fantastic caves including Hang En and the Tu Lan system are much more affordable and are also unbeatable experiences. The town itself is a sleepy place where the locals are extremely friendly and the sunrises and sunsets over the river are not to be missed. Alongside visits to the caves, there are some excellent cycling routes in the area that take in parts of the original Ho Chi Minh Trail.

Hang Son Doong It's so massive that skyscrapers could stand inside and it is home to its own forest in which monkeys and flying foxes have been spotted. Photographs of this natural wonder went viral in 2013 and 2014, helping to catapult the area into the limelight. The cave can only be accessed on a tour with Oxalis – see Tour companies, below.

Phong Nha Cave ⓘ *www.phongnhakebang.vn, boats leave from the Son River landing stage in Phong Nha*. Phong Nha Cave is a true speleological wonder. Visitors are taken upstream from Phong Nha before heading into the cave itself for around 600 m and then dropped off to explore. There are stalagmites and stalactites and those with a powerful torch can pick out the form of every manner of ghoul and god in the rocks. A team of British divers explored 9 km of the main cave system in 1990 but less than 1 km is accessible to visitors.

Thien Duong (Paradise Cave) ⓘ *120,000d*. Paradise Cave was the first cave to put this area on the map and prior to images of Son Doong going viral, this was the area's star attraction. It is a gargantuan cave, the first 1 km or so is well lit and there is a good walking trail along it. In places it reaches a width and height of 100 m and the formations it harbours are truly captivating. It is not to be missed.

Nuoc Mooc spring and eco trail ⓘ *50,000d*. A pretty trail through woodland leads down to gushing rapids that are formed by water that emerges in a large torrent from an unknown underground source. A series of wooden walkways leads across the rapids to a pleasant spot where it's possible to take a dip – you'll be forced to wear a life jacket and, given the current a few feet away from the swimming area, this is no bad thing. The road to to Nuoc Mooc is hilly, but it makes a great bike ride which can be combined with a trip to Dark Cave.

Dark Cave ⓘ *50,000d*. Another of the caves first explored by British cavers in the early 1990s, Dark Cave is over 5 km in length and reaches heights of around 80 m. A new, fun way to reach the cave mouth is to zip line in from a high tower. As the name suggests, this cave lacks natural light so those who venture in should do so with headlamps.

Tu Lan Cave System This series of caves was made famous by National Geographic photographer Carsten Peter. The river caves, with majestic formations, are only accessible on organized one, two or three day tours which involve plenty of exciting cave swimming. On overnight tours guests camp out on pebble beaches on lagoons filled by waterfalls surrounded by limestones cliff faces – see **Oxalis Adventure Tours**, page 96.

Dong Ha and the border with Laos

The **Demilitarized Zone** (DMZ), **Khe Sanh** and the **Ho Chi Minh Trail** lie to the south of Dong Hoi. These war-time sights are normally visited on a tour from Hué and are described in detail on page 111.

About 94 km south, at Dong Ha, Highway 9 branches off the main coastal Highway 1 and proceeds to the border with Laos at **Lao Bao** (Dansavanh in Laos, see box, page 545).

Dong Ha sits on the junction of Highways 1 and 9 and is prospering from the growth of trade with Laos. Dong Ha is a convenient overnight stop for those crossing into or coming from Laos. Buses now travel regularly to the border from Hué. Along this route is Khe Sanh (now also called Huong Hoa) – one of the most evocative names associated with American involvement in Vietnam (see page 111).

Close to Khe Sanh are parts of the famous **Ho Chi Minh Trail** along which supplies were ferried from the north to the south. Highway 9 has been extensively improved in recent years to provide land-locked Laos with an alternative access route to the sea. This **Lao Bao** crossing (2 km beyond Lao Bao village) to Savannakhet provides Laos visas on arrival.

Listings Dong Hoi and around

Where to stay

Dong Hoi

$ Quang Ly Guesthouse
6 Thuan Ly, T52-383 7268,
quanglyguesthouse@yahoo.com.
Clean and basic place with very friendly and helpful owners. Free internet, tour information and motorcycle and bike hire. Located close to the station.

Phong Nha

$$ Phong Nha Lakehouse Resort
1 km outside Phong Nha, T978-266326,
www.phongnhalakehouse.com.
In a lovely location overlooking a lake, this resort was adding some lakefront bungalows at the time of writing which look set to be some of the best digs in town. Also has a restaurant with great views serving a wide range of delicious dishes. As is often the case here in Phong Nha, the owners are extremely warm and welcoming.

$$-$ Phong Nha Farmstay
8 km from Phong Nha, T53-3675 135,
www.phong-nha-cave.com.
The setting of this Aussie/Vietnamese owned place couldn't be better, right on the edge of beautiful paddy fields in the countryside outside Phong Nha. Alongside a range of rooms from dorms to family options, there is a great restaurant and bar, plus a pool, a rooftop bar and terrace. The staff are extremely helpful and can provide plenty

of information on what to do. Bicycles available for hire. This is the kind of place people get stuck for way longer than planned. Highly recommended.

$ Easy Tiger
T53-3675 135, www.phong-nha-cave.com.
Owned by Bich and Ben of the Farmstay, this is the place of choice for backpackers, with clean dorms complete with animal fur pattern bed covers. Downstairs is a large bar/restaurant area that kicks off in the evenings. Also has a free pool table and an extremely good information desk. Runs tours and sells bus tickets.

$ Ho Khanh's Homestay
Beyond the Oxalis office, T9-1679 4506,
www.phong-nha-homestay.com.
This idyllic spot is owned by the family of Mr Ho Khanh, the man who led the British caving expedition to discover Son Doong cave, one of the world's largest. Right on the bank of the river, the views here are breathtaking, particularly on a calm, misty morning. Accommodation is simple, but charming and clean. Great breakfast pancakes too. Although their English is very limited, the hosts are wonderful and help to make this a very special place to stay.

$ Thanh Tam
T52-3677999, www.thanhtamhotel
phongnha.com.
A newly built *nha nghi* (guesthouse) that offers a host of extremely clean and cheap rooms, some with excellent river views.

Also has a good restaurant serving noodles and rice dishes. A good choice for those on a budget.

Dong Ha and the border with Laos

$ Melody Hotel
62 Le Duan St, T53-355 4664, www.melodyhoteldha.net.
25 rooms recently renovated rooms, all with ac. Offers tours to the DMZ, ticket booking and motorcycle hire.

Restaurants

Dong Ha and the border with Laos

$ Dong Que Restaurant
109 Le Duan St.
Typical Vietnamese fare catering for passing tourist trade.

Phong Nha
Alongside the places listed below, **Easy Tiger** and the **Farmstay** both have good kitchens. Phong Nha is seeing new places open on a regular basis to serve the growing number of visitors.

$ Bamboo Cafe
Main road, T52-367 8777.
Owned by the engaging Hai who also runs the fabulous eco tour of the area, **Bamboo Cafe** is a great spot to meet other travellers and enjoy Western or Vietnamese food, a good shake or an ice cold beer.

$ Best BBQ Pork in The World
Near the market – look for the wooden sign and the barbecue smoke.
This street-side barbecued pork joint also has a normal Vietnamese name, but it's the sign advertising the pork that draws in the crowds. And the sign does not lie – the barbecued pork here is outrageously good. The wonderful hosts also serve a range of Central Vietnamese dishes. Not to be missed.

$ Pub With Cold Beer
Just outside Phong Nha – see Easy Tiger for a map.
Perhaps the best grilled chicken in Vietnam served by a lovely family. The chicken comes with sublime peanut sauce that's made fresh on the premises. A gem.

$ Tuan Ngoc
Opposite Easy Tiger, T986-059441.
Run by the friendly Ngoc and her husband Tuan, this is a great place to sample some dishes local to Phong Nha and Hué. Recommended.

$ Vung Hué
Just off the main street, T942-071656.
This is where both locals and the expats head for the best Vietnamese food in town. The decor is as bare as can be, but the ribs are amazing and so is the fried beef.

What to do

Phong Nha
Oxalis Adventure Tours, *T52-367 7678, www. oxalis.com.vn/contact.* This highly professional outfit counts Howard and Deb Limbert of the British Cave Association among its staff. It is also the only operator to run tours to Son Doong. It offers a range of trips to the Tu Lan cave system for cave swimming and camping out on remote waterfall-filled lakes. A variety of options can be chosen, from 1-day to multi-night treks. One of the most exceptional treks on offer is to Hang En where trekkers camp on a beach inside an almighty cavern large enough to house a jumbo jet. Very highly recommended tours.
Phong Nha Adventure Cycling, *main road, T98-555 5827, www.phongnhacycling.jimdo. com.* Led by the inimitable Shi, a range of cycling tours are on offer, including trips to Dark Cave, villages, the **Pub With Cold Beer** and the original Ho Chi Minh Trail. A great way to see more of the area and learn about its past and present.

Transport

Dong Hoi
Air
Flights link Dong Hoi with **HCMC** and **Hanoi** – check **Vietnam Airlines** for the current schedule.

Bus
The bus station is on Tran Hung Dao St. Buses travelling up Highway 1 linking **HCMC** with **Hanoi** pass through Dong Hoi.

Train
Regular connections with **Hanoi** and **HCMC**.

Phong Nha
Local buses serve Phong Nha from Dong Hoi and it's also possible to take a taxi. It is also on the Boomerang bus route used by backpackers.

Dong Ha and the border with Laos
Bus
Sepon Travel, 189 Le Duan St, T53-385 5289, www.sepontour.com, runs buses to **Laos**. The bus station is at 425 Le Duan St, 1.5 km from the old one, T53-385 1488. Bus to **Vinh**, 12 hrs. Dong Ha is 74 km from **Hué**, buses every 30 mins 0630-1800 and 80 km from the Lao Bao border crossing; to **Huong Hoa** (Khe Sanh) every 30 mins, 0500-1800; to **Lao Bao** every 30 mins. To **Hanoi**, 1800.

For details of the border crossing between Lao Bao (Vietnam) and Dansavanh (Laos), see box, page 545.

Hué
& around

former royal capital bursting with history and culture

★Hué, an imperial city that housed generations of the country's most powerful emperors, was built on the banks of the Huong Giang (Perfume River), named after a scented shrub that is supposed to grow at its source.

Just south of the city are the last resting places of many Vietnamese emperors while the ancient Citadel complex offers a fascinating glimpse into its glorious past. A number of war relics in the Demilitarized Zone can be easily visited from Hué. Also in the region are the nearby Thuan An Beach, the charming Thanh Hoan Covered Bridge, the misty heights of Bach Ma National Park, the Lang Co Peninsula and the stunning Hai Van Pass.

Hué → *Colour map 3, B5.*

heaven for history buffs and architecture lovers

Imperial City
Entrance through the Ngo Mon Gate, 23 Thang 8 St, 0700-1730, 105,000d. Guides are available in languages including English, French, Russian, Mandarin and Japanese. Guiding can last until 1900 after the ticket desk closes.

The Citadel was built to a design of Vauban (France's 17th-century fortifications designer) and covers 520 sq ha. Its walls are 6.6 m high, 21 m thick and 10,000 m in circumference with 10 entrances topped by watch towers. Inside the Citadel, the Great Enclosure contains the Imperial City and Forbidden City.

The Imperial City is built on the same principles as the Forbidden Palace in Beijing. It is enclosed by 7- to 10-m-thick outer walls, the **Kinh Thanh**, along with moats, canals and towers. Emperor Gia Long commenced construction in 1804 after geomancers had decreed a suitable location and orientation for the palace. The site enclosed the land of eight villages (for which the inhabitants received compensation), and covers 6 sq km; sufficient area to house the emperor and all his family, courtiers, bodyguards and servants. It took 20,000 men to construct the walls alone. Not only has the city been damaged by war and

Essential Hué and around

Getting around

For the city itself, walking is an option – interspersed, perhaps, with the odd cyclo journey. Most guesthouses hire out bicycles and this is a very pleasant and slightly more flexible way of exploring Hué and some of the surrounding countryside. A motorbike provides even more flexibility: it makes it possible to fit so much more into a day.

Getting to and around the **Imperial Tombs** is easiest by motorbike or car as they are spread over a large area. Most hotels and tour operators organize tours. If cycling, set out early if you hope to see all the tombs in a day. It is also possible to go on the back of a motorcycle taxi. Boats can be chartered to sail up the river, but only a few of the tombs can be reached in this way.

Most visitors visit the sights of the DMZ, including Khe Sanh and the Ho Chi Minh Trail, on a tour. Buses do leave for the town of Huong Hoa (Khe Sanh) from the An Hoa bus station; the former site of the US base is 3 km from Huong Hoa bus station. From here it is possible to arrange transport to the Ho Chi Minh Trail and to other sights. A one-day tour of all the DMZ sights can be booked from any of Hué's tour operators.

Best restaurants

Le Jardin de la Carambole, page 104
Nina's Café, page 104
Omar Khayyam's, page 105

When to go

The rainy season runs from September to January and rainfall is particularly heavy between September and November; the best time to visit is therefore between February and August.

Time required

Two days for the temple and the main mausoleums.

Best places to stay

La Residence, page 103
Pilgrimage Village, page 103
Saigon Morin, page 103

Weather Hué

January	February	March	April	May	June
24°C 18°C 131mm	25°C 19°C 44mm	27°C 20°C 50mm	31°C 22°C 47mm	33°C 25°C 96mm	33°C 25°C 96mm

July	August	September	October	November	December
33°C 26°C 98mm	33°C 25°C 113mm	32°C 24°C 351mm	29°C 23°C 520mm	26°C 21°C 445mm	24°C 19°C 250mm

incessant conflict, but also by natural disasters such as floods which, in the mid-19th century, inundated the city to a depth of several metres.

Chinese custom decreed that the 'front' of the palace should face south (like the emperor) and this is the direction from which visitors approach the site. Over the outer moat, a pair of gates pierce the outer walls: the **Hien Nhon** and **Chuong Duc** gates. Just inside are two groups of massive cannon; four through the Hien Nhon Gate and five through the Chuong Duc Gate. These are the **Nine Holy Cannon (Cuu Vi Than Cong)**, cast in 1803 on the orders of Gia Long from bronzeware seized from the Tay Son revolutionaries. The cannon are named after the four seasons and the five elements, and on each is carved its name, rank, firing instructions and how the bronze of which they are made was acquired. They are 5 m in length, but have never been fired. Like the giant urns outside the Hien Lam Cac (see page 102), they are meant to symbolize the permanence of the empire. Between the two gates is a massive **flag tower**. The flag of the National

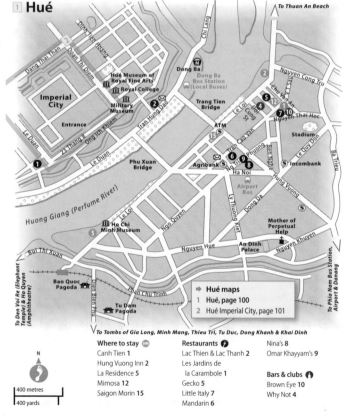

➡ **Hué maps**
1 Hué, page 100
2 Hué Imperial City, page 101

To Tombs of Gia Long, Minh Mang, Thieu Tri, Tu Duc, Dong Khanh & Khai Dinh

Where to stay 🛌
Canh Tien **1**
Hung Vuong Inn **2**
La Residence **5**
Mimosa **12**
Saigon Morin **15**

Restaurants 🍴
Lac Thien & Lac Thanh **2**
Les Jardins de
la Carambole **1**
Gecko **5**
Little Italy **7**
Mandarin **6**

Nina's **8**
Omar Khayyam's **9**

Bars & clubs 🍸
Brown Eye **10**
Why Not **4**

Liberation Front flew here for 24 days during the Tet Offensive in 1968 – a picture of the event is displayed in Hué's Ho Chi Minh Museum.

Northwards from the cannon, and over one of three bridges which span a second moat, is the **Ngo Mon (Royal Gate) (1)**, built in 1833 during the reign of Emperor Minh Mang. The ticket office is just to the right. The gate, remodelled on a number of occasions since its original construction, is surmounted by a pavilion from where the emperor would view palace ceremonies. Of the five entrances, the central one – the Ngo Mon – was only opened for the emperor to pass through. The other four were for procession participants, elephants and horses. UNESCO has thrown itself into the restoration of Ngo Mon with vigour and the newly finished pavilion, supported by 100 columns, atop the gate now gleams and glints in the sun; those who consider it garish can console themselves with the thought that this is how it might have appeared in Minh Mang's time.

② **Hué Imperial City**

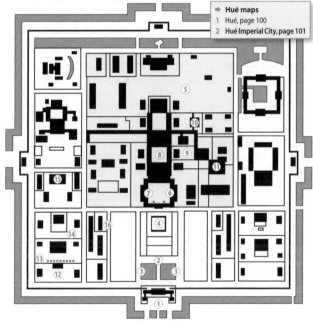

| ➡ **Hué maps** |
| 1 Hué, page 100 |
| 2 Hué Imperial City, page 101 |

100 metres
100 yards

1 Ngo Mon (Royal Gate)
2 Golden Water Bridge

3 Tanks
4 Dai Trieu Nghi (Great Rites Courtyard) & Thai Hoa Palace (Palace of Supreme Harmony)
5 ☐ Tu Cam Thanh (Purple Forbidden City)
6 Ta Pavilion

7 Huu Vu Pavilion
8 Central Pavilion, private apartments of the Emperor
9 Quang Minh Palace
10 Royal Reading Pavilion
11 Royal (East) Theatre

12 Hien Lam Cac
13 9 Bronze urns
14 Thé Temple (Temple of Generation)
15 Hung Temple
16 Waiting Pavilion (Huu Ta Dai Lam Vien)

North from the Ngo Mon, is the **Golden Water Bridge** (2) – again reserved solely for the emperor's use – between two **tanks** (3), lined with laterite blocks. This leads to the **Dai Trieu Nghi (Great Rites Courtyard)** (4), on the north side of which is the **Thai Hoa Palace (Palace of Supreme Harmony)** (4), constructed by Gia Long in 1805 and used for his coronation in 1806. From here, sitting on his golden throne raised up on a dais, the emperor would receive ministers, foreign emissaries, mandarins and military officers during formal ceremonial occasions. In front of the palace are 18 stone stelae, which stipulate the arrangement of the nine mandarinate ranks on the Great Rites Courtyard: the upper level was for ministers, mandarins and officers of the upper grade; the lower for those of lower grades. Civil servants would stand on the left, and the military on the right. Only royal princes were allowed to stand in the palace itself, which is perhaps the best-preserved building in the Imperial City complex. Its red and gold ironwood columns decorated with dragon motifs, symbol of the emperors' power, the tiled floor and fine ceiling have all been restored.

North of the Palace of Supreme Harmony is the **Tu Cam Thanh (Purple Forbidden City)** (5). This would have been reserved for the use of the emperor and his family, and was surrounded by 1-m-thick walls: a city within a city. Tragically, the Forbidden City was virtually destroyed during the 1968 Tet offensive. The two **Mandarin Palaces** and the **Royal Reading Pavilion** (see below) are all that survive.

At the far side of the Thai Hoa Palace, are two enormous **bronze urns (Vac Dong)** decorated with birds, plants and wild animals, and weighing about 1500 kg each. To either side of the urns are the **Ta** (6) and **Huu Vu** (7) pavilions – one converted into a souvenir art shop, the other a mock throne room in which tourists can pay to dress up and play the part of the emperor for five minutes. The **Royal Reading Pavilion** (10) has been renovated but, needless to say, has no books. On the far side of the palace are the outer northern walls of the citadel and the north gate.

Most of the surviving buildings of interest are to be found on the west side of the palace, running between the outer walls and the walls of the Forbidden City. At the southwest corner is the well-preserved and beautiful **Hien Lam Cac** (12), a pavilion built in 1821, in front of which stand nine massive **bronze urns** (13) cast between 1835 and 1837 on the orders of Emperor Minh Mang. It is estimated that they weigh between 1500 kg and 2600 kg, and each has 17 decorative figures, animals, rivers, flowers and landscapes representing between them the wealth, beauty and unity of the country. The central, largest urn is dedicated to the founder of the empire, Emperor Gia Long. Next to the urns walking northwards is **Thé Temple (Temple of Generations)** (14). Built in 1821, it contains altars honouring 10 of the emperors of the Nguyen Dynasty behind which are meant to be kept a selection of their personal belongings. It was only in 1954, however, that the stelae depicting the three Revolutionary emperors Ham Nghi, Thanh Thai, and Duy Tan were brought into the temple. The French, perhaps fearing that they would become a focus of discontent, prevented the Vietnamese from erecting altars in their memory. North of the Thé Temple is **Hung Temple** (15) built in 1804 for the worship of Gia Long's father, Nguyen Phuc Luan, the father of the founder of the Nguyen Dynasty. The temple was renovated in 1951.

Where to stay

Most hotels lie to the south of the Perfume River. Hué still suffers from a dearth of quality accommodation but this has improved in recent years and more properties are planned.

$$$$ La Residence Hotel & Spa
5 Le Loi St, T54-383 7475,
www.la-residence-Hué.com.
Anyone who knew this hotel before will be stunned at its fabulous makeover. For lovers of art deco, it is an essential place to stay and to visit. Home of the French governor of Annam in the 1920s, it has been beautifully and decadently restored with 122 rooms, restaurant, lobby bar, spa and swimming pool close to the Perfume River. The citadel can be seen from the hotel. The rooms in the original governor's residence are the most stylish, with 4-poster beds and lovely dark wood furnishings; other rooms are extremely comfortable too, with all mod-cons. The breakfasts are very filling; guests also enjoy free internet. The hotel has a fascinating collection of old colonial-era photographs that are hung along the corridors. Highly recommended.

$$$$ Pilgrimage Village boutique resort and spa
130 Minh Mang Rd, T54-388 5461,
www.pilgrimagevillage.com.
Tastefully designed rooms in a village setting ranging from honeymoon and pool suites to superior rooms. The rooms in small houses with private pools are gorgeous and recommended. There are 2 restaurants (see Restaurants), a number of bars, a beautiful and atmospheric spa (the Vietnamese aromatherapy massage is outstanding), open to outside guests also, and 2 inviting pools. Cooking and t'ai chi classes are available. There's a complementary shuttle service to and from town.

$$$$ Saigon Mor...
30 Le Loi St, T54-382 ...
www.morinhotels.co...
Recognizable as the fi...
built by the Morin brot...
Arranged around a cou...yard with a small pool, the rooms are large and comfortable. All come with a/c, satellite TV and hot water. The courtyard, lit with candles, is a delightful place to sit in the evening and enjoy a quiet drink. Service is friendly and the overall effect most agreeable. Recommended.

$ Hung Vuong Inn
20 Hung Vuong St, T54-382 1068,
hung.vuong.inn@gmail.com.
There are 9 double and twin rooms above the shop that are all spotlessly clean. Rooms have a TV and mini-bar and bathtubs; some have a balcony. It is quieter on the back side of the building. The restaurant of the same name is a very popular spot.

$ Vietnam Backpackers' Hostel
10 Pham Ngu Lao St, T54-382 6567,
www.vietnambackpackershostels.com.
Prices include breakfast. Happy hour 2000-2100. A great travellers' hostel with a bar downstairs and ultra clean rooms and dorms upstairs with a lovely balcony over the street for chilling. Tours offered too.

Guesthouses

The little *hem* (alley) opposite the **Century Riverside** has some really nice rooms in comfortable and cheerful guesthouses in what is easily the best value accommodation in Hué. Particularly recommended are:

$ Canh Tien Guesthouse
9/66 Le Loi St, T54-382 2772.
12 rooms that come with fan or a/c. Cheaper rooms have fans; the most expensive have a balcony. Wi-Fi.

..., 66) Le Loi St, T54-382 8068.
...e cheapest options in town. French
...poken when the owner is here. 8 rooms
with a/c, hot water and bathtub that are
quiet, simple and clean but very aged.
Rooms with fan are cheaper. Wi-Fi available.
A friendly bargain basement option.

Restaurants

The influence of the royal court on Hué
cuisine is evident in a number of ways:
there are a large number of dishes served,
with each dish being relatively light. Hué
food is delicately flavoured and requires
painstaking preparation in the kitchen:
in short, it's a veritable culinary harem
in which even the most pampered and
surfeited emperor could find something to
tickle his palate. Other Hué dishes are more
robust, notably the famed *bun bo Hué*,
round white noodles in soup with slices of
beef and laced with chilli oil of exquisite
piquancy. Restaurants for local people
usually close early; it's best to get there
before 2000. Traveller cafés and restaurants
tend to keep serving food until about 2200.

$$$-$$ Le Jardin de la Carambole
www.lesjardinsdelacarambole.com.
A beautiful restaurant housed in an old
villa, **Les Jardins** is universally popular and
a perfect place for a special, romantic meal.
The French and Vietnamese food are both
delightful and the waiting staff are attentive.
Don't miss the beef in banana leaf or the
goat cheese salad. A must-visit when in Hué.

$$ La Carambole
*19 Pham Ngu Lao St195, T54-381 0491, la_*
carambole@hotmail.com. Open 0700-2300.
One of the first restaurants catering to
foreigners in town, this remains one of
the most popular and deservedly so. It is
extremely touristy being located in the heart
of the hotel area, but it retains its charm
and serves up comforting food in a bustling

atmosphere. Make a reservation or be
prepared to wait.

$$ Little Italy
10 Nguyen Thai Hoc, T54-382 6928,
www.littleitalyHué.com.
Owned by the people behind **DMZ Bar**,
Little Italy has shifted location but kept the
same successful formula in place: filling
pizzas and pastas and friendly service.

$ Gecko
9 Pham Ngu Lao St, T98-668 9432.
New kid on the block, **Gecko** has a well-
designed open courtyard space with
bespoke furnishing and exposed brickwork.
Serves pizza, pasta and a small range of
Vietnamese classics. Very friendly young
staff and a good vibe.

$ Jardin de Y Thao
3 Thach Han St, T54-352 3018,
ythaogarden@gmail.com.
Rather touristy, this old house in a pretty
garden is nonetheless delightful.

$ Lac Thien
6 Dinh Tien Hoang St, T54-352 7348.
Lac Thien serves well-prepared Hué staples
at cheap prices. The owner is a gregarious
chap who introduces himself to all customers
when he is here. Each diner will also leave
with a little gift from the staff.

$ Mandarin
24 Tran Cao Van St, T54-382 1281,
www.mrcumandarin.com.
An old favourite run by Mr Cu, this café is
decorated with his own black and white
photos. Serves a variety of cheap, filling food.
Travel services and bike rental. Mr Cu is one
of the most helpful café owners in the whole
of Vietnam making this a good place to book
tours and get information.

$ Nina's Café
16/34 Nguyen Tri Phuong, T54-838 636,
www.ninascafe.jimdo.com.
Hidden at the end the guesthouse-filled
alley, this is a family-run outfit in the front
garden of their home. Superb versions of

many Hué specialities and great service. Ask about 'Nina's Tour' to the family village 30 km from town.

$ Omar Khayyam's
34 Nguyen Tri Phuong St, T54-382 1616.
Hué's most popular Indian restaurant for many years. Serves authentic tandoori dishes and curries.

Bars and clubs

Brown Eyes
56 Chu Van An, T54-382 7494.
On a busy night, **Brown Eyes** can get packed out and it stays open later than most. Loud music, cheap beers and plenty of backpackers. A sign states they 'open until the last person passes out'.

DMZ Bar
60 Le Loi St, T54-382 3414, www.dmzbar. com.vn. Open 0900-0200.
Hué's oldest bar, **DMZ** serves cheap cold beer and bargain cocktails making it a popular spot with budget travellers who gather to play on the free pool table. A good place to meet people and pick up tourist information.

Why Not?
46 Pham Ngu Lao, T54-3824 793, www.whynot.com.vn.
Alongside **DMZ**, this is one of the city's most busy bars. Trades on cheap drinks, music and a good atmosphere. Also serves a range of cheap food and has a pool table. Draws in a mixed crowd of travellers and locals.

Entertainment

Rent a dragon boat and sail up the Perfume River with your own private singers and musicians. Tour offices and major hotels will arrange groups.
See a Royal Court performance in the Imperial City's theatre or listen to performers during the Saigon Morin's occasional evening buffet.

Shopping

There is a much wider range of goods on sale in Hué now than was the case in the past, no longer just the *non bai tho* or poem hats. These are a form of the standard conical hat, *non lá*, which are peculiar to Hué. Made from bamboo and palm leaves, love poetry, songs, proverbs or simply a design are stencilled on to them, which are only visible if the hat is held up to the light and viewed from the inside. Shops on Le Loi and Pham Ngu Lao streets, sell ceramics, silk and clothes. There are a number of new art galleries. Perfectly decent stuff but not the range of Hoi An, where visitors are advised to shop.
No Vietnamese visitor would shake the dust of Hué off his feet without having previously stocked up on *me xung*, a sugary, peanut and toffee confection coated in sesame seeds: quite a pleasant energy booster to carry while cycling around the tombs, and with the significant advantage over Mars bars, that while it may pull your teeth out it won't melt in your pocket.

Healing the Wounded Heart Shop,
23 Vo Thi Sau St, T54-383 3694, www. spiralfoundation.org. Recycled products such as water bottles and electricity wires are fashioned into bags and homeware by disabled people. Profits fund heart surgery for poor children and support the livelihoods of Hué's disabled craftsmen.

What to do

Many hotels organize bus and boat tours to the Imperial Tombs. It is also possible to charter boats to the tombs (the most romantic way to visit them) and to Thuan An Beach. Local tour operators charge around private boat around US$15-20 return to visit Thien Mu Pagoda, Hon Chien Temple, Tu Duc, Minh Mang and Khai Dinh's Tombs, departing at 0800-0830, returning 1530-1630. Boats are available on the stretch of river bank between the Huong Giang Hotel and the Trang Tien Bridge and also from the dock behind the Dong Ba Market.

From Hué, there are also tours organized to some of the sights of the Vietnam War, taking in sights including Vinh Moc tunnels and museum, the Ho Chi Minh Trail and Khe Sanh. Those wishing to travel overland to Laos can arrange to be dropped off in Khe Sanh and pay less.

Tour operators

Almost every travellers' café acts as an agent for a tour operator and will take bookings but they do not run the tours themselves.
Café on Thu Wheels, *3/34 Nguyen Tri Phuong St, T54-383 2241, minhthuHué@yahoo.com.* Run by Minh, Toan and Thu – 3 siblings. Motorcycle tour of Hué (US$12) and Hoi An (US$45) DMZ (US$45). The formidable Thu allows you to tailor your own tour taking in the best pagodas and sites around Hué, with well-informed English-speaking guides. DMZ bus tours are US$18.
Hue Easy Rider, *147 A/27 Ngu Binh, T9-8432 6842 www.hueeasyridertour.com.* Hugley popular motorcycle tours of Hué, the DMZ and further afield.
Mandarin Café, *24 Tran Cao Van St, T54-382 1281, www.mrcumandarin.com.* This café offers many services and its staff are also helpful. Open Tour Buses arranged. All-day trip to the tombs, Bach Ma National Park and the DMZ. Also arranges sunset boat trips.
Stop and Go Cafe, *3 Huong Vuong St, T54-382 7051, T90-512 6767 (mob), stopandgocafe@ yahoo.com.* Known for its tours of the DMZ. 3 itineraries are on offer ranging from 7 to 11 hrs. Tours are led by ARVN veterans, which brings the landscape to life and an insight you won't get on a much cheaper tour. Run by the helpful Thien and his sister. City tours and Bach Ma National Park tours also on offer. Transport ticket booking service.
Tien Bicycles, *12 Nguyen Thien Ke St, T54-382 3507, www.tienbicycles.com.* Mr Tien has been running recommended bicycling tours for 10 years. He offers long-distance rides as well as tours to the DMZ.

Transport

Phu Bai airport is a 25-min drive south of the city. The 2 bus stations and 1 railway station are more central and there are connections to Hanoi and Ho Chi Minh City – and all points between. The trains fill up, so advance booking is recommended, especially for sleepers.

Air

There is an airport bus, 30 mins, 50,000d run by **Vietnam Airlines** from 20 Ha Noi St that leaves 1 hr 40 mins before the flight. Returns also after flights. Taxi US$10-15 depending on destination – meter taxis. Use **Mai Linh** (white and green) **Taxi Vang** (yellow).
   Airline offices Vietnam Airlines, 23 Nguyen Van Cu St, T54-382 4709, open 0715-1115, 1330-1630.

Bicycles

Bicycles can be hired from most hotels, guesthouses and cafés; bicycles are about 40,000d a day. **Try** Tien Bicycles (see Tour operators) for something more sturdy for longer trips.

Boat hire

Boats can be hired through tour agents and from any berth on the south bank of the river, east of Trang Tien Bridge or through travel cafés. Good for either a gentle cruise with singers in the evening, or a more attractive way of getting to some of the temples and mausoleums. Note that if you travel by boat to the tombs you will often have to pay a driver to take you to the tomb as they often a kilometre or so from the riverbank.

Bus and Open Tour Bus

The Ben Xe Phia Nam, 97 An Duong Vuong St, T54-382 5070, serves destinations mostly south of Hué: **Saigon** and **Dalat** and **Danang** but also services to **Savannakhet** Tue-Fri, Sun, 0830. Buses to **Vientiane** and Pakse several times per week. Book with tour operators, see above. Open Tour Buses can be booked to major destinations from hotels or tour agencies. Tourist buses to **Savannakhet**, Laos, via Lao Bao available from Sepon Travel.

The **Ben Xe Phia Bac station**, An Hoa Ward, T54-358 0562, is up at the northwest corner of the citadel and serves destinations north of Hué: **Dong Hoi** (for Phong Nha and the caves), **Dong Ha**, and many daily services to **Hanoi**. To **Khe Sanh** buses leave throughout the day. Also regular buses to **Lao Bao**, for Laos.

The **Dong Ba** station (by the central market) serves villages and **Thuan An Beach**.

Cyclos

Cyclos are available everywhere. They are pleasant for visiting the more central attractions. Cyclo drivers in Hué win the country's Oscar for persistence.

Motorbikes

Bikes can be hired from most hotels and guesthouses for around US$15-20 or more per day with a driver or US$5 without. *Xe om* are available everywhere. They are the speedier way to see the temples as the terrain south of town is quite hilly.

Mr Teo is a reliable and very safe driver – ask your hotel staff to arrange a booking with him on 091-447 8429 (mob).

Taxi

Mai Linh Taxi, T54-389 8989.

Train

The station is at the west end of Le Loi St, T54-382 2175, and serves all stations south to **HCMC** and north to **Hanoi**. The 4-hr journey to **Danang** is especially recommended for its scenic views. Booking office open 0700-2200.

Along the Perfume River and the Imperial tombs

opulent, fanciful and grand-scale mausoleums

As the geographical and spiritual centre of the Nguyen Dynasty, Hué and the surrounding area is the site of numerous pagodas and seven imperial tombs, along with the tombs of numerous other royal personages and countless courtiers and successful mandarins.

Each of the tombs follows the same stylistic formula, although at the same time they reflect the tastes and predilections of the emperor in question. The tombs were built during the lifetime of each emperor, who took a great interest in the design and construction – after all they were meant to ensure his comfort in the next life. Each mausoleum, variously arranged, has five design elements: a courtyard with statues of elephants, horses and military and civil mandarins (originally, usually approached through a park of rare trees); a stela pavilion (with an engraved eulogy composed by the emperor's son and heir); a Temple of the Soul's Tablets; a pleasure pavilion; and a grave. Geomancers decreed that they should also have a stream and a mountainous screen in front.

Thien Mu Pagoda

It is an easy 4-km bicycle (or cyclo) ride from the city, following the north bank of the river upstream (west).

Thien Mu Pagoda (the Elderly Goddess Pagoda), also known as the Thien Mau Tu Pagoda, and locally as the **Linh Mu Pagoda** (the name used on most local maps), is the finest in Hué. It is beautifully sited on the north bank of the Perfume River, about 4 km upstream from the city. It was built in 1601 by Nguyen Hoang, the governor of Hué, after an old woman appeared to him and said that the site had supernatural significance and should be marked by the construction of a pagoda. The monastery is the oldest in Hué, and the seven-storey **Phuoc Duyen** (Happiness and Grace Tower), built by Emperor Thieu Tri in 1844, is 21 m high, with each storey containing an altar to a different Buddha. The summit of the tower is crowned with a water pitcher to catch the rain, water representing the source of happiness.

Arranged around the tower are four smaller buildings one of which contains the **Great Bell** cast in 1710 under the orders of the Nguyen Lord, Nguyen Phuc Chu, and weighing 2200 kg. Beneath another of these surrounding pavilions is a monstrous **marble turtle** on which is a 2.6-m-high stela recounting the development of Buddhism in Hué, carved in 1715. Beyond the tower, the entrance to the pagoda is through a triple gateway patrolled by six carved and vividly painted guardians – two on each gate. The roof of the sanctuary itself is decorated with *jataka* stories. At the front of the sanctuary is a brass, laughing Buddha. Behind that are an assortment of gilded Buddhas and a crescent-shaped gong cast in 1677 by Jean de la Croix. The first monk to commit suicide through self immolation, Thich Quang Duc, came from this pagoda and the grey Austin in which he made the journey to his death in Saigon is still kept here in a garage in the temple garden.

In May 1993, a Vietnamese – this time not a monk – immolated himself at Thien Mu. Why is not clear: some maintain it was linked to the persecution of Buddhists; others that it was because of the man's frustrated love life.

Tomb of Emperor Gia Long
Daily 0630-1730, 80,000d for the upkeep of the tomb. Get there by bike or motorbike.

The Tomb of Emperor Gia Long is the most distant and the most rarely visited but is well worth the effort of getting there (see below). The tomb is overgrown with venerable mango trees, the only sound is bird call and, occasionally, the wind in the trees: otherwise a blessed silence. Devoid of tourists, touts and ticket sellers it is the most atmospheric of all the tombs, and as the political regime in Vietnam is not a fan of Gia Long it is likely to remain this way. However, given the historical changes that were to be wrought by the dynasty Gia Long founded, it is arguably the most significant tomb in Hué. It was built between 1814 and 1820. Being the first of the dynasty, Gia Long's mausoleum set the formula for the later tombs. There is a surrounding lotus pond and steps lead up to a courtyard with the Minh Thanh ancestral temple, rather splendid in its red and gold. To the right of this is a double, walled and locked burial chamber where Gia Long and his wife are interred (the Emperor's tomb is fractionally taller). The tomb is perfectly lined up with the two huge obelisks on the far side of the lake. Beyond this is a courtyard with five now headless mandarins, horses and elephants on each side; steps lead up to the stela eulogizing the Emperor's reign, composed, presumably, by his eldest son, Minh Mang, as was the custom. This grey monolith engraved in ancient Chinese characters remained miraculously undisturbed during two turbulent centuries.

Gia Long's geomancers did a great job finding this site: with the mountainous screen in front it is a textbook example of a final resting place. Interestingly, despite their getting first choice of all the possible sites, it is also the furthest tomb from the palace; clearly they took their task seriously.

Nguyen Anh, or Gia Long as he was crowned in 1802, came to power with French support. Back in 1787, Gia Long's son, the young Prince Canh, had caused a sensation in French salon life when, along with soldier/missionary Georges Pigneau de Béhaine, he had sought military support against the Tay Son from Louis XVI. In return for Tourane (Danang) and Poulo Condore (Con Dao), the French offered men and weapons – an offer that was subsequently withdrawn. Pigneau then raised military support from French merchants in India and in 1799 Prince Canh's French-trained army defeated the Tay Son at Quy Nhon.

Gia Long's reign was despotic – to his European advisers who pointed out that encouragement of industry would lead to the betterment of the poor, he replied that he preferred them poor. The poor were virtual slaves – the price for one healthy young buffalo was one healthy young girl. Flogging was the norm – it has been described as the 'bamboo's golden age'. One study by a Vietnamese scholar estimated that there were 105 peasant uprisings between 1802 and 1820 alone. For this, and the fact that he gave the French a foothold in Vietnam, the Vietnamese have never forgiven Gia Long. Of him they still say *"cong ran can ga nha"* (he carried home the snake that killed the chicken).

To get to the Tomb of Emperor Gia Long take Dien Bien Phu Street out of town past the railway station. After a couple of kilometres turn right at the T-junction facing pine-shrouded Dan Nam Giao Temple (where Vietnamese emperors once prayed for good weather) and take first left onto Minh Mang. Continue on, passing the sign marking your departure from Hué and taking the right-hand branch of the fork in the road. After a short distance the road joins the river bank and heads for some 2 km towards the river crossing (the new Hué bypass – Highway 1). Follow the riverbank directly underneath this bridge and continue straight on as the road begins to deteriorate. A few metres beyond the Ben Do 1-km milestone is a red sign reading Gia Long Tomb. Down a steep path a sampan is waiting to ferry passengers across this tributary of the Perfume River (bargain); on the far side follow the track upstream for about 1 km. By a café with two billiard tables turn right and then almost immediately turn left. Keep on this path (ask for directions along the way).

Tomb of Emperor Minh Mang
Daily 0630-1730, 80,000d. Get there by bicycle or motorbike and follow the instructions for Gia Long's tomb, but cross the Perfume River using the new road bridge; on the far side of the bridge turn immediately left.

The Tomb of Emperor Minh Mang is possibly the finest of all the imperial tombs. Built between 1840 and 1843, it is sited among peaceful ponds, about 12 km from the city of Hué. In terms of architectural poise, balance and richness of decoration, it has no peer in the area. The tomb's layout, along a single central and sacred axis (*Shendao*), is unusual in its symmetry; no other tomb, with the possible exception of Khai Dinh (see page 110), achieves the same unity of constituent parts, nor draws the eye onwards so easily and pleasantly from one visual element to the next. The tomb was traditionally approached through the **Dai Hong Mon**, a gate which leads into the ceremonial courtyard containing an array of statuary; today visitors pass through a side gate. Next is the stela pavilion in which there is a carved eulogy to the dead emperor composed by his son, Thieu Tri. Continuing downwards through a series of courtyards there is, in turn, the **Sung An Temple** dedicated to Minh Mang and his empress, a small garden with flower beds that once formed the Chinese character for 'longevity', and two sets of stone bridges. The first consists of three spans, the central one of which (**Trung Dao Bridge**) was for the sole use of the emperor. The second, single bridge leads to a short flight of stairs with naga balustrades, at the end of which is a locked bronze door (no access). The door leads to the tomb itself which is surrounded by a circular wall.

Tomb of Tu Duc
Daily 0630-1730, 80,000d.

The Tomb of Tu Duc is 7 km from the city and was built between 1864 and 1867 in a pine wood. It is enclosed by a wall, some 1500 m long, within which is a lake. The lake, with lotus and water hyacinth, contains a small island where the emperor built a number of replicas of famous temples – now rather difficult to discern. He often came here to relax, and from the pavilions that reach out over the lake, composed poetry and listened to music. The **Xung Khiem Pavilion**, built in 1865, has recently been restored with UNESCO help and is the most attractive building here. The tomb complex follows the formula described above: ceremonial square, mourning yard with pavilion and then the tomb itself. To the northeast of Tu Duc's tomb are the tombs of his empress, Le Thien Anh and adopted son, Kien Phuc. Many of the pavilions are crumbling and ramshackle – lending the tomb a rather tragic air. This is appropriate: although he had 104 wives, Tu Duc fathered no sons. He was therefore forced to write his own eulogy, a fact which he took as a bad omen. The eulogy itself recounts the sadness in Tu Duc's life. A flavour of its sentiment can be gleaned from a confession he wrote in 1867 following French seizure of territory. It was shortly after Tu Duc's reign that France gained full control of Vietnam.

Tomb of Khai Dinh
Daily 0630-1730, 80,000d. Get there by motorbike or bicycle. As for Gia Long's tomb, continue under the new river crossing, but turn immediately left, through a collection of small shops and head straight on, over a small crossroads and parallel to the main road. From the riverbank a return moto trip is 30,000d.

The Tomb of Khai Dinh is 10 km from Hué. Built between 1920 and 1931, it is the last of the mausoleums of the Nguyen Dynasty and, by the time Khai Dinh was contemplating the afterlife, brick had given way in popularity to the concrete that is now beginning to deteriorate. Nevertheless, it occupies a fine position on the Chau Mountain facing southwest towards a large white statue of Quan Am, also built by Khai Dinh. The valley, used for the cultivation of cassava and sugar cane, and the pine-covered mountains, make this one of the most beautifully sited and peaceful of the tombs. Indeed, before construction could begin, Khai Dinh had to remove the tombs of Chinese nobles who had already selected the site for its beauty and auspicious orientation. A total of 127 steep steps lead up to the Honour Courtyard with statuary of mandarins, elephants and horses. An octagonal Stela Pavilion in the centre of the mourning yard contains a stone stela engraved with a eulogy to the emperor. At the top of some more stairs are the tomb and shrine of Khai Dinh, containing a bronze statue of the Emperor sitting on his throne and holding a jade sceptre. The body is interred 9 m below ground level. The interior is richly decorated with ornate and colourful murals (the artist incurred the wrath of the emperor and only just escaped execution), floor tiles and decorations built up with fragments of porcelain. It is the most elaborate of all the tombs and took 11 years to build. Such was the cost of construction that Khai Dinh had to levy additional taxes to fund the project. The tomb shows distinct European stylistic influences; Khai Dinh himself toured France in 1922, three years before he died.

Amphitheatre and Elephant Temple
Free. To get there, head about 3 km west of Hué railway station on Bui Thi Xuan St; turn left up a paved track opposite 203 Bui Thi Xuan St; the track for the Elephant Temple runs in front of the amphitheatre (off to the right).

Ho Quyen (Amphitheatre) lies about 4 km upstream of Hué on the south bank of the Perfume River. The amphitheatre was built in 1830 by Emperor Minh Mang as a venue for the popular duels between elephants and tigers. Elephants were symbolic of emperors and strength whereas tigers were seen as anti-imperial beasts and had their claws removed before the fight. This royal sport was in earlier centuries staged on an island in the Perfume River or on the river banks, but by 1830 it was considered desirable for the royal party to be able to observe the duels without placing themselves at risk from escaping tigers. The amphitheatre is said to have been last used in 1904 when, as was usual, the elephant emerged victorious: "The elephant rushed ahead and pressed the tiger to the wall with all the force he could gain. Then he raised his head, threw the enemy to the ground and smashed him to death," wrote Crosbie Garstin in *The Voyage from London to Indochina*. The walls of the amphitheatre are 5 m high and the arena is 44 m in diameter. At the south side, beneath the royal box, is one large gateway (for the elephant) and, to the north, five smaller entrances for the tigers. The walls are in good condition and the centre is filled either with grass or immaculately tended rows of vegetables, depending on the season.

Den Voi Re, the Temple of the Elephant Trumpet, dedicated to the call of the fighting elephant, is a few hundred metres away. It is a modest little place and fairly run down with a large pond in front and contains two small elephant statues. Presumably this is where elephants were blessed before battle or perhaps where the unsuccessful ones were mourned.

North of Hué → *Colour map 3, B4/5.*

the place to head for an insight into Vietnam's war with the USA

The Demilitarized Zone (DMZ)

The incongruously named Demilitarized Zone (DMZ), scene of some of the fiercest fighting of the Vietnam War, lies along the **Ben Hai River** and the better-known **17th parallel**. The DMZ was the creation of the **1954 Geneva Peace Accord**, which divided the country into two spheres of influence prior to elections that were never held. Like its counterpart in Germany the boundary evolved into a national border separating communist (the northern Democratic Republic of Vietnam) from capitalist (South Vietnam), but unlike its European equivalent it was the triumph of communism that saw its demise. As nearly all war paraphernalia has been stripped from the DMZ the visit is more of a 'pilgrimage' than anything else.

Khe Sanh Khe Sanh is the site of one of the most famous battles of the war. The battleground lies along Highway 9 that runs west towards Laos, to the north of Hué, and south of Dong Hoi and is 3 km from the village of the same name. There a small **museum** at the remains of the Tacon military base, surrounded by military hardware.

Ho Chi Minh Trail The Ho Chi Minh Trail is another popular but inevitably disappointing sight, given that its whole purpose was to be as inconspicuous as possible. Anything you see was designed to be invisible – from the air at least; rather an artificial 'sight' but a worthy pilgrimage considering the sacrifice of millions of Vietnamese porters and the role it played in the American defeat. The trail runs close to Khe Sanh.

Vinh Moc ⓘ *20,000d.* These **tunnels** served a function similar to that of the better-known Cu Chi tunnels (see page 172). They evolved as families in the heavily bombed village dug themselves shelters beneath their houses and then joined up with their neighbours. Later the tunnels developed a more offensive role when Viet Cong soldiers fought from them. Some visitors regard these tunnels as more 'authentic' than the 'touristy' tunnels of Cu Chi. To get to the tunnels head 6 km north of Ben Hai River and turn right in Ho Xa village; Vinh Moc is 13 km off Highway 1.

Con Co Island This island was an important supply depot and anti-aircraft stronghold in the war. Life for ordinary peasants in the battlezone just north of the DMZ was terrifying; some idea of conditions (for revolutionary peasants at least) can be gained from the 1970 North Vietnamese film *Vinh Linh Steel Ramparts*.

Rock Pile This 230-m-high limestone outcrop, just south of the DMZ, served as a US observation post. An apparently unassailable position, troops, ammunition, Budweiser and prostitutes all had to be helicoptered in. The sheer walls of the Rock Pile were eventually scaled by the Viet Cong. Jon Swain, the war correspondent, describes in his memoirs, *River of Time*, how his helicopter got lost around the Rock Pile and nearly came to disaster in this severely contested zone. The **Hien Luong Bridge** crossing the Ben Hai River on the 17th parallel which marked the boundary between north and south is included in most tours. There's a striking national monument, police post, and meeting hall equipped with mannequins in meeting pose next to the bridge.

Other sights Private tours can also visit Doc Mieu Fire Base, Con Thien Fire Base and the Truong Son National Cemetery where there are more than 10,000 graves.

West of Hué → *Colour map 3, B5.*

peaceful countryside ideal for cycling

Thanh Toan Covered Bridge
Take a bicycle or motorbike as the route to the bridge, 8 km west of Hué, passes through beautiful countryside where ducks waddle along roads and paddy fields line the route. Best done in the glow of the late afternoon sun.

Thanh Toan Covered Bridge was built in the reign of King Le Hien Tong (1740-1786) by Tran Thi Dao, a childless woman as an act of charity hoping that God would bless her with a baby. The bridge, with its shelter for the tired and homeless, attracted the interest of several kings who granted the village immunity from a number of taxes. The original yin-yang tiles have been replaced with ugly green enamelled tube tiles, unfortunately, but the structure is still in good condition.

South of Hué → *Colour map 3, B5.*

stunning lagoons, wild national park land and a magnificent ocean-front mountain pass

Between Hué and Danang a finger of the Truong Son Mountains juts eastwards, extending all the way to the sea, dividing the country into two halves. This barrier to north–south communication has resulted in some spectacular engineering solutions: the railway line closely follows the coastline (fortunately it is single track and narrow gauge) sometimes almost hanging over the sea – while Highway 1 winds its way equally precariously over the Hai Van Pass. The coastline is stunning. The road used to be littered with broken-down trucks and buses for which the long haul up to the summit was just too much. Very few vehicles now use the pass following the opening of the 6-km Hai Van Tunnel.

The difficult terrain means that much remains wooded, partly because the trees are too inaccessible to cut down and partly because of government edicts preventing the clearance of steep slopes.

★ Bach Ma National Park and Hill Station

www.bachmapark.com.vn, national park entry 40,000d. Buses from Hué to Cau Hai village, which is 3 km from the park gates. If you are using your own transport, simply turn off at the small town of Cau Hai.

The hilly woodlands of Bach Ma National Park stretch from the Lao border right down to the coast and although little is virgin forest quite a lot of bird and animal life flourishes within its leafy branches. It is very worthy of a day or two of exploration for anybody interested in seeing Vietnam's nature. A lovely time to visit is in March and April for the rhododendron blossom.

The French established a great many hill stations in Vietnam. Dalat was the only one to really develop as a town. Others, like Sapa, were rejuvenated a few years ago and yet others, like Bach Ma, had been forgotten about until very recently. Now the ruins of villas have been uncovered and flights of steps unearthed and old gardens and ponds cleared.

> **Tip...**
>
> Beware of the leeches during the rainy season and the crowds on summer weekends. Bear in mind also that it is at least 7°C colder than the coastal plains.

Bach Ma was established as a hill station in 1932 when the construction of a road made it accessible. By the outbreak of the Second World War there were 139 villas and a hotel. Recognizing its natural beauty and biological diversity, the French gave it protected status. In 1991 the Vietnamese government classified it as a national park with 22,031 ha at its core and a further buffer zone of 21,300 ha. The area is rugged granite overlain in places by sandstone rising to an altitude of 1448 m at the summit of Bach Ma. There are a number of trails past cascades, through rhododendron woods and up the summit trail overlooking the remains of colonial villas.

The park is home to an array of mammals including the **red-shanked douc langur** and the buff-cheeked or **white-cheeked gibbon**. Birdlife here is particularly interesting. Four restricted range species are the **Annam partridge**, **crested argus**, **short-tailed scimitar babbler** and the **grey-faced tit babbler**. The most characteristic feature of Bach Ma's birdlife is the large number of pheasants. Of the 12 species of pheasant recorded in Vietnam, seven have been seen in the park. A subspecies of the silver pheasant lives here and Edwards' pheasant, believed extinct until it was rediscovered in 1996, was seen just outside the park buffer zone in 1998. There are many other species of interest including the red-collared woodpecker, Blyth's kingfisher and the coral-billed ground cuckoo.

Lang Co

The road from Hué to Lang Co passes through many pretty, red-tiled villages, compact and surrounded by clumps of bamboo and fruit trees which provide shade, shelter and sustenance. And, for colour, there's the bougainvillea – which through grafting produces pink and white leaves on the same branch. Just north of Hai Van Pass lies the once idyllic fishing village of Lang Co (about 65 km south of Hué) on a spit of land, which has a number of cheap and good seafood restaurants along the road. Shortly after crossing the Lang Co lagoon, dotted with coracles and fish traps, the road begins the long haul up to Hai Van Pass but the majority of traffic now diverts through the tunnel.

Apparently, in the first year of his reign, Emperor Khai Dinh visited Lang Co and was so impressed that he ordered the construction of a summer palace. This, it seems, was never carried out, not even by his son Bao Dai who was so fond of building palaces. There are several guesthouses and tourist resorts on Lang Co and the Banyan Tree Group's Laguna Lang Co complex with its five-star resorts, a spa, shops and a golf course on a 200-ha site.

Hai Van Pass

Hai Van Pass (Deo Hai Van, 'Pass of the Ocean Clouds' or, to the French, Col des Nuages) lies 497 m above the dancing white waves that can be seen at its foot. In historic times the pass marked the border between the kingdoms of Vietnam and Champa. The mountains also act as an important climatic barrier trapping the cooler, damper air-masses to the north and bottling it up over Hué, which accounts for Hué's shocking weather. They also mark an abrupt linguistic divide, with the Hué dialect (the language of the royal court) to the north, the source of bemusement to many southerners.

The pass is peppered with abandoned pillboxes and crowned with an old fort, originally built by the dynasty from Hué and used as a relay station for the pony express on the old Mandarin Road. Subsequently used by the French, today it is a pretty shabby affair. Looking back to the north, stretching into the haze is the lagoon of Lang Co. To the south is Danang Bay and Monkey Mountain.

Listings South of Hué

Where to stay

Bach Ma National Park and Hill Station
There are a variety of villas offering simple accommodation.

Lang Co

$$$$ Angsana Lang Co
T54-369 5800, www.angsana.com.
The less expensive of the 2 upscale properties on the Laguna development, the **Angsana** offers a host of different room options, many with large sea-view balconies and more decadent lodgings with private pools. Fantastic beachfront setting, massive swimming pools and a variety of wining and dining options.

$$$$ Banyan Tree Lang Co
T54-3695 888, www.banyantree.com.
Part of the massive **Laguna Lang Co** site, the **Banyan Tree** offers some of the most luxurious accommodation in the country with a small collection of seriously decadent and tasteful bungalows. The restaurant and spa are both of the highest order. Very pricey, but extremely sharp.

$$$$ Vedana Lagoon Resort and Spa
Zone 1, Phu Loc town, T54-381 9397, www.vedanaresorts.com.
A new resort of beautiful bungalows situated over the lagoon waters and run by the same folk as the **Pilgrimage Village**, 1 hr south of Hué city centre. This is a very quiet place to get away from it all for a night or 2.

$$$ Lang Co Beach Resort
T54-387 3555, www.langcobeachresort.com.
A large, full-service resort with pool, restaurant and bar. All rooms have a/c. There are some cheap budget rooms, but it is way better to go for an oceanfront villa with veranda, which is much larger with a better outlook than a garden-view villa. There are well-tended gardens here and a nice pool. The resort has certainly seen better days and can be almost eerily quiet, but it offers reasonable value and a great location.

Danang
& around

premier stretch of coast with UNESCO-listed sites

★Danang, Vietnam's third largest port and a commercial and trading centre of growing importance, has a fantastic location with excellent beaches right on its doorstep as well as the stunning Son Tra Peninsula with its heavily forested slopes and fine deserted beaches. There are also three UNESCO World Heritage Sites (Hué, Hoi An and My Son) within a short drive, plus a brilliant culinary culture.

Danang → *Colour map 2, B5.*

a friendly, forward-looking beach-side city with excellent cuisine

Danang Museum of Cham Sculpture
At the intersection of Trung Nu Vuong and Bach Dang streets, T511-357 2414, daily 0700-1730, www.chammuseum.danang.vn. Labels are in English. Guided tours are held 0800-1030 and 1400-1630.

The museum was established by academics of the École Française d'Extrême-Orient and contains the largest display of Cham art anywhere in the world. The museum buildings alone are worth the visit: constructed in 1916 in a beautiful setting, the complex is open-plan in design, providing an environment in which the pieces can be exhibited to their best advantage. There are a number of rooms each dedicated to work from a different part of Champa: **Tra Kieu**, **My Son** and **Dong Duong** and a new extension. Because different parts of Champa flowered artistically at different times from the fourth to the 14th centuries, the rooms show the evolution of Cham art and prevailing outside influences from Cambodia to Java. One problem with the display is the lack of any background information. The pieces are wonderful, but the visitor may leave the museum rather befuddled by the display.

Principal periods are: My Son E1 (early eighth century); Hoa Lai (early ninth century); Dong Duong (late ninth century); Late Tra Kieu (late 10th century); Thap Mam (12th to 13th century); Po Klong Garai (13th to 16th century).

Tra Kieu was the earliest Cham capital sacked by the Chinese in the fifth century. Some 40 km southwest of Danang, little remains today but the pieces on display at the museum testify to a lively and creative civilization. An altar is inscribed with scenes from the wedding story of Sita and Rama from the Ramayana, a Hindu epic.

Many pieces from My Son illustrate the Hindu trinity: Brahma the Creator, Vishnu the Preserver and Siva the Destroyer. Ganesh, the elephant-headed son of Siva, was a much-loved god and is well represented here.

At the end of the ninth century Dong Duong replaced My Son as the centre of Cham art. At this time Buddhism became the dominant religion of court although it never fully replaced Hinduism. The Dong Duong room is illustrated with scenes from the life of Buddha. From this period faces become less stylistic and more human and the bodies of the figures more graceful and flowing. The subsequent period of Cham art is known as the late Tra Kieu style. In this section there are *apsaras*, celestial dancing maidens whose fluid and animated forms are exquisitely captured in stone. Thereafter Cham sculpture went into artistic decline. The Thap Mam style (late 11th to early 14th century) sees a range of mythical beasts whose range and style is unknown elsewhere in Southeast Asia. Also in this room is a pedestal surrounded by 28 breast motifs. It is believed they represent Uroha, the mythical mother of the Indrapura (My Son, Tra Kieu, Dong Duong) nation, but its significance and that of others like it is unknown.

The museum has a new collection with objects from Quang Tri, Tra Kieu, Quang Nam, Thap Mam-Binh Dinh, An My, Chien Dan, Qua Giang-KHué Trung and Phu Hung in its extension. One of its most outstanding pieces is a bronze with golden eyes, perfect breasts and stretched earlobes. It is the Avalokites Vara, an image of the Bodhisattva of compassion and dates from the ninth century.

Other sights

Danang's **Cao Dai Temple** ⓘ *63 Haiphong St*, is the second largest temple in Vietnam. **Danang Cathedral** ⓘ *156 Tran Phu St, 0500-1700, Mass is held 6 times on Sun*, built in 1923, is single-spired with a sugary-pink wash. The stained-glass windows were made in Grenoble, in 1927, by Louis Balmet who was also responsible for the windows of Dalat Cathedral (see page 135).

Listings Danang

Tourist information

The Sinh Tourist
154 Bach Dang St, T511-384 3259,
www.thesinh tourist.vn.
Helpful and can book buses as well as help with information as can other tour operators, see page 118. The website www.indanang.com is worth consulting for news and events.

Where to stay

$$$ A La Carte
Vo Nguyen Giap, T511-3959 555,
www.alacarteliving.com.
This is a fantastic addition to the Danang seafront with exceptional rooms for the price, many of which have great sea views.

The rooftop pool is a treat and affords awesome views of the Son Tra Peninsula. Highly recommended.

$$$ Novotel Danang Premier Han River
36 Bach Dang, T511-3929 999,
www.novotel.com.
Situated right on the bank of the Han River, this striking new hotel offers excellent rooms – those on the upper floors have superb views of the city and its bridges, especially by night. Polished service, a quality gym and excellent dining options and sky bar.

$$ Chu Hotel
2-4 An Thuong 1 St, T511-395 5123,
www.chuhotel.com.
In a great location by the sea, **Chu Hotel** has a choice of four rooms furnished to a

very high standard, especially given the price. Exceptionally good service and good Italian coffees.

$ Funtastic Danang Hostel
115 Hai Phong, T90-356 1777, www.funtasticdanang.com.
A range of clean dorm rooms as well as a double and a twin. Great little chill out area with bean bags, a book exchange. Very friendly, welcoming staff. Motorbike and bicycle rental. The best backpacker choice in town.

Restaurants

Eating in Danang is a pleasure and makes it worth a visit in itself. There are many local specialities and the seafood is second to none. Bread in Danang is particularly good, which makes *banh mi ôp la* (fried eggs and bread) a great start to the day.

$$$ Furama Resort
See Where to stay.
Sublime thin-crust pizzas and perfect pasta.

$$$ The Green House
Hyatt Regency Danang, www.danang.regency.hyatt.com.
The Green House is 1 of 3 excellent restaurants at the **Hyatt Regency** overseen by executive chef, Frederik Farina. Expect superb Italian fare. The **Beach House** restaurant is another good option, especially for special lunch with sea views.

$$-$ Apsara
222 Tran Phu St, T511-356 1409, www.apsara-danang.com. Open 1000-1400, 1700-2100.
Besides the upmarket hotel options, this is the most elegant dining in town with crisp white linens on the table and attentive staff. There's a good spread of Vietnamese food on the menu.

$$-$ The Waterfront
150-152 Bach Dang St, T9-3507 5580, www.waterfrontdanang.com. Open 0900-2400.

Very cool 2-storey restobar serving innovative cuisine and top drawer cocktails. Great, minimalist design.

$ Bread of Life
12 Le Hong Phong St, T511-356 5185, www.breadoflifedanang.com.
Closed Sun. This is a restaurant that provides training and jobs to deaf people. It's a worthwhile cause to support and the pizzas are very tasty. Baked goods and other comfort food too. Motorbike rental also.

$ Bun Cha Ca
109 Nguyen Chi Thanh. Open 0900-1700.
Rice noodle and fish soup loaded with pineapple and tomato. Add a spritz of lime and chilli to taste and you'll be in heaven. A bargain.

$ Com Ga A Hai
96 Thai Phien.
A hugely popular spot with locals, this street-side eatery dishes up delectable grilled chicken with rice. Not to be missed.

Bars and clubs

Dimples Bar and Grill
My An Beach, Vo Nguyen Giap, T120-238 9110.
Popular with expats, **Dimples** has a cooling sea breeze, a free pool table and a decent menu of comfort foods.

Sky 36
See Novotel (Where to stay).
Set at the top of the **Novotel**, **Sky 36** is more of a club than a bar, with loud music and dancers. Prices are steep and there is a smart-casual dress code. The views are outstanding.

The Waterfront
See Restaurants.
Alongside an excellent menu, **The Waterfront** does a good line in beers, wines and cocktails. The most stylish bar in town.

Shopping

Marble carvings
Available from shops in town, but particularly from the stalls around the foot of Marble Mountains (see page 119).

Markets
The city has a fair array of markets. There is a covered **general market (Cho Han)** in a building at the intersection of Tran Phu and Hung Vuong streets. Another market, **Cho Con**, is at the intersection of Hung Vuong and Ong Ich Khiem streets. The stalls close by sell basketwork and other handicrafts. On Haiphong St, running east from the railway station, there is a **street market** selling fresh produce.

What to do

Asia Pacific Travel, *79 Thanh Long St, Haichau District, T511-6286088, www.asia pacifictravel.vn*. Arranges tours to Hoi An (biking and fishing tour) and My Son.
Funtastic Danang Hostel, *115 Hai Phong, T90-356 1777, www.funtasticdanang.com*. This new hostel also runs a very good tour desk with daily trips around Danang and also to Hoi An and the Tra Que vegetable village. This is also the best place to book the fantastic street tour with Summer, author of the superb local food blog, www.danangcuisine.com.
The Sinh Tourist, *154 Bach Dang St, T511-843259, www.thesinhtourist.vn*. Open Tour Buses stop at 1030 and 1530 to go to Hoi An, 1 hr, from 79,000d-89,000 in low season. To Hué at 0900 and 1400, 109,000 and 89,000 respectively. Ba Na Hill tour 850,000d including cable car and lunch.

Transport

Danang is extremely well connected. Along with the airport, it is on the north–south railway line linking Hanoi and Ho Chi Minh City, and there are also regular bus and minibus connections with all major cities in the south as far as Ho Chi Minh City, and in the north as far as Hanoi from the new bus station, 7 km north of the city. Open Tour Buses stop in the town centre.

Air
The airport, 2.5 km southwest, is on the edge of the city. Metered taxis run into town in 5-10 mins. There are connections with **Bangkok, Phnom Penh, Siem Reap, Singapore, Hong Kong** and most domestic airports.
    Airline offices Vietnam Airlines, 58 Bach Dang St, T511-381 1111.

Bicycle and motorbike
Bicycles are available from many hotels and hostels, including Funtastic (see Where to stay).
    Rent a Bike Vietnam, 80 Phan Thanh, T91-302 6878, www.rentabikevn.com. A new branch of this reliable Vietnamese/British run company which has been running in Hanoi for some years. Danny and Thu offer high quality motorbikes for rent and sale. Also a great source of local information. Good rates on longer term rentals.

Bus
Buses to **Hoi An** run from the station at the west end of Hung Vuong St, opposite Con Market. The **Ben Xe Trung Tam Danang** bus station is 7 km north of Danang and 15 km south of the Hai Van Tunnel. Buses to **Hanoi, Dong Hoi, Hué, HCMC, Buon Ma Thuot, Kontum** and **Pakse**. **Tickets** can be bought from agents in town. Sinh Tourist (see agents) also sells open tour tickets.

International connections It is possible to get a visa for Laos in Danang from the Lao consulate (see page 434) here. However, 30-day visas are available at the border on arrival, so there is no real need to do so. There are daily departures for the Lao town of **Savannakhet**, on the Mekong River from the **Hoa Minh station**. The road runs west from Dong Ha into the Annamite Mountains and crosses the border at Lao Bao, not far

from the former battlefield of Khe Sanh,
see page 111.

For details of the border crossing between
Mukdahan (Vietnam) and Savannakhet
(Laos), see box, page 544.

Taxi
There are many **taxi**s in town, including
Mai Linh. A taxi from Hoi An along the new
coastal road will cost around 500,000d.

Train
The train station is on Haiphong St, 2 km
west of town, T511-375 0666, and there are
express trains to and from **Hanoi**, **HCMC**
and **Hué**.

Around Danang → *Colour map 3, B5/6.*
endless white sands and a record-breaking national park cable car

Son Tra Peninsula
The Son Tra Peninsula makes an excellent day out from the city. Hire a motorbike or bicycle
(but beware of the hills) and take to the road that hugs the coastline right the way around
it. Climb to the top for amazing views of the city and toward Lang Co and the Hai Van Pass.
There are plenty of simple seafood restaurants and also enough beaches that, with a bit of
hunting, you are likely to find one all to yourself.

My Khe Beach (China Beach)
Once a fabled resort China Beach was the GI name for this US military R&R retreat during
the Vietnam War, but locals never refer to it as such – here it has always been My Khe.

Until recently, My Khe was a real 'undiscovered' asset, despite being only 20 minutes
from the centre of Danang. However, investors have now recognized that it has the
potential to transform Danang into the Rio de Janeiro of Asia. This once-abandoned, wild
stretch of beach is now nearly all taken up by resorts. Miles and miles of fine white sand,
clean water and a glorious setting (the hills of Monkey Mountain to the north and the
Marble Mountains clearly visible to the south) have attracted hotels such as the Nam Hai,
which has garnered several major international awards, see Where to stay. Only several
kilometres of a 30-km stretch between Danang and Hoi An remains public.

Marble Mountains (Nui Non Nuoc)
*12 km from Danang and 20 km from Hoi An. Many visitors stop off at Marble Mountain en route
to Hoi An, daily 0600-1700, 15,000d.*

The Marble Mountains overlook the city of Danang and its airfield, about 12 km to the
west. The name was given to these five peaks by the Nguyen Emperor Minh Mang on his
visit in 1825 – although they are in fact limestone crags with marble outcrops. They are
also known as the mountains of the five elements (fire, water, soil, wood and metal). An
important religious spot for the Cham, the peaks became havens for communist guerrillas
during the war owing to their commanding view over Danang airbase. From here, a force
with sufficient firepower could control much of what went on below, and the guerrillas
harried the Americans incessantly. The views from the mountain sides, overlooking
Danang Bay, are impressive. On the Marble Mountains are a number of important sights,
often associated with caves and grottoes formed by chemical action on the limestone rock.

At the foot of the mountains is a village with a large number of shops selling marble
carvings with a bewildering array of kitsch on offer.

Of the mountains, the most visited is **Thuy Son**. There are several grottoes and cave pagodas in the mountain that are marked by steps cut into the rock. The **Tam Thai Pagoda**, reached by a staircase cut into the mountain, is on the site of a much older Cham place of worship. Constructed in 1825 by Minh Mang, and subsequently rebuilt, the central statue is of the Buddha Sakyamuni (the historic Buddha) flanked by the Bodhisattva Quan Am (a future Buddha and the Goddess of Mercy), and a statue of Van Thu (symbolizing wisdom). At the rear of the grotto is another cave, the **Huyen Khong Cave**. Originally a place of animist worship, it later became a site for Buddhist pilgrimage. The entrance is protected by four door guardians. The high ceiling of the cave is pierced by five holes through which the sun filters and, in the hour before midday, illuminates the central statue of the Buddha Sakyamuni. In the cave are various natural rock formations which, if you have picked up one of the young cave guides along the way, will be pointed out as being stork-like birds, elephants, an arm, a fish and a face.

A few hundred metres to the south on the right is a track leading to **Chua Quan The Am**, which has its own grotto complete with stalactites, stalagmites and pillars. Local children will point out formations resembling the Buddha and an elephant.

Listings Around Danang

Where to stay

My Khe Beach (China Beach)

$$$$ Furama Resort
68 Ho Xuan Huong St, T511-384 7888, www.furamavietnam.com.
The first 5-star to open in the area, Furama is still going strong and many of its staff have been there since the beginning. Its 198 rooms and suites are beautifully designed and furnished. 2 pools, one of which is an infinity pool overlooking the beach. All facilities are first class. Water sports, diving, mountain biking, tennis and a health centre offering a number of massages and treatments. Operates a free and very useful shuttle to and from the town, Marble Mountains and Hoi An. Fantastic buffet breakfasts and good seafood barbecues in the evenings.

$$$$ Fusion Maia
T511-396 7999, www.maiadanang.fusion-resorts.com.
This innovative private pool villa resort has innovative concepts including an all inclusive spa treatments with the room rate and the chance to have your breakfast anytime and anywhere in the grounds. Very sleek design and very polished service. This is pure, unadulterated luxury. The only downside is you may not want to leave.

$$$$ Hyatt Regency Danang Resort
T511-398 1234, www.danang.regency.hyatt.com.
This massive hotel-cum-resort has been getting rave reviews since it opened for its sleek accommodation, fantastic dining and great service. A wide range of rooms on offer and frequent special offers and package deals.

$ Hoa's Place
215/214 Huyen Tran Cong Chua St, T511-396 9216, hoasplace@gmail.com.
A laid-back and very basic popular hangout that is a hit with those who want to kick back on a budget by the sand.

Hoi An
& around

enchanting town, ancient ruins, beautiful beaches

★Hoi An's tranquil riverside setting, its diminutive scale (you can touch the roof of many houses), friendly and welcoming people and its wide array of shops and galleries have made it one of the most popular destinations for foreign travellers. There is plenty to see of historical interest, there is a nearby beach and, as if that were not enough, it has superb and inexpensive restaurants and a fantastic street food culture.

Hoi An → *Colour map 3, B6.*

one of the prettiest towns in Asia

This ancient town lies on the banks of the Thu Bon River. During its heyday 200 years ago, when trade with China and Japan flourished, Hoi An became a prosperous little port. Much of the merchants' wealth was spent on family chapels and Chinese clan houses, which remain little altered today.

By the end of the 19th century the Thu Bon River had started to silt up and Hoi An was gradually eclipsed by Danang. Hoi An has, however, emerged as one of the most popular tourist destinations in Vietnam, and although Hoi An's historic character is being somewhat submerged by the rising tide of tourism, nevertheless, visitors to Hoi An are charmed by the gentleness of the people and the sedate pace of life.

Sights
Most of Hoi An's more attractive buildings and assembly halls (*hoi quan*) are found either on, or just off, Tran Phu Street. Tran Phu stretches west to east from the Japanese Covered Bridge to the market, running parallel to the river. Entrance to most historic buildings is by sightseeing ticket, 120,000d for up to five sites, on sale at the **Hoi An Tourist Offices**, see page 125.

Japanese Covered Bridge (Cau Nhat Ban) ⓘ *Tran Phu St, 1 token; keep your ticket to get back*. Also known as the Pagoda Bridge, the Faraway People's Bridge and, popularly, as the Japanese Covered Bridge, this is Hoi An's most famous landmark. The bridge was built in the 16th century. On its north side there is a pagoda, Japanese in style, for the protection

Essential Hoi An and around

Getting around

Hoi An is compact and is best explored on foot. Guesthouses hire out bicycles. Motorcycles are not needed unless you want to head further afield.

When to go

The **Full Moon Festival** is held on the 14th day of the lunar month. The town converts itself into a Chinese lantern fest and locals dress in traditional costume. Candles are lit and floated in plastic lotus flowers along the river – it is an exceptionally pretty sight.

Time required

At least a full day is needed to see all the historic sites, but most people stay far longer, whether they originally intended to or not.

Best excursions
An Bang Beach, page 130
Tra Que village, page 129
My Son, page 131

of sailors. At the west end of the bridge are statues of two dogs, and at the east end, of two monkeys – it is said that the bridge was begun in the year of the monkey and finished in the year of the dog. Some scholars have pointed out that this would mean a two-year period of construction, an inordinately long time for such a small bridge; they maintain that the two animals represent points of the compass, WSW (monkey) and NW (dog). Father Benigne Vachet, a missionary who lived in Hoi An between 1673 and 1683, notes in his memoirs that the bridge was the haunt of beggars and fortune tellers hoping to benefit from the stream of people crossing over it. Its popular name reflects a long-standing belief that it was built by the Japanese, although no documentary evidence exists to support this. One of its other names, the Faraway People's Bridge, is said to have been coined because vessels from far away would moor close to the bridge.

Hoi Quan (Assembly Halls)

Chinese traders in Hoi An (like elsewhere in Southeast Asia) established self-governing dialect associations or clan houses, which owned their own schools, cemeteries, hospitals and temples. The *hoi quan* (clan houses or assembly halls) may be dedicated to a god or an illustrious individual and may contain a temple but are not themselves temples. There are five *hoi quan* in Hoi An, four for use by people of specific ethnicities: Fukien, Cantonese, Hainan, Chaozhou and the fifth for use by any visiting Chinese sailors or merchants. Strolling east from the Covered Bridge down Tran Phu Street all the assembly halls can be seen.

Quang Dong Hoi Quan (Cantonese Assembly Hall) ⓘ *176 Tran Phu St, 1 'assembly hall' token.* Merchants from Guangdong would meet at this assembly hall. It is dedicated to Quan Cong, a Han Chinese general and dates from 1786. The hall, with its fine embroidered hangings, is in a cool, tree-filled compound and is a good place to rest.

Ngu Bang Hoi Quan All (Chinese Assembly Hall) ⓘ *64 Tran Phu St, free.* Unusually for an assembly hall (sometimes referred to as Chua Ba (Goddess Temple)), it was a mutual aid society open to any Chinese trader or seaman, regardless of dialect or region of origin. Chinese vessels tended to visit Hoi An during the spring, returning to China in the summer. The assembly hall would help ship-wrecked and ill sailors and perform the burial rites of merchants with no relatives in Hoi An. Built in 1773 as a meeting place for all five groups (the four listed above plus Hakka) and also for those with no clan house of their own, today it accommodates a Chinese School, Truong Le Nghia, where children of the diaspora learn the language of their forebears.

Phuc Kien Hoi Quan (Fukien Assembly Hall) ⓘ *46 Tran Phu St, 1 'assembly hall' token.* Founded around 1690, this served Hoi An's largest Chinese ethnic group, those from Fukien. It is an intimate building within a large compound and is dedicated to Thien Hau, goddess of the sea and protector of sailors. She is the central figure on the main altar, clothed in robes, who, together with her assistants, can hear the cries of distress of drowning sailors. Immediately on the right on entering the temple is a mural depicting Thien Hau rescuing a sinking vessel. Behind the main altar is a second sanctuary, which houses the image of Van Thien whose blessings pregnant women invoke on the lives of their unborn children.

Hai Nam Hoi Quan (Hainan Assembly Hall) ⓘ *10 Tran Phu St, 100 m east of the Fukien Assembly Hall, free.* With a rather more colourful history, this assembly hall was founded in 1883 in memory of the sailors and passengers who were killed when three ships were plundered by an admiral in Emperor Tu Duc's navy. In his defence the admiral claimed the victims were pirates and some sources maintain he had the ships painted black to strengthen his case.

Chaozhou (Trieu Chau Assembly Hall) ⓘ *362 Nguyen Duy Hieu St, 1 'assembly hall' token.* Exquisite wood carving is the highlight of this one. The altar and its panels depict images from the sea and women from the Beijing court, presumably intended to console homesick traders.

Merchants' houses
Phung Hung House ⓘ *4 Nguyen Thi Minh Khai St, 1 'old house' token.* Just west of the Japanese Bridge, this house was built over 200 years ago; it has been in the same family for eight generations. The house, which can be visited, is constructed of 80 columns of ironwood on marble pedestals. During the floods of 1964, Phung Hung House became home to 160 locals who camped upstairs for three days as the water rose to a height of 2.5 m.

Tan Ky House ⓘ *101 Nguyen Thai Hoc St, 1 'old house' token.* Built by later generations of the Tan Ky family (they originally arrived in Hoi An from China 200 years earlier), dating from the late 18th century, this house reflects not only the prosperity the family had acquired but also the architecture of their Japanese and Vietnamese neighbours, whose styles had presumably worked their influence on the aesthetic taste and appreciation of the younger family members.

Diep Dong Nguyen House ⓘ *80 Nguyen Thai Hoc St.* Two Chinese lanterns hang outside the once Chinese dispensary. The owner is friendly, hospitable and not commercially minded. He takes visitors into his house and shows everything with pride and smiles.

Quan Thang ⓘ *77 Tran Phu St, 1 'old house' token.* This is another old merchant's house, reputed to be 300 years old.

Tran Family Temple ① *on the junction of Le Loi and Phan Chu Trinh streets, 1 'old house' token.* Having survived for 15 generations, the current generation has no son, which means the lineage has been broken. The building exemplifies well Hoi An's construction methods and the harmonious fusion of Chinese and Japanese styles. It is roofed with heavy *yin* and *yang* tiling, which requires strong roof beams; these are held up by a triple-beamed support in the Japanese style (seen in the roof of the covered bridge). Some beams have Chinese-inspired ornately carved dragons. The outer doors are Japanese, the inner are Chinese. On a central altar rest small wooden boxes that contain the photograph or likeness of the deceased together with biographical details; beyond, at the back of the house, is a small, raised Chinese herb, spice and flower garden with a row of bonsai trees. As with all Hoi An's family houses guests are received warmly and courteously and served lotus tea and dried coconut.

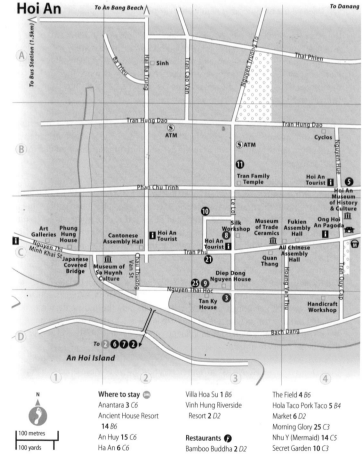

Hoi An

Tourist information

Tourist offices
*At the main entrance points to the old town,
see map for locations, T510-386 1327, www.
hoianworldheritage.org.vn. Open 0700-1730.*
The tourist kiosks provide a good map.

Seedlings **7** *D2*
Son **1** *B6*
Streets **11** *B3*

Dive Bar **9** *C3*
White Marble
Wine Bar **3** *D3*

Bars & clubs 🎵
Before and After **8** *C3*

Where to stay

There has been a dramatic increase in the
number of hotel rooms available in Hoi An
but it is still advisable to book in advance
as during peak times, rooms are scarce.

$$$$ Anantara Hoi An
*1 Pham Hong Thai St, T510-391 4555,
www.hoi-an.anantara.com.*
This colonial style resort is in an excellent
location right on the riverfront next to the
town. The rooms are spacious and extremely
comfortable. There's a restaurant, elegant
café and cosy bar complete with a huge cigar
collection on site. Excellent buffet breakfasts
– try and grab a table with a river view.
Fabulous staff. Highly recommended.

$$$$ The Nam Hai
*Hamlet 1, Dien Duong Village, 11 km north
of Hoi An, 30 km south of Danang on Ha My
Beach, T510-394 0000, www.ghmhotels.com.*
The Nam Hai is a stunning creation of 100
beachside villas overlooking the sea. Raised
platforms inside the villas create a special
sleeping and living space enveloped with
white silk drapes; egg-shell lacquered baths
in a black marble surround are incorporated
into the platform. The restaurants serve
excellent local as well as Indian food and
the breakfast is excellent, with free flow
bucks fizz and a cocktail that changes
daily. There are 2 restaurants flanking the
vast infinity pool. 3 excellent pools, a gym,
tennis, badminton and basketball courts. For
relaxing relaxation there's a lovely library and
spa. An organic garden nextdoor provides the
resort's vegetables.

$$$$ Victoria Hoi An Beach Resort
& Spa
*Cua Dai Beach, T510-392 7040,
www.victoriahotels-asia.com.*
A charming, resort right on the beach
with beautifully furnished rooms, many of
which face the sea. There is a large pool, the

L'Annam Restaurant, a couple of bars and live music and dancing. Charming service. A free shuttle bus runs between the hotel and the town. Also runs excellent tours, including fun days out in vintage sidecars.

$$$$-$$$ Ancient House Resort
377 Cua Dai St, T510-392 3377,
www.ancienthouseresort.com.
A beautiful, small hotel set around a pretty garden complete with a pool. Rooms have plenty of character and there is a free shuttle to town and the beach as well as free bicycles. Behind the hotel is a traditional house producing rice noodles. Breakfast included.

$$$$-$$$ Hoi An Riverside Resort
175 Cua Dai Rd, Cua Dai Beach, T510-386 4800, www.hoianriverresort.com.
A short, 5-min cycle ride from the beach and a 15-min pedal from town, this hotel faces the Thu Bon River. There is a pool set in landscaped gardens with hammocks. Standard rooms have balconies; and all rooms have showers. **Song Do** restaurant is the best place to be at sunset.

$$$ Ha An Hotel
6-8 Phan Boi Chau St, T510-386 3126,
www.haanhotel.com.
This is a lovely hotel with a flourishing courtyard garden. Rooms are decorated with ethnic minority accents; they are on the small side but they are bursting with character and the overall ambience is delightful. A great option in the heart of the town.

$$$ Villa Hoa Su
Hamlet 5, Cam Thanh Ward, T510-393 3933,
www.villahoasu.com.
Just 5 extremely well appointed, beautiful rooms at this brilliant boutique property set around a pool and fragrant frangipani garden. Be sure to book well ahead – this place is popular with expats holidaying from Hanoi and Saigon and books up fast. A truly exceptional place.

$$$ Vinh Hung Riverside Resort
11 Ngo Quyen, T510-386 4074,
www.vinhhungresort.com.
Absolutely wonderful riverfront property with beautiful rooms, impeccable service, delicious food and perhaps the best spa in town. Highly recommended.

$$ An Huy Hotel
30 Phan Boi Chau St, T510-386 2116,
www.anhuyhotel.com.
Courtyards that create a breeze and shutters that keep the noise out. Spacious rooms are beautifully decorated in Japanese style.

Restaurants

A Hoi An speciality is *cao lau*, a noodle soup with slices of pork and croutons, traditionally made with water from one particular well and lots of stalls sell it along the river at night. *Mi Quang* is another local treat – it is a delicious combination of noodles, pork, shrimp, rice crackers, peanuts and plenty of herbs. Overall, the quality of food in Hoi An, especially the fish, is outstanding and the value for money is unmatched. Bach Dang St is particularly pleasant in the evening, when tables and chairs are set up almost the whole way along the river.

$$$-$$ Bamboo Buddha
13 Nguyen Hoàng, T51-0392 5000,
www.bb-hoian.com.
Very sleek new French/Vietnamese-run restaurant and bar. Highlights include the Australian barbecued flap steak with *tam ky* pepper sauce and the lime leaf chicken skewers. Gourmet menu options include roast duck breast with passion fruit sauce and butter candied apple. Excellent wine list. Popular with the French expat crowd. 3rd-floor bar with some outdoor seating.

$$$-$$ Secret Garden
132/2 Tran Phu St, off Le Loi St, T510-391 1112,
www.secretgardehoian.com.
An oasis amid the shopping malestrom of downtown Hoi An. Superior and attentive

service in a delightful courtyard garden with delicious dishes. Try the sublime thin slices of beef with garlic and pepper, lemon juice, soya sauce, and black sesame oil or the star fruit soup. Live music is played nightly and there's a cooking school. Touristy, but recommended.

$$ The Field
Vong Nhi Hamlet, Cam Thanh Village, T510-392 3977.
Difficult to find, but worth the effort, **The Field** has a magical setting among the paddy fields outside Hoi An. Best visited at sunset. Serves a wide range of Vietnamese dishes.

$$ Nhu Y (aka Mermaid)
2 Tran Phu St, T510-386 1527, http://msvy-tastevietnam.com.
The now famous Miss Vy turns out all the local specialities as well as some of her own fantastic creations. The 5-course set dinner is particularly recommended.

$$ Seedlings
41 Nguyen Phuc Truc, T510-392 1565, www.seedlingshoian.com.
Just across the bridge on An Hoi with great views of the old town, Seedlings provides training to disadvantaged youths and excellent food to hungry tourists. Working in partnership with local youth NGO, **Reach**, the Seedlings model sees the restaurant graduates move on to the up-scale Laguna properties over the Hai Van Pass north of Danang. The beef rendang and banana flower salads are excellent. Also offers free bicycle rental to diners. The manager, Mai, is extremely welcoming. Soon to open rooftop bar.

$$ Streets Restaurant Café
17 Le Loi St, T510-391 1948, www.streetsinternational.org.
A professional training restaurant for disadvantaged youngsters (including a Hoi An specialities tasting menu)s that serves up very tasty Vietnamese and Western cuisine in a lovely old property. Trainee chefs complete an 18-month programme here. Recommended.

$$-$ The Market
3 Nguyen Hoang, The latest restaurant from the inimitable Ms Vs who is now something of a local celebrity.
A bright open courtyard space with beautiful floor tiling and wooden bench style seating is surrounded by various small cooking stations, each filling the air with enticing aromas. A superb place to try a wide range of Hoi An's special dishes.

$$-$ Son Restaurant
177 Cua Dai Rd, T98-950 1400, www. sonhoian.com. Open 0900-2200.
Now in a new location set back from the river, **Son** is still serving up excellent Vietnamese food Du. The extremely tasty fresh fruit smoothies are a serious contender for the best in the land. This is a top lunch spot and highly recommended.

$ Hola Taco Pork Taco
95000d.
Brad and Nhung came down from Hanoi in 2014 to open this excellent Mexican joint that serves superb tacos and burritos.

$ Morning Glory
106 Nguyen Thai Hoc St, T510-324 224 1555.
In an attractive building with a balcony serving up Vietnamese street food such as crispy mackerel and mango salsa, caramel fish in clay pot and spicy prawn curry. The restaurant is run by Miss Vy of **Mermaid** fame.

Bars and clubs

Before and Now
51 Le Loi, T510-910599.
Often livelier than most bars, particularly after around 2100 thanks to the good drinks offers and classic tunes on the stereo. A good spot to meet fellow travellers.

Dive Bar
88 Nguyen Thai Hoc, T510-391 0782.
A popular hang out for divers and backpackers alike, the **Dive Bar** has a DJ, free pool table and a good selection of cocktails.

Soul Kitchen
See Restaurants.
A great spot to lose an afternoon or evening right on An Bang Beach. Sun afternoons are particularly popular.

White Marble Wine Bar
98 Le Loi St, T510-391 1862, whitemarble@ visithoian.com. Open 1100-2300.
Well-stocked cellar and a modern aesthetic that somehow meshes well with the old town setting, **White Marble** is a fine place to share a bottle. Serves good food too.

Shopping

Hoi An is a shopper's paradise – Tran Phu and Le Loi sts being the main shopping areas. 2 items stand out: paintings and clothes. Hoi An is also the place to buy handbags and purses and attractive Chinese silk lanterns, indeed anything that can be made from silk. There is also a lot of quite nice chinaware available, mostly modern, some reproduction and a few antiques. There is blue and white and celadon green, the ancient Chinese pale green glaze, here often reproduced with fine cracks. Note, however, that it is illegal to take items more than 200 years old out of the country.

Countless galleries sell original works of art. Vietnamese artists have been inspired by Hoi An's old buildings and a Hoi An school of art has developed. Hoi An buildings are instantly recognizable even distorted into a variety of shapes and colours on canvas or silk. Galleries are everywhere but in particular the more serious galleries are to be found in a cluster on Nguyen Thi Minh Khai St west of the Japanese Bridge.

Books
Randy's BookXchange, *Cam Nam Island, T93-608 9483, randy@randysbookxchange. com.* Long-standing bookstore with a wide range of genres, including travel guides. It's a welcoming place to browse.

Handicrafts and jewellery
Memory, *96A Bach Dang St and 62 Le Loi St, T510-391 1483.* Wonderful, imaginative designs, with prices for simple ear rings starting from a few dollars ranging up to around US$70 for more intricate styles.
Reaching Out Handicrafts, *103 Nguyen Thai Hoc St, T510-391 0168, www.reachingout vietnam.com.* Arts and crafts, cards and notebooks, lovely jewellery, textiles and silk sleeping bags all made by disabled artisans living in Hoi An. The shop is a fair trade one and profits support the disabled community. There is usually someone at work in the shop so you can see what they are getting up to.

Tailors and fashion
Hoi An is famed for its tailors – there are now reckoned to be more than 140 in town – who will knock up silk or cotton clothing extremely quickly. However, bear in mind that if every visitor to Hoi An wants something made in 12-24 hrs, this puts an enormous strain on staff. Quite apart from the fact that the workers having to stay up all night, the quality of the finished garment will almost certainly suffer. So, if you are in Hoi An for a few days, give yourself time to accommodate 2nd or 3rd fittings, which may be necessary. Tailors themselves recommend a minimum 36-hr period. The quality of the stitching varies from shop to shop, but many tailors will now be honest and tell you they don't make the clothing on-site, but rather send it elsewhere – this means what you are really searching for is a good measurement service. Ideally, have one thing made and check it before committing to more. The range of fabrics is limited and quality can be poor. Many stores also now sell shoes offering everything from simple heals to outrageously

coloured suede boots and knock-off Nikes; again, the the quality tends to be quite poor.
Gingko, *59 Le Loi, T510-3910 796, www.ginkgo-vietnam.com.* A good choice of funky, quality cotton T-shirts with original designs as well as a more limited range of trousers and shorts. A good place to buy gifts.
Metiseko, *3 Chau Thuong Van, T510-3929 278, www.metiseko.com.* The most chic, high quality threads in town alongside interesting homewares.
O Collective, *85 Nguyen Thai Hoc, T128-327 6993.* A creative little boutique with a tempting range of fashion and homewares.

What to do

The **Hotel Hoi An** (see above) runs several activities including how to be a farmer, fisherman, make Chinese lanterns and visits to carpentry and pottery villages.

Boat rides
Boat rides are available on the Thu Bon River. You can either hire a boat and be paddles around or opt for a motorboat and head further upstream – both options are tranquil and relaxed ways of spending the early evening.

Cookery classes
The Market, *see Restaurants.* Housed in the restaurant of the same name, The Market offers a range of professionally run courses. The Masterclass option includes breakfast as well as hands-on tuition for 675,000d, while the Countryside Bicycle Tour and cooking class is 882,000d. Pick of the bunch, however, is the Gourmet Class with charismatic owner Ms Vy, a third generation chef, for 1,155,000 per person.
Red Bridge Cooking School, *run out of the Hai Café, 98 Nguyen Thai Hoc St, T510-386 3210.* Full-day and half-day courses on offer. Visit the market to be shown local produce, take a boat ride to the cooking school, visit a herb garden and learn to cook before enjoying a feast. This has been one of the

most popular and acclaimed **cooking courses** for many years.

Diving and snorkelling
Cham Island Diving Center, *88 Nguyen Thai Hoc St, T5103-910782, www.chamislanddiving.com.* A PADI dive centre. Its Cham Island excursion is recommended for snorkellers as it gives time to explore the village on Cham Island.

Therapies
Spa & Beauty, *Victoria Hoi An Beach Resort & Spa, Cua Dai Beach, T510-927040, www.victoria hotels-asia.com. Open 0900-2100.* A lovely, friendly spa centre covering a wide range of treatments from body wraps to facials. The reflexology treatment is especially good.
The Spa at the Nam Hai, *Hamlet 1, Dien Duong Village, Dien Ban District, 7 km from Cua Dai Beach, T510-394 0000 ext 7700, www.ghmhotels.com. Open 0900-2100.* This is one of the most gorgeous spas in Southeast Asia. Centred around a lotus pond with stilted buildings in the water, succumb to the delicious treatments on offer including massage, body polishes, facials and spa rituals. The spa's ritual treatment – 2 hrs of pampering – means submitting to an aromatherapy foot polish, aromatherapy massage, silk body scrub, honey and milk body masque and a rose and petal milk bath to complete the experience.

Tour operators
Heaven and Earth, *Hai Ba Trung St (opposite number 720), T510-386 4362, www.vietnam-bicycle.com.* A great local operator running hugely popular bicycle tours around Hoi An.
Hoi An Motorbike Adventures, *54A Phan Chau Trinh St, T91-823 0653, www.motorbike tours-hoian.com.* Highly respected and long-running outfit which runs excellent half-day to 5-day tours in the area.
Hoi An Travel, *Hotel Hoi An, 10 Tran Hung Dao St, and at Hoi An Beach Resort, T510-391 0911, www.hoiantravel.com. Open 0800-2000.* Offers a variety of tours including a visit to

Tra Que vegetable village, fishing at Thanh Nam, lantern making, visiting Kim Bong carpentry village, Thanh Ha pottery village, and visiting the Cham Islands.

Phattire ventures, *619 Hai Ba Trung St, T510-391 7839, www.ptv-vietnam.com.* Trekking, biking, rock climbing and more from this long-running outfit which began life in Dalat. Very friendly and helpful staff.

Victoria Hoi An Beach Resort & Spa, *T510-392 7040, www.victoriahotels-asia.com.* The hotel offers a variety of services priced by the hour including boating, kayaking, fishing, windsurfing, hobie-cat sailing, tennis court use, and a trip in a restored sidecar; you can also take an adventurous 5-day sidecar trip to the Laos border.

Transport

Air

Hoi An does not have an airport. A taxi from Danang airport to Hoi An will cost about 500,000d, 40 mins. Taxi from Hoi An to Danang is around US$10. Transport to Hoi An can also be arranged through operators. **Vietnam Airlines** agent, 10 Tran Hung Dao St, T510-391 0912.

Bicycle and motorbike

Hotels and tour operators have 2WD and 4WD vehicles for hire. Bicycle hire is free at many hotels and guesthouses or around 20,000d per day. Motorcycles can be hired all over town – simply ask at your reception and one will likely be delivered to your door.

Bus and Open Tour Bus

There are direct bus connections with Ho Chi Minh City, Hanoi, Hué and Nha Trang. The bus station is about 1 km west of the centre of town on Ly Thuong Kiet St. There are also regular connections with **Danang**, 1 hr, from 0530 until 1800. Open Tour Buses go north to **Hanoi** and south to **HCMC**. Book through local tour operators.

Taxi

Mai Linh, T510-391 4914.

Around Hoi An

miles of beaches and ancient Cham-era ruins

Cua Dai Beach and An Bang Beach

You must leave your bicycle (5000d) or moto (10000d) just before Cua Dai Beach in a car park unless you are staying at one of the beach resorts.

A white-sand beach with a host of simple restaurants and sun loungers, **Cua Dai Beach** is 4 km from Hoi An, east down Tran Hung Dao Street, and is a pleasant 25-minute bicycle ride or one-hour walk from Hoi An. Alternatively, a quieter route is to set off down Nguyen Duy Hieu Street. This peters out into a footpath which can be cycled. It is a lovely path past paddy fields and ponds. Nothing is signed but those with a good sense of direction will make their way back to the main road a kilometre or so before Cua Dai. Those with a poor sense of direction can come to no harm. Four kilometres north of Hoi An, off the dual carriageway, is **An Bang Beach** where a collection of popular beach bars and some very nice accommodation has opened up. It can be more pleasantly reached by cycling 2.5 km north past paddies on Hai Ba Trung Street (15 minutes). A Cua Dai-An Bang-Hoi An loop is a pleasant couple of hours' cycle ride.

The **Cham Islands** are 15 km from Cua Dai Beach and clearly visible offshore. There are seven islands in the group – Lao (pear), Dai (long), La (leaf), Kho (dry), Tai (ear), Mo (tomb) and Nom (east wind). Bird's nests are collected here. You can visit the fishing villages and snorkel and camp overnight (see **Cham Island Diving Center**, page 129).

★**My Son** → *Colour map 3, B5.*

Daily 0630-1630, 80,000d, around 45 mins from both Hoi An and Danang. Tour operators in Hoi An and Danang also offer tours here.

Declared a World Heritage Site by UNESCO in 1999, My Son is one of Vietnam's most ancient monuments. Weather, jungle and years of strife have wrought their worst on My Son. But arguably the jungle under which My Son remained hidden to the outside world provided it with its best protection, for more has been destroyed in the past 40 years than the previous 400. Today, far from anywhere, My Son is a tranquil archaeological treasure with some beautiful buildings and details to look at. My Son is located about 60 km south of Danang, 28 km west of Tra Kieu, and consists of more than 70 monuments spread over a large area.

Not many visitors have time to make an excursion to see it which makes it all the more appealing to those that do. The thin red bricks of which the towers and temples were built have been carved and the craftsmanship of many centuries remains obvious today. The trees and creepers have been pushed back but My Son remains cloaked in green; shoots sprout up and one senses that were its custodians to turn their backs for even a short time My Son would be reclaimed by the forces of nature.

Tra Kieu, My Son and Dong Duong are the three most important centres of the former Cham Kingdom (see page 470). The characteristic Cham architectural structure is the tower, built to reflect the divinity of the king: tall and rectangular, with four porticoes, each of which is 'blind' except for that on the west face. Because Cham kings were far less wealthy and powerful than the *deva-rajas* (god kings) of Angkor, the monuments are correspondingly smaller and more personal. Originally built of wood (not surprisingly, none remains), they were later made of brick, of which the earliest (seventh century) are located at My Son. These are so-called Mi-Son E1 – the unromantic identifying sequence of letters and numbers being given, uncharacteristically, by the French archaeologists who rediscovered and initially investigated the monuments in 1898. Although little of these early examples remains, the temples seem to show similarities with post-Gupta Indian forms, while also embodying Chen-La stylistic influences. Bricks are exactly laid and held together with a form of vegetable cement probably the resin of the day tree. It is thought that on completion, each tower was surrounded by wood and fired over several days in what amounted to a vast outdoor kiln.

It is important to see My Son in the broader context of the Indianization of Southeast Asia. Not just architecture but spiritual and political influences are echoed around the region. Falling as it did so strongly under Chinese influence it is all the more remarkable to find such compelling evidence of Indian culture and iconography in Vietnam. Indeed this was one of the criteria cited by UNESCO as justification for its listing. Nevertheless one of the great joys of Cham sculpture and building is its unique feel, its graceful lines and unmistakable form. Angkor in Cambodia is the most famous example but Bagan in Burma, Borobudur in Java and Ayutthaya in Thailand, with all of which My Son is broadly contemporaneous, are temple complexes founded by Hindu or Sivaist god kings. In all these places Buddhism appeared in the seventh century and by the 11th century was in the ascendent with the result that, My Son excepted, these are all widely regarded as Buddhist holy sites. The process whereby new ideas and beliefs are absorbed into a pre-existing culture is known as syncretism. The Hindu cult of *deva-raja* was developed by the kings of Angkor and later employed by Cham kings to bolster their authority. The king was the earthly representative of the god Siva. Sivaist influence at My Son is unmissable. Siva is one of the Hindu holy trinity, destroyer of the universe. Siva's dance of destruction is the very rhythm of existence and hence also of rebirth. Siva is often represented, as at My Son and other Cham relics throughout Vietnam, by the lingam, the phallus. My Son was obviously a settled city whose population is unknown but it seems to have had a holy or spiritual function rather than being the seat of power and it was, very probably, a burial place of its god kings.

Much that is known of My Son was discovered by French archaeologists from the École Française d'Extrême-Orient. Their rediscovery and excavation of My Son revealed a site that had been settled from the early eighth to the 15th centuries, the longest uninterrupted period of development of any monument in Southeast Asia. My Son architecture is notable for its use of red brick, which has worn amazingly well. Sandstone plinths are sometimes used, as are sandstone lintels, the Cham seemingly – like the Khmer of Angkor – never having learnt the art of arch building, one of the few architectural techniques in which Europe was centuries ahead of Asia. Linga and yoni, the female receptacle into which the carved phallus was normally inserted, are also usually made of sandstone. Overwhelmingly, however, brick is the medium of construction and the raw material from which Hindu, Sivaist and Buddhist images and ornaments are so intricately carved.

Unfortunately, My Son was a Viet Cong field headquarters and therefore located within one of the US 'free fire' zones and was extensively damaged – in particular, the finest sanctuary in the complex was demolished. Of the temple groupings, Groups A, E and H were badly damaged in the war. Groups B and C have largely retained their temples but many statues, altars and linga have been removed to the Cham Museum in Danang.

Listings Around Hoi An

Where to stay

An Bang Beach

$$$ An Bang Beach Hideaway
T91-769 8970, www.anbangbeach hideaway.com.
Just outside Hoi An in the village of An Bang, this small collection of rooms set across 3 buildings is truly special. Designed by the architect owner, the funky rooms are very homely, each with its own sitting area and outdoor space. An absolute gem of a place, with excellent service to boot. You won't want to check out.

Restaurants

An Bang Beach

$$ Soul Kitchen
An Bang Beach, T90-644 0320, www.soulkitchen.sitew.com.
This is a super laid-back spot with lounge seating, bean bags, day beds and more conventional tables leading from the bar area right down to the sand. The food is nothing exceptional, but the ambiance, location and music policy are all hard to beat, so this is a highly recommended spot for a chilled-out lunch that might well spill into an afternoon and evening.

Dalat

kitsch tourist town surrounded by flower gardens and orchards

Dalat is an attractive town situated on a plateau in the Central Highlands at an altitude of almost 1500 m. The town itself, a former French hill station, is centred on a lake – Xuan Huong – amid rolling countryside and is dotted with more than 2000 French villas. In the area are forests, waterfalls, and an abundance of orchids, roses and other temperate flora. *Colour map 4, B2.*

Sights

a wonderfully eclectic selection of sights

Dalat is the honeymoon capital of southern Vietnam and it is known as a city of romance and even, rather less explicably, the Paris of Vietnam. It also remains a hugely popular destination with Vietnamese tourists.

Essential Dalat

Getting around

Dalat is rather a large town and there are a number of hills. A plentiful selection of taxis is available as are the ubiquitous *xe om* drivers.

When to go

The best time to visit is from November to May when there is less rainfall and pleasant temperatures. At the weekends the centre is closed to traffic between 1900 and 2200 allowing for stalls to set up on Nguyen Thi Minh Khai Street.

Time required

A day or two is enough for most visitors to Dalat.

Xuan Huong Lake

Originally the Grand Lake, Xuan Huong Lake was renamed in 1954. It was created in 1919 after a small dam was constructed on the Cam Ly River. It is the attractive centrepiece of the town and a popular exercise area for the local inhabitants of whom many will, first thing in the morning, walk around the lake stopping every so often to perform t'ai chi exercises. Power-walking at dusk is also popular. The lake was drained in 2010 so as to remove accumulated silt and construct a new road across the centre. It should be refilled by the time you read this.

Dalat Flower Garden

Vuon Hoa Dalat, 2 Phu Dong Thien Vuong St, daily 0700-1800, 10,000đ.

At the northeast end of the lake is the Dalat Flower Garden. It supports a range of plants including orchids, roses, lilies and hydrangeas. Signs are not in English, only

Latin and Vietnamese; the one English sign directs visitors to the orchidarium. There are kiosks selling drinks and ice creams and there's a lake with pedaloes.

Colonial villas

Many of the large colonial villas – almost universally washed in pastel yellow – are 1930s and 1940s vintage. Some have curved walls, railings and are almost nautical in inspiration; others are reminiscent of houses in Provence. Many of the larger villas can be found along **Tran Hung Dao Street** and a number of these are now being converted into villa hotels. Sadly many of the villas have fallen into a very sorry state and are looking decidedly unloved. Given their architectural significance this is a great pity. Perhaps the largest and most impressive house on Tran Hung Dao is the former residence of the Governor General at 12 Tran Hung Dao Street – now the **Hotel Dinh 2**. The villa is 1930s in style, with large airy rooms and furniture and occupies a magnificent position set among mountain pines and overlooking the town and lake. The house is a popular place for domestic tourists to have their photographs taken. It is possible to

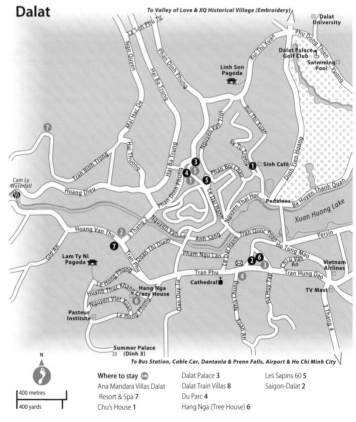

Dalat

To Valley of Love & XQ Historical Village (Embroidery)

Dalat University

Dalat Palace Golf Club

Swimming Pool

Linh Son Pagoda

Cam Ly Waterfall

Sinh Café

Pedaloes

Xuan Huong Lake

Yersin

Vietnam Airlines

Lam Ty Ni Pagoda

Hang Nga Crazy House

Tran Phu Cathedral

TV Mast

Pasteur Institute

Summer Palace (Dinh 3)

To Bus Station, Cable Car, Dantanla & Prenn Falls, Airport & Ho Chi Minh City

N

400 metres
400 yards

Where to stay
Ana Mandara Villas Dalat Resort & Spa 7
Chu's House 1

Dalat Palace 3
Dalat Train Villas 8
Du Parc 4
Hang Nga (Tree House) 6

Les Sapins 60 5
Saigon-Dalat 2

stay here although it is often booked up and is popular with members of Lam Dong People's Committee.

Dalat Cathedral
Tran Phu St. Mass is held twice a day Mon-Sat 0515 and 1715 and on Sun at 0515, 0700, 0830, 1600 and 1800. Has a good choir and attracts a large and enthusiastic congregation.

The single-tiered cathedral is visible from the lake and 100 m from the Novotel hotel. At the top of the turret is a chicken-shaped wind dial. It is referred to locally as the 'Chicken Cathedral'. Construction began in 1931, although the building was not completed until the Japanese 'occupation' in 1942. The stained-glass windows, with their vivid colours and use of pure, clean lines, were crafted in France by Louis Balmet, the same man who made the windows in Nha Trang and Danang cathedrals, between 1934 and 1940. Sadly, most have not survived the ravages of time. Lining the nave are blocks of woodcarvings of Christ and the crucifixion.

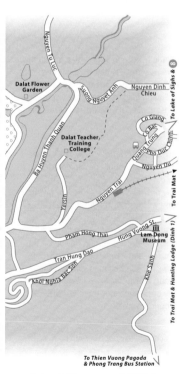

Restaurants 🍴
Bicycle Up Café **1**
Da Quy **4**
Hoa Binh **5**
La Rabelais **6**
Le Café de la Poste **2**
Tau Cao **7**
V Café **3**

To Thien Vuong Pagoda & Phong Trang Bus Station

Summer Palace (Dinh 3) and Dinh 1
Le Hong Phong St, T63-382 6858, 0730-1100 and 1330-1600, 10000d. Café, ice creams available.

Vietnam's last emperor, Bao Dai, had a Summer Palace on Le Hong Phong Street, about 2 km from the town centre and now known as Dinh 3. Built on a hill with views on every side, it is art deco in style both inside and out, and rather modest for a palace. The palace was built between 1933 and 1938. The stark interior contains little to indicate that this was the home of an emperor – almost all of Bao Dai's personal belongings have been removed. The impressive dining room contains an etched-glass map of Vietnam, while the study has Bao Dai's desk, a few personal ornaments and photographs, noticeably of the family who, in 1954, were exiled to France where they lived. One of the family photos shows Bao Dai's son, the prince Bao Long, in full military dress uniform. He died in July 2007 in France aged 71. Emperor Bao Dai's daughters are still alive and were, in a spirit of reconciliation, invited back to visit Vietnam in the mid-1990s. They politely declined (one of the reasons given was that as they were both in their 70s it would have been too much effort), although the grandchildren may one day return. The emperor's bedroom and bathroom are open to public scrutiny as is the little terrace from his bedroom where, apparently, on a clear night he would gaze at the stars. The family drawing room is open together with a little commentary on which chair was used by whom. The palace is very popular with rowdy Vietnamese tourists who have their photographs taken wherever they can. The gardens are colourful and well maintained, though have a carnival atmosphere. From the moon balcony you can see the garden has been arranged into the shape of the Bao Dai stamp.

Hang Nga Crazy House
3 Huynh Thuc Khang, T63-382 2070, daily 0700-1800.

The slightly wacky theme is maintained at the nearby Tree House leading many to wonder what they put in the water for this corner of Dalat to nurture so many creative eccentrics. Doctor Dang Viet Nga has, over a period of many years, built up her hotel in organic fashion. The rooms and gardens resemble scenes taken from the pages of a fairytale book. Guests sleep inside mushrooms, trees and giraffes and sip tea under giant cobwebs. There is a honeymoon room, an ant room and plenty more. It is not a particularly comfortable place to stay and the number of visitors limits privacy. (Dr Dang Viet Nga also built the Children's Centre at 38 Tran Phu Street.)

Dalat Market
At the end of Nguyen Thi Minh Khai St.

Dalat Market (Cho Dalat) sells a dazzling array of exotic fruits and vegetables grown in the temperate climate of the area – plums, strawberries, carrots, potatoes, loganberries, artichokes, apples, onions and avocados. The forbidding appearance of the market is masked by the riot of colour of the flowers on sale, including gladioli, irises, roses, gerbera, chrysanthemums and marigolds. Sampling the immense variety of candied fruit here is the highlight of any visit to Dalat.

Waterfalls
Cam Ly Waterfall ⓘ *2 km from the centre of town, T63-382 4145, daily 0700-1700*, is the closest waterfall to Dalat town centre. It is pleasant enough but should be avoided during the dry season. **Datanla Falls** ⓘ *along a track, 5 km out of town on Highway 20 towards HCMC, T63-383 1804, 0700-1700*, the path leads steeply downwards into a forested ravine; it is an easy hike there, but tiring on the return journey. However, the **Alpine Coaster**, a toboggan on rails, makes the journey faster and easier. The falls – really a cascade – are hardly spectacular, but few people come here except at weekends so it is usually peaceful.

   Prenn Falls ⓘ *12 km from Dalat, on the route to HCMC, next to the road, T63-353 0785, 0700-1700*, the falls were dedicated to Queen Sirikit of Thailand when she visited them in 1959. Though it underwent renovations a few years ago, the falls began to suffer pollution and degredation because dredged silt from Xuan Huong lake in Dalat was being dumped at the source of the falls. The falls are not particularly impressive, but there is a pleasant rope bridge that can be crossed and views of the surrounding area.

Dalat cable car (Cáp Treo)
It starts south of town off 3 April Rd, T63-383 7938, 40,000d – widely popular with both locals and tourists.

The journey from top to bottom takes about 15 minutes and leads to a Thien Vien Truc Lam Pagoda and Paradise Lake.

Tourist information

Dalat Travel Bureau
www.dalattourist.com.vn.
The state-run travel company for Lam Dong Province.

Where to stay

$$$$ Ana Mandara Villas Dalat Resort & Spa
Le Lai St, T63-355 5888,
www.anamandara-resort.com.
The previous owners, **Six Senses**, restored 17 French hillside villas built in the 1920s and 1930s. Each of the villas has a couple of bedrooms, a living room and dining room; guests have dedicated butlers. The furnishings are reminiscent of Shaker-style furniture; the beds are heavenly; the baths are on feet. **Nine Restaurant & Bar** at Villa 9 has beautiful tilework and a large central fireplace. French-style shutters open on to a small terrace. The heated pool, buried amid the secluded hillside villas, is lovely; a night swim in the cool air is invigorating and at night the air is enveloped with the smell of pine. There's a luxurious spa on site and a city excursion in a 1930s Citroen is a must.

$$$$ Dalat Palace Luxury Hotel
12 Tran Phu St, T63-382 5444.
This rambling old building, built in 1922 and restored to its former glory in 1995, is a wonderful hotel. Those that knew it before restoration will be amazed: the renovation is superb: curtains, furniture, statues, gilt mirrors and chandeliers adorn the rooms which are tastefully arranged as the French do best. The view over Xuan Huong Lake to the hills beyond is lovely and the extensive grounds of the hotel are beautifully laid out. The hotel offers guests special green fees on the nearby golf course.

$$$$-$$$ Saigon-Dalat Hotel
2 Hoang Van Thu, T63-355 6789,
www.saigondalathotel.com.
Now a 4-star hotel, this is one of the largest in the city. The striking white exterior, alpine-style roof is visible throughout western Dalat. The hotel has 2 restaurants and a bar, plus the **Moulin Rouge Restaurant** across the street.

$$$ Du Parc (formerly Novotel Dalat)
7 Tran Phu St, T63-382 5777.
First opened in 1932 this was completely restored in 1995. Rooms are nicely restored and comfortably furnished, now including complementary Wi-Fi. Meals are served at the atmospheric **Café de la Poste** across the street.

$$$ Hang Nga (Tree House)
Huynh Thuc Khang St, T63-382 2070.
If you fancy a fantasy night in a mushroom, a tree or a giraffe then this is the place for you. Prices have risen and the rooms tend to be ones visited by curious tourists and the furniture is sturdily made and not too comfortable.

$$ Dalat Train Villas
1 Quang Trung, T90-334 2442,
www.dalattrainvilla.com.
Housed in a beautifully restored colonial villa, this property boats the most characterful rooms in town. Just outside is a wonderful little café in a train carriage which is worth a visit in its own right.

$ Chu's House
65 Truong Cong Dinh, T63-382 5097,
www.chuhouse.com.
Right in the heart of town this is a friendly and very well appointed budget option.

$ Les Sapins 60
60 Truong Cong Dinh, T63-383 0839,
www.lessapins60dalathotel.com.
Family-run, this small central hotel feels brand new with sparkling clean rooms

which are very quiet thanks to the thick double glazed windows. Some rooms with small balconies. Simple decor and very homely. Welcoming and knowledgable staff. Also sells its own line of coffees including robusta, Arabica and weasel varieties. Motorcycle hire available.

Restaurants

$$$ Le Rabelais
12 Tran Phu St, T63-382 5444.
A superb dining room with views down to the lake. It serves French specialities. Excellent wine list. Smart dress is required.

$$$-$ Le Café de la Poste
12 Tran Phu St.
Adjacent to the Sofitel and under the same management. International comfort food at near-Western prices in an airy and cool building. The 3-course lunch menu is great value. The staff look a little uncomfortable in French-style outfits. A pool table dominates the café. Upstairs is a Vietnamese restaurant.

$ Da Quy (Wild Sunflower)
49 Truong Cong Dinh St, T63-351 0883.
This sweet little family-run business is very friendly and a delightful place to eat with maroon checked tablecloths and a tidy atmosphere. The menu is varied; try the sautéd beef and snow peas.

$ Dalat Train Café
1 Quang Trung, www.dalattrainvilla.com.
Housed in a railway carriage, this place is a characterful spot for a cheap bite to eat.

$ Hoa Binh 1
67 Truong Cong Dinh St.
An all-day eatery serving standard backpacker fare – fried noodles, vegetarian dishes and pancakes at very low prices.

$ Tau Cao
217 Phung St, close to the Mimosa Hotel, T63-382 0104.

This Chinese rice noodle restaurant serves up steaming soups with or without *wan tun*. Still going strong after many years.

$ V Café
1 Bui Thi Xuan, T63-352 0215, www.vcafedalatvietnam.com.
Hugely popular spot with live music every night and a menu of comfort food – think pork chop and mash, burgers and a smattering of Mexican options. By no means fine dining, but a cosy place.

Cafés

Bicycle Up Café
82 Truong Cong Dinh.
An old bicycle and bath tub full of flowers welcome visitors to this cosy, funky little spot run by Ms Indy. With a beautiful tiled floor, mix and match furnishings and an upright piano, this is one of the finer places in town to enjoy an espresso made using La Viet speciality coffee.

Stalls

There are *pho* and *banh mi* (bread) stalls on **Tang Bat Ho St**. Noodle soup, filled baguettes and pastries available from early morning until late. The streets around the university are also good places to find a cheap local Vietnamese meal.

Bars and clubs

Beepub
74 Truong Cong Dinh, T633-825576, www.beepub.vn.
A new and very small pub with a live band most nights. A popular spot with locals and the town's expats and a good place to meet people.

Escape Bar
4 Phan Boi Chau, T63-357 8888.
This is the liveliest bar in town with a rocking house band blasting out classic covers every night of the week. Great atmosphere on busier nights.

Larry's Bar
Du Parc Hotel, see Where to stay.
Open 1600-2400.
A rustic look for this basement bar with comfortable chairs, a pool table and TV room. It was named after Larry Hillblum of DHL fame, who in 1994 spent a fortune renovating the **Sofitel**, **Mercure** and the golf course. Good selection of drinks and bar food available, but sadly it is often eerily quiet.

Festivals

Dec-Mar is when most of the festivals of the local tribes take place. For specific information contact the provincial tourist offices.

Dec or Jan Celebrates the flower capital of Vietnam in peak season.

Shopping

Dalat produces some of the best handmade silk paintings in Vietnam. During your stay in Vietnam you are bound to see shops selling them. The original place to develop this was XQ in Dalat (www.tranhtheuxq.com). It is possible to see how these works of art are produced at the XQ Historical Village on the north side of town and the XQ showroom.

Local produce is plentiful and cheap and can be purchased in Dalat market. Dalat wine is the national standard and comes in red and white. Artichoke teas, jams and dried mushrooms are also a local favourite.

What to do

Swimming
There is an open-air swimming pool on Phu Dong Thien Vuong St (Hu Boi Nuoc Nong) next to the Dalat Flower Garden.

Therapies
L'Apothiquaire, *T63-382 5444, www.lapothiquaire.com*. In the eaves of the **Dalat Palace**.

Tour operators
Many of the hotels have tour desks, including **Chu Hotel** and **Le Sapine 60**, see Where to stay.
Original Dalat Easy Riders, *67 Truong Cong Dinh, www.dalateasyriders.vn*. Ben who now mans the office is the son of Mr Hong, one of the original easy riders from back in 1991. Hong and his team run a 1-day tour which takes in war sites as well as tea, coffee and vegetable farms, waterfalls and minority villages. Also offers trips from Dalat to Nha Trang, Hoi An on comfortable Honda Custom 250cc motorcycles. Prices from US$65 a day, including accommodation.
Phattire Adventures, *109 Nguyen Van Troi, T63-382 0331, www.ptv-vietnam.com*. Canyoning, from US$45; mountain biking, from US$37, with easy, medium and hard trails through pine forests; trekking from US$32 with options to visit Tiger Falls. Rafting on the La Ba river, where the white water can hit grade 3+ from Sep-Dec. One of the staff, Luet, is particularly helpful. High quality Giant bicycles for the cycle trips. A very professional agent.
Sinh Tourist, *22 Bui Thi Xuan St, T63-382 2663, www.thesinhtourist.vn*. Part of the nationwide **Sinh Tourist** tour operators. Primarily provides cheap travel to HCMC and Nha Trang. It can also arrange local tours and hotel bookings.

Transport

Air
There are daily flights from Ho Chi Minh City and Hanoi. **Vietnam Airlines**, No 2 and No 40 Ho Tung Mau St, T63-383 3499. Daily 0730-1130, 1330-1630. Closes 30 mins earlier at the weekend.

Bus and Open Tour Bus
There are plenty of local buses that plough the inter provincial routes of **Buon Ma Thuot**, **Pleiku**, **Kontum**, **Nha Trang**, **HCMC**, **Gia Nghia**, **Phan Rang**, **Phan Thiet**, **Danang**. Buses to Lak Lake, 5 hrs. Open Tour

Bus companies (**Phuong Trang** and **Sinh Tourist**) operate daily trips to **HCMC**, 7 hrs, **Nha Trang**, 7 hrs, and **Mui Ne**, 8 hrs.

Phuong Trang, 11A Le Quy Don St, T63-358 5858. Phuong Trang dominates southern Vietnam's bus services, and rightly so. The new Phuong Trang bus station is impressive, but more so is the top-quality service.

Car

Dalat is on Highway 20. It is possible to hire cars and taxis in Dalat. Many of the tour operators have cars for hire and there are many taxis. **Mai Linh Dalat**, 44/8 Hai Ba Trung St, T63-351 1511.

Motorbikes and bicycles

Xe oms are ubiquitous. Many places hire motorbikes including **Le Sapine 60** hotel (see Where to stay).

Train

Daily services run the 7 km between Dalat and **Trai Mat**.

Central
Highlands

coffee-growing country populated by minority groups

The Central Highlands, centred around the Truong Son Mountain Range, is commonly referred to as the backbone of Vietnam and is primarily an agrarian area; it is a huge source of flowers and vegetables with many tea and coffee plantations that supply the whole world. Tourism is an additional source of revenue for many of the inhabitants, but outside the main towns of Dalat, Buon Ma Thuot, Pleiku and Kontum the way of life remains largely unchanged.

Weather Central Highlands

January	February	March	April	May	June
25°C	27°C	30°C	31°C	29°C	26°C
13°C	13°C	18°C	18°C	20°C	20°C
18mm	18mm	33mm	60mm	177mm	228mm

July	August	September	October	November	December
20°C	26°C	26°C	27°C	26°C	26°C
19°C	19°C	19°C	17°C	16°C	13°C
230mm	403mm	177mm	80mm	72mm	6mm

a modern city with little for the tourist

Buon Ma Thuot is the provincial capital of Daklak Province. The city has changed from being a sleepy backwater town (similar to Kontum) to a thriving modern city, but it has little to draw visitors.

Buon Ma Thuot has now surpassed its illustrious and renowned neighbour of Dalat to be the main centre for tea and coffee production, and the area has become the second largest producer of coffee in the world. The creation of the Trung Nguyen coffee empire in 1997 and the subsequent franchise of the names have meant that Trung Nguyen coffee shops are to be found everywhere in Vietnam. It is good to see that some profits have been reinvested in the community (there are new schools, roads, hospitals aplenty). There is also a sports complex to rival any to be found in Ho Chi Minh City or Hanoi.

Around Buon Ma Thuot → *Colour map 4, B2.*

waterfalls and minority cultures

Dray Sap, Dray Nur and Gia Long waterfalls
T500-385 0123, daily 0700-1700, 30,000d for Dray Sap and Gia Long combined and another 30,000d for Dray Nur. 30 km south of Buon Ma Thuot, 2 km off Highway 14 heading in the direction of HCMC.

Essential Central Highlands

Getting around

Many buses go to Pleiku, Kontum, Nha Trang, Buon Ma Thuot, Phan Thiet, and Phan Rang. Open Tour Buses go to Nha Trang.

When to go

As different indigenous groups live in the Central Highlands, there are festivals all year round. Buffalo sacrifice ceremonies take place in Mnong, Sedang and Cotu communities after the spring harvest. Climatically the best time to visit is from November to April when there is little to no rain and the temperature is warm to hot.

Time required

To discover the national parks and minority villages around three days is required.

The waterfalls consist of several different cascades all next to each other. They form a 100-m-wide cascade and are particularly stunning in the wet season and justify the name of 'waterfall of smoke', although Dray Nur and Dray Sap are impressive even in the dry season. The best view of Gia Long is from the north side but you can't cross from the south to view it. In the wet season it may occasionally be closed, as the paths are too treacherous to use. There are two paths to take, one down by the river and the other on the high ground.

Dray Sap has been taken over by a private company. An Ede ceremonial house has been added along with a small, rather unpleasant zoo.

Lak Lake and M'nong villages
The serene **Lak Lake** is about 50 km south-east of Buon Ma Thuot. It is an attraction in its own right but all the more compelling a visit on account of the surrounding **M'nong villages**. Unfortunately, Lak Lake has been developed as a tourist attraction and Buon Jun is rather touristy now. For those going

Central Highlands

The Central Highlands have long been associated with Vietnam's hill tribes. French missionaries were active among the minorities of the Central Highlands (the colonial administration deterred ethnic Vietnamese from settling here) although with uneven success. Bishop Cuenot dispatched two missionaries from Quy Nhon to Buon Ma Thuot where they received a hostile reception from the Mnong, so travelled north to Kontum where among the Ba-na they found more receptive souls for their evangelizing. Today, many of the ethnic minorities in the Central Highlands are Roman Catholic, although some are Protestant (Ede around Buon Ma Thuot, for instance).

At the same time French businesses were hard at work establishing plantations to supply the home market. Rubber and coffee were the staple crops. The greatest difficulty they faced was recruiting sufficient labour. Men and women of the ethnic minorities preferred to cultivate their own small plots rather than accept the hard labour and slave wages of the plantation owners. Norman Lewis travelled in the Central Highlands and describes the situation in his book, *A Dragon Apparent*.

Since 1984 there has been a bit of a free-for-all and a scramble for land. Ethnic Vietnamese have encroached on minority land and planted it with coffee, pepper and fruit trees. From the air one sees neat rows of crops and carefully tended plots, interrupted only by large areas of scrub that are too dry to cultivate. The scene is reinforced at ground level where the occasional tall tree is the only reminder of the formerly extensive forest cover. The way of life of the minorities is at risk of disappearing with the forests.

The Mnong, Coho, Sedang and Bahnar people speak a language that stems from the Mon Khmer language. The language of the Ede, Giarai, Cham and Raglai originates from the Malayo-Polynesian language.

on a tour there is little choice as to where to go, but for the independent traveller on a motorbike there are plenty of villages, both ethnic Vietnamese and minority, to visit, but do not expect any English to be spoken.

Early-morning mists hang above the calm waters and mingle with the columns of woodsmoke rising from the longhouses. The M'nong Rlam at Buon Jun has been influenced by the Ede and so live in longhouses. However, most M'nong such as M'nong Chil, Noong, Gar and Bu-dang live in straw and mud- or wood-thatched homes. The lake can be explored by dugout. The canoes are painstakingly hollowed out from tree trunks by axe. The M'nong have been famed as elephant catchers for hundreds of years, although the elephants are now used for tourist rides rather than in their traditional role for dragging logs from the forest.

It is possible to stay overnight at a M'nong village, **Buon Jun** (Buon means village), indeed it is the only way to watch the elephants taking their evening wallow in the cool waters and to appreciate the tranquility of sunrise over the lake. The M'nong number about 50,000 and are matriarchal. An evening supping with your hosts, sharing rice wine and sleeping in the simplicity of a M'nong longhouse is an ideal introduction to these genial people. Between 1600 and 1730 every evening you can watch the men bring back the fish of the day to the lakeshore; the children are eager to help on the shore, buffalos are bathing and pigs are snorting around in the vegetation. Sup a beer at one of the cafés along the lakefront as the sun sets. For more information, see Where to stay, below.

Yok Don National Park

T500-378 3049, yokdonecotourism@vnn.vn. daily 0700-2200. Tours range from elephant riding (US$40 for 2 hrs) to elephant trekking and animal spotting by night. Trekking is another option. Accommodation is available (see Where to stay, below).

A 115,545-ha wildlife reserve about 40 km northwest of Buon Ma Thuot, Yok Don National Park (Vuon Quoc Gia Yok Don) contains at least 63 species of mammals, 17 of which are on the worldwide endangered list, and 250 species of bird. There are known to be around 50 Asian elephants, Samba deer, giant muntjac, leopard, the recently discovered golden jackal and green peafowl. The park is surprisingly flat – save Yok Don Mountain in the middle at 482 m and Yok Da Mountain (482 m) further north – and is, surprisingly, a less-than-dense deciduous forest which makes it easy to trek on an elephant though few wild animals congregate where elephant treks occur. There are 120 species of tree and 854 species of flora. Within its boundaries, also, there are 25 villages of different ethnic tribes who maintain a number of domesticated elephants. Trekking deep into the park and staying in tents near Yok Don Mountain is probably the only chance of seeing wildlife of any great rarity but, alas, the rare become rarer with each passing year. The less adventurous (or those with smaller elephant-trekking budgets) will have to make do with one-hour rides or simply watching one of the village's elephants at work. Note that the rainy season is from April to October.

Listings Around Buon Ma Thuot

Where to stay

Lak Lake and M'nong villages

$$-$ Bao Dai Villa
Lak Lake, T500-358 6184,
www.daklaktourist.com.vn.
Opt for the massive King's Room with portraits on the wall for a unique stay in the area. All 6 rooms have modern comforts and bathtubs. The villa is surrounded by beautiful magnolia trees. The restaurant features old black and white photos of the emperor and his elephant team.

$ Buon Jun longhouse
Buon Jun village.
Contact **Daklak Tourist** at the entrance to the village, T500-358 6184, laklake@daklaktourist.com.vn, for arrangements. It

costs US$12 to stay in a longhouse including breakfast. Longhouses vary between traditional wooden ones to concrete ones. If you don't like creepy crawlies opt for the concrete ones which also have their own bathrooms. Those nearer the lake are noisier.

$ Lak Lake Resort
Lien Son village, near Buon Jun, Lak Lake,
T500-358 6184, www.daklaktourist.com.vn.
There are 32 rooms with balconies in a great position overlooking the lake. Rooms have TV, a/c and bathtubs. Breakfast is included. There's a branch of **Daklak Tourist** on site.

$ Lak Lake Resort Longhouse.
2 longhouses in the grounds of the **Lak Lake Resort**, see above. The same price as the village longhouses, but the bathrooms are better.

Yok Don National Park

$ Park Guesthouse
T500-378 3049, yokdonecotourism@vnn.vn.
Park HQ has very simple rooms with 2 beds, a/c, fan, hot showers, TV with minimal reception and Wi-Fi.

Restaurants

Lak Lake and M'nong villages

$ Lak Resort floating restaurant
Lien Son village, near Buon Jun,
Lak Lake, T500-358 6184.

This restaurant juts out into the lake and is a pleasant place for a meal and a few beers in the shade with a cooling breeze.

Transport

Lak Lake and M'nong villages
There are hourly buses to and from Buon Ma Thuot to **Lak Lake**. Hourly buses to and from **Krong Kno** for the Dray Sap waterfall. Buses to **Dalat** from Lak Lake, 5 hrs.

Pleiku → *Colour map 4, A2.*

well and truly off the beaten path

Pleiku is the provincial capital of Gia Lai Province. It is located in a valley at the bottom of a local mountain, Ham Rong, clear to see from 12 km away. It is a rather forgettable place and does not attract visitors, other than those who are here for a stopover. During the monsoon the side streets turn into muddy torrents and chill damp pervades guesthouse rooms. The city itself is sprawling although there are six main streets on which you'll find all that you will need in terms of restaurants, shops, internet cafés and hotels.

Kontum → *Colour map 4, A2.*

low-key, backwater town with cultural variety

The town, 49 km north of Pleiku, has a population of 36,000, many of whom are from ethnic minorities. It is a small, sleepy market town and in itself is not remarkable except that it houses the Wooden Church, Tan Huong Church and the Bishop's Seminary. These alone are worth a trip to Kontum.

Despite being one of the larger provinces within Vietnam, Kontum is the least populated and one of the poorest. It was created in 1991 when it was decided to break up Gia Lai Province.

Sights
The main sights within Kontum are the Wooden Church, Tan Huong Church, the Bishop's Seminary, the provincial museum on the riverfront, the surrounding Ba-na villages, and Kontum prison.

Tan Huong Church ① *92 Nguyen Hué St (if the church is shut ask in the office adjacent and they will gladly open it).* The whitewashed façade bears an interesting depiction of St George and the dragon. It is not immediately evident that the church is built on stilts, but crouch down and look under one of the little arches that run along the side and the stilts, joists and floorboards are clear. The glass in the windows is all old, as the rippling indicates, although one of the two stained-glass windows over the altar has required a little patching up. Unfortunately the roof is a modern replacement, but the original style of fishscale tiling can still be seen in the tower. The interior of the church is exquisite, with dark wooden columns and a fine vaulted ceiling made of wattle and daub. The altar is a new, but rather fine addition, made of a jackfruit tree, as is the lectern. The original building was erected in 1853 and then rebuilt in 1860 following a fire. The current church dates from 1906.

Wooden Church Further east on the same street is the superb Wooden Church. Built by the French with Ba-na labour in 1913, it remains largely unaltered, with the original wooden frame and wooden doors. Unfortunately the windows are modern tinted-glass and the paintings on them depicting scenes from Christ's life as well as a couple of Old Testament scenes with Moses are a little crude. In the grounds stands a statue of Stephen Theodore Cuenot, the first Roman Catholic bishop of East Cochin China diocese. There is also an orphanage that is run by the church in the grounds that welcomes visitors.

Bishop's Seminary The architecturally remarkable and prominent building is set in lovely gardens with pink and white frangipani trees. It was completed in 1935; the seminary was founded by French missionary Martial Jannin Phuoc. The upstairs **exhibition room** ⓘ *Mon-Sat 0800-1130, by donation*, displays an eclectic collection of instruments, photos and scale models; some signs are in English.

Kontum Prison ⓘ *500 m along Truong Trong St, daily 0800-1100, 1400-1700*. Built in 1915, this was home to several prominent revolutionaries. It was abandoned by the French in 1933 and later left to collapse. There is a small museum in some new buildings and a memorial depicting malnourished prisoners. The labels are in Vietnamese only.

Ba-na villages There are scores of Ba-na villages around Kontum that can be reached by motorbike, and at least one that is easily accessible on foot. Plei To Nghia is at the westerly end of Phan Chu Trinh Street down a dusty track. Wattle and daub houses, mostly on stilts, can be seen and the long low white building on short stilts at the village entrance is the church. In the evening the elderly folk of the village go for communal prayers while the young people gather at the foot of their longhouses for a sunset chat. In and around the village are small fields heavily fortified with thorns and barbed wire, which seems a little strange considering the Ba-na do not lock their doors. In fact the defence is not against poachers but the village's large population of rooting, snuffling, pot-bellied pigs. Every family has a few pigs that roam loose. The pigs are sometimes given names and recognize the voice of their owner, coming when called.

Most houses are on stilts, with the animals living underneath. They are built from wattle and daub around a wooden frame, although brick is starting to appear as it is cheaper than declining wood resources, and modern tile is beginning to replace the lovely old fishscale tiling. Considering the tiny spaces in which most Vietnamese live, these houses are positively palatial. There is a large living room in the centre, a kitchen (with no chimney) at one end and bedroom at the other.

Kon D'Ri (Kon Jori) is a fine example of a community almost untouched by modern life (apart from Celine Dion's voice competing with the cows and cockerels!). A perfect *rong* communal house dominates the hamlet, and all other dwellings in the village are made from bamboo, or mud and reeds. The Ba-na *rong* is instantly recognizable by its tall thatched roof. The height of the roof is meant to indicate the significance of the building and make it visible to all. It is a focal point of the village for meetings of the village elders, weddings and other communal events. The stilt house close by is in fact a small Roman Catholic church.

Nearby **Kon Kotu** is similar. To get there follow Nguyen Hué Street and turn right into Tran Hung Dao Street, cross the suspension bridge (Kon Klor Bridge) over the Dakbla River (built in 1997 after a flood washed the old one away).

A lively Ba-na community can be found at **Kontum KoNam** (turn right off Nguyen Hué past the wooden church). Here the stilt houses are crowded close together and the village bustles with activity.

Around Kontum

Chu Pao Pass Twelve kilometres south of Kontum the road crosses the Chu Pao Pass. There is nothing to see in particular, but there are commanding views over the Kontum Plateau. The road descends past sugar cane plantations before crossing the Dakbla River. It is also possible to get to Kontum from Laos at the Bo-Y border crossing.

The border crossing Bo-Y is open to foreigners crossing into Laos. Lao visas should be available on arrival but it is safer to have obtained them beforehand. For details, see the box on page 545.

Listings Kontum

Tourist information

Kontum Tourist Office
2 Phan Dinh Phung St (ground floor of the Dakbla Hotel 1), T60-386 1626. Daily 0700-1100, 1300-1700.

Where to stay

$ Indochine (Dong Duong) Hotel
30 Bach Dang St, T60-386 3335, www.indochinehotel.vn.
The views from this hotel are fantastic. You can look right up the river to the mountains beyond. Decent-sized rooms with mod-cons including hairdryer.

$ Thinh Vuong
16B Nguyen Trai St, T60-391 4729.
The more expensive bedrooms have living area, fridge, TV and bathtubs in the windowless bathrooms. Cheaper rooms are quite spacious too. Very friendly and helpful staff make this place a very good choice.

Restaurants

There are many restaurants and cafés along Nguyen Hué St all of which are much of a muchness in terms of food, quality, choice, presentation and value. Tapioca noodles – *banh canh mi* – are excellent in Kontum.

$$ Dakbla Restaurant
Dakbla 1 Hotel, 2 Phung St, T60-386 3333.
Good selection of both Vietnamese and international cuisine. Quality and presentation are good and the service is friendly albeit a tad slow. The restaurant looks out onto the hotel courtyard.

$ Dakbla's Café
168 Nguyen Hué St, T60-386 2584, vandakbla@yahoo.com.
Filled with ethnic minority artefacts, it has the most interesting decor town. The pleasant staff are conversant in several languages (English, French and German) and there's a decent selection of reasonable food at cheap prices.

Cafés

Evacoffee
1 Phan Chu Trinh St, T60-386 2944, evacoffee@gmail.com.
A cool hideaway amid plants, sculptures and wooden furniture.

Bars and clubs

Basic beer joints are primarily found along Nguyen Hué St. For a mixed drink your best choice is one of the hotels or Evacoffee.

Festivals

Dec-Mar is when most of the festivals of the local tribes take place. For specific information contact the provincial tourist offices.

14 Nov Festival to celebrate **Bishop Cuenot**.

What to do

Kayaking and trekking
Kayaking, trekking and overnight stays with ethnic minorities can be arranged by **Kontum Tourist** (see below).

Tour operators
Highland Ecotours, *15 Ho Tung Mau T90-511 2037 (mob), www.vietnamhighlands.com.*
Mr Huynh speaks good English and is courteous and helpful. Formerly the manager of **Kontum Tourist**, Mr Nguyen Do Huynh now runs a private company offering river boat trips and hill tribe trecks in the surrounding province.

Kontum Tourist, *2 Phan Dinh Phung St (ground floor of the Dakbla Hotel), T60-386 1626.* The office arranges kayaking along the river, visits and overnight stays in the local Ba-na and Gia-rai villages, trekking and visits to the former battle sites and Ho Chi Minh Trail; it can also arrange tours starting and finishing from Danang, HCMC or Buon Ma Thuot.

Transport

Kontum is situated just off Highway 14 and is 44 km north of Pleiku. There are numerous local buses that plough the route from Pleiku and to a lesser degree from Buon Ma Thuot and Quy Nhon. Kontum does not have an airport but shares the airport with Pleiku, an hour's drive away.

Bus
There are daily departures from the bus station at 281 Phan Dinh Phung St, T60-386 2265, at 0700 and 0800 to **Pleiku**, **Buon Ma Thuot** and **Quy Nhon**. A bus runs from Quy Nhon via Kontum to **Laos** via the border at Bo-Y. For details of the border crossing between Bo-Y (Vietnam) and Yalakhuntum (Laos), see box, page 545.

Car and motorbike
Kontum Tourist rents cars and motorbikes. It will also organize transport to the border at Bo-Y (80 km, 1½ hrs) where you can cross to **Phu Kua** in Laos (nearest town **Attapeu**).

Nha Trang
& around

seaside city and tourist epicentre

Nha Trang is a seaside city with a long golden beach, which only a few years ago was remarkably empty. However, in recent years it has been massively developed and has become a major destination for both Russians and the growing number of domestic Vietnamese tourists. Huge international hotels now line the riverfront, while a construction boom in the hotel quarter is on-going.

An important Cham settlement, the area around Nha Trang retains distinguished and well-preserved Cham towers.

Nha Trang → *Colour map 4, B3.*

beaches, museums and plenty of nearby diversions

The beach

The beach and beachside promenade have been spruced up in recent years and it is now a pleasant place to relax. Beach beds are available, the nicest being in front of the Sailing Club and La Louisiane. There are fixed thatched umbrellas in the sand and public toilets.

Cham Ponagar temple complex

Open 0600-1800, 20,000d. The best time to visit the towers is late afternoon, 1600-1700. To get to the temple complex you can either walk or catch a cyclo. Follow 2 Thang 4 St north out of town; Cham Ponagar is just over the 2nd of 2 bridges (Xom Bong bridge), a couple of kilometres from the city centre.

On a hill just outside the city is the Cham Ponagar Temple complex, known locally as Thap Ba. Originally the complex consisted of eight towers, four of which remain. Their stylistic differences indicate they were built at different times between the seventh and 12th centuries. The largest (at 23 m high) was built in AD 817 and contains a statue of Lady Thien Y-ana, also known as Ponagar (who was the beautiful wife of Prince Bac Hai), as well as a fine and very large lingam. She taught the people of the area weaving and new agricultural techniques, and they built the tower in her honour. The other towers are dedicated to gods: the central tower to Cri Cambhu (which has become a fertility temple for childless couples); the northwest tower to Sandhaka (woodcutter and foster-father to Lady Thien Y-ana); and the south tower to Ganeca (Lady Thien Y-ana's daughter).

Getting around

Nha Trang is negotiable on foot – just. But there are bicycles and motorbikes for hire everywhere. Some hotels and the tour companies have cars for out-of-town excursions.

Time required

Those with a love of beaches or cham relics may linger here for up to a week, but others may simply travel through.

Tip...

There have been a reports of revellers being mugged at night. Don't carry huge sums of money or your valuables with you on a night out.

Cai River estuary and fishing boats

En route to the towers, the road crosses the Cai River estuary where there is a diversity of craft including Nha Trang's elegant fleet of blue fishing boats, lined with red and complete with painted eyes for spotting the fish, and coracles (*cái thúng*) for getting to the boats and mechanical fish traps. The traps take the form of nets that are supported by long arms; the arms are hinged to a platform on stilts and are raised and lowered by wires connected to a capstan which is turned, sometimes by hand but more commonly by foot.

Long Son Pagoda
23 Thang 10 St.

The best-known pagoda in Nha Trang is the Long Son Pagoda, built in 1963. Inside the sanctuary is an unusual image of the Buddha, backlit with natural light. Murals depicting the *jataka* stories decorate the upper walls. To the right of the sanctuary, stairs lead up to a 9-m-high white Buddha, perched on a hill top, from where there are fine views. Before reaching the white pagoda, take a left on the stairs. Through an arch behind the pagoda you'll see a 14-m-long reclining Buddha. Commissioned in 2003, it is an impressive sight.

The pagoda commemorates the monks and nuns who died demonstrating against the Diem government – in particular those who, through self-immolation, brought the despotic nature of the Diem regime and its human rights abuses to the attention of the public.

Nha Trang Cathedral
Mass Mon-Sat 0500 and 1630, Sun 0500, 0700, and 1630.

Granite-coloured (though built of concrete) and imposing, the cathedral was built between 1928 and 1933 on a small rock outcrop. It was not until 1961, however, that the building was consecrated as a cathedral for the diocese of Nha Trang and Ninh Thuan. The cathedral has a single, crenellated tower, a fine, vaulted ceiling, with stained glass in the upper sections of its windows and pierced metal in the lower. The windows over the altar depict Jesus with Mary and Joseph, Joan of Arc and Sainte Thérèse. Like the windows in Dalat and Danang cathedrals they were made in Grenoble by Louis Balmet. Fourteen rather fine pictures depict the stations of the cross: they look French but there is no attribution and no one seems sure of their provenance. The path to the cathedral runs off Nguyen Trai Street.

Alexandre Yersin Museum
10 Tran Phu St, T58-382 9540, Mon-Fri 0700-1130, 1330-1700, 28,000d.

The Yersin Museum is contained within the colonnaded **Pasteur Institute** founded by the great scientist's protégé, Dr Alexandre Yersin. Swiss-born Yersin first arrived in Vietnam in 1891 and spent much of the rest of his life in Nha Trang. The museum contains the lab equipment used by Yersin, his library and stereoscope through which visitors can see in 3-D the black-and-white slides, including shots taken by Yersin on his visits to the highlands.

Khanh Hoa Museum

16 Tran Phu St, T58-382 2277, Tue-Fri 0800-1100, 1400-1700, free. English-speaking curators will be pleased to show you around and should be tipped.

The Khanh Hoa Museum, which was renovated in 2010, contains a Dongson bronze drum and a Palaeolithic stone xylophone. There is a room of ethnographics and, of course, a Ho Chi Minh room that contains several items of interest.

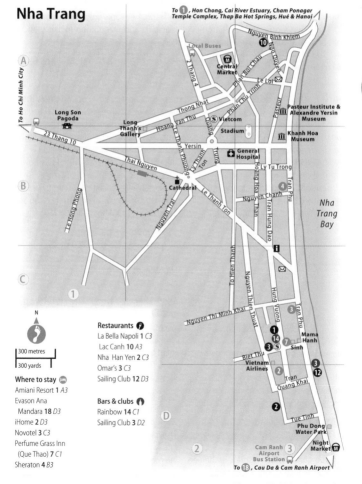

Nha Trang

To 1, Hon Chong, Cai River Estuary, Cham Ponagar Temple Complex, Thap Ba Hot Springs, Hué & Hanoi

To Ho Chi Minh City

Long Son Pagoda

Local Buses

Central Market

Le Loi

Nguyen Binh Khiem

Pasteur Institute & Alexandre Yersin Museum

23 Thang 10

Long Thanh's Gallery

Thong Nhat

Hoang Van Thu

Vietcom

Stadium

Khanh Hoa Museum

Thai Nguyen

Yersin

General Hospital

Ly Tu Trong

Cathedral

Le Thanh Ton

Nguyen Chanh

Tran Hung Dao

Nha Trang Bay

Nguyen Thai

Nguyen Thien Thuat

Nguyen Thi Minh Khai

Tran Phu

Hung Vuong

Biet Thu

Vietnam Airlines

Mama Hanh

Sinh

Tran Quang Khai

Phu Dong Water Park

Tue Tinh

Night Market

Cam Ranh Airport Bus Station

To 18, Cau Da & Cam Ranh Airport

N

300 metres

300 yards

Where to stay
Amiani Resort 1 A3
Evason Ana
  Mandara 18 D3
iHome 2 D3
Novotel 3 C3
Perfume Grass Inn
  (Que Thao) 7 C1
Sheraton 4 B3

Restaurants
La Bella Napoli 1 C3
  Lac Canh 10 A3
Nha Han Yen 2 C3
Omar's 3 C3
Sailing Club 12 D3

Bars & clubs
Rainbow 14 C1
Sailing Club 3 D2

Central market

The **Cho Dam** (central market) close to Nguyen Hong Son Street is a good place to wander and browse and it is quite well-stocked with useful items. In the vicinity of the market, along **Phan Boi Chau Street**, for example, are some bustling streets with old colonial-style shuttered houses.

Long Thanh's gallery

126 Hoang Van Thu St, not far from the railway station, T58-382 4875, www.longthanhart.com, open 0900-1900. Long Thanh is willing by pre-arrangement to meet photographers and organize photographic expeditions.

Long Thanh is one of Vietnam's most distinguished photographers and many of his famous pictures are taken in and around his native Nha Trang. He works only in black and white. Long Thanh has won a series of international awards and recognition for his work. He speaks English and welcomes visitors to his gallery.

Listings Nha Trang map p151

Tourist information

Khanh Hoa Tours
1 Tran Hung Dao St, T58-352 6753,
www.nhatrangtourist.com.vn.
Daily 0700-1130, 1330-1700.
The official city tour office, can arrange visa extensions, car and boat hire and tours of the area. It's also a **Vietnam Airlines** booking office. Not particularly helpful, but plenty of the tour operators in town have good information.

Where to stay

There has been a considerable increase in the number of hotel rooms available in Nha Trang with some huge projects built in the last few years.

$$$$ Amiana Resort
Pham Van Dong, T58-730 5555,
www.amianaresort.com.
An absolutely stunning resort north of the main town away from the crowds with superb rooms, excellent service and quality dining.

$$$$ Evason Ana Mandara Nha Trang
Tran Phu St, T58-352 2222,
www.sixsenses.com.
Nha Trang's finest beach resort. Unashamed and exquisite luxury. Simple but elegant designs are set against cool woods, wafting fans and icy a/c. The resort has sea view or garden villas that are all beautifully furnished with special touches and outdoor bathtubs. Every conceivable facilitiy is available in this enchanting retreat, including 2 pools, a tennis court, a large gym and more. Bicycles available. Fantastic dining. For those wanting further pampering there is the **Six Senses Spa**, see What to do, page 154.

$$$$ Novotel Nha Trang
50 Tran Phu St, T58-625 6900,
www.novotel-nhatrang.com.
Super smart rooms in this new hotel overlooking the beach.

$$$$ Sheraton Nha Trang Hotel & Spa
26-28 Tran Phu St, T58-388 0000,
www.sheratonnhatrang.com.
Excellent luxury hotel right across from the **main** beach. Very stylish with a wonderful pool. There are 6 restaurants and bars. The views are outstanding from the higher floors.

$$-$ Perfume Grass Inn (Que Thao)
4A Biet Thu St, T58-352 4286,
www.perfume-grass.com.
This long-running and and super friendly family hotel has 21 rooms. Restaurant and internet service downstairs. Good value for money. Book in advance.

$ iHome Nha Trang
172/19 Bach Dang, T915-973079,
www.ihomenhatrang.com.
The pick of the budget options in town,
iHome is small but perfectly formed with lots
of unique touches, comfy beds, a relaxing
common area and excellent, friendly staff.

Restaurants

There are a number of seafood restaurants
and cafés along the beach road and a wide
range of restaurants elsewhere, particularly
Indian and Italian. A local speciality is *nem
nuong*, which is grilled pork wrapped in
rice paper with salad leaves and *bun*, fresh
rice noodles. The bread in Nha Trang is
excellent. All of the major hotels/resorts
have good restaurants serving à la carte
and huge weekend brunches. Try the
Sofitel, Novotel and the Amiana (see Where
to stay).

$$$-$$ Sailing Club
72-74 Tran Phu St, T58-352 4628,
sailingnt@dng.vnn.vn. Open 0700-2300.
Although best known as a bar, this busy
and attractive beachfront area also serves a
variety of excellent cuisine and it is one of the
most attractive places to eat in town.

$$ La Mancha
78 Nguyen Thien Tuat St, T58-352 7978.
Open 1100-2400.
Great atmosphere, with Spanish and sangria
decor, barbecued meat and plenty of tapas
style dishes. Great decor.

$$ Nha Hang Yen
3/2A Tran Quang Khai, T93-376 6205.
This is a hugely popular and welcoming
place that has a nice buzz in the evenings.
A wide range of well executed Vietnamese
dishes. The waiting staff are friendly and
attentive and happy to give advice on what
to order. Packs out, so it is best to book
ahead. If this is full, try Lanterns at 34/6
Nguyen Thien Thuat St which does a similar
line in quality Vietnamese food.

$$-$ Café des Amis
2D Biet Thu St, T58-352 1009.
Good for breakfast, vegetarian and
seafood. Nice to sit outside for lunch.

$$-$ La Bella Napoli
6/0 Hung Vuong St, T58-352 7299,
labellanapoli@hotmail.com.
This long-running Italian favourite serves
up good wood-fired pizzas and the usual
range of pastas and salads. Friendly service.
Reasonable wine list.

$ Lac Canh
44 Nguyen Binh Khiem St, T58-382 1391.
Specializes in beef, squid and prawns
which you barbecue at your table. Smoky
atmosphere and it can be hard to get a table.
A good place to dine with the locals in a lively
atmosphere. Not a great place to dine alone.

$ Omar's Tandoori Cafe
89b Nguyen Thien Thuat St, T58-352 2459.
A popular Indian restaurant near the beach.
Indian chef, excellent and filling food.
Friendly, efficient service.

Stalls and seafood restaurants
For excellent and inexpensive beefsteak
there are a couple of *Bo Ne* restaurants at
the western end of Hoang Van Thu St (that
is, away from the beach) that serve beef
napoleon and chips. A little way from the
centre but worth a visit. There are also many
simple seafood restaurants lining the river
road across the bridge.

Bars and clubs

Around Nguyen Thien Thuat, Biet Thu
and Tran Phu there are now plenty of bars
which have a distinctly seaside feel, with
one of the most packed out aptly named
the Booze Cruise.

Happy hours are long and the prices
competitive. In many, the dress code seems
to be vest and flip flops. None of these bars
are particularly appealing, but there are a
few better options around town.

Louisiane Brewhouse
29 Tran Phu St, T58-352 1948,
www.louisianebrewhouse.com.vn.
This place has been transformed into a
restaurant and brewery but has maintained
its swimming pool so is popular with families
for lunch and is a polar bar in the evenings
with its lovely sea breeze.

The Rainbow
90a Hung Vuong St, T58-352 4351.
Open 0600-2400.
This popular bar, run by **Rainbow Divers**,
this is a popular spot. Dive information on
site too. They've got draft beers and provide
food in the shape of burgers and pizzas.

Sailing Club
74-76 Tran Phu St, T58-352 4628.
Open until late.
Lively bar, especially on Sat nights when
well heeled locals and visitors congregate to
enjoy the pool, cold beer, dancing and music.

Shopping

Nha Trang is now bursting with shops
selling clothing, with everything from
branded surf/beach wear to evening
dresses on offer. The main hotel area is
full of shops and larger malls now stand on
the main beach road. There are also tens
of jewellery shops in the hotel quarter.

What to do

Cookery classes
The **Ana Mandara Resort** offers a
morning market tour and cookery class.
Recommended.

Diving
The Evason Hideway, *Ninh Van Bay*. Has
opened a PADI dive centre and are working
with the Marine Protected Area Authority in
Nha Trang to improve fishing practices in the
area and to enlarge the protected area.
Rainbow Divers, *90A Hung Vuong St, T58-*
352 4351, www.divevietnam.com. It runs a
full range of training and courses including

the National Geographic dive courses.
Rainbow Divers receives good reports
regarding its equipment and focus on
safety. Qualified instructors speak a variety
of European languages. Top professional
operation. Rainbow also operates out of
Whale Island Resort.

Theme parks, waterparks and watersports
Vinpearl Land, *Tre Island, T58-359 8123,*
www.vinpearlland.com. This amusement and
water park is wildly popular with Vietnamese
tourists. Its Hollywood-style sign can be seen
from the shore. You can take the ferry or the
4 km long cable car. A 500,000d card gets
you entrance, rides and cable car ride.

Therapies
iResort, *19 Xuan Ngoc, T58-383 8838, www.i-*
resort.vn. The most modern and beautiful
hot spring and mud bath resort in the area.
Six Senses Spa, *Ana Mandara Resort, see*
Where to stay, above, www.sixsenses.com.
Offers an array of treatments – Japanese
and Vichy showers, hot tubs and massages,
exfoliations using fruit body smoothers in
beautiful and luscious surroundings.

Tour operators
As so often happens in Vietnam, every café
and guesthouse offers tours. Some tour
operators can arrange trips to Buon Ma
Thuot and the Central Highlands.
Khanh Hoa Tours, *1 Tran Hung Dao St,*
T58-352 6753, www.nhatrangtourist.com.vn.
Daily 0700-1130, 1330-1700. Official city tour
office. See also page 152.
Luxury Travel, *A/9 Quang Trung St, T58-35127*
9763. With offices around Vietnam, this agent
focuses on higher end tours. Books a variety
of trips including new boat tours around
the bay.
Sinh Tourist, *90C Hung Vuong St, T58-352*
4329, www.thesinhtouristvn. Offers the usual
Sinh Café formula and Open Tour tickets to
Nha Trang, Hoi An, Mui Ne, HCMC, Dalat, Hué
and Hanoi. **Sinh Tourist** buses arrive and

depart from here. It offers the island tour, a Central Highlands tour, city tour and arranges transport nearby attractions.

Transport

Air
Connections with **HCMC**, **Hanoi** and **Danang**. Hotels can arrange bus transfers from the airport at Cam Ranh, 34 km away, 30 mins. There is an airport bus the plentiful meter taxis are far easier.

Airline offices Vietnam Airlines, 91 Nguyen Thien Thuat St, T58-352 6768.

Bicycles
Bicycles can be hired from almost every hotel and café in Nha Trang and many guesthouses now offer then for free.

Bus and Open Tour Bus
The long-distance bus station (*ben xe lien tinh*) is west out of town at 23 Thang 10 St (23 October St). *Xe oms* take passengers into town. It has connections with **HCMC**, **Phan Rang**, **Danang**, **Quy Nhon**, **Buon Ma Thuot**, **Dalat**, **Hué** and **Vinh**. Note that inter-province buses do not go into Nha Trang, they drop off at junctions on Highway 1 from where a *xe om* will deliver you to your destination. Open Tour Buses arrive at and depart from their relevant operator's café or depot (see Tour operators, above).

Motorbike
Motorbikes can be hired from almost every hotel and every café in Nha Trang.

Taxi
Mai Linh, T58-391 0910. **Nha Trang Taxi**, T58-382 6000. From Cam Ranh Airport to town, 260,000d.

Train
The station is on Thai Nguyen St, T58-382 0666. Open 0700-1130, 1330-1700, 1800-2200. The town is on the main north–south railway line and there are trains to Ho Chi Minh City and Hanoi (and stops between).

Around Nha Trang

islands and long, windswept beaches

The islands
From Cau Da pier, boats can be taken to the islands in Nha Trang Bay. Prices vary according to the number of passengers.

These islands are sometimes known as the **Salangane islands** after the sea swallows that nest here in such profusion. The sea swallow (*yen* in Vietnamese) produces the highly prized bird's nest from which the famous soup is made (see box, page 23).

On **Mieu Island** you can relax on a beach away from the hubbub of Nha Trang and visit a laid back village. Another popular nearby island is **Hon Mun**. The best part is anchoring offshore and jumping into the cool water to snorkel.

Hon Tre Island is now taken over by the **Vinpearl Land amusement park** ⓘ *500,000d, www.vinpearlland.com*. The island can be reached by cable car or boat and the entry fee includes access to a huge water park with around 20 slides and a massive wave pool. There are also plenty of fairground rides and other kid-friendly attractions. A fun family day out.

Ho Chi Minh City

skyscrapers of glass dwarf shophouses of old

Ho Chi Minh City, the largest city in Vietnam, is frenetic, exciting, riddled with traffic and enlivened by great shops, bars and restaurants. This thoroughly dynamic city, in one of the fastest-growing regions of the world, is morphing before our eyes.

Despite government restrictions, thousands of young men and women make their way here every week in search of a better life. Only 25 years ago Tan Son Nhat, the airport, was right out at the edge of the city; it has been an inner suburb for years, long ago leapfrogged by the sprawl that is pushing outwards into former paddy fields with astonishing speed.

Visitors to Ho Chi Minh City shouldn't miss the heart of the downtown, taking in the grand opera house and old post office and the art deco buildings of Dong Khoi. A sense of adventure will be richly rewarded here, especially when getting lost among the temple-filled streets of the Chinese quarter. This is also a city for the tastebuds, with a diverse street food alongside a slew of first-rate international dining options and plenty of great rooftop bars to round-off your day of exploration.

Best for
Art ▪ Bars ▪ Food ▪ Walking tours

Footprint picks

★ **Notre Dame Cathedral**, page 161

Visit this grand landmark during a service when crowds gather on motorbikes out front.

★ **War Remnants Museum**, page 164

Harrowing, but informative and the best way to get an understanding of Vietnam's recent wars from a Vietnamese perspective.

★ **Fine Arts Museum**, page 168

Art fan or not, this cool and peaceful gallery housing many of the country's finest works is a magical place to spend an hour or two.

★ **Chinatown pagodas**, page 169

Ornate, peaceful and atmospheric, the pagodas of Cholon are not to be missed.

★ **Binh Tay Market**, page 171

Less visited that the famous Ben Thanh market, Binh Tay has a distinctly local feel and a vast array of wholesale goods.

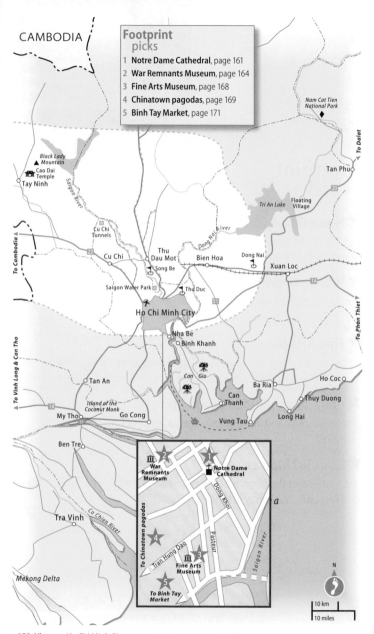

CAMBODIA

Footprint picks

1 **Notre Dame Cathedral**, page 161
2 **War Remnants Museum**, page 164
3 **Fine Arts Museum**, page 168
4 **Chinatown pagodas**, page 169
5 **Binh Tay Market**, page 171

Nam Cat Tien National Park

To Dalat

Black Lady Mountain
Cao Dai Temple
Tay Ninh

Saigon River

Tri An Lake
Floating Village

Tan Phu

Cu Chi Tunnels

To Cambodia

Cu Chi
Thu Dau Mot
Song Be
Bien Hoa

Dong Nai River

Dong Nai
Xuan Loc

Saigon Water Park
Thu Duc

Ho Chi Minh City

To Vinh Long & Can Tho

Nha Be
Binh Khanh

To Phan Thiet

Tan An

Can Gio

Ba Ria
Ho Coc

Island of the Coconut Monk
Go Cong

Can Thanh

Thuy Duong

My Tho

Vung Tau
Long Hai

Ben Tre

War Remnants Museum

Notre Dame Cathedral

Dong Khoi

Pasteur

Saigon River

Co Chien River

Tra Vinh

To Chinatown pagodas

Tran Hung Dao

Fine Arts Museum

Mekong Delta

To Binh Tay Market

N

10 km
10 miles

Sights

palaces, pagodas, paintings aplenty

From the majestic Notre Dame Cathedral, opera house and the old post office to the art deco buildings of Donh Khoi street, there are many sights from the French colonial era. The markets of Ben Thanh and the more local Binh Tay are great places to get a sense of the city. Ho Chi Minh City has a wealth of museums and galleries, while pagoda hunters could lose days in Chinatown alone.

City centre → Colour map 5, A/B3.

more elegant, less frenzied

The core of Ho Chi Minh City is, in many respects, the most interesting and historical. Remember, of course, that 'historical' here has a very different meaning from that in Hanoi. In Ho Chi Minh City a 100-year-old building is ancient – and, alas, increasingly rare. Still, a saunter down Dong Khoi Street, in District 1, the old rue Catinat can still give one an impression of life in a more elegant and less frenzied era. Much remains on a small and personal scale and within a 100-m radius of just about anywhere on Dong Khoi or Thai Van Lung streets there are dozens of cafés, restaurants and increasingly upmarket boutiques. However, the character of the street has altered with the opening of luxury chain names and the Times Square development. A little bit of Graham Greene history was lost in 2010 when the Givral Café in the Eden Centre, which featured in *The Quiet American*, was closed as Vincom Towers built another tower block on Lam Son Square.

Lam Son Square and around

Opera House (Nha Hat Thanh Pho) ⓘ *7 Lam Son Sq, T08-3832 2009, nhahat_ghvk@hcm. fpt.vn.* The impressive, French-era Opera House dominates Lam Son Square. It was built in 1897 to the design of French architect Ferret Eugene and restored in 1998. It once housed the National Assembly; nowadays, when it is open, it provides a varied programme of events, for example, traditional theatre, contemporary dance and gymnastics.

Continental Hotel North of the Opera House, now repainted, was built in 1880 and is an integral part of the city's history. Graham Greene stayed here and the hotel features in the novel *The Quiet American*. Old journalists' haunt Continental Shelf was, according to war journalist Jon Swain, "a famous verandah where correspondents, spies, speculators, traffickers, intellectuals and soldiers used to meet during the war to glean information and pick up secret reports, half false, half true or half disclosed. All of this is more than

Essential Ho Chi Minh City

Finding your feet

Virtually all of the sights visitors wish to see lie to the west of the Saigon River. To the east there are many large new developments, homes of the city's expat population and the growing Vietnamese middle class.

Most visitors head straight for hotels in Districts 1 (the historic centre) or 3. Cholon or Chinatown (District 5) is a mile west of the centre and is a fascinating place to wander. Port of Saigon is in districts 4 and 8. Few visitors venture.

All the sights of Central Ho Chi Minh City can be reached on foot in no more than 30 minutes from the major hotel areas of Nguyen Hue, Dong Khoi and Ton Duc Thang streets. Visiting all the sights described below will take several days. Quite a good first port of call, however, is the **Panorama 33 Café** on the 33rd floor of Saigon Trade Center, 37 Ton Duc Thang Street, Monday-Friday 1100-2400, Saturday-Sunday 0900-2400.

Best views

Chill Skybar, page 180
OMG bar, page 181
Saigon Saigon bar, page 181

Best pagodas and temples

Xa Loi, page 166
Phung Son Tu, page 168
Thien Hau, page 170
Quan Am, page 171

Getting around

The abundant transport is fortunate, because it is a hot, large and increasingly polluted city. Metered taxis, motorcycle taxis and a handful of cyclos vie for business in a healthy spirit of competition. Many tourists who prefer some level of independence opt to hire a bicycle or motorbike.

Tip...

Take care when carrying handbags and purses. Drive-by snatchings are on the increase.

When to go

Ho Chi Minh City is a great place to visit all year around.

Time required

The major sights can be seen in a weekend, but take a few days longer to soak up the city and explore it further.

Weather Ho Chi Minh City

January	February	March	April	May	June
31°C	32°C	33°C	34°C	33°C	32°C
21°C	22°C	23°C	24°C	25°C	24°C
15mm	8mm	23mm	63mm	183mm	261mm

July	August	September	October	November	December
31°C	31°C	31°C	31°C	31°C	31°C
24°C	24°C	24°C	23°C	23°C	22°C
257mm	249mm	270mm	255mm	156mm	65mm

enough for it to be known as Radio Catinat. I sometimes went there for a late evening drink among the frangipani and hibiscus blossom ... It was the reverse of the frenzy of the war, and a good place to think".

The **Continental** lines **Dong Khoi Street** (formerly the bar-lined Tu Do Street, the old Rue Catinat), which stretches down to the river. Many shops specialize in, or sell a mix of, silk clothes and accessories, jewellery, lacquerware and household goods and there are now a number of swanky cafés along the stretch.

Hotel Caravelle Facing the **Continental**, also adjoining Dong Khoi Street, is the Hotel Caravelle, which houses boutique shops selling luxury goods. The **Caravelle** opened for business in 1959. The 10th floor housed a famous **Saigon** bar, a favourite spot for wartime reporters, and during the 1960s the *Associated Press*, *NBC*, *CBS*, the *New York Times* and *Washington Post* based their offices here. The press escaped casualties when, on 25 August 1964, a bomb exploded in room 514, on a floor mostly used by foreign reporters. The hotel suffered damage and there were injuries but the journalists were all out in the field. It was renamed **Doc Lap** (Independence Hotel) in 1975 but not before a Vietnamese tank trundled down the rue Catinat to Place Garnier (now Lam Son Square) and aimed its turret at the hotel; to this day nobody knows why it did not fire. During the filming of Graham Greene's *The Quiet American*, actors Michael Caine and Brendan Fraser stayed at the hotel.

Nguyen Hue Boulevard At the northwest end of Nguyen Hue Boulevard is the yellow and white **City Hall**, formerly the French **Hôtel de Ville** built in 1897 and now the Ho Chi Minh City People's Committee building, which overlooks a **statue of Bac Ho** (Uncle Ho) offering comfort, or perhaps advice, to a child. This is a favourite spot for Vietnamese to have their photograph taken, especially newly-weds who believe old Ho confers some sort of blessing.

South of City Hall, the **Rex Hotel**, a pre-Liberation favourite with US officers, stands at the intersection of Le Loi and Nguyen Hue boulevards. This was the scene of the daily 'Five O'Clock Follies' where the military briefed an increasingly sceptical press corps during the Vietnam War. Its bar is now somewhat aged, but the view from it is still excellent so it is a worthwhile stop for an afternoon drink.

On weekend evenings thousands of young Saigon men and women and young families cruise up and down Nguyen Hue Boulevard (and Le Loi Boulevard and Dong Khoi Street) on motorbikes. There are now so many motorbikes on the streets of Ho Chi Minh City that intersections seem lethally confused. Miraculously, the riders miss each other (most of the time) while pedestrians safely make their way through waves of machines.

★ Notre Dame Cathedral
Visiting times are given as 0500-1100 and 1500-1730. Communion is celebrated here 7 times on Sun (drawing congregations Western churches can only dream of) and 3 times on weekdays.

North up Dong Khoi Street, in the middle of **Cong Xa Paris** (Paris Square), is the imposing, austere red-brick, twin-spired Notre Dame Cathedral, overlooking a grassed square in which a statue of the Virgin Mary stands holding an orb. The statue was the subject of intense scrutiny in 2006 as it was said that it had shed tears. The cathedral was built between 1877 and 1880 and is said to be on the site of an ancient pagoda. A number of the homeless sleep under its walls at night; unfortunately the signs asking Vietnamese men not to treat the walls as a public urinal do not deter this unpleasant but widespread practice. Mass times are a spectacle as crowds, unable to squeeze through the doors, listen to the service while perched on their parked motorbikes in rows eight or nine deep.

Independence Palace

135 Nam Ky Khoi Nghia St, T08-3822 3652, www.dinhdoclap.gov.vn, daily 0730-1100, 1300-1600, 15,000d, brochure 10000d, documentary 50,000d. Tours every 10 mins. The hall is sometimes closed for state occasions.

The Independence Palace (also known as the **Reunification Hall**) is in a large park to the southeast of Nguyen Thi Minh Khai Street and southwest of Nam Ky Khoi Nghia Street. The residence of the French governor was built on this site in 1868 and was later renamed the Presidential Palace. In February 1962, a pair of planes took off to attack Viet Cong

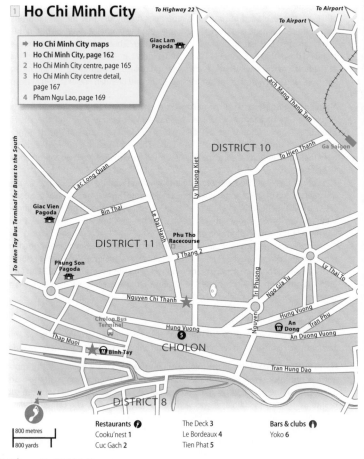

Ho Chi Minh City

➡ **Ho Chi Minh City maps**
1 Ho Chi Minh City, page 162
2 Ho Chi Minh City centre, page 165
3 Ho Chi Minh City centre detail, page 167
4 Pham Ngu Lao, page 169

To Highway 22
To Airport
To Airport

Giac Lam Pagoda

Cach Mang Thang Tam

DISTRICT 10

To Hien Thanh
Ga Saigon

Ly Thuong Kiet

Lac Long Quan

Giac Vien Pagoda

Bin Thai

Le Dai Hanh

Phu Tho Racecourse

DISTRICT 11

3 Thang 2

Phung Son Pagoda

Tri Phuong

Ngo Gia Tu

Ly Thai To

Nguyen Chi Thanh

Hung Vuong

An Dong

Tran Phu

Cholon Bus Terminal

Hung Vuong

An Duong Vuong

Thap Muoi

Binh Tay

CHOLON

Tran Hung Dao

DISTRICT 8

To Mien Tay Bus Terminal for Buses to the South

N

800 metres
800 yards

Restaurants 🍴
Cooku'nest 1
Cuc Gach 2

The Deck 3
Le Bordeaux 4
Tien Phat 5

Bars & clubs 🍸
Yoko 6

emplacements – piloted by two of the south's finest airmen – but they turned back to bomb the Presidential Palace in a futile attempt to assassinate President Diem. The president, who held office between 1955-1963, escaped with his family to the cellar, but the palace had to be demolished and replaced with a new building. (Diem was later assassinated after a military coup.) One of the two pilots, Nguyen Thanh Trung is a Vice President of **Vietnam Airlines** and still flies government officials around every couple of months to keep his pilot's licence current. One of the most memorable photographs taken during the war was of a North Vietnamese Army (NVA) tank crashing through the gates of the Palace on 30 April 1975 – symbolizing the end of South Vietnam and its government. The President of South Vietnam, General Duong Van Minh, along with his entire cabinet, was arrested in the Palace shortly afterwards. The hall has been preserved as it was found in 1975 and

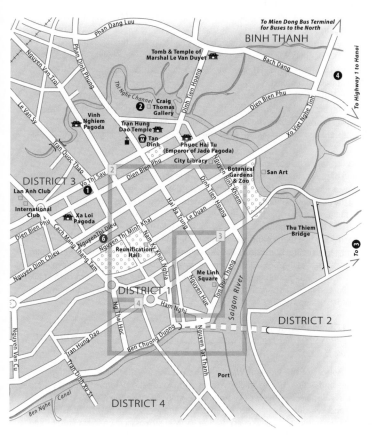

BACKGROUND

History of the city

Before the 15th century, the area was a small Khmer village surrounded by a wilderness of forest and swamp. By 1623 Ho Chi Minh City had become an important commercial centre, and in the mid-17th century it became the residence of the so-called Vice-King of Cambodia. In 1698, the Viets managed to extend their control this far south and finally Ho Chi Minh City was brought under Vietnamese control.

In the middle of the 19th century, the French began to challenge Vietnamese authority in the south of the country. Between 1859 and 1862, in response to the Nguyen persecution of Catholics in Vietnam, the French attacked and captured the city. They named it Saigon (Soai-gon – 'wood of the kapok tree'), and the Treaty of Saigon in 1862 ratified the conquest and created the new French colony of Cochin China. Saigon was developed in French style: wide, tree-lined boulevards, street-side cafés, elegant French architecture, boutiques and the smell of baking baguettes.

During the 1960s and early 1970s the city boomed and flourished under the American occupation (it was the seat of the South Vietnam government) until the fall or liberation – depending upon your point of view. Officially Ho Chi Minh City (HCMC) since 1975, it remains to most the bi-syllabic, familiar, old 'Saigon'.

visitors can take a guided tour. In the **Vice President's Guest Room**, there is a lacquered painting of the Temple of Literature in Hanoi, while the **Presenting of Credentials Room** contains a fine 40-piece lacquer work showing diplomats presenting their credentials during the Le Dynasty (15th century). In the basement there are operations rooms, military maps, radios and other paraphernalia. In essence, it is a 1960s-style building filled with 1960s-style official furnishings that now look very kitsch. Not only was the building designed according to the principles of Chinese geomancy but the colour of the carpets – lurid mustard yellow in one room – was also chosen depending on whether it was to calm or stimulate users of the rooms. Visitors are shown an interesting film about the Revolution and some fascinating photographs and memorabilia from the era. A replica of the tank that bulldozed through the gates of the compound heralding the end of South Vietnam is displayed in the forecourt.

★ War Remnants Museum

28 Vo Van Tan St, Q3, T08-3930 5587, www.baotangchungtichchientranh.vn, daily 0730-1200, 1330-1700, 15,000d.

All the horrors of the Vietnam War from the nation's perspective – photographs of atrocities and action, bombs, military tanks and planes and deformed foetuses – are graphically displayed in this well laid-out museum building. In the courtyard are tanks, bombs and helicopters, while the new museum, arranged in five new sections, records man's inhumanity. The display covers the Son My (My Lai) massacre on 16 March 1968, the effects of napalm and phosphorous, and the after-effects of Agent Orange defoliation (this is particularly disturbing, with bottled malformed human foetuses). This museum has gone through some interesting name changes in recent years. It began life as the

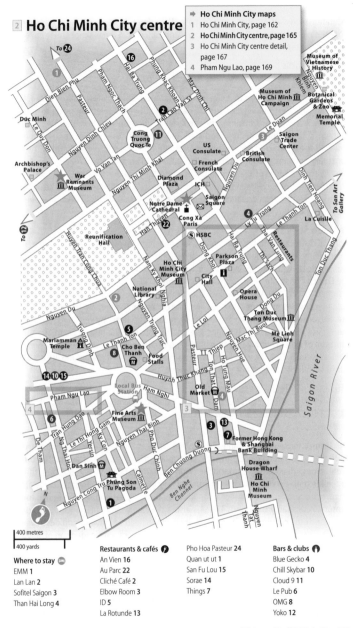

➡ **Ho Chi Minh City maps**
1 Ho Chi Minh City, page 162
2 Ho Chi Minh City centre, page 165
3 Ho Chi Minh City centre detail, page 167
4 Pham Ngu Lao, page 169

Where to stay 🛌
EMM **1**
Lan Lan **2**
Sofitel Saigon **3**
Than Hai Long **4**

Restaurants & cafés 🍴
An Vien **16**
Au Parc **22**
Cliché Café **2**
Elbow Room **3**
ID **5**
La Rotunde **13**

Pho Hoa Pasteur **24**
Quan ut ut **1**
San Fu Lou **15**
Sorae **14**
Things **7**

Bars & clubs 🎵
Blue Gecko **4**
Chill Skybar **10**
Cloud 9 **11**
Le Pub **6**
OMG **8**
Yoko **12**

Exhibition House of American and Chinese War Crimes. In 1990, 'Chinese' was dropped from the name, and in 1994 'American' was too. Since 1996 it has simply been called the War Remnants Museum.

Xa Loi Pagoda
89 Ba Huyen Thanh Quan St, daily 0630-1100, 1430-1700.

Ho Chi Minh City has close to 200 pagodas – far too many for most visitors to see. Many of the finest are in Cholon (see page 169), although there is a selection closer to the main hotel area in central Ho Chi Minh City. The Xa Loi Pagoda is not far from the War Remnants Museum and is surrounded by food stalls. Built in 1956, the pagoda contains a multi-storeyed tower, which is particularly revered, as it houses a relic of the Buddha. The main sanctuary contains a large, bronze-gilded Buddha in an attitude of meditation. Around the walls are a series of silk paintings depicting the previous lives of the Buddha (with an explanation of each life to the right of the entrance into the sanctuary). The pagoda is historically, rather than artistically, important as it became a focus of dissent against the Diem regime.

Le Duan Street
North of the cathedral is Le Duan Street, the former corridor of power with Ngo Dinh Diem's Palace at one end, the zoo at the other and the former embassies of the three major powers, France, the USA and the UK, in between. Nearest the Reunification Hall is the compound of the **French Consulate**. A block away is the **former US Embassy**. After diplomatic ties were resumed in 1995 the Americans lost little time in demolishing the 1960s building which held so many bad memories. The US Consulate General now stands on this site. A memorial outside, on the corner of Mac Dinh Chi Street, records the attack by Viet Cong special forces during the Tet offensive of 1968 and the final victory in 1975. At 2 Le Duan Street is the **Museum of Ho Chi Minh Campaign (Bao Tang Quan Doi)** ① *T08-3822 9387, Tue-Sun 0730-1100, 1330-1630, 15,000d*, with a tank and warplane in the front compound. It contains an indifferent display of photographs and articles of war.

Museum of Vietnamese History
2 Nguyen Binh Khiem St, T08-3829 8146, www.baotanglichsuvn.com, Tue-Sun 0800-1130, 1330-1700,15,000d. Labels in English and French. Water puppet shows (see also page 181) are held here daily.

The history museum (Bao Tang Lich Su Viet Nam) is an elegant building constructed in 1928 and is pagodaesque in style. It displays a wide range of artefacts from the prehistoric (300,000 years ago) and the Dongson periods (3500 BC-AD 100), right through to the birth of the Vietnamese Communist Party in 1930. Particularly impressive are the Cham sculptures, of which the standing bronze Buddha, dating from the fourth to sixth century, is probably the finest. There is also a delicately carved Devi (Goddess) dating from the 10th century as well as pieces such as the head of Shiva, Hindu destroyer and creator, from the eighth to ninth century and Ganesh, elephant-headed son of Shiva and Parvati, also dating from the eighth to ninth century.

There are also representative pieces from the Chen-la, Funan, Khmer, Oc-eo and Han Chinese periods, and from the various Vietnamese dynasties together with some hill tribe artefacts. Labelling is in English, French and Vietnamese.

Other highlights include the wooden stakes planted in the Bach Dang riverbed for repelling the war ships of the Mongol Yuan in the 13th century, a beautiful Phoenix head from the Tran dynasty (13th to 14th century) and an Hgor (big drum) from the Jarai people, made from the skin of two elephants. It belonged to the Potauoui (King of Fire) family in Ajunpa district, Gia Lai Province. There are some fine sandstone sculptures too including an incredibly smooth linga from Long An Province (seventh to eighth century) in the Mekong Delta. The linga represents the cult of Siva and signifies gender, energy, fertility and potency.

3 Ho Chi Minh City centre detail

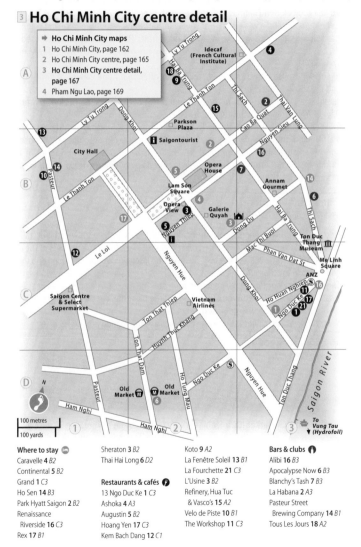

➡ **Ho Chi Minh City maps**
1   Ho Chi Minh City, page 162
2   Ho Chi Minh City centre, page 165
3   **Ho Chi Minh City centre detail,**
    page 167
4   Pham Ngu Lao, page 169

Near the History Museum is the **Memorial Temple** ① *Tue-Sun 0800-1130, 1300-1600*, constructed in 1928 and dedicated to famous Vietnamese.

Ben Thanh Market (Cho Ben Thanh)

A large, covered central market, Ben Thanh Market sits on a large and chaotic roundabout which, at the time of writing, was undergoing construction as part of the city's first metro line project. Ben Thanh is well stocked with cheap clothes (think souvenir T-shirts), household goods, and a wide choice of souvenirs, lacquerware, embroidery and so on, as well as some terrific lines in food, fresh and dried fruits. Rather touristy, it is still used by locals, but to get a more authentic sense of a busy city market, head to Binh Tay Market (see page 171).

Ben Thanh is also home to a food stall corner offering a huge variety of dishes from around the south of the country.

Outside the north gate (*cua Bac*) on Le Thanh Ton Street are some particularly tempting displays of fresh fruit and beautiful cut flowers.

The Ben Thanh Night Market has flourished since 2003. Starting at dusk and open until after midnight the night market is Ho Chi Minh City's attempt to recreate Bangkok's Patpong market. As the sun sinks and the main market closes stalls spring up in the surrounding streets. Clothes and cheap jewellery and an abundance of food stalls are the key attractions.

★ Fine Arts Museum
97A Pho Duc Chinh St, T08-3829 4441, daily 0900-1700.

Housed in an atmospheric colonial building which is slightly dishevelled but rather charming for it, the Fine Arts Museum is a very pleasant place to escape the heat of the city and take a look at some 20s architecture close up. The interior is wonderfully tiled and there is a courtyard to the rear, and an ancient iron lift. The art collection dates spans works from the fourth century right up to the contemporary era. The American War features heavily in the post-1975 work and the theme can become a little tiresome, but there is plenty of other art on offer, including some interesting Cham-era pieces. This is also a good place to pick up prints, with works by Vietnamese artists as well as propaganda posters on offer.

Phung Son Tu Pagoda
338 Nguyen Cong Tru St.

This is a small temple built just after the Second World War by Fukien Chinese; its most notable features are the wonderful painted entrance doors with their fearsome armed warriors. Incense spirals hang in the open well of the pagoda, which is dedicated to Ong Bon, the Guardian of Happiness and Virtue.

The **War Surplus Market (Dan Sinh)** ① *Yersin between Nguyen Thai Binh St and Nguyen Cong Tru St*, is not far from the Phung Son Tu Pagoda. Merchandise on sale includes dog tags and military clothing and equipment (not all of it authentic). The market is popular with Western visitors looking for mementoes of their visit, so bargain particularly hard.

Pham Ngu Lao

an area catering for the backpacker

Most backpackers arriving overland in Ho Chi Minh City are dropped off in this bustling district, a 10- to 15-minute walk from downtown. The countless hotels, guesthouses and rooms to rent open and close and change name or owner with remarkable speed. The area is littered with restaurants, cafés, bars, email services, laundries, tour agencies and money changers, all fiercely competitive; there are mini-supermarkets and shops selling rucksacks, footwear, DVDs, pirated software and ethnic knick-knacks.

Cholon (Chinatown)

trading district packed with temples and assembly halls

★This is the heart of Ho Chi Minh City's Chinese community. Cholon is an area of commerce and trade; not global but nevertheless international. In typical Chinese style it is dominated by small and medium-size businesses and this shows in the buildings' shop fronts (look for the Chinese characters on signs over the door). Cholon is home to a great many temples and pagodas – some of which are described below. As one would expect from a Chinese trading district, there is plenty of fabric for sale in the markets.

Cholon or Chinatown is inhabited predominantly by Vietnamese of Chinese origin. Despite a flow of Chinese out of the country post-1975, there is still a large population of Chinese Vietnamese living here. The area encompasses District 5 to the southwest of the city centre, and to the casual visitor appears to be the most populated, noisiest and in general the most vigorous part of Ho Chi Minh City, if not of Vietnam. It is here that entrepreneurial talent and private funds are concentrated; both resources that the government are keen to mobilize in their attempts to reinvigorate the economy.

Cholon is worth visiting not only for the bustle and activity, but also because the temples and assembly halls found here are the finest in Ho Chi Minh City. As with any town in Southeast Asia boasting a sizeable Chinese population, the early settlers established meeting rooms that offered social, cultural and spiritual support to members of a dialect group. These assembly halls (*hoi quan*) are most common in Hoi An and Cholon. There are

4 **Pham Ngu Lao**

Where to stay
Beautiful Saigon **4**
Chau Long Mini **1**
Long Hostel **2**

Restaurants & cafés
Café Zoom **9**
Good Morning
Vietnam **13**
Kim Café **4**

Not to scale

➡ **Ho Chi Minh City maps**
1 Ho Chi Minh City,
  page 162
2 Ho Chi Minh City centre,
  page 165
3 Ho Chi Minh City centre
  detail, page 167
4 **Pham Ngu Lao, page 169**

temples in the buildings, which attract Vietnamese as well as Chinese worshippers, and indeed today serve little of their former purpose. The elderly meet here occasionally for a natter and a cup of tea.

Nghia An Assembly Hall
678 Nguyen Trai St, not far from the Arc en Ciel Hotel.

A magnificent, carved, gold-painted wooden boat hangs over the entrance to the Nghia An Assembly Hall. To the left, on entering the temple, is a larger-than-life representation of Quan Cong's horse and groom. (Quan Cong was a loyal military man who lived in China in the third century.) At the main altar are three figures in glass cases: the central red-faced figure with a green cloak is Quan Cong himself; to the left and right are his trusty companions, General Chau Xuong (very fierce) and the mandarin Quan Binh respectively. On leaving, note the fine gold figures of guardians on the inside of the door panels.

Tam Son Assembly Hall
118 Trieu Quang Phuc St, just off Nguyen Trai St.

The temple, built in the 19th century by Fukien immigrants, is frequented by childless women as it is dedicated to Chua Thai Sanh, the Goddess of Fertility. It is an uncluttered, 'pure' example of a Chinese/Vietnamese pagoda – peaceful and quiet. Like Nghia An Hoi Quan, the temple contains figures of Quan Cong, his horse and two companions.

Thien Hau Temples
710 and 802 Nguyen Trai St.

The Thien Hau Temple at 710 Nguyen Trai Street is one of the largest in the city. Constructed in the early 19th century, it is Chinese in inspiration and is dedicated to the worship of both the Buddha and to the Goddess Thien Hau, the goddess of the sea and the protector of sailors. Thien Hau was born in China and as a girl saved her father from drowning, but not her brother. Thien Hau's festival is marked here on the 23rd day of the third lunar month. One enormous incense urn and an incinerator can be seen through the main doors. Inside, the principal altar supports the gilded form of Thien Hau, with a boat to one side. Silk paintings depicting religious scenes decorate the walls. By far the most interesting part of the pagoda is the roof, which can be best seen from the small open courtyard. It must be one of the finest and most richly ornamented in Vietnam, with the high-relief frieze depicting episodes from the Legends of the Three Kingdoms. In the post-1975 era, many would-be refugees prayed here for safe deliverance before casting themselves adrift on the East Sea. A number of those who survived the perilous voyage sent offerings to the merciful goddess and the temple has been well maintained since. On busy days it is very smoky. Look up on leaving to see over the front door a picture of a boiling sea peppered with sinking boats. A benign Thien An looks down mercifully from a cloud.

A **second temple** dedicated to Thien Hau is a couple of blocks away at 802 Nguyen Trai Street. Chinese migrants from Fukien Province built it in the 1730s, although the building on the site today is not old. The roof can be seen from the road and in addition to the normal dragons are some curious models of what appear to be miniature Chinese landscapes carried by bowed men. Inside it is less busy than the first Thien Hau temple but on good days worshippers hurry from one image of Thien Hau (depicted here with a black face) to another waving burning joss sticks in front of her. Whatever happens in these temples is not religious in the sense of worshipping a god but more a superstition, entreating the spirits for good fortune (hence the lottery ticket sellers outside) or asking them to stave off bad luck. Note that these are not pagodas in the sense that they are not a place for the worship of Buddha and you will see no Buddhist monks here and have no sense of serene or enlightened calm. This temple has some nicely carved stone pillars of entwined dragons and on the wall to the right of the altars is a frieze of a boat being swamped by a tsunami. The walls are festooned with calendars from local Chinese restaurants and gold shops.

Ming Dynasty Assembly Hall
380 Tran Hung Dao St.

The Ming Dynasty Assembly Hall (Dinh Minh Huong Gia Thanh) was built by the Cantonese community which arrived in Saigon via Hoi An in the 18th century. The assembly hall was built in 1789 to the dedication and worship of the Ming Dynasty although the building we see today dates largely from an extensive renovation carried out in the 1960s. There is some old furniture; a heavy marble-topped table and chairs that arrived in 1850 from China. It appears that the Vietnamese Emperor Gia Long used the Chinese community for cordial relations with the Chinese royal court and one of the community, a man called Trinh Hoai Duc, was appointed Vietnamese ambassador to the Middle Dynasty. In the main hall there are three altars which, following imperial tradition, are: the central altar dedicated to the royal family (Ming Dynasty in this case), the right-hand altar dedicated to two mandarin officers (military) and the left-hand altar dedicated to two mandarin officers (civil).

The hall behind is dedicated to the memory of the Vuong family who built the hall and whose descendants have lived here ever since. There is, in addition, a small side chapel where childless women can seek divine intercession from a local deity, Ba Me Sanh.

Quan Am Pagoda
12 Lao Tu St (just off Luong Nhu Hoc St).

The Quan Am Pagoda is thought to be one of the oldest in the city. Its roof supports four sets of impressive mosaic-encrusted figures, while inside, the main building is fronted with old, gold and lacquer panels of guardian spirits. The main altar supports a seated statue of A-Pho, the Holy Mother. In front of the main altar is a white ceramic statue of Quan Am, the Goddess of Purity and Motherhood (Goddess of Mercy). The pagoda complex also contains a series of courtyards and altars dedicated to a range of deities and spirits. Outside, hawkers sell caged birds and vast quantities of incense sticks to pilgrims.

★Binh Tay Market
While most tourists visit Ben Thanh Market, it is Binh Tay Market which is the more rewarding. Sandwiched between Thap Muoi and Phan Van Khoe streets, it is one of the most colourful and exciting markets in Ho Chi Minh City, with a wonderful array of noises, smells and colours and stalls that have past from generation to generation creating a rich sense of history and belonging among the stall holders. It sprawls over a large area and is contained in what looks like a rather decayed Forbidden Palace. Every conceivable space is used with stalls festooned with everything from spices to flip flops. This is also a good place to seek out a bowl of noodles or grab a cup of strong iced coffee and watch the madness unfold in front of you. A new high-rise market – the five-storey **An Dong Market** – opened at the end of 1991 in Cholon. It was built with an investment of US$5 million from local ethnic Chinese businessmen.

The Cu Chi Tunnels are the most popular day trip, followed closely by an excursion to the Mekong Delta, especially My Tho (see page 191). It is possible to get to the coast and back in a day by visiting Vung Tau, but this is not a particularly appealing destination for most. Ho Chi Minh City does, on the other hand, have several out-of-town sports facilities with three golf courses and the exhilarating Saigon Water Park all within less than an hour's drive (see page 184).

Cu Chi Tunnels

Most visitors reach Cu Chi on a tour or charter a car and include a visit to Tay Ninh – see below. Regular buses leave for Cu Chi town from the Mien Tay station (Cholon) and the Ham Nghi station; from Cu Chi it is necessary to take a taxi to the tunnels or the infrequent Ben Suc bus, 10 km. It is also possible to take a motorbike from Ho Chi Minh City and back but the road is becoming increasingly dangerous with fast and heavy traffic. Daily 0700-1630, 90,000d.

Cu Chi Tunnels are about 40 km northwest of Ho Chi Minh City. Cu Chi town is on the main road to Tay Ninh and the Cao Dai temple and both the tunnels and the temple can be visited in a single day trip. Dug by the Viet Minh, who began work in 1948, they were later expanded by the People's Liberation Armed Forces (PLAF, or Viet Cong, VC, see page 476) and used for storage and refuge, and contained sleeping quarters, hospitals and schools. Between 1960 and 1970, 200 km of tunnels were built. At the height of their usage, some 300,000 were living underground. The width of the tunnel entry at ground level was 22 cm by 30 cm. The tunnels are too narrow for most Westerners, but a short section of the 250 km of tunnels has been especially widened to allow tourists to share the experience. Tall or large people might still find it a claustrophobic squeeze.

Cu Chi was one of the most fervently communist of the districts around Ho Chi Minh City and the tunnels were used as the base from which the PLAF mounted the operations of the Tet Offensive in 1968. Communist cadres were active in this area of rubber plantations, even before the Second World War. Vann and Ramsey, two American soldiers, were to notice the difference between this area and other parts of the south in the early 1960s: "No children laughed and shouted for gum and candy in these hamlets. Everyone, adult and child, had a cold look" (*A Bright Shining Lie*, Sheehan 1989).

When the Americans first discovered this underground base on their doorstep (Dong Du GI base was nearby) they would simply pump CS gas down the tunnel openings and then set explosives. They also pumped river water in and used German Shepherd dogs to smell out air holes. The VC, however, smothered the holes in garlic to deter the dogs. They also used cotton from the cotton tree – kapok – to stifle the smoke from cooking; 40,000 VC were killed in the tunnels in 10 years. Later, realizing that the tunnels might also yield valuable intelligence, volunteer 'tunnel rats' were sent into the earth to capture prisoners.

Cu Chi district was a free-fire zone and was assaulted using the full battery of ecological warfare. Defoliants were sprayed and 20 tonne Rome Ploughs carved up the area in the search for tunnels. It was said that even a crow flying over Cu Chi district had to carry its own lunch. Later it was also carpet bombed with 50,000 tonnes dropped on the area in 10 years.

At **Cu Chi 1** (Ben Dinh) ① *90,000d*, visitors are shown a somewhat antique but nevertheless interesting film of the tunnels during the war before being taken into the tunnels and seeing some of the rooms and the booby traps the GIs encountered. The VC survived on just cassava for up to three months and at both places you will be invited to taste some dipped in salt, sesame, sugar and peanuts. You will also be invited to a firing range to try your hand with ancient AK47s at a buck a bang.

Cu Chi 2 (Ben Duoc), has a temple, the **Ben Duoc Temple**, in memory of the 50,000 Saigon dead; the exterior is covered in mosaic murals. It stands in front of a rather beautiful sculpture of a tear called *Symbol of the Country's Spiritual Soul*.

Near the tunnels is the Cu Chi graveyard for patriots with 8000 graves. It has a very interesting large and striking bas-relief of war images along the perimeter of the entrance to the cemetery.

Cao Dai Great Temple

Ceremonies are held each day at 0600, 1200, 1800 and 2400, visitors can watch from the cathedral's balcony. Visitors should not enter the central portion of the nave – keep to the side aisles – and also should not wander in and out during services. If you go in at the beginning of the service you should stay until the end (1 hr). Take a tour, or charter a car in Ho Chi Minh City. Regular buses leave for Tay Ninh, via Cu Chi, from Mien Tay station (2½ hrs) or motorbike.

Tay Ninh, the home of the temple, is 96 km northwest of Ho Chi Minh City and 64 km further on from Cu Chi town. It can be visited on a day trip from the city and can easily be combined with a visit to the Cu Chi tunnels. The idiosyncratic Cao Dai Great Temple, the 'cathedral' of the Cao Dai religion, is the main reason to visit the town.

The Cao Dai Great Temple, built in 1880, is set within a very large complex of schools and administrative buildings, all washed in pastel yellow. The twin-towered cathedral is European in inspiration but with distinct oriental features. On the façade are figures of Cao Dai saints in high relief and at the entrance is a painting depicting Victor Hugo flanked by the Vietnamese poet Nguyen Binh Khiem and the Chinese nationalist Sun Yat Sen. The latter holds an inkstone, symbolizing, strangely, the link between Confucianism and Christianity. Novelist Graham Greene in *The Quiet American* called it "The Walt Disney Fantasia of the East". Monsieur Ferry, an acquaintance of Norman Lewis, described the cathedral in even more outlandish terms, saying it "looked like a fantasy from the brain of Disney, and all the faiths of the Orient had been ransacked to create the pompous ritual...". Lewis himself was clearly unimpressed with the structure and the religion, writing in *A Dragon Apparent* that "This cathedral must be the most outrageously vulgar building ever to have been erected with serious intent".

Towards the Cambodian border

The province of Tay Ninh borders Cambodia and, before the 17th century, was part of the Khmer Kingdom. Between 1975 and December 1978, soldiers of Pol Pot's Khmer Rouge periodically attacked villages in this province, killing the men and raping the women. Ostensibly, it was in order to stop these incursions that the Vietnamese army invaded Cambodia on Christmas Day 1978, taking Phnom Penh by January 1979.

Travellers taking the bus to Phnom Penh from Ho Chi Minh City cross at **Moc Bai** (Bavet in Cambodia). Cambodian visas are available at the border; Vietnamese visas are not.
▸▸ *For border crossing details, see box, page 544.*

Tourist information

Tourist Information Center
92-96 Nguyen Hue St, T08-8322 6033,
www.ticvietnam.com. Daily 0800-2100.
Provides free information, hotel reservations,
an ATM and currency exchange.

Where to stay

City centre

$$$$ Caravelle
19 Lam Son Sq, T08-3823 4999,
www.caravellehotel.com.
Central and one of HCMC's top hotels, this
is a true heritage option having opened in
1959, although a new tower was added in
1998. Very comfortable with 335 rooms,
fitted out with all the mod cons, many
with incredible views and well-trained and
friendly staff. Breakfast is sumptuous and
filling and **Restaurant Nineteen**, see below,
serves a fantastic buffet lunch and dinner.
Saigon Saigon, see page 181, the rooftop bar, draws the crowds until the early
hours and offers knockout veiws. A suite
of boutique shops plus a pool and Qi Spa
complete the luxury experience.

$$$$ Continental
132-134, Dong Khoi St, T08-3829 9201,
www.continentalhotel.com.vn.
Built in 1880 and renovated in 1989, the
Continental has an air of faded colonial
splendour. There are now smarter options in
town in this price bracket, but few can match
it for history.

$$$$ Grand
8 Dong Khoi St, T08-3823 0163,
www.grandhotel.vn.
A 1930s building in the heart of the
shopping district that might look more
comfortable on Brighton's seafront than in
HCMC. It was renovated 10 years ago but
the stained glass and marble staircase have
largely survived the process. Lovely pool
(try to get a pool-side room) and a very
reasonably priced restaurant.

$$$$ Park Hyatt Saigon
2 Lam Son Sq, T08-3824 1234,
www.saigon.park.hyatt.com.
This striking hotel is in a class of its own. It
exudes elegance and style and its location
north of the Opera House is unrivalled.
Works of art are hung in the lobby, rooms are
classically furnished in French colonial style
but with modern touches; the pool area is
lovely; the wonderful lounge area features
a baby grand piano and there are a number
of very good restaurants. **Square One**, is an
excellent restaurant with open kitchens and
displays. There's also a fitness centre and spa.

$$$$ Renaissance Riverside
8-15 Ton Duc Thang St, T08-3822 0033,
www.marriott.com.
Overlooking the water, this upmarket option
offers some of the finest views in the city
in the riverside rooms. It also has Vietnam's
highest atrium. Several excellent restaurants
including Kabin Chinese restaurant and
attractive pool. Executive floors provide
breakfast and all-day snacks.

$$$$ Rex
141 Nguyen Hué Blvd, T08-3829 2185,
www.rexhotelvietnam.com.
A historically important hotel in the heart
of Saigon. During the Vietnam War the
American Information Service made its base
at the hotel and it became a base for daily
press briefings to foreign correspondents
known as the five o'clock follies. There is now
a newer fabulous side extension that has
become the principal entrance complete
with high-end shopping arcade. The original
lobby is decorated entirely in wood and
tastefully furnished with wicker chairs. New
wing premium rooms are very smart, if a
little business-like; cheaper 'Superior' rooms

in the old wing have small bathtub and are interior facing.

$$$$ Sheraton
88 Dong Khoi St, T08-3827 2828, www.sheraton.com/saigon.
This tall glass-clad hotel has certainly proved popular since it opened in late 2003. There is very good lunch and dinner on offer at the **Saigon Café**, and Level 23, with its brilliant views across HCMC, is recommended for a night-time drink. The hotel, with modern, stylish rooms is sandwiched into a downtown street and boasts boutique shops, a gorgeous pool, a spa and tennis courts.

$$$$ Sofitel Plaza Saigon
17 Le Duan St, T08-3824 1555, www.sofitel.com.
A smart, fashionable and comfortable hotel with a fantastic roof-top pool surrounded by frangipani plants. Gets rave reviews for its excellent service.

$$$ EMM Hotel Saigon
157 Pasteur, T08-3936 2100, www.emmhotels.com.
This is the first of what promises to be a new chain of funky modern hotels in Vietnam. Set over 2 floors, the rooms are very well furnished with modern touches and prints of the city. A good buffet breakfast is served in a cool restaurant space with an outdoor area offering great views. A reasonable gym and a travel desk for tour bookings.

$$$ Lan Lan Hotel 2
46 Thu Khoa Huan, T08-3822 7926, www.lanlanhotel.com.vn.
Excellent value rooms. Those on the upper floors have expansive views of the city. Helpful staff, buffet breakfast and in-room wifi. Has a 2nd location on the same road.

$$ Ho Sen
4B-4C Thi Sach St, T08-3823 2281, www.hosenhotel.com.vn.
This rather bland-looking hotel is nonetheless very clean and in a great location, so it's a good find. Rooms are very quiet and fairly spacious. Staff are friendly and helpful.

$$ Tan Hai Long 3
65 Ho Tung Mau St, T08-3915 1888, www.thlhotelgroup.com.
A well-positioned hotel with small rooms, good-sized bathrooms and good service. Great value.

Pham Ngu Lao

$$ Beautiful Saigon
62 Bui Vien St, T08-3836 4852, www.beautifulsaigonhotel.com.
A good addition to the backpacker zone replacing an old hotel, this is more for the flashpackers and welcome it is too. Very nice smart and tidy rooms all with mod cons, Wi-Fi and breakfast at fair prices and recommended by happy guests.

$ Chau Long Mini Hotel
185/8 Pham Ngu La, T08-3836 9667.
Simple, clean rooms, some with balconies. Family-run and welcoming. Great budget option.

$ Long Hostel
373/10 Pham Ngu Lao, T08-3836 0184, longhomestay@yahoo.com.
Run by the supremely friendly and charming Ms Long, a retired teacher who serves tea and fruit to guests on arrival, this hotel has spotless rooms, all with TV and a/c. Highly recommended. Book ahead.

Outer Ho Chi Minh City

$$$$ Thao Dien Village
195 Nguyen Van Huong St, Thao Dien Ward, Q2, T08-3744 6458, www.thaodienvillage.com.
A stylish boutique hotel and spa resort in the expat enclave. Lovely to escape the hustle of downtown. Popular restaurant. Also a great spa and pool.

Restaurants

HCMC has a rich culinary tradition and, as home to people from most of the world's imagined corners, its cooking is diverse. You could quite easily eat a different national cuisine every night for several weeks. French food is well represented and there are many restaurants from neighbouring Asian countries especially Japan, Korea, China and Thailand. The area between Le Thanh Ton and Hai Ba Trung streets has become a 'Little Tokyo' and 'Little Seoul' on account of the number of Japanese and Korean restaurants.

Pham Ngu Lao, the backpacker area, is chock-a-block with low-cost restaurants many of which are just as good as the more expensive places elsewhere. Do not overlook street-side stalls where staples include of *pho* (noodle soup), *bánh xeo* (savoury pancakes), *cha giò* (spring rolls) and *banh mi pate* (baguettes stuffed with pâté and salad), all usually fresh and very cheap. The major hotels all have gourmet shops selling bread and pastries. Eating out is an informal business; suits are not necessary anywhere, and in Pham Ngu Lao expect shorts and sandals.

The Ben Thanh night market (see page 168) is a major draw for Vietnamese and overseas visitors. Stalls are set up at dusk and traffic suppressed. There is a good range of inexpensive foodstall dishes and lots of noodles; it stays open until around 2300.

Tip...

If Japanese food is your thing, eat up. HCMC, it is said, has some of the cheapest Japanese food in the world.

City centre

$$$ An Vien
178A Hai Ba Trung St, T08-3824 3877. Daily 1200-2300.
Excellent and intimate restaurant that serves the most fragrant rice in Vietnam. Attentive service and rich decor. The *banh xeo* and crispy fried squid are recommended.

$$$ Hoa Tuc
74 Hai Ba Trung St, T08-3825 1676. Open 1000-2230.
Set in the buzzing Hai Ba Trung courtyard space. Dine amid the art deco accents on soft shell crab or a salad of pink pomelo, squid and crab with herbs. The desserts are tantalizing.

$$$ La Fourchette
9 Ngo Duc Ke St, T08-3829 8143. Daily 1200-1430, 1830-2230.
Truly excellent and authentic French bistro offering a warm welcome, well-prepared dishes and generous portions of tender local steak. Booking advised. Recommended.

$$$ San Fu Lou
76A le Lai St, T08-3823 9513, www.sanfulou.com.
Opened in 2014, this is an uber-cool venue with sharp service offering excellent dim sum with some classic dumplings and some unique creations. A buzzing joint. Best to dine with a group and try as much as possible.

$$$ Sorae Sushi
AB Tower, 76A Le Lai St, T08-3827 2372, www.soraesushi.com.
Outrageously slick space on the upper floors of the AB Tower affording awesome views through massive floor-to-ceiling windows, although the sleek interior means there is plenty for the eyes inside. The food is first-rate, as is the service. Truly high-end dining that would slot right in among London's finest. Expect to do some serious damage to your wallet if you arrive hungry or in the mood for a fine sake.

$$$-$$ The Refinery
74 Hai Ba Trung St, T08-3823 0509.
Open 1100-2300.
This former opium factory (through the arch and on the left) is a little understated in its reincarnation. It could equally be slotted into this guide's 'bar' section thanks to the great cocktails, but it also does some quality dishes such as the herb-encrusted steak and grilled barramundi. Always busy with a good atmosphere.

$$ Augustin
10D Nguyen Thiep St, T0890-382966, 294 8081. Mon-Sat 1100, 1130-1400 and 1800-2230.
Fairly priced and some of the best, unstuffy French cooking in HCMC; tables pretty closely packed, congenial atmosphere. Excellent onion soup, baked clams and rack of lamb.

$$ Elbow Room
52 Pasteur St, T08-3821 4327, www.elbowroom.com.vn.
Cosy, bare-brick American diner serving the best burgers in town and awesome shakes – don't miss the vanilla version.

$$ Guc Cach
10 Dang Tat, T08-4801 4410.
The 2nd restaurant run by a local architect, **Guc Cach** is known for its great atmosphere, old school Saigon decor and excellent Vietnamese fare. The soft shell crab is superb. Recommended.

$$ KOTO Saigon
151A Hai Ba Trung St, T08-3934 9151, www.koto.com.au.
KOTO stands for Know One, Teach One. It is a training restaurant for disadvantaged young people, plus it serves good food, so a visit here is a no brainer. Serves a selection of Vietnamese classics alongside other Southeast Asian options and a handful of Belgian dishes.

$$ Quan Ut Ut
168 Vo Van Kiet, T9-3914 4500, www.quanutut.com.
Set over 3 floors with canal views, this ever-buzzing joint is a temple for grilled meat lovers. Tender ribs cooked to pefection, first-rate mac and cheese and a burger that's a solid contender for the best in town. Also serves a very tasty pale ale. A top spot.

$$-$ Ashoka
17A/10 Le Thanh Ton St, T08-3823 1372. Daily 1100-1400, 1700-2230.
Indian restaurant popular with expats. Highlights are the mutton shami kebab, prawn vindaloo and kadhai fish – barbecued chunks of fresh fish cooked in *kadhai* (a traditional Indian-style wok with Peshwari ground spices and sautéed with onion and tomatoes).

$ 13 Ngo Duc Ke
15 Ngo Duc Ke St, T08-3823 9314. Daily 0600-2230.
Fresh, well cooked, honest Vietnamese fare. Chicken in lemongrass is a great favourite and *bo luc lac* melts in the mouth. Popular with locals.

$ Au Parc
23 Han Thuyen St, T08-3829 2772. Mon-Sat 0730-2230, Sun 0800-1700.
Facing on to the park in front of the old Presidential Palace, this stylish café serves a some delicious Greek and Turkish options, sandwiches, salads, juices and drinks. Also does a good Sunday brunch that's popular with the city's expats.

$ Hoang Yen
5-7 Ngo Duc Ke St, T08-3823 1101. Daily 1000-2200.
Plain setting and decor but absolutely fabulous Vietnamese dishes, as the throngs of local lunchtime customers testify. Soups and chicken dishes are ravishing.

$ Pho Hoa Pasteur
260C Pasteur St. Daily 0600-2400.
Probably the best known *pho* restaurant and packed with customers. The *pho* costs more than average, but it is good quality and there are around 10 varieties on the English menu.

Cafés

Cooku'nest Café
13 Tu Xuong St, Q3, T08-2241 2043.
This kooky venue looks like it has been hoiked off an Alpine slope. It's a pine cabin equipped with cuckoo clock. Sit upstairs on the floor next to tiny tables and mingle with the local student gang. There's live music every night. Wi-Fi available.

Kem Bach Dang
26-28 Le Loi Blvd.
On opposite corners of Pasteur St. A very popular café serving fruit juice, shakes and ice cream. Try the coconut ice cream (*kem dua*) served in a coconut.

La Fenêtre Soleil
2nd floor, 135 Le Thanh Ton St (entrance at 125 Nam Ky Khoi Nghia St), T08-3822 5209. Mon-Sat, café 0900-1900, bar 1900-2400.
Don't be put off by the slightly grimy side entrance; clamber up into the boho-Indochine world of this gorgeous café/bar, artfully cluttered with antiques, lamps, comfy sofas and home-made cakes, muffins, smoothies and other delights. The high-energy drinks of mint, passionfruit and ginger juice are lovely. Highly recommended.

Tous les Jours
180 Hai Ba Trung St, Q3, and also in several other locations including Diamond Plaza, T08-3823 8302. Open 0600-2300.
A smorgasbord of cakes and pastries awaits the hungry visitor.

Pham Ngu Lao
Nearly all these restaurants are open all day every day from early or mid-morning until 2230 or later – when the last customer leaves, as they like to say. All are geared to Westerners and their habits and tastes and in just about all of them there will be at least one person who speaks English and French. Most tend to be cheap but prices have risen in recent times; do check.

$$ Good Morning Vietnam
197 De Tham St, T08-3837 1894. Open 0900-2400.
One of the popular chain of Italian restaurants in southern Vietnam. Italian owned and run and serving up Italian flavours. Their pizzas are delicious and salads are good.

$ Cafe Zoom
169A De Tham St, T1222 993585, www.vietnamvespaadventure.com.
Laid-back vibe and venue serving top burgers and fries – look for the classic Vespas lined up out front.

$ Kim Café
268 De Tham St, T08-3836 8122. Open from early till late.
Wide range of food, popular with travellers.

Cholon
In Cholon you'll find a few cavernous Chinese restaurants and also lots of tiny street-side noodle stands.

$$ Tien Phat
18 Ky Hoa St, Q9, T08-3853 6217.
Conveniently located near the temples of Cholon. Open for breakfast and lunch. Specializes in dim sum. There is a good selection all freshly prepared, nice with hot tea.

Outer Ho Chi Minh City

$$$ The Deck
38 Nguyen U Di, An Phu, Q2, T08-3744 6322, www.thedecksaigon.com.
A very popular expat spot with tables on a deck right on the Saigon River. The food is, in the main, delicious and creative.

$$$-$$ Le Bordeaux
72 D2 St, Cu Xa Van Thanh Bac, Q Binh Thanh, T08-3899 9831, www.restaurant-lebordeaux. com.vn. Mon 1830-2130, Tue-Sat 1130-1330, 1830-2130.
Rather a tragedy that it is in such an awkward location. If you can find it you are in for a

treat. Lovely decor and warm atmosphere, receives high accolades for its French cuisine but it is not cheap.

Food stalls

For those staying centrally, a wander along Nguyen Thai Binh is recommended. At number 75 you'll find **Pho Phuong Bac** which sells good *pho* in the morning and a variety of great dished throughout the day and evening. All along this road there are small eateries selling everything from spring rolls to rice buffets (*com bing dan*), most of which are packed out with office workers during lunch time. Nearby at 40 Ton That Dam St, **Hu Tieu Nam Loi** is a long-running chicken and fish *hu tieu* joint that is worth seeking out. Just north of the centre on the south side of Tan Dinh is another good area to seek out food, including excellent *banh xeo*. The stalls in Benh Thanh shouldn't be overlooked; the *banh canh cua* (40,000d) and *nuoc mia* (sugarcane juice, 10,000d) at stall 1028 are delectable. Over in District 4, Vinh Kanh St is the place to head for roadside seafood. The great scallops and crab claws at **Can An Hien** (number 12) are mouth watering. **Anh Thu**, 49 Dinh Cong Trang St, and other stalls nearby on the south side of Tan Dinh market serve *cha gio, banh xeo* and *bi cuon*.

Cafés

A swathe of new thoughtfully designed, original, one-off cafés have opened, invigorating the city's caffeine scene. Alongside this, Starbucks has entered the fray alongside chains including **Gloria Jean's**, **Coffee Bean** and **Tea Leaf**.

A Cafe
15 Huynh Khuong Ninh.
Run by artist, Nguyen Thanh Truc, this is real find. The intimate café offers a peaceful place to enjoy a good book, quiet conversation and superb coffee. Beans are roasted on-site and the coffee can be brewed in every way imaginable. Well worth going out of your way for.

Cliché Café
20 Tran Cav Van, T08-3822 0412.
Open 0800-1030.
Head straight upstairs to take a seat among all manner of knick knacks in this popular café. Serves excellent, strong iced coffee and good value set lunches.

ID
34D Thu Khoa Huan. Open 0800-2230.
Plenty of comfortable seating, low lighting, vinyl nailed to the walls, and, like most cafés in this vein, a collection of retro audio equipment. A good place to relax.

La Fenêtre Soleil
44 Ly Tu Trong St, T08-3824 5994.
This place has moved and reinvented itself with a cool café vibe by day but regular DJ and salsa moves by night.

La Rotunde
77B Ham Nghi, T0983-889935.
More like somebody's Indochina apartment than a public café, this is a wonderfully unique café space that also serves an excellent Vietnamese buffet lunch.

L'Usine
151 Dong Khoi, District 1, T08-6674,
www.lusinespace.com.
Part café, part lifestyle store, **L'Usine** is an uber cool venue. Legendary cupcakes, delicious freshly cut sandwiches and perfect shakes. A hipster hangout. There is also now a 2nd branch on Le Loi.

Things
14 Ton That Dam. Open 0900-2200.
Shabby chic, with such oddities as a cupboard full of Converse and a bed in the corner. Friendly owner Linh (also a TV presenter) is a good source of what's new in town. Very quirky.

Velo de Piste
10 Pasteur.
By day this café is referred to as Heritage, but later in the afternoon tables made from suitcases perched on stools appear on the pavement and the place takes on a decidedly

Shoreditch-esque hipster vibe. Single speed bikes hang from the walls and a collection of old typewriters sit on shelves.

The Workshop
27 Ngo Duc Ke St.
An extremely sleek coffee shop that makes the very best of the period building that houses it, with exposed brick, huge windows and chunky wooden tables. Run by self-professed coffee nerds Dung and Duy with consultation from one of Asia's leading coffee minds, Will Frith. The first-rate coffee is roasted on the premises. Highly recommended.

Bars and clubs

Along with the influx of foreigners and the freeing up of Vietnamese society has come a rapid increase in the number of bars in HCMC and they cater to just about all tastes. Everything is on offer, from roadside plastic chair drinking to uber-chic sky bar cocktails with killer views.

Alibi
5A Nguyen Sieu St, T08-3825 6257, www.alibi.vn.
Goes on after hours and is a magnet for tourists and expats. Consistently popular and in a new location. Very smooth 2-floor venue decorated with deep reds and pictures of old Saigon. Remains under the tourist radar. Weekend DJs, a long wine list and a well-rounded menu to boot.

Apocalypse Now
2BCD Thi Sach St, T08-3825 6124.
Cover charges at weekends. Open until 0300/0400. This legendary venue remains one of the most popular and successful bars and clubs in HCMC. Draws a very wide cross section of punters of all ages and nationalities. DJs often spin a fun/cheesey selection of floor fillers. Can take on a slight meat market feel in the wee hours.

Blanchy's Tash
95 Hai Ba Trung, T09-0902 8293, www. blanchystash.com. Open 1100-late.
Upscale bar. Weekends are rammed downstairs where music blasts, while the rooftop terrace is more relaxed. Regular DJ nights, excellent cocktails, and an expensive, well-regarded restaurant.

Blue Gecko
31 Ly Tu Trong St, T08-3824 3483, www.bluegeckosaigon.com.
This bar has been adopted by HCMC's Australian community so expect cold beer and Australian flags above the pool table.

Chill Skybar
76A Le Lai, District 1, T09-3272 0730, www.chillsaigon.com. Open 1600-late.
With a view that has to be seen to be believed, a mixologist of international acclaim and the kind of crowd that means you'll want to dress your best (flip flops and shorts are not permitted), **Chill Skybar** is a rather pretentious, but worth a look to see Saigon's more lavish side. The cocktails are wallet-busting.

Cloud 9
2 Cong Truong Quoc Te, District 3, T08-0948-343399.
Another of the city's roof-top bars, **Cloud 9** is a chic nightspot with contemporary design and excellent drinks. Dress sharp.

La Habana
6 Cao Ba Quat, T08-3829 5180, www.lahabana-saigon.com.
Latin beats and mojitos make for a great night out, particularly on salsa nights when the dance floor fills with local talent keen to show off their skills. Serves the finest paella in town.

Le Pub
175/22 Pham Ngu Lao, T08-3837 7679. Open 0900-2400.
The no-nonsense pub formula here makes a good place for a cold beer although an awful music policy can sometimes make it impossible to bear. Western and Vietnamese food.

OMG bar

15 Nguyen An Ninh, T09-3720 0222.

While it will be a little heavy on the neon for some tastes, the reason to drink here isn't to enjoy the decor, but to enjoy the excellent view of downtown HCMC, looking right out across Ben Thanh market and the Bitexco Tower. Also serves food and holds regular party nights.

Pasteur Street Brewing Company

144 Paster St, T9-0551 4782.

The first craft beer establishment in town, this is a very cool operation run by beer geeks who have scoured Vietnam to come up with interesting locally brewed beers with bite. Sleek decor, a small menu of food designed to complement the beer and knowledgable staff make this a must for any beer connoisseur.

Rex Hotel Bar

See Where to stay, above.

An open-air rooftop bar which has a kitsch revolving crown. There are good views, cooling breeze, snacks and meals – and a link with history (page 161).

Saigon Saigon

10th floor, Caravelle Hotel, 19 Lam Son Sq, T08-3824 3999.

Breezy and cool, with large comfortable chairs and superb views by day and night. Excellent cocktails but not cheap.

Vasco's

74/7D Hai Ba Trung St, T08-3824 2888. Open 1600-2400.

A hugely popular spot in a great courtyard setting. A great place to kick off an evening out. Good happy hour offers.

Yoko

22A Nguyen Thi Dieu, T08-3933 0577. Open 1800-2400.

Ever busy live music venue. Slightly more rock and underground than the **Acoustic Cafe** over on Ngo Thoi Nhiem. An excellent night out. Arrive early to bag a seat.

Entertainment

Cinemas

French Cultural Institute (Idecaf), *31 Thai Van Lung, T08-3829 5451, www.idecaf.gov.vn.* Shows French films.

Lotte Cinema, *Diamond Plaza, 34 Le Duan St, www.lottecinemavn.com.* The cinema on the 13th floor of this shopping centre screens English-language films.

Traditional music and opera

Conservatory of Music (Nhac Vien Thanh Pho Ho Chi Minh), *112 Nguyen Du St, T08-3824 3774, www.hcmcons.vn.* Traditional Vietnamese music and classical music concerts are performed by the young students who study music here and sometimes by local and visiting musicians.

Opera House, *Lam Son Sq, T08-3832 2009, www.hbso.org.vn.* Regular classical concerts, opera and ballet. Check the website for upcoming shows.

Water puppetry

Golden Dragon Water Puppet Theatre, *55B Nguyen Thi Minh Khai St, T08-3930 2196, www.thaiduongtheatre.com.* A 50-min performance daily at 1700, 1830 and 1945.

Museum of Vietnamese History, *2 Nguyen Binh Khiem St, T08-3829 8146, www.baotanglichsuvn.com.* There are daily 15-min water puppetry performances in the tiny theatre in an outdoor, covered part of the museum, see page 166. The advantage of this performance over the Hanoi theatre is that the audience can get closer to the puppetry and there is better light.

Shopping

Antiques

Most shops are on **Dong Khoi**, **Mac Thi Buoi** and **Ngo Duc Ke** streets. For the knowledgeable, there are bargains to be found, especially Chinese and Vietnamese ceramics – however you will need an export permit to get them out of the country (see page 433). Also available are old watches, colonial bric-a-brac, lacquerware and carvings, etc. For the less touristy stuff, visitors would be advised to spend an hour or so browsing the treasure trove shops in **Le Cong Trieu St** (aka **Antique St**). It runs between Nam Ky Khoi Nghia and Pho Duc Chinh streets just south of Ben Thanh Market. Among the bric-a-brac and tat are some interesting items of furniture, statuary, stamps, candlesticks, fans, badges and ceramics. Bargaining is the order of the day and some pretty good deals can be struck.

Art galleries

Craig Thomas Gallery, *27i Tran Nhat Duat, T09-0388 8431, www.cthomasgallery.com. Tue-Sat 1200-1800, Sun 1200-1700.* Exhibitions of young, emerging and mid-career Vietnamese contemporary artists.
Galerie Quynh, *Dong Khoi, T08-3836 8019, www.galeriequynh.com. Tue-Sat 1000-1800.* Promotes a select group of Vietnamese artists and plays host to travelling international exhibitions.
San Art, *ground floor, 48/7 Pham Viet Chanh, T08-3840 0898, www.san-art.org. Tue-Sat 1030-1830.* Artist-run exhibition space and reading room. Regular programme of events, including lectures.

Bicycles

As well as the cheap shops along Le Thanh Ton St, close to the Ben Thanh Market there are now a handful of shops selling high quality international brands including **Saigon Cycles** which stocks Surly and Trek – Skygarden, Phu My Hung, www.xedapcaocap.com.

Books, magazines and maps

Books and magazines All foreigners around Pham Ngu Lao and De Tham streets are game to the numerous booksellers who hawk mountains of pirate books under their arms. The latest bestsellers together with enduring classics (ie *The Quiet American*) can be picked up for a couple of dollars.

Artbook, *43 Dong Khoi St, T08-3910 3518, www.artbookvn.com.* For art, architecture and coffee table books.
Fahasa, *40 Nguyen Hue Blvd, T08-3912 5358, www.fahasasg.com.* A very large store with dozens of English titles and magazines.

Maps HCMC has the best selection of maps in Vietnam, at stalls on Le Loi Blvd between Dong Khoi St and Nguyen Hue Blvd. Bargain hard – the bookshops are probably cheaper.

Western newspapers and magazines

Sold in the main hotels. Same day *Bangkok Post* and *The Nation* newspapers (English-language Thai papers), and up-to-date *Financial Times*, *Straits Times*, *South China Morning Post*, *Newsweek* and *The Economist*, available from larger bookshops.

Ceramics

Vietnam has a ceramics tradition going back hundreds of years. There has been a renaissance of this art in the past decade. Shops selling new and antique (or antique-looking ceramics) abound on the main shopping streets of **Dong Khoi** and **Le Thanh Ton**. There is a lot of traditional Chinese-looking blue and white and also very attractive celadon green, often with a crackled glaze. There are many other styles and finishes as local craftsmen brush the dust off old ideas and come up with new ones. **Nga Shop**, see Lacquerware, below, has a good range.

Clothing, silk and *ao dai*

Dong Khoi is home to many excellent boutiques. Vietnamese silk and traditional dresses (*ao dai*) are to be found in the shops on here. A number of shops in De Tham St sell woven and embroidered goods including bags and clothes.
Devon London, *151 Dong Khoi, www.devonlondon.com.* Modern clothing from one of Vietnam's most promising young designers.

Ipa Nima, *77-79 Dong Khoi St and in the New World Hotel, T08-3822 3277, www.ipa-nima. com.* Sister branch of the Hanoi store with sparkling bags and accessories.

Khaisilk, *107 Dong Khoi, T08-3829 1146.* Khaisilk belongs to Mr Khai's growing empire. He has a dozen shops around Vietnam. Beautifully made, quality silk products from dresses to scarves to ties can be found in this luxury outlet.

Department stores

Diamond Department Store, *Diamond Plaza 1st-4th floor, 34 Le Duan St, T08-3822 5500. Open 1000-1000.* HCMC's central a/c department store set over a couple of floors. It sells luxury goods, clothes with some Western brands, watches, bags and perfumes. There is also a small supermarket inside. A bowling alley complex and cinema dominate the top floor.

Parkson Plaza, *35 Bis-45 Le Thanh Ton St.* A high-end department store.

Foodstores

Shops specializing in Western staples, such as cornflakes, peanut butter and Marmite, abound on Ham Nghi St around Nos 62 and 64 (**Kim Thanh**). There are also now mini-marts, such as **Circle K**, on many of the streets downtown.

Annam Gourmet Hai Ba Trung, *16-18 Hai Ba Trung St, T08-3822 9332, www.annam-gourmet.com. Mon-Sat 0800-2100, Sun 1000-2000.* Local organic vegetables and other international delicacies at this new culinary emporium.

Gifts and handicrafts

Dogma, *43 Ton That Thiep, www.dogma. vietnam.com.* Sells propaganda posters, funky T-shirts and postcards.

Gaya, *1 Nguyen Van Trang St, corner of Le Lai St, T08-3925 2495, www.gayavietnam. com. Open 0900-2100.* A 3-storey shop with heavenly items: exquisitely embroidered tablecloths, bamboo bowls, ceramics and large home items such as screens; also

gorgeous and unusual silk designer clothes by, among others, Romyda Keth, based in Cambodia. If you like an item but it does not fit they will take your measurements but it could take a fortnight to make.

Mai Handicrafts, *298 Nguyen Trong Tuyen St, Q Tan Binh, T08-3844 0988.* A little way out of town but sells an interesting selection of goods, fabrics and handmade paper all made by disadvantaged people in small income-generating schemes.

Nagu, *132-134 Dong Khoi St (next to the Park Hyatt), www.zantoc.com.* Delicate embroidered silk products among other fashion, home and giftware.

Nguyen Freres, *2 Dong Khoi St, T08-3823 9459, www.nguyenfreres.com.* An absolute Aladdin's cave. Don't miss this – even if it's just to potter among the collectable items.

Saigon Kitsch, *43 Ton That Tiep St. Open 0900-2000.* This is the place to come for communist kitsch ranging from propaganda art posters to placemats and mugs. Also retro bags and funky jewellery on sale.

Jewellery

Jewellery is another industry that has flourished in recent years and there is something to suit most tastes. At the cheaper end there is a cluster of gold and jewellery shops around **Ben Thanh Market** and and also in the **International Trade Centre** on Nam Ky Khoi Nghia St. In these stalls because skilled labour is so cheap one rarely pays more than the weight of the item in silver or gold. At the higher end **Therese**, with a shop in the **Caravelle Hotel**, has established an international reputation.

Lacquerware

Vietnamese lacquerware has a long history, and a reputation of sorts. Visitors to the workshop can witness the production process and, of course, buy the products if they wish. Lacquerware is available from many of the handicraft shops on Nguyen Hue Blvd and Dong Khoi St. Also from the **Lamson Lacquerware Factory**, 106 Nguyen

Van Troi St (opposite **Omni Hotel**). Accepts Visa and MasterCard.

Duy Tan, *41 Ton That Thiep St, T08-382 3614. Open 1100-2000.* Pretty ceramics and lacquerware.

Nga Shop, *49-57 Dong Du St, T08-3823 8356, www.huongngafinearts.vn.* **Nga** has become one of the best-known lacquer stores as a result of her high-quality designs. Other top-quality rosewood and ceramic handicrafts suitable for souvenirs are available.

Linen

Good-quality linen tablecloths and sheets are avaliable from shops on Dong Khoi and Le Thanh Ton streets.

Outdoor gear

Vietnam produces a range of equipment for camping, such as walking boots, fleeces and rucksacks. Real and fake goods can be bought, especially from around Pham Ngu Lao and De Tham streets.

War surplus

From **Dan Sinh Market**, Yersin St, between Nguyen Thai Binh St and Nguyen Cong Tru St.

What to do

Cookery classes

Saigon Cooking Class, *held at the new Hoa Tuc (see Restaurants), 74 Hai Ba Trung St, T08-3825 8485, www.saigoncookingclass.com.* **Vietnam Cookery Center**, *362/8 Ung Van Khiem St, Q Binh Thanh, T08-3512 2764, www.vietnamese-cooking-class-saigon.com.* Offers short and in-depth courses for adults and children.

Swimming

Some hotels allow non-residents to use their pool for a fee. Decent pools are at the **Sofitel Plaza**, **Grand** and **Caravelle**.

International Club, *285B Cach Mang Thang Tam St, Q10, T08-3865 7695.*

Lan Anh Club, *almost next door to the International Club at 291 Cach Mang Thang Tam St, T08-3862 7144.* Pleasant with a nice pool and tennis courts.

Saigon Water Park, *Go Dua Bridge, Kha Van Can St, Q Thu Duc, T08-3897 0456. Mon-Fri 0900-1700, Sat and Sun 0900-2000.* Admission is charged according to height. A little way out but is enormous fun. It has a variety of water slides of varying degrees of excitement and a child's pool on a 5-ha site. It is hugely popular with the Vietnamese.

Therapies

L'Apothiquaire, *61-63 Le Thanh Ton St, T08-3822 1218, www.lapothiquaire.com.* Massages, chocolate therapy, spa packages and slimming treatments in this lovely spa.

Qi Salon and Spa, *Caravelle Hotel, www.qispa.com.vn.* You can indulge in everything from a 20-min Indian head massage to a blow-out 5-hr Qi Special.

Tour operators

Asian Trails, *9th floor, HMC Tower, 193 Dinh Tien Hoang St, T08-3910 2871, www.asiantrails.travel.* Southeast Asia specialist. Also has offices in Hanoi, Phnom Penh and Vientiane.

Buffalo Tours, *81 Mac Thui Buoi St, T08-3827 9170, www.buffalotours.com.* Organizes trips to the Mekong Delta, city tours, the Cu Chi tunnels and Cao Dai Temple. Staff are helpful. Good countrywide operator with longstanding reputation. Also has an office in the **EMM Hotel** (see Where to stay).

Exotissimo, *64 Dong Du St, T08-3827 2911, www.exotissimo.com.* An efficient agency that can handle all travel needs of visitors to Vietnam. Its local excursions are very well guided.

Handspan Adventure Travel, *F7, TitanCentral Park Building, 10th floor, 18A Nam Quoc Cang, 208 Nguyen Trai, Q1, T08-3925 7605, www.handspan.com.* Reputable and well-organized. Specializes in adventure tours.

Kim Café, *189 De Tham St, District 1, T08-3920 5552, www.kimtravel.com.* Organizes minibuses to Nha Trang, Dalat, etc, and tours of the Mekong. A good source of information. Backpacker friendly prices.

Sinh Tourist (formerly **Sinh Café**), *246-248 De Tham St, T08-3838 9597, www.thesinhtourist.vn.* **Sinh Tourist** now has branches and agents all over main towns in Vietnam. Its tours are generally good value and its open ticket is excellent value. For many people, especially budget travellers, **Sinh** is the first port of call. The company also deals with visa extensions, flight, train and hotel bookings and car rentals. This one is the HQ.

Sophie's Tour, *T0121-830 3742, www. sophiesarttour.com.* Run by Sophie, a long-term Saigon expat with a passion for the city and its art. Engaging 4-hr tour looking at the works of artists who studied, fought and witnessed major events in Vietnam's recent history from colonialism to the present. Highly recommended.

Vietnam Vespa Adventures, *Cafe Zoom, 169A De Tham St, T08-3920 3897, www. vietnamvespaadventure.com.* Half-day tours of the city, 3-day tours to Mui Ne and 8-day tours to Dalat and Nha Trang. The city tours are fun, insightful and recommended.

XO Tours, *T09-3308 3727, www.xotours.vn.* **XO** tours take clients around the city on the back of motorbikes ridden by women wearing traditional ao dai. The foodie tour introduces dishes and districts tourists don't normally see. Shopping and sightseeing tours also offered. Fun, different and highly rated.

Transport

Air
Airport information
HCMC may not be Vietnam's capital, but it is the economic powerhouse of the country and the largest city and thus well connected with the wider world – indeed, more airlines fly into here than into Hanoi.

Tan Son Nhat Airport, 49 Troung Son, Tan Binh, T08-3844 8358, www.saigonairport. com, is 30-40 mins northwest of the city, depending on the traffic. Airport facilities include banks and ATMs and locker rooms,

desks for airlines including **Vietnam Airlines** and VietJetAir, and an information desk. Lost and found, T08-3844 6665 ext 7461.

Bicycle and motorbike
If staying in HCMC for any length of time it might be a good idea to buy a bicycle (see Shopping, above, and page 182). Alternatively, bikes and motorcycles can be hired for cheaply around Pham Ngu Lao.

Bikes should always be parked in designated compounds (*gui xe*) for a small fee (don't lose your ticket!) or with a guard in front of businesses.

Bus
Local
The bus service in HCMC has now become more reliable and frequent. They run at intervals of 10-20 mins – depending on the time of day. In rush hours they are jammed with passengers and can run late. There are bus stops every 500 m or so. Most buses start from or stop by the Ben Thanh bus station opposite Ben Thanh Market, T08-3821 4444. A free map of all bus routes can also be obtained here in the chaotic waiting room.

Long distance
With the completion of a new ring road around HCMC, long-distance public buses, unless specifically signed HCMC or 'Ben Xe Ben Thanh' do not come into the city. Passengers are dropped off on the ring road at Binh Phuoc bridge. However, companies such as **Sinh Tourist** and **Phuong Trang** (futabuslines.com.vn) run services from Pham Ngu Lao.

From **Mien Dong Terminal**, north of the city, buses north to **Dalat**, **Hué**, **Danang** and all significant points on the road to Hanoi. The **Hoang Long** bus company runs deluxe buses daily to **Hanoi**. Has an office at 47 Pham Ngu Lao, T08-915 1818 and it is possible to book online at www. hoanglongasia.com.

From **Mien Tay Terminal**, some distance southwest of town, buses south to the

Mekong Delta towns. There is also a bus station in Cholon which serves destinations such as **Long An**, **My Thuan**, **Ben Luc** and **My Tho**.

International bus

Many tour operators run tours and transport to Cambodia (see Tour operators) crossing the border at **Moc Bai**. Visas for Cambodia can be bought at the border. **Sapaco Tourist**, 309-327 Pham Ngu Lao St, T08-3920 3623, www.sapacotourist.com, runs buses from Pham Ngu Lao to **Phnom Penh** from 0600-1400, 8 daily 6 hrs; to **Siem Reap**, US, 12 hrs. For details of the border crossing between Moc Bai (Vietnam) and Bavet (Cambodia), see box, page 544.

Cyclos

Cyclos are a peaceful way to get around the city. They can be hired by the hour or to reach a specific destination. Some drivers speak English. Each tends to have his own patch, which is jealously guarded. Expect to pay more outside the major hotels.

Cyclos are much rarer these days but can be found waiting in tourist spots. Some visitors complain of cyclo drivers in HCMC 'forgetting' the agreed price (though Hanoi is worse). Cyclos are being banned from more and more streets in the centre of HCMC, which may involve a longer and more expensive journey. This excuse is trotted out every time (particularly if extra money is demanded) and it is invariably true. If taking a tour agree a time and price and point to watches and agree on the start time.

Taxi

HCMC has quite a large fleet of meter taxis. There are many taxi companies fighting bitterly for trade. Competition has brought down prices so they are now reasonably inexpensive and for 2 or more are cheaper than cyclos or *xe om* (motorcycle taxi).

Not all taxis are trustworthy, but it is easy to avoid scams. Simply use one of these companies, which are all over town: **Mai Linh** (T08-3822 2666, www.mailinh.vn) or **Vinasun** (T08-3827 2727).

Xe om are the quickest way to get around town and cheaper than cyclos; agree a price and hop on the back. *Xe om* drivers hang around on most street corners. Short journeys run from around 15,000d but you may end up paying more.

Train

The station is 2 km from the centre of the city at 1 Nguyen Thong St, Q3, T08-3931 2795. Facilities for the traveller are much improved and include a/c waiting room, post office and bank (no TCs). Regular daily connections with **Hanoi** and all points north. Trains take between 29½ and 42½ hrs to reach Hanoi; hard and soft berths are available. Sleepers should be booked in advance.

There is now a **Train Booking Agency** at 275c Pham Ngu Lao St, T08-3836 7640, 0730-1830, which saves an unnecessary journey out to the station. Alternatively, for a small fee, most travel agents will obtain tickets. The railway timetable can be seen online at www.vr.com.vn.

Southern Vietnam

beaches, islands and riverine delta life

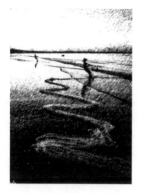

The Mekong Delta, the rice basket of Vietnam, comprises a great swathe of Southern Vietnam. At its verdant best the delta is a riot of greens – pale green rice seedlings deepen in shade as they sprout ever taller, while palm trees and orchards make up an unbroken horizon of green hues.

Formal sights are thin on the ground and travel can be slow. But herein lies the first contradiction of the delta, for the journey is often more fun than the destination. Boat trips along canals, down rivers and around islands hold more appeal than many of the towns and the main roads that are straggled with mile upon mile of homes and small, and increasingly large, industry. The southern end of Vietnam is also home to Mui Ne with its Sahara-like dunes and Phu Quoc island, Vietnam's largest. Also off the southern coast lies the wonderfully unspoiled former prison colony island of Con Dao.

Best for
Diving ▪ River trips ▪ Water sports

Footprint picks

⭐ **Can Tho floating markets**, page 197

All manner of food produce sold from boats and barges with a buzz like no other.

⭐ **Nui Sam (Sam Mountain)**, page 203

Climb past pagodas to the summit for magnificent vistas of paddy fields as far as the eye can see.

⭐ **Phu Quoc**, page 205

Vietnam's largest island with a forested interior and a great choice of amazing beaches.

⭐ **Con Dao**, page 210

Unspoilt archipelago with a beguiling former prison colony island at its heart.

⭐ **Mui Ne**, page 214

Kitesurfing capital and home to Sahara-like red and white dunes.

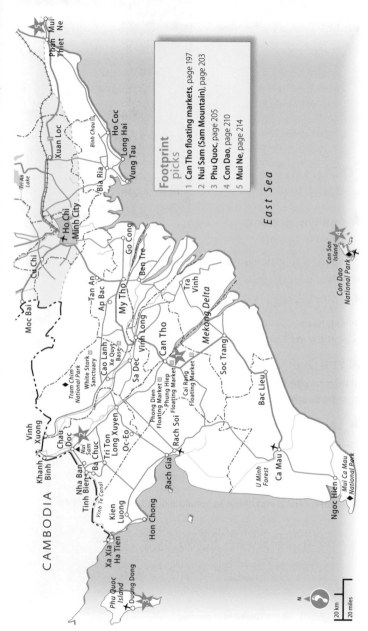

Footprint picks

1 **Can Tho floating markets**, page 197
2 **Nui Sam (Sam Mountain)**, page 203
3 **Phu Quoc**, page 205
4 **Con Dao**, page 210
5 **Mui Ne**, page 214

East Sea

CAMBODIA

Mekong Delta

Phan Thiet
Mui Ne
Ho Coc
Long Hai
Vung Tau
Bia Ria
Xuan Loc
Binh Chau
Tri An Lake
Ho Chi Minh City
Cu Chi
Moc Bai
Go Cong
Ben Tre
Tan An
Ap Bac
My Tho
Tra Vinh
Vinh Long
Can Tho
Cao Lanh
Xe Quyt Base
Sa Dec
White Stork Sanctuary
Tram Chim National Park
Phong Dien Floating Market
Phung Hiep
Cai Rang Floating Market
Soc Trang
Rach Soi Floating Market
Bac Lieu
Vinh Xuong
Khanh Binh
Chau Doc
Nui Sam
Tri Ton
Long Xuyen
Oc-Eo
Nha Ban
Ba Chuc
Tinh Bien
Vinh Te Canal
Kien Luong
Rach Gia
Ca Mau
U Minh Forest
Mui Ca Mau National Park
Ngoc Hien
Xa Xia
Ha Tien
Duong Dong
Hon Chong
Phu Quoc Island
Con Son Island
Con Dao National Park

20 km
20 miles
N

My Tho
& around

fruit orchards and local life

My Tho is an important riverside market town, 71 km southwest of Ho Chi Minh City and 5 km off the main highway to Vinh Long. It is the stepping-off point for boat trips to islands in the Tien River. Visitors enjoy the chance to wander among abundant fruit orchards and witness local industries at first hand. Around My Tho are the northern delta towns of Ben Tre, Vinh Long, Tra Vinh, Sa Dec and Cao Lanh.

Vinh Long at the end of the 19th century
Source: *The French in Indochina*, first published in 1884

Essential My Tho and around

Getting around

The much-improved Highway 1 is the main route from Ho Chi Minh City to My Tho, and there are regular connections with other main towns in the area. There is an efficient public bus service, taxis aplenty, a few river taxis and boats and *xe om*.

When to go

December to May is when the Mekong Delta is at its best. During the monsoon from June to November the weather is poor with constant background drizzle interrupted by bursts of torrential rain.

Time required

Ideal for a weekend.

Best sleeping and eating

A bowl of hu tieu my tho, page 194
Banh Xeo 46, page 194
A homestay on Cai Mon island, page 194

My Tho → *Colour map 5, B3.*
pagodas and military significance

The town has had a turbulent history: it was Khmer until the 17th century, when the advancing Vietnamese took control of the surrounding area. In the 18th century Thai forces annexed the territory, before being driven out in 1784. Finally, the French gained control in 1862. Today, it is much more peaceful destination.

Sights

On the corner of Nguyen Trai Street and Hung Vuong Street, and five minutes' walk from the central market, is My Tho church painted with a yellow wash with a newer, white campanile. The central market covers a large area from Le Loi Street down to the river. The river is the most enjoyable spot to watch My Tho life go by.

It is a long walk to **Vinh Trang Pagoda** ⓘ *60 Nguyen Trung Trac St, daily 0900-1200, 1400-1700 (best to go by bicycle or* xe om*)*. The entrance to the temple is through an ornate porcelain-encrusted gate. The pagoda was built in 1849 and displays a mixture of architectural styles: Chinese, Vietnamese and colonial. The façade is almost fairytale in inspiration. Two huge new statues of the Buddha now dominate the area.

Not far from My Tho is the hamlet of **Ap Bac**, the site of the communists' first major military victory against the ARVN. The battle demonstrated that without direct US involvement the communists could never be defeated. John Paul Vann was harsh in his criticism of the tactics and motivation of the South Vietnamese Army who failed to dislodge a weak VC position. As he observed from the air, almost speechless with rage, he realized how feeble his Vietnamese ally was; an opinion that few senior US officers heeded – to their cost (see *Bright Shining Lie* by Neil Sheehan).

Tourist information

Tien Giang Tourist
8 30 Thang 4 St on the river, Ward 1, T730-387 3184, www.tiengiangtourist.vn.
Boat trips, fishing tours and even nigh firefly watching tours. Also has a ticket office for transport. The staff are friendly and helpful and have a good command of several languages.

Where to stay

$$-$ Song Tien Annex
33 Trung Trac St, T0730-397 7883, www.tiengiangtourist.com.
This is a large 20-room hotel boasting big beds and bathtubs on legs. The large, renovated Song Tien around the corner is another good option if this is full.

$ Rang Dong
No 25, 30 Thang 4 St, T730-3874400, www.rangdonghotel.net.
Private mini hotel, near river with a/c, TV and hot water. Friendly staff are very helpful.

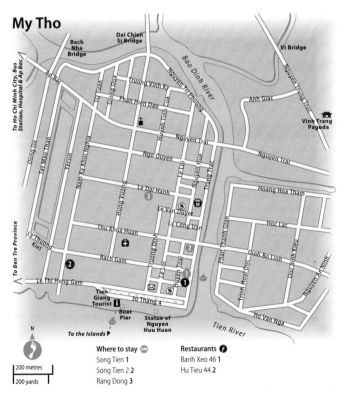

My Tho

Where to stay
Song Tien **1**
Song Tien 2 **2**
Rang Dong **3**

Restaurants
Banh Xeo 46 **1**
Hu Tieu 44 **2**

Restaurants

A speciality of the area is *hu tieu my tho* – a spicy soup of vermicelli, sliced pork, dried shrimps and fresh herbs. At night, noodle stalls spring up on the pavement on Le Loi St at the junction with Le Dai Han St.

$ Banh Xeo 46
11 Trung Trac St.
Serves *bánh xèo*, savoury pancakes filled with beansprouts, mushrooms and prawns; delicious.

$ Bo De Quan
69A Nguyen Trung Truc.
Just across the street from a pretty temple, this is a great veggie Vietnamese restaurant set in a verdant garden.

$ Hu Tien 44
44 Nam Ky Khoi Nghia St. Daily 0500-1200.
Specializes in *hu tien my tho.*

What to do

Ben Tre Tourist, *8, 30 Thang 4 St, T730-387 5070, www.bentretourist.vn.* Although this company operates island tours from My Tho, it would be best to use its specialist knowledge of Ben Tre province. Escape the My Tho crowds with homestays at Cai Mon and take a tour to the gardens and canals of this neigbouring province.

Tien Giang Tourist, *Dockside location is at No 8, 30 Thang 4 St, T730-387 3184, www. tiengiangtourist.com.* Dinner with traditional music on the Mekong, canoe and boat hire.

Transport

Boat
As in all Mekong Delta towns, local travel is often by boat to visit the orchards, islands and remoter places.

Bus
The bus station (Ben Xe My Tho) is 3-4 km from town on Ap Bac St towards HCMC with regular connections every 30 mins from 0430 to **HCMC**'s Mien Tay station (2 hrs); **Vinh Long** (2½ hrs); and **Cao Lanh** (2½ hrs). There are also buses to **Can Tho** and **Chau Doc**.

The islands

go in the afternoon when they are quieter

There are four islands in the Tien River between My Tho and Ben Tre: Dragon, Tortoise, Phoenix and Unicorn. The best way of getting to them is to take a tour. A vast pier and boat service centre has been built on 30 Thang 4 Street where all the tour operators are now concentrated. To avoid the hundreds of visitors now descending on these islands, go in the afternoon after the tour buses have gone. Hiring a private boat is not recommended due to the lack of insurance, the communication difficulties and lack of explanations. Prices vary according to the number of people and which islands you choose to visit.

Dragon Island

Immediately opposite My Tho is Dragon Island, Tan Long Island. It is pleasant to wander along its narrow paths. Tan Long is noted for its longan production but there are many other fruits to sample, as well as honey and rice whisky.

Phoenix Island

The Island of the **Coconut Monk**, also known as Con Phung (Phoenix Island), is about 3 km from My Tho. The 'Coconut Monk' established a retreat on this island shortly after the end of the Second World War where he developed a new 'religion', a fusion of Buddhism and

Christianity. He is said to have meditated for three years on a stone slab, eating nothing but coconuts – hence the name. Persecuted by both the South Vietnamese government and after reunification, the monastery has fallen into disuse.

Unicorn Island

Unicorn Island is a garden of Eden – stuffed with longan, durian, roses, pomelo and a host of other fruit trees. Honey is made on this island too.

Ben Tre → *Colour map 5, B3.*

appealing backwater delta town

Ben Tre is a typical Vietnamese delta town with a charming riverfront feel. The small bridge over the river is wooden slatted but with iron supports. Bountiful fruit stalls are laid out on the waterfront and locals sell potted plants on barges by the river. Small cargo ships pass dilapidated shacks falling into the muddy waters. It doesn't attract a lot of visitors. Its main claim to fame is that it is the birthplace of Nguyen Dinh Chieu, a blind and patriotic poet. In recent years, though, it has improved its tourism facilities.

Ben Tre is no longer an island province; a bridge links it from just outside My Tho. The province is essentially a huge island of mud at one of the nine mouths of the Mekong. It depends heavily on farming, fishing and coconuts although there are some light industries engaged in processing the local farm output and refining sugar. During the wars of resistance against the French and Americans, Ben Tre earned itself a reputation as a staunch Viet Minh/Viet Cong stronghold.

Can Tho
& around

floating markets and river trips

Can Tho is a large and rapidly growing commercial city lying chiefly on the west bank of the Can Tho River. Capital of Can Tho Province and the region's principal transport hub, it is also one of the most welcoming of the delta towns and launch pad for trips to see some of the region's floating markets. South of Can Tho are the towns of Soc Trang, Bac Lieu and Ca Mau.

Essential Can Tho and around

Getting around

Some of the sites, the floating markets for instance, are best visited by boat. There are also river taxis and an efficient public bus service.

When to go

As in all the other Mekong cities the best time is from December to April when the temperatures are warm and there is no rain. May to November is the monsoon season and as such is prone to flooding (although it does fare better than other cities).

Time required

Two days is enough.

Can Tho → Colour map 5, B2.
the largest city in the heart of the delta

A small settlement was established at Can Tho at the end of the 18th century, although the town did not prosper until the French took control of the delta a century later and rice production for export began to take off. Despite the city's rapid recent growth there are still strong vestiges of French influence apparent in the broad boulevards flanked by flame trees, as well as many elegant buildings. Can Tho was also an important US base.

Sights

Hai Ba Trung Street, alongside the river, is the heart of the town; at dusk families stroll in the park here in their Sunday best. Opposite the park is **Chua Ong Pagoda** ① *34 Hai Ba Trung St*, dating from 1894 and built by Chinese from Guangzhou. Unusually for a Chinese temple it is not free-standing but part of a terrace of buildings. The right-hand side of the pagoda is dedicated to the Goddess of Fortune, while the left-hand side belongs to General Ma Tien, who, to judge from his unsmiling statue, is fierce and warlike and not to be trifled with. The layout is a combination of typical pagoda – with a small open courtyard for the incense smoke to escape – and typical meeting house, complete with its language school, of the overseas Chinese in Southeast Asia.

The bustling market that used to operate on Hai Ba Trung Street along the bank of the river, and gave the town a bit of character, has been moved 1 km downriver. A new riverside promenade has been created. There's also a new crafts market building with a riverside restaurant, see Restaurants, page 198.

Munirang-syaram Pagoda ① *36 Hoa Binh Blvd (southwest of post office)*, was built just after the Vietnam War and is a Khmer Hinayana Buddhist sanctuary. **Bao Tang Can Tho** ① *Hoa Binh St, Tue-Thu 0800-1100, 1400-1700, Sat-Sun 0800-1100, 1830-2100*, in an impressive building, is the local history museum.

Binh Thuy Temple ① *7 km north along the road to Long Xuyen*, dates from the mid-19th century; festivals are held here in the middle of the fourth and 12th lunar months. Nearby, 500 m down Bui Huu Nghia Road, opposite Binh Thuy temple, visit **Nha Co Binh Thuy aka the ancient house** ① *10,000d to go inside the house* (also known as Vuon Lan if you get a moto to take you there), which was used as a setting in the film The Lover.

★Floating markets

The daily markets are busiest at around 0600-0900. Women with sampans to rent will approach travellers in Hai Ba Trung St near the market waving a book of testimonials from previous satisfied customers. A trip of at least 5 hrs is recommended to see the landscape at a leisurely pace. If you take a larger boat you will not be able to manoeuvre in and out of the market.

There are boat trips to the floating markets at Phung Hiep, 33 km away (an eight-hour round trip by sampan or take a bus to Phung Hiep and rent a boat there) and Phong Dien, 15 km down the Can Tho River (a five-hour trip). Cai Rang is 7 km away and is easy to visit for those with only a couple of hours to spare.

Bustling affairs, the vendors attach a sample of their wares to a bamboo pole to attract customers. Up to seven vegetables can be seen dangling from staffs – wintermelon, pumpkin, spring onions, giant parsnips, grapefruit, garlic, mango, onions and Vietnamese plums. Housewives paddle their sampans from boat to boat and barter, haggle and gossip in the usual way. At the back of the boats, the domesticity of life on the water is in full glare – washing is hung out and motors are stranded high above the water. Orchards and gardens abound; small sampans are best as they can negotiate the narrowest canals to take the visitor into the heart of the area, a veritable Garden of Eden. Phung Hiep also features yards making traditional fishing boats and rice barges.

Listings Can Tho

Where to stay

$$$$ Victoria Can Tho Resort
Cai Khe ward, T710-381 0111,
www.victoriahotels.asia.
A 92-room riverside hotel set in lovely, well-tended garden on its own little peninsula. It

is Victoria Hotel 'French colonial' style at its best with a breezy open reception area and emphasis on comfort and plenty of genuine period features. It has a pool, spa pavilion, tennis court and restaurant. The staff are multilingual and helpful. The a/c rooms are well decorated and have satellite TV, Wi-Fi, en suite facilities, decent-sized bathtub, well-stocked minibar and electronic safe in the room. Even if you decide to stay in a more centrally and somewhat cheaper hotel then a visit to the grounds and one of the restaurants would be a pleasant experience. The hotel offers a complimentary boat shuttle to the town centre.

$$ Kim Tho
14 Ngo Gia Tu St, T710-322 2228, www.kimtho.com.
A lovely if a little dated hotel with some rooms offering great river views. Very welcoming and plenty of character. The standout attraction is the roof-top café with fabulous views. Includes breakfast.

$ Saigon-Can Tho
55 Phan Dinh Phung St, T710-382 5831, www.saigoncantho.com.vn.
A/c, comfortable, central business hotel in the competent hands of Saigontourist. The staff are friendly and helpful. The rooms are well equipped with a/c, satellite TV, en suite facilities and minibar. There's a currency exchange, free internet and Wi-Fi for guests, sauna and breakfast included.

$ Tay Ho
42 Hai Ba Trung St, T710-382 3392, tay_ho@hotmail.com.
This lovely place has a variety of rooms and a great public balcony that can be enjoyed by those paying for back rooms. All rooms now have private bathrooms. River view rooms cost more. The staff are friendly.

Restaurants

Hai Ba Trung St by the river offers a good range of excellent and very well-priced little restaurants, and the riverside setting is an attractive one.

$$$-$$ Victoria Can Tho Spices
See Where to stay.
Excellent location on the riverbank where it's possible to dine alfresco or inside its elegant restaurant. The food is delicious and the service is excellent.

$$-$ Sao Hom
Nha Long Cho Co, T710-381 5616, http://saohom.transmekong.com.
This new and very busy restaurant on the riverfront serves plentiful food and provides very good service. Watching the river life and the floating pleasure palaces at night is a good way to spend an evening meal here. Shame about the illuminated billboards on the opposite bank. This place is popular with large tour groups that alter the character of the restaurant when they swarm in.

$ Mekong
38 Hai Ba Trung St.
Perfectly good little place near the river in this popular restaurant strip. Serves decent Vietnamese fare at reasonable prices.

$ Nam Bo
50 Hai Ba Trung St, T710-382 3908.
Excellent little place serving tasty Vietnamese and French dishes in an attractive French house on the corner of the street; try to get a table on the balcony. Small café downstairs.

What to do

Boat trips
Trans Mekong, *97/10 Ngo Quyen, P An Cu, T710-382 9540, www.transmekong.com.* Operates the *Bassac*, a converted 24-m wooden rice barge that can sleep 12 passengers in 6 a/c cabins with private bathrooms. Prices include dinner and breakfast, entry tickets to visited sites, a French- or English-speaking guide on board and access to a small boat, *Bassac II*, catering for 24 guests. The Victoria Can Tho operates the *Lady Hau*, an upmarket converted rice barge for trips to the floating markets.

Cookery classes
The Victoria Can Tho, *see Where to stay.* Offers a Vietnamese cooking class in the hotel, in a rice field, at the 'Ancient House'

or on its boat the *Lady Hau* with a trip to the local market.

Swimming
The Victoria Can Tho (see Where to stay, above) has a pool open to the public for a fee.

Therapies
The Victoria Can Tho boasts several massage cabins on the riverfront offering a host of treatments. Open to non-guests.

Tour operators
Can Tho Tourist, *20 Hai Ba Trung St, T710-382 1852, http://canthotourist.vn*. Organizes tours in small and larger boats – the latter not the best way to see the delta. The staff are helpful and knowledgeable. Tours include trips to Cai Rang, Phong Dien and Phung Hiep floating markets, to Soc Trang, city tours, canal tours, bicycle tours, trekking tours, stork sanctuary tour and homestays that involve working with farmers in the fields. General boat tours also arranged. Victoria Can Tho, *T710-381 0111, www. victoriahotels.asia*. Expensive tours to see delta sights; city tour; floating markets and Soc Trang offered. The *Lady Hau* cruises to Cai Rang floating market (breakfast on board). Sunset cruises also possible.

Transport

Air
Vietnam Airlines, 66 Chau Van Liem St. The airport is situated about 7 km from the city centre. Flights to **Hanoi**.

Bicycle
Bikes can be hired for from **Can Tho Tourist**, see Tour operators above.

Boat
A bridge has been built to Can Tho but ferries will still operate for direct routing as the bridge is 10 km from Can Tho. There are no public boats leaving Can Tho.

Bus
The bus station is about 2 km northwest of town along Nguyen Trai St, at the intersection with Hung Vuong St. Hourly connections to **HCMC**'s Mien Tay terminal, 4-5 hrs (**Phuong Trang** bus company, T710-376 9768, provides a good service), and other towns in the Mekong Delta: **Rach Gia**, 0400-1800, 5 hrs; **Chau Doc**, 8 daily, 4 hrs; **Long Xuyen**, 6 daily; **My Tho**, hourly; **Vinh Long**, hourly, 55,000d; **Ca Mau**, hourly Soc Trang. **Can Tho Tourist**, see Tour operators, above, will book a ticket for you for a small fee and include transfer from your hotel to the bus station.

Car
Cars with drivers can be hired from larger hotels.

Taxi
Mai Linh Taxi, T710-382 8282.

Chau Doc
& around

wetland bird sanctuary and a sacred, pagoda-dotted mountain

Chau Doc was once an extremely attractive riverside town on the west bank of the Hau. It still has a pretty riverfront, but the bustling market town is no longer as appealing as it once was. One of its biggest attractions is the nearby Nui Sam, which is dotted with pagodas and tombs. Across the river you can boat over to Cham villages and see the floating fish farms. South of Chau Doc the road passes the sorrowful Ba Chuc ossuary. There are also three international border crossings to Cambodia.

Chau Doc → *Colour map 5, B1.*

an important trading centre for the surrounding agricultural communities

The large market sprawls from the riverfront down and along Le Cong Thanh Doc, Phu Thu, Bach Dang and Chi Lang streets. It sells fresh produce and black-market goods smuggled across from Cambodia.

Near the market and the river, at the intersection of Tran Hung Dao Street and Nguyen Van Thoai Street, is the **Chau Phu Pagoda**. Built in 1926, it is dedicated to Thai Ngoc Hau, a former local mandarin. The pagoda is rather dilapidated, but has some fine carved pillars, which miraculously are still standing. A **Cao Dai temple**, which welcomes visitors, stands on Louise Street.

The **Vinh Te Canal**, north of town, is 90 km long and is a considerable feat of engineering, begun in 1819 and finished in 1824 using 80,000 workers. Its purpose was twofold: navigation and defence from the Cambodians. So impressed was Emperor Minh Mang in the achievement of its builder, Nguyen Van Thoai (or Thoai Ngoc Hau), that he named the canal after Thoai's wife, Chau Thi Vinh Te.

Listings Chau Doc

Where to stay

$$$$-$$$ Victoria Chau Doc
32 1 Le Loi St, T076-386 5010,
www.victoriahotels-asia.com.
This old, cream building with its beautiful
riverfront deck and pool complete with
loungers and view of the river confluence
is the perfect place location in which to
relax. All rooms are attractively decorated.
The hotel group runs a daily speedboat to
and from Phnom Penh. A refined place with
superb service.

$$$$-$$$ Victoria Nui Sam Lodge
Sam Mountain, www.victoriahotels.asia.
A fantastic addition to the area, this beautiful
resort offers 36 bungalows dotted across
the mountain offering knock-out views.
The service is excellent and the kitchen
is first rate. A fantastic hideaway in the
Mekong. Also has a wonderful swimming
pool with unobstructed views of the paddy
fields stretching as far as the eye can see.
Recommended.

$ Hai Chau hotel
63 Thuong Dang Le St.
A good budget option. The garish exterior
doesn't bode well, but the rooms are clean
and the a/c works well.

Restaurants

$$$ La Bassac
In Victoria Chau Doc.
The French and Vietnamese menus at this
suave riverside restaurant with stunning
terrace include buffalo paillard with shallot
confit, basa in banana leaf with saffron, rack
of lamb coated in Mekong herbs, sweet
potato puree and pork wine reduction or
spaghetti with flambéed shrimps in vodka
paprika sauce. The bar is a lovely spot for a
pre-dinner drink.

Essential Chau Doc

Getting around

Chau Doc itself is easily small enough to
explore on foot. By means of a bridge
or sampan crossing, some nearby Cham
villages can be reached and explored
on foot too. Nui Sam, the nearby sacred
mountain, can be reached by motorbike
or bus.

When to go

Chau Doc suffers not only from the
universal Mekong problem of the
monsoon floods, but also from the fact
that Nui Sam is one of the holiest sites in
southern Vietnam and, as such, attracts
vast numbers of pilgrims on auspicious
days. From a climatic viewpoint then the
best time to visit is December to April.

Time required

Ideal for two days of exploring.

$$ Thanh Thao
74 Trung Nu Vuong T073-869095.
Serves a huge selection of fresh seafood,
including crab, squid and lobster. A
no-nonsense eatery that's very popular
with locals.

$ Bay Bong
22 Thung Dang Le St, T076-386 7271.
Specializes in hot pots and soups and also
offers a good choice of fresh fish. The staff
are friendly.

$ Mekong
*41 Le Loi St, T076-386 7381, opposite Victoria
Chau Doc. Open for lunch and dinner.*
It is located right beside a in a lovingly
restored French villa. Good selection of food
including grilled prawns and fried rice dishes.
and the staff are friendly.

$ Sunrise Palace
Next to the tourist pier. Open 1100-2230.
The beef in Chau Doc is probably the best in Vietnam and here the *bo nuong* (grilled beef), served with herbs, is excellent. Good *de nuong* (goat) too. Serves delicious Russian live beer that goes perfectly with the food. The outdoor seating is best – inside is a wedding venue space.

Festivals

On all almost every weekend there is one festival or another. The busiest festivals are centred on Tet, 4 months after Tet and the mid-autumn moon festival.

What to do

Swimming
There is a swimming pool at the **Victoria Chau Doc**.

Therapies
A massage and fitness centre can be found at the **Victoria Chau Doc**. All the services are available to the general public.

Tour operators
Mekong Tours, *Vinh Phuoc Hotel, and 14 Nguyen Huu Canh St, T076-386 8222, and at Thanh Nam 2 hotel.* Local trips include the fish farms, floating markets and Cham village. Trips to Phu Quoc and boat trips to Phnom Penh (8-10 hrs or express boat 5 hrs; Cambodian visas can be bought at the border). A/c and public buses also booked to Ha Tien. Open Tour Bus ticketing and visa applications. Private boats can be arranged, but this is now rare so prices are not set.

Victoria Chau Doc, *32 Le Loi St, T76-386 5010, www.victoriahotels-asia.com.* Tours to Nui Sam, the city and a very interesting tour to the floating market, fish farms and Muslim village, cooking class, Tra Su forest tour, farming tour and Le Jarai cruise tour. Minimum 2 people for all tours.

Transport

It is possible (but expensive) to get to Chau Doc by boat from Can Tho (private charter only or by the Victoria Hotel group boat for guests only). Road connections with Can Tho, Vinh Long and Ho Chi Minh City are good.

Boat
There are daily departures to **Phnom Penh**. A couple of tour operators in town organize boat tickets, see Tour operators, above. **Victoria Hotel** speedboats go to Phnom Penh. Make sure you have a valid Vietnamese visa if you are entering the country as these cannot be issued at the border crossing; Cambodian visas can be bought at all the nearby crossings. For details of border crossings, see box, page 544.

Bus
The station is 3 km south from the town centre T76-386 7171. Minibuses stop in town on Quang Trung St. Connections with **HCMC** (6 hrs), hourly, 0600-2400; **Tra Vinh**; **Ca Mau**; **Long Xuyen**; **Can Tho**, every 30 mins; **Rach Gia**; and **Ha Tien**. There is an uncomfortable 10-hr bus ride from Chau Doc to Phnom Penh via Moc Bai, see page 173.

Mekong Tours, see Tour operators, runs a bus to **Phnom Penh** via Tinh Bien (see border crossings to Cambodia, page 173).

★ Nui Sam (Sam Mountain)
Take a bus (there is a stop at the foot of the mountain) or xe om.

This mountain, about 5 km southwest of town, was designated a 'Famed Beauty Spot' in 1980 by the Ministry of Culture and is one of the holiest sites in southern Vietnam. Rising from the flood plain, Nui Sam is a favourite spot for Vietnamese tourists who throng here, especially at festival time.

The mountain, really a barren, rock-strewn hill, can be seen at the end of the continuation of Nguyen Van Thoai Street. It is honeycombed with tombs, sanctuaries and temples. Most visitors come only to see Tay An Pagoda, Lady Xu Temple, and the tomb of Thoai Ngoc Hau (see below). But it is possible to walk or drive right up the hill for good views of the surrounding countryside: from the summit it is easy to appreciate that this is some of the most fertile land in Vietnam. At the top is a military base, formerly occupied by American soldiers and now by Vietnamese watching their Cambodian flank. Near the top the **Victoria Hotel** group has built a hotel used for conferences only.

Tay An Pagoda is at the foot of the hill, facing the road. Built originally in 1847, it has been extended twice and now represents an eclectic mixture of styles – Chinese, Islamic, perhaps even Italian. The pagoda contains a bewildering display of more than 200 statues.

A short distance on from the pagoda, to the right, past shops and stalls, is the **Chua Xu**. This temple was originally constructed in the late 19th century, and then rebuilt in 1972. It is rather a featureless building, though highly revered by the Vietnamese and honours the holy Lady Xu whose statue is enshrined in the new multi-roofed pagoda. The 23rd to the 25th of the fourth lunar month is the period when the holy Lady is commemorated, during which time, hundreds of Vietnamese flock to see her being washed and reclothed. Lady Xu is a major pilgrimage for traders and business from Ho Chi Minh City and the south, all hoping that sales will thereby soar and profits leap.

On the other side of the road is the **tomb of Thoai Ngoc Hau** (1761-1829); an enormous head of the man graces the entranceway. Thoai is a local hero having played a role in the resistance against the French but more for his engineering feats in canal building and draining swamps. He is also known as Nguyen Van Thoai and this name is given to one of Chau Doc's streets. The real reason to come here is to watch the pilgrims and to climb the hill.

Hang Pagoda, a 200-year-old temple situated halfway up Nui Sam, is worth visiting for several reasons. In the first level of the temple are some vivid cartoon drawings of the tortures of hell. The second level is built at the mouth of a cave which last century was home to a woman named Thich Gieu Thien. Her likeness and tomb can be seen in the first pagoda. Fed up with her lazy and abusive husband she left her home in Cholon and came to live in this cave, as an ascetic supposedly waited on by two snakes.

Nui Sam is the most expensive burial site in southern Vietnam. Wealthy Vietnamese and Chinese believe it is a most propitious last resting place. This is why the lower flanks are given over almost entirely to tombs.

Cham villages

There are a number of Cham villages around Chau Doc. **Phu Hiep**, **Con Tien** and **Chau Giang** are on the opposite bank of the Hau River. There are several mosques in the villages as the

Cham in this part of Vietnam are Muslim. At Chau Phong visitors can enjoy homestays. To reach the villages, take a sampan from the ferry terminal near the Victoria Chau Doc Hotel.

A visit to the floating fish farm villages (some 3000 floating houses), such as **Con Tien**, is a worthwhile and informative experience. A floating farm will have some 150,000 carp contained in a 6-m-deep iron cage beneath the house. Fish are worth around 600d for a baby and up to 25,000d for 500 g for a five-month-old fish. Catfish and mullet are also raised. (Chau Doc has a catfish monument on the riverfront promenade.) When the fish are ready for sale, boats with nets under them are used to transport the fish to Long Xuyen.

Border crossings to Cambodia

It is possible to cross the border to Cambodia north of Chau Doc at the **Vinh Xuong** (Omsano in Cambodia) boat crossing; just south of Chau Doc at **Tinh Bien** near Nha Ban (Phnom Den, Takeo, on the Cambodian side), and at **Xà Xía**, near Ha Tien (Prek Chak in Cambodia). It is possible to exit at Vinh Xuong and get a Cambodian visa but it's not possible to get a Vietnamese visa to enter Vietnam. At Tinh Bien you can buy a Cambodian visa but not a Vietnamese visa on entering. At Xà Xía, you can get a Cambodian visa but not a Vietnamese visa. There is a Vietnam consulate in Sihanoukville.

Phu Quoc Island

well worth visiting for a few days' relaxation

★Phu Quoc is Vietnam's largest island with beautiful sandy beaches and crystal-clear waters along much of its coastline and forested hills and pepper plantations inland. The arrival of numerous new resorts and the opening of the new international airport has seen some of its virgin land disappear under concrete, but, for the moment, it remains a wonderful place and still extremely under-developed in comparison to the major Thai islands. *Colour map 6, C2.*

Phu Quoc Island

Sights

Duong Dong is the main town on the island and many of the hotels and resorts are near here on **Truong Beach**. Millions of fish can be seen laid out to dry on land and on tables – all destined for the pot. Before being bottled they are fermented. At the **Khai Hoan fish sauce factory** ⓘ *free*, huge barrels act as vats, each containing fish and salt. If the sauce is made in concrete vats, the taste is lost and so the sauce is cheaper.

Coi Nguon Museum ⓘ *149 Tran Hung Dao St, T77-398 0206, www.coinguonphuquoc. com, daily 0700-1700, 1 English-speaking guide*, displays a huge amount of island creatures, fishing paraphernalia, old currency and Chinese ceramics from shipwrecked boats.

The island is also a centre for South Sea pearls, with 10,000 collected offshore each year. At the gloriously kitch **Phu Quoc Pearl Gallery** ⓘ *10 km south of Duong Dong, www.treasuresfromthedeep.com, daily 0800-1800*, a video demonstrates the farming operation, the tasting of pearl meat and pearl-making is illustrated in the gallery. Some 100 m south of the pearl farm on the coastal road there are two whale dedication

Essential Phu Quoc Island

Getting around

While some of the island's roads are surfaced many are still dirt tracks and so the best way to get around the entire island is by motorbike. There are plenty of motorbike taxis and motorbikes are easily available and cheap to hire. The only problem that visitors are likely to encounter is the very limited signposting, which can make some places pretty hard to find without some form of local assistance. Cars with drivers at fairly reasonable costs are available. Ask at hotels.

When to go

The best time to visit is December to May; during the monsoon seas on the east coast can be very rough.

Time required

Popular weekend destination, but take a few more days to fully explore the interior and take boat trips to outlying islands.

Best beaches

Ganh Dau, page 206
Bai Dai, page 206
Sao, page 206

temples, **Lang Ca Ong**. In front of one is a crude whale/dolphin statue.

Ganh Dau, at the northwest tip, is 35 km from Duong Dong. The townsfolk speak Khmer because refugees escaping the Khmer Rouge came here and settled with the locals. The Cambodian coast is 4-5 km away and can be seen, as can the last island of Vietnam. (The Cambodians actually claim Phu Quoc as their own.) The beach has a few palms and rocks to clamber on and there is a restaurant.

Bai Dai Beach, south of Ganh Danh, is a strip of white sand backed by casuarinas overlooking Turtle Island. Inland from here the area is heavily forested but the wood is protected by law. In this part of the island fish are laid out to dry on large trestle-tables or on the ground for use as fertilizer. South of Dai Beach is **Ong Lang Beach** where there are a couple of resorts, see Where to stay.

The dazzling white sands of **Sao Beach** on the southeast coast are stunning and worth visiting by motorbike. There are a couple of restaurants at the back of the beach.

The inland streams and waterfalls (Da Ban and Chanh streams) are not very dramatic in the dry season but still provide a relaxing place to swim and walk in the forests.

One of the biggest draws are the boat trips around the **An Thoi islands**, scattered islands, like chips off a block, off the southern coast, which offer opportunities for swimming, snorkelling, diving and fishing. It is also possible to stop off to visit an interesting fishing village at Thom Island.

Listings Phu Quoc Island *map p205*

Where to stay

During peak periods, such as Christmas and Tet, it is advisable to book accommodation well in advance. Most of the resorts lie along the west coast to the south of Duong Dong and are within a few kilometres of the airport. Others are on On Lang Beach.

$$$$ Chen Sea Resort & Spa
Ong Lang Beach, T077-399 5895,
www.centarahotelsresorts.com/cpv.
A very inviting resort with lovely villas set back from the yellow sand beach with sunken bathtubs on generous verandas and outdoor rain showers. The narrow strip of golden sand is dotted with paprika-coloured

umbrellas, and there's an infinity pool, spa, water sports and atmospheric restaurant. Excellent buffet breakfast – don't miss the addictive smoothies. Highly recommended.

$$$$ La Veranda
Tran Hung Dao St, Long Beach, T077-398 2988, www.laverandaresort.com.
A beautiful luxury resort with rooms and villas set in luscious gardens leading on to the main beach on the island. All rooms are beautifully furnished and come with TV, DVD player and Wi-Fi. De luxe rooms and villas come with gorgeous 4-poster beds and drapes. There's a spa, pool and the delicious food of the Pepper Tree Restaurant. The welcome and service is exceptional.

$$$$-$$$ Mai House Resort
Long Beach, T077-384 7003, maihouseresort@yahoo.com.
This is a beautiful resort run by the lovely Tuyet Mai and her husband. The architecture and design is all Mai's work – tasteful with plenty of attention to detail. Set in large flourishing gardens in front of a delicious slice of beach dotted with palms. The 20 a/c bungalows feature 4-poster beds, beamed roofs, pretty tiled bathrooms and balconies with carved balustrades. Sea-view rooms are bigger. Adjoining bungalows available for families. The open fronted small restaurant (with Wi-Fi access and places to lounge) overlooks the beach. One of the best places to eat on the island.

$$$$-$$$ Mango Bay Resort
Ong Lang Beach, T077-3981693 or T9-6968 1820 (mob), www.mangobayphuquoc.com.
A small and environmentally friendly resort located on the beach close to pepper farms. Some bungalows are made from rammed earth and are kitted out with bamboo furniture and tiled floors. There's information on birds and fish, and the restaurant provides a mixture of Vietnamese and Western food at very reasonable prices.

$$$ Bo Resort
Ong Lang Beach, T077-986142/3, www.boresort.com.
This feels like a great escape with 18 stilted bungalows set on a hillside amid flourishing gardens. Rooms come with large rustic bathrooms and alfresco showers. There's no road access to the wild stretch of beach where there are pines, hammocks, kayaks and a beach bar. There's Wi-Fi in the restaurant/bar and candlelight at night. The owners are warm and friendly.

$$$-$$ Freedomland
Ong Lang Beach, 10-12 mins' walk from beach, T01-226 586802, www.freedomlandphuquoc.com.
This laid-back resort creates a community vibe as all guests eat together at the large dinner table and around campfires. The food is excellent. Wooden stilt bungalows with thatched roofs are scattered around the grounds. Very friendly and highly recommended.

$$ Beach Club
Long Beach, T077-398 0998, www.beachclubvietnam.com.
Luscious golden sands and thatched beach umbrellas at this fantastic, highly rated small resort. The ochre-coloured rooms and 4 bungalows are all close to the sea. It's good value and so always booked up. Reserve well in advance.

$$ Lang Toi
Sao Beach, T09-82337477, langtoi_ restaurant@yahoo.com.vn.
With just 4 beautiful rooms complete with deep bathtubs, large balconies and tasteful wooden furnishings, this house is the best of the 2 options on the stunning Sao Beach. Beachfront restaurant serves all manner of seafood and simpler rice and noodle dishes. Recommened.

Restaurants

The food on Phu Quoc is generally very good, especially the fish and seafood. On the street in Duong Dong try the delicious *gio cuong* (fresh spring rolls). Along the river road a few restaurants also serve good Vietnamese dishes and seafood and are very popular with locals and Vietnamese tourists – Truong Duong at 30/4 Thanh Tu (T09-146 1419) is one of the best.

Most of the resorts mentioned have beachfront restaurants. The night market is a fantastic place to try lots of different local food in a buzzing atmosphere.

$$$-$$ Itaca Lounge
125 Tran Hung Dao, T0773-992022, www.itacalounge.com.
Chilled out open air place with heavy Greek influences on the menu. Spanish chef Mateu Batista has 25 years of experience and creates a range of creative dished that make this one of the island's must-visit options.

$$$-$$ The Pepper Tree
La Veranda Resort (see Where to stay).
Fine dining in a refined seafront setting with perfect service. The ideal place for a special romantic meal. The pork with local pepper sauce is a treat.

$$$-$$ The Spice House, Cassia Cottage
Ba Keo Beach, T0773-848395, www.cassiacottage.com.
In a lovely garden setting, this fine restaurant has gained a solid reputation for its excellent barbecued seafood and good curries.

$ Buddy's
26 Nguyen Trai St, T77-399 4181.
This is a traveller crowd favourite serving Kiwi ice creams, great shakes and big burgers. Also brews good *Lavazza*.

$ La Cafe
11 Tran Hung Dao St, T90-820 1102.
A tiny streetside cafe serving yoghurts, shakes and breakfasts on cute black-lacquered furniture under beige umbrellas.

Bars and clubs

The Dog Bar
88 Tran Hung Dao St, near the Thien Hai Son Resort, T90-381 4688.
Well-located beer den with cold drinks, pool and sports TV.

Rory's (formerly Amigos)
Next to Veranda, 118/10 Tran Hung Dao, T091-707 0456.
Run by an affable Aussie couple, this beachfront bar and restaurant has a huge deck for great sun set views. Pizzas and burgers, grilled seafood and a large range of cocktails. Good promos and dancing later till the small hours.

Shopping

If you have Vietnamese friends or family and return home without a bottle of the fish sauce you will be in trouble. However, you cannot take the sauce on a **Vietnam Airlines** flight. The Duong Dong market and also the night market are the best places to head for gifts.

Coi Nguon, *149 Tran Hung Dao, T0773-980206, www.coinguonphuquoc.com.* A well-stocked shop selling a wide variety of wares using pearls, conch shells and driftwood, **Coi Nguon** is also home to a good museum. **Treasures from the Deep**, *www.treasuresfromthedeep.com.* New Zealand jeweller, which is the best place to buy the pearls the island is famed for.

What to do

Most of the resorts are very happy to arrange tours and they are a good source of up-to-date information. Water sports, cycling tours, boat tours and walking can all be arranged.

Diving
Rainbow Divers, *Tran Hung Dao St, close to the market, T91-723 9433 (mob),*

www.divevietnam.com. Long-standing operation with a very good reputation.

Tour operators

John's Tours, *New Star Café, 143 Tran Hung Dao St, T091-910 7086, www.johnsislandtours. com*. Run by the super helpful and friendly John Tran out of the **New Star Caféa** office (next to the alley to La Veranda) and various kiosks on the beach as well as hotel desks. John can organize anything for any budget and knows the island like the back of his hand. Snorkelling, squid fishing, island tours and car hire can all be arranged. Car hire and motorbikes with drivers also arranged.

Tony Travel, *100 Tran Hung Dao St or based at the Rainbow Divers office on Tran Hung Dao St opposite the market, T0913-197334, phuquoctonytourravelpq@yahoo.com.vn.* Kiosks on the beach too. Tony knows Phu Quoc extremely well and speaks fluent English. He would be able to organize almost anything. In his stable are island tours, snorkelling to the south and north islands, deep-sea fishing excursions, car and motorbike rental and hotel and transport reservations. He also runs **Rainbow Divers**.

Transport

You can get to Phu Quoc by boat from Rach Gia or Ha Tien or by plane from Rach Gia and Ho Chi Minh City. Most hotels will provide a free pick-up service from the airport if accommodation is booked in advance. *Xe om* drivers and taxis meet the ferries.

Air

There are daily flights to **HCMC** and **Rach Gia**.

Airline offices Vietnam Airlines, 122 Nguyen Trung Truc St, Duong Dong, T77-399667.

Boat

Most ferries leave from Vong and Nam Ninh ports near the beaches of the same names. John of **John's Tours** (see page 209) can sell all tickets and can advise on schedules. An Thoi port in the south.

Hong Tam, at **John's Tours**, ferries to **Ha Tien** daily at 0830, 1½ hrs. **Superdong**, 1 Tran Hung Dao St, Duong Dong, T077-348 6180. Ferries to **Rach Gia** from Vong Beach at 0800 and 1300, 2½ hrs 1300 arriving 1535. Ferries for **Ha Tien** leave a 0800, 1½ hrs. **Savana**, 21 Nguyen Trai St, Duong Dong, T0773-992999, 1 ferry per day to **Rach Gia**, 1240, 2½ hrs.

Duong Dong Express leaves for **Rach Gia** at 1245 arriving 1515, www.duongdongexpress.com.vn.

Vinashin, 21 Nguyen Trai St, T077-260 0155, leaves 0810.

Cawaco from Ham Ninh to **Ha Tien** at 0830 arriving 1000. Also departs Bai Vong 1400 arriving 1520.

Car, bicycle and motorbike

Cars, motorbikes and bicycles can be rented from resorts.

Taxi

Mai Linh, No 10 30 Thang 4 St, Duong Dong, T77-397 9797. **Sasco**, 379 Nguyen Trung Truc St, T77-399 5599.

Con Dao

a true island paradise

★Con Dao is an archipelago of 14 islands and one of Vietnam's last relatively untouched wilderness areas with great possibilities for wildlife viewing and the country's best diving. The biggest and only permanently settled island is Con Son with a population of approximately 6000 people.

Sights → *Colour map 4, C3.*

The combination of mountains and islands, as well as its biodiversity, make Con Dao extremely special. It is also one of Vietnam's last relatively pristine areas. There are just a few main roads around Con Son and an unbelievable lack of traffic. The main hotels face out onto Con Son Bay behind the coastal road. The colourful fishing boats that used to bob and work the sea here have largely been moved to Ben Dam port although a few remain.

Essential Con Dao

Getting around

The main hotels offer a shuttle to the airport, but the best way to get around the island is by hiring a motorbike or a bicycle for shorter trips.

When to go

Between June and September is sea turtle nesting season (records show that the 1st and 15th of the month are best) although good weather is not guaranteed. February to April can be incredibly windy. The wet season lasts from May to November.

Time required

It's possible to see a lot of the island in two days, but three or four will allow you to truly enjoy it.

The prison system

The prison system operated between 1862 and 1975, first by the French and then by the Americans. **Prison Phu Hai**, which backs on to parts of the Saigon Con Dao Resort, was built in 1862 and is the largest prison on the islands with 10 detention rooms and 20 punishment cells. Inside, the chapel was built by the Americans in 1963. Next door is **Phu Son Prison** built in 1916. The third prison, **Phu Tho**, plus **Camp Phu Tuong** and **Camp Phu Phong** (built in 1962) contained the infamous 'tiger cages' where prisoners were chained and tortured; the enclosures still stand. Metal bars were placed across the roofs of the cells and guards would throw excrement and lime onto the prisoners. In addition, many prisoners were outside in areas known as 'sun-bathing compartments'. Not content on limiting torture methods, a cow manure enclosure was used to dunk prisoners in sewage up to 3 m deep. American-style tiger enclosures were built in 1971 at **Camp Phu Binh**. In total there were 504 tiger cages. Beyond the prisons, inland, is the **Hang Duong cemetery** where many of the victims of the prison are buried. The grave of Le Hong Phong, the very first General Secretary of the Communist Party in Vietnam (1935-1936) and Vo Thi Sau (1933-1952) can be seen among them.

A tour of the prisons and cemetery costs can be arranged through the museum, see below. There is an excellent and well-curated museum just outside the main town, which offers a fascinating if disturbing insight into the island's past. A visit here is highly recommended.

There is a small museum and explanatory displays at the **National Park office headquarters** ⓘ *see below, Mon-Fri 0700-1130, 1330-1700, Sat 0730-1100, 1400-1630.*

Con Dao National Park
29 Vo Thi Sau St, T64-383 0650, www.condaopark.com.vn.

There are a number of activities that can be organized in the national park, from snorkelling and swimming, to forest walks and birdwatching. Diving is available to see some of Con Dao's underwater features, such as its caves, as well as the coral reefs. In 1984 the forests on all 14 islands of the Con Dao archipelago were given official protection, and in 1993, 80% of the land area was designated a national park. In 1998 the park boundaries were expanded to include the surrounding sea.

In 1995, with support from the World Wildlife Fund, the park began a sea-turtle conservation project. Con Dao is the most important sea-turtle nesting site in Vietnam, with several hundred female green turtles (*Chelonia mydas*) coming ashore to lay their eggs every year. Occasionally the hawksbill turtle visits too. Park staff attach a tag to every turtle in order to identify returning turtles, and move the turtles' eggs if they are in danger of being flooded at high tide. The rest of the year the turtles migrate long distances. Recently, a turtle tagged in Con Dao was found in a fishing village in Cambodia – unfortunately the tag was insufficient protection to prevent it being eaten. Also in 1995, park staff identified the presence of dugongs (sea cows), which are mammals that feed on seagrass and can live to more than 70 years. Unfortunately, before the park was established dugongs were caught for meat so now the population in Con Dao is small and endangered.

The coral reefs surrounding the islands are among the most diverse in the country. Scientists have identified more than 200 species of coral and coral fish. In November 1997, typhoon Linda struck the islands and many of Con Dao's coral reefs were damaged.

In the forests scientists have identified more than 1000 plant species, of which several are unique to Con Dao and include many valuable medicinal and timber species. Bird life is also significant with rare species such as the pied imperial pigeon (*Ducula bicolor*) – Con Dao is the only place in Vietnam where you can see this bird – the red-billed tropicbird (*Phaethon aethereus*) – found on only a few islands in the world – and the brown booby (*Sula leucogaster*) – a rare sea bird that inhabits the park's most remote island, Hon Trung (Egg Island). Egg Island, a speedboat ride northeast of Con Son, is a rugged outcrop hosting thousands of seabirds including sooty and crested terns, white-bellied sea eagles, and the rare, in Vietnam, masked booby. Most of the threats to the islands' natural resources come from development in the form of new roads, houses and the new fishing port built in Ben Dam Bay – an area of once-beautiful coral reef and mangrove forest.

Beaches and bays
Ong Dung Beach can be reached by walking across Con Son Island downhill on a track through the jungle. Plenty of birds can be seen if you trek at the right time of day. You can

snorkel around 300 m offshore. There is a forest protection centre at the bay where you can buy food and drink and hire snorkelling gear and a boat. See also Where to stay, below.

Bai Nhat Beach, just before Ben Dam Bay, is a beautiful wild stretch of sand where good swimming is possible.

North of Con Son is **Tre Lon Island**, said to be one of the best places in the archipelago to see coral reefs and reef fish; this was also used as an isolated French prison. Le Duan, former General Secretary of the Communist Party, was imprisoned here from 1931-1936.

Close to the airport is one of the island's best and most wild beaches at **Dam Trau**. Golden sands in a tight curved bay backed by casuarinas can be found here but there are no island views. Signposted 'Mieu Cau' on the left just before the airport, it is a 15-minute walk, passing a pagoda flanked by two white horses.

Bay Canh Island is a major sea turtle nesting site; there is also a functioning French-built lighthouse dating from 1883. If you are interested in seeing the turtles arrange to stay overnight through the national park.

Cau Island, east of Bay Canh Island is the only other island in the archipelago with fresh water. It harbours the swifts that make the nests and turtles that come to lay their eggs. It was also an isolated French prison at one time. Pham Van Dong, a former prime minster of both North Vietnam and the reunited Vietnam (1955-1987), was incarcerated here for seven years, from 1929 to 1936.

For swimming, **Lo Voi Beach**, east of the hotels, is good for swimming as is **An Hai Beach** at the other end of the bay. Birdwatching is also possible around the freshwater lake – **Quang Trung** – swamps and tree-covered sand dunes near the park headquarters. Spotters could see the Brahminy kite (*Haliastur Indus*), white-bellied sea eagle, Javan pond heron and cinnamon bittern. On the way to Ong Dung you can see the white-rumped shama, greater racket-tailed drongo, the rare pied imperial pigeon and the even rarer red-billed tropicbird.

At **Dat Doc**, east of Con Son, is a very attractive and pristine bay backed by a sheer cliff face. The **Evason Hideaway & Six Senses Spa** company has built here.

Listings Con Dao

Where to stay

$$$$ Six Senses Con Dao
Dat Doc Beach, www.sixsenses.com.
One of the most fabulous resort in all of Southeast Asia, this is pure unadulterated luxury. The duplex villas stretch along a gorgeous stretch of sand which is bookended by a grand green hill. Each villa has its own private pool and personal butler service. The restaurant is absolutely first rate serving superb international and local flavours. The breakfast takes the 5-star experience to another level with delicious a la carte options (the Turkish poached eggs are amazing) as well as a buffet complete with a walk-in cold room. Highly expensive but highly recommended.

$$$ Con Dao Resort
8 Nguyen Duc Thuan St, T64-383 0939, www.condaoresort.com.vn.
Until **Six Senses** arrived on the scene, this was the best resort on the island. There are 41 rooms including some in villas on the beach. The rooms feature a/c bathtubs, TV and balconies. There's a pool and a tennis court. There's also a restaurant which is rather average. Staff can arrange walking and motorbike tours of the area.

$$$ Saigon Con Dao
18 Ton Duc Thang St, T64-383 0336, www.saigoncondao.com.

These buildings on the seafront may remind you of a Cornish seaside hotel from the 1980s, but they are clean and comfortable. The restaurant is not particularly good and the buffet breakfast caters to Vietnamese tastes.

$$-$ Con Dao Camping
Nguyen Duc Thuan St.

By the old pier, these simple A-frame huts offer beachfront digs for those on a budget. Rather dated, they are nonetheless clean and offer sea views at very cheap prices.

Restaurants

Until recently there was very little to choose from on Con Dao, but there are now a handful of good places in the main town. There are also plenty of places to grab a cheap bowl of noodles around the market and the night food street nearby features some noodle stands as well as some seafood. On the road to Con Dao Camping there are a number of Vietnamese seafood places catering to large groups.

$ Bar 200
Pham Van Dong, T064-363 0334.

This new addition to the town also houses **Senses Diving** school. It's run by 2 Brits and a South African who opened it up in part to satisfy their own food cravings. You can therefore find great Western options including salads and pizzas as well as good espresso. A great source of local information and very, very friendly. A good spot to meet fellow divers and travellers.

$ Infiniti
Pham Van Dong, T64-383 0083.

This is a very funky cafe which seems rather out of place in Con Dao's main town. Run by two friendly brothers, it serves pizza, excellent chicken burgers, sublime shakes,

beers and cocktails. Also does a barbecue party on weekends and regular specials. A great find.

$ Six Senses Con Dao
See Where to stay.

The restaurant here is first-rate, with superb grilled seafood and wide range of local and international flavours. Also has an exceptional wine list. Highly recommended for a treat.

What to do

Boat tours

The National Park organizes boat tours depending on the number of people and the weather. These include trips to Hon Tre Lon, Hon Tre No, Hon Bay Canh and Hon Cau as well as points around Con Son Island.

Diving

This is the premier place to dive in Vietnam. Courses are offered by **Senses Diving** based at **Bar 200** (see Restaurants). This is a very professional outfit run by highly experienced diver masters.

> **Tip...**
>
> To see the turtles hatching on Con Dao's beaches, visit May-October.

Transport

Air

Con Dao Airport, T64-383 1973. There are regular flights to and from **Ho Chi Minh City**. Weekly schedules vary throughout the year.

Boat

It is possible to reach Con Dao by boat, but the journey is a nightmare by all accounts and not recommended at all.

Phan Thiet
& Mui Ne

Sahara-like dunes, kitesurfing beaches and fishing villages

Phan Thiet is a fishing town at the mouth of the Ca Ty River. For the traveller the real attraction lies east of town in the form of the 20-km sweep of golden sand of Mui Ne. Here some of Vietnam's finest coastal resorts can be found with some excellent water sports and two of the country's most attractive golf courses. The town has become hugely popular with both kitesurfers and Russians, with plenty of businesses catering to both markets.

Phan Thiet → *Colour map 4, C2.*

Despite its modest appearance, Phan Thiet is the administrative capital of Binh Thuan Province. Its main attraction is the 18-hole golf course, designed by Nick Faldo. It is regarded as one of the best in Vietnam, and golfers come from all around the region to play it.

The most distinctive landmark in town is the municipal **water tower** completed in 1934. It is an elegant structure with a pagoda-like roof; built by the infamous 'Red Prince' and first president of Laos. The tower icon features in the logos of many local businesses and agencies. There are a few Ho Chi Minh relics, including a museum on Nguyen Truong To Street and the Duc Thanh school next door, where Ho Chi Minh taught in 1911, but otherwise nothing of interest at the museum.

Van Thuy Thu Temple ⓘ *20A Ngu Ong St, 0730-1130 and 1400-1700,* is the oldest whale temple (built in 1762) in Vietnam. The temple houses more than 100 whale skeletons, including one specimen more than 22 m in length. Like all whale temples, it was originally built by the sea but, as sea levels have receded, this temple is now stranded in the middle of the neighbourhood.

★Mui Ne → *Colour map 4, C2.*

Mui Ne is the name of the famous sandy cape and the small fishing village that lies at its end. Mui Ne's claims to fame are its *nuoc mam* (fish sauce) and its beaches where it is possible to do a host of water sports including kiteboarding, for which it is justly famous. Body boarding and surfing are better December to January when there are more waves. The wind dies down at the end of April, and May has virtually no wind. The cape is dominated by some impressive sand dunes; some are golden but in other parts quite red, a reflection of the underlying geology.

Both motorbike taxis and Mai Linh car taxis abound in the town and along the Mui Ne strip.

The weather in Phan Thiet always seems nice. It is, of course, better in the dry season, December through April. Phan Thiet is most popular with overseas visitors (and the growing number of package tour operators) in the Christmas to Easter period when prices at the some of the better hotels rise by 20% or more. From December to March, Mui Ne loses portions of its beach to the sea.

Kitesurfers can linger for weeks here, but for the rest two to four days will be ample.

The red dunes, page 218
The white dunes, page 218
Fairy Stream, page 218

Around the village visitors may notice a strong smell of rotting fish. This is the unfortunate but inevitable by-product of fish sauce fermenting in wooden barrels. The *nuoc mam* of Phan Thiet is made from anchovies, as *ca com* on the label testifies. The process takes a year but to Vietnamese palates it is worth every day. *Nuoc mam* from Phan Thiet is regarded highly but not as reverentially as that from the southern island of Phu Quoc.

There are still significant numbers of Cham (50,000) and Ra-glai (30,000) minorities who, until a century ago, were the dominant groups in the region. There are many relics of the Champa kingdom here in Binh Thuan Province, the best and easiest to find being **Po Shanu**, two Cham towers dating from the late eighth century on a hill on the Mui Ne road. They are now somewhat broken down but the road leading up to them makes a nice evening ride; you can watch the sun set and from this vantage point you'll see the physical make-up of the coastal plain and estuaries to the south and the central highlands to the north. Driving up the long climb towards Mui Ne the towers are on the right-hand side of the road and quite unmissable. Like Cham towers elsewhere in this part of the country they were constructed of brick bound together with resin of the day tree. Once the tower was completed timber was piled around it and ignited; the heat from the flames melted the resin, which solidified on cooling.

Hon Rom and around

Hon Rom, about 15 km by motorbike or bicycle from Mui Ne, is the name of the undeveloped bay north of Mui Ne and is accessible only from Mui Ne. North of Hon Rom are **Suoi Nuoc**, **Binh Thien Village** and **Turtle Island**. The Full Moon Beach Resort runs the Full Moon Villas and Jibe's II at Suoi Nuoc.

Tourist information

Binh Thuan Tourist
82 Trung Trac St, T62-381 6821,
www.binhthuan-tourist.com.
Arranges tours and car rentals.

Where to stay

Phan Thiet

$$$$ DuParc Phan Thiet Ocean Dunes & Golf Resort
1 Ton Duc Thang St, T62-382 2393,
www.vietnamgolfresorts.com.
On the beach just outside Phan Thiet, this is set behind lovely gardens. 123 comfortable rooms (although some of these are showing their age) in a bland building and new well-appointed villas with beach views. Good facilities, 2 pools, 2 restaurants with tasty food, bar, tennis courts and gym. Guests enjoy a 30% discount on green fees at the adjacent 18-hole champion golf course, the **Ocean Dunes Golf Club**.

Mui Ne

Weekends tend to be busier as Mui Ne is a popular escape for expats from HCMC. There has been a great construction boom and there are now many places to stay at a range of prices. Fortunately supply has kept up with demand so Mui Ne offers good value. Advisable to book ahead as the popular places fill up fast particularly around Christmas and Tet and Vietnamese public holidays.

$$$$ Anantara Mui Ne Resort and Spa
Nguyen Dinh Chieu, T062-374 1888,
www.anantara.com.
A fantastic 5-star resort with impeccable service, good restaurant, sea-view rooms and a great slice of beach. The wine cellar is very well stocked and there is also an excellent gym.

$$$$ Mia Mui Ne
T62-384 7440, www.miamuine.com.
This is a gorgeous resort. Designed in the most charming style its bungalows and rooms are simple and cool and surrounded by dense and glorious vegetation. For inspiration and good taste it ranks among the best in Vietnam. Its pool has been extended and the bathrooms for the superior rooms enlarged. It has an excellent restaurant and bar. A good buffet breakfast is included.

$$$$ Victoria Phan Thiet Beach Resort & Spa
T62-381 3000, www.victoriahotels-asia.com.
Part of the **Victoria Group**, the resort has 59 upgraded thatched bungalows without outdoor rain showers and 3 villas, built in country-house style in an attractive landscaped setting. It is well equipped with restaurants, bar, 2 pools, sports facilities, a children's club and a spa. A great place to bring kids who love the donkey that's available for rides in the grounds. Very friendly staff and a good buffet breakfast.

$$$$-$$$ Coco Beach (Hai Duong)
T62-384 7111-3, www.cocobeach.net.
The European owners live here and the place is well run. Not luxurious but friendly and impeccably kept. 28 wooden bungalows and 3 wooden, 2-bedroom 'villas' facing the beach. Beautiful setting, lovely pool and relaxing. Excellent restaurant and a beachclub. **Coco Beach** was the first resort on Mui Ne and it is pleasing how it remains easily among the best.

$$$ Full Moon Beach
T62-384 7008, www.windsurf-vietnam.com.
Visitors are assured of a friendly reception by the French and Vietnamese couple who own and run the place. Accommodation is in a variety of types: some rooms are spacious, others a little cramped, some brick, some bamboo. The most attractive rooms have a sea view and constant breeze. There is

a good restaurant. They also run the **Full Moon Village** along the coast in Suoi Nuoc which is a very tranquil spot away from all the other resorts.

$$$-$$ Saigon Mui Ne
T62-384 7303, www.saigonmuineresort.com.
This is a Saigon tourist resort, perfectly professional but lacking flair and imagination. Bungalows, pool, jacuzzi, restaurant, spa, fitness centre and kiteboarding classes.

$$-$ Hiep Hoa
T62-384 7262, T090-812 4149 (mob), hiephoatourism@yahoo.com.
This is an attractive place. Now with 15 a/c rooms. It's quiet, clean and with its own stretch of beach. Popular and should be booked in advance. Its rates are excellent value for Mui Ne; they go down in the low season.

$$-$ Mui Ne Backpackers Resort
88 Nguyen Dinh Chieu, T062-384 7047, www.muinebackpackers.com.
One of the best options for those on a budget and one of the longest standing in the area. There is a small swimming pool and a variety of different room options to choose from. Located right on the beach, the sea view.

Restaurants

Mui Ne
Of the hotel restaurants the **Mia** and **Victoria** stand out. Many hotels do good barbecues at the weekend. There are many local seafood joints along the main road either side of the resort strip where the catch of the day is grilled – it's best to wander along and pick the busiest place.

$$ El Latino
Nguyen Dinh Chieu, T62-3743 5950.
A very welcoming little spot serving up some quality Mexican fare including great tacos and burritos, although the servings are on the small side. Has some coaches for laid-back dining in a funky open-air space.

$$ Forest Restaurant
7 Nguyen Dinh Chieu St, T62-384 7589.
Local dishes and lots of seafood, this garden-jungle setting puts on live music throughout the evening. Popular with the town's expats recommend this place for the good food, despite the touristy vibe.

$$-$ Jibe's Beach Club
T62-384 7405. Open 0700-late.
Popular chill-out bar serving burgers, salads and food with a French bent thanks to theowner, Pascal. In the daytime there is a kitesurf school cafe vibe, but in the evenings white linens come out and there is a more sophisticated ambiance. Recommended.

$$-$ Shree Ganesh
57 Nguyen Dinh Chieu, T62-374 1330.
This popular Omar's franchise serves North Indian and Tandoori cuisine. One of the best in Mui Ne with consistently high reviews for many years.

Bars and cafés

Mui Ne

Jibe's Beach Club
See Restaurants.
A laid back bar with quieter tunes, some good wine and a beachfront setting.

Joe's Cafe
139 Nguyen Dinh Chieu St, T62-374 3447, joescafemuine.com.
Ever popular and always busy spot with live music every night in a garden setting.

Pogo
www.thepogobar.com.
Just down from **Sinh Tourist** with cocktails, and local and international food. Keeps going later than most thanks to the roaring bonfires.

Wax
68 Nguyen Dinh Chieu St, T62-384 7001.
Located beside the beach at Windchamp Resort, **Wax** is dance-part central, especially during holidays.

Shopping

Mui Ne
There is now a large selection of shops in Mui Ne spanning the west end of the beach. Almost anything can be found, from beachwear, water sports equipment, pearls and jewellery to lacquerware and crocodile leather.

What to do

Mui Ne
The dunes and Fairy Stream
Tours to the red and white sand dunes and the Fairy Stream are top of most people's list when they visit Mui Ne and with very good reason. It's possible to hire a motorbike and venture out solo. The red dunes are very close to town and the white dunes are about an hour further on. Every motorbike hire place will be able to provide a map. The dunes are spectacular and best visited in the late afternoon. Kids hiring out plastic boards for sliding down the steep sand banks can be rather persistent. If you travel to the white dunes in the heat of the day, be sure to take enough fuel for the return leg and plenty of water for the dunes themselves. All tour operators offer trips to these dunes, some including jeep transport and rides on quad bikes.

Therapies
The Village, *Victoria Phan Thiet Beach Resort & Spa, see Where to stay, above.* The hotel's own on-site centre offers the best massage in town by the most experienced therapists.

Water sports
Mui Ne is the water sports capital of Vietnam. The waters can be crowded with windsurfers and kiteboarders. The combination of powerful wind and waves attract huge numbers of kitesurfers. Equipment and training is offered by numerous centres. Jibe's Beach Club, *T62-384 7405, T091-316 2005 (mob), www.windsurf-vietnam.com.*

There are plenty of places offering lessons in town, but this is the original centre, which is part of and close to Full Moon Beach Resort. **Jibe's** is the importer of sea kayaks, windsurfers, surfboards, sailboats, SUP (stand-up paddle) and kitesurf equipment. Equipment is available for purchase or for hire by the hour, day or week. Hourly windsurf lessons, multi-day kite-surf lessons and boogie board and kayak hire.

Tour operators
Sinh Tourist, *144 Nguyen Dinh Chieu St, T62-384 7542, muine@thesinhtourist.vn.* A branch of the tour operator good for **Open Tour Bus** tickets and local tours to the sand dunes, fishing village and Phan Thiet city tour. Transport rented.
Victor Tours & Coco Cafe, *121A Nguyen Dinh Chieu, across from Full Moon Resort, T98-959 1599.* **Victor Tours** offers a full range of tour to all the local sites and books bus transport throughout Vietnam. Customs tours and unique outings are also available.

Transport

Bicycles and motorbikes
Xe oms are abundant in Phan Thiet town, as are reputable taxis. Bikes and motorbikes can be rented from hotels or tour operators, see **Victor Tours**, tour operators, above, and are the best way to explore the vicinity.

Bus and Open Tour Bus
The bus station is on the east side of town. Connections with all neighbouring towns. A local bus plies the nearby **Phan Thiet Coop** supermarket to Mui Ne route, as do taxis. Phuong Trang and Sinh Tourist Open Tour Buses drop off and pick up from all resorts on Mui Ne. The **Sinh Tourist** bus departs from its resort and Phuong Trang from its central office. To **Nha Trang** and **HCMC** twice a day at 1300 and 2345 (also 0800 to HCMC) 5½ hrs, both journeys. To **Dalat**, 7 hrs.
 Phuong Trang, *97 Nguyen Dinh Chieu St, T62-374 3113, www.phuongtrangdalat.com.*

Cambodia is perhaps the most beguiling of all the countri
of Southeast Asia. Long associated with the brutal Khmer
Rouge, the country has risen above its blood-tinted history to
finally take its place as one of the region's pre-eminent tourist
destinations. Home to a truly rich mix of travel experiences from
ancient monuments and powdery beaches to remote ethnic
minority villages and city life, Cambodia never fails to excite
the senses.

Ancient Cambodia produced one of world's greatest
civilizations at Angkor. But Angkor Wat is merely one temple
lying at the heart of a thousand others. The capital, Phnom
Penh, retains the sort of landscape most travellers dream of: a
skyline punctuated by spires, turrets and pinnacles of royal and
religious origin rather than by office blocks.

Further south is Sihanoukville, Cambodia's most popular
beach-side town, characterized by long, palm-fringed beaches,
comfy deckchairs and gentle, lapping waters. More adventurous
souls will be impressed by the outlying islands, which provide
the perfect backdrop for snorkelling, diving or fishing trips.
Decrepit colonial ruins scattered through a Garden of Eden
landscape make Kep the real gem of the south, however.
Infinitely more low key than Sihanoukville, the small coastal
town, with its blossoming flowers, trees laden with fruit and
freshly cooked crab speciality, is truly a slice of paradise.

In stark contrast to the laid-back beaches are the northeastern
provinces. Here, tracts of red earth cut through hills, carpeted in
jungle and speckled with the thatched huts that are home to a
miscellany of minority groups. Elephant rides are the call of the
day around Sen Monorom, while those looking for adventure
in Ban Lung won't be disappointed by the waterfalls, boat rides
and the stunning, bottle-green waters of Yaek Lom Lake.

Phnom Penh
& around

With its colonial heyday long gone Phnom Penh is re-emerging as one of Southeast Asia's most charming and dynamic capital cities. The wide boulevards remain and the beautiful French buildings are regaining some of their former glory.

Thankfully the dusty, fly-blown post-civil war atmosphere of decay is being replaced with burgeoning economic development and whilst the arrival of giant air-conditioned shopping malls might not suit the fantasies of Western travellers, Khmers are rightly feeling proud of the advances their capital city is making.

Phnom Penh is still a city of contrasts: East and West, poor and rich, serenity and chaos. Monks' saffron robes lend a splash of colour to the capital's streets, and stylish restaurants and bars line the riverside and many of the back streets in the city centre. However, the memory of the war is never far away, an enduring reminder of Cambodia's tragic story. Perhaps the one constant in all the turmoil of the past century has been the monarchy – the splendid Royal Palace, visible to all, remains as a symbol of the monarchy's once undimmed authority, something even the Khmer Rouge had to treat with caution.

Best for
Architecture▪History▪Restaurants▪Shopping

Phnom Penh

Footprint
picks

★ **Royal Palace and Silver Pagoda**, pages 225 and 227
Highlights of the capital's 19th-century concoction of temples,
summerhouses and palaces.

★ **National Museum of Cambodia**, page 230
A magnificent collection of Khmer sculpture, mostly from the
Angkor period.

★ **Central Market**, page 233
With its art deco dome, this is the place to pick up silverware, gold
and gems.

★ **Tuol Sleng Museum**, page 234
A former high school used as the Khmer Rouge's S-21 interrogation
centre – a chilling reminder of the country's recent history.

★ **Choeung Ek**, page 235
Now a peaceful place but once the scene of Cambodia's notorious
'killing fields'.

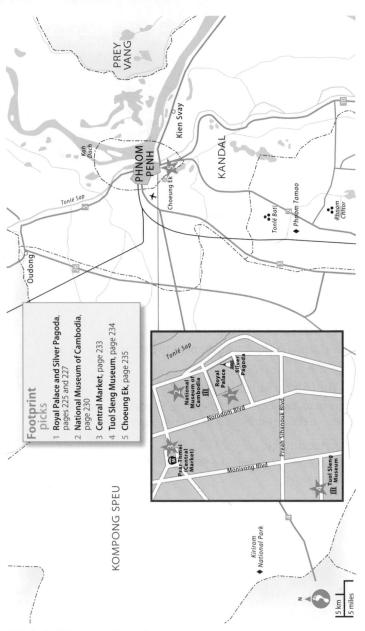

KOMPONG SPEU

PREY VANG

Kien Svay

PHNOM PENH

KANDAL

Koh Dach

Tonlé Sap

Oudong

Choeung Ek

Phnom Tamao

Tonlé Bati ◆ Phnom Tamao

Phnom Chisor

Kirirom National Park

Footprint picks

1 Royal Palace and Silver Pagoda, pages 225 and 227
2 National Museum of Cambodia, page 230
3 Central Market, page 233
4 Tuol Sleng Museum, page 234
5 Choeung Ek, page 235

Tonlé Sap

National Museum of Cambodia 2

Royal Palace

Silver Pagoda 1

Norodom Blvd

Preah Sihanouk Blvd

Psar Thmei (Central Market) 3

Monivong Blvd

Tuol Sleng Museum 4

5 km
5 miles

N

Sights
Phnom Penh

The Royal Palace area, with its glittering spires, wats, stupas, National Museum and broad green spaces, is perfectly situated alongside the river and is as pivotal to the city as the city is to the country.

Historic centre
the heart of the city: all the top sights are here

★ Royal Palace

Entrance on Samdech Sothearos Blvd, www.phnompenh.gov.kh/phnom-penh-city-royal-palace-125.html. Daily 0730-1100, 1400-1700. US$3, plus US$2 for camera or US$5 for video camera.

Of all the cultural sights in Phnom Penh, the Royal Palace is the most impressive. The scale of the palace (and adjoining Silver Pagoda) dwarfs the others and, given the rather gloomy recent history that pervades most of the city's sights, the Royal Palace holds nothing nasty in store for its visitors. Built mainly by the French in 1866, on the site of the old town, the entrance is on Samdech Sothearos Boulevard via the Pavilion of Dancers (or Chan Chaya Pavilion). Opposite the entrance are the walls of the royal residence (closed to the public) and the stable of the white elephant (a highly auspicious and sacred animal treasured as a symbol of royal beneficence).

Throne Hall The main building facing the Victory Gate, the Throne Hall was built in 1917 in Khmer style; it has a tiered roof and a 59-m tower, influenced by Angkor's Bayon Temple. The steps leading up to it are protected by multi-headed nagas. It is used for coronations and other official occasions such as the reception of foreign ambassadors when they present their official credentials. Scenes from the Ramayana adorn the ceiling. Inside stand the sacred gong and French-style thrones only used by the sovereign. Above the thrones hangs Preah Maha Svetrachatr, a nine-tiered parasol, which symbolizes heaven. A huge carpet fills the hall. Woven into the carpet is the pattern found in the surrounding tiles and the steps leading up to the building. There are two chambers for the king and queen at the back of the hall, which are used only in the week before a coronation when the royal couple were barred from sleeping together. The other adjoining room is used to house the ashes of dead monarchs before they are placed in a royal stupa. Only the main throne room is open to the public. Here there are Buddha images in the left nave, before which the kings would pray each day. The chairs closest to the entrance were reserved for high officials and the others were for visiting ambassadors. The yellow chairs were used by visiting heads of state.

Essential Phnom Penh and around

Finding your feet

Navigating Phnom Penh is reasonably straightforward. Every street is numbered but some major thoroughfares have names too.

Streets
The key to unlocking Phnom Penh's geography is the simple fact that the horizontal streets (east–west) are evenly numbered while odd numbers (north–south) are used for the vertical ones.

Main roads
Monivong and Norodom boulevards are the main roads running north–south, while east–west are Confederation de Russie, Kampuchea Krom and Preah Sihanouk boulevards.

Best places to stay
Amanjaya Pancam, page 235
Anise, page 237
Paragon Hotel, page 237

Orientation
All Phnom Penh lies to the west of the rivers Tonlé Sap and Bassac which run north–south. The best French colonial architecture is on streets 53, 114, 178, Norodom Boulevard and Samdech Sothearos Boulevard. Sisowath Quay, the street which runs along the riverbank, has the highest concentration of restaurants.

Best restaurants
Pop Café de Giorgio, page 239
Romdeng, page 239
Asia Europe Bakery, page 240

Getting around

Hotels can arrange car hire around town and surrounding areas. When travelling on any form of public transport in Phnom Penh, be wary of bag snatchers. For transport details, see page 242.

Tuk-tuk
Fleets of tuk-tuks (*lomphata* in Khmer) provide the nearest thing to taxis.

Motodop
Most visitors use the local *motodops* (motorbike taxis where you ride on the back) as a quick, cheap and efficient way of getting around. Be advised that riding a moto can be risky; wear a helmet.

Public bus
Public buses started operating in Phnom Penh in 2014.

When to go

November to March is best, although it can be cool at higher elevations. Temperatures peak in April. The rainy season is May to October.

Time required

It takes at least a day to see the main sights.

Weather Phnom Penh

Jan	Feb	Mar	Apr	May	Jun	Jul	Aug	Sep	Oct	Nov	Dec
31°C	32°C	34°C	35°C	34°C	33°C	32°C	32°C	31°C	30°C	30°C	30°C

Immediately to the south of the Throne Hall is a small unremarkable building which contains a collection of knick-knacks, curios, swords, small silver ornaments and costumes. There is also a display of the different coloured costumes worn by staff at the Royal Palace each day of the week.

Royal Treasury and Napoleon III Pavillion Built in 1886, the Royal Treasury and the Napoleon III Pavillion – or summerhouse – are to the south of the Throne Hall. The latter was presented by Napoleon III to his Empress Eugenie as accommodation for the princess during the Suez Canal opening celebrations. She later had it dismantled and dispatched it to Phnom Penh as a gift to the king. The elegant building is constructed around a slender wrought-iron frame and is packed with bric-a-brac. Programmes of long-forgotten, but no doubt memorable, royal command dance performances are strewn in glass cases. Upstairs there are some decidedly third-rate portraits and some rather more interesting historical photographs of the royal family. The prefabricated folly was renovated and refurbished in 1990 and its ersatz marble walls remarbled – all with French money – but the graceful building is still showing signs of age and is much in need of more money. "Floor condition is under deterioration" reads one melancholy warning sign. Next to the villa are rooms built in 1959 by Sihanouk to accommodate his cabinet. Beyond is the north gate and the Silver Pagoda enclosure.

★Silver Pagoda
Daily 0730-1100, 1400-1700. US$3, plus US$2 for camera or US$5 for video camera.

Often called the Pagoda of the Emerald Buddha or Wat Preah Keo Morokat after the statue housed here, the Silver Pagoda houses something of a magpie collection. The wooden temple was originally built by King Norodom in 1892 to enshrine royal ashes and then rebuilt by Sihanouk in 1962. The pagoda's steps are of Italian marble, and inside, its floor comprises more than 5000 silver blocks (mostly carpeted over to protect them from the bare feet of visitors) which together weigh nearly six tonnes. All around are cabinets filled with presents from foreign dignitaries. The pagoda is remarkably intact, having been granted special dispensation by the Khmer Rouge, although 60% of the Khmer treasures were stolen from here. In the centre of the pagoda is a magnificent 17th-century emerald Buddha statue made of Baccarat crystal. In front is a 90-kg golden Buddha studded with 9584 diamonds, dating from 1906. It was made from the jewellery of King Norodom and its vital statistics conform exactly to his – a tradition that can be traced back to the god-kings of Angkor. The gold Buddha image is flanked by bronze and silver statues of the Buddha. Under a glass cover is a golden lotus – a Buddhist relic from India. At the back of the room there is a jade Buddha and a palanquin used for coronations which required 12 porters to carry it.

The 600-m-long wall enclosing the Silver Pagoda is galleried; its inward face is covered in frescoes, painted in 1903-1904 by 40 local artists, which depict epic scenes from the Ramayana and numerous scenes of the Silver Pagoda and Royal Palace itself – the story starts by the east gate. The lower part of the fresco has deteriorated alarmingly under the combined assault of children's fingers and rising damp. To the east of the Silver Pagoda is a statue of King Norodom on horseback (it is in fact a statue of Napoleon III with the head replaced with that of the Cambodian monarch). Beyond the statue is a stupa containing the ashes of King Ang Duong (1845-1859). Beyond the stupa, on the south wall, are pavilions containing a footprint of the Buddha (to the east) and a pavilion for royal celebrations (to the west). Next to Phnom Mondap, an artificial hill with a building covering the Buddha's

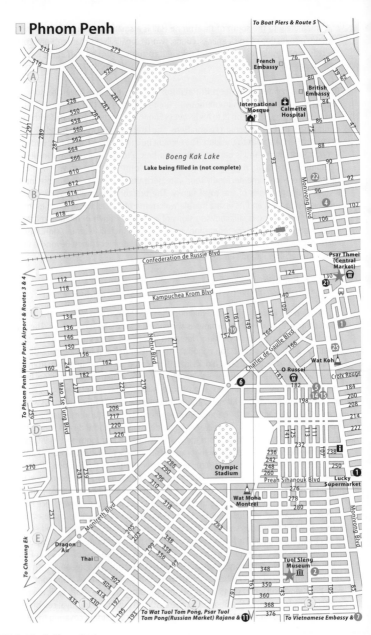

1 Phnom Penh

To Boat Piers & Route 5

French Embassy

British Embassy

International Mosque
Calmette Hospital

Boeng Kak Lake
Lake being filled in (not complete)

Monivong Blvd

Psar Thmei (Central Market)

Confederation de Russie Blvd

Kampuchea Krom Blvd

Nehru Blvd

Charles de Gaulle Blvd

Wat Koh

O Russei

Croix Rouge

Mao Tse Tung Blvd

Olympic Stadium

Preah Sihanouk Blvd

Wat Moha Montrei

Lucky Supermarket

To Phnom Penh Water Park, Airport & Routes 3 & 4

Monireth Blvd

To Choeung Ek

Dragon Air

Thai

Tuol Sleng Museum

To Wat Tuol Tom Pong, Psar Tuol Tom Pong(Russian Market) Rajana &

To Vietnamese Embassy &

To Route 6

Japanese Friendship Bridge

→ **Phnom Penh maps**
1 Phnom Penh, page 228
2 Sisowath Quay, page 231

N

200 metres
200 yards

US Embassy

Tonlé Sap

Wat Phnom

To Siem Reap

Sisowath Quay

Tropical & Travellers Medical Clinic

Psar Chas (Old Market)

Wat Ounalom

National Museum of Cambodia

Royal Palace

Silver Pagoda

Samdech Sothearos Blvd

Sisowath Quay

Norodom Blvd

Samdech Sothearos Blvd

Vietnam Airlines

Monument Books

International SOS Medical & Dental Clinic

Silk Air

Independence Monument

Air France

Lao Airlines

Wat Lang Ka

Vietnam Lao Embassy

To Lao Embassy   To   To   Former US Embassy, Route 1 & Vietnam

Phnom Penh's inhabitants

The population of Phnom Penh seems rural in character and tends to vary from season to season: in the dry season people pour into the capital when there is little work in the countryside but go back to their farms in the wet season when the rice has to be planted.

Phnom Penh has long faced a housing shortage – two-thirds of its houses were damaged by the Khmer Rouge between 1975 and 1979 and the rate of migration into the city exceeds the rate of building. Apart from the sheer cost of building new houses and renovating the crumbling colonial mansions, there has been a severe shortage of skilled workers in Cambodia: under Pol Pot 20,000 engineers were killed and nearly all the country's architects.

Exacerbating the problem is the issue of land ownership as so many people were removed from their homes. These days there are many more qualified workers but sky-rocketing property prices coupled with the confusing issue of land title has created a situation where a great land grab is occurring with people being tossed out of their homes or having them bulldozed to make way for profitable developments.

footprint, in the centre of the south wall is a stupa dedicated to Sihanouk's favourite daughter who died of leukaemia in 1953. On the west wall is a stupa of King Norodom Suramarit with a bell tower in the northwest corner. Beyond the bell tower on the north wall is the mondap (library), originally containing precious Buddhist texts. The whole courtyard is attractively filled with urns and vases containing flowering shrubs.

★National Museum of Cambodia
Entrance is on the corner of streets 13 and 178. Daily 0800-1700. US$3. French- and English-speaking guides are available, mostly excellent.

The National Museum of Cambodia was built in 1920 and contains a collection of Khmer art – notably sculpture – throughout the ages (although some periods are not represented). Galleries are arranged chronologically in a clockwise direction. Most of the exhibits date from the Angkor period but there are several examples from the pre-Angkor era (that is from the kingdoms of Funan, Chenla and Cham). The collection of Buddhas from the sixth and seventh centuries includes a statue of Krishna Bovardhana found at Angkor Borei showing the freedom and grace of early Khmer sculpture. The chief attraction is probably the pre-Angkorian statue of Harihara, found at Prasat Andat near Kompong Thom. There is a fragment from a beautiful bronze statue of Vishnu found in the West Baray at Angkor, as well as frescoes and engraved doors.

Sisowath Quay is Phnom Penh's Left Bank. A broad pavement runs along the side of the river and on the opposite side of the road a rather splendid assemblage of colonial buildings looks out over the broad expanse of waters. The erstwhile administrative buildings and merchants' houses today form an unbroken chain –

2 Sisowath Quay

→ **Phnom Penh maps**
1 Phnom Penh, page 228
2 Sisowath Quay, page 231

N

| 50 metres |
| 50 yards |

Where to stay
Amanjaya Pancam
  & K-West Restaurant **1**
Bougainvillier **2**
Bright Lotus Guesthouse **3**
Dara Reang Sey **9**
Foreign Correspondents
  Club of Cambodia (FCCC)
  & Fresco **12**
Indochine 2 **5**
Paragon **6**
Quay **13**

Restaurants
Cantina **3**
Fortune Pho **15**
Friends **5**
Khmer Borane **9**
La Croisette **10**
Le Wok **18**
Metro **12**
Pop Café de Giorgio **8**
Rising Sun **13**
Veiyo **16**

Bars & clubs
Memphis Pub **17**
Riverhouse Lounge **14**

PHNOM PENH

Background

Phnom Penh lies at the confluence of the Sap, Mekong and Bassac rivers and quickly grew into an important commercial centre. Years of war have taken a heavy toll on the city's infrastructure and economy, as well as its inhabitants. Refugees first began to flood in from the countryside in the early 1950s during the First Indochina War and the population grew from 100,000 to 600,000 by the late 1960s. In the early 1970s there was another surge as people streamed in from the countryside again, this time to escape US bombing and guerrilla warfare. On the eve of the Khmer Rouge takeover in 1975, the capital had a population of two million, but soon became a ghost town. On Pol Pot's orders it was forcibly emptied and the townspeople frog-marched into the countryside to work as labourers. Only 45,000 inhabitants were left in the city in 1975 and a large number were soldiers. In 1979, after four years of virtual abandonment, Phnom Penh had a population of a few thousand. People began to drift back following the Vietnamese invasion (1978-1979) and as hopes for peace rose in 1991, the floodgates opened yet again: today the population is approaching one million.

Phnom Penh has undergone an economic revival since the Paris Peace Accord of 1991. Following the 1998 coup there was a brief exodus of businesses and investors but by 2014 money was pouring back into the city with large developments, including office space, housing and even shopping malls on the rise.

about a kilometre long – of bars and restaurants, with the odd guesthouse thrown in. While foreign tourist commerce fills the street, the quayside itself is dominated by local Khmer families who stroll and sit in the cool of the evening, served by an army of hawkers.

Wat Ounalom
North of the National Museum, at the junction of St 154 and Samdech Sothearos Blvd, facing the Tonlé Sap.

This is Phnom Penh's most important wat. The first building on this site was a monastery, built in 1443 to house a hair of the Buddha. Before 1975, more than 500 monks lived at the wat but the Khmer Rouge murdered the Patriarch and did their best to demolish the capital's principal temple. Nonetheless it remains Cambodian Buddhism's headquarters. The complex has been restored since 1979 although its famous library was completely destroyed. The stupa behind the main sanctuary is the oldest part of the wat.

Wat Phnom and around
a tranquil park and stunning art deco market

The Wat Phnom stands on a small hill and is the temple from which the city takes its name. Be careful when visiting after dark; there have been muggings and bag snatchings.

Wat Phnom ⓘ *Blvd Tou Samouth where it intersects St 96, US$1* was built by a wealthy Khmer lady called Penh in 1372. The sanctuary was rebuilt in 1434, 1890, 1894 and 1926.

The main entrance is to the east; the steps are guarded by nagas and lions. The principal sanctuary is decorated inside with frescoes depicting scenes from Buddha's life and the *Ramayana*. At the front, on a pedestal, is a statue of the Buddha. There is a statue of Penh inside a small pavilion between the vihara and the stupa, with the latter containing the ashes of King Ponhea Yat (1405-1467). The surrounding park is tranquil and a pleasant escape from the madness of the city. Monkeys with attitude are in abundance but they tend to fight among themselves.

West of Wat Phnom is the **National Library** ⓘ *0800-1100 and 1430-1700*, exemplifying the refinement of French colonial architecture. Original construction began in 1924, and the resplendent building was set in blossoming gardens. Not surprisingly and somewhat sacrilegiously, the Khmer Rouge ransacked the building, transforming it into, of all things, a stable. Books were either burnt or thrown out on to the streets. Fortunately many of the discarded books were grabbed by locals who kindly returned them to the library after 1979. There are some antiquated palm-leaf manuscripts, photo documentation from earlier years and some fascinating artworks.

★ Central Market (Psar Thmei)

The stunning Central Market is a perfect example of art deco styling and one of Phnom Penh's most beautiful buildings. Inside, a labyrinth of stalls and hawkers sell everything from jewellery to curios. Those who are after a real bargain are better off heading to the Russian Market where items tend to be much cheaper.

Boeng Kak Lake
10- to 15-min walk northeast of the Central Market.

Boeng Kak Lake will appeal to backpackers as it's well supplied with cheap food and guesthouses. The lakeside setting with the all-important westerly aspect – ie sunsets instead of the sunrises of Sisowath Quay – appeals strongly to the nocturnal instincts of guests (some bars and restaurants open 24 hours a day). The lake was quite beautiful but close to the guesthouses it becomes more like a floating rubbish tip and, with not much lake left, it looks more like a canal. On the water not much differentiates one guesthouse from another – all are of the same ilk. In the eyes of the law, the places on the lake are considered 'squatted' so their future is unsure. The lake has been partially filled and families are being evicted from this area to make way for new development, but many bars and guesthouses are still standing. Local guesthouse owners estimate that it will take another two years to fill the lake completely, but only time will tell how fast it will develop.

South of the centre

gruesome reminders of the recent past

Independence Monument
South of the Royal Palace, between St 268 and Preah Sihanouk Blvd.

The Independence Monument was built in 1958 to commemorate independence but has now assumed the role of a cenotaph. Wat Lang Ka, on the corner of Sihanouk and Norodom boulevards, was another beautiful pagoda that fell victim to Pol Pot's architectural holocaust. Like Wat Ounalom, it was restored in Khmer style on the direction of the Hanoi-backed government in the 1980s.

Wat Lang Ka
Corner of Sihanouk and Norodom Blvd (close to Independence Monument).

Another beautiful pagoda that fell victim to Pol Pot's architectural holocaust but, like Wat Ounalom, it was restored in Khmer style on the direction of the Hanoi-backed government in the 1980s. It is a really soothing get-away from city madness and the monks here are particularly friendly. They hold a free meditation session every Monday and Thursday night at 1800 and anyone is welcome to join in.

★Tuol Sleng Museum (Museum of Genocide)
Southwest from Independence Monument, St 113 (close to St 350), Tue-Sun 0800-1100, 1400-1700; public holidays 0800-1800. US$2; free film at 1000 and 1500.

After 17 April 1975 the classrooms of Tuol Svay Prey High School became the Khmer Rouge main torture and interrogation centre, known as Security Prison 21 – or just S-21. More than 20,000 people were taken from S-21 to be executed at Choeung Ek extermination camp. Countless others died under torture and were thrown into mass graves in the school grounds. Only seven prisoners survived because they were sculptors or artists and could turn out countless busts of Pol Pot.

Classrooms were subdivided into small cells by means of crude brick walls (now liable to topple over). In some rooms there is a metal bedstead and on the wall a fuzzy black and white photograph showing how the room was found in 1979 with a body manacled to the bed. Walls on the stairways often have holes knocked in them and one can all too easily imagine the blood and filth that poured down the stairs making these outlets necessary. The school was converted into a 'museum of genocide' by the Vietnamese (with help from the East Germans who had experience in setting up the Auschwitz Museum). One block of classrooms is given over to photographs of the victims. All the Khmer Rouge victims were methodically numbered and photographed. The pictures on display include those of foreigners who fell into the hands of the Khmer Rouge but the vast majority are Cambodians – men, women, children and babies – all of whom were photographed. Some have obviously just been tortured or raped and stare with loathing and disgust into the camera, while others appear to be unaware of the fate that awaits them. The photographs are quite easily the most poignant and painful part of the museum. One block contains the simple but disturbing weapons of torture. It is a chilling reminder that such sickening violence was done by such everyday objects.

Former US Embassy
Intersection of Norodom and Mao Tse Tung boulevards.

The former US Embassy is now home to the Ministry of Fisheries. As the Khmer Rouge closed in on the city from the north and the south in April 1975, US Ambassador John Gunther Dean pleaded with Secretary of State Henry Kissinger for an urgent airlift of embassy staff. But it was not until the very last minute (just after 1000 on 12 April 1975, with the Khmer Rouge firing mortars from across the Bassac River onto the football pitch near the compound which served as a landing zone) that the last US Marine helicopter left the city. Flight 462, a convoy of military transport helicopters, evacuated the 82 remaining Americans, 159 Cambodians and 35 other foreigners to a US aircraft carrier in the Gulf of Thailand. Their departure was overseen by 360 heavily armed marines. Despite letters from the ambassador to all senior government figures, offering them places on the helicopters, only one, Acting President Saukham Khoy, fled the country. The American airlift was a deathblow to Cambodian morale. Within five days, the Khmer Rouge had taken the city and within hours all senior officials of the former Lon Nol government were executed on the tennis courts of the embassy.

★Choeung Ek
Southwest on Monireth Blvd, about 15 km from town. US$2. Return trip by tuk-tuk US$5-10.

Now in a peaceful setting surrounded by orchards and rice fields, Choeung Ek was the execution ground for the torture victims of Tuol Sleng – the Khmer Rouge interrogation centre, S-21 (see opposite page). It is referred to by some as the **'killing fields'**. Today a huge glass tower stands on the site, filled with the cracked skulls of men, women and children exhumed from 129 mass graves in the area (which were not discovered until 1980). To date 8985 corpses have been exhumed from the site, although researchers believe the number of victims buried is closer to double that figure. The site, once an orchard, is peaceful now, with only the odd bird or quacking duck to break the silence – and rather more numerous children begging. Signs attempt to explain the inexplicable: "The method of massacre which the clique of Pol Pot criminals was carried upon the innocent people of Kampuchea cannot be described fully and clearly in words because the invention of this killing method was strangely cruel. So it is difficult for us to determine who they are for they have the human form but their hearts are demons' hearts …". The really sad part is that Choeung Ek is just one of 4973 grave sites uncovered by the Documentation Centre, dedicated to investigating Khmer Rouge atrocities.

Listings Phnom Penh *maps p228 and p231*

Where to stay

There is now a full range of accommodation options in Phnom Penh with the numerous mid-range 'boutique'-style properties being the best represented. The backpacker area near Boeung Kak Lake has now completely disappeared. Street 182 offers a selection of cheaper alternatives. The websites www.booking.com and www.agoda.com are good starting points for reservations and the cheapest rates. For longer stays contact the properties directly as most are open to negotiating rates. Rates vary according to season.

$$$$ Amanjaya Pancam
Corner of St 154 and Sisowath Quay, T023-219579, www.amanjaya-pancam-hotel.com.
Gorgeous rooms full of amenities, beautiful furniture and creative finishing touches. The balconies have some of the best views on the river. Service can be a little ragged – you'll be asked to pay in full when you check-in – but

they get enough right to make this probably the best place by the river. Free Wi-Fi and awesome breakfast are both included in the room rate. Good location. Recommended.

$$$$ Le Royal
St 92, T023-981888, www.raffles.com/phnom-penh.
A wonderful colonial-era hotel built in 1929 that has been superbly renovated by the Raffles Group. The tasteful renovation incorporates many of the original features and something of the old atmosphere. The hotel has excellent bars, restaurants and a delightful tree-lined pool. 2-for-1 cocktails daily 1600-2000 at the **Elephant Bar** are a must.

$$$$-$$$ Central Mansions
No 1A, St 102, T023-986810, www.centralmansions.com.
Almost brand new and excellent-value serviced apartment block. The rooms are actually 1- or 2-bedroom stylish apartments, complete with cooking facilities and

washing machines. Service is excellent, there's free Wi-Fi, 2 decent-sized swimming pools, and the breakfast (included) at the attached café is very good. Rates vary according to length of stay.

$$$$-$$$ The Quay
277 Sisowath Quay, T023-224894, www.thequayhotel.com.
Another hotel from the FCC people set on the riverfront in a remodelled colonial property. It aspires to create a designer feel, which it partly pulls off, although this is slightly undone by a patchy cheap finish. But there are big tubs, flatscreen TVs, a/c, free Wi-Fi and it's a good location. Also claims to be an 'eco-hotel'.

$$$$-$$$ Sunway
No 1, St 92, T023-430333, www.phnompenh. sunwayhotels.com.
Overlooking Wat Phnom, this is an adequate hotel in an excellent location. 140 ordinary though well-appointed rooms, including 12 spacious suites, provide comfort complemented by facilities and amenities to cater for the international business and leisure traveller.

$$$ Almond Hotel
128F Sothearos Blvd, T023-220822, www.almondhotel.com.kh.
Stylish hotel in an upmarket part of town that offers good value. The more expensive rooms offer the best deal and have huge balconies; the cheaper ones have no windows. A/c, en suite and TV throughout. Breakfast and Wi-Fi included.

$$$ Aram
St 244, T023-211376, www.boddhitree.com.
Nice little guesthouse tucked away in a small street near the palace. The stylish rooms are a bit miniscule and a tad overpriced.

$$$ Bougainvillier Hotel
277G Sisowath Quay, T023-220528, www.bougainvillierhotel.com.
Lovely riverside boutique hotel, rooms decorated in a very edgy, modern Asian theme, with a/c, safe, cable TV and minibar. Good French restaurant.

$$$ Foreign Correspondents Club of Cambodia (FCCC)
363 Sisowath Quay, T023-210142, www.fcccambodia.com.
Known locally as the FCC, this well-known Phnom Penh landmark has 3 decent-sized and stylish rooms, some with balconies overlooking the river.

$$$ Juliana
No 16, St 152, T023-880530, www.julianahotels.com/phnompenh.
A very attractive resort-style hotel with 91 rooms, and decent-sized pool in a secluded garden that provides plenty of shade; several excellent restaurants.

$$$ La Rose Boutique Hotel and Spa
164b Norodom Bvld, T023-211130, www.larose.com.kh.
Great little hotel with sumptuous rooms, excellent and very friendly service, free Wi-Fi and breakfast. The restaurant is a bit hit and miss but the spa treatments are very good. Location on busy Norodom is not for everyone but that shouldn't detract from this being one of the best mid-range options in town.

$$$ The Pavilion
No 227, St 19, T023-222280, www.thepavilion.asia.
A popular and beautiful, 10-room hotel set in a French colonial villa. Each room is different with a/c, en suite and TV. The restaurant serves decent food.

$$$ Rambutan
No 29, St 71, T017-992240, www.rambutanresort.com.
Priding itself as LGBT-friendly, this small hotel is set on a quiet backstreet and has neat, well-designed rooms, all en suite; the pricier ones have bathtubs and balconies. Free Wi-Fi and saltwater pool.

$$$-$$ Amber Villa
No 1A, St 57, T023-216303, www.amber-kh.com.

This friendly, family-run small hotel is often full so book ahead. Rooms include breakfast, laundry and internet; all have a/c and en suite facilities. The best have TV/DVD and balconies.

$$$-$$ La Safran La Suite
No 4, St 282, T023-217646,
www.lesafranlasuite.com.
Stylish, well-designed and well-lit rooms all with a/c, en suite facilities, internet and cable TV. Arty, designer vibe. Small pool outside. Formerly known as the Scadinavian Hotel.

$$ Billabong
No 5, St 158, T023-223703,
www.thebillabonghotel.com.
Reasonably new hotel with well-appointed rooms. Breakfast included. Swimming pool, poolside bar and deluxe rooms with balconies overlooking the pool. Internet.

$$ Dara Reang Sey Hotel
45 Corner St of St 13 and 118 Phsar Chas,
T023-428181, www.darareangsey.com.
Busy hotel with popular local restaurant downstairs, clean rooms with hot water and some rooms have baths.

$$-$ Alibi Villa Guesthouse
Just off Sothearos Blvd (behind Song Tra Ice Cream), T023-987890,
www.alibiguesthouse.com.
Homely city villa with 10 spotless and en suite rooms. Friendly and in a great location. Free Wi-Fi.

$$-$ Anise
No 2C, St 278, T023-222522,
www.anisehotel.com.kh.
Excellent value in the heart of a busy area. All rooms are en suite with cable TV and a/c. Pay a little more and you'll get a room with a bath and private balcony. Included in the price is laundry, internet and breakfast. Recommended.

$$-$ Boddhi Tree Umma
No 50, St 113, T016-865445,
www.boddhitree.com.
A tranquil setting. Lovely old wooden building with guest rooms offering simple

amenities, fan only, some rooms have private bathroom. Great gardens and fantastic food. Very reasonable prices.

$$-$ Bright Lotus Guesthouse
No 22, St 178 (near the museum), T023-990446, www.thebrightlotus1.com.
Fan and a/c rooms with private bathroom and balconies. Restaurant.

$$-$ Golden Gate Hotel
No 9, St 278 (just off St 51), T023-427618,
www.goldengatehotels.com.
Very popular and comparatively good value for the facilities offered. Clean rooms with TV, fridge, hot water and a/c. Within walking distance of restaurants and bars. Visa/MasterCard accepted.

$$-$ Indochine 2 Hotel
No 28-30, St 130, T023-211525,
www.indochine2hotel.com.
Great location and good, clean, comfortable rooms.

$$-$ New York Hotel
256 Monivong Blvd, T023-214116,
www.newyorkhotel.com.kh.
The rooms aren't going to set the world on fire but the facilities are good for the price – massage centre, sauna, restaurant and in-room safe.

$$-$ Paragon Hotel
219b Sisowath Quay, T023-222607,
www.paragonhotel-cambodia.com.
The **Paragon** gets the simple things right – it's a well-run and friendly hotel. The best and priciest rooms have private balconies overlooking the river. The cheaper rooms at the back are dark but still some of the best value in this part of town. Colour TV, hot water and private shower or bath, a/c or fan. Recommended.

$$-$ Walkabout Hotel
Corner of St 51 and St 174, T023-211715,
www.walkabouthotel.com.
A popular Australian-run bar, café and guesthouse. 23 rooms ranging from small with no windows and shared facilities to

large a/c rooms with en suite. Rooms and bathrooms are OK but lower-end rooms are a little gloomy and cell-like. 24-hr bar.

$ Capitol
No 14, St 182, T023-217627,
www.capitolkh.com.
As they say, 'a Phnom Penh institution'. What in 1991 was a single guesthouse has expanded to 5 guesthouses all within a stone's throw. All are aimed at the budget traveller and offer travel services as well as a popular café and internet access.

There are a number of other cheap guesthouses in close proximity, such as **Happy Guesthouse** (next door to **Capitol Guesthouse**) and **Hello Guesthouse** (No 24, St 107).

Restaurants

Most places are relatively inexpensive (US$3-6 per head). There are several cheaper cafés along Monivong Blvd, around the lake, Kampuchea Krom Blvd (St 128) in the city centre and along the river. Generally the food in Phnom Penh is good and the restaurants surprisingly refined.

$$$ Bougainvillier Hotel
See Where to stay.
Upmarket French and Khmer food. Good home-made ice cream.

$$$ Foreign Correspondents Club of Cambodia (FCCC)
See Where to stay.
2nd-floor bar and restaurant that overlooks the Tonlé Sap. Extensive menu with an international flavour – location excellent, food patchy.

$$$ K-West
Amanjaya Hotel, see Where to stay.
Open 0630-2200.
Beautiful, spacious restaurant offering respite from the outside world. Khmer and European food plus extensive cocktail menu.

$$$ Metro
Corner of Sisowath and St 148.
Open 1000-0200.
Huge, affordable tapas portions make this a great spot for lunch or dinner.

$$$ Yi Sang
Ground floor of Almond Hotel, see Where to stay. Open daily.
Serves excellent Cantonese food in 3 sittings: 0630-1030 dim sum and noodles; 1130-1400 dim sum and à la carte; 1730-2200 seafood and à la carte. Some of the best grub in town. Very good quality and great value.

$$ Baan Thai
No 2, St 306, T023-362991. Open 1130-1400 and 1730-2200.
Excellent Thai food and attentive service. Popular restaurant. Garden and old wooden Thai house setting with sit-down cushions.

$$ Boddhi Tree Umma
See Where to stay.
A delightful garden setting and perfect for lunch, a snack or a drink. Salads, sandwiches, barbecue chicken. Very good Khmer food.

$$ Cantina
347 Sisowath Quay, T023-222502,
www.cantinacambodia.com.
Great Mexican restaurant and bar opened by long-time local identity, Hurley Scroggins III. Fantastic food made with the freshest of ingredients. The restaurant attracts an eclectic crowd and can be a source of great company.

$$ The Deli
Near corner of St 178 and Norodom Blvd T012-851234.
Great cakes, bread, salads and lunch at this sleek little diner. Sandwich fillings, for the price, are a bit light, though.

$$ Gasolina
No 56/58, St 57, T012-373009. Open 1100-late.
Huge garden and decent French-inspired food await in this friendly, relaxed restaurant. The owner also arranges t'ai chi and capoeira

classes. They normally have a barbecue at the weekends.

$$ Khmer Borane
99 Sisowath Quay, www.borane.net.
Excellent Khmer restaurant with wide selection of very well-prepared Khmer and Thai food. Try the Amok.

$$ La Croisette
241 Sisowath Quay, T023-882221.
Authentically French and good-value hors d'oeuvres and steak. Good selection of wines.

$$ La Marmite
No 80, St 108 (on the corner with Pasteur), T012-391746. Wed-Mon.
Excellent-value French food – some of the best in town. Extremely large portions.

$$ Le Wok
No 33, St 178, T09-821857. Daily 0800-2200.
French-inspired Asian food served in this friendly little restaurant located on fashionable street 178. Daily fixed lunch menus and à la carte.

$$ Ma Ma
St 51, T023-692 2813.
Very popular with the Thai community for good reason, this family-run Thai eatery sells some of the most authentic Thai food in town.

$$ Mount Everest
No 63, St 294, T012-706274. Open 1000-2200.
Has served acclaimed Nepalese and Indian dishes for several years, attracting a loyal following. There's also a branch in Siem Reap.

$$ Pop Café de Giorgio
371 Sisowath Quay, T012-562892. Open 1100-1430 and 1800-2200.
Almost perfect, small, Italian restaurant sited next door to the FCC. Owned and managed by expat Giorgio, the food has all the panache you'd expect from an Italian. The home-made lasagne is probably one of the best-value meals in town. Recommended.

$$ Pyong Yang Restaurant
400 Monivong Blvd, T023-993765.
This North Korean restaurant is an all-round experience not to be missed. The food is exceptional but you need to get there before 1900 to get a seat before their nightly show starts. All very bizarre: uniformed, clone-like waitresses double as singers in the nightly show, which later turns into open-mic karaoke.

$$ Rising Sun
No 20, St 178 (just round the corner from the FCC).
English restaurant with possibly the best breakfast in town. Enormous roasts and excellent iced coffee.

$$ Romdeng
No 74, St 174, T092-2153 5037, romdeng@ mithsamlanh.org. Open 1100-2100.
Sister restaurant to **Friends** (see below), helping out former street kids. Serves exclusively Khmer foods. Watch out for specials like fried tarantula with chilli and garlic. Highly recommended.

$$ Veiyo (River Breeze)
237 Sisowath Quay, T012-847419.
Pizza and pasta, along with Thai and Khmer cuisine.

$ 53
St 370. Open lunchtime-late.
Big open-plan friendly Khmer restaurant with decent Khmer food. This is where the locals eat and the place can be noisy and rammed full on a busy evening. Good value.

$ Fortune Pho
St 178, just behind the FCC. Open 0800-2100.
This small shop offers great Vietnamese, with an authentic and amusingly brusque service.

$ Friends
No 215, St 13, T023-426748.
Non-profit restaurant run by street kids being trained in the hospitality industry. The food is delicious and cheap.

$ Sam Doo
56 Kampuchea Krom Blvd, T023-218773. Open until 0200.

Late-night Chinese food and the best and cheapest dim sum in town.

$ The Shop
No 39, St 240, T012-901964. 0900-1800.
Deli and bakery serving sandwiches, juices, fruit teas, salads and lunches.

Cafés and bakeries
Several café and bakery chains have opened up across Phnom Penh. **Brown Coffee**, www.browncoffee.com.kh, is locally owned and has several oulets selling great coffee, decent cakes and snacks. Another is the Singaporean **Ya Kun Coffee and Toast** on St 322 and at the new Aeon shopping mall.

Asia Europe Bakery
No 95 Sihanouk Blvd, T012-893177.
One of the few Western-style bakery/cafés in the city. Delicious pastries, cakes and excellent breakfast and lunch menu. Recommended.

Fresco
365 Sisowath Quay, just underneath the FCC, T023-217041.
Same owners as FCC. Has a wide selection of sandwiches, cakes and pastries of mixed quality and high price.

Garden Centre Café
No 23, St 57, T023-363002.
Popular place to go for lunch and breakfast. Perhaps not surprisingly, the garden is nice too.

Jars of Clay
No 39 St 155 (beside the Russian Market).
Fresh cakes and pastries.

Java
No 56 Sihanouk Blvd.
Contenders for best coffee in town. Good use of space, with open-air balcony and pleasant surroundings. Delightful food. Features art and photography exhibitions on a regular basis.

La Gourmandise Bleue
159 St 278, T023-994019. Tue-Sun 0700-2000.
Sweet little French/North African bakery serving almost perfect cakes and coffee. Famous for its macaroons and also does couscous dishes.

T&C Coffee World
Numerous branches – 369 Preah Sihanouk Blvd; Sorya Shopping Centre; 335 Monivong Blvd.
Vietnamese-run equivalent of Starbucks, but better. Surprisingly good food and very good coffee. Faultless service.

Bars and clubs

Blue Chilli
No 36, St 178, T012-566353. Open 1800-late.
Gay bar with DJ and dancing. Drag show on Sat.

Elephant Bar
Le Royal Hotel, see Where to stay.
Open until 2400.
Stylish and elegant bar in Phnom Penh's top hotel, perfect for an evening gin. 2-for-1 happy hour every day with unending supply of nachos, which makes for a cheap night out in sophisticated surroundings. Probably the best drinks in town.

Foreign Correspondents Club of Cambodia (FCCC)
See Where to stay.
Perfect location overlooking the river, with satellite TV and pool. *Bangkok Post* and *The Nation* both available for reading here. Happy hour 1700-1900.

Heart of Darkness
No 26, St 51. Open late.
Reasonable prices and friendly staff. Has been Phnom Penh's most popular hangout for a number of years. Full of prostitutes, but your best bet for a night of dancing. There have been many violent incidents here, so it is advisable to be on your best behaviour in the bar as they do not tolerate any provocation.

Metro

See Restaurants. Open 1000-0200.
Serves fine grub and is home to a fabulous bar. Popular with wealthy Khmers and expats. Recommended.

Riverhouse Lounge

No 6, St 110 Sisowath Quay. Open 1600-0200.
Upmarket cocktail bar and club. Views of the river and airy open balcony space. Live music (Sun) and DJs (Sat).

Sharkys

No 126, St 130.
"Beware pickpockets and loose women", it warns. Large, plenty of pool tables and food served until late. Quite a 'blokey' hangout.

Talking to a Stranger

No 21, St 294, T012-798530.
Great cocktails, relaxed atmosphere. Recommended.

Entertainment

Pick up a copy of the Cambodia Daily and check out the back page for details of up-and-coming events.

Dance

National Museum of Cambodia, *St 70.* Folk and national dances are performed by the National Dance group as well as shadow puppets and circus. Fri and Sat 1930, US$4.

Live music

Memphis Pub, *St 118 (off Sisowath Quay)*, open until 0200. Small bar off the river, very loyal following from the NGO crowd. Live rock and blues music from Tue-Sat.
Riverhouse Lounge, *see Bars and clubs.* Usually has a guest DJ at weekends and live jazz on Tue and Sun.

Shopping

Art galleries

Reyum Institute of Arts and Culture, *No 4, St 178, T023-217149, www.reyum.org. Open 0800-1800.* This is a great place to start for those interested in Cambodian modern art. Some world-class artists have been mentored and exhibit here.

Handicrafts

Many non-profit organizations have opened stores to help train or rehabilitate some of the country's under-privileged.
Bare Necessities, *No 46 St 322, T023-996664.* Selling a range of bras and underwear which fit Western sizes, from maternity to sporty to sexy. A social enterprise raising money to support awareness and treatment of breast cancer for poor, rural Cambodian women.
Disabled Handicrafts Promotion Association, *No 317, St 63.* Handicrafts and jewellery made by people with disabilities.
The National Centre for Disabled People, *3 Norodom, T023-210140.* Great store with handicrafts such as pillow cases, tapestries and bags made by people with disabilities.
Nyemo, *No 71 St 240 between St 63 and Monivong Blvd, www.nyemo.com.* Supports vulnerable women and children by teaching skills such as sewing and weaving, which are then sold to raise funds. Also runs a restaurant and hotel.
Orange River, *361 Sisowath Quay (under FCCC), T023-214594.* Has a selection of beautifully designed decorative items and a very good stock of fabrics and silks which will leave many wishing for more luggage allowance. Pricier than most other stores.
Rajana, *No 170, St 450, next to the Russian Market.* Traditional crafts.
Silk & Pepper, *33 St 178 (next door to Le Wok, see Restaurants).* Sleek, Khmer-inspired fashions and silks. Also sells Kampot pepper in little china pots.

Markets

Psar Thmei (Central Covered Market), *just off Monivong Blvd.* Distinguished by its central art deco dome (built 1937), it is mostly full of stalls selling silver and gold jewellery, old coins and assorted fake antiques. Around the main building more mundane items are for sale, including, of course, *kramas,* the famous Cambodian checked scarf. The main gates into the Central Market are lined with stalls selling touristy items.

Tuol Tom Pong, *between St 155 and St 163 to east and west, and St 440 and St 450 to north and south.* Known to many as the Russian Market. Sells a huge range of goods, fabrics and an immense variety of tobacco – an excellent place for buying souvenirs, especially silk. Most things at this market are about half the price of the Central Market.

Shopping centres

Aeon Mall, *Sothearos Bvld, next to the Russian Embassy, www.aeonmallphnompenh.com.* Cambodia's first full-blown, gargantuan shopping mall. For Western travellers it might not represent their fantasy of what 'authentic Khmer culture' looks like but this is shaping up to be THE spot where young Phnom Penhites want to be seen. Lots to eat, lots to buy – worth a look.

Sorya Shopping Centre, *St 63, beside the Central Market.* 7-floor, a/c shopping centre. It even has a skating rink.

Silverware and jewellery

Old silver boxes, belts, antique jewellery can be found along **Monivong Blvd** (the main thoroughfare). **Samdech Sothearos Blvd**, just north of St 184, has a good cluster of silver shops.

Supermarkets

Sharky Mart, *No 124, St 130 (below Sharkys Bar), T023-990303.* 24-hr convenience store.

Cookery courses

Cambodia Cooking Class, *No 14, St 285, T023-882314, www.cambodia-cooking-class.com.*

Language classes

The Khmer School of Language, *No 529, St 454, Tuol Tumpung 2, Chamcar Morn, T023-213047, www.cambcomm.org.uk/ksl.*

Tour operators

Asia Pacific Travel, *www.asiapacifictravel.vn.* Operates tours throughout Vietnam, Cambodia and Laos.

Asian Trails, *No 22, St 294, PO Box 621, Sangkat Boeng Keng Kong I, Khan Chamkarmorn, T023-216555, www.asiantrails.travel.* Offers a broad selection of tours: Angkor, river cruises, remote tours, biking trips.

Capitol Tours, *No 14, St 182 (see Capitol Guesthouse), T023-217627, www.bigpond.com. kh/users/capitol.* Cheap tours around Phnom Penh's main sites and tours around the country. Targeted at budget travellers.

Exotissimo Travel, *6th floor, SSN Center No 66 Norodom Blvd, T023-218948, www.exotissimo. com.* Wide range of day trips and classic tours covering mainstream destinations.

PTM Tours, *No 333B Monivong Blvd, T023-219161, www.ptm-travel.com.* Reasonably priced package tours to Angkor and around Phnom Penh. Offers cheap hotel reservations.

RTR Tours, *No 54E Charles de Gaulle Blvd, T023-210468, www.rtrtours.com.kh.* Tours and travel services. Friendly and helpful.

Air

Siem Reap Airways and the national carrier, **Cambodia Angkor Air**, have connections with Siem Reap. Book in advance. All departure taxes are now included in the ticket price.

Bicycle

Hire from guesthouses for about US$1 per day.

Boat

Fast boats to **Siem Reap** depart from the tourist boat dock on Sisowath Quay at the end of 106 St (5 hrs, US$35). Ferries leave from wharves on the river north of the Japanese Friendship Bridge. All boats leave early, 0700 or earlier. Most hotels will supply ferry tickets.

Bus

Long distance Most buses leave southwest of Psar Thmei (Central Market) by the Shell petrol station. All the companies mentioned here run a service between **Siem Reap** and Phnom Penh. **Capitol Tours**, T023-217627, departs from its terminal, No 14, St 182. **GST**, T012-895550, departs from the southwest corner of the Central Market (corner of St 142). **Phnom Penh Public Transport Co** (formerly Ho Wah Genting Bus Company), T023-210359, departs from Charles de Gaulle Blvd, near the Central Market. To **Kratie**, 1 bus per day (US$4); **Capitol Tours** runs a bus to **Kampot**, 0700 and 1300, US$3.50. There are also frequent departures from the Central Market (Psar Thmei) bus terminal. **Phnom Penh Bus Co** to **Sihanoukville**, 5 times daily. **GST** buses leave 4 times daily, 4 hrs. To **Siem Reap**, see page 281. **Virak Buntham Express Travel**, St 106, on the riverfront opposite the Night Market, T012-322302, runs buses to and from **Koh Kong**, 0800. To **Stung Treng** the Soyra bus, Central Bus Station, T023-210359, leaves Phnom Penh at 0715, US$10. The **Soyra** bus also leaves for **Banlung**, Ratanakiri at 0700.

International Buses from Phnom Penh to **Ho Chi Minh City** depart daily (**Phnom Penh Public Transport Co, Capitol Tour, Soyra, Mekong Express**), 8 hrs, US$9-12. The **Soyra** bus company and **Mekong Express** run a daily bus to **Bangkok** from Phnom Penh, 0630 and 0730, US$9. The **Soyra** bus company also runs frequent routes to Laos and leaves Phnom Penh for **Pakse** every morning at 0645, US$27.

Car

Car Rental, T012-950950. Chauffeur-driven cars are available at most hotels from US$25 per day upwards. Several travel agents will also hire cars. Prices increase if you're venturing out of town.
Phnom Penh Taxi Driver, T016-886544, www.phnompenhtaxidriver.com. Great little tour and taxi company run by the super-friendly Mr Ben. He speaks good English, has superb knowledge of Cambodia, offers excellent rates (no real need to haggle) and does everything from airport runs to full tours of the country. Highly recommended.

Cyclo

Plentiful but slow. Fares can be negotiated but are not that cheap – a short journey should be no more than 1000 riel. A few cyclo drivers speak English or French. They are most likely to be found loitering around the big hotels and can also be hired for the day (around US$5).

Moto

'Motodops' are 50-100cc motorbike taxis and the fastest way to get around Phnom Penh. Standard cost per journey is around US$0.50 for a short hop but expect to pay double after dark. If you find a good, English-speaking moto driver, hang on to him and he can be yours for US$8-10 per day.

Shared taxi

These are either Toyota pickups or saloons. For the pickups the fare depends upon whether you wish to sit inside or in the open; vehicles depart when the driver has enough fares. Psar Chbam Pao, just over Monivong Bridge on Route 1, for **Vietnam**. For **Sihanoukville** and **Siem Riep**, shared taxis from the Central Market (Psar Thmei) leave 0500-0600. Shared taxi to **Kampot** takes 2-3 hrs, US$4, leaving from Doeum Kor Market on Mao Tse Tung Blvd.

Taxi

There are only a few taxis in Phnom Penh. It is possible to get a taxi into town from the airport and 1 or 2 taxi companies can be reached by telephone but don't expect to flag one down on the street. Phnom Penh hotels will organize private taxis to Sihanoukville for US$40-50.
Global Taxi, T011-311888, T092-889962, is Phnom Penh's 1st meter taxi service. US$1 at flagfall for 1st 2 km then US$0.10 per km. On call 24/7. **Taxi Vantha**, T012-855000/T023-982542, 24 hrs.

Angkor
& Central Cambodia

finest Khmer site with simple floating villages

A vast and elaborately detailed complex, the ancient temple city of Angkor Wat has remained the heart and soul of Cambodia for almost two millennia. And, despite the ever-growing throngs of visitors, this historical site still exceeds expectation.

Included in the gargantuan complex lie legions of magical temples which attest to the ability of bygone artisans. Visitors also flock to jungle-clad Ta Prohm, where tenatacle-like foliage entwined around the temple provides an insight into how earlier explorers would have discovered it.

The town of Siem Reap has graduated from Angkor's service centre to an international tourist hub, teeming with modern restaurants and upmarket hotels. Fortunately the settlement still retains much if its original charm. A short trip from Siem Reap is the Tonlé Sap, Southeast Asia's largest freshwater lake, scattered with many floating villages.

If you travel by road from Phnom Penh to Angkor you'll pass through Kompong and Cambodia's Central Region. You will be rewarded with amazing temples, beautiful jungle scenery and some of the friendliest villages in the country.

Best for
Architecture ▪ History ▪ Restaurants ▪ Shopping

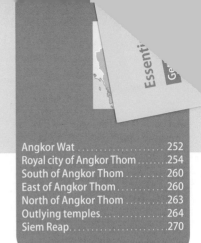

Footprint
picks

★ **Angkor Wat**, page 252
The largest religious monument
in the world.

★ **Angkor Thom**, page 254
With its spectacular Bayon, this was the last capital of the
Angkorian empire.

★ **Ta Prohm**, page 260
One of the most enchanting temples, surrounded by fig trees
and creepers.

★ **Preah Khan**, page 263
A sprawling monastic complex in the middle of nowhere.

★ **Banteay Srei**, page 266
Angkor's most beautiful and intricate carvings.

★ **Tonlé Sap**, page 270
Supporting numerous floating villages, Tonlé Sap is the largest
freshwater lake in Southeast Asia.

Getting around

Angkor Thom is in the centre of the temple complex, about 4 km away from Angkor Wat and Preah Khan. One road connects the temples. Most of the temples within the Angkor complex (except the Roluos Group) are located in an area 8 km north of Siem Reap, with the area extending across a 25-km radius. The Roluos Group is 13 km east of Siem Reap and further away is Banteay Srei (32 km).

Snapshot

Cambodia Angkor Air offers several daily flights between Siem Reap and Phnom Penh. (There are also now thrice-weekly flights to/from Sihanoukville.) From July-March daily **river ferries** ply the Tonlé Sap river and lake between Phnom Penh and Siem Reap.

Bicycle Bicycle hire, US$2-3 per day from most guesthouses, represents a nice option for those who feel reasonably familiar with the area. The **White Bicycles** scheme, www. thewhitebicycles.org, set up by Norwegian expats, offers bikes for US$2 per day with US$1.50 of that going straight into local charities and no commission to the hotels. If you only have a day or two to explore you won't be able to cover many of the temples on a pedal bike due to the searing temperatures and sprawling layout. Angkor Wat and Banteay Srei have official bicycle parking sites (1000 riel) and at the other temples you can quite safely park and lock your bikes in front of a drink stall.

Car with driver and guide These are available from larger hotels for US$25-30 per day plus US$25 for a guide. An excellent service is provided by **Mr Hak**, T012-540336, www.angkortaxidriver.com, who offers packages and tours around Angkor and the surrounding area. The **Angkor Tour Guide Association** and most other travel agencies can also organize this.

Elephant These are stationed near the Bayon or at the South Gate of Angkor Thom during the day. In the evenings, they are located at the bottom of Phnom Bakheng, taking tourists up to the summit for sunset.

Helicopter You can also charter a helicopter, see page 279.

Moto Expect to pay US$10-12 per day for a moto unless the driver speaks good English, in which case the price will be higher. This price will cover trips to the Roluos Group of temples but not to Banteay Srei. No need to add more than a dollar or two to the price for getting to Banteay Srei unless the driver is also a guide and can demonstrate that he is genuinely going to show you around.

Tuk-tuk have appeared in recent years and a trip to the temples on a motorbike-drawn cart is a popular option for two people, U$14-17 a day.

Guides

Guides can be invaluable when navigating the temples. Most hotels and travel agents will be able to point you in the direction of a good guide. The **Khmer Angkor Tour Guide Association**, on the road to Angkor, T063-964347, www.khmerangkortourguide.com, has well-trained and well-briefed guides; some speak English better than others. The going rate is US$20-25 per day.

Temple fees and hours

The **Angkor Pass** can only be bought at official ticket booths, which are on the road from Siem Reap to Angkor Wat. The checkpoint on the road from the airport to Angkor Wat and the checkpoint at Banteay

Srei also have one-day Angkor Passes, but not three-day and seven-day passes.

A **one-day** pass costs US$20, three-day pass US$40, **seven-day** pass US$60 (free for children under 12) and must be paid in cash (US dollars, Cambodian riel, Thai baht or euro accepted). Passes for **three** and **seven days** are issued with a photograph, which is taken on location. The seven-day pass is valid for any seven days (they don't have to be consecutive) one month from the purchase date. Most people will be able to cover the majority of the temples within three days. If you buy your ticket after 1715 the day before, you get a free sunset thrown in. The complex is open daily 0500-1800.

You will need to pay additional fees if you wish to visit Beng Melea (US$5), Phnom Kulen (US$20) or Koh Ker (US$10); payable at the individual sites.

Beating the crowds

Avoiding traffic within the Angkor complex is difficult but achievable. If you reverse the order of the standard tours, peak hour traffic at major temples is dramatically reduced. As many tour groups troop into Siem Reap for lunch this is an opportune time to catch a peaceful moment in the complex, just bring a packed lunch.

To avoid the masses at the draw-card attraction, Angkor Wat, try to walk around the temple, as opposed to through it. Sunset at Phnom Bakheng has turned into a circus fiasco, so aim for Angkor or the Bayon at this time as they are both quiet in comparison.

Security

Landmines planted on some outlying paths have nearly all been cleared, but it is still safer to stick to well-used paths. Be wary of snakes in the dry season. The very poisonours Hanuman snake (lurid green) is fairly common in the area.

Sunrise is still relatively peaceful at Angkor, grab yourself the prime position behind the left-hand pond (you need to depart Siem Reap no later than 0530), though there are other stunning early morning options, such as Srah Srang or Bakong. Bakheng gives a beautiful vista of Angkor in the early-mid morning.

When to go

November-February (the driest and coolest time of year, which can still be unbearably hot). This is the peak visitor season and so can be crowded. The monsoon is from June to October/November. At this time it can get very muddy but it's a great time to photograph the temples as the foliage is lush and there is less dust. April can be furnace-like and unpleasantly dusty.

Tip...

Everybody wants to visit Angkor Wat and Angkor Thom, but do visit Ta Prohm, which has been left in an unrestored state; you will certainly get the atmosphere, especially if you go late afternoon.

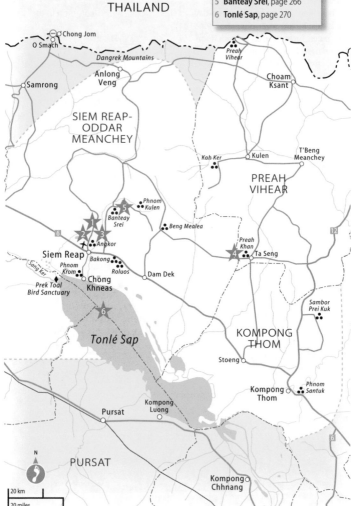

THAILAND

Chong Jom

O Smach

Dangrek Mountains

Preah Vihear

Samrong

Anlong Veng

Choam Ksant

SIEM REAP-
ODDAR
MEANCHEY

Koh Ker

Kulen

T'Beng Meanchey

PREAH VIHEAR

Phnom Kulen

5 *Banteay Srei*

Beng Mealea

Angkor

Siem Reap

Bakong

Preah Khan

Ta Seng

12

Phnom Krom

Roluos

Dam Dek

Sang Ker

Prek Toal Bird Sanctuary

Chong Khneas

Sambor Prei Kuk

6

Tonlé Sap

KOMPONG THOM

Stoeng

Kompong Thom

Phnom Santuk

Kompong Luong

Pursat

PURSAT

6

Kompong Chhnang

N

20 km
20 miles

Sights
Angkor

The huge temple complex of Angkor, the ancient capital of the powerful Khmer Empire, is one of the archaeological treasures of Asia and the spiritual and cultural heart of Cambodia. Angkor Wat is arguably the greatest temple within the complex, both in terms of grandeur and sheer magnitude. After all, it is the biggest religious monument in the world, its outer walls clad with one of the longest continuous bas-relief ever created. The diverse architectural prowess and dexterity of thousands of artisans is testified by around 100 brilliant monuments in the area. Of these, the Bayon (with its beaming smiles), Banteay Srei (which features the finest intricate carvings) and the jungle temple of Ta Prohm are unmissable. However, some people prefer the understated but equally brilliant temples of Neak Pean, Preah Khan and Pre Rup.

The temples are scattered over an area in excess of 160 sq km. There are three so-called 'circuits'. The **Petit Circuit** takes in the main central temples including Angkor Wat, Bayon, Baphuon and the Terrace of the Elephants. The **Grand Circuit** takes a wider route, including smaller temples like Ta Prohm, East

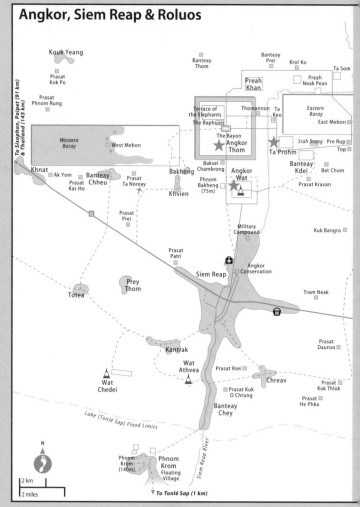

Angkor, Siem Reap & Roluos

Mebon and Neak Pean. The **Roluos Group Circuit** ventures further afield still, taking in the temples near Roluos: Lolei, Preah Ko and Bakong. Here are some options for visiting Angkor's temples:

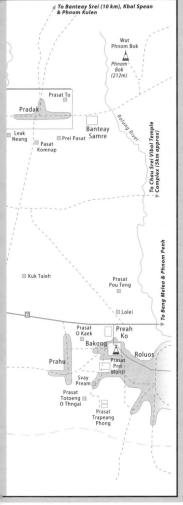

Half day
South Gate of Angkor Thom, Bayon, Angkor Wat.

One day Angkor Wat (sunrise or sunset), South Gate of Angkor Thom, Angkor Thom Complex (Bayon, Elephant Terrace, Royal Palace) and Ta Prohm. This is a hefty schedule for one day; you'll need to arrive after 1615 and finish just after 1700 the following day.

Two days The same as above but with the inclusion of the rest of the Angkor Thom, Preah Khan, Srah Srang (sunrise) and, at a push, Banteay Srei.

Three days **Day 1** Sunrise at Angkor Wat; morning South Gate of Angkor Thom, Angkor Thom complex (aside from Bayon); Ta Prohm; late afternoon-sunset at the Bayon.

Day 2 Sunrise Srah Srang; morning Banteay Kdei and Banteay Srei; late afternoon Preah Khan; sunset at Angkor Wat.

Day 3 Sunrise and morning Roluos; afternoon Ta Keo and sunset either at Bakheng or Angkor Wat.

Those choosing to stay one or two days longer should try to work Banteay Samre, East Mebon, Neak Pean and Thomannon into their itinerary. A further two to three days warrants a trip to Prasat Kravan, Ta Som, Beng Melea and Kbal Spean.

★The awe-inspiring sight of Angkor Wat first thing in the morning is something you're not likely to forget. Constructed between 1113 and 1150, it is believed to be the biggest religious monument ever built and certainly one of the most spectacular. British historian Arnold Toynbee said in his book *East to West* that: "Angkor is not orchestral; it is monumental." That sums it up. The temple complex covers 81 ha and is comparable in size to the Imperial Palace in Beijing. Its five towers are emblazoned on the Cambodian flag and the 12th-century masterpiece is considered by art historians to be the prime example of Classical Khmer art and architecture. It took more than 30 years to build and is contemporary with Nôtre-Dame in Paris and Durham Cathedral in England. The temple is dedicated to the Hindu god Vishnu, personified in earthly form by its builder, the god-king Suryavarman II, and is aligned east to west.

Construction and orientation

Angkor Wat differs from other temples primarily because it is facing westward, symbolically the direction of death, leading many to believe it was a tomb. However, as Vishnu is associated with the west, it is now generally accepted that it served both as a temple and a mausoleum for the king. The sandstone was probably quarried from a far-away mine and floated down the Siem Reap river on rafts. Like other Khmer temple mountains, Angkor Wat is an architectural allegory, depicting in stone the epic tales of Hindu mythology. The central sanctuary of the temple complex represents the sacred Mount Meru, the centre of the Hindu universe, on whose summit the gods reside. Angkor Wat's five towers symbolize Meru's five peaks; the enclosing wall represents the mountains at the edge of the world and the surrounding moat, the ocean beyond.

Angkor Wat was found in much better condition than most of the other temples in the complex because it seems to have been continuously inhabited by Buddhist monks after the Thais invaded in 1431. They were able to keep back the encroaching jungle. A giant stone Buddha was placed in the hall of the highest central tower, formerly sacred to the Hindu god, Vishnu. Three modern Buddhist monasteries flank the wat.

The complex

The temple complex is enclosed by a **square moat** – more than 5 km long and 190 m wide – and a high, galleried wall, which is covered in epic bas-reliefs and has four ceremonial tower gateways. The main gateway faces west and the temple is approached by a 475-m-long road, built along a **causeway**, which is lined with **naga balustrades**. There are small rectangular barays on either side of the roadway. To either side of the balustrades are two isolated buildings, thought to have been **libraries** – there are two more pairs of them within the temple precincts on the first and second terraces.

At the far end of the causeway stands a **cruciform platform**, guarded by stone lions, from which the devaraja may have held audiences; his backdrop being the three-tiered central sanctuary. Commonly referred to as the **Terrace of Honour**, it is entered through the colonnaded processional gateway of the outer gallery. The transitional enclosure beyond it is again cruciform in shape. Its four quadrants formed galleries, once stocked full of statues of the Buddha. Only a handful of the original 1000-odd images remain. Each gallery also had a basin which would originally have contained water for priests'

ritual ablution. The second terrace, which is also square, rises from behind
Thousand Buddhas. It has a tower at each corner.

The cluster of **central towers**, 12 m above the second terrace, is reach
stairways which represent the precipitous slopes of Mount Meru. Many his
that the upwards hike to this terrace was reserved for the high priests an... ...mself.
Today, anyone is welcome but the difficult climb is best handled slowly by stepping
sideways up the steep incline. The five lotus flower-shaped sandstone towers – the first
appearance of these features in Khmer architecture – are believed to have once been
covered in gold. The eight-storey towers are square, although they appear octagonal,
and give the impression of a sprouting bud. Above the ascending tiers of roofs – each
jutting gable has an elaborately carved pediment – the tower tapers into a circular roof.
A quincunx shape is formed by the towers with four on each corner and another marking
the centre. The central tower is dominant, and is the Siva shrine and principal sanctuary,
whose pinnacle rises more than 30 m above the third level and 55 m above ground level.
This sanctuary would have contained an image of Siva in the likeness of King Suryavarman
II, as it was his temple-mountain. But it is now a Buddhist shrine and contains statues of the
Buddha. The steps leading up to the third level are worn and very steep. On the south side
the steps have a hand rail (not recommended for vertigo sufferers).

Bas-reliefs

Over 1000 sq m of bas-relief decorate the temple. Its greatest sculptural treasure is the
2-m-high bas-relief, around the walls of the outer gallery. It is the longest continuous bas-
relief in the world. In some areas traces of the paint and gilt that once covered the carvings
can still be seen. Most famous are the hundreds of figures of devatas and apsaras in niches
along the walls. The apsaras – the celestial women – are modelled on the god-king's own
bevy of bare-breasted beauties and the sculptors' attention to detail provides an insight
into the world of 12th-century haute couture. Their hair is often knotted on the crown and
bejewelled – although all manner of wild and exotic coiffures are depicted. Jewelled collars
and hip-girdles also are common and bracelets worn on the upper arms. Sadly many of the
apsaras have been removed in recent years.

The bas-reliefs narrate stories from the *Ramayana* and *Mahabharata*, as well as legends
of Vishnu, and are reminiscent of Pallava and Chola art in southeast India. Pious artisans
and peasants were probably only allowed as far as Angkor Wat's outer gallery, where they
could admire the bas-reliefs and pay homage to the god-king. In the open courtyards,
statues of animals enliven the walls. Lions stand on guard beside the staircases. There were
supposed to be 300 of them in the original building. Part of the bas-reliefs were hit by
shrapnel in 1972, and some of its apsaras were used for target practice.

Temple surrounds

One of the great delights of Angkor, particularly at Angkor Wat, are the glorious trees. Huge
tropical trees grow in Angkor's forests – a reminder of how much of Cambodia used to look.
Driving out to Angkor from Siem Reap, the flat landscape is largely bare of trees but inside
the protected area forests flourish. High in the treetops birds sing and call to each other all
day. The wildlife, whose motto seems to be 'always watching: always waiting', is an integral
part of Angkor. Keeping the prising tentacles and smothering creepers at bay requires
constant vigilance and a sharp blade. A great deal of archaeology is still concealed in the
embrace of the forest and exploring the less beaten paths often reveals some unknown
and unmapped ruin.

Anti-clockwise around the bas-reliefs

1 Western gallery The southern half represents a scene from the *Mahabharata* of a battle between the Pandavas (with pointed head dresses, attacking from the right) and the Kauravas. The two armies come from the two ends of the panel and meet in the middle. The southwest corner has been badly damaged – some say by the Khmer Rouge – but shows scenes from Vishnu's life.

2 Southern gallery The western half depicts Suryavarman II (builder of Angkor Wat) leading a procession. He is riding a royal elephant, giving orders to his army before leading them into battle against the Cham. The rank of the army officers is indicated by the number of umbrellas. The undisciplined, outlandishly dressed figures are the Thais.

3 Southern gallery The eastern half was restored in 1946 and depicts the punishments and rewards one can expect in the after life. The damned are depicted in the bottom row, while the blessed, depicted in the upper two rows, are borne along in palanquins surrounded by large numbers of bare-breasted apsaras.

4 Eastern gallery The southern half is the best-known part of the bas-relief – the churning of the sea of milk by gods and demons to make ambrosia (the nectar of the gods which gives immortality). In the centre, Vishnu commands the operation. Below are sea animals and above, apsaras.

5 Eastern gallery The northern half is an unfinished representation of a war between the gods for the possession of the ambrosia. The gate in the centre was used by Khmer royalty and dignitaries for mounting and dismounting elephants.

★Royal city of Angkor Thom

the empire's massive administrative centre contains the imposing Bayon

Construction

Construction of Jayavarman VII's spacious walled capital, Angkor Thom (which means 'great city'), began at the end of the 12th century: he rebuilt the capital after it had been captured and destroyed by the Cham. Angkor Thom was colossal – the 100-m-wide moat surrounding the city, which was probably stocked with crocodiles as a protection against the enemy, extended more than 12 km. Inside the moat was an 8-m-high stone wall, buttressed on the inner side by a high mound of earth along the top of which ran a terrace for troops to man the ramparts.

The area within the walls was more spacious than that of any walled city in medieval Europe – it could easily have encompassed the whole of ancient Rome. Yet it is believed that this enclosure, like the Forbidden City in Beijing, was only a royal, religious and administrative centre accommodating the court and dignitaries. The rest of the population lived outside the walls between the two artificial lakes – the east and west barays – and along the Siem Reap River.

6 Northern gallery Represents a war between gods and demons. Siva is shown in meditation with Ganesh, Brahma and Krishna. Most of the other scenes are from the *Ramayana*, notably the visit of Hanuman to Sita.

7 Western gallery The northern half has another scene from the *Ramayana* depicting a battle between Rama and Ravana who rides a chariot pulled by monsters and commands an army of giants.

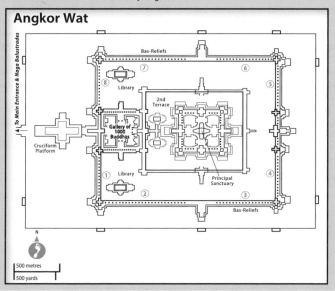

Angkor Wat

Four great gateways in the city wall face north, south, east and west and lead to the city's geometric centre, the Bayon. The fifth, Victory Gate, leads from the Royal Palace (within the Royal Enclosure) to the East Baray. The height of the gates was determined by the headroom needed to accommodate an elephant and howdah complete with parasols. The flanks of each gateway are decorated by three-headed stone elephants and each gateway tower has four giant faces, which keep an eye on all four cardinal points.

Five causeways traverse the moat, each bordered by sculptured balustrades of nagas gripped, on one side, by 54 stern-looking giant gods and on the other by 54 fierce-faced demons. The balustrade depicts the Hindu legend of the churning of the sea (see box, above).

Some stone buildings survived the sacking of the city by the Cham, such as the temples of Phimeanakas and Baphuon, and these were incorporated by Jayavarman in his new plan. He adopted the general layout of the royal centre conceived by Suryavarman II.

Inside Angkor Thom

The **South Gate** provides the most common access route to Angkor Thom, predominantly because it sits on the path between the two great Angkor complexes. The gate is a wonderful introduction to Angkor Thom with well-restored statues of asuras (demons) and gods lining the bridge. The figures on the left, exhibiting serene expression, are the gods, while those on the right, with grimaced, fierce-looking heads, are the asuras. The significance of the naga balustrade, across the moat, is believed to be symbolic of a link between the world of mortals, outside the complex, to the world of gods, inside the complex. The 23-m-high gates feature four faces in a similarly styled fashion to those of the Bayon.

The Bayon

The Bayon is one of Angkor's most famous sights and most people visiting Cambodia are familiar with the beaming faces before even stepping foot in the temple. The Bayon was Jayavarman VII's own temple-mountain, built right in the middle of Angkor Thom; its large faces have now become synonymous with the Angkor complex. It is believed to have been built between the late 12th century to early 13th century, around 100 years after Angkor Wat. Unlike other Khmer monuments, the Bayon has no protective wall immediately enclosing it. The central tower, at the intersection of the diagonals city walls, indicates that the city walls and the temple were built at the same time.

The Bayon is a three-tiered, pyramid temple with a 45-m-high tower, topped by four gigantic carved heads. These faces are believed to be the images of Jayavarman VII as a Bodhisattra, and face the four compass points. They are crowned with lotus flowers, symbol of enlightenment, and are surrounded by 51 smaller towers each with heads

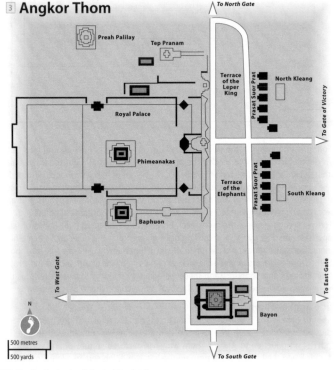

3 **Angkor Thom**

facing north, south, east and west. There are over 2000 large faces carved throughout the structure. Although the Bayon seems a complex, labyrinthine structure, its overall layout is quite basic. The first two of the three levels feature galleries of bas-relief (which should be viewed clockwise); a circular central sanctuary dominates the third level.

When Pierre Loti, the French writer, first saw these towers in 1912 he was astounded: "I looked up at the tree-covered towers which dwarfed me, when all of a sudden my blood curdled as I saw an enormous smile looking down on me, and then another smile on another wall, then three, then five, then 10, appearing in every direction". The facial features are striking and the full lips, curling upwards at the corners, are known as 'the smile of Angkor'.

Even the archaeologists of the École Française d'Extrême Orient were not able to decide immediately whether the heads on the Bayon represented Brahma, Siva or the Buddha. There are many theories. One of the most plausible was conceived in 1934 by George Coedès, an archaeologist who spent years studying the temples at Angkor. He postulated that the sculptures represented King Jayavarman VII in the form of Avaloketsvara, the Universal Buddha, implying that the Hindu concept of the god-king had been appended to Buddhist cosmology. Jayavarman VII, once a humble monk who twice renounced the throne and then became the mightiest of all the Khmer rulers, may be the smiling face, cast in stone, at the centre of his kingdom. The multiplication of faces, all looking out to the four cardinal points, may symbolize Jayavarman blessing the four quarters of the kingdom. After Jayavarman's death, the Brahmin priests turned the Bayon into a place of Hindu worship.

The Bayon has undergone a series of facelifts through its life, a point first observed in 1924 by Henri Parmentier – a French archaeologist who worked for L'École Française d'Extrême Orient – and later excavations revealed vestiges of a former building. It is thought that the first temple was planned as a two-tiered structure dedicated to Siva, which was then altered to its present form. As a result, it gives the impression of crowding – the towers rise right next to each other and the courtyards are narrow without much air or light. When Henri Mouhot rediscovered Angkor, local villagers had dubbed the Bayon 'the hide and seek sanctuary' because of its labyrinthine layout.

Bayon bas-reliefs

The bas-reliefs which decorate the walls of the Bayon all seem to tell a story but are much less imposing than those at Angkor Wat. The sculpture is carved deeper but is more naive and less sophisticated than the bas-reliefs at Angkor Wat. They vary greatly in quality, which may have been because the sculptors' skills were being overstretched by Jayavarman's ambitious building programme. The reliefs on the outer wall and on the inner gallery differ completely and seem to belong to two different worlds. The relief on the outside depicts historical events; those on the inside are drawn from the epic world of Hindu gods and legends, representing the creatures who were supposed to haunt the subterranean depths of Mount Meru. In fact the reliefs on the outer wall illustrating historical scenes and derring-do with marauding Cham were carved in the early 13th century during the reign of Jayavarman; those on the inside were carved after the king's death when his successors turned from Mahayana Buddhism back to Hinduism. In total, there are over 1.2 km of bas-reliefs, depicting over 11,000 characters.

Two recurring themes in the bas-reliefs are the powerful king and the Hindu epics. Jayavarman is depicted in the throes of battle with the Cham – who are recognizable thanks to their unusual and distinctive headdress, which looks like an inverted lotus flower.

The naval battle pictured on the walls of Banteay Chhmar are almost identical. Funnily enough, there's a bas-relief in the north section of the west gallery depicting a huge fish eating a deer, a complimentary inscription says 'the deer is its food', an artistic directive, which the carver obviously forgot to remove. The other bas-reliefs give an insight into Khmer life at the time: the warrior elephants, oxcarts, fishing with nets, cockfights and skewered fish drying on racks; vignettes show musicians, jugglers, hunters, chess-players, people nit-picking hair, palm readers and reassuringly down-to-earth scenes of Angkor citizens enjoying a drink. In the naval battle scenes, the water around the war canoes is depicted by the presence of fish, crocodiles and floating corpses.

Royal Enclosure

The Royal Enclosure, to the north of the Bayon, had already been laid out by Suryavarman I: the official palace was in the front with the domestic quarters behind, its gardens surrounded by a laterite wall and moat. Suryavarman I also beautified the royal city with ornamental pools. Jayavarman VII simply improved his designs.

Terrace of the elephants In front of the Royal Enclosure, at the centre of Angkor Thom, Suryavarman I laid out the first Grand Plaza with the recently renovated Terrace of the Elephants (also called the Royal Terrace). The 300-m-long wall derives its name from the large, lifelike carvings of elephants in a hunting scene, adorning its walls. The 2.5-m wall also features elephants flanking the southern stairway. Believed to once be the foundations for the royal reception hall, lead tiles were found here in more recent years. This discovery corroborates Chinese diplomat Chou Ta-kuan's evidence that "the tiles of the king's main apartment are made of lead". Royalty once sat in gold-topped pavilions at the centre of the pavilion, and here there are rows of garudas (bird-men), their wings lifted as if in flight. They were intended to give the impression that the god-king's palace was floating in the heavens like the imagined flying celestial palaces of the gods. At the end of the terrace is an impressive sculpture of a five-headed horse.

North and South Kleangs Also in front of the Royal Enclosure are the stately North and South Kleangs, which sit on the east side of the central square (opposite the Terrace of the Elephants). Although Kleang means 'storeroom', a royal oath of allegiance carved into one of the doorways indicates that they may have served as reception areas for foreign envoys. The North Kleang was originally constructed in wood under Rajendravarman II; Jayavarman V reconstructed it with stone and Jayavarman VII later added 12 laterite victory towers, called the **Prasat Suor Prat**. The function of the towers is steeped in controversy. While some say they were intended as anchors for performing acrobats and clowns, Chou Ta-kuan stated that they were used to settle disputes between performing men (to see who could last the longest seated on a tower without illness or injury). Henri Mauhot disagreed with both theories, suggesting that the towers were created to hold the crown jewels.

Terrace of the Leper King At the northeast corner of the 'central square' is the 12th-century Terrace of the Leper King, which may have been a cremation platform for the aristocracy of Angkor. Now rebuilt it is a little too fresh and contemporary for some tastes. The 7-m-high double terrace has bands of bas-reliefs, one on top of the other, with intricately sculptured scenes of royal pageantry and seated apsaras as well as nagas and garudas which frequented the slopes of Mount Meru. Above is a strange statue from an earlier date, which probably depicts the god of death, Yama, and once held a staff in its right hand. The statue's naked, lichen-covered body gives the terrace its name – the lichen gives the uncanny impression of leprosy.

Opposite the Terrace of the Elephants, on the south side of the Terrace of the Leper King, are the remains of an earlier wall, carved with bas-reliefs of demons. These reliefs were found by French archaeologists and had been intentionally concealed. This illustrates the lengths to which the Khmers went to recreate Mount Meru (the home of the gods) as faithfully as possible. According to Hindu mythology, Mount Meru extended into the bowels of the earth; the bas-relief section below ground level was carved with weird and wonderful creatures to symbolize the hidden depths of the underworld. The second layer of carving is the base of Mount Meru on earth. Flights of steps led through these to the lawns and pavilions of the royal gardens and Suryavarman's palace.

The Phimeanakas

The Phimeanakas (meaning Celestial or Flying Palace in Sanskrit) inside the Royal Enclosure was started by Rajendravarman and used by all the later kings. The structure stands close to the walls of the Royal Palace, none of which exists today. Suryavarman I rebuilt this pyramidal temple when he was renovating the Royal Enclosure. It rises from the centre of the former Royal Palace. Lions guard all four stairways to the central tower which was originally covered in gold, as the Chinese envoy Chou Ta-kuan related in 1296. The Phimeanakas represented a genuine architectural revolution: it was not square, but rectangular and on the upper terrace, surrounding the central tower, there was a gallery with corbelled vaults, used as a passageway.

The Srah Srei, or the women's bath, to the north of Phimeanakas is also within the walled enclosure. Chou Ta-kuan appears to have enjoyed watching Angkor's womenfolk bathe, noting that, "To enter the water, the women simply hide their sex with their left hand". The Phimeanakas is linked by the **Avenue of Victory** to the Eastern Baray.

South of the Royal Enclosure

South of the Royal Enclosure and near the Terrace of the Elephants is the Baphuon, built by Udayadityavarman II. The temple was approached by a 200-m-long sandstone causeway, raised on pillars, which was probably constructed after the temple was built. The platform leads from the temple-mountain itself to the east gopura – an arched gateway leading to the temple courtyards. The Baphuon is not well preserved as it was erected on an artificial hill which weakened its foundations. Only the three terraces of its pyramidal, Mount Meru-style form remain and these give little indication of its former glory: it was second only to the Bayon in size. Chou Ta-kuan reported that its great tower was made of bronze and that it was "truly marvellous to behold". With extensive restoration, the temple is starting to shape-up. Most of the bas-reliefs were carved in panels and refer to the Hindu epics. Some archaeologists believe the sculptors were trying to tell stories in the same way as the shadow plays. It is believed that the fourth level wall on the western side was originally created in the form of a large, reclining Buddha, though it is hard to make out today. There is a wonderful view from the summit. South of the Baphuon returns you back to the Bayon.

Preah Palilay

Preah Palilay, just outside the north wall of the Royal Enclosure, was also built by Jayavarman VII. Just to the east of this temple is **Tep Tranam**, the base of a pagoda, with a pool in front of it. To the east of Tep Tranam and the other side of the Northern Avenue is the **Preah Pithu Group**, a cluster of five temples.

elephants take tourists up to the summit of Phnom Bakheng for sunset

Phnom Bakheng and Baksei Chamkrong

To get up to the ruins, either climb the steep and uneven hill where the vegetation has been cleared (slippery when wet), ride an elephant to the top of the hill (US$15) or walk up the gentle zig-zag path the elephants take.

Phnom Bakheng, Yasovarman's temple-mountain, stands at the top of a natural hill, 60-m high, affording good views of the plains of Angkor. There is also a roped off Buddha's footprint to see. It is just outside the south gate of Angkor Thom and was the centre of King Yasovarman's city, Yasodharapura – the 'City Endowed with Splendour'. A pyramid-temple dedicated to Siva, Bakheng was the home of the royal lingam and Yasovarman's mausoleum after his death. It is composed of five towers built on a sandstone platform. There are 108 smaller towers scattered around the terraces. The main tower has been partially demolished and the others have completely disappeared. It was entered via a steep flight of steps which were guarded by squatting lions. The steps have deteriorated with the towers. Foliate scroll relief carving covers much of the main shrine – the first time this style was used. This strategically placed hill served as a camp for various combatants, including the Vietnamese, and suffered accordingly. Today the hill is disfigured by a radio mast.

Baksei Chamkrong was built by Harshavarman I at the beginning of the 10th century and dedicated to his father, Yasovarman I. It lies at the foot of Phnom Bakheng (between Bakheng and Angkor Thom), the centre of Yasovarman's city, and was one of the first temples to be built in brick on a stepped laterite base. An inscription tells of a golden image of Siva inside the temple.

if you have the time, Ta Prohm is well worth the effort

★ Ta Prohm

For all would-be Mouhots and closet Indiana Joneses, the temple of Ta Prohm, to the south of Ta Keo, is the perfect lost-in-the-jungle experience. Unlike most of the other monuments at Angkor, it has only been minimally cleared of undergrowth, fig trees and creepers and so retains much of its mystery. Widely regarded as one of Angkor's most enchanting and beautiful temples, it is an absolute 'must-see'.

Ta Prohm was built to house the divine image of the Queen Mother and was consecrated in 1186 – five years after Jayavarman VII seized power. The outer enclosures are somewhat obscured by dense foliage but reach well beyond the temple's heart (1 km by 650 m). The temple proper consists of a number of concentric galleries featuring corner towers and the standard gopuras. Other buildings and enclosures were built on a more ad hoc basis. The temple marked the end of an architectural style in which the temple's structure lay on a single plane with rising towers alluding to the notion of elevation rather than comprising multiple levels.

It underwent many transformations and an inscription gives detailed information on the complex. Within the complex walls lived 12,640 citizens. It contained 39 sanctuaries or prasats, 566 stone dwellings and 288 brick dwellings. Ta Prohm literally translates as the Royal Monastery and that is what it functioned as, home to 18 abbots and 2740 monks. By the 12th century temples were no longer exclusively places of worship – they also had to accommodate monks so roofed halls were increasingly built within the complexes. According to contemporary inscriptions, the temple required 79,365 people for its upkeep, relying on the income of 3140 villages to subsidize the 2740 officials and 615 dancers. The list of property it owned was on an equally impressive scale. It included 523 parasols, 35 diamonds and 40,620 pearls.

The French writer Elie Lauré wrote: "With its millions of knotted limbs, the forest embraces the ruins with a violent love". Creepers entwine themselves around ancient stones like the tentacles of a giant octopus. Trunks and roots pour off temple roofs like lava flows. It was decided by the École Française d'Extrême Orient to leave the temple in its natural state. The trees are predominantly the silk-cotton tree and the aptly named strangler fig. The plants are believed to have spawned in the temple's cracks from seeds blown in or dropped by birds. Naturally, the roots of the trees have descended towards the soil, prying their way through foundations in the process. As the vegetation has matured it has forced its way further into the temple's structure, damaging the man-built base and causing untold destruction. This has created a situation where the structures now rely on the trees for support. Herein lies the dilemma – if the trees die or are damaged, the now-damaged and loose temple walls could easily crumble or collapse. Venerable trees weighing several tonnes growing on temple roofs also cause unimaginable stress, slowly shattering the stones.

In recent years a colossal tree was struck by lightening and fell on a gallery, causing quite serious damage. This reignited a campaign to 'save Ta Prohm' and a project is underway to prune some of the smaller trees and larger branches.

Banteay Kdei, Srah Srang and Prasat Kravan

Banteay Kdei The massive complex of Banteay Kdei, otherwise known as 'the citadel of cells', is 3 km east of Angkor Thom and just to the southeast of Ta Prohm. Some archaeologists think it may be dedicated to Jayavarman VII's religious teacher. The temple has remained in much the same state it was discovered in – a crowded collection of ruined laterite towers and connecting galleries lying on a flat plan, surrounded by a galleried enclosure. It is presumed that the temple was a Buddhist monastery and hundreds of buried Buddha statues have been excavated from the site. In recent times a community of monks has used the site but this is less common now due to the strict restrictions imposed by temple management. The temple area is enclosed by a large laterite wall, 700 m by 500 m, and has three main enclosures. Like Ta Prohm it contains a Hall of Dancers (east side), an open roof building with four separate quarters. The second enclosure runs around the perimeters of the inner enclosure. The third, inner enclosure contains a north and south library and central sanctuary. The central tower was never finished and the square pillars in the middle of the courtyard still cannot be explained by scholars. There are few inscriptions here to indicate either its name or purpose, but it is almost certainly a Buddhist temple built in the 12th century, about the same time as Ta Prohm. It is quite similar to Ta Prohm in design but on a much smaller scale. Historians Freeman and Jacques believe that it was probably built over the site of another temple. The temple is being restored, slowly but surely. However, the 13th-century vandalism of Buddha images (common to most of Jayavarman's temples) will prove a little more difficult to restore. This temple offers a few good examples of Mahayanist Buddhist frontons and lintels that escaped the desecration.

Srah Srang The lake or baray next to Banteay Kdei is called Srah Srang ('Royal Bath') and was used for ritual bathing. The steps down to the water face the rising sun and are flanked with lions and nagas. This sandstone landing stage dates from the reign of Jayavarman VII but the lake itself is thought to date back two centuries earlier. A 10th-century inscription reads "this water is stored for the use of all creatures except dyke breakers", ie elephants. This design is believed to be characteristic of that adopted in the Bayon. The Baray, which measures 700 m by 300 m, has been filled with turquoise-blue waters for over 1300 years. With a good view of Pre Rup across the lake, some archaeologists believe that this spot affords the best vista in the whole Angkor complex. The green landscape around the baray and beautiful views offer a tranquil and cool resting place, perfect for a picnic lunch.

Prasat Kravan On the road between Angkor Wat and Banteay Kdei, on the small circuit, is Prasat Kravan. The temple, built in AD 921, means 'Cardamom Sanctuary' and is unusual in that it is built of brick. (By that time brick had been replaced by laterite and sandstone.) It consists of five brick towers arranged in a line. The bricklayers did a good job, especially considering they used a vegetable composite as their mortar. The temple's bas-reliefs are considered a bit of an anomaly as brick was hardly ever sculpted upon. In the early 10th century, temples were commissioned by individuals other than the king; Prasat Kravan is one of the earliest examples. It was probably built during the reign of Harshavarman I.

The Hindu temple, surrounded by a moat, is positioned in a north-south direction. Two of the five decorated brick towers contain bas-reliefs (the north and central towers). The central tower is probably the most impressive and contains a linga on a pedestal. The sanctuary's three walls all contain pictures of Vishnu; the left-hand wall depicts Vishnu disguised as Vamana the dwarf. The incarnation of Vamana was used to dupe the evil demon king, Bali, into letting the unassuming dwarf take a small space to meditate. Instead the mighty Vishnu rose up, taking three important steps – from a pedestal, across the ocean, to a lotus – in order to reclaim the world from the evil demon king. On the right-hand wall again is the mighty Vishnu riding his Garuda. Common to both the bas-reliefs is the four-armed Vishnu waving around a number of objects: disc, club, conch shell and ball – these are all symbolic of his personal attributes and power. On the opposing wall is Vishnu, this time with eight arms standing between six rows of people meditating above a giant reptile.

The Northern tower is devoted to Lakshimi, Vishnu's wife. Like her consort, she is also baring her personal attributes. The best light to view the relief is in the morning.

The Cardamom Sanctuary is named after a tree that grew on the grounds. Ironically, its ruin has been largely due to the roots of trees growing beneath it. The French have been involved in the temple's reconstruction. The temple's twin, Prasat Neang Khamau (the Black Lady Sanctuary), can be found outside Phnom Penh.

Pre Rup
Northeast of Srah Srang is Pre Rup, the State Temple of King Rajendravarman's capital. Built in AD 961, the temple-mountain representing Mount Meru is larger, higher and artistically superior than its predecessor, the East Mebon, which it closely resembles. In keeping with the tradition of state capitals, Pre Rup marked the centre of the city, much of which doesn't exist today. The pyramid-structure, which is constructed of laterite with brick prasats, sits at the apex of an artificial, purpose-built mountain. The temple is enclosed by a laterite outer wall (127 m by 117 m) and inner wall (87 m by 77 m) both which contain gopuras in the centre of each wall. The central pyramid-level consists of a three-tiered, sandstone platform, with five central towers sitting above. This was an important innovation at Pre Rup and East Mebon, that the sanctuary at the top was no longer a single tower – but a group of five towers, surrounded by smaller towers on the outer, lower levels. This more

complicated plan reached its final development at Angkor Wat 150 years later. The group of five brick towers were originally elaborately decorated with plaster, but most of it has now fallen off. However, the corners of each of the five towers contain guardian figures – as per tradition, the eastern towers are female and the western and central towers are male. The shrine has fine lintels and columns on its doorways. But the intricate sandstone carvings on the doors of the upper levels are reproductions. The upper levels of the pyramid offer a brilliant, panoramic view of the countryside.

North of Angkor Thom

head north for Jayavarman VII's first capital

★Preah Khan

Northeast of the walled city of Angkor Thom, about 3.5 km from the Bayon, is the 12th-century complex of Preah Khan. One of the largest complexes within the Angkor area, it was Jayavarman VII's first capital before Angkor Thom was completed. The name Preah Khan means 'sacred sword' and probably derives from a decisive battle against the Cham, which created a 'lake of blood', but was inevitably won by Jayavarman VII.

Preah Khan is not uniform in style. It is highly likely that Jayavarman VII's initial very well-organized and detailed city plans went slightly pear-shaped during the working city's life. A number of alterations and buildings were added, in addition to a vast civilian habitation (huts and timber houses), which all came together to create a complex labyrinth of architectural chaos. It is similar in ground plan to Ta Prohm (see page 260) but attention was paid to the approaches: its east and west entrance avenues, leading to ornamental causeways, are lined with carved stone boundary posts. Evidence of 1000 teachers suggests that it was more than a mere Buddhist monastery but most likely a Buddhist university. Nonetheless an abundance of Brahmanic iconography is still present on site. Around the rectangular complex is a large laterite wall surrounded by large garudas wielding the naga (each over 5 m in height). The theme continues across the length of the whole 3-km external enclosure, with the motif dotted every 50 m. Within these walls lies the surrounding moat.

The city is conveniently located on the shores of its own baray, Jayataka (3.5 km by 900 m). Some foundations and laterite steps lead from the reservoir, where two beautiful gajasimha lions guard the path. It is best to enter the temple from the baray's jetty in order to experience the magnificence of the divinities and devas of the Processional Way (causeway leading across the moat).

The construction's four walls meet in the centre creating two galleries and likewise, two enclosures. The outer enclosure contains the traditional four gopuras (adorned with stately bas-reliefs) and the Hall of Dancers. This hall contains an elaborate frieze of dancing apsaras and was used, in recent times, to host charity performances to help fund the area's restoration. Within the enclosure there are also a few ponds, libraries and supplementary buildings, most notably, a two-storey pavilion (north of the performance hall) which is believed to have housed the illustrious 'sacred sword'.

The second and innermost walls run so closely together that it is possible to pass through the following enclosure without realizing you had entered it (this is probably due to an expansion undertaken very early on in the piece to offer additional protection to the shrines).

The inner enclosure is a bewildering array of constructions and shrines. Holes in the inner walls of the central sanctuary of Preah Khan suggest they may once have been decorated with brass plates – an obvious target for looters. One inscription implies that up to 1500 tonnes was used within the edifice. The temple was built to shelter the statue of

Jayavarman VII's father, Dharanindravarman II, in the likeness of Bodhisattva Avatokitsvara, which has now probably been smashed. A stela was discovered at the site glorifying the builder, Jayavarman VII and detailing what it took to keep the place ticking over. The inventory mentions that for Preah Khan's upkeep, the services of 97,840 men and women, 444 chefs, 4606 footmen and 2298 servants were required. Preah Khan's inscriptions also refer to the existence of 515 other statues, 102 royal hospitals of the kingdom, 18 major annual festivals and 10 days' public holiday a month.

The temple was starting to deteriorate, but clearing and careful conservation have helped remedy this. During the dry season, the World Monuments Funds (WMF), based in New York, undertakes archaeological site conservation activities here.

Preah Neak Pean, Ta Som and Krol Ko

To the east of Preah Khan and north of the Eastern Baray are two more Buddhist temples built by Jayavarman VII: Preah Neak Pean (the westernmost one) and the ruins of Ta Som.

Neak Pean This exquisite temple was also a fountain, built in the middle of a pool, representing the paradisiacal Himalayan mountain-lake, Anaavatapta. Two nagas form the edge of the island and their tails join at the back. In modern Khmer it is known as the Preasat neac pon – the 'tower of the intertwined dragons'. The colossal image of the horse is the compassionate Bodhisattva who is supposed to save sailors from drowning. The temple pools were an important part of the aesthetic experience of Preah Khan and Neak Pean – the ornate stone carving of both doubly visible by reflection. Such basins within a temple complex were used for religious ritual, while the larger moats and barays were used for bathing, transport and possibly for irrigation.

Ta Som Located north of the East Baray is the pretty Ta Som. This mini temple has many of the same stylistic and design attributes of Ta Prohm and Banteay Kdei but on a much smaller scale. Unlike the larger constructions of Jayavarman VII, Ta Som's layout is extremely simple – three concentric enclosures and very few annex buildings. The main entrance is to the east, which would indicate some urbanization on the eastern side of the temple. The two inner enclosures are successively offset to the west. The outer (third) enclosure (240 m x 200 m) is pierced by two cruciform gopuras; the eastern one is preceded by a small terrace bound by naga balustrades. The current entry is through the western gopura as this faces the road between East Mebon and Preah Neak Pean and cuts across the moat.

Krol Ko North of Preah Neak Pean and about 2 km past Ta Som, Krol Ko was built in the late 12th to early 13th century. Referred to as the Oxen Park, Krol Ko is a single, laterite tower which is about 30 m sq. The two frontons represent bodhisattva Lokesvara, to whom it is believed the temple is dedicated.

Outlying temples

plenty to discover here if you are not already templed-out

The Roluos Group

The Roluos Group, some 16 km southeast of Siem Reap, receives few visitors but is worth visiting if time permits. Jayavarman II built several capitals including one at Roluos, at that time called Hariharalaya. This was the site of his last city and remained the capital during the reigns of his three successors. The three remaining Hindu sanctuaries at Roluos are

Preah Ko, **Bakong** and **Lolei**. They were finished in AD 879, AD 881 and AD 893 respectively by Indravarman I and his son Yashovarman I and are the best preserved of the early temples.

All three temples are built of brick with sandstone doorways and niches. The use of human figures as sculptural decoration in religious architecture developed around this time – and examples of these guardian spirits can be seen in the niches of Preah Ko and Lolei. Other sculptured figures which appear in the Roluos Group are the crouching lion, the reclining bull (Nandi – Siva's mount) and the naga. The gopura – an arched gateway leading to the temple courtyards – was also a contemporary innovation in Roluos. Libraries used for the storage of sacred manuscripts appeared for the first time, as did the concentric enclosures surrounding the central group of towers. Preah Ko and Lolei have characteristics in common: both were dedicated to the parents and grandparents of the kings who built them. Neither temple has a pyramid centre like Bakong as the pyramid temples were built exclusively for kings.

Preah Ko Meaning 'sacred ox', Preah Ko was named after the three statues of Nandi (the mount of the Hindu god, Siva) which stand in front of the temple. Orientated east-west, there is a cluster of six brick towers arranged in two rows on a low brick platform, the steps up to which are guarded by crouching lions while Nandi, looking back, blocks the way. The front row of towers was devoted to Indravarman's male ancestors and the second row to the female. The ancestors were represented in the image of a Hindu god. Only patches remain of the once magnificent stucco relief work, including a remnant of a kala – a motif also found on contemporary monuments in Java.

Bakong Indravarman's temple-mountain, Bakong, is a royal five-stepped pyramid temple with a sandstone central tower built on a series of successively receding terraces with surrounding brick towers. It may have been inspired by Borobudur in Java. Indravarman himself was buried in the temple. Bakong is the largest and most impressive temple in the Roluos Group by a long way. A bridge flanked by a naga balustrade leads over a dry moat to the temple. The central tower was built to replace the original one when the monument was restored in the 12th century and is probably larger than the original. Local children will point out to you that it is just possible to catch a glimpse of Angkor Wat from the top. The Bakong denotes the true beginning of classical Khmer

> **Tip...**
> It is possible to visit the other ancient Khmer sites dotted around the main temples at Angkor; most can be reached by moto or by car.

architecture and contained the god-king Siva's lingam. The most important innovations of Indravarman's artists are the free-standing sandstone statues – such as the group of three figures, probably depicting the king with his two wives, who are represented as Siva with Uma, a Hindu goddess and consort of Siva, and Ganga, goddess of the Ganges River. The corners of the pyramid are mounted with statues of elephants and the steps guarded by crouching lions. Nandi watches the steps from below. The heads of all the figures are now missing but the simplicity of the sculpture is nonetheless distinctive; it is a good example of early Khmer craftsmanship. The statues are more static and stockier than the earlier statues of Chenla. There is now a Buddhist monastery in the grounds – originally it was dedicated to Siva.

Lolei Built by Yashovarman I in the middle of Indravarman's baray, Lolei's brick towers were dedicated to the king's ancestors, but over the centuries they have largely disintegrated; of the four towers two have partly collapsed. Much of the decoration has worn away but the inscriptions carved in the grey sandstone lintels and door jambs remain in good condition.

★Banteay Srei ('Citadel of Women')
25 km from Ta Prohm along a decent road and about 35-40 mins by motorbike. The way is well signed. There are lots of food and drink stalls.

Banteay Srei, to the north of Angkor, is well worth the trip. This remarkable temple was built by the Brahmin tutor to King Rajendravarman, Yajnavaraha, grandson of Harshavarman (AD 900-923), and founded in AD 967. The temple wasn't discovered until 1914, its distance from Angkor and concealment by overgrown jungle meaning that it wasn't picked up in earlier expeditions. At the time of discovery, by geographic officer Captain Marec, the site was so badly damaged that mounds of dirt had covered the main structure and foliage had bored its way through much of the site. It wasn't until 1924 that the site was cleared and by 1936 it had been restored.

Banteay Srei translates as 'Citadel of Women', a title bestowed upon it in relatively recent years due to the intricate apsara carvings that adorn the interior. While many of Angkor's temples are impressive because of their sheer size, Banteay Srei stands out in the quality of its craftsmanship. The temple is considered by many historians to be the highest achievement of art from the Angkor period. The explicit preservation of this temple reveals covered terraces, of which only the columns remain, which once lined both sides of the primary entrance. In keeping with tradition, a long causeway leads into the temple, across a moat, on the eastern side.

The main walls, entry pavilions and libraries have been constructed from laterite and the carvings are in pink sandstone. The layout was inspired by Prasat Thom at Koh Ker. Three beautifully carved tower-shrines stand side by side on a low terrace in the middle of a quadrangle, with a pair of libraries on either side enclosed by a wall. Two of the shrines, the southern one and the central one, were dedicated to Siva and the northern one to Vishnu. Both had libraries close by, with carvings depicting appropriate legends. The whole temple is dedicated to Brahma and many believe this temple is the closest to its Indian counterparts. Beyond this inner group of buildings was a monastery surrounded by a moat.

In 1923 controversy surrounded the temple when it was targeted by famous French author André Lalraux for a major looting expedition. The author of *The Royal Way* (1930) shamefully attempted to pillage Banteay Srei of its treasures, having read that the temple not only contained a series of brilliant carvings in excellent condition but that it was also unexcavated (which he took to mean abandoned). He travelled to Angkor and proceeded to cut out one tonne of the finest statues and bas-reliefs. Fortunately, he was arrested trying to leave the country with the treasures and was sentenced to three years in prison (a term that he did not serve). One of the best known statues from this site is a sculpture of Siva sitting down and holding his wife, Uma, on his knee: it is in the National Museum of Arts in Phnom Penh.

Having been built by a Brahmin priest, the temple was never intended for use by a king, which goes some way towards explaining its small size – you have to duck to get through the doorways to the sanctuary towers. Perhaps because of its modest scale Banteay Srei contains some of the finest examples of Khmer sculpture. Finely carved pink sandstone ornaments, roofs, pediments and lintels, all magnificently decorated with tongues of flame, serpents' tails, gods, demons and floral garlands.

Background
Angkor

Khmer Empire

Under Jayavarman VII (1181-1218) the complex stretched more than 25 km east to west and nearly 10 km north to south, approximately the same size as Manhattan. For five centuries (ninth-13th), the court of Angkor held sway over a vast territory. At its height Khmer influence spanned half of Southeast Asia, from Burma to the southernmost tip of Indochina and from the borders of Yunnan to the Malay Peninsula. The only threat to this great empire was a river-borne invasion in 1177, when the Cham used a Chinese navigator to pilot their canoes up the Mekong. Scenes are depicted in bas-reliefs of the Bayon temple.

The kings and construction – the temples and the creators

Jayavarman II (AD 802-835) founded the Angkor Kingdom, then coined Hariharalaya to the north of the Tonlé Sap, in the Roluos region (Angkor), in AD 802. Later he moved the capital to Phnom Kulen, 40 km northeast of Angkor, where he built a Mountain Temple and Rong Shen shrine. After several years he moved the capital back to the Roluos region.

Jayavarman III (AD 835-877) continued his father's legacy and built a number of shrines at Hariharalaya. Many historians believe he was responsible for the initial construction of the impressive laterite pyramid, Bakong, considered the great precursor to Angkor Wat. Bakong, built to symbolize Mount Meru, was later embellished and developed by Indravarman. **Indravarman** (AD 877-889) overthrew his predecessor violently and undertook a major renovation campaign in the capital Hariharalaya. The majority of what stands in the Roluos Group today is the work of Indravarman. A battle between Indravarman's sons destroyed the palace and the victor and new king **Yasovarman I** (AD 889-900) moved the capital from Roluos and laid the foundations of Angkor itself. He dedicated the temple to his ancestors. His new capital at Angkor was called Yasodharapura, meaning 'glory-bearing city', and here he built 100 wooden *ashramas* (retreats – all of which have disintegrated today). Yasovarman selected Bakheng as the location for his temple-mountain and after flattening the mountain top, set about creating another Mount Meru. The temple he constructed was considered more complex than anything built beforehand, a five-storey pyramid with 108 shrines. A road was then built to link the former and present capitals of Roluos and Bakheng. Like the kings before him, Yasovarman was obliged to construct a major waterworks and the construction of the reservoir – the East Baray (now completely dry) – was considered an incredible feat.

After Yasovarman's death in AD 900 his son **Harshavarman** (AD 900-923) assumed power for the next 23 years. During his brief reign, Harshavarman is believed to have built Baksei Chamkrong (northeast of Phnom Bakheng) and Prasat Kravan (the 'Cardamom Sanctuary'). His brother, **Ishanarvarman II** (AD 923-928), resumed power upon his death but no great architectural feats were recorded in this time. In AD 928, **Jayavarman IV** moved the capital 65 km away to Koh Ker. Here he built the grand state temple Prasat Thom, an impressive seven-storey, sandstone pyramid.

Following the death of Jayavarman, things took a turn for the worst. Chaos ensued under Harshavarman's II weak leadership and over the next four years, no monuments were known to be erected. Jayavarman's IV nephew, **Rajendravarman** (AD 944-968), took control of the situation and it's assumed he forcefully relocated the capital back to

Angkor. Rather than moving back into the old capital Phnom Bakheng, he marked his own new territory, selecting an area south of the East Baray as his administrative centre. Here, in AD 961 he constructed the state temple, Pre Rup, and constructed the temple, East Mebon (AD 953), in the middle of the baray. Srah Srang, Kutisvara and Bat Chum were also constructed, with the help of his chief architect, Kavindrarimathana. It was towards the end of his reign that he started construction on Banteay Srei, considered one of the finest examples of Angkorian craftsmanship in the country. Rajendravarman's son **Jayavarman V** (AD 968-1001) became the new king in AD 968. The administrative centre was renamed Jayendranagari and yet again, relocated. More than compensating for the unfinished Ta Keo was Jayavarman's V continued work on Banteay Srei. Under his supervision the splendid temple was completed and dedicated to his father.

Aside from successfully extending the Khmer Empire's territory King **Suryavarman I** (1002-1049), made a significant contribution to Khmer architectural heritage. He presided over the creation of a new administrative centre – the Royal Palace (in Angkor Thom) – and the huge walls that surround it. The next in line was **Udayadityavarman II** (1050-1066), the son of Suryavarman I. The Baphuon temple-mountain was built during his relatively short appointment.

After overthrowing his Great-Uncle Dharanindravarman, **Suryavarman II** (1112-1150), the greatest of Angkor's god-kings, came to power. His rule marked the highest point in Angkorian architecture and civilization. Not only was he victorious in conflict, having beaten the Cham whom couldn't be defeated by China, he was responsible for extending the borders of the Khmer Empire into Myanmar, Malaya and Siam. This aside, he was also considered one of the era's most brilliant creators. Suryavarman II was responsible for the construction of Angkor Wat, the current-day symbol of Cambodia. Beng Melea, Banteay Samre and Thommanon are also thought to be the works of this genius. He has been immortalized in his own creation – in a bas-relief in the South Gallery of Angkor Wat the glorious King Suryavarman II sitting on top of an elephant. After a period of political turmoil, which included the sacking of Angkor, **Jayavarman VII** seized the throne in 1181 and set about rebuilding his fiefdom. He created a new administrative centre – the great city of Angkor Thom. The mid-point of Angkor Thom is marked by his brilliant Mahayana Buddhist state temple, the Bayon. It is said that the Bayon was completed in 21 years. Jayavarman took thousands of peasants from the rice fields to build it, which proved a fatal error, for rice yields decreased and the empire began its decline as resources were drained. The temple, which consists of sculptured faces of Avolokiteshvara (the Buddha of compassion and mercy) are often said to also encompass the face of their great creator, **Jayavarman VIII**. He was also responsible for restoring the Royal Palace, renovating Srah Srang and constructing the Elephant Terrace, the Terrace of the Leper King and the nearby baray (northeast of Angkor Thom), Jayatataka reservoir. At the centre of his reservoir he built Neak Pean. Jayavarman VII adopted Mahayana Buddhism; Buddhist principles replaced the Hindu pantheon, and were invoked as the basis of royal authority. This spread of Buddhism is thought to have caused some of the earlier Hindu temples to be neglected. The king paid tribute to his Buddhist roots through his monastic temples – Ta Prohm and Preah Khan.

The French at Angkor

Thai ascendency and eventual occupation of Angkor in 1431, led to the city's abandonment and the subsequent invasion of the jungle. Four centuries later, in 1860, Henri Mouhot – a French naturalist – stumbled across the forgotten city, its temple towers enmeshed in the forest canopy. Locals told him they were the work of a race of giant gods. Only the stone temples remained; all the wooden secular buildings had decomposed in the intervening centuries. In 1873 French archaeologist Louis Delaporte removed many of Angkor's finest statues for 'the cultural enrichment of France'. In 1898, the École Française d'Extrême Orient started clearing the jungle, restoring the temples, mapping the complex and making an inventory of the site. Delaporte was later to write the two-volume *Les Monuments du Cambodge*, the most comprehensive Angkorian inventory of its time, and his earlier sketches, plans and reconstructions, published in *Voyage au Cambodge* in 1880 are without parallel.

Angkor temples

The temples at Angkor were modelled on those of the kingdom of Chenla (a mountain kingdom centred on northern Cambodia and southern Laos), which in turn were modelled on Indian temples. They represent Mount Meru – the home of the gods of Indian cosmology. The central towers symbolize the peaks of Mount Meru, surrounded by a wall representing the earth and moats and basins representing the oceans. The *devaraja*, or god-king, was enshrined in the centre of the religious complex, which acted as the spiritual axis of the kingdom. The people believed their apotheosized king communicated directly with the gods.

The central tower sanctuaries housed the images of the Hindu gods to whom the temples were dedicated. Dead members of the royal and priestly families were accorded a status on a par with these gods. Libraries to store the sacred scriptures were also built within the ceremonial centre. The temples were mainly built to shelter the images of the gods – unlike Christian churches, Moslem mosques and some Buddhist pagodas, they were not intended to accommodate worshippers. Only priests, the servants of the god, were allowed into the interiors. The 'congregation' would mill around in open courtyards or wooden pavilions.

The first temples were of a very simple design, but with time they became more grandiose and doors and galleries were added. Most of Angkor's buildings are made from a soft sandstone which is easy to work. It was transported to the site from Phnom Kulen, about 30 km to the northeast. Laterite was used for foundations, core material, and enclosure walls, as it was widely available and could be easily cut into blocks. A common feature of Khmer temples was false doors and windows on the sides and backs of sanctuaries and other buildings. In most cases there was no need for well-lit rooms and corridors as hardly anyone ever went into them. That said, the galleries round the central towers in later temples, such as Angkor Wat, indicate that worshippers did use the temples for ceremonial circumambulation when they would contemplate the inspiring bas-reliefs from the important Hindu epics, *Ramayana* and *Mahabharata* (written between 400 BC and AD 200).

Despite the court's conversion to Mahayana Buddhism in the 12th century, the architectural ground-plans of temples did not alter much – even though they were based on Hindu cosmology. The idea of the god-king was simply grafted onto the new state religion and statues of the Buddha rather than the gods of the Hindu pantheon were used to represent the god-king. One particular image of the Buddha predominated at Angkor in which he wears an Angkor-style crown, with a conical top encrusted with jewellery.

The nearest town to Angkor, Siem Reap is a bustling tourism hub with a growing art and fashion crowd. The town has developed quite substantially in the past few years and, with the blossoming of hotels, restaurants and bars, and is now a pleasant place in its own right. It's a popular base for volunteers, and visitors exhausted by the temple trail might care to while away a morning or afternoon in Siem Reap itself. However, without the temples, it's true to say that few people would ever find themselves here.

Sights

The town is laid out formally and, because there is ample land on which to build, it is pleasantly spacious. Buildings are often set in large overgrown grounds resembling mini-wilderness. However, hotel building has pretty much kept pace with tourist arrivals and the current level of unprecedented growth and development is set to continue, so this may not be the case in the future. The growth spurt has put a great strain on the city's natural resources.

Old Market This area is the most touristy part of town. There is a sprinkling of guesthouses in this area, recommended for independent travellers and those staying more than two or three days. Otherwise, there's a much greater selection of accommodation just across the river, in the **Wat Bo** area. It's not as crowded as the market area and there is less traffic than the airport road.

> **Tip...**
>
> In Siem Reap visit the market and buy black peppercorns to take home.

Angkor National Museum ⓘ *On the road to the temples, www.angkornational museum. com, daily 0830-1800, US$12.* The museum is a short walk from the town centre. Due to the high entry fee it is usually empty and it does seem rather incongruous that the artefacts on display here are not actually still in-situ at the temples themselves. Having said that, it isn't a bad museum and you can gather a lot of useful information about the development of Angkor. There are also some intriguing background details such as the 102 hospitals built during the reign of Jayavarman VII and the 1960 boxes of haemorrhoid cream that were part of their annual provisions. There are also some displays on the clothes the average Angkorian wore but it's a shame there isn't more about the daily lives of these ancients.

★ Tonlé Sap

The Tonlé Sap, the Great Lake of Cambodia, is one of the natural wonders of Asia. Uniquely, the 100-km-long Tonlé Sap River, a tributary of the mighty Mekong, reverses its flow and runs uphill for six months of the year. Spring meltwaters in the Himalaya, coupled with seasonal rains, increase the flow of the Mekong to such an extent that some is deflected up the Tonlé Sap River. From June the lake begins to expand until, by the end of the rainy season, it has increased in area four-fold and in depth by up to 12 m. At its greatest extent, the lake occupies nearly a seventh of Cambodia's land area, around 1.5 million ha, making it the largest freshwater lake in Southeast Asia. From November, with the onset of the dry season, the Tonlé Sap River reverses its flow once more and begins to act like a regular tributary – flowing downhill into the Mekong. By February the lake has shrunk to a fraction of its wet-season size and covers 'just' 300,000 ha.

This pattern of expansion and contraction has three major benefits. First, it helps to restrict flooding in the Mekong Delta in Vietnam. Second, it forms the basis for a substantial part of Cambodia's rice production. And third, it supports perhaps the world's largest and richest inland fishery, yielding as much as 10 tonnes of fish per square kilometre. It is thought that four million people depend on the lake for their subsistence and three out of every 4 kg of fish caught in the country come from the Tonlé Sap.

Because of the dramatic changes in the size of the lake some of the fish, such as the 'walking catfish', have evolved to survive several hours out of water, flopping overland to find deeper pools. *Hok yue* – or elephant fish – are renowned as a delicacy well beyond Cambodia's borders. Large-scale commercial fishing is a major occupation from February to May and the fishing grounds are divided into plots and leased out. Recent lack of dredging means the lake is not as deep as it was and fish are tending to swim downstream into the Mekong and Tonlé Sap rivers. The annual flooding covers the surrounding countryside with a layer of moist, nutrient-rich mud which is ideal for rice growing. Farmers grow deep-water rice, long stalked and fast growing – it grows with the rising lake to keep the grain above water and the stem can be up to 6 m long. The lake also houses people, with communities living in floating villages close to the shore.

Chong Khneas ⓘ *Boats can be hired and trips to floating villages are offered, expect to pay about US$10-15 per hr; take a moto from Siem Reap (10 km, US$2); boats from Phnom Penh berth at Chong Khnea.* Chong Khneas consist of some permanent buildings but is a largely floating settlement. The majority of the population live in houseboats and most services – including police, health, international aid agencies, retail and karaoke – are all provided on water. A trip around the village is testimony to the ingenuity of people living on this waterway with small kids paddling little tubs to each other's ouses.

Chong Khneas gets hundreds of visitors every day. For a more authentic, less touristy experience head out a bit further, 25 km east, to the village of **Kompong Phluk**. Costs to get to these villages are pretty high (up to US$50 per person) but are brought down if there are more passengers on the boat. See **Terre Cambodge** or **Two Dragons Guesthouse** under What to do to organize a tour.

Tip...

If you want to visit a school and orphanage, go to Savong's School (savong.com), a genuine success story.

Prek Toal Biosphere Also on the Tonlé Sap Lake is the Prek Toal Biosphere – a bird sanctuary which is home to 120 bird species, including cranes, stalks and pelicans. Boats can be organized from Chong Kneas to visit the Prek Toal Environment Office, US$30 return, one hour. From here you can arrange a guide and another boat for around US$20. **Terre Cambodia**, www.terrecambodge.com, runs boat tours upwards of US$80, as do **Osmose**, T012- 832812, osmose@bigpond.com.kh, and the **Sam Veasna Center for Wildlife and Conservation**, T063-761597, info@samveasna.org. There is basic accommodation at the Environment Office.

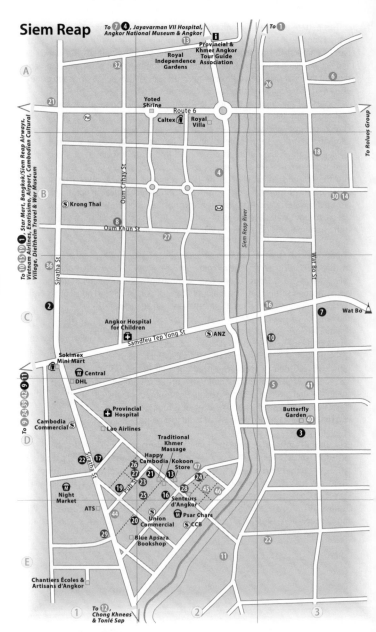

Siem Reap

To ⑦ ❹ , Jayavarman VII Hospital,
Angkor National Museum & Angkor

To ❶

Provincial &
Khmer Angkor
Tour Guide
Association

Royal
Independence
Gardens

⑬

㉜

㉖

⑥

Yoted
Shrine

Route 6

Caltex

Royal
Villa

⑱

④

Krong Thai

Oum Chhay St

Oum Khun St

⑧

㉗

Siem Reap River

Wat Bo St

㉚ ⑭

To ⑩⑮⑲❶ , Star Mart, Bangkok/Siem Reap Airways,
Vietnam Airlines, Exotissimo, Airport, Cambodian Cultural
Village, Diethelm Travel & War Museum

Sivatha St

㊱

❷

⑯

⑦ Wat Bo

Angkor Hospital
for Children

Samdfeu Tep Yong St

ANZ

⑩

Sokimex
Mini Mart

Central

DHL

To ⑨❷❸❾⑪

Provincial
Hospital

Cambodia
Commercial

Lao Airlines

⑤

⑭

Butterfly
Garden

㊵

❸

Traditional
Khmer
Massage

㉒

⑰

Happy
Cambodia

Kokoon
Store

㊼

㉖

㉑

⑬

㉔

Night
Market

⑲

㉕

Pub St

Sivatha St

⑯

㉘

㊺

㊻

ATS

㊹

Senteurs
d'Angkor

Psar Chars

⑳

Union
Commercial

CCB

㉙

Blue Apsara
Bookshop

⑪

㉒

Chantiers Écoles &
Artisans d'Angkor

To ⑫ ,
Chong Khneas
& Tonlé Sap

To ⑥

⑯

Star

To Roluos Group

```
N
```

100 metres
100 yards

Where to stay 🛏
Angkor Village Resort **1** *A3*
Bopha **5** *D3*
Borann **6** *A3*
Bou Savy **19** *A1*
Casa Angkor **8** *B1*
Earthwalkers **10** *C1*
FCC Angkor **4** *B2*
Home Sweet Home **14** *B3*
Jasmine Lodge **15** *B1*
La Noria **26** *A3*
La Résidence d'Angkor **16** *C3*
Le Meridien Angkor **7** **2** *A2*
Mahogany Guesthouse **18** *B3*
Mekong Angkor Palace **36** *C1*
Molly Malone's **44** *E1*
Neth Socheata **45** *D2*
Park Hyatt Siem Reap **9** *C1*
Passaggio **22** *E2*
Raffles Grand d'Angkor **13** *A2*
Rambutan Resort **11** *E2*
Sala Bai **39** *C3*
Shadow of Angkor I **46** *D2*
Shadow of Angkor II **40** *D3*
Shinta Mani **27** *B2*
Sokha Angkor **21** *A1*
Soria Moria **41** *D3*
Steung Siem Reap **47** *D2*
Suorkear Villa **12** *D1*
Two Dragons
 Guesthouse **30** *B3*
Victoria Angkor **32** *A1*
The Villa **42** *C3*

Restaurants 🍴
Abacus **1** *A1*
Barrio **2** *C1*
Blue Pumpkin **13** *D2*
Butterflies Garden **3** *D3*
Chez Sophea
 and Matthiu **4** *A2*
Khmer Kitchen **16** *D2*
Le Malraux **17** *D1*
Red Piano **19** *D1*

Singing Tree **20** *E1*
Soup Dragon **21** *D2*
Sugar Palm **9** *C3*
Tell Steakhouse **22** *D1*
Viroth's **7** *C3*

Bars & clubs 🍸
Angkor What? **23** *D2*
Fresh at Chili Si Dang **10** *C3*
Laundry **24** *D2*
Linga **25** *D2*
Miss Wong **26** *D1*
Temple Club **27** *D1*
Warehouse **28** *D2*
X Rooftop Bar **29** *E1*
Zone One **11** *C3*

Tourist information

There is a tourist office at the far end of
Sivatha St (towards the crocodile farm),
0730-1100 and 1430-1700.

Where to stay

It is not uncommon for taxi, moto and
tuk-tuk drivers to tell new arrivals that
the guesthouse they were booked into is
now 'closed' or full. They will try to take
you to the place where they get the best
commission. One way around this is to
arrange for the guesthouse or hotel to pick
you up from either the bus station or other
arrival point – many offer this service for
free or a small fee.

\$\$\$\$ Angkor Village Resort
*1 km north of Siem Reap, Phum Treang,
T063-963561, www.angkorvillage.com.*
The resort contains 40 rooms set in Balinese-
style surroundings. Traditional massage
services, 2 restaurants, theatre shows and
lovely pool. Elephant, boat and helicopter
rides can be arranged. Recommended.

\$\$\$\$ La Résidence d'Angkor Hotel
*River Rd, T063-963390,
www.residencedangkor.com.*
This is a hotel to aspire to. With its beautifully
laid out rooms all lavishly furnished with
marble and hardwoods,
it is reassuringly expensive. Each room
has a huge free-form bath – the perfect
end to a day touring the temples.

\$\$\$\$ Le Meridien Angkor
*Main road towards the temples, T063-963900,
www.lemeridien.com/angkor.*
From the outside this 5-star hotel is severe
with angled architecture and small, dark
slits for windows. Walk into the lobby and it
is immediately transformed into space and
light. Rooms are nicely designed and sized
and all come with a/c, en suite and cable
TV. Other facilities include spa, restaurants

and pool. The garden is a lovely spot to take breakfast. Recommended.

$$$$ Park Hyatt Siem Reap
Sivutha Blvd, T063-211234, www.siemreap. park.hyatt.com.
This is probably Siem Reap's best-value luxury hotel. The rooms offer simple contemporary design with giant bathtubs and plump bedding – all with a/c and cable TV. The pool is a maze of plinths and greenery and makes for a perfect spot to laze. Can feel a bit urban for Siem Reap but still a great hotel. Recommended.

$$$$ Raffles Grand Hotel d'Angkor
1 Charles de Gaulle Blvd, T063-963888, www.raffles.com/siem-reap.
Certainly a magnificent period piece from the outside, Siem Reap's oldest (1930) hotel fails to generate ambience, the rooms are sterile and the design of the huge new wings is uninspired (unforgivable in Angkor). Coupled with this is a history of staff lock-outs and mass sackings that have caused the Raffles brand damage. However, it does have all the mod cons, including sauna, tennis, health and beauty spa, lap pool, gym, 8 restaurants and bars, nightly traditional performances, landscaped gardens, 24-hr valet service and in-house movie channels.

$$$$ Shinta Mani
Junction of Oum Khun and 14th St, T063-761998, www.shintamani.com.
This 18-room luxury, boutique hotel is wonderful in every way: the design, the amenities, the food and the service. The hotel also offers a beautiful pool, library and has mountain bikes available. Provides vocational training to underprivileged youth.

$$$$ Sokha Angkor Resort
Sivatha St, T063-969999, www.sokhahotels. com/siemreap.
One of the few Cambodian-owned 5-star hotels in the country, the rooms and services here are top notch, even if the decor is a little gaudy (if you can't afford to stay here, come and check out the incredibly over-the-top

swimming pool, complete with faux temple structures and waterfalls). Also home to an excellent Japanese restaurant.

$$$$ Victoria Angkor Hotel
Route 6, T063-760428, www.victoriahotels-asia.com.
Perfection. A beautiful hotel, with that 1930s East-meets-West style that exemplifies the French tradition of *art de vivre*. The superb decor makes you feel like you are staying in another era. Each room is beautifully decorated with local fabrics and fantastic furniture. Swimming pool, open-air salas, jacuzzi and spa. It's the small touches and attention to detail that stands this hotel apart from the rest. Highly recommended.

$$$$-$$$ FCC Angkor
Near the post office on Pokambor Av, T063-760280, www.fcccambodia.com.
The sister property of the famous **FCC Phnom Penh**, this hotel is set in the grounds of a restored, modernist villa. Rooms offer contemporary luxury and plenty of space but be warned – there is a massive generator at one end of the complex running 24/7 so make sure you are housed well away from here. Also tends to trade more on its reputation so service, food, etc, can be ropey.

$$$$-$$$ Steung Siem Reap Hotel
St 9, T063-965167, www.steungsiemreaphotel.com.
This pleasant rooms in this colonial-style hotel come with cooling wooden floors and many overlook a very quiet pool. There are all the trimmings you'd expect in this price range, including gym, sauna, free Wi-Fi, free breakfast, a/c, huge bathtubs. Service and food average but still a good spot.

$$$$-$$$ Suorkear Villa
Sala Kamroeuk village, T063-764156, www.suorkearvilla.com.
Set in a very peaceful, private garden compound a couple of kilometres east of town, this 17-room/suite 'boutique' resort is unpretentious yet stylish. There's free breakfast, Wi-Fi, a restaurant and

complimentary transfers to and from town. The pool is cute as well. All rooms are, of course, a/c with TV and en suite hot-water facilities. Recommended.

$$$-$$ Casa Angkor
Corner of Chhay St and Oum Khun St, T063-966234, www.casaangkorhotel.com.
This is a good-looking, pleasant and well-managed 21-room hotel. 3 classes of room, all a decent size, well appointed and with cool wooden floors. Friendly reception and efficient staff. Restaurant, beer garden and reading room.

$$$-$$ La Noria
On the road running along the east side of the river, just past the 'stone' bridge, T063-964242, www.lanoriaangkor.com.
Almost perfect riverside setting for this gorgeous small resort. Tranquil gardens, a small pool and a real away-from-it-all vibe seduces guests who stay in brightly coloured a/c and en suite rooms each with their own balcony. No TV, very quiet and decent restaurant. Recommended.

$$$-$$ Molly Malone's
Old Market area, T063-963533, www.mollymalonescambodia.com.
Fantastic rooms with 4-poster beds and good clean bathrooms. Irish pub downstairs. Lovely owners. Recommended.

$$$-$$ Passaggio
Near the Old Market, T063-760324, www.passaggio-hotel.com.
15 double and 2 family rooms, spacious, a/c, minibar and cable TV, internet, laundry service, bar and restaurant, outdoor terrace.

$$$-$$ Soria Moria
Wat Bo Rd, T063-964768, www.thesoriamoria.com.
Excellent, well-run small hotel with a roof-top bar and a decent restaurant. Rooms – all en suite, with contemporary Asian flourishes, a/c and TVs – are quiet; the upper ones have nice airy views over the town. The enlightened owners have now

transferred half the ownership to their Khmer staff as part of an ongoing project to create sustainable, locally owned hotels in the area. Highly recommended.

$$ Borann
On the eastern side of the river, north of NH 6, just behind La Noria, T063-964740, www.borann.com.
This is an attractive hotel in a delightful garden with a pool. It is secluded and private. 5 small buildings each contain 4 comfortable rooms; some have a/c, some fan only.

$$ Mekong Angkor Palace Hotel
21 Sivatha St, T063-963636, www.mekongangkorpalaces.com.
Excellent mid-range, great-value hotel in a good central location. All the spotless rooms are trimmed with a contemporary Khmer vibe, free Wi-Fi, a/c, hot-water bathrooms and TVs. Room rates also include breakfast and there's an excellent pool. Recommended.

$$ Shadow of Angkor II
Wat Bo Rd, T063-760363, www.shadowofangkor.com.
Set on a quiet road this is the sister guesthouse of **Shadow of Angkor I** located on the market side of the river. Also offers well-located, good-value, well-run mid-range accommodation. As well as being clean and comfortable most rooms have balconies and all have a/c, free Wi-Fi, TV and hot water.

$$ The Villa
153 Taphul St, T063-761036, www.thevillasiemreap.com.
From the outside this place looks like a funky little guesthouse but some of the rooms are small and dark. All have a/c, TV and shower while the more expensive deluxe rooms are spacious and spotless.

$$-$ Bopha
On the east side of the river, T063-964928, www.bopha-angkor.com.
Stunning hotel. Good rooms with all the amenities, decorated with local furniture

and fabrics. Brilliant Thai-Khmer restaurant. Highly recommended.

$$-$ Home Sweet Home
Wat Bo area, near the Royal Palace garden, T063-760279, www. homesweethomeangkor.com.
Popular, and a favourite of the moto drivers (who get a kickback). Regardless, it's still got quite good, clean rooms, some with TV and a/c.

$$-$ Jasmine Lodge
Airport Rd near to town centre, T012-784980, www.jasminelodge.com.
One of the best budget deals in town, **Jasmine** is often fully booked, and with good reason. The super-friendly owner Kunn and his family go out of their way to make this a superlative place to stay; there's free Wi-Fi, breakfast can be included in the rate on request, there are huge shared areas for sitting, a book exchange, tour bookings, bus tickets, etc. There is a huge spread of rooms from basic ones with a fan and shared facilities to sparkling new accommodation with a/c, TV and hot-water bathrooms. Highly recommended.

$$-$ Rambutan Resort
Wat Damnak area (past Martini Bar), T012-885366, www.rambutans.info.
Good, clean rooms and decent restaurant.

$$-$ Sala Bai
155 Taphul Rd, T063-963329, www.salabai.com.
Part of an NGO programme that trains disadvantaged young Cambodians to work in the hospitality industry. The rooms are decent enough, in a good location and the suite is an excellent deal. Cheaper rooms have fan, pricier ones a/c, all have private hot-water showers. Gets booked up so reserve in advance. See also Restaurants, below

$$-$ Two Dragons Guesthouse
Wat Bo Village, T012-868551, www.twodragons-asia.com.
Very pleasant, clean rooms. Good little Thai restaurant. The owner, Gordon, is very well informed and runs www.talesofasia.com. He can organize a whole range of exciting tours around the area.

$ Bou Savy
Just outside town off the main airport road, T063-964967, www.bousavyguesthouse.com.
One of the best budget options in town, this tiny and very friendly family-owned guesthouse is set in soothing gardens and offers a range of rooms with fan or a/c. Also offers breakfast, internet and has some nice public areas. Recommended.

$ Earthwalkers
Just off the airport road, T012-967901.
Popular European-run budget guesthouse. Good gardens and pool table. Bit far out of town.

$ Mahogany Guesthouse
Wat Bo St, T063-963417/012-768944, proeun@bigpond.com.kh.
Fan and some a/c. An attractive and popular guesthouse, lovely wooden floor upstairs (try to avoid staying downstairs), coffee-making facilities and friendly atmosphere.

$ Neth Socheata
10 Thnou St, directly opposite the Old Market, T063-963294, www.nethsocheatahotel.com.
One of the Siem Reap's best deals, this small budget guesthouse, tucked away down a quiet alley opposite the market, has very nice, clean, pleasantly decorated rooms. All have en suite hot-water facilities and either a/c or fan. The best rooms have small balconies while others are windowless. There's free Wi-Fi and a friendly welcome. Recommended.

Restaurants

Near the moat there are a number of cheap food and drink stalls, bookshops and a posse of hawkers selling film, souvenirs, etc. Outside the entrance to Angkor Wat is a larger selection of cafés and restaurants including the sister restaurant to **The Blue Pumpkin** (see below), serving good sandwiches and breakfasts, ideal for takeaway.

$$$ Abacus
Route 6 to the airport, turn right at Acleda bank, T063-763660, www.cafeabacus.com.
A little further out from the main Old Market area, this place is considered one of the best restaurants in town. Offering French and Cambodian, everything is fantastic here. The fish is superb, the steak is to die for. Recommended.

$$$ Barrio
Sivatha St, away from the central area, T012-756448.
Fantastic French and Khmer food. A favourite of expats. Recommended.

$$$ Chez Sophea and Matthiu
Outside Angkor Wat, T012-858003.
A great place in the evening serving Khmer and French cuisine. Romantic setting. It closes around 2100, but later if you want to stay for a digestif or 2.

$$$ Le Malraux
Sivatha Blvd, T063-966041, www.le-malraux-siem-reap.com. Daily 0700-2400.
Sophisticated French cuisine served in this excellent restaurant. Also offers Khmer and Asian dishes, great wine list and good cognacs. Patio or indoor seating.

$$$-$$ Sala Bai Restaurant School
See Where to stay. Open for breakfast and lunch only.
Taking in students from the poorest areas of Cambodia, **Sala Bai** trains them in catering skills and places them in establishments around town. Service is not the best as students are quite shy practising their English, but a little bit of patience will help them through. Highly recommended.

$$$-$$ Soria Moria Fusion Kitchen
See Where to stay, above. Open 0700-2200.
Serves a range of local, Scandinavian and Japanese specialities. Wed night is popular, when all tapas dishes and drinks, including cocktails, cost US$1 each.

$$ The Blue Pumpkin
Old Market area, T063-963574, www.tbpumpkin.com.
Western and Asian food and drinks. Sandwiches, ice cream, pitta, salads and pasta.

$$ Bopha
See Where to stay, above.
Fantastic Thai/Khmer restaurant in a lovely, tranquil garden setting. One of the absolute best in town. Highly recommended.

$$ Butterflies Gardens
Just off Wat Bo Rd, T063-761211, www. butterfliesofangkor.com. Daily 0800-2200.
Tropical butterflies flit around a koi-filled pond in this slightly odd eatery. The food is Khmer/Asian and is average but the setting is well worth a visit.

$$ Molly Malone's
See Where to stay, above, T063-963533.
Lovely Irish bar offering classic dishes such as Irish stew, shepherd's pie, roasts, and fish and chips.

$$ Red Piano
341 St 8, northwest of the Old Market, T063-963240, www.redpianocambodia.com.
An institution in Siem Reap, based in a 100-year-old colonial building. Coffee, sandwiches, salad and pastas. Cocktail bar offering a range of tipples, including one dedicated to Angelina Jolie (who came here while working on *Tomb Raider*).

$$ Singing Tree Café
Alley West St, Old Market area, T09-263 5500, www.singingtreecafe.com. Tue-Sun 0800-2100.

Brilliant diner/community centre. Tasty European and Khmer home cooking, with plenty of veggie options. Also hosts a DVD library and a fairtrade shop.

$$ Soup Dragon
No 369, St 8, T063-964933.
Serves a variety of Khmer and Vietnamese dishes but its speciality is soups in earthenware pots cooked at the table. Breezy and clean, a light and colourful location. Upstairs bar, happy hour 1600-1930.

$$ The Sugar Palm
Taphul Rd, T063-964838, www.the sugarpalm.com/spsr. Closed Sun.
Sophisticated Khmer restaurant, with immaculate service and casual ambience.

$$ Tell Steakhouse
374 Sivatha St, T063-963289.
Swiss/German/Austrian restaurant and bar. Branch of the long-established Phnom Penh restaurant. Serves excellent fondue and raclette, imported beer and sausages. Reasonable prices and generous portions.

$$ Viroth's Restaurant
246 Wat Bo St, T012-826346, www.viroth-restaurant.com.
Upmarket place offering very good modern Khmer cuisine plus a few Western staples. Looks more expensive than it actually is and is good value.

$ Khmer Kitchen
Opposite Old Market and Alley West, T063-964154, www.khmerkitchens.com/siemreap.
Tasty cheap Khmer dishes service can be a little slow, but the food is worth waiting for. Sit on the alley side for good people-watching. Try the pumpkin pie (more of an omelette than a pie).

Bars and clubs
Pub Street may sound a bit brash by name but it has several good bars and restaurants.

Angkor What?
Pub St, T012-490755.
Friendly staff, popular with travellers and young expats.

Fresh at Chilli Si Dang
East River Rd, T017-875129. Open 0800-late.
Laid-back atmosphere, friendly service away from the tourist drag. Happy hour between 1700 and 2100.

Laundry
Near the Old Market, turn right off 'Pub St', T012-246912. Open till late.
Funky little bar.

Linga
Pub St Alley, T012-246912, www.lingabar.com.
Gay-friendly bar offering a wide selection of cocktails. Great whisky sours.

Miss Wong
The Lane (behind Pub St), T092-428332, www.misswong.net. Open 1700-0100.
Cute little bar serving sharp cocktails in an Old Shanghai setting.

Temple Club
Pub St, T015-999909.
Popular drinking hole, dimly lit, good music. Not related to its seedier namesake in Phnom Penh.

The Warehouse
Opposite Old Market area, T063-964600, www.thewarehousesiemreap.com. Open 1000-0300.
Popular bar, good service and Wi-Fi.

X Rooftop Bar
Sok San Rd, top of Sivataha St (you'll see the luminous X from most high-rise buildings in town), T012-263271, http://xbar.asia. Open 1600-sunrise.
The latest-closing bar in town. Happy hour 1600-1730.

Zone One
Taphul Village, T012-912347. Open 1800-late.
The place to experience local nightlife.

Entertainment

Music

A popular Sat evening attraction is the one-man concert put on by **Dr Beat Richner** (Beatocello), founder of the Jayavarman VII hospital for children. Run entirely on voluntary donations the 3 hospitals in the foundation need US$9 million per year in order to treat Cambodian children free of charge. He performs at the hospital, on the road to Angkor, at 1915, 1 hr, free admission but donations gratefully accepted. An interesting and worthwhile experience.

Shadow puppetry

This is one of the finest performing arts of the region. The **Bayon Restaurant**, Wat Bo Rd, has regular shadow puppet shows in the evening. Local NGO, **Krousar Thmey**, often tours its shadow puppet show to Siem Reap. The show is performed by underprivileged children (who have also made the puppets) at **La Noria Restaurant** (Wed 1930 but check as they can be irregular). Donations accepted.

Shopping

Outside Phnom Penh, Siem Reap is about the only place whose markets are worth browsing for genuinely interesting souvenirs. Old Market (Psar Chars) is not a large market but stall holders and keepers of the surrounding shops have developed quite a good understanding of what tickles the appetite of foreigners: Buddhist statues and icons, reproductions of Angkor figures, silks, cottons, *kramas*, sarongs, silverware, leather puppets and rice paper rubbings of Angkor bas-reliefs are unusual mementos. In the night market area, off Sivatha St, you'll find bars, spas and cafés. The original night market, towards the back, has more original stalls, but is slightly more expensive.

Boutique Senteurs d'Angkor, *opposite Old Market, T063-964801, www.senteurs dangkor.com*. Sells a good selection of handicrafts, carvings, silverware, silks, handmade paper, cards, scented oils, incense, pepper and spices.

Chantiers Écoles, *Stung Thmey St, down a short lane off Sivatha St, T063-963330*. A school for orphaned children that trains them in carving, sewing and weaving. Products are on sale under the name **Les Artisans d'Angkor** and raise 30% of the school's running costs.

What to do

Helicopter and balloon rides

For those wishing to see Angkor from a different perspective it is possible to charter a helicopter. In many ways, it is only from the air that you can really grasp the size and scale of Angkor and a short flight will certainly be a memorable experience. A cheaper alternative for a good aerial view is to organize a balloon ride above the temples. The tethered balloons float 200 m above Angkor Wat for about 10 mins, US$10 per trip. The balloon company is based about 1 km from the main gates from Angkor Wat, on the road from the airport to the temples.

Helicopters Cambodia, *65 St Hup Quan, near Old Market, T063-963316, www. helicopterscambodia.com*. A New Zealand company offering chartered flights around the temples from US$75 per person.

Therapies

Khmer, Thai, reflexology and Japanese massage are readily available. Many masseuses will come to your hotel.

Frangipani, *24 Hup Guan St, near Angkor Hospital for Children, T063-964391, www. frangipanisiemreap.com*. Professional masseuse offers aromatherapy, reflexology and other treatments.

Mutita Spa, *Borei Angkor Resort and Spa, Route 6, T063-964406*. Offers unique J'Pong therapy, which is a traditional Cambodian heat and relaxation treatment using herbal steam.

Seeing Hands, *324 Sivatha St*. Massage by sight-impaired individuals. US$3 per hr. Highly recommended.

Tour operators

Asia Pacific Travel, *No 100, Route 6, T063-760862, www.angkortravelcambodia.com*. Tours of Angkor and the region.

Buffalo Tours, *556 Tep Vong St, Khum Svay Dangkom, T063-965670, www.buffalotours. com*. Wide range of customized tours.

Exotissimo Travel, *No 300, Route 6, T063-964323, www.exotissimo.com*. Tours of Angkor and sites beyond.

Hidden Cambodia Adventure Tours, *T012-655201, www.hiddencambodia.com*. Specializes in dirt-bike tours to remote areas and off-the-track temple locations. Recommended for the adventurous.

Journeys Within, *on the outskirts of Siem Reap towards the temples, T063-966463, www.journeys-within.com*. Customized tours, visiting temples and experiencing the everyday lives of Cambodians.

Khmer Angkor Tour Guide Association, *on the road to Angkor, T063-964347, www. khmerangkortourguide.com*. The association has well-trained and well-briefed guides; some speak English better than others. The going rate is US$20-25 per day.

Mr Hak, *T012-540336, www.angkortaxidriver. com*. Provides an excellent service offering packages and tours around Angkor and the surrounding area. Recommended.

Terre Cambodge, *Huap Guan St, near Angkor Hospital for Children, T092-476682, www. terrecambodge.com*. Offers tours with a twist, including cruises on an old sampan boat. Not cheap but worth it for the experience.

Two Dragons Guesthouse, *see Where to stay, above*. Can organize off-the-beaten-track tours. Owner Gordon Sharpless is a very knowledgeable and helpful fellow.

WHL Cambodia, *Wat Bo Rd, T063-963854, www.angkorhotels.org*. Locally run website for booking hotels and tours with a responsible tourism approach.

World Express Tours & Travel, *St No 11 (Old Market area), T063-963600, www. worldexpresstour.com*. Can organize tours all over Cambodia. Also books local and international air/bus tickets. A good place to extend visas. Friendly service.

Transport

For information on transport between Siem Reap and Angkor, see page 246.

Airport

Siem Reap Airways and the national carrier **Cambodia Angkor Air** have connections with **Phnom Penh**. Book in advance. All departure taxes are now included in the ticket price. **Siem Reap Airport**, 7 km from Siem Reap, T063-963148, is the closest to the Angkor ruins. A moto into town is US$1, a taxi US$7. Guesthouse owners often meet flights. Visas can be issued upon arrival US$20 (₡1000), photo required.

Bicycle

The **White Bicycles** scheme, www. thewhitebicycles.org, set up by Norwegian expats (see page 246). Recommended. **Khemara**, opposite the Old Market, T063-964512, rents bicycles for US$2 per day.

Boat

The ferry docks are at Chong Khneas, 15 km south of Siem Reap on the Tonlé Sap Lake, near Phnom Krom. Taxis, tuk-tuks and motodops wait at the dock; a motodop into town will cost US$2. Tickets and enquiries, T012-581358. To **Phnom Penh**, US$35, 5-6 hrs. It is a less appealing option in the dry season when low water levels necessitate transfers to small, shallow draft vessels. In case of extremely low water levels a bus or pickup will need to be taken for part of the trip. The mudbank causeway between the lake and the outskirts of Siem Reap is hard to negotiate and some walking may be necessary (it's 12 km from Siem Reap to Bindonville harbour). Boats depart Siem Reap at 0700 from Chong Khneas about 12 km away on the Tonlé Sap Lake (a motodop will cost US$2 to get here) arriving in Phnom Penh Port at Sisowath Quay (end of 106 St). Tickets and enquiries, T012-581358.

Bus

Different companies use different bus stations. The Chong Kov Sou station is 7 km west of Siem Reap. Motodops into town cost US$1.50-2, tuk-tuks US$3. Others arrive near the Old Market.

A/c buses are one of the most convenient and comfortable ways to travel from Siem Reap to **Phnom Penh**, US$6-13, 6 hrs. At the time of going to press the road between Siem Reap and Phnom Penh was undergoing a massive redevelopment and consequently parts of it have been reduced to a rutted, dirt-track. Until it is completed expect increased journey times. Almost every guesthouse or hotel sells tickets although it is easy enough to pick up from the bus stations/terminal. In peak periods, particularly Khmer New Year, it is important to purchase tickets a day or two prior to travel. **Neak Krorhorm Travel**, **GST**, **Mekong Express** and **Capitol** depart Siem Reap (from near the Old Market) between 0630 and 0800, and the same from Phnom Penh bus station.

Taxi

A shared taxi to **Phnom Penh** will cost US$10.

GOING FURTHER

Battambang

Cambodia's second largest city lies 40 km west of the Tonlé Sap at the centre of a fertile plain on the lovely Sangkei River. It retains a lot of charming early 20th-century buildings as well as 16 wats, some – so it is said – dating back to the Angkor period, which are scattered around the city and surrounding lush countryside. The town itself is quite beautiful, with a number of old colonial buildings sitting around the misty, river area. A large number of NGOs working in the northwest region have offices here so the town has quite good amenities and restaurants. With its proximity to the Thai border and the trade opportunities that come with that, Battambang is slowly emerging as a prosperous, very liveable provincial city. There's a new university, the streets are mostly clean and well kept and there is a discernible feeling of pride emanating from the city's leafy streets. More notably, some of the riverside colonial buildings are now being beautifully restored, something which only adds to the relaxed upbeat vibe. Battambang, which translates as 'disappearing stick', is named after a magical stick that the king used to ensure his power.

Transport

Boat

Daily connections by boat provide the most scenic and enjoyable way to get between Battambang and Siem Reap and if you take a slow boat it's a perfect way to enjoy the bucolic charms of the Cambodian countryside. The trip is best in the wet season (May-October) when the river is high. During the late dry season it can take considerably longer.

The boat to Siem Reap leaves daily from the pier just east of Route 5 river crossing. Departs at 0700, 3-4 hours, US$15. In the dry season the boat can take up to seven hours, or longer, and includes a one-hour trip in the back of a pickup, when the river becomes too low. From the boat to any hotel a moto should cost US$1.

Northeastern Cambodia

follow the Mekong to Laos or trek in the Highlands

A wild and rugged landscape, comprising the provinces of Ratanakiri and Stung Treng, greets any visitor to the remote Northeast region.

Vast forested swathes of sparsely inhabited terrain spread north and eastwards toward Vietnam and Laos and are home to several distinct ethnic groups. The thick jungles also provide sanctuary to the majority of Cambodia's few remaining tigers.

During the civil war, the Northeast was cut off from the rest of the country. Then came years of bad transport links, with only the most committed making the arduous run up from Phnom Penh. Yet the Northeast is now developing. A Chinese-built road, including a road bridge over the river in Stung Treng, now forms a strong link between Cambodia and Laos, cutting hours off the journey time.

Framing its western edge, and cutting it off from the rest of the country, is the Mekong River. It bifurcates, meanders and braids its way through the country and represents in its width a yawning chasm and watery superhighway that connects the region with Phnom Penh. Stung Treng and Kratie are located on this mighty river and despite the lack of any kind of riverboat service are still excellent places to view the elusive Irrawaddy river dolphin.

The dust-blown and wild frontier town of Ban Lung, the capital of Ratanakiri, is emerging as a centre of trekking and adventure travel.

Best for
Ecotourism ■ Landscapes ■ Trekking ■ Wildlife

Footprint
picks

★ **Irrawaddy dolphins**, page 285

Kampi Pool, near Kratie, is one of the few places in the world to spot these endangered creatures.

★ **Yaek Lom**, page 290

The crystal-clear waters of this perfectly circular volcanic lake are a good spot for a dip (Cambodia's biggest swimming pool).

★ **Gibbon spotting**, page 293

The experience of seeing these apes swinging through the jungle is memorable.

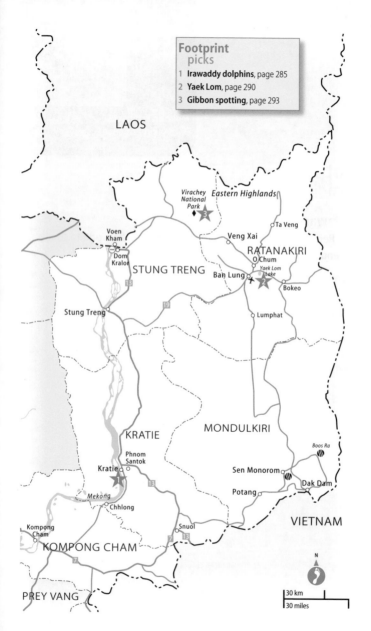

Footprint
picks
1 **Irawaddy dolphins**, page 285
2 **Yaek Lom**, page 290
3 **Gibbon spotting**, page 293

LAOS

Virachey
National
Park
Eastern Highlands

Ta Veng

Voen
Kham
Veng Xai

Dom
Kralor
RATANAKIRI

O Chum

STUNG TRENG
Ban Lung
Yaek Lom
Lake

Bokeo

Stung Treng

Lumphat

KRATIE
MONDULKIRI

Phnom
Santok
Boos Ra

Kratie
Sen Monorom
Dak Dam

Mekong
Potang

Chhlong

VIETNAM
Snuol

Kompong
Cham
KOMPONG CHAM

PREY VANG

N

30 km
30 miles

Kompong Cham, Kratie and Stung Treng make up the Mekong Provinces. Despite the Mekong River, its waterway and perpetual irrigation, these provinces are surprisingly economically unimportant and laid back. But with the new Chinese-built road now open and fully functioning – it's easily one of the best in the country – the Northeast's provincial charms may start to diminish.

Kompong Cham and around

Kompong Cham, the fourth largest town in Cambodia, is a town of some commercial prosperity owing to its thriving river port and also, it is said, as a result of preferential treatment received from local boy made good: the prime minister Hun Sen. Town and province have a combined population of more than 1.5 million people. There is nothing in or around Kompong Cham to detain the visitor for long, most merely pass through en route for Stung Treng and the Northeast, but it is a pleasant enough town to rest awhile.

A new road linking Kompong Cham and Kratie, and passing just outside Chhlong, has been built. This shaves about 90 minutes off the original journey time and may place Chhlong on a new travellers' route.

Chhlong

Chhlong, between Kompong Cham and Kratie, is one of Cambodia's best-kept secrets. The small town, nestled on the banks of the Mekong, 41 km from Kratie and 82 km from Kompong Cham, is one of the few places that survived the Khmer Rouge's ransacking and boasts a multitude of French colonial buildings and traditional wooden Khmer houses. Of particular interest are the foundations of 120 antique houses and a 19th-century wooden Khmer house supported by 100 columns. Formerly a base for workers in surrounding rubber plantations, it is easy to feel nostalgic for a bygone era in Chhlong, with its wats and monasteries, an old school and charming market set in a colonial-style building. There are a couple of basic guesthouses on the riverfront road if you want to stop here for a night or two. There's also a small market with a few stalls selling noodle and rice dishes.

★Kratie

Kratie (pronounced 'Kratcheay') is a port town on the Mekong roughly halfway between Phnom Penh and Laos. In many ways it is a delightful place with a relaxed atmosphere and some good examples of shophouse architecture, but there is a discernible nefarious undercurrent due to Kratie's reputation as a centre of organized crime and corruption. With the murky majesty of the Mekong dominating the town, sunset is a real highlight in Kratie, as the burning red sun descends slowly below the shore line.

Kratie's main claim to fame are the **Irrawaddy dolphins** that inhabit this portion of the Mekong (Kampi Pool), 15 km north of the town on the road to Stung Treng. The best time to glimpse these rare and timid creatures is at sunrise or sunset when they are feeding. Motos from the town are US$4-5 return, boats then cost US$9 per person or US$7 per person for three or more people.

Koh Trong Island ⓘ *Directly opposite Kratie town*. The island has a lovely 8-km stretch of sandy dunes (in the dry season) where you can swim and relax. Aside from the beach, the

Essential Northeastern Cambodia

Getting around

Well-surfaced roads now connect Phnom Penh and the Northeast, with buses and shared taxis running to Kompong Cham and all points north including Kratie, Stung Treng and Ban Lung. With the new road opening, boats are no longer used as a main form of transport. Away from the main highways, roads can disintegrate to dirt tracks at times and journey times can be long. Local transport is by moto, tuk-tuk or taxi. Shared taxis are also available.

Most guesthouses and hotels in Sen Monorom can recommend an English-speaking guide/moto driver for around US$15; more if lengthy trips are required.

When to go

The dry season (November-March) is the most comfortable time to visit, with January and February the driest. After the rainy season the waterfalls are at their best. The rainy season (May-October) makes travel in isolated areas hard going.

Time required

At least a week to explore the remote villages or go trekking or gibbon spotting in Ratanakiri. Allow extra time for transport delays.

Weather Ban Lung

Jan	Feb	Mar	Apr	May	Jun
23°C	25°C	27°C	28°C	27°C	27°C
☀	☀	☀	☁	☁	🌧

Jul	Aug	Sep	Oct	Nov	Dec
27°C	27°C	27°C	26°C	25°C	23°C
🌧	🌧	🌧	🌧	☁	☀

island consists of small market farms and a simple, laid-back rural lifestyle – highly recommended for those who want to chill out. On the south side is a small Vietnamese floating village.

Kampi Rapids ① *3 km north of Kampi Dolphin Pool, also known as Kampi Resort, 1000 riel.* This is a refreshing and picturesque area to take a dip in the clear Mekong waters (during the dry season). A bridge leads down to a series of scenic thatched huts which provide shelter for the swimmers.

Sambor ① *21 km north of the Kampi Pool.* Sambor is a pre-Angkorian settlement, but today, unfortunately, not a single trace of this ancient heritage exists. The highlight of a trip to Sambor is as much in the journey, through beautiful countryside, as in the temples themselves. Replacing the ancient ruins are two temples. The first and most impressive is the 100-column pagoda, rumoured to be the largest new pagoda in the country. It is a replica of the 100-column wooden original, which was built in 1529. During the war, Pol Pot operated out of the complex, killing hundreds of people and destroying the old pagoda. The new one was built in 1985 (perhaps the builders were slightly overzealous – it features 116 columns). Some 300 m behind the gigantic pagoda sits a much smaller and arguably more interesting temple. The wat still contains many of its original features, including a number of wooden pylons that date back 537 years.

Stung Treng

Yet another eponymous provincial capital set at the point where the Sekong River cuts away from the Mekong, Stung Treng is just 40 km from Laos and a stopping-off place on the overland route to Ratanakiri. The town still maintains a wild frontier feel despite losing much of its edge due to the building of the mammoth Chinese road and a striking bridge that has created good links to Laos (see page 289), for details on how to reach Laos). Pigs, cows and the odd ox-cart still wander through the town's busy streets but there isn't a lot for tourists. It's a friendly place though and tour guides can organize boat runs to a local river dolphin project, cycling trips along the river banks and excursions to some waterfalls. **Lbak Khone**, the 26-km rocky area that the Mekong rapids flow through en route to the Laos border, is one of the country's most stunning areas.

Listings Mekong Provinces

Where to stay

Kompong Cham and around

$$-$ Monorom 2 VIP Hotel
Mort Tunle St, waterfront, T092-777102,
www.monoromviphotel.com.
With a perfect Mekong setting, this new hotel is easily the best in town. Get a room at the front and you'll have a balcony overlooking the river – each comes with bathtub, hot water, cable TV, tea-making facilities and there's free Wi-Fi for guests on the ground floor. Recommended.

$ Chaplins Guesthouse
Riverfront Rd, T012-627612,
www.chaplinsguesthouse.com.
Cosy guesthouse with clean comfortable rooms, free parking and Wi-Fi. Restaurant and bar on site. 15-min walk from the central market.

$ Rana Homestay
Srey Siam, T012-696340, www.rana-ruralhomestay-cambodia.webs.com.
Set in a small village just outside Kampong Cham, this is an engaging homestay programme well run by Kheang and her American husband, Don. Set up more for educational purposes than as a business, you can get a real insight into rural life here. Rates include full board but accommodation is basic. Free moto pick-up from Kampong Cham if you book for 2 or more nights. Recommended.

Kratie

$ Balcony Guesthouse
Corner Preah Soramarit St and St 5, riverfront,
T016-604036, www.balconyguesthouse.net.

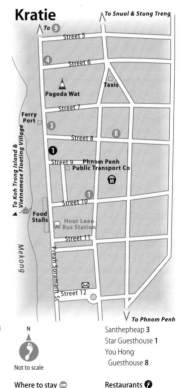

Kratie

To Snuol & Stung Treng
To 9
Street 5
4
Street 6
Taxis
Pagoda Wat
Street 7
Ferry Port
3
Street 8
8
1
Street 9 — Phnom Penh Public Transport Co
To Koh Trong Island & Vietnamese Floating Village
M
1
Street 10
Food Stalls
Hour Lean Bus Station
Street 11
Preah Soramarit St
Mekong
Street 12
To Phnom Penh

N
Not to scale

Santhepheap **3**
Star Guesthouse **1**
You Hong
Guesthouse **8**

Where to stay 🛏
Balcony Guesthouse **9**
Oudom Sambath **4**

Restaurants 🍴
Red Sun Falling **1**

There are several airy, clean and basic rooms in this villa overlooking the river. There is, as the name suggests, a giant, communal balcony which is a great place to lounge and watch Mekong sunsets. Bar, restaurant and internet as well.

$ Oudom Sambath Hotel
439 Preah Suramarit St, riverfront, T072-971502.
Well-run place with a friendly English-speaking Chinese/Khmer owner. The rooms are huge, with a/c, TV, hot water, etc. The more expensive rooms have large baths and regal-looking furniture. The huge rooftop balcony has the best views in town, out over the Mekong. There are rooms up here as well but these fill quickly. Also has a decent and very cheap restaurant. Recommended.

$ Santepheap Hotel
Preah Suramarit St, riverfront, T072-971537.
Rooms are adequate in this reasonable hotel. It has a quiet atmosphere and the clean and airy rooms come with attached bathrooms, fridge, fan or a/c.

$ Star Guesthouse
Beside the market, T072-971663.
This has gained the reputation of being the friendliest guesthouse in town. It is very popular with travellers and rooms are nicely appointed.

$ You Hong Guesthouse
No 91, St 8, between the taxi rank and the market, T012-957003.
Clean rooms with attached bathroom and fan. US$1 extra gets you cable TV. Friendly, helpful owners. The restaurant is often filled with drunk backpackers.

Stung Treng

$$-$ Hotel Golden River
Riverfront, T012-980678,
www.goldenriverhotel.com.
4-storey hotel with splendid river views and the only lift in northeastern Cambodia. Each spotless and comfortable room has a hot-water bathtub, cable TV and a/c; the ones at the front offer the river as backdrop. Friendly service and a bargain given the location. Recommended.

$$-$ Ly Ly Guesthouse
Opposite the market, T012-937859.
Decent Chinese-style hotel with varying types of rooms – all come with private shower/toilet and cable TV. The ones at the back of the building have balconies and are the best value. A/c or fan throughout. Friendly with some English spoken. Recommended.

$$-$ Stung Treng Hotel and Guest House
On main road near the river, T016-888335.
Decent enough rooms in a good location.

Restaurants

Kompong Cham and around

$$ Ho An Restaurant
Monivong St, T042-941234.
Large, Chinese restaurant with a good selection of dishes. Friendly service.

$$-$ Lazy Mekong Daze
On the riverfront.
British owner Simon provides alcohol, cakes, fish and chips, and Khmer food from this friendly riverside establishment. He also has a free pool table and you can watch the latest football on his TV.

$ Fresh Coffee
Same block as Monorom 2 VIP Hotel on the riverfront. Open 0700-2100.
Small new coffee shop selling burgers, cakes and some Khmer food.

$ Smile Restaurant
No 6, St 7, same block as Monorom 2 VIP Hotel on the riverfront. Open 0630-2200.
Huge Khmer menu with some Western dishes in this excellent NGO-connected eatery that helps orphans and kids with HIV. Free Wi-Fi. Recommended.

Kratie

There are a number of foodstalls along the river at night serving fruit shakes. The market also sells simple dishes during the day.

$$-$ Balcony Guesthouse
See Where to stay, above.
Serves up an excellent fried British breakfast and various other Western and Khmer dishes from its huge balcony overlooking the river. Good spot for a drink as well. Recommended.

$$-$ Red Sun Falling
Preah Soramarit St, riverfront. Mon-Sat.
Offers a variety of Western dishes and a few Asian favourites.

$$-$ Star Guesthouse
See Where to stay, above.
A decent enough menu but sometimes the prices (almost US$1 for a squeeze of honey) and quality let the place down. Western food, and the home-made bread is excellent.

Stung Treng

$ Prochum Tonle Restaurant
At the Sekong Hotel on the riverfront.
Some of the best Khmer food in town at this locally renowned restaurant.

$ Sophakmukal
Near the market.
Beer garden-style restaurant with very good, cheap Cambodian food, curry, amok, soup (all under US$1). Very friendly owner. Recommended.

$ Ponika's Palace
In a side street near the market.
Daily 0630-2100.
Very friendly owners, fresh decor and good food make this place one of the best spots in town. Great burgers and pizza supplement excellent Khmer food; decent breakfasts too. Recommended.

Kompong Cham and around
Bus
The town is 120 km northeast of Phnom Penh via the well-surfaced Routes 5, 6 and 7. There are regular connections with **Phnom Penh** by shared taxi and numerous bus companies run regular services. Buses also connect to all points north including **Chhlong**, **Kratie**, **Stung Treng** and **Ban Lung**.

Moto, tuk-tuk, taxi and boat
Local transport is by moto, tuk-tuk or taxi. A moto for a day is between US$6-8 and 500-1000 riel for short trips. Local tuk-tuk driver and guide Mr Vannat has an excellent reputation and is fluent in French and English, T012-995890. US$20 a day for a boat ride.

Kratie
Bus
Roughly 4 buses a day run to **Phnom Penh**, US$5/US$8, 4-5 hrs, stopping off at **Kompong Cham** en route. Stung Treng is served by regular minibuses 0800-1400, US$6, 2 hrs, and at least 1 daily bus, US$4, 2½ hrs; while there is at least 1 minibus a day to **Ban Lung**, US$12, 6 hrs. Many of these buses depart from the bus stand near the river, but you might want to ask at your accommodation if this has changed.

Motodop
Local transport by motodop US$1 per hr or US$6-7 per day.

Taxi
You can find shared taxis plying routes to all destinations though prices fluctuate according to season, road condition and fuel prices.

Stung Treng
Before the bridge opened in 2008, Stung Treng used to be the staging post for travel to Laos with regular boats plying the few kilometres upriver to the border. Nowadays,

most travellers heading south from Pakse in Laos, no longer stop in Stung Treng, preferring instead to take through buses directly to Kratie and Phnom Penh.

Most hotels can organize tickets. Alternatively, you can go directly to the taxi/bus rank. At present there is at least 1 bus a day to **Pakse** (Laos), 4½ hrs, US$6, and onward tickets to **Vientiane** (changing in Pakse) are also available, US$35, should you wish to connect directly to the Laos capital. There are a couple of buses to **Phnom Penh,** daily, 9 hrs, US$7.50; and the same bus will stop at **Kratie,** US$5. Plenty of minibuses also ply this route.

Pickups and shared taxis connect regularly with Phnom Penh via Kratie, and with recent road construction the roads should be OK to travel along (if a little bumpy). Shared taxis to **Phnom Penh** leave at 0600 from the taxi rank near the river, 7 hrs, US$15. To **Ban Lung** at 0700 from the taxi rank and the trip takes 4-5 hrs, US$10.

Ratanakiri Province

great trekking, ecotourism and ethnic minority homestays

The name Ratanakiri means 'jewel mountains' in Pali, and presumably comes from the wealth of gems in the hills, but it could just as easily refer to the beauty of the landscape.

With the main road in and out of Ratanakiri now fully paved, the otherworldly feel of the province is slowly disappearing. However, outdoor enthusiasts won't be disappointed, with waterfalls to discover, elephants to ride, river trips to take and the beautiful Yaek Lom volcanic lake to take a dip in.

Ban Lung and around

Ban Lung has been the dusty provincial capital of Ratanakiri Province ever since the previous capital Lumphat was flattened by US bombers trying to 'destroy' the footpaths and tracks that made up the Ho Chi Minh Trail. The dirt tracks that used to suffocate the town with their dry season dust and wet season mud have now been mostly paved, making a visit here more feasible. The town is situated on a plateau dotted with lakes and hills, many of great beauty, and serves as a base from which visitors can explore the surrounding countryside. With the Vietnamese in the east building a road from the nearby Le Thanh/O Yadao border crossing, plans to pave the existing roads into and out of Ban Lung, and a burgeoning tourist market, mark this part of Cambodia for dramatic change. At present you'll find basic guesthouse accommodation, and food and drink can be obtained in town.

★Yaek Lom

US$1 and a parking charge of 500 riel, all of which goes into a fund to promote the conservation of the area.

Yaek Lom is a perfectly circular volcanic lake about 5 km east of town and easily reached by motorbike. The crystalline lake is rimmed by protected forest dominated by giant emergents (dipterocarps and shoreas) soaring high into the sky. Around the feet of these giant trees is a dense tangle of smaller woods and bamboos which filters the late afternoon sun into gorgeous hues of green and dappled patterns of light and shade. It takes about one hour to walk around the lake: in doing so you will find plenty of secluded bathing spots and a couple of small jetties; and, given the lack of water in town, it is not surprising that most locals and visitors bathe in the wonderfully clear and cool waters. There is a visitor centre which serves as an ethnic minority museum with a collection of instruments, baskets, tools and other curios.

Waterfalls

2000 riel each, follow Highway 19 out of town and branch off 2 km out on the main road in the first village out of Ban Lung: Chaa Ong Falls are 9 km northwest at the intersection, turn right at the village and head for about 5 km to Katien Waterfall (follow the signs), the same road leads to Kachaang Waterfall.

Waterfalls near Ban Lung There are three waterfalls in close proximity to Ban Lung town. **Kachaang Waterfall** is 6 km away. The 12-m-high waterfall flows year round and is surrounded by magnificent, pristine jungle and fresh mist rising from the fall. **Katien Waterfall** is a little oasis 7 km northwest of Ban Lung. Believed to have formed from volcanic lava hundreds of years ago, the 10-m plunging falls are sheltered from the outside world by a little rocky grotto. It is one of the better local falls to swim in as it is very secluded (most people will usually have the area to themselves), the water is clean and the bunches of vines hanging from the summit provide good swinging potential. Amongst the dotted ferns, rocky boulders and large meandering fig trees, the 40-m-wide pool peters off into a delicate brook, an offshoot of the Koutung Stream. Katien flows all year round and is a favourite of elephant trekkers. However, the best waterfall is arguably **Chaa Ong Falls**, with the 30-m falls plunging into a large pool. Those game enough can have a shower behind the crescent-shaped ledge.

Ou'Sean Lair Waterfall ⓘ *35 km from Ban Lung.* This is a wonderful day excursion offering a fantastic cross-section of what are essentially Ratanakiri's main attractions (without the riverside element). From Ban Lung, fields of wind-bent, spindly rubber trees provide a canopy over the road's rolling hills, a legacy left from the French in the 1960s. Punctuating the mottled natural vista is an equally diverse range of ethnic minority settlements. Tampeun and Kreung villages are dotted along the road and about half way (17 km from Ban Lung), in a lovely valley, is a tiny Cham village. The perfect end to the journey is the seven-tiered Ou'Sean Lair falls. The falls were reportedly 'discovered' some years ago by a Tampeun villager, who debated as to whether he should tell the Department of Tourism of their existence. In return for turning over the falls, they were named after him. The falls are most spectacular in the wet season but are still pretty alluring during the dry season.

Listings Ratanakiri Province

Where to stay

Ban Lung and around

$$-$ Borann Lodge
800 m east of market, T012-959363, www. borannlodge.blogspot.co.uk.
This huge chalet-style villa set down a Ban Lung sidestreet comes with 6 rooms of varying sizes though each has a/c and fan and en suite bathroom with hot water. The owners and staff are very friendly and

Borann feels more like a homestay than a guesthouse. Massive wooden model of Angkor and various over-the-top wooden furniture items add to the character. Affiliated with **Yaklom Hill Lodge** (see below). Recommended.

$$-$ NorDen House
On road to Yaklom Lake, T012-880327, www.nordenhouseyaklom.com.
The nearest accommodation to Yaklom Lake. You'll find a collection of spotless, well-

appointed bungalows here each with a/c, TV and en suite hot-water facilities. There are some attractive gardens, a decent restaurant, free Wi-Fi plus they can arrange bus tickets. They also rent out the best motorbikes in town. Swedish and Khmer owners. Recommended.

$$-$ Yaklom Hill Lodge
Near Yaklom Lake, 6 km east of Ban Lung, T011-725881 or T097-699 9146, www.yaklom. blogspot.co.uk.

Set in a private forest this rustic ecolodge is a bit out of town. Bungalows have balconies and hammocks and are well decorated with local handicrafts and fabrics. They also have fan, mosquito net and attached bathroom with shower; power is supplied via generator and solar panels. The friendly owner, Sampon, arranges all manner of tours and treks and is the only operator in the area who uses local ethnic minority people as guides. Affiliated with **Borann Lodge** (see above). The food is a bit ropey but still this place is recommended.

$ Sopheap Guest House
Next to the market, T012-958746.

Clean rooms complete with hot water, fan or a/c, cable TV and a noisy and lively central location. Get one with a balcony and you'll have a great view of the market life unfolding below you.

$ Tree Top Eco-Lodge
Phum Nol, Laban Seak Commune, T012-490333, www.treetop-ecolodge.com.

Lovely set of large wooden bungalows overlooking a valley on the edge of town. Interiors are well decorated and each room has a huge balcony and en suite hot-water bathroom. There are some good communal areas and verandas, a restaurant/bar and free transfers to the bus station. Recommended.

Restaurants

Ban Lung and around
Food options are improving in Ban Lung with a greater range of fresh fruit and other produce on sale at the market and various small bakeries offering Khmer-style cakes and breads opening up.

$ A' Dam
On the same road as Borann Lodge and Tree Top Eco-Lodge, T012-411115. Open 1100-2200.

It's understandable why A'Dam is popular with both Ban Lung locals and expat NGO workers. Great Khmer and Western food is piled high and served cheap by the friendly Khmer owners. Also doubles as a bar. Recommended.

$ Apocalypse Bar
East of the market, near Borann Lodge (see Where to stay, above).

You can get decent coffee and tea plus breakfasts at this small eatery attached to the **DutchCo** tour agency.

$ Café Alee
No 25, Rd 78A, Chey Chomneas Village, T089-473767.

Relaxed café/restaurant/bar serving typical Cambodian dishes with some home comfort Western and vegetarian options. Knowledgeable owner. Good coffee.

$ Tree Top Eco-Lodge
See Where to stay, above.

Great location for both dinner and a drink but the food isn't all that it could be. It has the best setting but you can eat better at other places.

What to do

Ban Lung and around
DutchCo Trekking Cambodia, *R78A (the road east of the market), T099-531745, www. ecotourismcambodia.info.* This is a small ecotourism outfit offering well-equipped, upmarket and pricey tours to various destinations in northeast Cambodia.
Yaklom Hill Lodge, *see Where to stay, above.* Offers a variety of tours and other adventures. Uses its own local ethnic minority guides.

ACTIVITY

★Gibbon spotting

Many have heard of the Gibbon Experience in Laos, but now Cambodia offers a gibbon experience of its own. While it doesn't offer ziplines and treetop accommodation, it does allow small, environmentally conscious groups of visitors to view and track wild gibbons in their natural habitat within **Veun Sai-Siem Pang Conservation Area (VSSPCA)**.

Set up as a community-based ecotourism project by **Gibbon Spotting Cambodia** (www.gibbonspottingcambodia.com), this scheme offers a two-day/one-night trek as well as a one-night express trek which includes an incredible morning spent with the semi-habituated gibbons. Experiencing them swinging in the jungle with their spellbinding call is very memorable.

Visits are limited to a maximum of six people at a time and tours cost US$199-399 per person, depending on numbers. This includes entrance fees, guide fees, homestays and camps, and all meals. Community funds are used for conservation and development initiatives so this is a very worthwhile way to contribute to wildlife conservation and community development in northeast Cambodia.

Responsible tour operators working to promote this new gibbon project include the following: **Gibbon Spotting Cambodia** (UK T+44 (0)203 6178 711, Cambodia T+855 (0)63 966 355, www.gibbonspottingcambodia.com), Cambodia's first ever gibbon experience. **Terres Rouge** (www.ratanakiri-lodge.com), Ratanakiri-based hotelier and trekking operator working with walk-in visitors in Ban Lung. **See Asia Differently** (UK T+44 (0)208 1505 150, Cambodia T+855 (0)63 966 355, www.seecambodiadifferently.com), a UK/Cambodia-based tour operator working with overseas agents or independent travellers.

Note Due to the limited number of treks to the area we strongly recommend pre-booking a long way in advance.

Transport

Ban Lung and around
Ban Lung is 9-11 hrs from Phnom Penh. It is better to break your journey in Kratie and Stung Treng and take a pickup/taxi from there.

Bus
Local bus services are sporadic. Regular daily buses to **Stung Treng**, 3 hrs, US$6; **Kratie**, 5-6 hrs, US$7; **Kompong Cham**, 6-8 hrs, US$9; **Siem Reap**, 14 hrs, change in **Skon**, US$16; **Phnom Penh**, 9-11 hrs, US$9-14; and to the **Vietnamese border**, 2½ hrs, US$10. All ar available in a variety of mini and larger buses. Shared and private taxis are also available with prices fluctuating depending on the season, road conditions and price of fuel; ask at your guesthouse/hotel for price approximations on arrival.

Car
Cars with driver can be hired for US$40-50 a day.

Motorbike
The chief mode of transport in Ban Lung is the motorbike, which comes with a driver, or not, as required.
NorDen House (see Where to stay, above) has a few top-class 250cc and 400cc dirt bikes for rent, from US$25 to US$50 per day.

Southern Cambodia

white sandy beaches, beautiful islands and good seafood

With the opening of the Vietnamese border near Kampot at Ha Tien, southern Cambodia is now firmly grasping its tourist potential as a staging post for overland travellers.

Yet, in many ways it manages to encompass the worst and best of what tourism can offer to a developing country such as Cambodia. Take Sihanoukville, which not so long ago was a sleepy port with idyllic beaches. Now, with human waste pouring directly into the sea from dozens of generic backpacker shanty bars and flophouses, this town could almost offer a textbook study in environmental catastrophe.

Travel down the coast to Kep and Kampot, and things couldn't be more different. An old French trading port overlooking the Prek Kamping Bay River and framed by the Elephant Mountains, low-key Kampot is filled with decrepit dusty charm. Just outside Kampot is Kep, the resort of choice for France's colonial elite, which is now slowly reasserting its position as a place for rest and recuperation.

Northwest from Sihanoukville is Koh Kong Province, a vast and untamed expanse of jungle that smothers the stunning Cardamom Mountain range in a thick green blanket. There's a sealed road through here linking Sihanoukville with Thailand. With logging companies waiting in the wings, this area is facing an uncertain future.

Best for
Beaches ■ Seafood ■ Walking ■ Wildlife

Footprint
picks

★ **Cardamom Mountains**, page 305
Home to most of Cambodia's large mammals and half of the country's birds.

★ **Koh Kong Island**, page 306
Stunning powdery white beaches; a little utopia.

★ **Kampot**, page 307
A charming riverside town with tree-lined streets and crumbling French colonial architecture.

★ **Bokor Hill Station**, page 308
An abandoned hill station with a tormented history, surrounded by forest walks and waterfalls.

★ **Kep**, page 311
A quiet alternative to Sihanoukville, Kep is a wonderful coastal town with beautiful gardens.

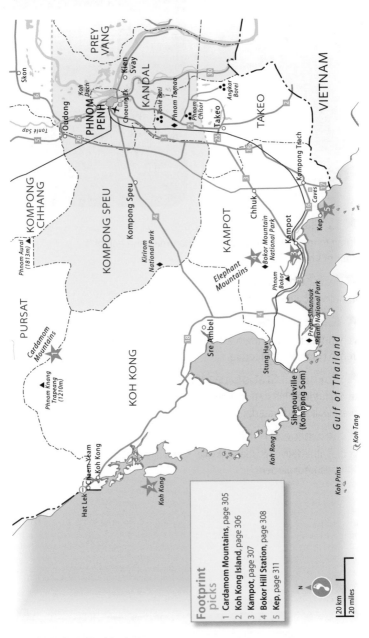

Footprint picks

1 **Cardamom Mountains**, page 305
2 **Koh Kong Island**, page 306
3 **Kampot**, page 307
4 **Bokor Hill Station**, page 308
5 **Kep**, page 311

fabulous beaches, some now sadly spoilt and littered

If Sihanoukville was being tended with care it would occupy a lovely site on a small peninsula whose knobbly head juts out into the Gulf of Thailand. The first-rate beaches, clean waters, trees and invigorating breezes are slowly being replaced with human effluvia, piles of rubbish and nasty flophouses. Cambodia's beaches could be comparable to those in Thailand but are slowly being horribly degraded. Most people head for beaches close to the town which, starting from the north, are Victory, Independence, Sokha, Ochheauteal and, a little further out, Otres. Sihanoukville's layout is unusual, with the 'town' itself acting as a satellite to the roughly equidistant main beaches. The urban area is pretty scattered and has the distinct feel of a place developing on an ad hoc basis.

Sights

Victory Beach A thin, 2-km-long beach on the north of the peninsula, just down from the port with reasonably secluded beaches at its extremes. Beach hawkers are ubiquitous and outnumber tourists at a ratio of about three to one. The area does afford a good sunset view, however.

Independence Beach At one time the sole preserve of the once bombed and charred – and now beautifully restored – **Independence Hotel**. The location of the hotel is magnificent and the grounds are a reminder of the place's former grandeur.

Sokha Beach Mostly privately owned but with a small public area, Sokha Beach is arguably Sihanoukville's most beautiful beach. The shore laps around a 1-km arc and even though the large **Sokha Beach Resort** has taken up residence it is very rare to see more than a handful of people on the beach. It is a stunning and relatively hassle-free beach, with white sand and gentle waters, ideal for swimming.

Ochheauteal Beach To the south of Sihanoukville, this is, bizarrely, the most popular beach with hordes of backpackers. What was once a sparkling stretch of white sand has been reduced to an unending dustbin of rickety, badly planned budget bars, restaurants and accommodation. Several of these places have now been cleared out and this stretch of beach is attempting to move upmarket. Along the beachfront road here keep a look out for Hun Sen's massive and impregnable residence. Watch your stuff as theft is also common here.

Serendipity Beach At the very north end of Ochheauteal, the beach commonly referred to as Serendipity Beach is basically Ochheauteal-like. This little strand has gained flavour with travellers due in part to being the first beach in Sihanoukville to offer a wide range of budget accommodation. At the time of publication, the many guesthouses and restaurants lining the shore of Serendipity and the extended Ochheauteal Beach area were at the centre of a land dispute with developers hankering to clear the budget accommodation to make way for large Thai-style resorts.

Otres Beach A couple of kilometres south of Ochheauteal, Otres is, at least for the moment, relatively quiet and undeveloped. The stretch of sand here is probably

Essential Southern Cambodia

Getting around

Bus
Good bus services link Phnom Penh and Sihanoukville (four hours), the gateway to southern Cambodia. There is a fledgling bus service linking Sihanoukville to Kampot and Kep, but this can depend on the season; however, there are plentiful buses from Phnom Penh to these coastal jewels.

Best places to stay
Reef Resort, Sihanoukville, page 301
Apex Koh Kong, Koh Kong City, page 306
Molieden, Kampot, page 309

Car
You can travel to Koh Kong via the brand new road from Sihanoukville or Hat Lek, Thailand. With the new road and bridges finally completed, there is no longer a public boat from Sihanoukville to Koh Kong.

Moto, tuk-tuk and motorcycle
Getting around Most people use motodops (US$0.25-1 depending on distance) or tuk-tuks, which can be rented by the day. It is possible to rent motorcycles though there do seem to be periodic bans for tourists using these. If a ban is in force we have heard reports of fines and even motorcycles being seized. If you do rent a motorcycle, always wear a helmet.

Best restaurants
Cabbage Garden, Sihanoukville, page 302
Café Laurent, Koh Kong, page 307
Rusty Keyhole, Kampot, page 310

When to go

November-February are the best months, with December and January offering ideal beach weather with warm days, clear skies, no rain, light breezes and cool evenings.

Visibility in Bokor Mountain National Park is low during the rainy season as it is swathed in low cloud, but the waterfalls are at their best during this time.

Time required

At least a day in Kampot, with a day in either the seaside town of Kep, Sihanoukville's beaches or exploring Bohor Mountain National Park.

Best beaches
Sokha Beach, Sihanoukville, page 297
Lazy Beach, Koh Rong Salaam, page 304
Southwestern Beach, Koh Rong, page 304

Weather Kampot											
Jan	Feb	Mar	Apr	May	Jun	Jul	Aug	Sep	Oct	Nov	Dec
31°C	31°C	32°C	32°C	32°C	31°C	31°C	30°C	30°C	31°C	30°C	30°C
☀	☀	⛅	⛅	⛅	⛅	⛅	⛅	⛅	⛅	⛅	☀

Sihanoukville

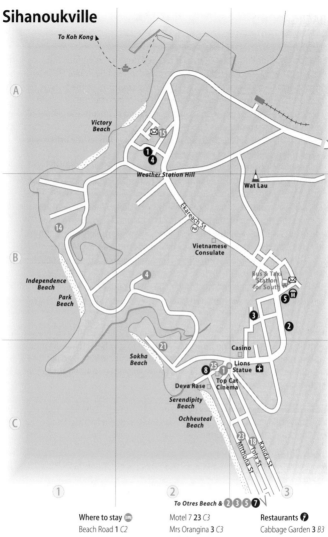

To Koh Kong ►

Victory Beach

Weather Station Hill

Wat Lau

Kareach St

Pol

Vietnamese Consulate

Independence Beach

Park Beach

Bus & Taxi Station for South

M

Sokha Beach

Casino

Lions Statue

Serendipity Beach

Deva Rase

Top Cat Cinema

Ochheuteal Beach

Minhoa St

Tola St

Kanda St

To Otres Beach & ② ③ ⑤ ⑦

N

200 metres
200 yards

Where to stay
Beach Road **1** *C2*
Castaways/
 Cantina del Mar **2** *C3*
Chez Claude **4** *B2*
Independence
 Boutique **14** *B1*
Mealy Chenda **15** *A2*

Motel 7 **23** *C3*
Mrs Orangina **3** *C3*
Orchidée Guesthouse **18** *C3*
Otres Lodge **5** *C3*
Reef Resort **25** *C2*
Sokha Beach Resort **21** *C2*

Restaurants
Cabbage Garden **3** *B3*
Cantina del Mar (Otres)
Chez Mari-yan **1** *A2*
Holy Cow **2** *B3*
Le Vivier de la Paillote ◄
Mick & Craig's **8** *C2*
Starfish Café **5** *B3*

BACKGROUND
Sihanoukville

Sihanoukville (or Kompong Som as it is called during the periods the king is in exile or otherwise 'out of office') was founded in 1964 by Prince Sihanouk to be the nation's sole deep-water port. It is also the country's prime seaside resort. In its short history it has crammed in as much excitement as most seaside towns see in a century – but not of the sort that resorts tend to encourage. Sihanoukville was used as a strategic transit point for weapons used in fighting the US, during the Vietnam War. In 1975, the US bombed the town when the Khmer Rouge seized the container ship *SS Mayaguez*.

Sihanoukville has now turned a corner, however, and with rapid development has firmly secured its place in Cambodia's 'tourism triangle', alongside Phnom Penh and Angkor Wat. Not much of this development is sustainable and incredibly tacky and overpriced resorts have already been built. While a liberal attitude towards the smoking of marijuana attracts a youthful crowd, no amount of intoxicants can cover up the fact that Sihanoukville is rapidly becoming an environmental stain on this already horribly scarred country. Massive offshore sand-dredging has also had an impact on this fragile coastline; the beaches are slowly being eroded with high tides swamping many of the beachside bars and restaurants. If it all becomes too much, the nearby Preah Sihanouk 'Ream' National Park (see below) is a welcome retreat.

Sihanoukville's longest and it is easy to find a spot for yourself. There are now a number of budget guesthouses opening up should you wish to stay here. To reach Otres you'll need to take a moto or tuk-tuk (US$3-4). Be careful of walking the long road out here or passing through the local fishing village, as several tourists have been robbed, threatened and even a stabbing has been reported.

Fishing port There is also a small fishing port, 2 km north of the Sihanoukville ferry dock. Here, the motley collection of wharves comes alive at daybreak, when colourful fishing boats dock and the fish are sorted and bought by wheeling dealing merchants.

Preah Sihanouk 'Ream' National Park
T012-875096, daily 0700-1715. Boat trip US$30 for 4 people. Nature trek with a guide (3-5 hrs), US$5 per person.

This beautiful park is a short 30-minute drive from Sihanoukville, hugging the coastline of the Gulf of Thailand. It includes two islands and covers 21,000 ha of beach, mangrove swamp, offshore coral reef and the Prek Tuk Sap Estuary. Samba deer, endangered civet species, porcupines and pangolin are said to inhabit the park, as well as dolphins. To arrange a guided tour visit the park office or arrange one through a guesthouse in Sihanoukville.

Where to stay

Places on the relatively undeveloped Otres Beach may appear and disappear quickly. Check with other travellers to see what is open.

$$$$ The Independence Boutique Resort and Spa
Independence Beach, T034-934300, www.independencehotel.net.
Once the most gorgeous hotel in town, the charms of this hotel are fading and the rooms are beginning to look tatty. Great sea views from the hilltop perch, with pleasing gardens and a pool.

$$$$-$$$ Sokha Beach Resort and Spa
St 2 Thnou, Sangkat 4, Sokha Beach, T034-935999, www.sokhahotels.com.
A deluxe, 180-room beachfront resort and spa, set amid an expansive 15 ha of beachfront gardens and fronting a pristine white sandy beach. Guests have a choice between hotel suites or private bungalows dotted in the tropical gardens. The hotel has fantastic facilities including a landscaped pool, tennis court, archery range, children's club and in-house Filipino band at night. Rooms are impressive. The hotel has very low occupancy, so check for discounts as it's always running special deals.

$$$-$ Beach Road Hotel
Serendipity Rd, T012-995175, www.beachroad-hotel.com.
Excellent value, well-run and maintained hotel with a large range of rooms to fit most budgets; prices drop during low season. All rooms are en suite, with TV, a/c, free Wi-Fi and hot water. The clincher is the gorgeous pool. Decent bar.

$$ Chez Claude
Between Sokha Beach and Independence Beach, T034-934100, www.claude cambodge.com.
A beautiful hillside spot with 9 bungalows representing a cross-section of indigenous housing. The restaurant has fantastic views.

$$ Reef Resort
Serendipity Beach, T012-315338, www.reefresort.com.kh.
Well-run, small hotel at the top of the hill near the garish Golden Lions roundabout. Rooms are a touch overpriced but there is a nice pool and breakfast is included. Bar and restaurant. Probably the best mid-range place in town. Book ahead. Recommended.

$$-$ Orchidée Guesthouse
Tola St, T034-933639, www.orchidee-guesthouse.com.
Well run, clean and well-aired rooms, with a/c and hot water. Restaurant with Khmer and Western seafood. Nice pool area, a 5-min walk to Ochheauteal Beach.

$ Castaways
Otres Beach, T097-861785.
Friendly place with basic bungalows and rooms directly on the beach; all are en suite and have fans. Good electricity supply that should be 24 hrs in high season.

$ Mealy Chenda
On the crest of Weather Station Hill, T012-419219.
Very popular hotel offering accommodation to suit a wide range of budgets from dorm rooms through to a/c doubles. Sparkling clean with fantastic views from the restaurant.

$ Motel 7
Ochheuteal Beach, T015-207719.
Set just back from the beach on the road, this is a stylish and simple guesthouse. All rooms have en suite facilities, cable TV and free Wi-Fi; the pricier ones also have a/c and hot water. Friendly owners were planning to set up a small coffee and ice cream parlour.

$ Mrs Orangina
Otres Beach, T017-820 4237.
Funky bungalow operation on the beach.
Cute, clean bungalows and relaxing vibe.

$ Otres Lodge
Otres Beach.
Decent bungalow-style huts, outdoor pool
and Khmer and Western food served at this
laid-back and popular spot.

Restaurants

$$$ Chez Mari-yan
Victory Beach area.
Good seafood restaurant with probably the
nicest setting in Sihanoukville.

$$$-$$ Le Vivier de la Paillote
Top of Weather Station Hill.
This is the finest dining establishment in
town and one of the best in the country.
The service can't be surpassed and it is
high on atmosphere.

$$ Holy Cow
Ekareach St, on the way out of town.
Ambient restaurant offering a selection of
healthy Western meals such as pasta, salads,
baked potatoes. The English owner is a long-
term resident and a very good source of local
information. To his credit he has created a
lovely atmosphere and provides impeccable
working conditions for his staff.

$$ Mick and Craig's
Ochheauteal Beach.
Thankfully the menu here is a lot more
creative than the venue's name. Sufficiently
large meals with a bit of pizzazz including
pizzas, burgers and houmous. The restaurant
also offers 'themed food nights', Sun roast,
barbecue and 'all-you-can-eat' nights.

$$ Starfish Café
*Behind Samudera supermarket, T034-952011,
www.starfishcambodia.org.*
Small café-cum-bakery in a very peaceful
garden setting. Here you can eat great food,

while knowing that you are supporting a
good cause. The organization was originally
established to help rehabilitate people with
disabilities and has extended its services to
cover a range of poverty-reducing schemes.
A very positive place that oozes goodness
in its food, environment and service – good
Western breakfasts, cakes, sandwiches,
salads and coffees. A non-profit massage
business has also opened on the premises.

$$-$ Cabbage Garden
*Down a back lane between Golden Lions and
town centre, T011-940171. Open 1000-2300.*
This restaurant is rightly famous with both
locals and resident expats for its incredible
Khmer food. The spicy shrimp mango salad
is essential. It's a little tricky to find (see
map) but a real discovery when you do.
Highly recommended.

$$-$ Cantina del Mar
Otres Beach.
Same owners as the sister restaurant in
Phnom Penh. You should find authentic
Mexican food and cold Mexican beer.

Bars and clubs

Most resorts, guesthouses and hotels
are also home to some kind of bar. In the
Serendipity/Ochheuteal Beach area, 2 of
the most infamous night-time hangouts
are **Monkey Republic** and **Utopia**. For
a Khmer alternative head to one of the
Khmer restaurants near the Golden Lions
roundabout where you will very likely be
serenaded by Khmer singers.

What to do

Diving
Scuba Nation Diving Centre, *Weather
Station Hill, T012-604680, www.dive cambodia.
com.* This company has the best reputation
in town and is the longest-established PADI
dive centre. An Open Water course is US$350,
dive trips are US$70.

Fishing

Tradewinds Charters, *at The Fishermen's Den Sports Bar, T01-270 2478, a couple of blocks opposite from the Marlin Hotel on Ekareach St.* Runs daily fishing trips. If you have caught something worth eating, the proprietor, Brian, will arrange for the restaurant to prepare a lovely meal from the catch.

Massage

Seeing Hands Massage, *next to Q&A Book Café on Ekareach St. Open 0900-2100.* US$6 per hr. Soothing Japanese-style shiatsu massages from trained blind masseurs.

Transport

Air

Sihanoukville Airport is roughly 14 km east of town, www.kos.aero. A shuttle into town costs US$6.

Cambodia Angkor Air, www.cambodiaangkorair.com, now flies 6 times a week between **Siem Reap** and Sihanoukville, 1 hr, from US$80 each way.

Bus

All buses depart from the main bus station near the new market unless otherwise stated.

Many guesthouses and local tour operators also offer minibus services but these vary according to the season. Around Khmer New Year and during the peak season you will need to book tickets the day before travel. Phnom Penh Sorya and Paramount both run services to **Phnom Penh** in comfortable, well-maintained, a/c coaches approximately every 30 mins 0700-1400, US$4-5; luxury **Mekong Express** at 0745, 1430, US$7. Route 4 is quick and comfortable and the trip takes about 4 hrs.

Bus services to **Koh Kong** are developing; there are roughly 2 morning departures a day, 4 hrs, US$13. The Thai border is open until 2000 and buses depart until 2330 from **Trat** to **Bangkok** (see page 307).

Minibuses to **Kampot/Kep** are run on an ad hoc basis by local guesthouses – check for information locally.

Taxi

Seats in shared taxis are available to **Phnom Penh** (US$7), **Koh Kong** (US$9) and **Kampot** (US$5). All depart from the taxi stand near the bus station.

Private taxis are available and vary according to the quality of the car: **Phnom Penh** (US$55-60), **Koh Kong** (US$60) and **Kampot** (US$25). You can also travel to Koh Kong via the new road from Sihanoukville or **Hat Lek**, Thailand.

Sihanoukville's islands

crystal-clear water makes for good diving and snorkelling

More than 20 beautiful islands and pristine coral reefs lie off Sihanoukville's coastline. Most of the islands are uninhabited except Koh Russei (Bamboo Island), Koh Rong Salaam and a few others that contain small fishing villages. Some of the islands mentioned now have guesthouses and hotels, see page 305 for details.

Diving and snorkelling around the islands is pretty good. The coast offers an abundance of marine life including star fish, sea anemones, lobsters and sponge and brain coral. Larger creatures such as stingrays, angel fish, groupers, barracuda, moray eels and giant clams are ubiquitous. Baby whale sharks and reef sharks also roam the waters. More elusive are the black dolphins, pink dolphins, common dolphins and bottle-nosed dolphins but they are sighted from time to time. It is believed that further afield (closer to Koh Kong) are a family of dugongs (sea cows). No one has sighted these rare creatures except for one hotel owner who sadly saw a dugong head for sale in Sihanoukville's market.

The islands are divided into three separate groups: the Kampong Som Group, the Ream Group and the Royal Islands. During winter (November to February) the Ream Islands are the best group to visit as they are more sheltered than some of the other islands but they are a lot further out.

Kampong Som Islands

The Kampong Som Islands are the closest to Sihanoukville and have quite good beaches. Here the visibility stretches up to 40 m. **Koh Pos** is the closest island to Sihanoukville, located just 800 m from Victory Beach. Most people prefer **Koh Koang Kang** also known as **Koh Thas**, which is 45 minutes from shore. This island has two beautiful beaches (with one named after Elvis) and the added attraction of shallow rocky reefs, teeming with wildlife, which are perfect for snorkelling.

Rong Islands

More rocky reefs and shallow water can be found at the Rong Islands. **Koh Rong** is about two hours west of Sihanoukville and has a stunning, 5-km-long sand beach (on the southwest side of the island). To the south of Koh Rong is **Koh Rong Salaam**, a smaller island that is widely considered Cambodia's most beautiful. There are nine fantastic beaches spread across this island, including west-facing **Lazy Beach** (stunning sunsets), and on the east coast, a lovely heart-shaped bay. It takes about 2½ hours to get to Koh Rong from Sihanoukville. **Koh Kok**, a small island off Koh Rong Salaam, is one of the firm favourite dive sites, warranting it the nickname 'the garden'; it takes 1¾ hours to get there.

Ream Islands

The Ream Islands encompass those islands just off the Ream coast: **Prek Mo Peam** and **Prek Toek Sap**, which don't offer the clearest waters. The islands of **Koh Khteah**, **Koh Tres**, **Koh Chraloh** and **Koh Ta Kiev** are best for snorkelling. Giant mussels can be seen on the north side of Koh Ta Kiev. Some 50 km out are the **Outer Ream Islands** which, without a doubt, offer the best diving in the area. The coral in these islands though has started to deteriorate and is now developing a fair bit of algae. **Kondor Reef**, 75 km west of Sihanoukville, is a favourite diving spot. A Chinese junk filled with gold and other precious treasures is believed to have sunk hundreds of years ago on the reef and famous underwater treasure hunter, Michael Archer, has thoroughly searched the site but no one can confirm whether he struck gold.

Royal Islands

The Royal Islands, Koh Tang, Koh Prins and Paulo Wai are seven hours away to the southwest. These islands are believed to have visibility that stretches for 40 m and are teeming with marine life; they are recommended as some of the best dive sites. It is believed that **Koh Prins** once had a modern shipwreck and sunken US helicopter but underwater scavengers looking for steel and US MIA guys have completely cleared the area. Large schools of yellowfin tuna are known to inhabit the island's surrounding waters. **Koh Tang** is worth a visit but is quite far from the mainland so an overnight stay on board might be required. Many local dive experts believe Koh Tang represents the future of Cambodia's diving. The island became infamous in May 1975 when the US ship *SS Mayaguez* was seized by the Khmer Rouge just off here. The area surrounding **Paulo Wai** is not frequently explored, so most of the coral reefs are still in pristine condition.

Koh Sdach

Closer to Thailand lies Koh Sdach (King's Island), a stop off on the boat ride between Sihanoukville and Koh Kong. This undeveloped island is home to about 4000 people, mostly fishing families. The beaches are a bit rocky but there is some fabulous snorkelling. There are now a couple of resorts and a simple guesthouse on the island.

$$$$ Belinda Beach Lovely Resort
Koh Sdach, T017-517517,
www.belindabeach.com.
Set in tropical gardens with panoramic views, rooms are spacious and well appointed with private balcony, rainshower and Wi-Fi. 2 restaurants on site. There's a private beach area, though the pool area is a better place to hang out.

$$ Lazy Beach
Koh Rong Salaam, booking office is just past Seahorse Bungalows, T016-214211, www.lazybeachcambodia.com.

Simple, clean bungalows by a stunning beach. It costs US$10 per person per single boat transfer to reach the island. Serves a good array of food as well.

$ Koh Ru
Koh Russie Island, booking office just past Seahorse Bungalows, T012-366660.
This is a quaint collection of simple fan bungalows and dorm rooms in a lovely beachside location. Totally relaxed and quiet, this is a decent spot to really get away from it all. Also serves food and drinks. Boat transfers US$10.

Koh Kong and around

a 'Wild West' town, virgin wilderness and powdery white beaches

Dusty Koh Kong is better known for its brothels, casinos and 'Wild West' atmosphere than for lying at the heart of a protected area with national park status (granted by Royal Decree in 1993). It is also often confused with its beautiful offshore namesake Koh Kong Island. The town is also reputed to have the highest incidence of HIV infection of anywhere in Cambodia and is a haven for members of the Thai mafia trying to keep their heads down and launder large sums of money through the casino. The place is only really used by travellers as a transit stop on the way to and from Thailand or two of the most scenic places in Cambodia – Koh Kong Island and the Cardamom Mountains. Due to its border location most people in Koh Kong will accept Thai baht as well as the usual US dollars and Cambodian riel.

★Central Cardamoms Protected Forest

The area remains relatively inaccessible but over the next few years it is anticipated that ecotourism operators will flock to the area. For now, it is best to make short trips into the park as the area is sparsely populated and heavily mined (so stay on clearly marked paths). Take a motorbike (with an experienced rider) or a boat. The latter option is more convenient in Koh Kong. There are usually several men with boats willing to take the trip down the Mohaundait Rapids, cutting through the jungled hills and wilderness of the Cardamoms. The cost of the trip is US$25-30.

In 2002, the government announced the creation of the Central Cardamoms Protected Forest, a 402,000-ha area in Cambodia's Central Cardamom Mountains. With two other wildlife sanctuaries bordering the park, the total land under protection is 990,000 ha –

the largest, most pristine wilderness in mainland Southeast Asia. The extended national park reaches widely across the country, running through the provinces of Koh Kong, Pursat, Kompong Speu and Battambang. Considering that Cambodia has been severely deforested and seen its wildlife hunted to near-extinction, this park represents a good opportunity for the country to regenerate flora and fauna. The Cardamoms are home to most of Cambodia's large mammals and half of the country's birds, reptiles and amphibians. The mountains have retained large populations of the region's most rare and endangered animals, such as the Indochinese tigers, Asian elephants and sun bears. Globally threatened species like the pileated gibbon and the critically endangered Siamese crocodile, which has its only known wild breeding population here, also exist. Environmental surveyors have identified 30 large mammal species, 30 small mammal species, more than 500 bird species, 64 reptile species and 30 amphibian species. Conservationists are predicting they will discover other animals that have disappeared elsewhere in the region such as the Sumatran rhinoceros. With virgin jungles, waterfalls, rivers and rapids this area has a huge untapped ecotourism potential. However, tourist services to the area are still quite limited.

★ Koh Kong Island
About 1-1½ hrs by boat from Koh Kong town. Boats from town usually charge ฿1000 per round trip.

The island (often called Koh Kong Krau) is arguably one of Cambodia's best. There are six white powdery beaches each stretching kilometre after kilometre, while a canopy of coconut trees shade the glassy-smooth aqua waters. It's a truly stunning part of the country and has been ear-marked by the government for further development, so go now, while it's still a little utopia. There are a few frisky dolphin pods that crop up from time to time. Their intermittent appearances usually take place in the morning and in the late afternoon. You could feasibly camp on the island though would likely need to bring all supplies with you, including drinking water.

Listings Koh Kong and around

Where to stay

With the road to Phnom Penh and Sihanoukville now completed, accommodation and other facilities in Koh Kong are improving.

$$-$ Apex Koh Kong
St 8, T016-307919, www.apexkohkong.com.
With a pool, free Wi-Fi, friendly staff and good food this is easily one of the best places to stay in Koh Kong. The bright, fresh rooms, all set around a courtyard, have cable TV, hot water and a/c. Excellent value. Recommended.

$$-$ Asean Hotel
Riverfront, T012-936667.
Good rooms with a/c, bathtubs, cable TV. The ones at the front have balconies and river views. There's a decent internet café downstairs. Friendly owners and well run. Recommended.

$$-$ Koh Kong City Hotel
Riverfront, T035-936777.
This biggish hotel by the river has decent, clean rooms, the best of which have great river views. Staff are a little indifferent but it is a good place to stay. Rooms are a/c with cable TV and hot-water en suite facilities throughout.

Restaurants

There are several places around town that sell Thai food. Most of the Khmer-owned hotels listed in Where to stay, above, also serve food or have a restaurant attached. The market is also a good place to pick up fruit and street food.

$$$ Dug Out
Main St, T016-650325.
Great Western breakfasts. Also serves other meals but at it's best first thing.

$$$-$ Café Laurent
Next to Koh Kong City Hotel, T011-590168. Mon-Sat 0700-2400.
This bistro serves excellent breakfasts, pastas and pizzas. The coffee and bread are also superb and the pastries are not bad either. Highly recommended.

$$-$ Aqua Sunset Bar and Restaurant
Riverfront, T016-637 8626. Open 0700-2400.
Average Thai, Western and Khmer food. Runs island and dolphin tours. It's a great spot to sip a sundowner.

Transport

Boat
At time of publication the boat service between Koh Kong and Sihanoukville was suspended and unlikely to be reinstated.

Bus
Bus tickets are available from most main guesthouses and hotels with buses departing from the bus station 1 km out of town, down St 3. There are 2-3 departures a day to/from **Sihanoukville** (US$6-10, 4 hrs) and **Phnom Penh** (US$8-10, 5 hrs).
   To Thailand The border crossing is 12 km from Koh Kong, across the river (15-20 mins). The trip to the border at Cham Yem inside Cambodia costs ฿60 by moto, ฿50 by shared taxi and US$6 with own taxi. The border is open 0700-2000. There are public minibuses on the Thai side to **Trat** (84 km), 1¼ hrs, until 1800, ฿150. You can find private taxis after 1800 but bidding will start at ฿1000. From Trat buses run to **Pattaya**, **Bangkok** and **Bangkok airport**.

Taxi
Shared taxis (6 per car) to **Sihanoukville** leave from the market, 4 hrs, US$10 person, from 0600 onwards, leaves when full. Private taxi, US$60.

Kampot and around
cool, riverside location and an abandoned 'station climatique' high in the mountains

★Kampot is a charming riverside town that was established in the 19th century by the French. The town lies at the base of the Elephant Mountain Range, 5 km inland on the River Prek Thom and was famed not only for the high-grade peppercorns grown by the former French colonialists but also for the salt pans to the south and east of the town.

On one side of the river are tree-lined streets, crumbling mustard yellow French shopfronts while on the other side you will find locals working in the salt pans. Kampot's sleepy riverside charm is slowly being replaced with a bustling market-town feel, as the riverfront is developed into a run of bars, eateries and guesthouses. A perfect example of this is the colonial-era indoor market facing onto the river that was abandoned and derelict for decades – it's now been turned into a lively gaggle of bars and pop-up shops. Yet, with its smattering of Chinese architecture and overall French colonial influence (many of its grand old colonial villas are also being restored), the handsome provincial town still has the feel of another era. Life in Kampot is laid-back and the town has become an expat retreat with Phnom Penh-ites ducking down here for the fresh air and cooler climate.

★Bokor Mountain National Park
42 km (90 mins) from Kampot, US$5. A moto and driver for the day will cost around US$15 or a car around US$30. The new road to Bokor is now open to visitors.

Although the atmospheric abandoned French casino resort has been replaced with a giant and garish Chinese-style casino and resort, you can still visit the abandoned French building and the views are still spectacular. Bokor Mountain National Park's plateau, at 1040 m, peers out from the southernmost end of the Elephant Mountains with a commanding view over the Gulf of Thailand and east to Vietnam. Bokor Hill (Phnom Bokor) is densely forested and in the remote and largely untouched woods scientists have discovered 30 species of plant unique to the area. Not for nothing are these called the Elephant Mountains and besides the Asian elephant there are tigers, leopards, wild cows, civets, pigs, gibbons and numerous bird species. At the peak of the mountain is **Bokor Hill Station**, where eerie, abandoned, moss-covered buildings sit in dense fog. The hill station was built by the French who, attracted by Bokor's relative coolness, established a 'station climatique' on the mountain in the 1920s. In 1970 Lon Nol shut it down and Bokor was quickly taken over by Communist guerrillas; it later became a strategic military base for

Kampot

To Bokor Mountain National
Park (42 km) & Sihanoukville

To Phnom Penh
(Route 3) & Caves

Prekthom

Sok Lim Tours

Kepler's Books

Riverside Walk

Old Market

Canadia

Obelisk Roundabout

Kampot 5 Seeing Hands Massage

Kampot Music School

Acleda Bank

Ministry of Tourism

Taxis

Naga Statue

Chinese School

Statue of 3 Soldiers

To Kep (25 km) & Caves

| 200 metres |
| 200 yards |

Where to stay
Bodhi Villa **6**
Bokor Mountain Lodge **9**
Borey Bokor 1 **1**
Les Manguiers **12**

Long Villa **13**
Mea Culpa Guesthouse **2**
Molieden **7**

Restaurants
Epic Arts Centre **2**
Jasmine **3**
Rusty Keyhole **4**

the Khmer Rouge. In more recent years there was a lot of guerrilla activity in the hills, but the area is now safe, with the exception of the danger – ever-present in Cambodia – of landmines. The ruins are surprisingly well preserved but bear evidence of their tormented past. There is a double waterfall called **Popokvil Falls**, a 2-km walk from the station, which involves wading through a stream, though in the wet season this is nigh on impossible.

Kbal Romeas caves and temple

Ten kilometres outside Kampot, on the roads to both Phnom Penh and to Kep, limestone peaks harbour interesting caves with stalactites and pools. It is here that you can find one of Cambodia's hidden treasures: an 11th-century temple slowly being enveloped by stalactites and hidden away in a cave in **Phnom Chhnok**, next to the village of Kbal Romeas. The temple, which is protected by three friendly monks, was discovered by Adhemer Leclere in 1866. Many motos (US$3-4) and cars (US$10) now offer trips.

Listings Kampot and around *map p308*

Where to stay

$$$-$$ Bokor Mountain Lodge
Riverfront, T033-932314,
www.bokorlodge.com.
Old colonial property on the riverfront that has had several incarnations and was once even an HQ for the Khmer Rouge. It's getting rather run-down but has bags of atmosphere and is probably the best spot in town for an icy sundowner. All rooms are en suite with a/c and cable TV.

$$$-$$ Les Manguiers
2 km north of town, T092-330050,
www.mangokampot.com.
Cute little French-run guesthouse. Set by the river amidst paddies and swaying tropical trees, this is a relaxing place to spend a couple of days. Good bungalows with fans or a/c; some rooms also in main building. Free use of bicycles for guests.

$$-$ Borey Bokor Hotel 1
T092-978168, boreybokorhotel@yahoo.com.
In an ostentatious style with all rooms offering a/c, fridge and comfy beds.

$ Bodhi Villa
2 km northwest of town on Teuk Chhou Rd,
T012-728884, www.bodhivilla.com.
Cheap, friendly, well-run and popular guesthouse in a good location just outside

town, on the river bank. Owners seem well intentioned, linking into local volunteer projects, though some might consider that the hedonistic atmosphere and roaring speedboat which they've introduced to the peaceful river detracts from their efforts. Basic rooms, simple bungalows and US$1 a night dorm.

$ Long Villa
No 75, St 713, T012-210820.
Very friendly, well-run guesthouse. The unspectacular though functional rooms vary from en suite with a/c and TV through to fan with shared facilities.

$ Mea Culpa Guesthouse
Just behind the town hall and river front road,
T012-504769, www.meaculpakampot.com.
Pick of the bunch at this friendly well-run and well-designed guesthouse. Rooms are en suite, with a/c, TV and free Wi-Fi.

$ Molieden
A block from the main bridge, T012-820779.
A surprisingly good find, its hideous facade gives way to a very pleasant interior. Large, tastefully decorated modern art deco rooms with TV and fan. The rooftop restaurant also serves some of the best Western food in town. Very good value with free Wi-Fi.

Restaurants

You can now find lots of street food in and around the night market and on the bridge road near the riverside.

$$$ Molieden Restaurant
See Where to stay.
On the roof of the guesthouse. Extensive selection of pastas, soup and Italian seafood dishes. Fantastic food. Recommended.

$$ Bokor Mountain Lodge
See Where to stay.
Great sandwiches made with the best ingredients – the fish and chicken amok is also divine. Recommended.

$$ Jasmine
Waterfront.
A riverside eatery set up by a Khmer woman (Jasmine) and her American photographer partner. They offer a slightly more upmarket experience than many of the other places along the riverfront, Khmer and Western dishes. Recommended.

$$ Rusty Keyhole Bar and Restaurant
River Rd, past Bamboo Light.
Run by the very down-to-earth and super-friendly Mancunian, Christian, Rusty's is now something of a local legend. Western food served. Friendly and the best place to watch football in town. The barbecue seafood and ribs come highly recommended.

$ Epic Arts Café
67 Oosaupia Muoy, centre of Kampot, T092-922069, www.epicarts.org.uk.
A brilliant little NGO-run establishment set up as a project to employ local disabled people. Delicious cakes.

What to do

Massage
There are a couple of great blind massage places in town.

Kampot 5 Seeing Hands, *just back from the river near the Bokor Mountain Lodge.* Best place in town. The people here are incredibly

warm and friendly and, at US$4 per hr, it's a great way to relax.

Pepper farm
Kadode Pepper Farm Shop, *just over the new bridge on the opposite side to the town, turn first right down a small road for about 100 m, T033-690 2354, www.farmlink-cambodia.com. Mon-Fri, 0730-1130 and 1330-1630.* Well worth a visit. Kampot is presently trying to restore its reputation for growing premier peppercorns and you'll find several varieties on sale here as well as palm sugar and a chance to find out about how farming is helping local communities prosper.

Tour operators
Cheang Try, T012-974698, is a local Khmer who runs both a motorcycle rental outlet in the centre of Kampot town and also does guided tours. At 17, Mr Try's entire family was murdered by the Khmer Rouge and he was forced to live alone in the jungle on Elephant Mountain, near Bokor for 18 months. He then returned to fight the Khmer Rouge. If you take a tour to Bokor with Mr Try his experiences will really bring the place alive and you'll come away with some evocative and powerful memories. Highly recommended.

Transport

Cheang Try tour operator (see above) sells tickets to bus services out of Kampot. He also runs a minibus on demand to Sihanoukville.

Bus
There are 2 buses in both directions run by the Phnom Penh Sorya Transport Co between Kampot and Phnom Penh. These services also stop in Kep. They depart the bus station on Blvd Charles de Gaulle near the central market in Phnom Penh at 0730 and 1315, returning at 0730 and 1230 from Kampot bus stand, US$4.

Minibuses to/from Sihanoukville are run on an ad hoc basis by guesthouses – check for information locally.

Taxi

To **Phnom Penh**, US$3-4, 3 hrs, vehicles leave from the truck station next to the Total gas station at 0700-1400, private taxi US$35-40. Coming from Phnom Penh, taxis to Kampot leave from Doeum Kor Market on Mao Tse Tung Blvd and not the central market. To **Sihanoukville**, US$4, private US$20-25, 2 hrs. To **Kep**, US$8, return US$14-15.

Kep

try the freshly caught crab and palm wine

★Whilst Kep remains under the radar of many tourists it is slowly being developed. There is now a promenade, the Crab Market area has permanent restaurants and a substantial pier has been built from where you can rent boats to take you to nearby islands. It is also very popular on weekends with holidaying Cambodians who enjoy the beautiful gardens and lush green landscape juxtaposed against the blue waters.

Tucked in on the edge of the South China Sea, Kep was established in 1908 by the French as a health station for their government officials and families. The ruins of their holiday villas stand along the beachfront and in the surrounding hills. They were largely destroyed during the civil war under Lon Nol and by the Khmer Rouge and were then further ransacked during the famine of the early 1980s when starving Cambodians raided the villas for valuables to exchange for food.

The town itself only has one major beach, a pebbly murky water pool that has been buttressed with softer, whiter sands trucked in from nearby Sihanoukville but decent beaches can be found on almost all of the 13 outlying islands where you can snorkel and dive (although this is better around the islands off Sihanoukville). Kep is considerably more laid-back than Sihanoukville and is rightly famous for the freshly caught crab and the *tik tanaout jiu*, palm wine. From Kep it is possible to hire a boat to **Rabbit Island** (Koh Toensay) from the main pier. Expect to pay about US$25 to hire a boat for the day. There are four half-moon beaches on this island which have finer, whiter sand than Kep beach.

Tip...

From July to October Kep is subject to the southeast monsoon, occasionally rendering the beach dangerous for swimming because of the debris brought in.

Listings Kep

Where to stay

$$$$ Knai Bang Chatt Resort
Phum Thmey, Sangkat Prey Thom, T036-210310, www.knaibangchatt.com.
Set in a restored 20th-century modernist villa, this property seeks to recreate an elitist and colonial atmosphere. Whilst it is in a gorgeous location and has some of the trappings of luxury it doesn't quite manage to pull it off. Service is patchy and rooms are overpriced.

$$$-$ Veranda Resort and Bungalows
Next door to N4, further up Kep Mountain, T033-399035, www.veranda-resort.com.
Superb accommodation. Large wooden bungalows, each with a good-sized balcony, fan, mosquito net and nicely

decorated mosaic bathroom. The more expensive of these include very romantic open-air beds. The restaurant offers the perfect vista of the ocean and surrounding countryside. Epicureans will love the variety of international cuisines including poutine of Quebec, smoked ham linguini and fish fillet with olive sauce (all under US$3). Recommended.

$$ The Beach House
33 A, Thmey village, opposite Srey Sor Beach T012-712750, www.thebeachhousekep.com.
Arguably the nicest spot to stay in Kep. Great rooms, nearly all of which look out onto the mesmeric ocean; all have a/c, hot water and TV. There is a small pool and soothing chill-out area. Unpretentious and good value. The staff can sometimes appear to be half-asleep but are very friendly when provoked. Recommended.

Restaurants

There are scores of seafood stalls on the beach that specialize in freshly caught crab. The Crab Market area is home to a row of restaurants serving crab, shrimp and fish. Nearly every hotel or guesthouse serves food; see Where to stay, above.

$$$-$$ Sailing Club
Adjacent to Knai Bang Chatt hotel (see Where to stay). Open 1100-late.
Bar/eatery in an airy seafront spot. Good cocktails and wine list, tasty burgers, ribs and steaks. Snooker table, kayaks for rent.

$$-$ Srey Pou
At Crab Market. Open 1100-late.
One of the best of the small restaurants in this location, popular with locals. Great seafood that is so fresh it's almost still wriggling on your plate. There's a wine selection, sea views and even free Wi-Fi.

Transport

Kep is only 25 km from **Kampot**. The road is good and the journey can be made in 30-45 mins. A large white horse statue marks the turn-off to Kep. Buses now run twice a day between Kep/Kampot and **Phnom Penh** (see Kampot Transport, page 310).

This is
Laos

Laos satisfies all the romantic images of perfumed frangipani trees, saffron-robed monks, rusty old bicycles and golden temples, all set amongst a rich tapestry of tropical river islands, ethnic minority villages, cascading waterfalls and vivid, green rice paddies, and bound together by the mighty Mekong River, the country's lifeline.

The vernacular architecture that other countries have swept away in a maelstrom of redevelopment survives in Laos. Simple wooden village homes, colonial-era brick-and-stucco shophouses and gently mouldering monasteries mark Laos out as different.

Traditional customs are also firmly intact: incense wafts out of streetside wats, monks collect alms at daybreak and the clickety-clack of looms weaving richly coloured silk can be heard in most villages.

As compelling as these sights and sounds are, the lasting impression for most visitors is of the people and their overwhelming friendliness.

Many believe the best thing about Laos is the constant call of *sabaidee* its people. This is a land that endures the terrible legacy of being the most bombed country per capita in the world, yet its people transform bomb casings into flower pots and bomb craters into fish ponds. Regardless of their history and their poverty, people here radiate a sunny, happy disposition.

Life is simple in Laos but the people radiate an infectious joie de vivre that ensures that good food and great company are the pinnacle of enjoyment. If you're seeking a relaxed pace of life and a warm welcome, you've come to the right place.

Vientiane & around

In 1563, King Setthathirat made the riverine city of Vientiane the capital of Laos. Or, to be more historically accurate, Wiang Chan, the 'City of the Moon', became the capital of Lane Xang.

In those days it was a small fortified city with a palace and two wats, which had grown prosperous from the surrounding fertile plains and the taxes levied from trade going upriver.

Today Vientiane is the sleepiest of all Southeast Asia's capital cities. Snuggled into a curve of the Mekong and cut off from the outside world for much of the modern period, its colonial heritage remains largely intact. While the last few years have brought greater activity, it is still a quiet city of golden temples, crumbling mansions and tree-lined boulevards, but with the benefits of excellent restaurants, wine bars and a £31 million riverfront development.

Around Vientiane are several places of interest. Phou Khao Khouay is one of Laos' most accessible protected areas, while Vang Vieng is a popular stopover for the adventure crowd on the way to Luang Prabang.

Best for
Museums ▪ Restaurants ▪ Riverfront walks

Vientiane

Footprint
picks

⭐ **That Luang**, page 319

This gleaming gold wat is the national symbol of Laos and the country's holiest site.

⭐ **Wat Phra Kaeo**, page 325

Formerly home to the Emerald Buddha, Wat Phra Kaeo has some of the finest sculpture in Laos.

⭐ **Lao National Museum**, page 328

The place to swat up on some history before visiting the rest of the country.

⭐ **Phou Khao Khouay Protected Area**, page 341

Accessible yet seldom visited park, with jungle-covered mountains, waterfalls and wild elephants.

⭐ **Vang Vieng caves**, page 344

Former party town reinventing itself as a centre for outdoor and adrenalin activities.

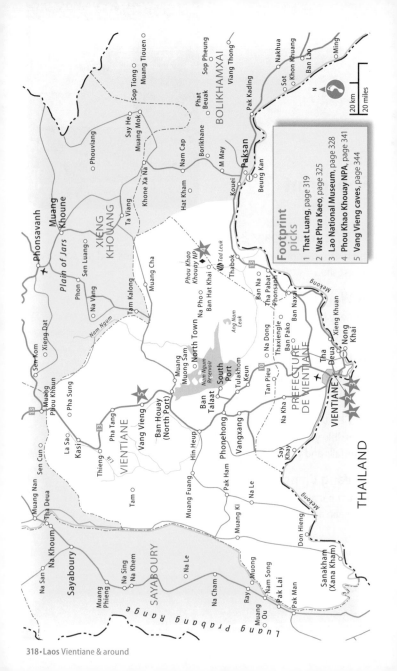

Footprint picks

1 That Luang, page 319
2 Wat Phra Kaeo, page 325
3 Lao National Museum, page 328
4 Phou Khao Khouay NPA, page 341
5 Vang Vieng caves, page 344

20 km
20 miles
N

BOLIKHAMXAI

Muang Tiouen
Sop Tiong
Nakhua
Ming
Sop Pheung
Phat
Sot
Khon Nhuang
Ban Lao
Viang Thong
Muang Mok
Say He
Phouviang
Borikhane
Pak Kading
Nam Cap
M May
Phat Beuak
Phouviang
Ta Viang
Khone Xa Na
Kouei
Paksan
Beung Kan
Hat Kham
Hat Kham

XIENG KHOUANG

Phonsavanh
Muang Khoune
Plain of Jars
Sen Luang
Phon
Na Vang
Muang Cha
Tam Kalong
Muang Sam
Phou Khao
Khouay NP
Tad Leuk
Thabok
Ban Na
Tha Pabat Phonsanh
Ban Naxai

Xieng Dat
Sen Kom
Muang Phou Khoun
Pha Sung
Na Pho
Ban Hat Khai
Ang Nam Leuk
Na Dong
Ban Pako
Tha Deua
Xieng Khuan
Nong Khai

PREFECTURE DE VIENTIANE

Muang
Muong Sam
North Town
Na Pho
Thakhek
Thaxiengle
Na Kha
VIENTIANE

La Sao
Kasi
Pha Tang
Vang Vieng
Ban Houay (North Port)
Hin Heup
Phonehong
Vangxang
Tan Pieu
Na Kha
Say Khay

Thieng
Sen Cun
VIENTIANE
Tam
Muang Fuang
Pak Ham
Na Le
Muang Ki
Na Le

SAYABOURY

Muang Nan
Tha Deua
Na Khoum
Na Sing
Na Khem
Muang Phieng
Na Le
Na Cham
Ray
Muong
Nam Song
Pak Lai
Pak Man
Muang Ou
Sanakham (Xana Kham)
Don Hieng

Na San

THAILAND

Mekong

Luang Prabang Range

Vientiane

Vientiane's appeal lies in its largely preserved fusion of Southeast Asian and French colonial culture. Baguettes, filter coffee and Bordeaux wines coexist with spring rolls, noodle soup and papaya salad. Colourful tuk-tuks scuttle along tree-lined boulevards, past old Buddhist temples and cosmopolitan cafés. Hammer-and-sickle flags hang at 10-pin bowling discos and chickens wander the streets. But, as in the rest of Laos, the best thing about Vientiane, is its people. Take the opportunity to stroll around some of the outlying *bans* (villages) and meet the wonderful characters who make this city what it is. *Colour map 1, C3.*

Sights

wide boulevards, crumbling French buildings and a handful of wats

Most of the interesting buildings in Vientiane are of religious significance. All tour companies and many hotels and guesthouses will arrange city tours and excursions to surrounding sights but it is just as easy to arrange a tour independently with a local tuk-tuk driver; the best English speakers (and thus the most expensive tuk-tuks) can be found in the parking lot beside Nam Phou and also beside Wat Mixay. Those at the Morning Market (Talaat Sao) are cheaper. Most tuk-tuk drivers pretend not to carry small change, so make sure you have the exact fare with you before taking a ride.

★ That Luang

That Luang Rd, 3.5 km northeast of the centre; daily 0800-1200 and 1300-1600 (except 'special' holidays); small entry charge. A booklet about the wat is on sale at the entrance.

That Luang is Vientiane's most important site and the holiest Buddhist monument in the country. The golden spire looks impressive at the top of the hill and dominates the skyline in the northeast of the city.

According to legend, a stupa was first built here in the third century AD by emissaries of the Moghul Emperor Asoka; it is supposed to have contained the breast bone of the Buddha. Excavations on the site, however, have located only the remains of an 11th- to 13th-century Khmer temple, making the earlier provenance doubtful in the extreme. The present monument, encompassing the previous buildings, was built in 1566 by King Setthathirat,

Essential Vientiane

Finding your feet

Vientiane is small and manageable. The core of the city is negotiable on foot, while outlying hotels and places of interest are accessible by bicycle. Although traffic has increased, cycling remains the best and most flexible way to tour the city, with tuk-tuks, scooters, motorbikes and taxis available for longer trips.

The city is divided into *bans* or **villages**, mainly centred on their local wats, and larger *muang* or **districts**: Muang Sikhottabong lies to the west, Muang Chanthabouli to the north, Muang Xaisettha to the east and Muang Sisattanak to the south. There are few street signs, but because the city is so small and compact it doesn't take long to get to grips with the layout. The names of major **streets** or *thanon* usually correspond to the nearest wat, while traffic lights, wats, monuments and large hotels serve as directional landmarks. When giving directions to a tuk-tuk it is better to use a map with Lao script or say the name of a nearby landmark, as street names still leave locals a little bewildered. A good quality free city map can be picked up in almost every hotel and tourist-friendly restaurant.

Best restaurants

Côte d'Azur, page 331
Le Silapa, page 331
Pimenton, page 331
La Terrasse, page 331
Lao Kitchen, page 332

When to go

November to February is the most comfortable time with warm sunny days. From March to May it can be debilitatingly hot, with some very humid days as the southwest monsoon hits in May/June. Rains continue until October when the northeast monsoon brings drier cooler weather. Average annual rainfall in Vientiane is 1700 m.

Best places to stay

Green Park Boutique Hotel, page 328
Settha Palace Hotel, page 328
Lao Orchid Hotel, page 329
Hotel Day Inn, page 329
Villa Manoly, page 329
Mali Namphu Guesthouse, page 330

Time required

Two to three days would allow a leisurely visit of the capital but those pressed for time often pass through in 24 hours, preferring to head straight up to Vang Vieng or Luang Prabang.

Weather Vientiane

January	February	March	April	May	June
28°C 17°C 15mm	30°C 16°C 18mm	31°C 18°C 35mm	33°C 21°C 90mm	32°C 23°C 191mm	31°C 23°C 259mm

July	August	September	October	November	December
30°C 23°C 295mm	30°C 23°C 344mm	30°C 22°C 253mm	29°C 20°C 119mm	28°C 18°C 52mm	27°C 14°C 20mm

whose statue stands outside. Plundered by the Thais and the Chinese Haw in the 18th century, it was restored by King (Chao) Anou at the beginning of the 19th century. He added the cloister and the Burmese-style pavilion containing the That Sithamma Hay Sok. The stupa was restored by l'École Française d'Extrême-Orient (whose conservators were also responsible for the restoration of parts of Angkor Wat at the start of the 20th century) but was rebuilt in 1930 because many Lao disapproved of the French restoration.

The reliquary is surrounded by a square cloister, with an entrance on each side, the most famous on the east. There is a small collection of statues in the cloisters, including one of the Khmer king Jayavarman VII. The cloisters are used as lodgings by monks who travel to Vientiane for religious reasons and especially for the annual **Buon That Luang festival** (see page 335). The base of the stupa is a mixture of styles, Khmer, Indian and Lao – and each side has a *hor vay* (small offering temple). This lowest level represents the material world, while the second tier is surrounded by a lotus wall and 30 smaller stupas, representing the 30 Buddhist perfections. Each of these originally contained smaller golden stupas but they were stolen by Chinese raiders in the 19th century. The 30-m-high spire dominates the skyline and resembles an elongated lotus bud, crowned by a banana flower and parasol. It was designed so that pilgrims could climb up to the stupa via the walkways around each level. It is believed that originally over 450 kg of gold leaf was used on the spire.

There used to be a wat on each side of the stupa but only two remain: Wat Luang Nua to the north and Wat Luang Tai to the south. The large new wat-like structure is the headquarters of a Buddhist organization. The outer walls are used to stage art exhibitions.

Although That Luang is considered to be the most important historical site in Vientiane, most visitors will feel that it is not the most interesting, impressive or beautiful, largely because it seems to have been constructed out of concrete. Wat Sisaket and Wat Phra Kaeo (see pages 324 and 325) are certainly more memorable buildings. Nonetheless, it is important to appreciate the reverence in which That Luang is held by most Lao, including the many millions of Lao who live across the border in Thailand. The *that* is the prototype for the distinctive Lao-style angular *chedi*, which can be seen in northeast Thailand, as well as across Laos.

Revolutionary Monument

Also known as the Unknown Soldier's Memorial, this hilltop landmark is just off Phon Kheng Road and visible from the parade ground (which resembles a disused parking lot) in front of That Luang. Echoing a *that* in design, it is a spectacularly dull monument, built in memory of those who died during the revolution in 1975. The **Pathet Lao Museum**, to the northwest of That Luang, is only open to VIPs and never to the public but there are a few tanks, trucks, guns and aircraft used in the war lying in the grounds: these can be seen from the other side of the fence.

Patuxai
Junction of That Luang Rd and Lane Xang Av. Daily 0800-1200 and 1300-1630, small charge.

At the end of That Luang is the Oriental answer to Paris's Arc de Triomphe and Vientiane's best-known landmark, the monstrous Victory Monument or Patuxai. It was originally called Anou Savali, officially renamed the Patuxai or Victory Monument, but is affectionately known by locals as 'the vertical runway'. It was built by the former regime in memory of those who died in the wars before the Communist takeover, but the cement ran out before its completion. Refusing to be beaten, the regime diverted hundreds of tonnes of cement, part of a US aid package to help with the construction of runways at Wattay Airport, to finish off the monument in 1969. In 2004, the Chinese funded a big concrete park area surrounding the site, including a musical fountain; it's a pity they didn't stretch the budget to finance the beautification of the park's centrepiece.

A small sign explains that, although Patuxai might look grand from a distance, on closer inspection "it appears like a monster of concrete". The top affords a bird's eye view of

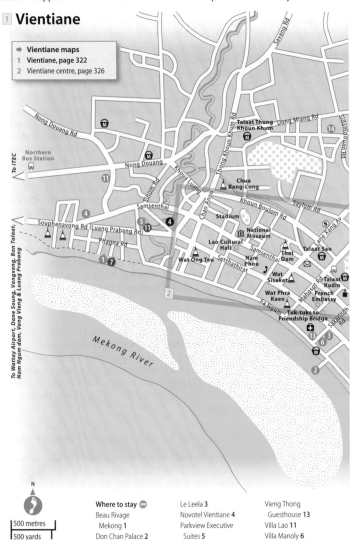

1 Vientiane

➡ Vientiane maps
1 Vientiane, page 322
2 Vientiane centre, page 326

Where to stay
Beau Rivage
  Mekong **1**
Don Chan Palace **2**

Le Leela **3**
Novotel Vientiane **4**
Parkview Executive
  Suites **5**

Vieng Thong
  Guesthouse **13**
Villa Lao **11**
Villa Manoly **6**

the leafy capital, including the distant glittering, golden dome of the old Russian circus, now the rarely used National Circus. The interior of the monument is reminiscent of a multi-storey car park (presumably as a counterpoint to the parade ground next to the Revolutionary Monument), with graffiti sporadically daubed on top of unfinished Buddhist bas-reliefs in reinforced concrete. The frescoes under the arches at the bottom represent

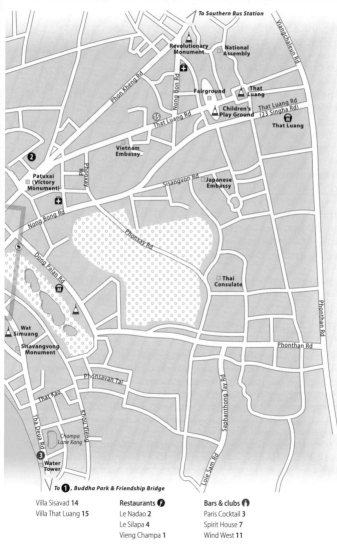

BACKGROUND
Vientiane

Vientiane is an ancient city. There was probably a settlement here, on a bend on the left bank of the Mekong, in the 10th century but knowledge of the city before the 16th century is thin and dubious. Scholars do know, from the chronicles, that King Setthathirat decided to relocate his capital here in the early 1560s. It seems that it took him four years to build the city, constructing a defensive wall (hence 'Wiang', meaning a walled or fortified city), along with Wat Phra Kaeo and a much-enlarged That Luang.

Vieng Chan, as it was called, remained intact until 1827 when it was ransacked by the Siamese; this is why many of its wats are of recent construction. Francis Garnier in 1860 wrote of "a heap of ruins" and having surveyed the "relics of antiquity" decided that the "absolute silence reigning within the precincts of a city formerly so rich and populous, was ... much more impressive than any of its monuments". A few years later, Louis de Carné wrote of the vegetation that it was like "a veil drawn by nature over the weakness of man and the vanity of his works".

The city was abandoned for decades and erased from the maps of the region. It was only conjured back into existence by the French, who commenced reconstruction at the end of the 19th century. They built rambling colonial villas and wide tree-lined boulevards, befitting their new administrative capital, Vientiane. At the height of American influence in the 1960s, it was renowned for its opium dens and sex shows.

mythological stories from the Lao version of the *Ramayana*, the *Phra Lak Pralam*. Until 1990 there was a bar on the bottom floor; today Vientiane's youth hang out on the parapet.

Wat Sisaket
Junction of Lane Xang Av and Setthathirat Rd. Daily 0800-1200 and 1300-1600, small charge. No photographs in the sim.

Further down Lane Xang is the Morning Market or Talaat Sao (see page 337). A major waterpark has been constructed in the park just behind Talaat Sao. Beyond the market, where Setthathirat meets Lane Xang, is one of Vientiane's two national museums, Wat Sisaket. Home of the head of the Buddhist community in Laos, Phra Sangka Nagnok, it is one of the most important buildings in the capital and houses over 7000 Buddha images. Wat Sisaket was built in 1818 during the reign of King Anou. A traditional Lao monastery, it was the only temple that survived the Thai sacking of the town in 1827-1828 (possibly out of respect for the fact that it had been completed only 10 years before the invasion), which now makes it the oldest building in Vientiane. Sadly, it is seriously in need of restoration.

The main sanctuary, or *sim*, with its sweeping roof, shares many stylistic similarities with Wat Phra Kaeo (see below): window surrounds, lotus-shaped pillars and carvings of deities held up by giants on the rear door. The *sim* contains 2052 Buddha statues (mainly terracotta, bronze and wood) in small niches in the top half of the wall. There is little left of the Thai-style *jataka* murals on the lower walls but the depth and colour of the originals can be seen from the few remaining pieces. The ceiling was copied from temples King

Today Vientiane is a quiet capital with an urban population of around 460,000 (up from 70,000 in 1960). There are around 695,500 inhabitants (about 10% of the population of Laos) in the Vientiane municipality but this extends far beyond the physical limits of the city. Before 1970 there was only one set of traffic lights in the whole city and, even with the arrival of cars and motorbikes from Thailand in recent years, the streets are a far cry from the congestion of Bangkok. Unlike Phnom Penh and Ho Chi Minh City, there are only scattered traces of French town planning; architecture is a mixture of east and west, with French colonial villas and traditional wooden Lao buildings intermingled with Chinese shophouses and more contemporary buildings. Some locals worry that foreign investment and redevelopment will ruin the city – already some remarkably grotesque buildings are going up – but officials seem to be aware that there is little to be gained from creating Bangkok in microcosm.

Vientiane's citizens are proud of their cultural heritage and are usually very supportive of the government's attempts to promote it. The government has tried, by and large, to maintain the national identity and protect its citizens from harmful outside influences. This is already starting to change; with the government reshuffle in 2006 came a gradual loosening of the cultural stranglehold. Elections in 2011 saw just one independent (non-party) candidate elected as well as 33 women. President Sayasone, born 1936, was re-elected.

In 2013, Vientiane saw the completion of a US$31-million redevelopment project, which has transformed the riverfront from a dirt road lined with basic restaurants to a dual-lane road and concrete river bank including public gardens and recreation area, especially popular at dawn and dusk.

Anou had seen on a visit to Bangkok. The standing image to the left of the altar is believed to have been cast in the same proportions as King Anou. Around the *sim*, set into the ground, are small *bai sema* or boundary stones. The *sim* is surrounded by a large courtyard, which originally had four entrance gates (three are now blocked). Behind the *sim* is a large trough, in the shape of a *naga*, used for washing the Buddha images during the **Boun Ok Phansa** festival (see page 334).

The cloisters were built during the 1800s and were the first of their kind in Vientiane. They shelter 120 large Buddhas in the attitude of subduing Mara, plus a number of other images in assorted *mudras*, and thousands of small figures in niches, although many of the most interesting Buddha figures are now in Wat Phra Kaeo. Most of the statues date from the 16th to 19th centuries but there are some earlier images. Quite a number were taken from local monasteries during the French period.

The whole ensemble of *sim* plus cloisters is washed in a rather attractive shade of caramel, and combined with the terracotta floor tiles and weathered roof presents a most satisfying sight. An attractive Burmese-style library, or *hau tai*, stands on Lane Xang outside the courtyard. The large casket inside used to contain important Buddhist manuscripts.

Just behind Wat Sisaket is a complex of colonial houses in a well-maintained garden.

★ Wat Phra Kaeo
Setthathirat Rd, daily 0800-1200 and 1300-1600 (closed public holidays), small entry charge. No photographs in the sim.

Almost opposite Wat Sisaket is the other national museum, Wat Phra Kaeo, also known as Hor Phra Kaeo. It was built by King Setthathirat in 1565 to house the Emerald Buddha (or Phra Kaeo), now in Bangkok, which he had brought from his royal residence in Chiang Mai. It was never a monastery but was kept instead for royal worship. The Emerald Buddha was removed by the Thais in 1779 and Wat Phra Kaeo was destroyed by them in the sacking of Vientiane in 1827. (The Thais now claim the Emerald Buddha as the most important icon in their country.) The whole building was in a bad state of repair after the sackings, with only the floor remaining fully intact. Francis Garnier, the French explorer who wandered

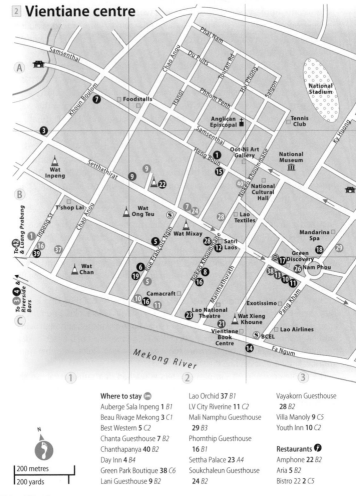

2 Vientiane centre

Where to stay	Lao Orchid **37** *B1*	Vayakorn Guesthouse
Auberge Sala Inpeng **1** *B1*	LV City Riverine **11** *C2*	**28** *B2*
Beau Rivage Mekong **3** *C1*	Mali Namphu Guesthouse	Villa Manoly **9** *C5*
Best Western **5** *C2*	**29** *B3*	Youth Inn **10** *C2*
Chanta Guesthouse **7** *B2*	Phornthip Guesthouse	
Chanthapanya **40** *B2*	**16** *B1*	**Restaurants**
Day Inn **4** *B4*	Settha Palace **23** *A4*	Amphone **22** *B2*
Green Park Boutique **38** *C6*	Soukchaleun Guesthouse	Aria **5** *B2*
Lani Guesthouse **9** *B2*	**24** *B2*	Bistro 22 **2** *C5*

through the ruins of Vieng Chan in 1860, describes Wat Phra Kaeo "shin[ing] forth in the midst of the forest, gracefully framed with blooming lianas, and profusely garlanded with foliage". Louis de Carné in his journal, *Travels in Indochina and the Chinese Empire* (1872), was also enchanted, writing when he came upon the vegetation-choked ruin that it "made one feel something of that awe which filled men of old at the threshold of a sacred wood".

The building was expertly reconstructed in the 1940s and 1950s and is now surrounded by a garden. During renovations, the interior walls were restored using a plaster made of sugar, sand, buffalo skin and tree oil.

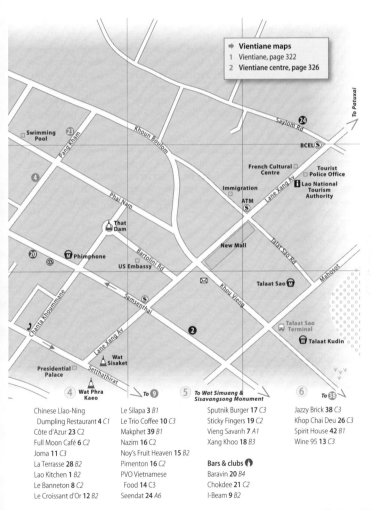

➡ **Vientiane maps**
1 Vientiane, page 322
2 Vientiane centre, page 326

Chinese Llao-Ning
  Dumpling Restaurant **4** *C1*
Côte d'Azur **23** *C2*
Full Moon Café **6** *C2*
Joma **11** *C3*
La Terrasse **28** *B2*
Lao Kitchen **1** *B2*
Le Banneton **8** *C2*
Le Croissant d'Or **12** *B2*

Le Silapa **3** *B1*
Le Trio Coffee **10** *C3*
Makphet **39** *B1*
Nazim **16** *C2*
Noy's Fruit Heaven **15** *B2*
Pimenton **16** *C2*
PVO Vietnamese
  Food **14** *C3*
Seendat **24** *A6*

Sputnik Burger **17** *C3*
Sticky Fingers **19** *C2*
Vieng Savanh **7** *A1*
Xang Khoo **18** *B3*

Bars & clubs 🍸
Baravin **20** *B4*
Chokdee **21** *C2*
I-Beam **9** *B2*

Jazzy Brick **38** *C3*
Khop Chai Deu **26** *C3*
Spirit House **42** *B1*
Wine 95 **13** *C3*

The *sim* stands on three tiers of galleries, the top one surrounded by majestic. lotus-shaped columns. The tiers are joined by several flights of steps and guarded by *nagas*. The main, central (southern) door is an exquisite example of Lao wood sculpture with carved angels surrounded by flowers and birds; it is the only notable remnant of the original wat. (The central door at the northern end, with the larger carved angels, is new.)

The *sim* now houses a superb assortment of Lao and Khmer art and some pieces of Burmese and Khmer influence, mostly collected from other wats in Vientiane.

★Lao National Museum
Samsenthai Rd, opposite the National Culture Hall. Daily 0800-1200 and 1300-1600, small entry charge. No photographs allowed.

This place was formerly called the Revolutionary Museum but in these post-revolutionary days it has been redesignated the National Museum. The museum's collection has grown over the last few years and now includes a selection of historical artefacts from dinosaur bones and pre-Angkorian sculptures to a comprehensive photographic collection on Laos' modern history. The rhetoric of these modern collections has been somewhat toned down from the old days, when photographic descriptions would refer to the 'running dog imperialists' (Americans).

One of the highlights of the museum is a dazzling array of personal effects from the revolutionary leader Kaysone including his exercise machine, a spoon he used and even the coconut he once had a sip from. Downstairs there is a collection of ancient artefacts, including stone tools and quite poignant burial jars. Upstairs the museum features a range of artefacts and busts as well as a small exhibition on ethnic minorities. The final section of the museum comprises mostly photographs tracing the country's struggle against the 'brutal' French colonialists and American 'imperialists'.

Listings Vientiane maps p322 and p326

Tourist information

Lao National Tourism Authority
Lane Xang (towards Patuxai), T021-212251, www.tourismlaos.org. Mon-Fri 0830-1200 and 1300-1600.
Provides information on ecotourism operators and trekking opportunities in provincial areas. This is a good starting point if you want to organize a trip to Phou Khao Khouay NPA. The English-language *Vientiane Times* runs items of Lao news, plus snippets translated from the local newspapers and listings.

Where to stay

$$$$ Green Park Boutique Hotel
248 Khouvieng Rd, T021-264097, www.greenparkvientiane.com.

Designed in a modern East-meets-West style, this hotel is set alongside Vientiane's primary park. Beautiful rooms with all the mod cons, Wi-Fi and super-duper bathtubs. Beautiful garden and excellent pool. The only drawback is that it's further out from the city centre and river, but still within walking distance and makes a fantastic luxury option. Recommended.

$$$$ Settha Palace Hotel
6 Pang Kham Rd, T021-217581, www.setthapalace.com.
The stunning **Settha Palace** was built in 1936 and opened as a hotel in 1999. Its French architecture, period furniture, plush rooms complete with black marble sinks and bathtubs and tropical gardens and pool sit more easily with the essence of

Vientiane than the other top-level hotels. It is considered by those in search of a little old world charm to be the best hotel in town. Recommended.

$$$$-$$$ Best Western Vientiane
2-12 François Ngin Rd, T021-216906, www.bestwesternvientiane.com.
The service here is hard to fault and facilities are good: restaurant, bar, basic gym, small pool and free airport pick-up. Now far better equipped than when it was the **Tai Pan** hotel, the rooms offer the level one would expect from **Best Western**, but there are more charming places to stay.

$$$ Lao Orchid Hotel
Chao Anou, T021-264134, www.lao-orchid.com.
Beautiful spacious rooms with stunning modern furnishings, polished floorboards and large showers. Outstanding value (4½-star accommodation for a 3-star price) and popular with business travellers. Advanced bookings imperative in peak season. Includes breakfast and Wi-Fi. Recommended.

$$ Auberge Sala Inpeng
063 Unit 06, Inpeng St, T021-242021, www.salalao.com.
An absolute gem for a capital city. 9 very attractive bungalows set in a small garden in a quiet street. Breakfast included.

$$ Beau Rivage Mekong
Fa Ngum Rd, T021-243350, www.hbrm.com.
One of the 1st Western-style boutique hotels in Vientiane has somewhat quirky, dated decoration in shades of pink. Nonetheless it has a great riverside location: outside of the centre but just a 5-min walk to the hustle and bustle. Some rooms have river views; garden view rooms are cheaper. Includes breakfast which is served at the popular **Spirit House** next door.

$$ Chanthapanya
Nokeo Khoummane Rd, T021-244284, www.chanthapanyahotel.com.

A well-located hotel that offers good value for money and interesting (if quirky) interiors. Furnished with modern Lao wooden furniture, comfy beds, fridge, TV, hot water, phone, a/c. Includes breakfast.

$$ Hotel Day Inn
059/3 Pang Kham Rd, T021-222985, dayinn@laopdr.com.
Run by a friendly Cambodian, Ms Ly, this renovated villa (the former Indian embassy) is in a good position in a quiet part of town, just to the north of the main concentration of bars and restaurants. Attractive rooms are large, airy and clean with a/c and excellent bathrooms; good breakfast and complimentary airport transfer included. Wi-Fi available. Recommended.

$$ Lani Guesthouse
281 Setthathirath Rd, T021-214919, www.lanigh.laotel.com.
This lovely old-style Vientiane building is in a charming location and is run by pleasant staff. Rooms are tad more expensive in the main house.

$$ LV City Riverine Hotel
48 Fa Ngum Rd, Mixay, T021-214643, www.lvcitylaos.com.
A good central choice. The suite has a 4-poster bed, textile decor and a good-sized bathroom. The deluxe rooms have beds raised on small platforms but with smaller bathrooms; standard rooms are very good with thoughtful extras like a clothes stand. Very helpful staff. Wi-Fi and breakfast included.

$$ Villa Manoly
Ban Phyavat, T021-218907, manoly20@hotmail.com.
A wonderful ramshackle French colonial villa crowded with objets d'art, curios, books and ancient TV sets. It's like a rambling private house. There's a pool in the garden. 12 rooms are in the main building and 8 rooms in a new block with small patios out front overlooking the pool. Recommended.

$$-$ Vayakorn Guesthouse
*91 Nokeo Khoummane Rd, T021-241911,
www.vayakorn@yahoo.com.*
Central and clean, with friendly staff.
Wonderful airy rooms, tastefully decorated
with polished floors and modern furniture.
Hot water, a/c and TV. Breakfast isn't included
but is excellent value. Recommended. The
Vayakorn Inn is also good and can be found
just around the corner. Wi-Fi available.

$ Chanta Guesthouse
*Setthathirat Rd (opposite Mixay Temple),
T021-243204.*
The shabby foyer doesn't do this place
justice. Rooms are homely, with polished
floorboards, TV, good bathrooms, wooden
furniture and great cotton bedclothes.
Cheaper rooms have shared facilities;
more expensive ones are en suite with a/c.

$ Mali Namphu Guesthouse
*114 Pang Kham Rd, T021-215093,
www.malinamphu.com.*
Difficult to spot as it looks like a small
shopfront but the façade is deceiving, as the
foyer opens onto a beautifully manicured
courtyard surrounded by quaint terraced
rooms. Some of the rooms are way better
than others so if possible ask to see a few.

$ Phornthip Guesthouse
72 Inpeng Rd, T021-217239.
A quiet, family-run and very friendly
guesthouse, but perhaps a little overpriced.
Rooms are large with en suite bathrooms,
some have a/c. There's a courtyard at the
back of the guesthouse, but no garden.
Bicycle hire available. Some room deals
include breakfast.

$ Soukchaleun Guesthouse
*121 Setthathirat Rd (opposite Mixay temple),
T021-218723, soukchaleun_gh@yahoo.com.*
Quaint guesthouse with a range of rooms,
from fan-cooled with shared bathroom
through to a/c en suite. Comfortable and
homely. Clean, friendly and good value.

$ Vieng Thong Guesthouse
*Ban Phiawat, opposite Wat Phiavat in a side
street, T021-212095.*
Family-style house, plus modern extension,
in a nice garden with a café. Super-friendly
staff. Large rooms with thick duvets, rattan
furniture, TV, china tea-sets and hot water
showers. Pleasant but a little expensive,
especially for the older rooms. The newer
rooms are much more attractive.

$ Youth Inn
*29 Fa Ngum Rd; also on François Ngin Rd;
T021-217130, youthinn@hotmail.com.*
A Vietnamese-run operation with 2 locations
in the heart of town. The standard-sized
rooms are spotlessly clean and are compact
with a/c. The owners are sometimes friendly
and sometimes not.

Serviced apartments

$$$$ Parkview Executive Suites
*Av Souphanouvong (near the Novotel),
T021-250888, www.parkviewexecutive.com.*
Serviced residence complex of 116 units,
catering for both long- and short-term stays.
Fitness centre, pool, sauna, jacuzzi, tennis
court, office space and secretarial support.
A bit off the beaten track.

Restaurants

Lao food stalls can be found at the Dong
Palane Night Market, on Dong Palane, and
the night markets near the corner of Chao
Anou and Khoun Boulom Rd. There are
various other congregations of stalls and
vendors around town, most of which set
up shop around 1730 and close by 2100.
Be sure to sample Lao ice cream with
coconut sticky rice.

The Chinese quarter is around Chao
Anou, Heng Boun and Khoun Boulom
and is now home to ever more Korean,
Vietnamese and Japanese restaurants,
though some of the smaller, old Chinese
noodle and tea houses remain. This is a
lively spot in the evenings. There are a

number of noodle shops here, all of which serve a palatable array of vermicelli, *muu daeng* (red pork), duck and chicken.

The Korean-style barbeque, *sindat*, is extremely popular, especially among the younger Lao, as it is a very social event and very cheap.

In terms of Western dining, there are some very fine options in town.

$$$-$$ Bistro 22
22 Samsenthai Rd, T055-527286.
Thoroughly French and thoroughly good. The lamb shank is supremely good. A place to treat yourself.

$$$-$$ Côte d'Azur
62/63 Fa Ngum Rd, T021-217252, jmdazur@laotel.com. Daily 1100-1400, 1800-2230. Closed Sun lunch.
A fine selection of dishes from the south of France, plus excellent wood-fired pizzas and delicious seafood dishes. Recommended.

$$$-$$ Le Silapa
17/1 Sihom Rd, T021-219689. Daily 1130-1400, 1800-2200; closes for a month during the rainy season and for a week over Lao New Year.
Anthony and Frederick provide a fantastic French-inspired menu and intimate atmosphere for fine dining without blowing the budget. The innovative modern meals (such as tilapia with a vegetable marmalade, lime and black olives sauce) would be as at home in the fine dining establishments of New York and London as they are here. Great-value set lunch menu. Part of the profits are donated to disadvantaged families, usually for expensive life-saving surgical procedures. Wine degustation evenings are occasionally held. Highly recommended.

$$$-$$ Pimenton
6 Nokeo Khoummane, T021-215506, www.pimentonrestaurant-vte.com.
This is a truly excellent addition to the culinary scene. A cool, minimalist industrial interior and a mouthwatering menu of steaks with various cuts from various continents all cooked to perfection. Also has some fantastic salads to complement the meat alongside a well-curated wine list and delectable cocktails. Well worth your money.

$$ Xang Khoo
68 Pangkham Rd, T021-219314.
A very charming little restaurant with tiled floor, beamed ceiling and a casually refined air. Offers a fantastic value lunch deal with excellent savoury crêpe and good pasta dishes. The French owner is a great person to ask for other food and drink suggestions. Good value Prosecco and superb coffee from the local **Le Trio** roasters.

$$-$ Amphone
Off Setthathirat Rd on Soi Wat Xieng Gneun, T020-7771 1138.
Offers Lao and international food in a lovely alfresco garden setting just off the main drag.

$$-$ Aria
8 Rue François Ngin, T021-222589.
Divine ice cream, a 16-page wine list, and a long mouthwatering menu of home-made pastas, ravioli, risottos and pizzas with real buffalo mozarella. The best place in town for pizza. The very welcoming owner is an Italian expat.

$$-$ Chinese Liao-ning Dumpling Restaurant
Fa Ngum Rd, T021-240811. Daily 1100-2230.
No-frills Chinese joint that's all about the food. Fabulous steamed or fried dumplings and a wide range of vegetarian dishes. Not somewhere to linger, but great a good place to get your dumpling hit.

$$-$ La Terrasse
55/4 Nokeo Khoummane Rd, T021-218550. Mon-Sat 1100-1400 and 1800-2200.
Large fail-safe menu offering French, European, Lao and some Moroccan food. Great 1970s-style comfort food, including an excellent 'plat du jour' each day. Good desserts, especially the chocolate mousse, and a wide selection of French wine. Fantastic service. Recommended.

$$-$ Lao Kitchen
Heng Boun, T021-254332,
www.lao-kitchen.com.
A must visit, **Lao Kitchen** serves up the best
of Lao food in a funky environment. It's best
to dine in a group and share dishes including
the grilled fish, Lao sausage, and the Luang
Prabang stew. Delicious.

$$-$ Nazim
39 Fa Ngum Rd, T021-223480.
Daily 1000-2230.
Authentic Indian (north and south) and Halal
food, very popular, with indoor and outdoor
seating. They have another restaurant in Vang
Vieng as well as a branch in Luang Prabang.

$$-$ Seendat
Sihom Rd, T021-213855. Daily 1730-2200.
This restaurant has been going for well
over 20 years and is a favourite amongst
the older Lao for its good food (*sindat*)
and atmosphere. Recommended.

$ Full Moon Café
François Ngin Rd, T021-243373.
Daily 1000-2300.
Huge pillows, good lighting and great music
make this place very relaxing. Asian fusion
cuisine and Western favourites. Fantastic
chicken wrap and good Asian tapas. The
Ladybug shake is a winner. Also offers a
book exchange and free Wi-Fi.

$ Makphet
In a new location behind Wat Ong Teu, T021-
260587, www.friends-international.org.
Fantastic Lao non-profit restaurant that helps
raise money for street kids and is run by former
street kids. Modern Lao cuisine with a twist.
Selection of delectable drinks such as the iced
hibiscus with lime juice. Beautifully decorated
with modern furniture and painting by the
kids. Also sells handicrafts and toys produced
by the parents from vulnerable communities.

$ PVO Vietnamese Food
San Phiavat, T021-214444.
A firm favourite that's been going strong
for years. Full menu of freshly prepared

Vietnamese food and also superb baguettes
stuffed with your choice of pâté, salad,
cheese, coleslaw, vegetables and meats.

$ Sputnik Burger
Setthathirath Rd, T030-937 6504.
It's hard to miss this place thanks to the sawn
in half VW Beetle out front. Each half contains
a table for two making this a fun place to
dine. The interior is cool too and the chefs
do a very good line in American burgers and
great fries on the side.

$ Sticky Fingers
François Ngin Rd, T021-215972.
Tue-Sun 1000-2300.
Not as popular as it once was, this is still a
solid choice for a laid-back meal. The Lao and
international menu includes everything from
Middle Eastern through to modern Asian.
Comfort food, including pasta and burgers,
fantastic salads and filling breakfasts.
Deliveries available.

$ Vieng Savanh
Heng Boun, T021-213990. Open 1000-1000.
Always busy with long queues forming in
the early evening for takeaways, this simple
restaurant is not a place to come for the
decor – red plastic chairs and kitsch pictures
are the order of the day here. The roll-your-
own fresh rolls are great fun and delicious.
A local institution, but don't expect service
with a smile…

Cafés, patisseries and juice bars

Joma
Setthathirat Rd, T021-215265.
Mon-Sat 0700-2100.
Hugely popular. A modern, café with other
branches in Hanoi and Luang Prabang. A good
selection of tasty pastries, bagels, sandwiches,
pastas, salads, pizzas, yoghurts and coffee.

Le Banneton
Nokeo Khoumanne Rd, T021-217321,
bpricco@laopdr.com.
Sister café to the Luang Prabang outlet, this
classy French café-cum-boulangerie serves a

range of excellent cakes, breads and quiches. Very cool a/c interior with cream walls and old black and white prints. A great place to escape the heat.

Le Croissant d'Or
Top of Nokeo Khoummane Rd, T021-223741. Daily 0700-2100.
French bakery with a small selection of pastries including good cheap croissants.

Le Trio Coffee
Setthathirat Rd, near Nam Phou, T020-2339 4020, letriocoffee@gmail.com.
Beautiful, tiny coffee shop. Much of the space is taken up by the **Le Trio** roasting machine which is used by Micka to produce a variety of excellent roasts. Also sells a range of quality coffee paraphernalia. A place for serious coffee drinkers.

Noy's Fruit Heaven
Heng Boun, T030-526 2369.
Fresh fruit is piled high at the entrance to this friendly, relaxed juice bar that can create just about any shake you can think of. Noy is lovely and will go out of her way to make her customers happy. She also serves good breakfasts and lunches. A great spot.

Bars and clubs

One of the highlights of Vientiane is to stroll along the Mekong watching the sunset, followed by a *Beerlao* at one of the bars on the waterfront.

Bars

Baravin
265 Samsenethai Rd, T021-217700.
A 'very, very French' wine bar for real wine lovers, it has the air of an undiscovered gem. The decor is wine-heavy, with racks lining the walls. Recommended.

Chokdee Belgian Beer Bar
Fa Ngum, T027-263847.
A huge selection of Belgian brews in this small, cosy bar. Also does good food. Grab a seat at the bar or on the small balcony on the 1st floor. A great addition to the capital's drinking scene

I-Beam
Setthathirath Rd, opposite Ong Tue temple, T021-254528. Open 1800-1200.
A sleek bar with a solid range of cocktails and some good tapas. Live music events on weekends sees the place packed out with a friendly buzz. A nice option after dinner is to go to **I-Beam** for a glass of wine and order a dessert from **Le Silapa** above it (see Restaurants).

Jazzy Brick
Setthathirat Rd, next to Le Trio Coffee (see above).
Very sophisticated, modern den, serving delectable cocktails, with jazz cooing in the background. Decorated with an eclectic range of quirky and kitsch artefacts. Very upmarket and perhaps a bit pretentious.

Khop Chai Deu
Setthathirat Rd (near the corner with Nam Phou).
Probably the most popular bar for tourists in Vientiane. Casual setting and nightly band. Also serves food, but it is better to eat elsewhere.

Paris Cocktail
Th Tha Deua, T021-353919.
This intimate drinking den is so named because the owner and head mixologist, Tony, spent years pouring well-executed cocktails in the French capital. A little bit of a wander from the action, it's worth the stroll, especially for the happy hour from 1700-2000.

Spirit House
Follow Fa Ngum Rd past the Mekong River Commission, T021-243795, www.thespirithouselaos.com.
Happy hour 1700-2000, so it's perfect for a sundowner. Beautiful wooden bar in perfect river location for sunsets. Good range of snacks including burgers and a delicious Cumberland sausage. Some of the best cocktails in the city. Popular with expats. Wi-Fi.

Wind West
By traffic lights, Luang Prabang Rd.
The place to join a fun bunch of locals for drinks and live music. It has an unfortunate name and looks pretty dim from the outside, but it's actually quite fun.

Wine 95
Setthathirat Rd (next to Jazzy Brick), T020-5550 2957, wine95vientiane@gmail.com.
Wine 95's long bar is a great place to pull up a bar stool, sample some excellent wine and chat with fellow patrons; however, it is an extremely pricey place to do so. Upstairs is a refined lounge area with comfortable high-backed chairs. Upmarket.

Entertainment

Cinema
French Cultural Centre, *Lang Xang Rd, T021-215764, www.if-laos.org*. Shows exhibitions, screens French films and also hosts the **Southeast Asian Film Festival**. Check the *Vientiane Times* for up-to-date details or pick up its quarterly programme.
Lao-International Trade Exhibition & Convention Center (ITECC), *T4 Rd – Ban Phonethane Neua, T021-416002, www.laoitecc.info*. Shows international films.

Exhibitions
Keep an eye on the *Vientiane Times* for upcoming international performances at the **Lao Cultural Centre** (the building that looks like a big cake opposite the museum).

COPE Visitors' Centre, *National Rehabilitation Centre, Khou Vieng Rd (signposted), www.copelaos.org. Open 0900-1800, free*. **COPE (Cooperative Orthotic and Prosthetic Enterprise)** has set up an interesting exhibition on UXO (unexploded ordnance) and its effects on the people of Laos. It includes a small movie room, photography, UXO and a range of prosthetic limbs (some, which are crafted out of UXO). The exhibition helps raise money for the work of COPE, which includes the production of prosthetic limbs and rehabilitation of.
T'Shop Lai, *Vat Inpeng St (behind Wat Inpeng), T021-223178, www.artisanslao.com. Mon-Sat 0800-2000, Sun 0800-1500*. Exhibitions of crafts made by disadvantaged people, as well as a great shop.

Live music
Bands will perform almost every night at **Khop Chai Deu** and at the **Music House**, on Fa Ngum, T021-212123. The **French Cultural Centre**, on Lang Xang, hosts a variety of musical performances, from local bands through to hip-hop ensembles.

Occasionally, music concerts and beauty pageants are held at the **Lao National Culture Hall**, opposite the National Museum. No official notice is given of forthcoming events but announcements sometimes appear in the *Vientiane Times* and large banners will flank the building.

Traditional dance
Lao National Theatre, *Manthathurath Rd, T020-550 1773*. Daily shows of traditional Lao dancing. Tickets available at the theatre. Performances are less regular in low season.

Festivals

1st weekend in Apr Pi Mai (Lao New Year) is celebrated with a 3-day festival and a huge water fight. It is advisable to put your wallet in a plastic bag and invest in a turbo water pistol. There are numerous *bacis* (good luck celebrations) and the traditional greeting at this time of year is 'Sok Dee Pi Mai' (good luck for the New Year).
Sep/Oct Boun Ok Phansa is a beautiful event on the night of the full moon at the end of Buddhist Lent. Candles are lit in all homes and candlelit processions take place around the city's wats and through the streets. Then, thousands of banana-leaf boats holding flowers, tapers and candles are floated out onto the river. The boats represent your bad luck floating away.

ON THE ROAD

Baci

The *baci* ceremony is a uniquely Lao *boun* (festival) and celebrates any auspicious occasion – marriage, birth, achievement or the end of an arduous journey, for instance. It dates from pre-Buddhist times and is animist in origin. It is centred on the *phakhouan*, a designer tree made from banana leaves and flowers (or, today, some artificial concoction of plastic) and surrounded by symbolic foods. The most common symbolic foods are eggs and rice – symbolizing fertility. The *mophone* hosts the ceremony and recites memorized prayers, usually in Pali, and ties cotton threads (*sai sin*) around the wrists of guests symbolizing good health, prosperity and happiness. For maximum effect, these strings must have three knots in them. It is unlucky to take them off until at least three days have elapsed, and custom dictates that they never be cut. Many people wear them until, frayed and worn, they fall off through sheer decrepitude. All this is accompanied by a *ramvong* (traditional circle dance), in turn accompanied by traditional instruments – flutes, clarinets, xylophones with bamboo crosspieces, drums, cymbals and the *kaen*, a hand-held pipe organ that is to Laos what the bagpipes are to Scotland.

Sep/Oct **Boun Souang Heua**, the boat-racing festival, is held towards the end of the rainy season. Boat races (*souang heua*) take place with 50 or so men in each boat; they power up the river in perfect unison. An exuberant event, with plenty of merrymaking.

12 Oct **Freedom of the French Day** is a public holiday.

Nov (date varies each year) **Boun That Luang** is celebrated in all of Vientiane's *thats* but most notably at That Luang (the national shrine). Originally a ceremony in which nobles swore allegiance to the king and constitution, it amazingly survived the Communist era. On the festival's most important day, **Thak Baat**, thousands of Lao people pour into the temple at 0600 and again at 1700 to pay homage. Monks travel from across the country to collect offerings and alms from the pilgrims. It is a really beautiful ceremony, with monks chanting and thousands of people praying. Women who attend should invest in a traditional *sinh* (traditional skirt). A week-long carnival surrounds the festival with fireworks, music and dancing. Recommended.

Shopping

Books

Book Café, *53/2 Heng Boun Rd, T020-689 3741.* Owned and operated by the expat author of *Laos, the Lao... and you* (a recommended read), this small shop has a good range of fiction and books on SEA. Operates a book swap scheme.

Monument Books, *124/1 Nokeo Khoummane Rd, T021-243708, www.monument-books.com.* The largest selection of new books in Vientiane, including Southeast Asian speciality books as well as coffee-table books. A good place to pick up Lao-language children's books to distribute to villages on your travels.

Vientiane Book Center, *32/05 Fa Ngum Rd, T021-212031, vientianebookcenter@yahoo.com.* A limited but interesting selection of used books in a multitude of languages.

Clothing, fashion, and textiles

Every hue and design is available in the **Talaat Sao** (Morning Market). For cheaper (but still good quality) fabric, pop across the road to **Talaat Kudin**; the fabric section is in the covered area at the back of the market. A *sinh*, the traditional Lao skirt, can be made within the day – just pick the length of fabric and the patterned band for the bottom of the skirt.

Cama Craft, *Mixay Rd, T021-501271*. Handmade clothes in Hmong styles.

Couleur d'Asie Concept Store, *Nokeo Khoummane Rd, T020-2815 7690*. Sells clothes, jewellery, accessories, furniture and decorations designed by the owner, Viviane Althey Inthavong. Also has a space for exhibitions and a good café-cum-restaurant.

Lao Cotton, *Luang Prabang Rd, out towards Wattay Airport, approximately 400 m on right from Novotel, T021-215840*. Good range of material, shirts and handbags; ask to have a look at the looms. Another branch on Samsenthai.

Lao Textiles by Carol Cassidy, *Nokeo Khoummane Rd, T021-212123, www.laotextiles. com. Mon-Fri 0800-1200 and 1400-1700, Sat 0800-1200*. Exquisite silk fabrics, including ikat and traditional Lao designs, made by an American in a beautifully renovated colonial property. Dyeing, spinning, designing and weaving all done on site. It's pricey, but many of the weavings are real works of art; custom-made pieces available on request.

Laoderm, *Samsenthai Rd, T021-254769. Mon-Sat 0800-1800*. Boutique selling original designs. Shirts, blouses and dresses weaved from linen, cotton and silk in muted tones

Sao Ban, *Chao Anou Rd, T025-5100034, www. saobancrafts.com*. A wonderful range of well-designed good-quality cotton and silk products as well as bags, bamboo ware and recycled bomb products. This is a very easy place to spend money, not only because of the excellent stock, but because it is a member of PADETC, a Lao NGO that integrates socially sustainable programs in education, agriculture, micro-finance, handcrafts and community leadership. Highly recommended.

Satri Laos, *Setthathirat, T021-244387, www.satrilao.laopdr.com*. If Vientiane had a Harrods this would be it. Upmarket boutique retailing everything from jewellery, shoes, clothes, furnishings and homeware. Beautiful stuff, though most is from China, Vietnam and Thailand.

Galleries

The main shops are along Setthathirat, Samsenthai and Pang Kham. The **Morning Market (Talaat Sao)** is also worth a browse, with artefacts, such as appliquéd panels, decorated hats and sashes, basketwork both old and new, small and large wooden tobacco boxes, sticky-rice lidded baskets, axe pillows, embroidered cushions and a wide range of silverwork. The likelihood of finding authentic antiques is pretty low. **Talaat Kudin** offers cheaper artefacts and silks but not as great a selection as Talaat Sao.

Camacraft, *Nokeo Khoummane, T020-556 1660*. NGO which retails handicrafts produced by the Hmong people. Embroidery, mulberry tea, Lao silk.

Indochine Handicrafts, *Samsenthai Rd next to the big wine barrel, T021-263619, maiphone@ hotmail.com*. Larger size collectibles, not really suitable for the suitcase shopper.

MaiChan Fine Arts & Handicrafts, *Samsenthai Rd, T021-263619, www.maichan handicraft.wordpress.com*. This is a neat little shop with lots of treasures including a wide range of scarves and hangings.

Oot-Ni Art Gallery, *Samsenthai Rd, T021-214359, www.ootni-yenkham.laopdr.com*. This is an Aladdin's Cave of serious objets d'art.

T'Shop Lai, *Wat Inpeng Soi, www.laococo. com*. As well as very high-quality handicrafts, this fantastic and delightfully scented shop sells wonderful furniture as well as shampoos, face creams and the like, all of which are 100% natural and organic.

Jewellery and silverware

Many of the stones sold in Vientiane are of dubious quality, but silver and gold are more reliable. Gold can be good value. Silver is cheap but not necessarily pure silver; nevertheless, the selection is interesting, with amusing animals, decorated boxes, old coins, earrings and silver belts. There's a wide selection in the **Morning Market** (**Talaat Sao**). Silver, gold and gem shops on Samsenthai are concentrated along the stretch opposite the **Asian Pavilion Hotel**; there are also gold shops further west towards the Chinese quarter. There are also a couple of shops around the fountain selling interesting designs and also wallet-friendly costume jewellery.

Sao Ban, *Chao Anou Rd, T025-510 0034, www.saobancrafts.com.* Sells a great range of silver jewellery and is a member of PADETC, a Lao NGO that integrates socially sustainable programs in education, agriculture, micro-finance, handcrafts and community leadership.

Markets and shopping malls

Vientiane has several excellent markets.

Morning Market (Talaat Sao), *off Lane Xang Av.* Busiest in the mornings (from around 1000), but operates all day. There are money exchanges here (quite a good rate), and a good selection of foodstalls selling Western food, soft drinks and ice-cream sundaes. It sells imported Thai goods, electrical appliances, watches, DVDs and CDs, stationery, cosmetics, a selection of handicrafts (see above), an enormous choice of Lao fabrics, and upstairs there is a large clothing section, silverware, gems and gold and a few handicraft stalls. There is also a modern shopping-centre addition to the Morning Market. It is pricier and less popular, and stocked with mostly Thai products sold in baht. On the 2nd floor, there is a reasonable food court. Next to it, the most enormous shopping mall should be open by the time you read this.

Talaat Kudin, *on the other side of the bus stop.* This is a ramshackle market with an interesting produce section. It offers many of the same handicrafts and silks as the Morning Market but is a lot cheaper.
Talaat Thong Khoun Khum, *on the corner of Khoun Khum and Dong Miang roads.* The largest produce market. It is sometimes known as the **Evening Market** but it's busiest in the mornings.
Talat Sao Mall, *www.talatsaomall.com.* 8 storeys of shops, restaurants, cinema, gym, disco and hotel.

What to do

Cooking
Villa Lao, *see Where to stay, T021-242292.* Cooking classes, covering all aspects of meal preparation, from purchasing the ingredients to eating the meal.

Cycling
Bicycles can be hired from several places in town, see Transport, page 339. A good outing is to cycle downstream along the banks of the Mekong. Cycle south on Tha Deua Rd until Km 5 (watch the traffic) and then turn right down one of the tracks towards the river. A path, suitable for bicycles, follows the river from Km 4.5. There are monasteries and drink sellers en route.

Language courses
Vientiane College, *Singha Rd, T021-414873, www.vientianecollege.com.*

Massage, saunas and spas
The best massage in town is given by the blind masseuses in a street off Samsenthai Rd, 2 blocks down from **Simuang Minimart** (across from Wat Simuang). There are 2 blind masseuse businesses side-by-side and both are fantastic: **Traditional Clinic**, T020-5565 9177, and **Porm Clinic**, T020-562 7633 (no English spoken). They are indicated by blue signs off both Khou Vieng and Samsenthai roads. Recommended.

Mandarina, *74 Pang Kham, T021-218703.*
A range of upmarket treatments costing
US$5-30. Massages, facials, body scrubs,
mini-saunas, oils and a jacuzzi.
Oasis Spa Massage & Beauty, *18/01 François
Ngin Rd, T021-243579.* Provides very good,
strong massages (*keng* – means strong
in Lao).
Papaya Spa, *opposite Wat Xieng Veh, T020-
561 0565, www.papayaspa.com.* **Papaya**
is a favourite with locals looking to spoil
themselves. You feel more relaxed the
minute you walk through the gates. Offers
massage, sauna, facials. Lovely gardens.
Recommended.
Wat Sok Paluang, *Sok Paluang.* Peaceful
leafy setting in the compound of Wat Sok
Paluang. Herbal sauna, followed by herb tea
(2000 kip) and massage by 2 young male
masseurs (4000 kip); very relaxing but some
women have reported groping. Vipassana
meditation is held every Sat 1600-1730, free,
T021-216214. To get there, walk through the
small stupas to the left of the wat; the sauna
is a rickety building on stilts on the right-
hand side, recognizable by the blackened
store underneath.

Sports clubs and swimming pools

Several hotels in town permit non-residents
to use their fitness facilities for a small fee,
including the **Tai Pan** (rather basic), **Lao
Plaza**, **Lane Xang**, **Don Chan** and **Novotel**.
See Where to stay.

Australia Club Recreation Centre, *Km 3,
Tha Deua Rd, T021-314921.* A beautiful setting,
with one of the nicest pools in Vientiane.
It's a lovely place for a swim followed by a
glass of wine as the sun sets. Also has a small
restaurant and a squash court. Short-term
membership available but cheaper if you get
a member to sign you in; loiter around some
of the expat drinking holes and you might
find someone willing. A tuk-tuk to the centre
is 20,000-30,000 kip.
Sengdara, *77/5 Phonthan Rd, T021-414058.
Daily 0500-2200.* Modern fitness centre with

gym, pool and sauna. US$5 for use of all the
facilities for a day, massage extra.

Thak Baat

Every morning at daybreak (0530-0600)
monks flood out of the city's temples, creating
a swirl of orange on the streets, as they collect
alms. It is truly beautiful to see the misty,
grey streets come alive with the robe-clad
monks. Foreigners are more than welcome
to participate and it feels much less intrusive
doing so here than in Luang Prabang. Just
buy some sticky rice or other food from the
vendors and kneel beside others.

Tour operators

For general travel information on getting
to Phou Khao Khouay, visit the **National
Tourism Authority** (see page 328). Most tour
operators will include 'eco' somewhere in
their name but this doesn't necessarily mean
very much.

Asian Trails Laos, *Unit 10, Ban Khounta
Thong, Sikhottabong District, T021-263936,
www.asiantrails.travel.* A Southeast Asian
specialist and very professional outfit.
Exotissimo, *6/44 Pang Kham Rd, T021-241861,
www.exotissimo.com.* Various tours and travel
services. Excellent but pricey.
Green Discovery, *Setthathirat Rd, next to Kop
Chai Deu, T021-223022, www.greendiscovery
laos.com.* Specializes in ecotours and
adventure travel. Recommended.

Yoga

Vientiane Yoga Studio, *Sokpaluang Rd,
Soi 1 (1st soi on the right after you turn
onto Sokpaluang from Kuvieng Rd), www.
vientianeyoga.weebly.com.* Various style
of yoga and pilates classes, plus dance.

Transport

Air
Wattay International Airport, T021-512012,
is 6 km west of town and has international
connections with **Cambodia**, **Vietnam** and
Thailand. It is also the hub of Laos' domestic

airline system, and to travel from the north to the south or vice versa it is often necessary to change planes here. Both international and domestic terminals have restaurants, telephone, taxi service and information booth. The international terminal also has ATMs, a post office, hotel desk and internet (upstairs).

Bicycle and motorbike

For those energetic enough in the hot season, bikes are the best way to get around town. Many hotels and guesthouses have bikes available; there are also bike hire shops dotted around town. Expect to pay about 20,000 kip per day. Markets, post offices and government offices usually have 'bike parks' where it is advisable to leave your bike. A small minding fee is charged.

First One Motorbikes, Rue François Ngin, T020-555 2899, k.naphaivong@gmail.com. For choice and experience, this place is hard to beat. Run since 2000 by avid biker, Mr Joy, here you can rent small automatic or semi-automatic bikes, 400cc choppers and 250cc off road machines. Prices range from about 80,000 kip up to US$50 or more.

Bus

Buses service outlying areas, but not the city itself. These buses run from the station next to the Talaat Sao/Central bus station, next to the Morning Market (see below).

Almost every guesthouse in town can sell you private bus tickets to the most of the following destinations and they clearly display times and prices on boards outside. Many will also offer a pick-up service direct from your hotel. However, if you want to go your own way, you'll need to venture out to one of the 3 main public bus terminals: Southern, Northern and Central bus station (next to the Morning Market).

VIP buses are very comfortable allowing you to sleep during the trip. For night journeys, book a double if you don't want to be stuck sleeping next to a stranger. Robberies have been reported on the night buses so keep valuables secure.

Southern bus station Route 13, 9 km north of the city centre (T021-740521). Public buses depart daily for destinations in southern Laos. Prices change fairly regularly, but they are clearly posted on official boards in the stations. The southern bus station has a range of stores and a pharmacy. To **Paksan** (150 km), 5 per day throughout the morning, 1½ hrs. To **Lak Sao** (for the Vietnamese border, 335 km), 8 hrs, 3 morning services. To **Thakhek** (360 km), 3 daily, 5-6 hrs plus a VIP bus in the early afternoon. To **Savannakhet** (483 km), 8 daily in the early morning, 8 hrs. To **Pakse** (736 km), 8 daily, 13 hrs; there are also overnight express buses to Pakse, 11 hrs. Buses to **Hanoi** also run from here, but it is far easier to book these from a guesthouse.

Northern bus station Route 2, towards the airport 3.5 km from the centre of town, T021-261905. Northbound buses leave regularly and have a/c. For the more popular routes, there are also VIP buses. To **Luang Prabang** (400 km), standard buses, 8 daily, 10 hrs; VIP buses 2 daily in the early morning, 8 hrs. To **Udomxai** (550 km), standard buses 2 daily, 13 hrs; 1 VIP bus in the afternoon. To **Luang Namtha** (648 km), daily, 19 hrs. To **Phongsali** (815 km), daily, 26 hrs. To **Houei Xai** (895 km), daily, 25-30 hrs. To **Sayaboury** (485 km), 2 daily, 12-15 hrs. To **Xam Neua** (850 km), 3 per day, 30 hrs. To **Phonsavanh** (365 km), 4-5 per day, 12+ hrs.

Central (Talaat Sao) bus station Across the road from Talaat Sao (Morning Market), in front of Talaat Kudin, on the eastern edge of the city centre, T021-216507. Destinations, distances and fares are listed on a board in English and Lao. Most departures are in the morning and can leave as early as 0400, so travellers on a tight schedule should check departure times the night before. There is a useful map at the station, and bus times and fares are listed in Lao and English. Staff at the ticket office speak only a little English so ask in the planning office if you need help. The times listed below depend on the weather and number of stops.

To the **Southern bus station**, 0600-1800 every 30 mins. To the **Northern bus station**, catch the Nongping bus (5 daily) and ask to get off at 'Thay Song'. To **Wattay Airport**, every 30 mins 0640-1800. To **Vang Vieng**, 5 daily, 3½ hrs.

Numerous buses criss-cross the province; most aren't very useful for tourists. To **Barksarp**, 6 daily. To **Ban Keun** (via Ban Thabok for Phou Khao Khouay), 9 daily. To **Xieng Khuan**, bus No 14 every 15 mins, 1 hr. To **Nam Ngum**, daily, 3 hrs. To **Vang Vieng**, 3 daily, but the VIP buses and minivans are preferable – this is for those who are flat broke only. To **Thakek**, 3 daily. To **Savannakhet**, 3 daily. To the **Friendship Bridge** (Lao side), every 15 mins. To **Nong Khai** (Thai side of the Friendship Bridge), 6 daily 0730-1800, about 1 hr including immigration. To **Udon Thani**, 6 daily 0800-1800.

To Thailand The Friendship Bridge is 20 km southeast of Vientiane; catch the Thai-Laos international bus from the Talaat Sao terminal, 90 mins at 0730, 0930, 1240, 1430, 1530 and 1800 to Nong Khai bus station. Or take one of the Friendship Bridge tuk-tuks from town. The border is open daily 0730-1800. Shuttle minibuses cross the bridge every 20 mins, stopping at the Thai and Lao immigration posts, where an overtime fee is charged at weekends and public holidays. Allow up to 1½ hrs to get to the bridge and through formalities on the Lao side. Tuk-tuks wait to take people to Nong Khai (10 mins);

Udon Thani is another hour further on and has good connections with Bangkok.

Car

Avis, Settathirath Rd, opposite Rue François Ngin, T021-223867, www.avis.la. Everything from a compact to a 4WD. Drivers can be hired and airport pick-up/drop-off is available. Operates in all areas of Laos PDR and cross border into Thailand, Vietnam and China.

Train

Trains cross the Friendship Bridge into Thailand and run to **Bangkok**, thus avoiding the need to change trains to cross the border (though you will still need to change trains in Nong Khai).

Tuk-tuks

Tuk-tuks usually congregate around tourist destinations: **Nam Phou**, **Talaat Sao** and **Talaat Kudin**. Tuk-tuks can be chartered for longer out-of-town trips or for short journeys of 2-3 km within the city. There are now fares to the most popular destinations posted clearly at the main pick-up points so there is no need to haggle.

There are also shared tuk-tuks, on regular routes on main streets. Tuk-tuks run to the **Friendship Bridge**, see under Bus, above, although if you buy your ticket from an agent, a pick-up is invariably included and takes the hassle out of the journey.

Around
Vientiane

There are plenty of short trips from Vientiane, ranging from the popular backpacker hotspot of Vang Vieng, through to the stunning Phou Khao Khouay National Protected Area. Vang Vieng has become very popular with action sports enthusiasts, with kayaking, caving and rock climbing all on offer.

Phou Khao Khouay National Protected Area
one of Laos' most beautiful and accessible nature reserves

★Phou Khao Khouay (pronounced *poo cow kway*) National Protected Area is one of Laos' premier national protected areas. The area extends across 2000 sq km and incorporates an attractive sandstone mountain range. It is crossed by three large rivers, smaller tributaries and two waterfalls at Tad Leuk and Tad Sae, which weave their way into the Ang Nam Leuk reservoir, a stunning man-made dam and lake on the outskirts of the park. Within the protected area is an array of wildlife, including wild elephants, gibbons, tigers, clouded leopards and Asiatic black bears.

The visitor centre at Tad Leuk rents out tents, mattresses, mosquito nets and sleeping bags. Toilets and washing facilities are on site. It is also possible to organize a homestay in one of the surrounding villages or stay overnight in the Elephant Observation Tower near Ban Na. Ban Hatkai and Ban Na also offer homestay accommodation. Trips are organized by the **National Tourism Administration** ⓘ *T021-212251, www.trekkingcentrallaos.com*, in Vientiane, opposite the French Language Centre, near the Morning Market. This centre also has an exhibition about Phou Khaou Khouay.

Vang Vieng and around
spectacular setting for adventure activities, surrounded by towering karst mountains

The drive to Vang Vieng, on the much improved Route 13, follows the valley of the Nam Ngum River north to Phonhong and then climbs steeply onto the plateau where Vang Vieng is located, 160 km north of Vientiane. The surrounding area is inhabited by the Hmong and Yao hill peoples and is particularly picturesque: craggy karst limestone scenery, riddled with caves, crystal-clear pools and waterfalls. In the early morning the views are reminiscent of a Chinese Sung Dynasty painting.

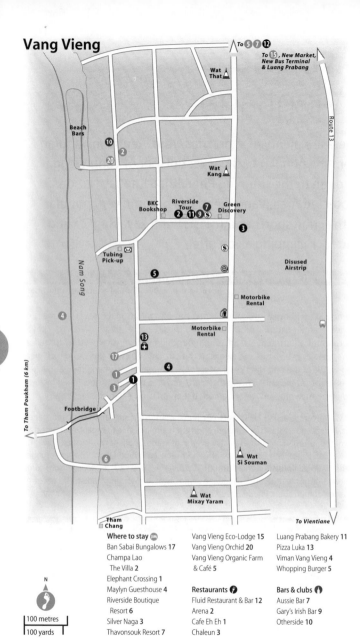

Vang Vieng

Wat That

To ⑤ ⑦ ⑫

To ⑮ , New Market,
New Bus Terminal
& Luang Prabang

Route 13

Beach
Bars

⑩
②
⑳

Wat
Kang

BKC
Bookshop

Riverside
Tour
② ⑪ ⑨ ⑤

Green
Discovery

③

Tubing
Pick-up

$

⑤

@

Disused
Airstrip

Motorbike
Rental

Motorbike
Rental

⑬

⑰

① ❶

③

④

Nam Song

④

To Tham Poukham (6 km)

Footbridge

⑥

Wat
Si Souman

Wat
Mixay Yaram

To Vientiane

Tham
Chang

N

100 metres

100 yards

Where to stay 🛏		
Ban Sabai Bungalows 17	Vang Vieng Eco-Lodge 15	Luang Prabang Bakery 11
Champa Lao	Vang Vieng Orchid 20	Pizza Luka 13
The Villa 2	Vang Vieng Organic Farm	Viman Vang Vieng 4
Elephant Crossing 1	& Café 5	Whopping Burger 5
Maylyn Guesthouse 4		
Riverside Boutique	**Restaurants 🍴**	**Bars & clubs 🍸**
Resort 6	Fluid Restaurant & Bar 12	Aussie Bar 7
Silver Naga 3	Arena 2	Gary's Irish Bar 9
Thavonsouk Resort 7	Cafe Eh Eh 1	Otherside 10
	Chaleun 3	

The town itself is nestled in a valley on the bank of the Nam Song River. It enjoys cooler weather and offers breathtaking views of the mountains of Pha Tang and Phatto Nokham. There are a number of 16th- and 17th-century monasteries in town; the most notable are Wat That at the northern edge of the settlement and Wat Kang, 100 m or so to the south.

Tip...

Hobo Maps produces a remarkably detailed map of the town and surrounding area with caves, paths and walks all marked. It sells for 25,000 kip from most guesthouses. It is well worth the purchase, especially if you want to explore much of the surrounding area that is not marketed by tour operators.

The town's laid-back feel and the tubing craze that kicked off here in the early 2000s made it a haunt for backpackers and it became a must-visit stop on the party banana pancake trail for many years. The late-night river bars and 'happy pizzas' have since been clamped down on and while it continues to pull in a good flow of backpackers, it is, thankfully, a far calmer place than it once was.

While the drop in 'happy pizza' eating backpacker numbers may have hurt some businesses in the short term, it has left the town a more pleasant place and the surrounding landscape has helped to establish Vang Vieng as a centre for those seeking to get into the great outdoors, with excellent cycling, walking, rock climbing, caving, and kayaking on offer. This is one of the most stunning and easily accessible parts of Laos. It is hoped that with the passing of the tubing scene and all that came with it, Vang Vieng will go from strength to strength by capitalizing on its abundance of beautiful spots.

Safety Laos is a very safe country for tourists but a disproportionate number of accidents and crimes seem to happen in Vang Vieng. Theft is routinely reported here, ranging from robberies on the river to the opportunist theft of items from guests' rooms. It is usually advisable to hand in any valuables to the management of your guesthouse or to padlock your bag and leave cash stashed in a very good hiding spot. Another major problem in the past was the sale of illegal drugs, but this is being clamped down on to some extent. **Vang Vieng Hospital** is on the road parallel to the river; in most cases it is much better to go to Vientiane or Thailand, see page 555. ▶▶ *For details of the significant safety risks involved in adventure activities, see Tour operators, page 348.*

Nam Song River

Vang Vieng has become synonymous with tubing down the Nam Song and today, now that many of the bars are shut, it is a very pleasant experience. There are still enough bars to have a good time, but not so many as to destroy the piece and create the feeling of an invasion that one hung over the town. Tubes can be picked up from the Old Market area where the tubing company has formed a cartel. Without stops the 3-km tubing from the Organic Farm back to town can take one to two hours if done quickly, but most people do it in three to four hours or take all day, choosing to stop along the way to drink, play volleyball or use the flying fox swings at the many bars dotted along the river on the way into town.

Many tour operators offer kayaking trips as well. Popular routes include kayaking down the Nam Song to the caves, especially Tham Nam (Water Cave), see below. ▶▶ *See What to do, page 348.*

★Caves

Vang Vieng is known for its limestone caves, sheltered in the mountains flanking the town. Pretty much every guesthouse and tour operator offers tours to the caves (the best of these is **Green Discovery**) and, although some caves can be accessed independently, it is advisable to take a guide to a few as they are dark and difficult to navigate. Often children from surrounding villages will take tourists through the caves for a small fee. Don't forget to bring a torch, or even better a headlamp, which can be picked up cheaply at the market both in Vang Vieng and Vientiane. Many of the larger caves have an entrance fee of around 10,000 kip and many have stalls where you can buy drinks and snacks. You can buy the **Hobo** map from the town which clearly gives the location of the best sites.

In addition to those listed below, there are many more caves in the vicinity of Vang Vieng, most to the west and north. It is possible to hire a bicycle or motorcycle in Vang Vieng, take it across the river and cycle to the caves and villages on the other side of the Nam Song as all the sites are between 2 km and 15 km from Vang Vieng. ▶▶ *See What to do, page 348.*

Tham Chang ⓘ *Access via the Vang Vieng Resort south of town (see Where to stay).* Of Vang Vieng's myriad caves, this is the most renowned. It passes right under a mountain and is fed by a natural spring, perfect for an early morning dip. From the spring, it is possible to swim into the cave for quite a distance (bring a waterproof torch, if possible). The cave is said to have been used as a refuge from Chinese Haw bandits during the 19th century and this explains its name: *chang* meaning 'loyal'. The entrance fee includes electric illumination of the cave. Although the cave is not the most magnificent of Vieng Vang's caves, it serves as a superb lookout point.

Tham Poukham ⓘ *7 km from Vang Vieng, 10,000 kip.* Another popular cavern, Tham Poukham is often referred to as the 'Cave of the Golden Crab' while the extremely pretty swimming hole outside it is called the Blue Lagoon. It's believed that if you catch a golden crab you will have a lifetime of fortune. To get there, cross the footbridge near the Villa Nam Song, and then follow the road for a further 6 km until you reach the village of Ban Nathong. From the village, the cave is a short climb up a steep hill. Mossy rocks lead the way into the main cavern where a large bronze reclining Buddha is housed. Here there is an idyllic lagoon with glassy green-blue waters, perfect for a dip.

Tham None ⓘ *4 km north of Vang Vieng, 10,000 kip,* is known locally known as the 'Sleeping Cave' because 2000 villagers took refuge there during the war. The large cave is dotted with stalagmites and stalactites, including the 'magic stone of Vang Vieng', which reflects light. There are also lots of bats residing in the grotto. This cave is very popular with tour groups and rock climbers.

Tham Xang (Elephant Cave) ⓘ *14 km north of Vang Vieng on the banks of the Nam Song, 10,000 kip,* also known as the 'Elephant Cave', is named after the stalagmites and stalactites that have created an elephant formation on a ledge. The cave also contains some Buddha images, including the footprint of Buddha. Although the cave itself is relatively nondescript the bell used by monks is made of a former bomb.

Tham Nam (Water Cave) ⓘ *15 km from town, follow the signposted path from Tham Xang, 10,000 kip,* a long spindly cave that is believed to stretch for at least 7 km. It takes about two hours to explore the cavern and at the entrance there is a crystal-clear pool, perfect for a dip. This is one of Vang Vieng's most interesting caves and in the wet season needs to be explored with an inner tube or by wading, while pulling yourself along a rope, although tour operators will take you beyond the roped area too. It's not easy and should not be attempted alone. At times the cavern is an extremely tight fit and commando-type crawling is required; a hard helmet with lamp attached is necessary. In spite of the difficulties, it is an incredible caving experience. To get to these two caves follow Route 13 north and turn left at Km 14, then follow this dirt road for 1 km until you reach the river. Boats charge 10,000 kip to cross the river to see Tham Xang, from which you can walk to Tham Nam.

Kasi → Colour map 1, B3.

Kasi sits on a road connecting Kasi with Nan district in Luang Prabang Province. This road provides an alternative way of getting to the World Heritage town of Luang Prabang for travellers coming from Vientiane or Vang Vieng, bypassing the Phoukhoun mountain pass and shortening the journey. This is a good option for those heading to Sayabouly or those who want to visit the massive Khoun Lang Cave. There is a narrow entrance but it opens to a single large passageway of 250 m in length which is full of stalactites, stalagmites and flowstone. The Khoun Lang Nature Park is also home to waterfalls and dense forest.

Listings Vang Vieng and around *map p342*

Tourist information

There is now an official tourist information office on the main road.

Where to stay

The town's popularity has ensured a uniformity among almost all places catering to budget tourists. However, there are now also a few good mid-range options and some very good upmarket resorts. Accommodation in the centre of town is usually cheaper, but try to get a room with a view of the river, as it is stunning. The bamboo bridge leads across the river bungalow on the far shore, but note that in the rainy season the only bridges in operation are the Namsong bridge (small charges apply) and the high bridge leading past the Vang Vieng Orchid to the island bars.

$$$$-$$$ Riverside Boutique Resort
On the river, T023-511729, www.riversidevangvieng.com.
By far and away the best lodgings in town. Swish rooms are well furnished with tasteful

decorations and drawings. The suites come with gigantic balconies and sunloungers; the ultimate – the Tai Deng – has the best views in Vang Vieng. Worth every penny. Good-sized pool and a spa due to open. Mediocre restaurant.

$$$ Silver Naga
On the river bank, T023-511822, www.silvernaga.com.
Very tasteful rooms with wooden floors and large comfortable beds. Rooms facing the river have fantastic views – those from the higher floors are truly exceptional. Breakfast is served on a lovely deck right on the river. There is a great pool, also with knockout views. Recommended.

$$$-$$ Ban Sabai Bungalows
On the banks of the river, T023-511088, www.xayohgroup.com.
A lovely complex of bungalows with balconies in a spectacular location, with all the modern fittings. However, the rooms are not well lit, the water is not very hot, the bathroom is badly designed with the sink in the shower compartment and the breakfast service is very unpolished. Rooms 1-4 are

near the laundry room and although not too noisy, light sleepers will be disturbed. Bungalows closer to the river are a bit more expensive. Those happy with the less glamorous side of rustic will love it here, but luxury lovers will not. The views from the balconies are top drawer and the staff are extremely friendly.

$$$-$$ Thavonsouk Resort
On the river, T023-511096,
www.thavonsouk.com.
Offers 5 different styles of accommodation across a sprawling riverfront premises. Rooms are much more attractive on the outside than they are inside. Standard rooms come with tacky wood-imitation tiles. Some mid-range bungalows are great value with massive balconies fitted with sunbeds. There is a traditional Lao house, decorated with Lao furnishings, suitable for a family or big group, plus suites (TV, fridge, bath, a/c) and standard accommodation. Fantastic restaurant. Keep your eye out for local home-grown pop star, Aluna and her father, Alom, who run this family business.

$$ Elephant Crossing
On the Nam Song River, T023-511232,
www.theelephantcrossinghotel.com.
Looking a little tired, this is nonetheless a good mid-range option with great views. Australian-run riverfront hotel classically decorated with modern wooden furnishings.

$ Champa Lao the Villa
Khemsong St, northern end of town,
T020-5501 8501, www.champa-lao.com.
What this place lacks in views it more than makes up for in character. An 80-year-old Lao stilt house with plenty of comfy, ethnic fabric covered seating and bamboo hammocks to kick back in. Run by a super-friendly husband and wife team who offer good service and sound advice. Alongside the main house a couple of small bungalows are set in the lush, dense garden. If this is full try **Champa Lao Bungalow** run by the same people.

$ Maylyn Guesthouse
On the opposite side of the river to town,
T020-5560 4095.
Easily the best place to stay on the 'other side', these simple bungalows are set in a well-kept garden and the owners help make it a great place to unwind for a few days. A good base from which to explore the caves.

$ Vang Vieng Orchid
On the river road, T023-511172.
Very comfortable rooms with fan or a/c, hot water in the bathrooms and clean tiled floors. The rooms with private balconies are well worth the few extra dollars because you will have a phenomenal view. The proximity to the infamous **Bucket Bar** makes this place quiet noisy.

Out of town
The places on the outskirts of town are great for those who wish to escape into a more natural landscape. The lack of facilities and transport in the area ensures tranquillity but also makes it quite difficult to get to town.

$$-$ Vang Vieng Eco-Lodge
7 km north of town, T021-413370,
www.vangvieng-eco-lodge.com.
Although this isn't an ecolodge it is still a beautiful place to stay and ideal for those who want to enjoy the scenery around Vang Vieng and not venture into the town itself. Set on the banks of the river with stunning gardens and beautiful rock formations, it is a perfect place to get away from it all. The bungalows are naturally ventilated but also come with fans. The rooms are special, with wood-beamed ceilings, Lao fabrics and 4-poster beds. Bathrooms are all unique and some have sunken tubs. Good Lao restaurant. Activities arranged.

$ Vang Vieng Organic Farm
3 km north of town in Ban Sisavang,
T023-511174, www.laofarm.org.
Now that the noise from the tubing bars has subsided, the farm's tranquillity has been restored. Run by Mr T (who inadvertently

started the tubing craze) who does great community work, promotes organic growing raises money for school buses. This is a very worthwhile place to lay your head. The accommodation is quite basic, but it is clean and the location is good. Also runs volunteering projects. Well worth a visit even if you don't stay here. Hugely popular restaurant, serving great starfruit wine and famous mulberry pancakes.

Kasi

Rooms are available at several guesthouses in town.

$ Somchith
Route 13, Main Rd.
The most popular place is this small guesthouse above a restaurant in the centre of town.

Restaurants

There is a string of eating places on the main road through town, with the same menu in almost every establishment – generally hamburgers, pasta, sandwiches and basic Asian.

$$-$ Arena
A couple of doors down from the Luang Prabang bakery, T020-7818 1171. Open all day.
Glass walls enclose this restaurant-cum-cafe that, in typical Vang Vieng style, serves a bit of everything. It's clean and has fast Wi-Fi and is a decent option for a light lunch and to escape the heat. Popular with backpackers.

$$-$ Luang Prabang Bakery Restaurant
Just off the main road.
One of the more expensive places in town serving a wide range of cakes and ice creams in the daytime and popular for cocktails in the evening. The standards aren't as high as the prices, but this remains a popular spot and is often busy when everywhere else is dead. Good Wi-Fi.

$ Cafe Eh Eh
Right next to the Elephant Crossing alley.
This newcomer to the scene is a funky little space knocking out excellent shakes, good

sandwiches and some delicious cakes – the cheesecake is a highlight. Also sells a nice range of gifts and cards. Recommended.

$ Chaleun
Opposite Green Discovery on the main road, T023-254335.
The decor is basic in the extreme, but this is probably the best of the restaurants clustered around this part of town, particularly for the quality of the Lao dishes.

$ Fluid
2 km outside town, www.vangvieng.biz.
Fantastic views, laid-back vibe, good staff and good food. Well worth the trip outside town. Highly recommended.

$ Organic Farm Café
Further down the main road from Fluid (see above).
Small café offering over 15 fruit shakes and a fantastic variety of food. Mulberry shakes and pancakes are a must and the harvest curry stew is delicious. Try the fresh spring rolls, with pineapple dipping sauce as a starter.

$ Pizza Luka
Signposted near the hospital. Open from 1800.
Freshly made Italian-style pizza with a range of quality toppings, this is the best pizza joint in town, hands-down. Friendly service and a relaxed vibe. The house red isn't bad either. Recommended.

$ Viman Vang Vieng
Near the Silver Naga, T020-5892 6695.
Great restaurant run by Kaz, a German-Thai gentleman who came to Vang Vieng as a tourist years ago and returned to set up shop here. He prides himself on making the best schnitzel this side of Bavaria; it's excellent and comes served with great fried potatoes. Kaz also does some quality Lao dishes and some Thai classics. His own artwork hangs on the walls. He is very passionate about the area and full of information. Well worth a visit.

$ Whopping Burger
1 block south of Arena (see above), whoppingburger@hotmail.co.jp.

This place does exactly what it says on the tin. Huge buns, huge patties and a decent portion of hand-cut fried on the side. Nice wooden seating, friendly owners and normally bustling.

Bars and clubs

Now that the party scene has died down, nightlife is a little lacklustre for those who come here expecting a wild night. However, there are a few bars on the road toward the tubing pick-up point that still get busy later on in the evenings, notably Gary's Irish Bar and the Aussie Bar.

For something a little more local, it's worth taking a look at some of the Lao joints that line the road on which the buses travel. These are open-air beer terraces with *Beerlao* flags string around them. Find a busy one and you'll likely have a good night. Down by the bamboo bridge there are a couple of bars with low tables and cushions on the ground that make great places for sundowners. The Otherside (on the main street by the river) is also a good spot for sunset beers and does a reasonable range of food. The most notable place is Fluid Bar (www.vangvieng.biz) which is 2 km outside town on the river. Here the lovely owners care a lot about the local area and are keen to promote longer stays here following the decline in visitors post-tubing craze days. This is a lovely spot to go and swing in a hammock, enjoy some good drinks and maybe a shisha.

Shopping

BKC Bookshop, *T023-5118694*. A reasonable range of second-hand books and guides to buy and exchange.
New Market, *2 km north of town*. Has the greatest selection of goods.

What to do

Ballooning
Ballooning above the beautiful karst landscape of Vang Vieng is simply awe-inspiring. Flights (US$70, child US$40) operate twice a day and can be booked via most agents including **Green Discovery**.

Kayaking and rafting
See also Tour operators, below. Kayaking is very popular around Vang Vieng and competition between operators has become fierce. Options range from day trips on calm waters to a trip to the Nam Lik River to kayak its rapids and see more far flung villages such as the Thai Dam village of Ban Vang Mon.

Rock climbing
Vang Vieng is the best established rock-climbing area in the country, and there are now 200 routes ranging from 4a to 8b. Many of the climbs were bolted by **Adam's Climbing School** or people associated with it. Adam's is the longest running outfit in town. Both **Adam's** and **Green Discovery** (see Tour operators, below) offer climbing courses almost every day in high season. The best climbing sites include: **Sleeping Cave**, which offers 14 separate routes; **Sleeping Wall**, a tough 20-m crag, which features 19 separate climbs, including a few ascents requiring some tricky manoeuvring and steep overhangs.

Tour operators
Tour guides are available for hiking, rafting, and visiting the caves and minority villages, from most travel agents and guesthouses. Safety issues need to be considered when taking part in any adventure activity. There have been fatalities in Vang Vieng from boating, trekking and caving accidents. The Nam Xong River can flow very quickly during the wet season (Jul and Aug) and tourists have drowned here. Make sure you wear a life-jacket and ensure you are not on the river after dark. Make sure all equipment is in

a good state of repair. A price war between operators has led to cost cutting, resulting in equipment that is not well maintained or non-existent. The more expensive, companies are usually the best (see also Tour operators, page 338).

Adam's Climbing School, *near the Silver Naga hotel, T020-5010832, www.laos-climbing.com.* The friendly owner, Adam, believes himself to be the first Lao rock climber – he's been climbing since 1997. He began in the rock climbing Mecca of Krabi, Thailand, before a stint in Germany and setting up in Laos in 2005. He and his team are super-encouraging so this is a great place for novices to learn. The huge variety of rock on offer also means it's a good place for more experienced climbers. Half-day to 3-day courses. Also rents motorbikes and can arrange ballooning trips. Highly recommended.

Green Discovery, *main road, T023-511440, www.greendiscoverylaos.com.* Caving, kayaking, hiking and rock climbing plus motorbike tours and mountain bike tours. Very professional and helpful. Recommended.

VLT Natural Tours, *near Ban Sabai (see Where to stay), T023-511369, T020-5520 8283, www.vangviengtour.com.* A long-running outfit, this company offers a huge variety of options including cooking tours, fishing and camping trips. Also runs combined trekking, caving, tubing and kayaking tours.

Tubing

Floating slowly along the Nam Song is an ideal way to take in the stunning surroundings of misty limestone karsts, jungle and rice paddies. The drop-off point is 3 km from Vang Vieng, near the Organic Farm. The tubing rental company in town still charges 55,000 kip. A deposit of 60,000 kip must also be paid. Rental begins at 0800 and it is best to start early to make the most of your trip down-river.

Transport

Vang Vieng is on Route 13 between Vientiane and Luang Prabang so a bus between Vientiane and anywhere up north (or vice versa) will pass through even if it is not on the itinerary. The journey to/from the capital takes about 3-4 hrs and from Luang Prabang around 5-7 hrs. See also Vientiane Transport, page 338.

Bicycle and motorbike hire

There are many bicycles for rent in town. There are also a few motorbike rental places, one of the best is opposite the **Silver Naga** hotel where a friendly young family rent out everything from automatic scooters to fully manual 250cc off-road bikes. Prices from around 60,000 kip, but it gets cheaper the longer you rent for.

Bus

Buses leave from the bus terminal at the New Market, 2 km north of town. There are toilets, shops and cafés. Almost every guesthouse and tour agency in Vang Vieng sells bus tickets. The minivan service is great because it includes a pick-up at your guesthouse.

Private minivan transport and VIP buses

To **Vientiane**: minivans leave at 0900 and there are 3 VIP buses per morning, 3 hrs. To **Luang Prabang**: minivans leave at 0900 and sometimes again at 1400, up to 9 hrs depending on the state of the road. VIP buses at 0900. To **Phonsavanh**: 1 per morning, 7 hrs.

Tuk-tuk

Tuk-tuks are available for hire for trips to the cave. It is best to ask at your guesthouse for the standard going rate and ideally ask them to arrange a tuk-tuk for you – this is much easier than trying to negotiate yourself.

Kasi
Bus/truck

There are connections south to **Vang Vieng** (2 hrs) and north to **Luang Prabang** (4 hrs).

Northern Laos

dense forests, hilltribes and river adventures

Much of Laos' northern region is rugged and mountainous, a remote borderland with a significant minority population of hill peoples.

Until recently, in some areas at least, the only way to travel was by boat, along one of the rivers – many fast-flowing – which have cut their way through this impressive landscape. Today road travel is much improved, though still not easy in some more remote parts.

The key centre of the north is the old royal capital of Luang Prabang, one of the world's most beautiful cities and a World Heritage Site. To the east is the Plain of Jars, the Nam Et-Phou Louey National Protected Area and Vieng Xai, a former stronghold of the Pathet Lao, while to the north is a string of small towns that are becoming increasingly popular places to visit. Eco-resorts in peaceful forest settings, treks to upland villages, night river safaris and graphic insights into the country's recent history are among the highlights of this region.

Best for
Caves ▪ Homestays ▪ Temples ▪ Trekking

Footprint
picks

★ **Luang Prabang**, page 353
Golden temples, charming cafés and boutique hotels.

★ **Tad Kuang Si**, page 364
Spectacular waterfalls, best appreciated in the wet season.

★ **Nam Ou River and Muang Ngoi Neua**, page 378
An ideal spot to laze in a hammock and soak up the scenery.

★ **Vieng Phouka**, page 387
A great base for trekking and exploring local caves.

★ **The Gibbon Experience**, page 393
Explore the jungle canopy of Bokeo Nature Reserve by zipline.

★ **Phonsavanh and Plain of Jars**, pages 398 and 402
Mysterious stone jars in a landscape scarred by war.

★ **Pathet Lao caves at Vieng Xai**, page 405
Fascinating cave city used as a revolutionary base during the war.

★ **Nam Nern Night Safari**, page 408
Venture up the river on a long-tail boat to spot rare animals.

Luang Prabang
& around

★In terms of size, Luang Prabang hardly deserves the title 'city' (the population is around 40,000) but in terms of grandeur the appellation is more than deserved. Luang Prabang is the town that visitors often remember with the greatest affection. Its rich history, incomparable architecture, easygoing atmosphere, good choice of restaurants, friendly population and stunning position, surrounded by a crown of mountains, mark it out as exceptional.

Anchored at the junction of the Mekong and Nam Khan rivers, the former royal capital was founded on Mount Phousi – a small rocky hill with leafy slopes – and has been a mountain kingdom for over 1000 years. Despite a few welcome concessions to modern life, including great food, and electricity, Luang Prabang still oozes the magic of bygone days. In the 18th century there were more than 65 wats in the city; many have been destroyed over the years but over 30 remain intact. UNESCO have not only designated the city as a World Heritage Site, but also the best-preserved traditional city in Southeast Asia.

Yet for all its magnificent temples, this royal 'city' feels more like a provincial town: in the early evening children play in the streets, while women cook; old men lounge in wicker chairs and young boys play *takraw*. The town's timelessness can be observed by simply walking the ancient streets. *Colour map 1, B2.*

Essentials Luang Prabang

Finding your feet

Luang Prabang is a small town and the best way to explore is either on foot or by bicycle. Bicycles can be hired from most guesthouses for 20,000 kip per day. For longer journeys, such as out to the waterfalls, tuk-tuks and *saamlors* are available for hire. Motorbikes here are more expensive than elsewhere in Laos, costing up to 16,000 kip per day. Expect to leave your passport as deposit.

Best restaurants

3 Nagas, page 369
L'Éléphant, page 369
Café Toui, page 369
Khai Phaen, page 369
Dyen Sabai, page 370

When to go

Luang Prabang lies 300 m above sea level on the upper Mekong, at its confluence with the Nam Khan. The most popular time to visit the town is during the comparatively cool months of November and December but the best time to visit is from December to February. After this the weather is hotting

Tip...

Luang Prabang is a great place to pick up textiles made in nearby ethnic communities– try **Ock Pop Tok** (see page 372) or **TAEC Boutique** (see page 373). Also well worth a visit is the **Traditional Arts and Ethnology Centre** (see page 363).

Tip...

Many of the excellent restaurants in Luang Prabang offer cookery courses where you learn how to prepare local staples such as *jaew bawng* (chilli salsa) or *mok pa* (fish steamed in banana leaves). **Tamarind** restaurant (see page 370) is highly recommended for its enchanting jungle garden school.

up and the views are often shrouded in a haze, produced by shifting cultivators using fire to clear the forest for agriculture. This does not really clear until May or, sometimes, June. During the months of March and April, when visibility is at its worst, smoke can cause soreness of the eyes, as well as preventing planes from landing.

In terms of festivals, on the October full moon, the delightful **Lai Heua Fai** (Fireboat Festival) takes place (see page 372).

Tip...

The two-day journey along the Mekong between Luang Prabang and Houei Xai/Pakbeng remains hugely popular and is considered a rite of passage in Southeast Asia. See page 374 for details.

Time required

The main sights in Luang Prabang could be seen in a couple of days but you could easily spend four or five. It's a beautiful place to hang out, eat well and wander the streets.

Luang Prabang is a small town and the sights are conveniently close together, the majority dotted along the main Sakkaline, Sisavangvong and Souvanna Khampong roads. Most are walkable – the important ones can be covered within two leisurely days – but a bike is the best way to get around. To begin with it may be worth climbing Mount Phousi or taking a stroll along the Mekong and Nam Khan river roads to get a better idea of the layout of the town. Most of Luang Prabang's important wats are dotted along the main road, Phothisarath. When visiting the wats it is helpful to take a guide to obtain entry to all the buildings, which are often locked for security reasons. Without a guide, your best chance of finding them open is early in the morning.

Royal Palace

Sisavangvong Rd, daily 0800-1100 and 1330-1600 (closed Tue), small admission charge. Shorts, short-sleeved shirts and strappy dresses prohibited; shoes should be removed and bags must be put in lockers. No photography.

Also called the **National Museum**, the Royal Palace is right in the centre of the city on the main road, Sisavangvong, which runs along the promontory and allowed royal guests ready access from the Mekong. Unlike its former occupants, the palace survived the 1975 revolution and was converted into a museum the following year. It replaced a smaller wooden palace on the same site.

Construction of the palace started in 1904, during the reign of Sisavang Vong, and took 20 years. It was built by the French for the Lao king, in an attempt to bind him and his family more tightly to the colonial system of government. Although most of the construction was completed by 1909, the two front wings were extended in the 1920s and a new, more Lao-style roof was added. These later changes were accompanied by the planting of the avenue of palms and the filling in of one of two fish ponds. Local residents regarded the ponds as the 'eyes' of the capital, so the blinding of one eye was taken as inviting bad fortune by leaving the city unprotected.

The subsequent civil war seemed to vindicate these fears. The palace is Khmer in style, cruciform in plan and mounted on a small platform of four tiers. The only indication of French involvement can be seen in the two French lilies represented in stucco on the entrance, beneath the symbols of Lao royalty. There are a few Lao motifs but, in many respects, the palace is more foreign than Lao: it was designed by a French architect, with steps made from Italian marble; built by masons from Vietnam; embellished by carpenters from Bangkok; and funded by the largesse of the colonial authorities. While the palace itself is modest, its contents are spectacular.

The museum now contains a collection of 15th- to 17th-century Buddha statues and artefacts from wats in Luang Prabang such as the ancient bronze drums from Wat Visoun. Notable pieces include an ancient Buddha head, an offering from Indian dignitaries, and a reclining Buddha with the unusual addition of mourners. The most important piece is the **Golden Buddha**, from which the city derives its name. Some believe that the original is kept in a bank vault in Vientiane or Moscow, although most dispel this as rumour. It is 90% solid gold, stands 83 cm high and weighs around 53 kg. Reputed to have come from Ceylon, and to date from between the first and ninth centuries, the statue was brought to Cambodia in the 11th century, given to King Phaya Sirichanta, and then taken to Lane Xang by King Fa Ngum, who had spent time in the courts of Angkor and married into Khmer royalty.

Entrance Hall The main entrance hall of the palace was used for royal religious ceremonies, when the Supreme Patriarch of Lao Buddhism would oversee proceedings from his gold-painted lotus throne.

King's Reception Room The room to the immediate right of the entrance was the King's Reception Room, also called the **Ambassadors' Room**. It contains French-made busts of the last three Lao monarchs, a model of the royal hearse (which is kept in Wat Xieng Thong) and a mural by French artist Alex de Fontereau, depicting a day in the life of Luang Prabang in the 1930s.

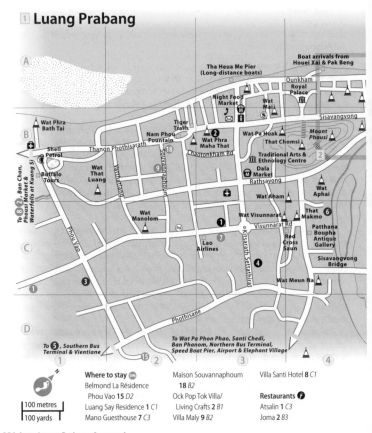

1 Luang Prabang

Where to stay
Belmond La Résidence
Phou Vao **15** *D2*
Luang Say Residence **1** *C1*
Mano Guesthouse **7** *C3*

Maison Souvannaphoum
18 *B2*
Ock Pop Tok Villa/
Living Crafts **2** *B1*
Villa Maly **9** *B2*

Villa Santi Hotel **8** *C1*

Restaurants
Atsalin **1** *C3*
Joma **2** *B3*

Coronation Room (Throne Room) To the rear of the entrance hall, the Coronation Room was decorated between 1960 and 1970 for Sisavang Vatthana's coronation, an event which was interrupted because of the war. The walls are a brilliant red with Japanese glass mosaics embedded in a red lacquer base with gilded woodwork. They depict scenes from Lao festivals, such as boat racing. The carved throne has a gold three-headed elephant insignia; on one side is a tall pot to hold the crown. To the right of the throne, as you face it, are the ceremonial coronation swords and a glass case containing 15th- and 16th-century crystal and gold Buddhas, many from inside the 'melon stupa' of Wat Visoun. Because Luang Prabang was constantly raided, many of these religious artefacts were presented to the king for safekeeping. At the back, to the right of the entrance, is the royal *howdah*, a portable throne was used during battle. The throne is covered with shields to protect it.

Private Apartments In comparison to the state rooms, the royal family's private apartments are modestly decorated. They have been left virtually untouched since Sisavang Vatthana and family left for exile in Xam Neua Province. The **King's Library** backs onto the Coronation Room: Sisavang Vatthana was a well-read monarch, having studied at the École de Science Politique in Paris. Behind the library, built around a small inner courtyard are the queen's modest bedroom, the king's bedchamber and the royal yellow bathroom, with its two regal porcelain thrones standing side by side. These rooms are cordoned off but you can still see them. The king's bed is a marvellous construction with a three-headed elephant insignia. The remaining rooms include a small portrait gallery, dining room and the children's bedroom, which is decorated with musical instruments and headdresses for *Ramayana* actors. In the hallway linking the rooms is a miscellany of interesting objects, including an intricately patterned *sinh*, worn by the queen, and a royal palanquin, which would have been tied to an elephant. Domestic rooms, offices and library are located on the ground floor beneath the state apartments.

Other reception rooms To the left of the entrance hall is the reception room of the **King's Secretary**, and beyond it, the **Queen's Reception Room**, which together house an eccentric miscellany of state gifts from just about every country except the UK. Of particular note is the moon rock presented to Laos by the USA following the

Mekong River

Tourist Boats to Pak Ou

Souvanna Khampong

Sakkaline

Nam Khan

Nam Khan

Wat Tao Hai

➡ **Luang Prabang maps**
1 Luang Prabang, page 356
2 Luang Prabang detail, page 360

To Pak Ou, Northern Bus Terminal & Xang Hai

To Airport, & Ban Hat Hien

⑤

⑥

Pizza Phan Luang **4** *C3*

Yensabai **3** *C1*

Bars & clubs 🎵
Dao Fa Nightclub **5** *D1*
Utopia **6** *C4*

BACKGROUND

Luang Prabang

According to legend, the site of Luang Prabang was chosen by two resident hermits. Buddha was believed to have glanced in Luang Prabang's direction, saying a great city would be built there. Details are sketchy regarding the earliest inhabitants of Luang Prabang but historians imply the ethnic Khmu and Lao Theung groups were the initial settlers. They named Luang Prabang, 'Muang Sawa', which literally translates as Java, hinting at some kind of cross-border support. By the end of the 13th century, Muang Sawa had developed into a regional hub.

A major turning point in the city's history came about in 1353, when the mighty Fa Ngum travelled up the Mekong, backed by a feisty Khmer army, and captured Muang Sawa. Fa Ngum imported Khmer traditions including Theravada Buddhism and great architecture, but his constituents and army, wary of his warmongering ways, exiled him in 1373, and his son, Oun Heuan, then assumed the throne.

In 1478 the city was invaded by Vietnamese. After several years occupying and ransacking the place, they were driven out and the kingdom embarked upon a massive reconstruction campaign. During this period some of Luang Prabang's finest monuments were built, including Wat Xieng Thong. Luang Prabang's importance diminished in the 18th century, following the death of King Souligna Vongsa and the break-up of Lane Xang, but it remained a royal centre until the Communist takeover in 1975. During the low point of Laos' fortunes in the mid-19th century, when virtually the whole country had become tributary to Bangkok (Siam), only Luang Prabang retained a semblance of independence. Luang Prabang didn't suffer as much as other provincial capitals during the Indochina wars, narrowly escaping a Viet Minh capture in 1953. During the Second Indochina War, however, the Pathet Lao cut short the royal lineage, forcing King Sisavang Vatthana to abdicate and sending him to a re-education camp in northeastern Laos where he, his wife and his son died from starvation.

Fortunately, UNESCO's designation of Luang Prabang as a World Heritage Site has restricted redevelopment. The old town – essentially the promontory – is protected while elsewhere only limited building is permitted (no building, can be higher than three storeys). Although the new road went ahead, the authorities built a bypass to ensure that the town wasn't disrupted.

Apollo 11 and 17 lunar missions. Also in this room are portraits of the last King Sisavang Vatthana, Queen Kham Phouy and Crown Prince Vongsavang, painted by a Soviet artist in 1967.

King's Chapel On the right wing of the palace, next to the King's Reception Room, is the king's private chapel, which houses the Pra Bang. It also contains four Khmer Buddhas, ivories mounted in gold, bronze drums used in religious ceremonies and about 30 smaller Buddha images from temples all over the city.

Haw Prabang This small ornate pavilion is located in the northeast corner of the palace compound, to the right of the entrance to the Royal Palace. It was designed by the Royal Architect of the time to house the Pra Bang and was paid for by small donations sent in from across the country. The Pra Bang should move here sometime in the future.

Other buildings In the left-hand corner (south) of the compound, is the **Luang Prabang Conference Hall**, built for the official coronation of Savang Vatthana, which was terminally interrupted by the 1975 revolution. The southwestern corner of the compound is now used as the **Royal Theatre**, where traditional performances are held.

Wat Mai
Sisavangvong Rd, daily 0800-1700, admission 20,000 kip.

Next to the Royal Palace is Wat Mai. This royal temple, inaugurated in 1788, has a five-tiered roof and is one of the jewels of Luang Prabang. It took more than 70 years to complete. It was officially called Wat Mai Souvanna Phommaram and was the home of the Buddhist leader in Laos, Phra Sangkharath, until he moved to That Luang in Vientiane. Auguste Pavie and his crew took up residence here while trying to win Luang Prabang over from the Siamese who controlled the Lao court at the time. The Siamese thought that detaining Pavie in the compound would keep him out of their way but the Frenchman struck up a friendship with a local abbot, who acted as a runner between the king and Pavie. The temple housed the Pra Bang from 1894 until 1947 and, during Pi Mai (New Year), the Pra Bang is taken from the Royal Palace and installed at Wat Mai for its annual ritual cleansing, before being returned to the palace on the third day.

Today, Wat Mai is probably the most popular temple after Wat Xieng Thong. The façade is particularly interesting: a large golden bas-relief tells the story of Phravet (one of the last reincarnations of the Gautama or historic Buddha), with village scenes, including wild animals, women pounding rice, and people at play. The interior is an exquisite amalgam of red and gold, with pillars similar to those in Wat Xieng Thong and Wat Visoun. The temple is indicative of Luang Prabang architecture, aside from the roofed veranda, whose gables face the sides rather than the front. The central beam at Wat Mai is carved with figures from the Hindu story of the birth of Ravanna and Hanuman. Behind the temple is a new construction where two classical racing boats are kept, ready to be brought out for Pi Mai (Lao New Year) and the August boat-racing festival. ▸▸ *See Festivals, page 372.*

Mount Phousi
The western steps lead up from Sisavangvong Rd, daily 0700-1800. If you want to watch the sun go down, get there early, but expect to have to jostle for position. Arrive at dawn and you are likely to be one of a handful there.

Directly opposite the Royal Palace is the start of the climb up Mount Phousi, the spiritual and geographical heart of the city and a popular place to watch the sunset over the Mekong. Luang Prabang was probably sited at this point on the Mekong, in part at least, because of the presence of Phousi. Many capitals in the region are founded near sacred hills or mountains, which could become local symbols of the Hindu Mount Mahameru or Mount Meru, the abode of the gods and also the abode of local tutelary spirits.

As you start the ascent, to the right is **Wat Pa Huak** ⓘ *daily 0800-1800*. It is worth visiting because the monastery has some fine 19th-century murals, depicting classic scenes along the Mekong. There are a few Buddha images here that date from the same period and a fine carved wooden mosaic on the temple's exterior, depicting Buddha riding Airavata, the three-headed elephant from Hindu mythology.

From Wat Pa Huak, 328 steps wind up Phousi, a gigantic rock with sheer forested sides, surmounted by a 25-m-tall *chedi*, **That Chomsi**. The *chedi* was constructed in 1804, restored in 1914 and is the starting point for the colourful Pi Mai (New Year) celebrations in April (see Festivals, page 372). Its shimmering gold-spired stupa rests on a rectangular base, ornamented by small metal Bodhi trees. Next to the stupa is a little sanctuary, from which the candlelit procession descends at New Year, accompanied by effigies of Nang Sang Khan, the guardian of the New Year, and naga, protector of the city. The drum, kept in the small *haw kong* on the east side of the hill, is used on ceremonial occasions. The summit of Phousi affords a panoramic view of Luang Prabang and the mountains. The Mekong lies to the north and west, with the city laid out to the southeast.

A path next to the *ack-ack* cannon leads down to **Wat Tham Phousi**, which is more like a car port than a temple, but which is home to a rotund Buddha, Kaccayana (also called Phra Ka Tiay). At the top of the steps leading out of the wat are two tall cacti, planted defiantly in the empty shell casings of two large US bombs – the monks' answer to decades of war.

Wat Sene (Wat Saen)
Further up the promontory, Wat Sene was built in 1718 and was the first *sim* in Luang Prabang to be constructed in Thai style, with a yellow and red roof. The exterior may lack subtlety, but the interior is delicate and refined, painted red, with gold patterning on every conceivable surface. *Sene* means 100,000 and the wat was built with a local donation of 100,000 kip from someone who discovered 'treasure' in the Nam Khan river. At the far end of the wat compound is a building containing a large, gold, albeit rather crudely modelled, image of the Buddha in the 'calling for rain' *mudra* (standing, arms

Luang Prabang detail

Where to stay
3 Nagas **4** *B3*
Ammata Guesthouse **20** *A3*
Apsara **1** *B4*
Apsara Rive Droite **15** *B4*
Mekong Riverview **2** *A5*
Oui's Guesthouse **21** *B5*

Nam Khan Riverside **3** *B2*
Pa Phai **8** *A2*
Pack Luck **7** *A3*
Sokdee Residence **5** *A2*
Villa Ban Lakkham **10** *B5*

Restaurants
3 Nagas **3** *B3*
Big Tree Café & Gallery **4** *A2*
Café Ban Vat Sene **1** *B2*
Café Toui **9** *A2*
Couleur Café **6** *B2*
Dyen Sabai **12** *B2*

held stiffly down). Note the torments of hell depicted on the façade of the building (top, left). The temple was restored in 1932, with further renovations in 1957. One of Laos' most sacrosanct abbots, the recently deceased Ajahn Khamchan, was ordained at the temple in 1940.

Wat Xieng Thong
Xiengthong Rd, daily 0800-1700, 20,000 kip.

Wat Xieng Thong Ratsavoraviharn, usually known as just Wat Xieng Thong, is set back from the road, at the top of a flight of steps leading down to the Mekong. It is arguably the finest example of a Lao monastery, with graceful, low-sweeping eaves, beautiful stone mosaics and intricate carvings. The wat has several striking chapels, including one that houses a rare bronze reclining Buddha and another sheltering a gilded wooden funeral chariot. The back of the temple is encrusted with a stunning glass mosaic depicting a Bodhi tree, while inside, resplendent gold-stencilled pillars support a ceiling with *dharma* wheels. The temple's tranquility is further enhanced by beautiful gardens of bougainvillea, frangipani and hibiscus, shaded by banyan and palm trees.

This monastery was a key element in Luang Prabang's successful submission to UNESCO for recognition as a World Heritage Site. The striking buildings in the tranquil compound are decorated in gold and post-box red, with imposing tiled roofs, intricate carvings, paintings and mosaics, making this the most important and finest royal wat in Luang Prabang. It was built by King Setthathirat in 1559, and is one of the few buildings to have survived the successive Chinese raids that marked the end of the 19th century. It retained its royal patronage until 1975 and has been embellished and well cared for over the years: even the crown princess of Thailand, Mahachakri Sirindhorn, has donated funds for its upkeep.

The sim The *sim* is a perfect example of the Luang Prabang style, with its low, sweeping roof in complex overlapping sections. The roof is one of the temple's most outstanding features and is best viewed at a distance. Locals believe that the roof has been styled to resemble a bird, with its wings stretched out to protect her young. The eight central wooden pillars have stencilled motifs in gold and the façade is finely decorated. The beautiful gold-leaf inlay is predominantly floral in design but a few of the images illustrate *Ramayana*-type themes and the interior stencils depict *dharma* wheels and the enigmatic King Chantaphanit.

In an ancient form of the modern-day Mousetrap game, a serpent-like aqueduct sits above the right-hand side of the main entrance. During Lao New Year water is poured into the serpent's tail, causing it to gush along to its mouth and tip onto the Buddha image below. The water then filters

➡ **Luang Prabang maps**
1 Luang Prabang, page 356
2 Luang Prabang detail, page 360

down a drain, flowing under the floor and eventually spouting out of the mouth of the mirrored elephant on the exterior wall.

At the rear of the *sim* is a mosaic representation of the thong copper 'Tree of Life' in glass inlay. This traditional technique can also be seen on the 17th-century doors of That Inheng, near Savannakhet in central Laos (see page 431).

Side chapels Behind the *sim* are two red *haw song phra* (side chapels): the one on the left is referred to as **La Chapelle Rouge** (the Red Chapel) and houses a rare Lao reclining Buddha in bronze, dating from the 16th century, which was shown at the 1931 Paris Exhibition. The image was kept in Vientiane and only returned to Luang Prabang in 1964. Several other Buddha images, of varying styles, dates, and materials, surround the altar. The exterior mosaics on the *haw song phra*, which relate local tales, were added in 1957 to honour the 2500th anniversary of the Buddha's birth, death and enlightenment. Somewhat unusually, the fresco features a heroic character from local Lao folklore, Siaw Sawat. The other *haw song phra*, to the right of the *sim*, houses a standing image of the Buddha which is paraded through the streets of the city each New Year and doused in water. A small stone chapel with an ornate roof stands to the left of the *sim*.

Chapel of the Funeral Chariot The **haw latsalot** (chapel of the funeral chariot) is diagonally across from the *sim* and was built in 1962. The centrepiece is the grand 12-m-high gilded wooden hearse, with its seven-headed serpent, which was built for King Sisavang Vong, father of the last sovereign, and used to carry his urn to the stadium next to Wat That Luang (see below) where he was cremated in 1959. It was built on the chassis of a six-wheel truck by the sculptor Thid Tan. On top of the carriage sit several sandalwood urns, none of which contain royal ashes. Originally the urns would have held the bodies of the deceased in a foetal position until cremation. The mosaics inside the chapel were never finished but the exterior is decorated with some almost erotic scenes from the *Ramayana* (or local *Phalak Phalam*), sculpted in enormous panels of teak wood and covered with gold leaf. Glass cabinets feature several puppets that were once used in royal performances.

Wat Visounnarat (Wat Wisunarat)
Daily 0800-1700, 20,000 kip.

This is better known as Wat Visoun and is on the south side of Mount Phousi. It is a replica of the original wooden building, constructed in 1513, which had been the oldest building in Luang Prabang, until it was destroyed by marauding Chinese tribes. Louis Delaporte's sketches from the 1860s show the original temple as boat- or coffin-shaped. The wat was rebuilt in 1898 and, in keeping with the original style, renovators tried to ensure that the brick and stucco construction resembled the original medieval shapes of the lathed wood. The arch on the northwest side of the *sim* is original and the only remaining piece of the 16th-century building.

The *sim* is virtually a museum of religious art, with numerous 'Calling to the Rain' Buddha statues: most are more than 400 years old and have been donated by locals. One of the biggest philanthropists was Prince Phetsarat who donated them in order to redeem the temple after the Haw invasion. Wat Visoun also contains the largest Buddha in the city and old stelae engraved with Pali scriptures (called *hin chaleuk*).

The big stupa, commonly known as **That Makmo** ('melon stupa'), was built by Queen Visunarat in 1504. It is of Sinhalese influence with a smaller stupa at each corner, representing the four elements. The stupa originally contained hundreds of small Buddha images, many of which were pilfered by the Haw. The remaining images were relocated to the Royal Museum for safe-keeping.

Wat Phra Maha That

Close to the **Hotel Phousi** on Phothisarath Road, this is a typical Luang Prabang wat, built in the 1500s and restored at the beginning of this century. The ornamentation of the doors and windows of the *sim* merit attention, with their graceful golden figures from the *Phalak Phalam* (the *Ramayana*). The pillars, ornamented with massive *nagas*, are also in traditional Luang Prabang style and reminiscent of certain styles adopted in Thailand. The front of the *sim* was renovated in 1991. The monastery contains a stupa, holding the ashes of Prince Phetsarath and his younger brother Prince Souvanna Phouma.

Wat Manolom

South of Wat That Luang (between Phou Vao and Kisarath Settathirat), Wat Manolom was built by the nobles of Luang Prabang to entomb the ashes of King Samsenthai (1373-1416) and is notable for its large armless bronze Buddha statue, one of the oldest Lao images of the Buddha, which dates back to 1372 and weighs two tonnes. Locals maintain that the arm was removed during a skirmish between Siamese and French forces during the latter part of the 19th century. The Lao have replaced the missing appendage with an unsuccessful concrete prosthetic. The monastery has an attractive weathered look and the usual carved doors and painted ceilings. While it is not artistically significant, the temple – or at least the site – is thought to be the oldest in the city, dating back, it is said, to 1375 and the reign of Fa Ngum. Close by are the ruins of an even older temple, **Wat Xieng Kang**, dating from 1363.

Wat Pa Phon Phao and Santi Chedi

3 km northeast of town, near Ban Phanom, daily 0800-1000 and 1300-1630, entry by donation.

Outside town, **Wat Pa Phon Phao** is a forest meditation centre renowned for the teachings of its famous abbot, Ajahn Saisamut, one of the most popular monks in Lao history. Better known to tourists, though, is **Santi Chedi**, known as the Peace Pagoda. It looks as though it is made of pure gold from a distance and it occupies a fantastic position. The wat's construction, funded by donations from Lao living abroad and from overseas Buddhist federations, was started in 1959 but was only completed in 1988; the names of donors are inscribed on pillars inside. It is modelled on the octagonal Shwedagon Pagoda in Yangon (Rangoon) and its inner walls are festooned with gaily painted frescoes of macabre allegories. The lurid illustrations depict the fate awaiting murderers, adulterers, thieves, drunks and liars who break the five golden rules of Buddhism. Less grotesque paintings, extending up to the fifth floor, document the life of the Buddha. On the second level, it is possible to duck through a tiny opening to admire the Blue Indra statues and the view of Luang Prabang.

Traditional Arts and Ethnology Centre

Ban Khamyong, T071-253364, www.taeclaos.org, Tue-Sun 0900-1800, 25,000 kip.

This fantastic museum is dedicated to the various ethnic groups that inhabit Laos. It is a non-profit centre with a permanent exhibition featuring interesting photographs, religious artefacts, clothing, traditional household objects and the various handicrafts practised by the different groups. Within the exhibition there is a focus on the Hmong and their New Year celebrations; the Khmu, their baskets and the art of backstrap looms; the Mien Yao embroidery and Lanten Taoist religious ceremonies; the Tai Dam bedding and Tai Lue culture. This museum is well worth a visit – particularly for anyone who is planning to venture further north to go trekking.

Attached to the centre is a handicraft shop selling beautiful silks with a large proportion of the profits directly supporting ethnic artisan communities. There's also a café and a small library.

Around Luang Prabang

Pak Ou Caves

The Pak Ou caves are perhaps the most popular excursion from Luang Prabang and are located 25 km upstream from the city, set in a limestone cliff opposite the mouth of the Nam Ou tributary (Pak Ou means 'Mouth of the Ou'). For many, it is the boat ride, rather than the caves themselves that make this a worthwhile day out. The two caves are studded with thousands of wood-and-gold Buddha images – 2500 in the lower cave and 1500 in the upper – and are one of the main venues for Pi Mai in April, when hundreds make the pilgrimage upriver from Luang Prabang. During the dry season the river shrinks, exposing huge sandbanks, which are improbable gold fields. Families camp out on the banks of the Mekong and pan for gold, most of which is sold to Thailand.

Exploring the caves Many restaurants, hotels, guesthouses and tour companies in Luang Prabang will arrange this boat trip, which is the best way to reach the caves. Otherwise, boats can be chartered from Tha Heua Me or from one of the stairways leading down to the river along Manthatourath, where boatmen wait for business. Boats will often stop at Xang Hai (see below) and Ban Pak Ou, across the water from the caves, where enterprising villages have set up thatched stalls serving sticky rice, barbecued Mekong fish and *tam maak houng* (spicy green papaya salad), plus cold drinks and snacks. It is also possible to take a tuk-tuk to the caves, but that option is far less fun.

Torches are available but candles make it possible to see reasonably well after your eyes have become accustomed to the dark. The lower cave, really a deep overhang, is named **Tham Ting**, while the upper, an enervating climb up 100 or so slippery steps, is called **Tham Phum**. A carved wooden frieze, supporting two massive wooden doors flanks the entrance of the cave. Aside from the numerous Buddha images, the cave features a statue of one of Buddha's disciples and a carved wooden water channel for the ceremonial washing of the sculptures. The cave is around 54 m long and the sculptures range from 10 cm to 1.5 m in height. Many of the images are in the distinctive attitude of the Buddha calling for rain (the arms held by the side, with palms turned inwards).

★Tad Kuang Si

30 km south Luang Prabang; admission 20,000 kip. Travel agents run tours or you can charter a tuk-tuk for about US$22 (make sure you agree how long you want to spend at the falls). Slow boats take 1 hr downriver and 2 hrs back, via Ban Ou (a pretty little village), where it is necessary to take a tuk-tuk (or walk) the last 6 km to the waterfalls. A 3rd possibility is to take a speedboat from either Tha Heua Xieng Keo (3 km downstream from Luang Prabang) or Ban Don, a few kilometres upstream.

These waterfalls are 30 km south of Luang Prabang on a tributary of the Mekong. The trip to the falls is almost as scenic as the cascades themselves, passing through small Hmong and Khmu villages and vivid green, terraced rice paddies.

BACKGROUND
Pak Ou caves

The two sacred caves were supposedly discovered by King Setthathirat in the 16th century but it is likely that the caverns were associated with spirit (*phi*) worship before the arrival of Buddhism in Laos. For years the caves, which locals still believe to be the home of guardian spirits, were inhabited by monks. The king visited them every New Year, staying at Ban Pak Ou on the opposite bank of the Mekong, where there is a royal wat with beautiful old murals on the front gable. The famous French traveller, Francis Garnier, also visited the caves on his travels in the 1860s.

Some of the Buddha images in the caves are thought to be more than 300 years old, although most date from the 18th and 19th centuries. In the past, gold and silver images were in abundance but these have all been stolen; now the Buddha images are crafted from wood, copper or stone.

The falls are stunningly beautiful, misty cascades flowing over limestone formations, which eventually collect in several tiered, turquoise pools. Originally the waterfall's surroundings were inhabited by numerous animals, including the deer that give the falls their name, Kuang Si. However, the only wildlife you're likely to see today are some Asiatic black bears, rescued from poachers, in enclosures halfway between the entrance and the falls. The United Nations Development Programme (UNDP) has cleared a path to the falls which winds right up to the top. The bottom level of the falls has been turned into a park and viewing area, with a small platform that affords good photo opportunities. The local village's economy seems increasingly to depend on the tourist business, so you'll find a large number of vendors selling snacks and drinks and some souvenirs. The site also has public toilets and changing rooms.

Although the waterfall is impressive year round, in the summer, the water cascades so gently over the various tiers of the falls that it's possible to scramble behind the curtains of water without getting wet. In the rainy season, the gallons of water roaring down the mountain catch the imagination and could form the backdrop for any Indiana Jones or James Bond adventure. Best of all, and despite appearances, it's still possible to take the left-hand path halfway up the falls and strike out through the pouring torrents and dripping caves to the heart of the waterfall. The pools above the falls are sheltered and comparatively private and make a wonderful spot for a swim; the second tier is best for a dip. If you follow the water either upstream or downstream there are plenty of other shady swimming spots. Note that swimming is only permitted in designated pools and, as the Lao swim fully clothed, you should wear modest swimwear and bring a sarong (this is a very popular area for Lao people to come and picnic).

Tourist information

Luang Prabang Tourist Information Centre
Sisavangvong Rd, T071-212487.
Aside from provincial information, it offers a couple of good ecotourism treks (which support local communities). The office also has informative displays on Lao culture and its ethnic groups.

Where to stay

Accommodation in Luang Prabang is generally high quality, with some extremely tasteful converted houses featuring dark woods and crisp white linens. The restored colonial villas on the peninsula and along Phou Vao Rd tend to get booked up, particularly during national holidays. For the more upmarket options, advance bookings are recommended at all times except in the wet season.

Around Lao New Year, hotels and guesthouses can almost charge what they like but during the wet season prices tend to be a lot lower, with smaller establishments dropping prices by around a 3rd and more expensive hotels knocking off about 20%. Internet rates are considerably cheaper than rack rates for hotels in the upper price range.

Some of the best-value accommodation can be found toward the tip of the peninsula around Wat Xieng Thong, and also among the quiet streets around Phou Vao. Another option is to stay slightly out of the old town where your money will go a lot further.

$$$$ 3 Nagas Alila
Sakkaline Rd, T071-253888,
www.alilahotels.com/3nagas.
Housed in a beautifully restored building, this boutique hotel is a beauty. Attention to detail is what sets it apart from the rest: from the 4-poster bed covered with local fabrics to the large deep-set bathtub with natural handmade beauty products. There's a lovely sitting area in each room, plus traditional *torchis* walls and teak floors. The **3 Nagas** restaurant opposite the hotel is also excellent.

$$$$ Maison Souvannaphoum
Phothisarath, T071-212200,
www.angsana.com.
Formerly Prince Souvannaphouma's residence, this place really is fit for royalty. There are 4 spacious suites and 23 rooms. Great location close to the night market. The service is top notch.

$$$$ Mekong Riverview
At the very tip of the peninsula, T071-254900,
www.mekongriverview.com.
This relative newcomer is an excellent addition to the town. Rooms with polished wood floors are individually decorated and come with gorgeous wooden furniture including writing bureaux in the suites. Riverview rooms have huge, very private balconies complete with wicker chairs, perfect for an afternoon snooze. Breakfast is served al fresco. Refined.

$$$$ Xieng Thong Palace
Next to Wat Xieng Thong, T071-213200,
www.xiengthongpalace.com.
Housed in the last residence of the royal family, this is a true luxury property. The 2-storey suites are the highlight, with their private indoor plunge pools. A fantastic buffet breakfast is served overlooking the river. Superb service and a top-end spa.

$$$$-$$$ The Belle Rive
Souvannakhamphong Rd, T071-260733,
www.thebellerive.com.
Sumptuous well-equipped rooms occupy elegant colonial-style buildings facing the Mekong on a quiet part of the peninsula.

Watch boats drifting past from the garden patio of the hotel's restaurant. The attraction of this hotel lies in its nostalgic charm; you almost expect to find Graham Greene or Noel Coward staying here. A Luang Prabang classic.

$$$$-$$$ Villa Maly
Souvannaphoum Rd, T071-253903, www.villa-maly.com.
This is a gorgeous boutique hotel set around a beautiful pool with ivory-coloured umbrellas in a leafy garden. A former royal residence, it is stylish and petite, and the rooms are suitably plush. The bathrooms, however, are a little on the small side. The service here remains impeccable and polished.

$$$$-$$$ Villa Santi Hotel
Sisavangvong Rd, T071-252157, www.villasantihotel.com.
Almost an institution in Luang Prabang, this is a restored house from the early 20th century that served as the private residence of the first King Sisavangvong's wife and then Princess Manilai. It's a charming place, full of character and efficiently run, and it has recently received a facelift. There are 6 heavenly suites in the old building, and 14 newer rooms, with baths and showers, in a stylish annexe.

$$$ The Apsara
Kingkitsarath, T071-254670, www.theapsara.com.
Ivan Scholte, wine connoisseur and antique collector, has done a perfect job on this establishment. It oozes style. The stunningly beautiful rooms are themed by colour, with 4-poster beds, changing screen, big bathtub and lovely balcony. Very romantic with a modern twist. The rooms in the 2nd building are also magnificent with *terrazzo* showers you could fit an elephant in. The foyer and lovely restaurant (see Restaurants, below) are decorated with Vietnamese lanterns, Burmese offering boxes and modern art.

Its sister hotel, **Apsara Rive Droite**, across the river, is also a gorgeous place to stay.

$$$-$$ Villa Ban Lakkham
Souksasuem Rd, T085-7125 2677, www.villabanlakkham.com.
Dark woods, deep reds, black-and-white photography and river-view rooms with pretty panelled French doors lend this hotel an old world charm. Low season 'hot deals' are great value. Lao, Vietnamese and Western breakfasts. Free bikes. Very welcoming.

$$ Ammata Guesthouse
37 Khunsua Rd, T071-212175, phetmanyp@yahoo.com.au.
Very popular guesthouse with largish rooms decorated simply and stylishly with wooden furniture and polished floorboards. Hot water and en suite bathroom.

$$ Nam Khan Riverside
Kingkitsarath Rd, T020-9721 8789, namkhanriverside@gmail.com.
Not as plush as some of the options along the Nam Khan, this hotel nonetheless wins out thanks to the lower prices and the balconies overlooking the water on which breakfast can be served. Managed by the friendly Mr Minh Duc, aka Ben, who is happy to give advice on what to see and do. Prices drop substantially in low season.

$$ Oui's Guesthouse
At the end of the peninsula in Ban Khili on Sukkaserm, T071-252374, ouisguesthouse@gmail.com.
Run by 3 sisters, this is a charming little guesthouse with sparkling new rooms and polished floorboards, hot water, TV and fridge. Nicely decorated with local artefacts.

$$ Pack Luck
Ban Vat Nong, opposite L'Éléphant, T071-253373, packluck@hotmail.com.
This boutique hotel has 5 rooms that you couldn't swing a cat in but are very tastefully decorated with beautiful fabrics. The luxurious bathrooms have deep slate bathtubs. Lots of character.

$$ Sokdee Residence
Just off Ounkham Rd, T071-252555,
www.sokdeeresidence.com.
Down a quiet, pleasant sidestreet,
this small hotel offers clean rooms with
wooden floors and comfortable beds
plus individual outdoor seating areas.
Good value in a great location.

$ Mano Guesthouse
Phamahapasaman Rd, T071-253112.
A clean guesthouse, with a tiled ground floor
and wood upstairs, this is a charming, family-
run option, with some a/c. A large chess
board is carved into a stone table outside.
The owners speak English and some French.

$ Pa Phai
Opposite Wat Pa Phai.
For those looking for a very cheap option with
plenty of authenticity, this is a good choice.
The old traditional house has seen very little
in the way of renovation – think bamboo
walls, no a/c and rock hard beds. Still, it's
clean, well located and the price is right. Also
offers a laundry service and bike hire.

Outside of town

$$$$ Belmond La Résidence Phou Vao
4 km east of the airport, T071-212 5303,
www.residencephouvao.com.
A stunning location with expansive views
over the green hills. Every detail in this hotel
is perfect, from the fragrance of frangipani
that wafts through the foyer to the carefully
lit infinity pool. Rooms are huge with
beautiful décor, lounge area and simply
divine bathrooms. This is a luxury hotel
through and through. In the low season
rates drop substantially. A real treat.

$$$$ Grand Luang Prabang Hotel &
Resort
Ban Xiengkeo, 4 km from town, T071-253851,
www.grandluangprabang.com.
Beautifully restored hotel in the former
Prince Phetsarath's residence. Simple,
classically decorated rooms set in lovely
gardens. Try to get a room with a view

of the river. An extremely relaxing place to
hole-up for a few days.

$$$$ Kiridara
Ban Naviengkham, 5-min tuk-tuk ride from
town, T0871-261888, www.snhcollection.com.
Set on a hill, the **Kiridara** offers breathtaking
views over Luang Prabang, a beautiful pool
and a range of tasteful rooms and suites
making this a wonderful choice for those
seeking out-of-town lodgings. The pick-up/
drop-off service is very handy and the service
and buffet breakfasts are first-rate.

$$$$ Luang Say Residence
Just off the Phou Vao Rd, a few
mins from town, T071-260891,
www.luangsayresidence.com.
Stunning, all-suite property with the air of a
sprawling colonial country club and a future
classic. 4-poster beds, huge, well-appointed
bathrooms, deep arm chairs and private
verandas with mountain views all combine
to make these rooms rather special. Also has
a fantastic restaurant, bar serving tapas and
the best pool in town.

$$$ Ock Pop Tok Villa
125/10 Ban Saylom, Living Craft Centre,
T071-212597, www.ockpoptok.com/stay.
4 individually designed rooms are on offer
in a fabulous villa overlooking the Mekong.
Breakfast is served in the beautiful café on the
river. This is a very tranquil and special option.
Guests are eligible for a discount on the
weaving classes in the **Living Craft Centre**.

Restaurants

Note that Luang Prabang has a curfew;
most places won't stay open past 2400.
   Luang Prabang produces a number of
culinary specialities that make interesting
souvenirs. The market is a good starting
point for buying these, although
restaurants have also latched onto their
popularity. The most famous is *khai pehn*,
dried river weed from the Nam Khan, mixed
with sesame and fried. *Cheo bong*, a spicy,
smoky purée made with buffalo hide, is also

popular. Other delicacies include: *phak nam* (a watercress that grows around waterfalls and used in soups and salads), *mak kham kuan* (tamarind jam) and *mak nat kuan* (pineapple jam).

One of the best local culinary experiences is to eat at the Lao food stalls that run on a lane off the night market on Sisavangvon Rd, 1600-2200. Here you can pick up fresh spring rolls (*nem dip*) papaya salad (*tam som*), sticky rice (*khao niao*), the local delicacy Luang Prabang sausage (*sai oua*), barbecue chicken on a stick (*gai*) or fish (*pa*), dried buffalo (*sin savanh*) and dried seaweed. For meat and fish, we recommend one of the stalls closest to the river end run by the rather rotund and serious looking Lao grill master and his smiling wife. There are also a number of cheap buffets where you can get a selection of local curries and dishes. If you don't want your food too spicy ask for '*bo pet*'.

$$$ Tangor
63 Sisavangvong Rd, T071-260761, www.letangor.com.
Justly popular French-run restaurant that's a hit not only with tourists, but with Luang Prabang's expat set. Creative and well-executed fusion cuisine and classics. Superb presentation and attentive service. An all-round winner. Don't miss the *ceviche* or the pork skewers and try the excellent tarte tatin for pudding. Delectable.

$$$-$$ 3 Nagas
Opposite the hotel of the same name, Sakkaline Rd, T071-253888.
The food here is both Lao and Western and highly recommended. The restaurant also has an exemplary wine list and its own unique concoctions of cocktails.

$$$-$$ The Apsara
See Where to stay.
Lao/Thai/Western fusion restaurant offering dishes such as braised pork belly and pumpkin, and great fish cakes. Try their

delicious red curry cream soup with lentils and smoked duck or braised beef shin Chinese style. Good value.

$$$-$$ Couleur Café/Restaurant
Ban Vat Nong, T020-55621064.
The French expats in town still have nothing but praise for this place with its French and Lao meals and chic setting. Good wine list and great steaks.

$$$-$$ L'Éléphant
Ban Vat Nong, T071-252482, contact@elephant-restau.com.
Upmarket and utterly delectable cuisine in a fantastic ambiance. The French dishes are excellent (try the lamb shank) and so are the faithful renditions of Lao classics. A good place to treat yourself. Highly recommended.

$$ Café Toui
Sisavangatthana Rd, T020-5657 6763, www.cafetoui.com.
Run by the lovely Toui, this small, intimate café-cum-restaurant is perhaps the best place to enjoy Lao food in a comfortable setting. Recommended dishes include the red fish curry, sublime Luang Prabang sausage and the buffalo steak. If you can't decide, the tasting platter is also a solid choice. Those who eat here once are highly likely to return. A gem.

$$ Khai Phaen
Sisavang Vatana Rd, T030-515 5221, www.tree-alliance.org.
Opened in 2014, this is a sister restaurant to the other Friends International NGO establishments, including the excellent **Makphet** in Vientiane. As such, it runs as a training restaurant for former street youth. Managed by Anousin aka 'Noy'; this latest addition to the chain is every inch as good as the others. Don't miss the Sandan's cashew nut crusted banana fritter with kaffir lime and coconut ice cream, nor the crispy cinnamon pork belly. Delectable dining with a feel-good factor. Highly recommended.

$$ Ock Pok Tock Silk Road Café
2 km out of town at the Living Crafts Centre,
T071-212597, www.ockpoptok.com/eat.
Closed for dinner.
A free tuk-tuk service whisks guests out to
this café right on the banks of the Mekong in
a wonderfully peaceful spot. The brunches
with granola and fresh yoghurt make for a
healthy late start to the day. For lunch, try the
lemongrass chicken or the fried river weed –
a local speciality.

$$ Pizza Phan Luang
Phan Luang, across the Nam Khan,
T020-5692 2529.
Best visited in the dry season when it's
possible to wander across the bamboo
bridge, **Pizza Phan Luang** serves good
quality, wood-fired pizzas in a romantic
candlelit atmosphere.

$$ Tamarind
Facing Wat Nong, T020-7777 0484, www.
tamarindlaos.com. Mon-Sat 1100-1800.
Pretty restaurant offering brilliant modern
Lao cuisine. The sampling platter is a
fantastic way to try a few different Lao
classics. On Fri nights the fish BBQ dinner is a
lively affair with a large selection of Lao dips
and information about Lao food and eating
customs. The owners, Joy and Caroline, have
received many accolades and can give you
lots of information on the area. Their cooking
classes are also a hit.

$$-$ Dyen Sabai
Ban Phan Luang, T020-5510 4817.
Depending on the season, guests reach
this cosy restaurant with pretty lighting via
a bamboo bridge or a short paddle boat
ride across the river. The unusual cocktails
and Lao food are not to be missed, nor
the amazing sunset views. This is a highly
recommended spot.

$$-$ Tum Tum Cheng
Just off Sakkaline Rd, T071-252019.
Lao food prepared by a Hungarian expat.
Tasty fusion-style meals. Very comfortable

outdoor seating. Also offers classes in Lao
cooking and classical Lao dancing.

$ Atsalin Restaurant
Visunnarat Rd, T020-999 9933.
For those looking for a quick hit of Lao food
on a budget, this no-frills joint is hard to
beat. Absolutely delicious slow-cooked pork
topped rice and a range of other Lao staples.
Not a place to linger, but a fine place to eat
well, very cheaply.

$ Thai Food Restaurant
Opposite the school.
This pavement restaurant has no name or
phone number, just a simple sign advertising
'Thai Food'. Serves a very good *pad ka prao*
and a superb *pad thai*. Tasty and cheap and
very friendly owners, although limited English
is spoken. Good option for a quick lunch.

Cafés and bakeries

Big Tree Café and Gallery
46 Ban Vat Nong, T020-7777 6748,
www.bigtreecafe.com. Open 0730-2100.
Small, cosy café serving excellent, bitter
espresso. Large photography prints of
Laos line the walls. Beautiful views from
the seats across the road on the river.
Also serves some good Korean food
thanks to the Korean owner.

Café Ban Vat Sene
Sakkhaline Rd, opposite Wat Sene.
A very pleasant option, with a breezy, colonial
atmosphere, the white walls contrasting with
the polished dark wooden floors, tables and
chairs. Great for breakfast. The French food is
a treat. Good place for coffee or tea. Outside
tables offer excellent views of the school
opposite and the noise of the kids playing at
lunch add to the excellent atmosphere. An
easy place to lose an afternoon.

Joma
Sisavangvong Rd near Nam Phou fountain,
T071-252292.
With several other branches in Hanoi,
Joma serves an array of comfort foods

including sandwiches, quiche and bagels alongside Western coffees and a big range of shakes. Now has a 2nd branch along the Nam Khong River.

La Banneton
Sakkhaline Rd, T020-5973 2608, dricker@yahoo.fr. Open 0730-2000.
Beautiful open-fronted French café with views of Wat Sop Sickharam. Superb pastries and a simple menu of classics including *feuillete*, croque monsieur and salads.

L'Étranger
Kingkitsarath Rd, near Hive Bar, T020-5547 1736.
Great little bookshop-cum-café. The upstairs is exceptionally comfortable with cushions and low tables. This is the perfect place to wind down, grab a book and have a cuppa. Outstanding breakfasts. A movie is shown daily at 1900.

Bars and clubs

A sunset beer at one of the many restaurants overlooking the river is divine – just take a wander along the Mekong and see which one takes your fancy. After everything closes most locals head to Dao Fa or Yensabai and finish the night with noodles on Phou Vao Rd. The other popular late-night drinking option is the bowling alley; ask any tuk-tuk driver and they'll be able to get you there.

Chez Matt
Opposite Icon Klub, T020-7777 9497.
The French owner, Matthieu, takes his wine very seriously, ensuring this is one of the best (if not *the* best), places in town to order by the glass or bottle. Established late 2013, this chic, open-fronted space boasts attentive staff and a fine selection of charcuterie and cheese boards.

Dao Fa nightclub
On the way to the Southern bus station.
Extremely popular with locals and plays Asian dance music at deafening volumes. Standing room only. Fun to try once.

Hive Bar
Kingkitsarath Rd, next to L'Étranger, T020-5999 5370.
One of the first bars to open on what has become something of a strip, **Hive** is still going strong and draws in crowds with its fashion shows and dance performances. Also a decent spot for some Western fodder, such as pizzas.

Icon Klub
Just off of Sisavangvong Rd near the Khan River, T071-254905, www.iconklub.com. Open 1730-2400.
Run by the lovely Elizabeth since 2009, **Icon** is a tiny bar that's perfect for well-made cocktails and interesting conversation with your fellow patrons and the owner herself. Good music. Don't miss the *Old Fashioned*.

Lao Lao Garden
Kingkitsarath Rd.
A tiered landscaped terrace, with low lighting and cheap cocktails many featuring *lao lao*), that's become a favourite backpacker haunt. A bonfire keeps you cosy in the winter months. The Lao-style barbecue is great.

Red Bul Bar
In the bar area opposite Hive, www.redbulbarluangprabang.com.
Popular with locals, expats and backpackers alike, this bar has a pool table, table football and a party atmosphere when it fills up. A good place to meet new people.

Utopia
On the Khan River in Ban Aphay.
Landscaped gardens, a sand volleyball court popular with locals as well as tourists, and a long wooden deck overlooking the Khan. Great for a drink at sunset.

Yensabai
Phou Vao Rd. Open 2100-late.
Normally the last bar standing, this is the place to head to when **Dao Fa** has closed its doors. Popular with locals and the odd backpacker. The late-night noodle shop opposite is an institution.

Entertainment

Theatre and dance

Traditional dance performances, influenced by the *Ramayana*, are held at the **Theatre Phalak Phalam** in the Royal Palace compound, T071-253705, Mon, Wed and Sat at 1800, 75,000-180,000 kip. The traditional dance of Luang Prabang, which is incorporated into most shows, is more than 600 years old.

An ethnic fashion show is held at **Hive** bar most nights in conjunction with Kop Noi.

Festivals

Apr Pi Mai (Lao New Year; movable) is the time when the tutelary spirits of the old year are replaced by those of the new. It has special significance in Luang Prabang, with some traditions that are no longer observed in Vientiane. In the past, the king and queen would clean the principal Buddha images in the city's main wats, while masked dancers pranced through the streets re-enacting the founding of the city by 2 mythical beasts. People from all over the province descend on the city. The newly crowned Miss New Year (Nang Sang Khan) is paraded through town, riding on the back of the auspicious animal of the year.

May Vien Thien (movable), the candlelit festival.

Aug Boat races (movable). Boats are raced by the people living in the vicinity of each wat.

Oct Lai Heua Fai (Fireboat Festival). Each village creates a large boat made of bamboo and paper and decorated with candles and offerings. These are paraded down the main street to Wat Xieng Thong where they are judged and sent down into the Mekong River to bring atonement for sins. Temples and houses are decorated with paper lanterns and candles. People also make their own small floats to release in the Mekong.

Dec Luang Prabang Film Festival, www.lpfilmfest.org, showcases Southeast Asian cinema. The project also produces educational activities for young Lao.

Shopping

Books

L'Étranger, *see Cafés, above*. Perhaps the best bookshop in the country.

Monument Books, *Thou Gnai Thai Rd (near the Mekong)*, T071-254954, www.monument-books.com. Part of a small chain that began in Cambodia back in 1993, **Monument** stocks most books written on Laos in both English and French.

Yensabai Books & Art, *Ratsavong Rd (opposite the Phousi steps)*, T020-2299 9917. A charming little bookstore that also sells a range of cards and offers art classes.

Fashion and textiles

Kin Thong Lao Silk, *48/3 Sakkaline Rd (opposite the school)*, T020-5554 6184. Run by the informative Mrs Kin Thong who hails from Sam Tay village near Sam Neua – an area well known for its silk weaving and from where she sources all her stock. Prices range from 150,000 kip right up to 5,000,000 kip for a large hanging. A huge range of beautiful designs.

Ock Pop Tok, *near L'Éléphant restaurant*, T071-253219. Specializes in naturally dyed silk. Clothes, furnishings and hangings made mostly made at the dedicated **Living Crafts Centre** just outside of town. Alongside traditional designs, a popular range of **Ock Pop Tok** originals are created. A new outlet, the **Ock Pop Tok Boutique**, is located on Sisavanvong opposite Vat Sene. Recommended.

Satri Lao Silk, *Sisavangvong Rd*, T071-219295. Beautiful silks and handicrafts. The quality is reflected in high prices.

Ma Te Sai, *42 Ban Aphai*, T071-260654. A lovely place to buy gifts for those back home, with everything from scarves and bags to photo frames and cosmetics on offer. **Ma Te Sai** means 'where is it from' in Lao, reflecting the fact that the owner sources everything from within Laos and works directly with many local artisans.

TAEC Boutique, *Sisavangvong Rd, near Vat Sene, T071-253364, www.taeclaos.org.* Run by the **Traditional Arts & Ethnology Centre**, this is a fantastic little shop with items ranging from table runners and scarves to hangings in both 100% silk and natural-dye cottons. A large percentage of the profits goes directly to the rural ethnic minority villages where the products are made. Very helpful and knowledgeable staff. Highly recommended.

Galleries

Fibre2Fabric, *71 Ban Vat Nong (next door to Ock Pop Tok), T071-254761, www.fibre2 fabric.org.* A fantastic gallery exhibiting textiles of different ethnic groups. Local weavers are often on hand to explain the weaving processes.

Friends Visitor Centre, *Kitsalat Rd, www. fwab.org/laos.* A fantastic photography gallery is housed on the 3rd floor of this building which also acts as the training centre for the new **Lao Friends Hospital For Children**. Photography has been donated from a raft of respected artists including Paul Wager and Kenro Izu. Well worth a visit.

Kinnaly Gallery, *Sakkaline Rd, T020-55557737.* Opened in 2006, this French-run gallery specializes in black-and-white photography.

Kop Noi, *Ban Aphay, www.kopnoi.com.* This little shop has a rotating exhibition on the 2nd floor. It also exhibits work by renowned Lao photographer SamSisombat.

Handicrafts

The night market is a great place for handicrafts, as are **Ma Ta Sei**, **Ock Pop Tok** and **TAEC Boutique**.

Jewellery

Naga Creations, *Sisavangvong Rd, T071-212775.* Lao silver with semi-precious stones. Contemporary and classic pieces available, including innovative work by the jeweller **Fabrice**.

Markets

Night market, *sprawling across several blocks of Sisavangvong Rd. Daily 1700-2230.* Hundreds of villagers flock to the market to sell their handicrafts, ranging from silk scarves to embroidered quilt covers and paper albums. It shouldn't be missed.

Phousi market, *1.5 km from the centre of town.* This is now the place to head for cheap goods rather than quality.

Talat Dala, *housed in market building in the middle of town on the corner of Setthathirat Rd and Chao Sisophon Rd.* Alongside sports clothes and mobile phone shops a few artisans and jewellers remain, but be prepared to haggle.

Silver

One of Luang Prabang's traditional crafts is silversmithing. Most tourists buy silver from either the **night market** or **Talat Dala**; however, many of these pieces are made elsewhere. A few expert silversmiths still ply their trade in the lanes that run toward the river from the Nam Phou Fountain.

Cookery classes

Bamboo Tree, *Soukhaserm Rd, T020-2242 5499.* A relative newcomer to the cookery class scene, **Bamboo Tree** has a great setting by the river with plenty of outdoor space. After an optional visit to the local market to buy fresh ingredients learners can choose which dishes to cook before enjoying a feast together. Popular options are the stuffed lemongrass, the river fish and the paw paw salad.

Tamarind, *facing Wat Nong, T020-7777 0484, www.tamarindlaos.com.* This successful restaurant runs specialized classes for groups in their enchanting jungle garden school outside of town. Recommended.

Elephant tours and activities

Elephant Village, *15 km from Luang Prabang (visits and activities can be organized through*

their office on Sisavangvong Rd), T071-252417, www.elephantvillage-laos.com. Established in conjunction with **Tiger Trails** in Luang Prabang, old working elephants are given a home here. To keep the elephants active, the operators run activities for tourists, including experiencing life as a *mahout* (elephant keeper). Sauna and massage **L'Hibiscus Spa**, *45 Sakkaline, no phone*. Housed in an atmospheric old building with gorgeous floor tiles and filled with a wonderful scent. **L'Hibiscus** offers a good range of treatments including hot stone massage and traditional Lao massage in a supremely relaxing setting.
Maison Souvannaphoum, *see Where to stay*. A spa with a range of luxurious and expensive treatments. For sheer indulgence.
Red Cross Sauna, *opposite Wat Visunnarat, reservations T071-212303. Daily 0900-2100 (1700-2100 for sauna)*. This is a no-frills massage outfit that's very popular with locals. Visitors can opt for an hour of massage and follow it up with a Lao herbal sauna. Profits go to the Lao Red Cross.
The Spa *at La Résidence Phou (see Where to stay), T071-212530, www.residencephouvao. com*. Offers very expensive 3-hr massage courses. This includes a 1-hr massage for each person, the class, a handbook and oils.
Spa Garden, *Ban Phonheauang, T071-212325, spagardenlpb@hotmail.com*. Tucked away in a very quiet and peaceful location, the mid-range **Spa Garden** offers many massage and beauty treatments including Lao massage, aromatherapy massage and facials.

Tour operators

Buffalo Tours, *8/40 Ban Nongkham, T071-254395, www.buffalotours.com*. Very well-regarded operator with offices throughout Southeast Asia. Managed by Mr Touy, this office can arrange local tours around Luang Prabang, cooking classes in local villages and also travel throughout the whole of Laos. Very helpful.
Green Discovery, *Sisavangvong Rd, T071-212093, www.greendiscoverylaos.com*. Rafting

and kayaking trips that pass through grade I and II rapids. Also cycling tours around Luang Prabang, homestays and trips to Pak Ou caves. Great staff.
Tiger Trail, *Sisavangvong Rd, T071-252655, www.laos-adventures.com*. Adventure specialists: elephant treks, biking, rafting and much more.

Weaving classes

Ock Pop Tock Weaving Centre, *2 km out of town on the river, bookings at Ock Pop Tock shop*. A variety of 1- to 3-day weaving classes are offered with learners being taught one-on-one by master weavers. Also has a great on-site café and peaceful accommodation.

Transport

Air

Luang Prabang International Airport (LPQ), 4 km northeast of town, T071-212172/3, is a small airport but has a couple of places to eat, handicraft shops, ATMs and a foreign exchange desk. You can get a tuk-tuk into town, but many guesthouses will arrange to pick you up if you ask in advance. **Lao Airlines**, Phamahapasaman Rd, T071-212172, has daily connections with **Vientiane** and **Pakse**. International services to **Siem Reap**, **Phnom Penh**, **Hanoi**, **Singapore**, **Chiang Mai**, **Bangkok**, and **Jinghong**.

Bicycle hire

Bikes can be rented for 20,000 kip per day from most guesthouses.

Boat

Most boats leave from the 2 docks behind the Royal Palace. For boat times and destinations, either consult the board at the main pier on the Mekong or ask at one of the many travel agents in town.
To Houei Xai/Pakbeng The 2-day boat trip down the Mekong between Houei Xai and Pakbeng has become a rite of passage for travellers in Southeast Asia. There are options to suit everyone, from

speedboats (not recommended as they are noisy and can be dangerous, and remove the charm of the voyage) and slow boats, to the most luxurious way to make the trip which is on the **Luangsay Cruise** (office on Sisavangvong Rd, T071-252553, www. luangsay.com) which makes the trip in 2 days and 1 night, stopping over at Pak Ou caves en route and staying overnight at their lodge in Pakbeng (see page 394).

To Nong Khiaw and Muang Khoua Due to the new Chinese-built dam, this once hugely popular journey is no longer possible in one hit. It is possible to arrange a van and boat combination, but it is very expensive and not simple. It's now much better to take the bus, which follows much of the same course and is also spectacular.

Bus/truck

There are 2 main bus stations, the northern and the southern, each generally serving destinations in the respective direction. Tuk-tuks are readily available to take passengers into town. Check which terminal your bus is using, as unscheduled changes are possible. Buses can be booked at many of the travel agents in town.

Local buses head to **Nong Khiaw**, **Xam Neua**, **Phongsali** and **Houy Say**. Large, comfortable buses depart for **Vang Vieng**, 6 hrs, and **Vientiane**, 9 hrs. The road south to Vang Vieng is extremely twisty and rarely flat, making for a spectacular journey, but a difficult one for those suffering from motion sickness. The stop-off point halfway is one of the most dramatic in the world, let alone Laos.

Minivans are a good option as they include pick-up at your accommodation and can often also be booked there. Vans depart for **Nong Khiaw**, 0830, 4 hrs; **Vang Vieng**, 0800 and 1400, 5 hrs; **Phonsavanh**, 0830, 7 hrs; **Luang Namtha**, 0800, 7 hrs; and **Udomxai**, 0800, 5 hrs.

International buses can be booked to **Vietnam** (Vinh, Hanoi, Danang and Hué), **Thailand** (Chiang Mai and Chiang Rai) and various destinations in **China**.

North of
Luang Prabang

The stunning settlements of Nong Khiaw and Neua in the north of Luang Prabang Province have become firm favourites with the backpacker set. Both places have an idyllic setting and have thankfully avoided becoming Vang Vieng-like party towns, their serenity still intact despite the influx of tourists. The gently undulating journey to this part of Laos follows the beautiful route of the Nam Ou past mountains, teak plantations and dry rice fields. There is plenty to do, including trekking to waterfalls, kayaking, rock climbing, village visits and cycling. However, this is also a great part of the country in which to enjoy a good book, swing in a hammock and sink into the wonderfully slow pace of life.

Nong Khiaw, Ban Saphoun and around → *Colour map 1, B3.*
scenic and laid-back riverside villages, well set-up for adventure tourism

Nong Khiaw lies 22 km to the northeast of Nam Bak and is a delightful little village on the banks of the Nam Ou, surrounded by limestone peaks and flanked by misty mountains – the largest of which is the aptly named Princess Mountain. The remote little town is one of Laos' prettiest destinations. There are, in fact, two settlements here: Ban Saphoun on the east bank of the Nam Ou, and Nong Khiaw on the west. Of the two, Ban Saphoun (the old village) offers the best views and has the best riverside accommodation. Confusingly, the combined village is known by both names and sometimes Muang Ngoi which is actually another town to the north and also the name of the district.

The road trip between Udomxai and Xam Neua is one of the most spectacular in Laos, moving through stunning scenery dotted with remote villages. Nong Khiaw sits by the bridge where Route 1 crosses the river. It is a beautiful spot – the sort of place where time stands still, journals are written, books read and stress is a deeply foreign concept.

It is possible to swim in the river (women should wear sarongs) or walk around the town or up the cliffs. The bridge across the Nam Ou offers fine views and photo opportunities.

A new trail has been created by the local community to the top of Pa Daeng Mountain – it's a tough hike, but it affords absolutely wonderful views across the town and the river valley. More strenuous sections of the path have ropes to help you haul your way up. Be sure to take plenty of water. A small fee is payable at the entrance to the trail to help maintain it.

Around Nong Khiaw

The most obvious attractions in the area are the caves used by locals when the US bombed the area. **Tham Pha Thok** ⓘ *2.5 km southeast of the bridge, 30-min trek to Tham Pha Thok: ask at any tour company or restaurant for directions, or better yet, take a guide who can give you some background information and history as no information displayed*, was a Pathet Lao regional base during the civil war. It was divided into sections – a hospital section, a police section and a military section. Old remnants exist, including campfires and ruined beds, but other than that there is little evidence of it being the PT headquarters until you see the bomb crater at the front. To get there you walk through beautiful rice paddies. There is also a second cave, **Tham Pha Kwong**, but this was closed at the time of writing.

A further 2 km along the road, at Ban Nokien, is the **Than Mok waterfall**. To get there, you can either walk or charter a boat (negotiate the price with the boatman at the pier); remember to agree a return time. There's a small fee to see the waterfall. It's difficult to find on your own, so consider a guide. The best time to go is in the morning, so as not to have to rush the climb up to the falls or cut short your time there before dark.

If you go to the boat landing it is sometimes possible to organize a fishing trip with one of the local fishermen, for very little money. You might need someone to translate for you.

Essential North of Luang Prabang

Best places to stay

Mandala Ou, Nong Khiaw, page 378
Nong Kiau Riverside Resort, Ban Saphoun, page 378
Manotham Guesthouse, Muang Khua, page 381

Finding your feet

Boat services have become irregular following road improvements. Nong Khiaw and Muang Khua can be reached from Luang Prabang by a combination of van and boat, but it's better (and just as scenic) to take the bus. You may find a boat service between Muang Khua and Nong Khiaw, along the beautiful Nam Ou River, surrounded by mountainous scenery. Buses and *songthaew* run to most towns and villages, but timetables are not always accurate. It is often a matter of asking at the bus station or waiting by the main road for hours and flagging down a bus on its way through. For shorter distances *songthaew* are more regular.

Tip ...

To help you feel even more relaxed while you're in Nong Khiaw, the massage place attached to **Sabai Sabai** restaurant is excellent.

★ Muang Ngoi Neua → *Colour map 1, B3.*

The town of Muang Ngoi Neua lies 40 km north of Nong Khiaw, along the Nam Ou River. This small town now has electricity and many of the dirt paths have been paved, but it remains surrounded by ethnic villages and retains its charm. Its increased popularity means that backpackers seem to outnumber tourists in peak times, nevertheless, Muang Ngoi Neua is a small slice of utopia, set on a peninsula at the foot of Mount Phaboom, shaded by coconut trees, with the languid river breeze wafting through the town's small paths. Most commonly known as **Muang Ngoi**, the settlement has had to embellish its name to distinguish it from Nong Khiaw, which is also often referred to as Muang Ngoi (see above). It's the perfect place to go for a trek to surrounding villages, or bask the day away swinging in your hammock.

Listings Nong Khiaw, Ban Saphoun and around

Where to stay

Most places offer Wi-Fi internet access.

Nong Khiaw

$$$ Mandala Ou
Near the bus station, T030-537 7332, www.mandala-ou.com.
A newcomer to the seen, this special resort is full of personal touches thanks to the lovely German/Thai couple who run it. Gorgeous setting with many wonderfully decorated rooms offering river and mountain views from a large veranda. Excellent food including fantastic home-baked bread. There is also a small swimming pool with a bar with knock-out views. An ultra-relaxing spot. Highly recommended.

Ban Saphoun

$$$ Nong Kiau Riverside Resort
Turn off right beside the bridge, T020-5570 5000, www.nongkiau.com.
Stunning bungalows and restaurant. The upscale rooms are beautifully decorated in modern Asian East-meets-West style, with 4-poster beds, mosquito nets and tiled hot-water bathrooms. For those looking for something a little more upmarket than the average guesthouse, this exquisite place fits the bill perfectly. The restaurant has a great selection of wines, and internet is available.

Book in advance as it is a favourite of the tour groups. Recommended.

$$ Sunset Guesthouse
Down a lane about 100 m past the bridge, T071-810033, sunsetgh2@hotmail.com.
Definitely trading on the views, given the prices and rather basic rooms, but the fact is you couldn't ask for a better setting from which to watch the sunset. The charming, sprawling bamboo structure looks out onto various levels of decking that serve as a popular restaurant in the evenings, although service can be a little slack. The rooms vary in quality, so ask to see a few.

$ Nam Noun Guesthouse
Just back from the river, T020-5577 4462.
At the lower end of the price range in town, these bungalows are nonetheless some of the best as they are set back from the river. Clean and complete with small verandas and hammocks. A top choice if the purse strings are tight.

Muang Ngoi Neua

$ Lattanavongsa Guesthouse
Northern side of the main road, T030-514 0770.
2 cluster bombs line the steps leading up to these attractive bungalows, which face onto garden. There are polished floorboards, large beds and reasonably lit rooms with bathroom.

$ Ning Ning Guesthouse
Behind the boat landing, T030-514 0863.
This place has a restaurant with a great view for sunset. Double and twin bungalows, with separate Western-style toilet and hot shower; the smarter rooms have large comfy double beds with super-white linen andmosquito nets; breakfast included. The food in the adjoining restaurant is great and the owner speaks good English. A popular spot.

Restaurants

Most of the guesthouses have cafés attached. For more expensive options head for either the Riverside which has a good wine list, or Mandala Ou which offers well-thought-out meals and fine views. For a cheap local fix try the noodle stall next to the bridge on the Ban Saphoun side of town. For something more local, opt for one of the simple places on the road toward the lookout climb.

Nong Khiaw

$ Chennai
Main road on the Nong Khiaw side,
T020-9559 9786.
One of 2 Indian restaurants right next to each other. There is little to choose between them as it seems the close proximity keeps the standard very high in both. Fantastic food and smooth service. Recommended.

Ban Saphoun

$ Alex Restaurant
100 m before the bridge.
A family-run place, this restaurant does some decent Lao food and also some reasonable Western dishes. Very warm and welcoming, there is always a good atmosphere which keeps people coming back night after night.

$ Sabai Sabai
Near the turn off for Sunrise and Alex,
T020-5858 6068.

Run by Mr Ken, this garden restaurant serves traditional Lao food. Try the pumpkin soup with coconut milk and egg served with fresh bread or in the evening opt for the Lao barbecue featuring chicken, pork and beef. The massage place attached is the best in town by a country mile.

Muang Ngoi Neua
Aside from the many guesthouse restaurants, which serve good-quality Lao food, there are also a number of places to eat along the main road. Most have exactly the same food on offer; in fact, many of them just copy their competitors' menus. The fruitshake stands in the centre of town are good value.

$$-$ Sainamgoi Restaurant & Bar
In the centre of the village.
Tasty Lao food in a pleasant atmosphere, with good background music. There's a bar – the only one in town – in the next room.

$ Nang Phone Keo Restaurant
On the main road.
All the usual Lao food plus some extras: try the 'falang roll' for breakfast (a combination of peanut butter, sticky rice and vegetables).

$ Sengdala Restaurant & Bakery
Along the main road.
Very good, cheap Lao food, terrific pancakes and freshly baked baguettes.

$ Sky Bar & Restaurant
See Where to stay, above.
Ambient in the evening although the food is not great.

What to do

Good-quality bicycles can be rented from NK Adventure. There's a movie house on the main road marked 'Cinema' but it was closed at the time of writing.

Nong Khiaw and Ban Saphoun
Green Discovery, *on the Ban Saphoun side,*
T071-819 0081, www.greendiscoverylaos.com.

Managed by the affable Tom, this branch of the nationwide tour operator offers everything from half-day ambles to multi-day treks including cycling, hiking and long-tail boat rides.

Jewel Travel Laos, *T071-253910, www.jeweltravellaos.com*. This is the agent to contact for rock climbing, with 1- to 3-day packages on offer and training available for complete novices. The climbing is on Deer Wall which offers routes from grades 5a-6b (French system).

Motorbike Rental Donkham, *T020-5888 8995*. Rents automatic and semi-automatic bikes and can advise on routes for you to explore solo.

NK Adventure, *main road, Nong Khiaw side, T020-5868 6068, bounhome68@hotmail.com*. Run by the very helpful Mr Boun Home and his friend Mang, both of whom were born in the town, this small tour company offers a one-day boat trip to Khmu villages or a trek to Tad Mok waterfall through rice paddies followed by a 2-hr kayak trip back. 2-day trips include a trek through forest to a Hmong/Khmu homestay followed by a trek to the river to kayak back to town. Active travellers should check out the new bicycle/kayak tour option, cycling out to a waterfall trek and returning via the river.

Muang Ngoi Neua

Trekking, hiking, fishing, kayaking, trips to the waterfalls and boat trips can be organized through most guesthouses.

Transport

Nong Khiaw and Ban Saphoun
Boat

Boat services have become irregular following road improvements, although you may find a service to **Muang Ngoi Neua**, 1 hr, from the boat landing. Otherwise, most local agents run day trip boats and it is often possible to jump on one of those. There are no regular boats to **Luang Prabang** following the

construction of the dam; however, if enough people wish to make the trip it is possible to arrange a boat to the dam and then a van from there to Luang Prabang. Speak to **NK Travel** (see Tour operators, above).

Bus/truck

Buses en route from surrounding destinations stop in Nong Khiaw briefly. Basic timetables are offered but buses can be hours early or late, so check details on the day. It is often a matter of waiting at the bus station for hours and hoping to catch the bus on its way through. Plonking yourself in a restaurant on the main road usually suffices but you will need to flag down the bus as it passes through town. To **Luang Prabang**, 3-4 hrs. Also several departures daily to **Nam Bak**, 30 mins, and on to **Udomxai**, 4 hrs.

Alternatively, you could take one of the more regular *songthaew* to **Pak Mong**, 1 hr, where there is a small noodle shop-cum-bus station on the west side of the bridge, and then catch another vehicle on to **Udomxai/Vientiane**.

Travelling east on Route 1, there are buses to **Vieng Kham**, 0900, 2 hrs, and a village 10 km from **Nam Nouan**, where you can change and head south on Route 6 to **Phonsavanh** and the **Plain of Jars**. There are direct buses north to **Xam Neua** and the village near Nam Nouan (useful if you are heading for the Nam Nern Night Safari, see box, page 408), which can be caught from the toll gate on the Ban Saphoun side of the river when it comes through from Vientiane, but it's usually quite crowded.

Muang Ngoi Neua
Boat

From the landing at the northern end of town, slow boats travel north along the beautiful Nam Ou River, surrounded by mountainous scenery, to **Muang Khua**, 5 hrs. Slow boats also go south (irregularly) to **Nong Khiaw**, 1 hr. Departure times vary and depend on there being sufficient passengers.

halfway house in a charming riverside spot

Muang Khua is nestled into the banks of the Nam Ou, close to the mouth of the Nam Phak, in the south of Phongsali Province. Hardly a destination in itself, it's usually just a stopover between Nong Khiaw and Phongsali although it is increasingly used as an overnight stop by travellers heading to Dien Bien Phu in Vietnam. Muang Khua is a great place to kick back for a few days if you want to take a break from the well-worn travellers' path. Rather scruffy around the edges, the town nonetheless has a certain charm and has a bank, post office and Telecom office. Take a wander across the rickety old bridge and walk along the river past small villages or sit in the market and enjoy some local food.

Located at the junction of two rivers and on Route 4 to Vietnam, Muang Khua has long been a crossroads between Vietnam and Laos. A French garrison was based in Muang Khua until 1954, when it was ousted by Vietnamese troops in the aftermath of the battle at Dien Bien Phu. For a brief period from 1958, Polish and Canadian officials of the Comité International de Contrôle were quartered in the town to monitor the ceasefire between the Pathet Lao and the Royal Lao government. Nowadays, Muang Khua is home to a burgeoning market in Vietnamese goods, trucked in from Dien Bien Phu. The border with Vietnam has now opened to tourists but the road is still under construction on the Lao side; a steady and increasing trickle of tourists seem to be making their way through on this route.
▶▶ *For details of the border between Sop Hun (Laos) and Tay Trang (Vietnam), see box, page 544.*

Listings Muang Khua

Where to stay

$ Manotham Guesthouse
Across the old bridge, T020-5588 0058.
The owner makes this place one to seek out. A cheery elderly man, he'll likely invite you to a communal dinner and gently encourage the drinking of *lao lao* after feeding you massive portions of home-cooked food. He will also help guests arrange transport on to Vietnam. Clean, very simple rooms. Recommended.

$ Nam Ou Guesthouse & Restaurant
Follow the signs at the top of the hill, T020-2283 3789.
Looking out across the river, this guesthouse is a good ultra-budget option and very popular with backpackers. Singles, twins and doubles, some with hot water en suites, and 3 rooms with river views.

Restaurants

This is a small town with very few eateries, although what it lacks in restaurants, it makes up for in pool tables; very small children show a frightening aptitude and you should be prepared to have an instant audience if you try your hand. Noodles and baguettes are available in the market and most guesthouses serve food.

$ Nam Ou Guesthouse & Restaurant
See Where to stay.
An incomparable location for a morning coffee overlooking the river; it has an English menu and friendly staff. This is the most reliable place to eat in town.

$ Saifon
By the river.
A basic restaurant with a small selection of

dishes translated into English on the menu. Service can be a little haphazard.

Boat

Road travel is now more popular but irregular boats still sometimes travel south on the Nam Ou River to **Muang Ngoi Neua**, 3 hrs, and **Nong Khiaw**, 4 hrs. Boats also run north to **Phongsali**, via the river port of **Hat Xa**, 20 km northeast of Phongsali, 3-5 hrs, 90,000-100,000 kip per person, minimum 10 people. From Hat Xa, it is a 1-hr pickup ride to Phongsali, but there are no services after mid-afternoon so you may have to stay the night.

Boats from Muang Khua are scheduled to leave at 0900-1000 but won't leave without enough passengers; it's best to get to the dock early and wait. In the low season, there may not be any scheduled boats but you could gather up a few more interested tourists and charter a boat – ask at the **Nam Ou Guesthouse**.

Bus/truck/pickup

You can also travel to **Phongsali** by road; the buses can get crowded but the scenery is superb. Buses run 3 times per day and take approximately 3½ hrs.

There is a direct bus from Muang Khua to **Dien Bien Phu** (Vietnam), which stops at the border to complete paperwork. The bus leaves from the opposite side of the river bank to Muang Khua at 0600, so allow plenty of time to get across the river. Most guesthouses can help with information.

GOING FURTHER
Phongsali

High up in the mountains at an altitude of 1628 m, this northern provincial capital provides beautiful views and an invigorating climate. It is especially stunning from January to March, when wildflowers bloom in the surrounding hills. The town can be cold at any time of the year, so take some warm clothes. Mornings tend to be foggy and it can also be very wet. There is an end-of-the-earth feel in the areas surrounding the main centre, with dense pristine jungle surrounded by misty mountains.

Phongsali was one of the first areas to be liberated by the Pathet Lao in the late 1940s. The town's architecture is a strange mix of Chinese post-revolutionary concrete blocks, Lao wood-and-brick houses with tin roofs, and bamboo or mud huts with straw roofs. The most attractive part of town is a series of shophouses that wind away from the **Phongsaly Hotel** towards Hat Xa. The town itself is home to about 20,000 people, mostly Lao, Phou Noi and Chinese, while the wider district is a potpourri of ethnicities, with around 25 different minorities inhabiting the area.

Northwest
Laos

Northwestern Laos comprises dramatic, misty mountainous scenery, clad with thick forests and peppered with small villages. This area is home to a variety of ethnic minority groups including the Akha, Hmong, Khmu and Yao and is a firm favourite with trekkers. The mighty Mekong forges its way through picturesque towns, such as Pakbeng and Houei Xai, affording visitors a wonderful glimpse of riverine life.

Udomxai (Oudom Xai) and around → *Colour map 1, B2.*

major travel hub somewhat lacking in charm

Udomxai, the capital of Udomxai Province, is a hot and dusty town that is used as a pit-stop but the local tourist board, with the help of a German NGO, have done a lot promote the area's other attractions, see below. Udomxai was razed during the war and the inhabitants fled to live in the surrounding hills; what is here now has been built since 1975, which explains why it is such an unattractive settlement. Since the early 1990s, the town has been experiencing an economic boom – as a result of its position at the intersection of roads linking China, Vietnam, Luang Prabang and Pakbeng – and commerce and construction are thriving. It also means that Udomxai has a large Chinese and Vietnamese population, a fact that appears to rile the locals.

Listings Udomxai (Oudom Xai) and around

Tourist information

Provincial Tourism Office
Near the river on the main road in the centre of town, T081-212482, www.oudomxay.info. Oct-Mar Mon-Fri 0800-1200 and 1330-1600, Apr-Sep Mon-Fri 0730-1200 and 1330-1600.
Offers helpful advice.

Where to stay

$$$$-$$$ Kamu Lodge
Ban Nyong Hay, Udomxai Province; book via the office in Luang Prabang at 44/3 Ban Wat Nong, Kham Kong Rd, T071-260319, T020-5603 2365 (mob), www.kamulodge.com. On the banks of the Mekong, 2½ hrs upstream from Luang Prabang and accessible only by boat.

Essential Northwest Laos

Finding your feet

There are airports at Udomxai and Luang Namtha with connections to Vientiane for those short on time. With the development of overland links, river transport has languished, but the route upstream from Luang Prabang to Houei Xai via Pakbeng, on the border with Thailand, remains hugely popular and is well worth doing (see page 374). Note that the boats can get very busy in peak season. There are good bus connections to most towns, the main transport hubs being Udomxai, Luang Namtha and Houei Xai.

Best places to stay

Boat Landing Guesthouse and Restaurant, page 388
Luangsay Lodge, page 394

When to go

December to February.

Time required

Allow at least a week to take in the main sights of Northwest Laos, longer if you want to take the boat or do the Gibbon Experience.

Best restaurants

Boat Landing Guesthouse and Restaurant, page 388
Forest Retreat's Bamboo Lounge, page 388
Taileu Guesthouse and Restaurant, page 392

Accommodation is in modern canvas tents, decorated with local furnishings. The Lao restaurant is set amongst the paddy fields. Also runs treks and activities, such as gold panning, rice planting and archery. This is a place to truly get away from it all as there is no internet. The price includes boat transfer.

$ Villa Keoseumsack
2 doors down from the Sinphet Restaurant, T081-312170, seumsack@hotmail.com.
'Villa' is perhaps a little overstated, but this is still perhaps the best option in town with its polished floors, large double beds, desks, wardrobes and hot-water showers. Fan rooms are cheaper.

Restaurants

As well as those listed below, Litthavixay Guesthouse (see Where to stay) can whip up some good dishes, including Western-style pancakes and breakfasts. There are a number of restaurants on the 1st left turn after the bridge; all do good Lao and Chinese food. Noodle soup shops are scattered throughout town and stalls in front of the market sell beer and tasty snacks from nightfall.

$ Kanya Restaurant
Just off the main street not far from the tourist office.
This is popular with Lao tour guides and has a menu in English offering the usual staples. The pork vermicelli is tasty and the iced coffees are served long.

Tip...

A more luxurious option for travelling by boat between Luang Prabang and Houei Xai is to take the two-day **Luangsay Cruise**, www.luangsay.com, which stops en route to visit riverside villages. See page 395.

$ Sinphet Restaurant
On the main road, opposite
Linda Guesthouse.
One of the best options in town. English menu, delicious iced coffee with Ovaltine, great Chinese and Lao food. Try the curry chicken, *kua-mii* or yellow noodles with chicken. Also does sandwiches, fruit shakes and pancakes.

Transport

Air
The airport is close to town and has flights to **Vientiane**. **Lao Airlines** has an office at the airport, T081-312047.

Boat
One of the nicest ways to get to **Luang Prabang** or **Houei Xai** is to take a bus from Udomxai to **Pakbeng** (see page 393) and catch a boat from there.

Bus/truck/songthaew
Udomxai is the epicentre of northern travel. If arriving in Udomxai to catch a connecting bus, it's better to leave earlier in the day as transport tends to peter out in the afternoon.

The bus station is 1 km east of the town centre from where buses leave for **Nong Khiaw**, 3 hrs; **Pak Mong**, 2 hrs; **Luang Prabang**, 5 hrs; **Vientiane**, 15 hrs; **Luang Namtha**, 4 hrs; and **Boten** (the Chinese border) 82 km. You will need to check if you are eligible for a visa at the Boten border as this is subject to change.

There are services north on Route 4 to **Phongsali**, 9-12 hrs. This trip is long so bring something soft to sit on and try to get a seat with a view.

There are plenty of *songthaew* on standby waiting to make smaller trips to destinations like **Pak Mong** and **Nong Khiaw**; if you miss one of the earlier buses, it may be worthwhile bargaining with the drivers; if they can get enough money, or can round up enough passengers, they will make the extra trip.

Luang Namtha and around → *Colour map 1, A2.*

sleepy, remote town that serves as a good base for exploring

The provincial capital was obliterated during the war and the concrete structures erected since 1975 have little charm. As in other towns in the north of Laos, the improvement in transport links with China and Thailand has led to burgeoning trade. The area has established itself as a major player in Laos' ecotourism industry, primarily due to the Nam Ha National Protected Area (see page 387) and the environmentally friendly **Boat Landing Guesthouse** (see page 388). Facilities such as banks, ATMs and Wi-Fi are widely available in town.

Sights
The **Luang Namtha Museum** ⓘ *near the Kaysone Monument, Mon-Fri 0800-1130, 1300-1600, 10,000 kip*, is worth a visit. The museum houses a collection of indigenous clothing and artefacts, agricultural tools, weapons, textiles and a collection of Buddha images, drums and gongs.

In the centre of town is a good **night market** with a range of food stalls and some handicrafts – this can be a good place to meet others in the evening.

The old **That Poum Pouk** ⓘ *3 km west of the airfield, 5000 kip, take a tuk-tuk from the market*, sits in a ruinous state on a hill. Local sources suggest that the stupa was built as part of a competition between the Lanna Kingdom (in northern Thailand) and the Lane Xang Kingdom to prove which of the two kingdoms had the most merit. Severe damage due to bombing in 1964 led local villagers and monks to reconstruct the stupa but this proved a fruitless exercise as further bombing in 1966 dislodged the stupa, parts of which can still be seen lying on the ground. Incredibly, much of the original stucco and an encrypted stelae survived the attacks. A new stupa has been built behind the ruined one. The trip to That Poum Pouk is most pleasant in the afternoon.

Villages around Luang Namtha

Luang Namtha Province has witnessed the rise and decline of various Tai kingdoms and now over 30 ethnic groups reside in the province, making it the most ethnically diverse province in the country. Principal minorities residing here include Tai Lue, Tai Dam, Lanten, Hmong and Khamu. There are a number of friendly villages around the town of Luang Namtha. As with all other minority areas, you should only visit the villages with a local guide or endorsed tourism organization.

Ban Nam Chang is a Lanten village 3 km along a footpath outside Luang Namtha; just ask the way. **Ban Lak Khamay** is quite a large Akha village 27 km from Luang Namtha on the road to Muang Sing. It was resettled from a nearby location higher in the hills in 1994 as part of a government programme to protect upland forests. The community now grows teak and rubber trees. The village chief speaks Lao. The settlement features a traditional Akha entrance; if you pass through this entrance you must visit a house in the village, or you will be considered an enemy. Otherwise you can simply pass to one side of the gate, but be careful not to touch it. Other features of interest in Akha villages are the swing, which is located at the highest point in the village and used in the annual swing festival (you must not touch the swing), and the meeting house, where unmarried couples go to court and where newly married couples live until they have their own house. There is another, smaller Akha village a few kilometres on towards Muang Sing.

Ban Nam Dee is a small bamboo paper-making Lanten village located about 6 km northeast of Luang Namtha. The name of the village means 'good water' and, not surprisingly, if you continue on from Ban Nam Dee for 1 km, you will come to a waterfall. The trip to the village is particularly scenic, passing through verdant green rice paddies dotted with huts. A motorbike rather than a bicycle will be necessary to navigate these villages and sights as the road is very rocky in places and unsuitable for cyclists. Villagers usually charge for access to the waterfall.

The small Tai Lue village of **Ban Khone Kam** is also worth a visit. The settlement is

Luang Namtha

To ❶ ❸, Muang Sing & Udomxai

Luang Namtha Museum 🏛
Kaysone Monument

NIT
Lao Telecom ☎

Luang Namtha
Provincial Tourism Office & Eco Guide Unit ❹

Bike Rental 🚲 ❹ ❺

Green Discovery 🏢

Night Market Ⓜ

@ KNT

❷

Intra-Provincial Bus Station 🚌

To ⑫, Boat Landing, Airport, Lao Airlines, That Poum Park, Inter-Provincial Bus Station & Houei Xai

Where to stay 🛏
Boat Landing Guesthouse & Restaurant 12
Manychan Guesthouse 4
Phou Lu III 1
Thoulasith Guesthouse 3

N
100 metres
100 yards

Restaurants 🍴
Baw Pen Yang 1
Forest Retreat's Bamboo Lounge 2
Lai's Place 3
Yamuna 4

based on the banks of the Nam Tha, halfway between Luang Namtha and Houei Xai, and is only accessible by boat or by foot. The friendly villagers offer **homestays** here, for one or two nights, providing an interesting cultural insight into the daily lives of the region's boatmen and rice farmers.

Ban Vieng Nua, 3 km from the centre of town, is a Tai Kolom village famous for its traditional house where groups can experience local dancing and a good luck *baci* ceremony. Contact the tourism office (see page 388) for further information and to make bookings. ▶▶ *For advice on visiting an ethnic minority village, see box, page 19.*

★ Vieng Phouka and around

Before the roads in the region were upgraded, Vieng Phouka was the place to stay overnight when travelling between Luang Namtha or Muang Sing and the Mekong. Located south of Luang Namtha (and 125 km north of Houei Xai), the town is surrounded by a variety of minority villages – Akha, Hmong, Lahu and Khmu, with the Khmu comprising about 90% of the population.

The local tourism authority, **Vieng Phouka Eco Guide Service** ⓘ *T081-212400 (T020-5598 5289 mob), www.luangnamtha-tourism.org*, organizes treks in the surrounding area, which is not as busy as Luang Namtha and recommended by trekkers. ▶▶ *See What to do, page 389.*

The 5-km-long **Nam Aeng Cave**, 12 km north of Vieng Phouka, is famous locally for an annual ceremony held on 13 January, when elders call up the large fish that inhabit part of the cave. The **Nom Cave**, a four-hour walk from the town, was once home to a famous sacred Buddha, but this has now been pilfered. During the revolution the Nom Cave served as a hideout. Around the area are a few scattered remains of the wall from the ancient city of Kuvieng, much of which has been dismantled by local villagers at the government's insistence.

Both Luang Namtha and Vieng Phouka make great bases from which to venture into the **Nam Ha National Protected Area**, one of a few remaining places on earth where the rare black-cheeked crested gibbon can be found (see below). If you're lucky, you can hear the wonderful singing of the gibbons in the morning.

Nam Ha National Protected Area (NPA)

This area has firmly established itself as a major player in Laos' ecotourism industry, primarily due to the **Nam Ha Ecotourism Project**, which was established in 1993 by NTA Lao and UNESCO to help preserve Luang Namtha's cultural and environmental heritage in the Nam Ha National Protected Area. The Nam Ha NPA is one of the largest protected areas in Laos and consists of mountainous areas dissected by several rivers. It is home to at least 38 species of large mammal, including the black-cheeked crested gibbon, tiger and clouded leopard, and over 300 bird species, including the Blythe's kingfisher. The Nam Ha project has won a UN development award for its outstanding achievements in the area.

The organization currently leads one- to five-day treks in the area and can arrange extended treks on special request. The treks offer the chance to visit traditional villages, explore various forest habitats, take river trips, stay in a jungle camp and support local conservation efforts. Check with the **Luang Namtha Eco Guide Unit** (see page 389) or **Green Discovery** (see Tour operators, page 389) for departures; an information session about the trek is given at the guide's office. Prices cover the cost of food, water, transportation, guides, lodging and the trekking permit. All the treks utilize local guides who have been trained to help generate income for their villages. Income for conservation purposes is also garnered from the fees for trekking permits into the area.

Tourist information

Luang Namtha Provincial Tourism Office
T086-211534, luangnamtha-tourism-laos.org.
Better than it once was, but for the best information it is still best to head for **Green Discovery** (see page 389).

Where to stay

There has been a sudden rush of guesthouses popping up here over the last few years but the Boat Landing, the best ecotourism venture in the country is still the stand-out choice in the area.

$$ Boat Landing Guesthouse & Restaurant
Ban Kone, T086-312398, www. theboatlanding.laopdr.com.
Further out of town than most other guesthouses, this place is located right on the river. Time stands still here. It's an eco-resort that has got everything just right: pristine surroundings, environmentally friendly rooms, helpful service and a brilliant restaurant serving northern Lao cuisine. The rooms combine modern design with traditional materials and decoration; breakfast included. The gardens brim with butterflies and birds; the best time, weather-wise, is Oct/Nov. Recommended.

$ Phou Lu III
A 5-min walk from the main strip on the river, T020-004400.
Pretty, spacious rattan bungalows line the river and provide the prettiest place to stay on a tight budget.

$ Thoulasith Guesthouse
Off the main road, T086-212166, thoulasithguesthouse@gmail.com.
Beautiful wooden building with a wrap-around balcony set in a compound with a garden, tables and chairs, making it a good

spot to meet fellow travellers. Rooms come with TV, desk, hot-water bathroom (3 rooms have bathtubs) and free Wi-Fi. Friendly management. There's a decent restaurant and it's very close to the night market for your evening meal. A top choice in this budget range.

Vieng Phouka
There are a few basic guesthouses in the southern part of town and there is little to choose between them. **Bo Kung** ($) is a decent option with very simple rooms.

Restaurants

$$-$ Boat Landing Guesthouse & Restaurant
See Where to stay, T086-312398. Open 0700-2100.
The best place to eat in town, with a beautiful dining area and exceptionally innovative cuisine: a range of northern Lao dishes made from local produce that supports local villages. Highly recommended.

$$-$ Forest Retreat's Bamboo Lounge
Main road, T020-6668 0031, www.bambooloungelaos.com.
A small 'gourmet café' run by a super-friendly Kiwi couple who serve up good pizza and a solid range of drinks in a warm and welcoming environment. This is an excellent place to eat and to get up-to-date information on what to do in the local area. They can also arrange treks and various tours. Recommended.

$ Baw Pen Yang Restaurant and Art Gallery
Down the sidestreet by Lai's.
Opened in 2014, this is a very welcome addition to the town, providing comfortable seating, a good range of hearty breakfasts and also artwork by a local artist which is available for purchase.

$ Lai's Place
On the main road.
A fantastic little spot with great owners serving very tasty Lao food. A place you're likely to return to.

Bakeries, cafés and street stalls
There is a bakery and cake shop near the market that sells mouthwatering treats; try the green tea cake. There are a few *feu* stalls by the main market. At night, food vendors gather at the night market, selling meat on a stick and waffles from pretty, candlelit stalls.

Shopping
The **night market** sells textiles woven by the women of Luang Namtha and warm clothes for travellers who've forgotten that it's cold in the mountains. There is an ever-growing range of other handicrafts on offer making this quite a pleasant place to do some gift shopping.

What to do

Massage and sauna
There are a few herbal saunas in town; bring your own towels.

Tour operators
If you want to trek from Luang Namtha and you're travelling solo or as a couple, it's expensive. Try to hook up with people before you get there or at your guesthouse. Agencies also put up boards requesting more takers. The larger the group, the cheaper the price.

Forest Retreat Laos, *see Restaurants*. Kiwi-owned, this company has an ethical focus and looks to plough profits back into local communities and promote responsible trekking. Offers kayaking, cycling, trekking or a mix of all 3. These folk are wonderfully passionate about the National Protected Area and Luang Namtha itself.
Green Discovery, *main road, T086-211484, www.greendiscoverylaos.com. Office open*

daily 0730-2100. Offers 1- to 7-day kayaking/rafting, cycling and trekking excursions into the Nam Ha NPA. Excellent guides.
Luang Namtha Eco Guide Unit, *T086-211534, www.luangnamtha-tourism.org.* Information on 1- to 4-day treks into the Nam Ha NPA. Biking tours, boat trips and tuk-tuk tours also possible. The tourism office has also set up an **Eco Guide** unit at Muang Nalea.

Vieng Phouka
The local tourism office runs 4 different treks of 1 to 3 days around the local villages, the Nam Ha National Park and caves, including food, camping and accommodation with a host family. The guides (trained by the LNTA and the EU) are usually Khmu and Akha from the surrounding villages. Contact the **Vieng Phouka Eco Guide Service Unit**, *T084-212400. Daily 0800-1200, 1330-1700.*

Transport

Air
Luang Namtha's airport is 6 km south of the city centre. Shared tuk-tuks wait outside the terminal for arriving flights and run to anywhere in town. There are 3 flights a week direct to **Vientiane** with Lao Airlines, T086-212072, which has an office south of town on the main road.

Bicycle/motorbike
Bicycles and motorcycle are available for hire from various places around town, but the place in front of **Zuela Guesthouse** has the best choice and very helpful staff. Motorbike tours of up to 5 days can also be arranged here.

Boat
Slow boats are the best and most scenic travel option but their reliability will depend on the tide and, in the dry season (Jan-May) they often won't run at all as the water level is too low. There isn't really a regular boat service from **Luang Namtha**, so you will

have to charter a whole boat or hitch a ride on a boat making the trip already. The **Boat Landing Guesthouse** is a good source of information about boats; if arrangements are made for you, a courtesy tip is appreciated.

Bus/truck/songthaew

The inter-provincial bus station and its ticket office are 10 km south of town. A newer intra-provincial bus station is on the main road, 100 m south of the town strip. From the intra-provincial bus station: to **Muang Sing**, 3 daily, 1½ hrs, additional pickups may depart throughout the rest of the day, depending on demand.

From the inter-provincial bus station: to **Udomxai**, several daily, 4 hrs; to **Houei Xai**, 0900 and 1330, 4 hrs. Take this service

for **Vieng Phouka**. To **Luang Prabang**, 1 morning departure, 8 hrs. To **Vientiane**, morning and afternoon, 21 hrs. To get to **Nong Khiaw**, you need to go via Udomxai (leave early).

To China The bus service from Luang Namtha to **Boten** (Chinese border) is variable, 2 hrs. The border is open 0800-1600. Laos visas are available at the border but it's best to organize a Chinese visa in advance at Vientiane.

Vieng Phouka

Buses and *songthaew* depart for **Houei Xai**, a few times daily from the market, usually in the morning, 5 hrs. It is also possible to catch buses to **Luang Namtha**, 4 hrs, and **Udomxai**.

Muang Sing → Colour map 1, A2.
friendly town amid gorgeous scenery with accessible hilltribe communities

Many visitors consider this peaceful valley to be one of the highlights of the north. Lying at the terminus of the highway in the far northwest corner of Laos, it is a natural point to stop and spend a few days recovering from the rigours of the road, before either heading south or moving on to China. This area is a border region that has been contested by the Chinese, Lao and Thai at various points in the last few centuries. While it is now firmly Lao territory, there is a sense that the Chinese have invaded by stealth as their economic presence is extremely evident. There are also several NGOs, as well as bilateral and multilateral development operations in the area. The only way to get to Muang Sing is by bus or pickup from Luang Namtha. The road is asphalt and the terrain on this route is mountainous with dense forest.

Sights

Muang Sing itself is little more than a supremely picturesque village, situated on an upland plateau, where golden rattan huts glow among misty blue-green peaks. The town features some interesting old wooden and brick buildings and, unlike nearby Luang Namtha and several other towns in the north, it wasn't bombed close to oblivion during the struggle for Laos. The **old French fort**, built in the 1920s, is off limits to visitors, as it is occupied by the Lao army, but the relocated market is certainly worth a look if you're up very early in the morning; it starts about 0600 and begins to wind down after 0800. Along with the usual array of plastic objects, clothes and pieces of hardware, local silk and cotton textiles can be purchased. Numerous hill peoples come to the market to trade, including Akha and Hmong tribespeople, along with Yunnanese, Tai Dam and Tai Lue.

The **Muang Sing Ethnic Museum** ① *in the centre of town, daily 0800-1200 and 1300-1600*, is a beautiful old wooden and brick building. It houses a range of traditional tools, ethnic clothes, jewellery, instruments, religious artefacts and household items, like the loom. The building was once the royal residence of the Cao Fa (Prince), Phaya Sekong. Most Buddhist monasteries in the vicinity are Tai Lue in style. The most accessible is **Wat Sing Chai**, on the main road.

Around Muang Sing

From Muang Sing, trek uphill past **Stupa Mountain Lodge** for 1 km to reach **That Xieng Tung**, the most sacred site in the area. The stupa was built in 1256 and is believed to contain the Buddha's adam's apple. It attracts lots of pilgrims in November for the annual **full moon festival**. Originally a city was built around the stupa but everyone migrated down to lower lands. There is a small pond near the stupa, which is believed to be auspicious: if it dries up it is considered bad luck for Muang Sing. It is said that the pond once dried up and the whole village had no rice and starved. Most tourism operators will run treks up to the stupa and a stop at **Nam Keo waterfall**, a large cascade with a 10-m drop, 7 km from the guesthouse. It's a nice place for a picnic. The local tourism authority runs treks to the falls. Bring good shoes.

Listings Muang Sing

Tourist information

Muang Sing Tourism Office
Ban Xiengchai, T086-400015, www. luangnamtha-tourism-laos.org. Mon-Fri 0800-1130 and 1330-1700, Sat-Sun 0800-1000 and 1500-1700.
Offers a wide variety of treks. There is a small bank opposite the market. Internet is available at the tourism office and Wi-Fi is becoming more widely available at guesthouses.

Where to stay

$ Adima Guesthouse
Near Ban Oudomsin, 8 km north of Muang Sing towards the Chinese border, 600 m off the main road, T020-2239 3398.
A little hard to get to but the location is extremely scenic with views over the paddy fields and hills. Peaceful bungalows constructed in traditional Yao and Akha style (some with shared bathroom), bathrooms with squat toilets, plus a lovely open-air restaurant serving good food. A place to get away from it all.

$ Phou Lu Bungalows
At the southern end of town, T030-5511 0326.
Spacious wooden double bungalows with 4-poster beds, small balconies with bamboo

seats, set around a grassy compound with restaurant and massage service.

$ Taileu Guesthouse
On the main road, T030-511 0354.
Above the restaurant there are 8 very basic rattan rooms with bamboo-style, 4-poster beds (the rickety backpacker version not the romantic type), squat toilets and temperamental hot water heated by solar power. The guesthouse owners are lovely people, speak good English and run one of the best places to eat in town.

Restaurants

It is highly recommended that you eat some of the delicious ethnic food while you're in Muang Sing as there aren't many other places where you will be able to sample these meals.

$$-$ Adima Guesthouse
See Where to stay.
Western offerings, such as the usual backpacker pancakes or fried eggs, as well as some Lao-inspired meals.

$ Muang Sing View Restaurant
Just off the main road.
A bamboo walkway leads to this rustic restaurant which enjoys the best views in Muang Sing overlooking the paddy

fields and the valley. All the usual Lao staples are served.

$ Taileu Guesthouse and Restaurant
See Where to stay, T081-212375.
The most popular place to eat due to its indigenous Tai Lue menu. Try baked aubergine with pork, soy mash and fish soup. Try their local piña colada with *lao lao*, their *sa lo* (Muang Sing's answer to a hamburger) or one of the famous *jeow* dishes. The banana flower soup is fantastic. This is an eating experience you won't find elsewhere in Laos. Noi, the owner, is very friendly. Highly recommended.

What to do

Trekking
Trekking has become a delicate issue around Muang Sing as uncontrolled tourism was beginning to have a detrimental effect on some of the minority villages. Luckily some sensible procedures have been put in place to ensure low-impact tourism. The **Muang Sing Tourism Office** (see Tourist information, above) has a wide variety of treks on offer from 1 to 3 days.

Exotissimo, *T086-400016, akhaexp@gmail. com, www.exotissimo.com.* In cahoots with

GTZ, a German aid agency, **Exotissimo** has launched more expensive but thoroughly enjoyable treks such as the 'Akha Experience', which include tasty meals prepared by local Akha people. Advertised as a 3-day trek, it can be organized as a 1- and 2-day trek too.

Transport

Bicycle
Available for rent from a couple of guesthouses in town – to go further afield a mountain bike is definitely preferable. Bikes are usually set out the front when they are available, so keep an eye out for the better ones.

Boat
It is sometimes possible to charter boats from **Xieng Kok** downstream on the Mekong to **Houei Xai**, 3-4 hrs, but the price can be rather steep.

Bus/truck/songthaew
The bus station is across from the new morning market, 500 m from the main road. To **Luang Namtha**, by bus or pickup, 2 hrs. It is also possible to charter a *songthaew* or tuk-tuk to Luang Namtha. *Songthaew* to **Xieng Kok**, 3 hrs. To **Muang Long**, 2 hrs.

Along the Mekong

border region, ideal for nature lovers

Houei Xai (Houay Xai) → *Colour map 1, B1.*
Most passengers arrive at the passenger ferry pier, close to the centre. The vehicle ferry pier is 750 m further north (upstream). The bus station is at the Morning Market, 3 km out of central Houei Xai. The immigration office is at the boat terminal and the airport, daily 0800-1800.

This town is in the heart of the Golden Triangle and used to derive its wealth from the narcotics trade on the heroin route to Chiang Mai in Thailand. Today trade still brings the town considerable affluence, although it is rather less illicit: timber is ferried across the Mekong from Laos to the Thai town of Chiang Khong and, in exchange, consumer goods are shipped back. Sapphires are mined in the area and, doubtless, there is also still some undercover heroin smuggling.

Houei Xai is a popular crossing point for tourists travelling to and from Thailand and a considerable amount of money flows in from the numerous guesthouses and restaurants that have been built here. However, few people spend more than one night in the town.

★Bokeo Nature Reserve Gibbon Experience

Office on the main Sekhong Rd in Houay Xai, T084-212021, www.gibbonexperience.org.

Most visitors who stick around Houei Xai do so to visit the Gibbon Experience, a thrilling, exciting and unmissable three-day trip into Bokeo Nature Reserve where a number of treehouses have been built high in the jungle canopy and linked with a course of interconnected ziplines. The experience of staying in one of these treehouses and being awoken by singing soprano gibbons is truly awe-inspiring, as is ziplining through the mist high above the jungle canopy.

In the morning well-trained guides take visitors for hikes to see if they can spot the elusive gibbons and other animal and plant species. Such species include the giant squirrel, one of the largest rodents in the world, and the Asiatic black bear, whose numbers are in decline due to hunting for their bile and gall bladders.

First and foremost this is a very well-run conservation project. It was started to help reduce poaching, logging, slash-and-burn farming and the destruction of primary forest by working with villagers to transform the local economy by making a non-destructive living from their unique environment. Already the Gibbon Experience has started to pay dividends: the forest conservation and canopy visits can generate as much income year on year as a local logging company could do only once.

Alongside the 'Classic' experience there is now a 'Waterfall Gibbon Experience' which takes people deeper into the reserve, trekking for two to three hours per day along the Nam Nga River. The waterfall tree house has a freshwater swimming hole at the bottom, the other shows sunsets overlooking several valleys. This option gets consistently excellent feedback from guests.

Pakbeng → *Colour map 1, B2.*

This long thin strip of a village is perched halfway up a hill, with fine views over the Mekong. Its importance lies in its location at the confluence of the Mekong and Nam Beng rivers. There is not much to do here but it's a good place to stop (and is the obligatory stop) on the slow boat between Houei Xai and Luang Prabang. The village is worth a visit for its traditional atmosphere and the friendliness of the locals, including various minorities. Just downstream from the port is a good spot for swimming in the dry season, but be careful as the current is strong. There are also a couple of monasteries in town. The locals organize guided treks to nearby villages. Electricity is now available 24 hours and internet is widely available.

Listings Along the Mekong

Tourist information

Lao National Tourism State Bokeo
On the main street up from immigration, T084-211162. Mon-Fri 0800-1130 and 1330-1600.
Can offer limited advice.

Where to stay

Houei Xai

$ BAP Guesthouse
On the main Sekhong Rd, T084-211083, bapbiz@live.com.
One of the oldest guesthouses in town consisting of a labyrinth of additions and add-ons as their business has grown over the

years. A range of rooms; the newer tiled ones with hot-water bathrooms are the best.

$ Sabaydee
On the riverfront, T020-5692 9458.
Big, tiled rooms, with en suite hot showers and Western toilets.
Good value and recommended.

$ Taveensinh Guesthouse
Northwest end of the town, T084-211502.
A good budget choice with clean rooms and great communal balconies overlooking the river and friendly family in charge.

Pakbeng
During peak season, when the slow boat arrives from Luang Prabang, about 60 people descend on Pakbeng at the same time. As the town doesn't have an endless supply of great budget guesthouses, it is advisable to get someone you trust to mind your bags, while you make a mad dash to get the best room in town. There are a number of shack-like bamboo lodgings running up the hill.

$$$$-$$$ Pakbeng Lodge
On the hillside above the river, T081-212304, www.pakbenglodge.com.
A wooden and concrete construction, built in traditional Lao style, this stunning guesthouse includes 20 rooms with fan, toilet and hot water. Good restaurant and wonderful views. Breakfast is included. 10 new deluxe rooms were due to open at the time of writing. Wi-Fi available. Elephant activities can be arranged.

$$$ Luangsay Lodge
About 1 km from the centre of town, www.mekong-cruises.com.
This is the most beautiful accommodation in Pakbeng. An attractive wooden pathway curves through luscious tropical gardens to several wooden bungalows with fantastic balconies and large windows overlooking the river and misty mountains. Hot-water bathrooms and romantic rooms make this a winner. Great restaurant. Book in advance

as it tends to get booked up by customers on the **Luangsay Cruise** especially in high season but Sun and last-minute deals are possible. Breakfast and dinner is included. Highly recommended.

$ Monsovanh Guesthouse
On the main road.
One of the most popular choice and rightly so thanks to the good location, clean rooms and welcoming owner. Very good breakfasts at the **Monsovanh** bakery across the road.

Restaurants

Houei Xai

$$-$ Riverside
Just off the main road, near the Houay Xai Guesthouse, T084-211064.
Huge waterfront restaurant on large platform. Perfect position for taking in the sunset. Great shakes. Extensive menu that's a mixture of Lao and Thai food. The curries are quite good. Usually live music is played here, some of it decidedly off-key.

$ BAP Guesthouse
See Where to stay.
Wide range of dishes including pancakes, croissants and eggs.

$ Nutpop
On the main road, T084-211037.
A pleasant little garden restaurant, set in an atmospheric lamp-lit building. Good Lao food – fried mushrooms and good curry. Excellent fish.

Pakbeng
Restaurants serve breakfast (baguettes, pancakes and coffee) really early. The eco-lodges have pretty upscale restaurants, and there are several more modest restaurants lining the main road towards the river; all seem to have the same English menu, basic Lao dishes, eggs and freshly made sandwiches. The local market has an array of dishes from *feu* through to frogs.

$ Kopchaideu Restaurant
Overlooking the Mekong.
This restaurant has a wide selection of Indian dishes with a few Lao favourites thrown in. Great shakes, naan bread and fantastic service – the pick of the bunch.

What to do

Houei Xai
Tour operators
Gibbon Experience, *T084-212021, www.gibbonexperience.org.* This unique ecotourism operation provides the rare opportunity to see or hear the soprano-singing, black-cheeked crested gibbons. See page 393 for details.

Pakbeng
Elephant trekking
Contact **Pakbeng Lodge**, *see Where to stay.*

Massage
Massage is offered in several places around town.

Transport

Houei Xai
Lao National Tourism State Bokeo (see page 393) can advise on the sale of boat, bus, pickup and other tickets but limited English is spoken. You are better off approaching the travel agencies around the immigration centre many of which sell bus and boat tickets. See page 374 for information on boat travel between Houei Xai and **Luang Prabang**.

Boat
The passenger ferry pier is close to the centre of town. The vehicle ferry pier is 750 m further north (upstream). The **BAP Guesthouse** is a good place to find out about boat services.

The 2-day trip down the Mekong to **Luang Prabang** is a Southeast Asian rite of passage. The slow boat to **Pakbeng** is raved about by

many travellers. However, in peak season it can be packed. Bring something soft to sit on, a good book to read and a packed lunch. If you can get enough people together you can charter your own boat – ask for advice at the tourist office as they may be able to arrange it much more cheaply than if you go direct. The trip in reverse usually has fewer passengers.

For a luxury option there is the lovely **Luangsay Cruise**, T084-212092, www.luangsay.com, opposite Lao immigration, which makes a 2-day/1-night cruise down the river in comfort with cushioned deckchairs, a bar, wooden interior, and plenty of food. Stops are made to visit riverside villages. Guests stay at the beautiful **Luangsay Lodge** in Pakbeng. Accommodation and meals are included.

Speedboats are a noisy, dangerous alternative to the slow boats.

Bus/truck/songthaew
The bus station is at the Morning Market, 3 km out of central Houei Xai. Trucks, buses and minivans run to **Vieng Phouka**, 5 hrs; **Luang Namtha**, 7 hrs; **Udomxai**, 12 hrs; **Luang Prabang**, 12 hrs; and **Vientiane**, 20 hrs.

To Thailand There is a Friendship Bridge 10 km south of Houei Xai which crosses to Chiang Khong in Thailand. To reach the bridge, take a tuk-tuk to the Laos immigration office from where a shuttle bus will deliver you to the Thai immigration office on the other side. Thai immigration is open daily 0800-1800. A 1-month Thai visa is available at the border. Buses and taxis travel from Chiang Kong to Chiang Rai Airport where there are connections to Bangkok. From Chaing Khong there are regular buses to Chiang Rai, 0600-1700, and Chiang Mai, 0630. Crossing into Laos, immigration is open daily 0730-1730, but expect to pay a small overtime fee at the weekend or after 1600. Tourist visas (30 days) are available at the border. There is also a bank at the Lao border (daily 0830-1600).

Pakbeng

Boat

Times and prices are always changing so it's best to check before you travel. There is a slow boat to **Houei Xai** and **Luang Prabang**. You can also take a boat downriver to **Tha Suang**, 2 hrs and then catch a *songthaew* from here to **Hongsa** or arrange a private pickup through the **Jumbo Guesthouse** in Hongsa, see Where to stay.

Bus/truck/songthaew

Buses and *songthaew* leave about 2 km from town in the morning for the route north to **Udomxai**, 6-7 hrs. Direct *songthaew* to Udomxai are few and far between, so take one to Muang Houn and then catch a more frequent service from there. The road to Udomxai passes through spectacular scenery.

Xieng Khouang
Province

Apart from the historic Plain of Jars, Xieng Khouang Province is best known for the pounding it took during the war. Many of the sights are battered monuments to the plateau's violent recent history. Given the time it takes to make the return trip and the fact that the jars themselves aren't as visually arresting as some sights in Laos, many travellers consider the destination a stretch too far. However, for those interested in modern history and seeing some of the country's less visited areas, it's one of the most fascinating areas of Laos and gives a real insight into the resilient nature of the Lao people. The countryside, particularly towards the Vietnam border, is very beautiful – among the country's best – and the jars, too, are interesting by dint of their very oddness and the mystery that surrounds them. In the late afternoon light the sight of them spread out across the rolling landscape is nothing less than other-worldly.

⭐Phonsavanh is the main town of the province today – old Xieng Khouang having been flattened – and its small airstrip is a crucial transport link in this mountainous region. Surrounding the town are huge mountains, among them Phu Bia, one of the country's highest. The town itself is notable mainly for its ugliness. It was established in the mid-1970s and sprawls out from a heartless centre with no sense of plan or direction. While Phonsavanh will win no beauty contests, it does have a rather attractive 'Wild West' atmosphere.

South of Phonsavanh, on two small hills, a pair of white and gold monuments can be seen. (The road to the memorials is marked Ban Yone Temple.) It is worth the short hike up, if only for the views they afford of the surrounding countryside.

The **Vietnamese war memorial**, on the west side, was built to commemorate the death of over one million Vietnamese troops during the war against the anti-Communists. It contains the bones of Vietnamese soldiers and is inscribed 'Lao Vietnamese Solidarity Forever'. It is the more interesting of the two for its golden socialist statues in strident pose and socialist murals in relief.

The UK-based **Mines Advisory Group (MAG) UXO Visitor Information Centre** ① *on the main road in the centre of town, Mon-Fri 0800-2000, Sat-Sun 1600-2000*, is currently engaged in clearing the land of Unexploded Ordnance. It has an exhibition of bombs, interesting photographs and information on the bombing campaign and ongoing plight of Laos with UXO. Usually there are members of staff on hand to explain exactly how the bombs were used. All T-shirts sold here help fund the UXO clearance of the area and are a very worthwhile souvenir.

Opposite the MAG centre is the **Xieng Khuang UXO Survivors Center** ① *www.laos.worlded.org, daily 0900-2100*, detailing the work of World Education Laos in preventing UXO accidents and aiding UXO survivors.

Just before the bus station on the way into town is **Mulberries** ① *Route 7, T020-5552 1408, www.mulberries.org, tours Mon-Sat 0800-1600*, where you can visit a silk farm, see the sericulture process in action and buy a wide range of exquisite silk goods in the shop.

Essential Xienh Khouang Province

Finding your feet

The region's main town is Phonsavanh, which has an airport and is a good base from which to explore the surrounding area. The most direct route by road from Luang Prabang to Xieng Khouang Province is to take Route 13 south to Muang Phou Khoun and then Route 7 east. You might want to take travel sickness tablets as it's quite a bumpy trip. An alternative, scenic, albeit convoluted, route is via Nong Khiaw (see page 376), from where there are pickups to Pak Xeng and Phonsavanh via Vieng Thong on Route 1 or Nam Nouan. Public transport throughout the province is limited and sporadic. A car with driver is the easiest way of touring the area.

When to go

It is cold at higher elevation, such as Phonsavanh, from November to March. Several jumpers and a thick jacket are required.

BACKGROUND

Xieng Khouang Province

Xieng Khouang Province has had a murky, blood-tinted, war-ravaged history. The area was the most bombed province in the most bombed country, per capita, in the world, as it became a crucial strategic zone that both the US and Vietnamese wanted to control. The town of Phonsavanh has long been an important transit point between China to the north, Vietnam to the east and Thailand to the south and this status historically made the town a target for neighbouring countries. What's more, the plateau of the Plain of Jars is one of the flattest areas in northern Laos, rendering it a natural battleground for the numerous conflicts that ensued from the 19th century to 1975. As a result, the region holds immense appeal for those interested in the modern history of the country.

Today, hundreds of thousands of bomblets – and equally lethal impact mines, which the Lao call *bombis* – remain buried in Xieng Khouang's grassy meadows. Because the war was 'secret', there are few records of what was dropped where, and even when the unexploded ordnance (UXO) has been uncovered their workings are often a mystery – the Americans used Laos as a testing ground for new ordnance so blueprints are unavailable.

Uncle Sam has, however, bequeathed to local people an almost unlimited supply of twisted metal. Bombshells and flare casings can frequently be seen in Xieng Khouang's villages where they are used for everything from cattle troughs and fences, to stilts for houses and water-carriers. In Phonsavanh steel runway sheets make handy walls, while plants are potted out in shell casings.

Xieng Khouang remains one of the poorest provinces in an already wretchedly poor country. The whole province has a population of only around 250,000, a mix of different ethnic groups, predominantly Hmong, Lao and a handful of Khmu. Government attempts to curtail shifting cultivation and encourage the Hmong to settle have not been very successful, largely because there are no alternative livelihoods available. Travelling through the province there is a sense not just that the American air war caused enormous suffering and destruction, but that the following decades have not provided much in the way of economic opportunities.

Listings Phonsavanh

Tourist information

Xieng Khouang Provincial Tourism *Department, 2 km from the town centre, signposted, T061-312217, xkgtourism@yahoo.com.* Some members of staff speak a bit of English. As well as having the largest collection of bomb paraphernalia in town, the office has interesting displays and can provide useful leaflets, as well as up-to-date bus timetables.

Where to stay

$$ The Hillside Residence (aka Nearn Phou) *On the track to the Vansana Resort, T061-213300, www.the-hillside-residence.com.*

Family-run guesthouse. Rooms are decorated with textiles and some offer great views. The 1st-floor balcony is a great place to kick back and the restaurant is reasonable. A nice option.

$$ Maly Hotel
Down the road from local government offices, T061-312031.
All rooms have hot water and are furnished with a hotchpotch of local artefacts, including a small cluster bomb casing on the table. The more expensive, much larger rooms on the upper floors have satellite TV, out-of-place baths in large bathrooms, a sitting area, fireplace and hairdryers. There is also a restaurant and tour desk. The former owner spent his teenage years in a cave at Xam Neua.

$$ Vansana Resort
On a hill about 1 km out of town, T061-213170, www.vansanahotel-group.com.
Rather dated, but offers big rooms equipped with telephone, TV, minibar, and tea/coffee-making facilities, and has good views of the countryside. The best room is the smart suite with polished wooden floors and textile decoration, or opt for one of the rooms upstairs, which have free-form bathtubs and picturesque balcony views. The restaurant offers Lao and international cuisine.

$ Nice Guesthouse
On the main road, T020-5561 6246, naibhoj@hotmail.com.
Clean, decent-sized rooms with hot water and comfortable beds. Offers reasonable value and friendly service.

Restaurants

$$-$ Craters
Main street, T020-7780 5775.
Modern, Western-style restaurant offering range of burgers, pizza and sandwiches. Comfortable cane sofas, good music, attentive service. Also has delectable but pricey cocktails.

$ Bamboozle! Restaurant and Bar
Main street opposite Nice Hotel, T020-779 928 959.
A top choice for Lao or Western fair in a good atmosphere. Along with **Craters**, this is one of the most ocular options in town.

$ Nisha Indian
Main street.
Great Indian restaurants can be found in the oddest of place in Laos, and this is no exception. A very good choice of north and south Indian food. The service can be rather slow, but the wait is worth it.

$ Simmaly
Main street, T061-211013.
What this place lacks in atmosphere it makes up tenfold with food. Great service and massive portions.

Shopping

There are a multitude of shops at the town's market. The dry market is beside the town bus station and sells a good selection of local handicrafts including textiles and silver. Most everyday items, from shoes to biscuits can also be purchased here. West of the centre of town is the Chinese market, which stocks a good variety of ethnic clothes and jewellery as well as lots of cheap tacky imported products. Behind the post office is a fresh produce market with a gamut of fruit and vegetables on offer. The Navang Craft Center, behind the new hilltop Phou Vieng Kham hotel, daily 0730-2000, specializes in crafts made of Fijian cypress wood. Silk goods are sold at Mulberries, see page 398, a silk farm on the outskirts of Phonsavanh.

Festivals

Dec National Day on 2 Dec is celebrated with horse-drawn drag-cart racing. Also in Dec is **Hmong New Year** (movable), which is celebrated in a big way in this area. Festivities centre on the killing of a pig and then offering the head to the spirits. Boys give cloth balls, known as *makoi*, to girls they've taken a fancy to.

What to do

Tour operators
There is no shortage of tour operators in Phonsavanh and most guesthouses can also arrange tours and transport. Most of the travel agencies are located within a block of each other on the main road.

Indochina Travel, *on the main road, T061-312409, www.indochinatravelco.com*. This is a comparatively expensive but well-regarded company offering minivan tours. It works out a lot cheaper if you can organize a group.

Transport

Air
Xienh Khouang Airport is 4 km from Phonsavanh. **Lao Airlines**, T061-312027 (airport T061-312177), runs flights to **Vientiane**, daily; check www.laoairlines.com for current schedules.

Bus
The bus station is 4 km west of Phonsavanh on Route 7, T030-517 0148; a tuk-tuk to/from the centre costs 10,000 kip. From the main bus station outside of town (T030-517 0148): to **Luang Prabang**, 8 hrs; **Vientiane**, 6 daily, 9-10 hrs, also a VIP bus (with a/c and TV) daily; **Vang Vieng**, 6 VIP buses daily, 14 hrs; and **Xam Neua**, daily, 10 hrs. Buses also travel to **Vinh** (Vietnam), 10 hrs, and **Hanoi**, 18 hrs.

Buses leave from the new market (T061-312178): to **Muang Kham**, 1 hr.

Buses from the Namngam market (near the tourist office, T020-5587 5207): to **Muang Khoun**, 45 mins; and **Nam Nouan**, 4 hrs (change here for transport west to **Nong Khiaw**).

Car with driver/songthaew
Hiring a car with driver is the easiest way of touring the area. A full car to the **Plain of Jars** will could be combined with a trip to the hot springs, west of Muang Kham.

Motorbike
Happy Motorbike for Rent (next to Craters), rents motorbike and also bicycles.

⭐The undulating plateau of the Plain of Jars (also known as Plaine de Jarres, or **Thong Hai Hin**), stretches for about 50 km east to west, covering an area of 1000 sq km at an altitude of 1000 m. In total there are 136 archaeological sites in this area, containing thousands of jars, discs and deliberately placed stones. Of these only three are currently open to tourists. Note that the plateau can be cold from December to March.

Tip...

Due to unexploded ordnance, visitors are strongly advised to stay within the boundaries of the MAG marker bricks.

It is recommended that you hire a guide, for at least a day, to get an insight into the history of the area and take you around the jar sites. There are many places in Phonsavanh offering tours of the jars and it is possible to either join together with a group or pay extra for your own private tour – the latter is recommended if you want to see everything at your own pace.

Site One

Some 334 jars survive, mainly scattered on one slope at so-called 'Site One' or **Thong Hai Hin**, 10 km southwest of Phonsavanh. This site is closest to Phonsavanh and has the largest jar – along with a small café. A path, cleared by MAG, winds through the

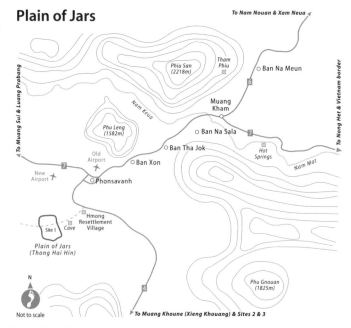

Plain of Jars

To Nam Nouan & Xam Neua

To Muang Sui & Luang Prabang

To Nong Het & Vietnam border

Phiu San (2218m)

Tham Phiu

Ban Na Meun

Nam Keua

Muang Kham

Phu Leng (1582m)

Ban Na Sala

Ban Tha Jok

Hot Springs

Nam Mot

Old Airport

Ban Xon

New Airport

Phonsavanh

Hmong Resettlement Village

Cave

Site 1

Plain of Jars (Thong Hai Hin)

Phu Gnouan (1825m)

N

Not to scale

To Muang Khoune (Xieng Khouang) & Sites 2 & 3

BACKGROUND
Plain of Jars

Most of the jars are between 1 m and 2.5 m high, around 1 m in diameter and weigh about the same as three small cars. The largest are about 3 m tall. The jars have long presented an archaeological conundrum, leaving generations of theorists nonplussed by how they got there and what they were used for. Local legend relates that King Khoon Chuong and his troops from southern China threw a stupendous party after their victory over the wicked Chao Angka and had the jars made to brew outrageous quantities of *lao lao*. However attractive this alcoholic thesis, it is more likely that the jars are in fact 2000-year-old funeral urns. The larger jars are believed to have been for the local aristocracy and the smaller jars for their minions.

site, with a warning not to walk away from delineated areas as UXO are still around. There are also information boards on UXO in the area. Each of the jars weighs about a tonne, although the biggest, called **Hai Cheaum**, is over 2 m tall and weighs over six tonnes. Folklore suggests that the jar is named after a Thai-Lao liberator, who overthrew Chao Angka. Further downhill is another smattering of jars, some of which feature carvings. The smallish cave in the hill to the left was used by the Pathet Lao as a hideout during the war and may have been the ancient kiln in which the jars were fired (see box, above). People leave cigarettes burning here in memory of those who lost their lives and it can be quite a poignant experience to visit it.

Site Two
True jar lovers should visit Site Two, known as **Hai Hin Phu Salatao** (literally 'Salato Hill Stone Jar Site'), and Site Three (see below). Site Two is 25 km south of Phonsavanh and features 90 jars spread across two hills. The jars are set in a rather beautiful location, affording scenic 360-degree views over the surrounding countryside. Most people miss this site, but it is in fact the most atmospheric because of the hilltop location. On the second hill, trees have grown through the centre of the jars, splitting them four ways; butterflies abound here.

Site Three
A further 10 km south of Site Two, Site Three, also called **Hai Hin Laat Khai**, is the most peaceful of all the sites, set in verdant green rolling hills, Swiss-cheesed with bomb craters.

To get to the site you have to walk through some rice paddies, past a burbling brook and cross the small bamboo bridge. There are more than 130 jars at this site, which are generally smaller and more damaged than at the other sites. There's also a very small, basic restaurant here, serving *feu*.

Close by is **Ban Xieng Dee**, a friendly village, home to a monastery featuring some Buddha images, which were badly damaged during the war. Villagers will lead treks to the nearby **Lang waterfall**.

Tip...

If you have time, try to visit at least two of the sites. Site One has the largest concentration of jars, as well as the biggest, but also sees the most visitors; Site Two spread is spread over two hills and has great views; Site Three is the most peaceful site, atop a small hill with views of farmland and villages.

Hua Phan
Province

Hua Phan Province is one of the most isolated areas of the country. More than 20 ethnic groups, mostly mountain-dwellers, inhabit the province.

Hua Phan is spectacularly beautiful but largely overlooked by tourists. Local authorities hope that the area's large tourism potential will help to alleviate poverty here and they have teamed up with NGOs to develop tourism infrastructure. The Nam Nern Night Safari in the Nam Et-Phou Louey National Protected Area is one of the very best tours in the country and together with the US-Based Wildlife Conservation Trust, the local authorities are looking to open more tours to the area. The recently opened Indochina War Airbase, known as Lima Site 36, looks set to attract those who are interested in the country's recent history.

★The village of Vieng Xai lies 31 km east of Xam Neua on a road that branches off Route 6 at Km 20. The trip from Xam Neua is possibly one of the country's most picturesque journeys, passing terraces of rice, pagodas, copper- and charcoal-coloured karst formations, dense jungle with misty peaks and friendly villages dotted among the mountains' curves.

The village area is characterized by lush tropical gardens, a couple of smallish lakes and spectacular limestone karsts, riddled with natural caves that proved crucial in the success of the left-wing insurgency in the 1960s and 1970s.

Although it takes only one day to see the caves, it is worth spending some more time exploring the area and at least staying overnight. The valley contains many other poignant reminders of the struggle, although the war debris is less obvious here than in Xieng Khouang.

Visiting the caves
There are six main caves open to visitors, five of which were formerly occupied by senior Pathet Lao leaders (Prince Souphanouvong, Kaysone Phomvihan, Nouhak Phounsavanh, Khamtai Siphandon and Phoumi Vongvichit). The sixth cave is the hospital cave. The caves have a secretive atmosphere, with fruit trees and frangipani decorating the exteriors. Each one burrows deep into the mountainside and features 60-cm-thick concrete walls, encompassing living quarters, meeting rooms, offices, dining and storage areas.

All the caves are within walking distance of the village, but it is best to cycle. Tickets are sold at the **Vieng Xai Caves Visitor Centre** ⓘ *on the edge of town, signposted, T064-314321, daily 0800-1200 and 1300-1600; guided tours are conducted in English at 0900 and 1300, with compulsory guide.* If you arrive outside of these hours, you can pay extra for your own tour. Tours last between three and four hours and are usually conducted by bicycle, which can be rented from the office.

A new set of excellent 90-minute audio tours, including personal memories of local people, has been launched. A taster can be heard on www.visit-viengxay.com. The visitor centre has historical information, photographs and Communist gifts on display.

Tham Souphanouvong
Off the small roads that head out of town towards the caves, is a mossy path flanked by large grapefruit trees which leads to Tham Souphanouvong. This cave was home to Prince Souphanouvong, the 'Red Prince' and son of the Queen of Luang Prabang. To the right of the path stands a pink stupa, the tomb of the prince's son, who was beaten to death with a hammer by infiltrators a few kilometres away in 1967, at the age of 28. Souphanouvong's stunning garden, bursting with a rainbow of flowers and dripping with fruit, was planted in 1973-1974 and is a memorial to his son and a metaphor for the war. An old bomb crater has been ingeniously concreted into a pool, referred to as the broken heart; a head, shoulders and neck have been landscaped around the heart. The whole area is surrounded by a sea of red plants, to symbolize all the blood lost during the war. Be careful near the far entrance of the cave as

> **Tip...**
>
> Most visitors make a day trip to see the caves, but this is a great shame, for Vieng Xai is a wonderful place for an early morning bike ride and to watch the sun go down over the karst scenery.

occasionally rocks have fallen. Souphanouvong and Phoumi's caves both feature a 'garage cave' at the base of the karst, a cavity in the limestone large enough to accommodate a car.

Tham Kaysone Phomvihane

Kaysone Phomvihane's cave is reached by mossy steps cut into the cliff face and is over 100 m long. The cavern is surrounded by blossoming bushes and large frangipani trees. Like the other caves here, it has a suite of rooms, including a bedroom, meeting room and library. A few of Kaysone's books are on display; it's no surprise that the collection includes Lenin, Marx, Engels, Ho Chi Minh and an economic text from Vietnam. Also on display are a few gifts from foreign dignitaries, including a lacquer-ware vase from Vietnam and a bust of Lenin (a framed picture of Che Guevara given to Kaysone by Fidel Castro has been removed due to water damage).

The cave's construction started some time prior to 1963 but Kaysone and Co moved in in 1974. Kaysone rarely left the cave and allowed only the most important of visitors inside, mostly other Communist leaders. About 10 people lived in the cave: Kaysone, his children, a doctor, intelligence officer, cook and bodyguards. At the start of the war Kaysone's wife relocated to Yunnan, China, where she was head of a school. These days she lives in Vientiane. The Americans knew of Kaysone's whereabouts but were unable to attack the cave directly or infiltrate it, due to its position and to the large numbers of Pathet Lao soldiers that were mounted on the summit. The cave remained Kaysone's official residence until 1973, when he relocated to the building in front of the cave. In 1975 he left the cave and moved to Vientiane.

An interesting feature of Kaysone's cave is a long, narrow passage which connects the living quarters to a large meeting area which includes emergency accommodation for dozens of guests.

Tham Than Khamtai Siphandon

Khamtai Siphandone's cave, the former military headquarters, is slightly different from the others. The first thing you'll notice is a set of three bomb craters within metres of the entrance to the cave. The craters, now overgrown, are so close together they almost touch. Possibly inspired by their arrival, the entrance is shielded by an enormous, tapering slab of concrete, 4.5 m high and nearly 2 m wide at the base. Inside, the cave is darker and more claustrophobic than the others, with no outside areas. The attendant may or may not lead you through a thick steel door at the bottom of some stairs well inside the cave. It gives access to a staircase which descends steeply before ending in a sheer drop of several metres, and connects to a number of military caves including the army administration. There is a longish tunnel which connects to **Tham Xang Lot** (Elephant Cave) but this is sometimes inaccessible.

Tham Xang Lot

A small distance from Khamtai's cave and included in its entry price, is the large and obvious entrance to what is known as Tham Xang Lot, or 'cave that an elephant can walk through'. Once used as an enclosure to keep animals such as elephants and monkeys, during the war this natural cavern was also used as a theatre, complete with stage, arch, orchestra pit and a concrete floor with space for an audience of several hundred. At the opposite end from the stage, a long passage featuring a number of stalactites and lit by daylight connects to the theatrette below Khamtai's cave. It is hard to imagine now, but this damp, dark area once entertained numerous dancers, symphonies, circuses and foreign dignitaries from Romania, Bulgaria, Vietnam and China. As one local recalls: "I snuck in for a look and an orchestra was playing. I got so excited but was trying to contain myself because I was worried that the grenade in my pocket would go off." At times up to 2000 soldiers were hidden in the two caves.

Other caves
The **Artillery Cave**, set halfway up a hillside, offers phenomenal views. The cave was a military installation purposefully set up to conceal fighters who would return fire during US bombing raids. **Phoumi Vongvichid's Cave**, home to the former Minister of Education and Public Health, also houses the enclosure of Sithon Kommadam, of the Lao Theung minority, who was reputedly immune to bullets. **Nouhak Phoumsavan's Cave** has been recently opened to the public. The cave was home to the former President of Laos.

Vieng Xai village
The village itself was built in 1973, when the bombing finally stopped and the short-lived Provisional Government of National Union was negotiated. Today the former capital of the liberated zone is an unlikely sight: surrounded by rice fields at the dead end of a potholed road, it features street lighting, power lines, sealed and kerbed streets and substantial public buildings. Nonetheless it is truly one of the most beautiful towns in Laos. The 'Garden of Eden'-type village is dotted with fruit trees and hibiscus and is flanked by amazing karst formations and dotted with man-made lakes (reputedly formed from bomb craters).

Just before the market and truck stop, a wonderful socialist-realist statue in gold-painted concrete pays tribute to those three pillars of the revolution: the farmer, the soldier and the worker; the worker has one boot firmly planted on a bomb inscribed 'USA'.

The police station is situated just behind the disused department store on the town square. ATMs located near the market. The small hospital is on the main road into town.

Around Vieng Xai
There is a spectacular **waterfall** and another cave site, 8 km before Vieng Xai. About 3 km after the turn-off from Route 6, a swift stream passes under a steel and concrete bridge. A path just before the bridge leads off to the left, following the river downstream. It takes just a few minutes to reach the top of the waterfall, but the path leads all the way to the bottom, about 20 minutes' walk. Swimming is not advised.

Listings Vieng Xai (Viengsay)

Where to stay

$ Naxay Guesthouse
Close to Prince Souphanouvong's cave,
T064-314336.
Now re-built, these are large, smart bungalows, well located for visiting the caves.

$ Naxay Guesthouse 2
Opposite Vieng Xai Cave Visitor Centre,
T064-314336.
The best option with 11 clean if a little aged bungalows with warm showers, comfortable

beds and Western-style toilet, set in a leafy compound. If nobody is there when you arrive, try around the corner at **Naxay Guesthouse** where the staff are normally found. Recommended.

$ Say Mon Yen/Xailomyen Guesthouse
By the lake, T030-516 1399.
13 small somewhat tired rooms over the lake with tiny bathrooms. There are lovely views from the vast restaurant which may or may not be serving food.

Restaurants

There are a few basic food stalls scattered around town offering noodle soup, *larb khoai* (buffalo) or *larb ngoa* (beef). Several of the guesthouses have restaurants, including **Xailomyen,** which does a range of fish, pork, noodle and egg dishes and also offers a lovely view over the lake. A very tasty *pho* is served at an outdoor joint complete with *pétanque* pitch about 100 m north of the school – look for orange and blue chairs and the *pétanque* area.

$ Nha Hang Viet
Just down the road from Sabaidee, T064-5550 9874.
This basic Vietnamese joint serves up fairly average food including fried rice, fried beef and stir fried morning glory.

$ Sabaidee Restaurant
On the corner by the market, T064-5557 7202.
Run by the very affable Prakash since 2012, this Indian and Lao restaurant offers excellent Indian dishes and also some Lao staples. Highlights include the *masala papad*, 'chilly' chicken and a sublime *brinjal bharta*. Be prepared for a long wait for the Indian dishes however, as everything is prepared fresh. Also rents bicycles. Recommended.

Transport

Pickups and passenger trucks leave from in front of the market in Vieng Xai to **Xam Neua** throughout the day, but the service is haphazard. You may be able to charter your own truck – ask at the Indian restaurant, **Sabaidee,** for help. A taxi from to Xam Neua will cost around 150,000 kip.

To Vietnam To catch the bus to the border, wait at the main road and cross your fingers that there is a seat free. For details of the border crossing with Vietnam, see box, page 544.

West on Route 1

few sights as such, but abundant natural beauty

Vieng Thong (aka Muang Hiam)
Vieng Thong, also known as Muang Hiam, lies 158 km west of Xam Neua on Route 1 and is a reasonable stopover for those journeying to or from Nong Khiaw. The town itself has little to offer but the surrounding countryside is nothing short of spectacular. The Nam Khan River flows through the town, straight from Luang Prabang, so it's a shame no tour operators have yet capitalized on what could be an amazing journey between the two areas.

Vieng Thong Tourist Information Office ⓘ *opposite the bus station*, can book accommodation and arrange a guide for the Nakout Historical Area. There is a bank next to **Heungkhamxay guesthouse** which has an ATM and money exchange service.

Nam Et-Phou Louey National Protected Area
Just 10 km beyond Vieng Thong is Laos' largest protected area, the Nam Et-Phou Louey National Protected Area. Camera trap studies conducted in recent years by the Wildlife Conservation Society have discovered a vast array of large mammals here, including tiger, guar, bear, leopard, macaque, wild pig and deer.

★**Nam Nern Night Safari** The Nam Nern Night Safari was set up by the Wildlife Conservation Society together with the local authorities in 2012 and has since won awards for its responsible tourism model and been featured in the *New York Times* Top 52 things to do in 2014. It is one of the top two-day experiences available in Laos.

ON THE ROAD

The Indochina War base Lima Site 26

Until 2014 this former secret airbase was off-limits to tourists and many maps did not show the road leading to it. However, it has been opened up in the hope of bringing more people to this little visited part of Laos.

The French first used the wide Nakhang Valley to construct an airstrip during the First Indochina War, but it was during the Second Indochina War (Vietnam War) that the site saw most of the action when it functioned as an important support centre for the Royal Lao Government (RLG) supported by the USA and Hmong paramilitaries – also referred to as the 'Secret Army'.

The base was known by the Americans as Lima Site 36 and it was used by the CIA's Air America for its covert operations to attack Pathet Lao controlled areas in the northern provinces, particularly Hou Panh. After continuous attacks during February 1969 which weakened defences, North Vietnamese forces approached the base from a completely unanticipated direction that caught the defenders by surprise, and on 1 March 1969, the base was captured.

Evidence of the former military base can still be found. The airstrip is still clearly visible, and around it there are three 10,000-litre fuel tanks and the remains of road work equipment. Further north, hidden in the overgrowth, a shell launcher is located. The area is highly contaminated with UXO, including land mines and stocks of ammunition that were not destroyed, and unexploded ordnance left over from the shelling of the site and ground battles.

Visiting Lima Site 26

It is now possible to stay in the fascinating village of Ban Nakout where the locals have constructed a simple but comfortable village lodge. Ban Nakout was established in 1865 when seven families moved there from Xieng Khouang. The village is 100% Tai Phuan and practises Buddhism.

In 1964, when the Nakhang area became an important military base, the villagers abandoned their homes and hid in the forest. When they returned they rebuilt their village using leftovers from the war, including oil drums and bomb shells. Tours can be booked via the tourism office in Vieng Thong (see opposite page).

It begins in the small village of Son Loua (aka Nam Nerm 2) which is most easily reached from Vieng Thong. After learning about the endangered wildlife in the Nam Et-Phou Louey National Protected Area and the efforts being made to stop illegal poaching, visitors are taken up the Nam Nern River in a long-tail boat. When the river is higher in October and November this river journey is quite exciting in itself, thanks to the rapids the boat is expertly guided over. Along the way there is an abundance of birdlife, including eagles and kingfishers.

After lunch at the base camp, the boat forges further upstream to a salt lick where you may spot animals such as deer. After collecting firewood and local plants to cook with dinner, visitors dine on the bank of the river next to a roaring fire.

The boat is then guided downstream with the engines cut, as the guides use head torches to point out wildlife such as sambar deer, slow loris and monitor lizards. Floating silently downstream in the pitch darkness is an unbeatable experience.

The next morning a tour of the base camp village precedes breakfast which is followed by a final thrilling journey back to the village to end the trip.

Back on dry land guests fill out a form detailing the wildlife seen; this relates directly to the bonus the participating villages will receive from the tour. The theory is that by paying more depending on the volume of wildlife seen, poaching will decrease and wildlife populations will begin to build.

Many local agents, including **Tiger Trail**, **Buffalo Tours** and **Green Discovery**, can book this tour (see Tour operators, page 374), or it can be booked direct in Vieng Thong at the NPA visitor centre or the tourist office by the bus station. Full details at www.namet.org.

Listings West on Route 1

Where to stay

Vieng Thong

$ Dokkhoun Guesthouse
Right next to Heungkhamxay, T064-810017.
Offers a similar level of accommodation to **Heungkhamxay**. Good quality for the price and well located.

$ Heungkhamxay Guesthouse
Near the market, T064-810033.
Basic, but clean en suite rooms and a strong internet connection. The owners have limited English but are very welcoming.

Restaurants

Vieng Thong
The small places around the bus station serve sticky rice and various dishes which you can peruse and order by the plate, including vegetables, beef and chicken.

$ Nha Hang 669
Opposite Heungkhamxay guesthouse near the market.
This is a ramshackle noodle and rice shop run by a Vietnamese woman. Serves reasonable fried beef in the evening and a good beef noodle soup in the morning.

$ Tontavenh
Opposite the market, T020-5557 9975.
Serves Lao food and is popular with the few tourists that come through town.

> **Tip...**
>
> For drinks and a light meal with a view, head to the bar down the track at the end of the bridge as you enter town. It's run by a very welcoming husband and wife team and offers a great vista overlooking the paddy fields and ice cold beers.

Transport

Vieng Thong
The bus station is on the road opposite the market. It is home to 3 or 4 small eateries where basic Lao food can be found. Buses leave from here for **Xam Neua**, 5-6 hrs; **Nong Khiaw**, 5 hrs, and **Luang Prabang**, 8-9 hrs.

The routes in both directions out of town are classic northern Laos, with seemingly no flat or straight sections as the road undulates through fantastic scenery. Try and bag a window seat and enjoy the fine vistas.

Central Laos

some of the country's best scenery, without the crowds

Laos' central provinces, sandwiched between the Mekong (and Thailand) to the west and the Annamite Mountains (and Vietnam) to the east, are some of the least visited in the country.

Travellers entering Laos from Vietnam cross the border via Lak Xao or Xepon but few choose to linger. This is a shame because the scenery here is stunning, with dramatic limestone karsts, enormous caves, beautiful rivers and forests. In particular, the upland areas to the east, off Route 8 and Route 12, are a veritable treasure trove of attractions, mottled with scores of caves, lagoons, rivers and unusual rock formations.

Tourists will require some degree of determination to explore this part of the country, as the infrastructure is still being developed, but it is far better than it was just a few years ago.

The Mekong towns of Thakhek and Savannakhet are also elegant and relaxed. If you are short on time, Thakhek is the best stopover point for the central provinces, and there is also some fantastic rock climbing nearby.

Best for
Caves ▪ Rock climbing ▪ Wilderness

Footprint picks

★ **Boat trip through Kong Lor Cave**, page 416

Float along the Nam Hinboun River as it travels through this awe-inspiring cave.

★ **The limestone caves off Route 12**, page 422

Explore underground caverns in the limestone landscape, especially the beautiful Buddha Cave.

★ **Savannakhet**, page 426

Enjoy the town's crumbling colonial charm, great local food and relaxed Mekong riverfront.

★ **Song Sa Kae sacred forest**, page 431

Trek to the sacred forest and cemetery within Dong Phou Vieng National Protected Area.

Footprint picks

1 **Boat trip through Kong Lor Cave**, page 416
2 **The limestone caves off Route 12**, page 422
3 **Savannakhet**, page 426
4 **Song Sa Kae sacred forest**, page 431

Paksan to
Lak Xao

East of Paksan adventurous visitors will encounter some of the county's most stunning landscapes. This region contains a maze of limestone karst peaks, studded with thousands of caves, and a beautiful river flanked by pristine jungle. The magical Kong Lor Cave, a river cave running straight through the centre of a mountain for 6 km and the principal tourist attraction in the region, could be straight out of *Lord of the Rings*.

East on Route 8

a colossal cave amid some of Laos' most stunning scenery

Ban Na Hin (Ban Khoun Kham)

Ban Na Hin, also known as Khoun Kham ('Gateway to Kong Lor') is a real end-of-the-earth town, low on charm but redeemed by the phenomenal landscapes surrounding it. Its two raisons d'être are as a transit point for Nam Theun II dam operations and for visitors to Kong Lor cave to the south. Ban Na Hin has quite a large market where you can buy fresh fruit and vegetables, bread and other supplies; if you haven't got a torch, it's a good idea to pick one up here. There are also a few cheap *feu* shops dotted around the market's periphery.

There isn't a whole lot more here but just outside of town is **Namsanam waterfall**. Take the signposted path on the left-hand side of Route 8, beside a colourful monastery. The trek to the falls is roughly 3 km through pleasant countryside. The two-tiered, 70-m-tall falls are magnificent and flow year round. There are reputed to be wild elephants in the area around the falls but the likelihood of seeing one is very slim. The provincial tourism office has built an **information centre** on Route 8, just before the turn-off to the waterfall. Apparently local guides do exist but you will probably find the waterfall before you find a guide.

Towards Tham Kong Lor

From Ban Na Hin it is possible to travel to Tham Kong Lor by boat or by road; both journeys pass through stunning scenery.

The boat trip starts in **Ban Napur**, a couple of kilometres south of Ban Na Hin, and runs along the Nam Hinboun River to either **Ban Phonyang**, where ecolodge Sala Hin Boun is located (see Where to stay, opposite) or to **Ban Kong Lor**, the closest village to the caves, where you can find a homestay and the new Sala Kong Lor Lodge (see page 417).

Route 13 is the main north–south road which hugs the Mekong and the border with Thailand, south of Vientiane. The other main highway in this region is Route 8, which runs from Ban Lao to the Vietnamese border at Nam Phao, (see box, page 545, for details) passing through the dramatic karst scenery of the Annamite Mountains. Daily buses from Vientiane ply this route. Paksan is the main town and transport hub with buses passing through every couple of hours.

Best place to stay

Sainamhai Resort, Ban Na Hin, page 417

When to go

November to March is the cool, dry season, with visitor numbers peaking November/December when the rivers are high enough to make river travel easy but it is not too hot. The towns along the Mekong south of Vientiane receive less rain than other parts of the country. The Fireball Festival, at the Phonsane Temple in Paksan takes, place in October.

It's a fascinating journey with excellent views of impressive limestone cliffs along the way and classic riverside scenes with people fishing and bathing. Take some padding as the wooden seats, even if they are cushioned, can be uncomfortable. Beyond Ban Phonyang the river route to Tham Kong Lor is gorgeous, with small fish skipping out of the water, languid buffalo bathing, kids taking a dip and ducks floating by – all surrounded by a *Lord of the Rings* fantasyland of cliffs and rocky outcrops.

Ban Kong Lor can also be reached by pickup or *songthaew* from Ban Na Hin but the road sometimes gets flooded.

★ Tham Kong Lor (Kong Lor Cave)

Entrance fee at cave site 5000 kip; 100,000 kip to go through the cave (maximum 3 people per boat). See Towards Tham Kong Lor, above, and Transport, opposite page, for information on getting to Tham Kong Lor.

Tham Kong Lor is sensational and should not be missed. The Nam Hinboun River has tunnelled through the mountain, creating a giant rocky cavern, 6 km long, 90 m wide and 100 m high, which opens out into blinding bright light at Ban Natan on the other side. The cave is apparently named after the drum makers who were believed to craft their instruments here. It is also home to possibly the largest living cave-dwelling spider in the world, the giant huntsman, which has a leg span of 30 cm. However, it is unlikely you will have a run in with the massive arachnid as they are very rare. Fisherman will often come into the cave to try their luck as it is believed that 20-kg fish lurk below the surface.

At the start of the cave, you will have to scramble over some boulders while the boatmen carry the canoe over the rapids, so wear comfortable shoes with a good grip. A torch or, better still, a head-lamp, is also recommended. It is eerie travelling through the dark, cool cave, with water splashing and bats circulating. There are a few minuscule rapids inside and the cave's surface is riddled with nooks and crannies. About two-thirds of the way through the cave is an impressive collection of stalagmites and stalactites.

It is possible to continue from Ban Natan, on the other side of Kong Lor, into the awesome Hinboun gorge. This is roughly 14 km long and, for much of the distance, vertical cliffs over 300 m high rise directly from the water on both sides. The discovery of some valuable religious documents indicates the historical significance of the gorge both during the Vietnamese War and much earlier. There is no white water but the river frequently flows quite fast. More impressive scenery then follows until the village of **Paktuk**, close to Route 13 where any journey can be continued. ▸▸ *The cave can also be visited as part of the 400-km 'loop' from Thakhek, see page 424.*

▸▸ *The cave can also be visited as part of the 400-km 'loop' from Thakhek, see page 424.*

Listings East on Route 8

Where to stay

Ban Na Hin

$ Inthapanya Guesthouse
At the far end of the village.
This wooden built guesthouse has reasonable clean rooms, a/c and internet. A decent budget option.

$ Sainamhai Resort
4 km outside town, T020-2249 8989.
Set on the river next to a small village, this welcoming little resort offers accommodation set among beautiful gardens along the Namhai River. There are 8 well-kept bungalows with great views. Friendly staff run a very good restaurant on-site. This is a great place for families, with a play area and a *pétanque* pitch. Call the resort for free pick-up from Ban Na Hin. They can also arrange trips to Kong Lor Cave. Recommended.

Towards Tham Kong Lor

There are 2 guesthouses on Route 13 in Ban Lao, just past the Route 8 intersection, which are passable. Homestays are available in Ban Kong Lor and Ban Natan.

$$-$ Sala Hin Boun
Ban Phonyang, 10 km from Kong Lor Cave, T020-7775 5220, www.salalao.com.
The best option. It enjoys a scenic location on the riverbank amongst karst rock formations and has 10 well-equipped and very pleasant rooms in 2 bungalows. The manager will arrange for a boat to pick you up in Ban Na Hin (aka Ban Khoun Kham) advance notice.

A tour to Kong Lor for 2-3 people with picnic lunch can be arranged.

$$-$ Sala Kong Lor Lodge
1.5 km from Kong Lor Cave, near Ban Tiou, T020-7776 1846, www.salalao.com.
Lodge with 4 small huts with twin beds and several superior rooms.

Transport

Ban Na Hin
Bus/songthaew
There is a small transport terminus at the Route 13/Route 8 intersection in **Ban Lao** (also known as Tham Beng or Vieng Kham) for north–south buses between Vientiane and Thakhek, Savannakhet or Pakse. *Songthaew* generally pass through here from early in the morning to well into the afternoon to Ban Na Hin. This trip along Route 8 is about 60 km.

To get to **Kong Lor Cave** cave from Ban Na Hin, a pickup is usually on hand to take passengers as far as **Ban Kong Lor**, the closest village to the caves, from where it's possible to hire a boat to take you into the cave. There is also one public *songthaew* a day making the journey to Ban Kong Lor.

Boat
To **Kong Lor Cave**, boats run from **Ban Napur**, a couple of kilometres south of Ban Na Hin, to **Ban Phonyang**, 2-3 hrs, or **Ban Kong Lor** (closer to the cave), and onto the cave, a further 1 hr.

If you are staying at **Sala Hin Boun**, see Where to stay, they will send a boat to Ban Napur to collect you.

Thakhek
& around

Thakhek is sometimes translated as Indian (*khek* or *khaek*) Port (*tha*), although it probably means Guest (*khaek*) Port after the large number of people who settled here from the north. During the royalist period through to the mid-1970s it was a popular weekend destination for Thais who came here in droves to gamble. After the Communist victory, when Laos effectively shut up shop, everything went very quiet. The recent recovery of commercial traffic has brought some life back to this small settlement, though it remains a quiet town. The third Friendship Bridge to Thailand was completed here in 2011 making the town a major international border point.

Thakhek is the most popular stopover point in the central provinces, although it is still not considered a primary tourist destination. However, the region encompasses some of the most beautiful scenery in Laos: imposing jagged mountains, bottle-green rivers, lakes and caves. Tourism infrastructure is improving and a trip to this area will prove a highlight of most visitors' holidays to Laos, particularly the stunning karst scenery and impressive trip out to Buddha Cave, or the popular route known as the 'Loop' (see page 424). Rock climbing has also taken off here thanks to the opening of the Green Climber's Home. *Colour map 3, B2.*

Sights

There are few officially designated sights in Thakhek but many visitors consider it to be a gem of a settlement. Quiet and elegant, with some remaining Franco-Chinese architecture, including a simple fountain square, it has a fine collection of colonial-era shophouses, a breezy riverside position and a relaxed ambience. What locals regard as the central business district at the river end of **Kouvoravong Road** is wonderful for its faded elegance. Other visitors, in contrast, look more critically at the dusty streets, seeing pockets of squalor, dilapidated buildings and an uncharacteristic atmosphere of disinterest among the locals.

Thakhek is small enough to negotiate on foot or by bicycle. A number of places organize motorbike hire (see Transport, page 422). ▸▸ *For details of the town's three markets, see Shopping, page 421.*

That Sikhot
6 km south of Thakhek, daily 0800-1800, 5000 kip.

That Sikhot or **Sikhotaboun** is one of Laos' holiest sites. It overlooks the Mekong and the journey downstream from Thakhek, along a quiet country road, reveals bucolic Laos at its best. The *that* was restored in 1956 but is thought to have been built by Chao Anou at the beginning of the 15th century, around the same time as That Inheng in Savannakhet Province (see page 431). The *that* houses the relics of Chao Sikhot, a local hero, who founded the old town of Thakhek.

That Sikhot consists of a large gold stupa raised 29 m on a plinth, with a viharn upstream commissioned in 1970 by the last King of Laos.

Kong Leng lake
33 km northeast of Thakhek.

This stunning lake is usually incorporated into hikes as there isn't direct road access to the site. It is steeped in legend, for locals believe an underground kingdom lies beneath the surface. As a result, you must request permission to swim in this lake from the local village authority and you can swim only in the designated swimming zone. Fishing is not

Essential Thakhek and around

Finding your feet

It takes four to five hours to travel from Paksan to Thakek along the north–south Route 13. The other major road is Route 12 which heads east from Thakhek and connects with Vietnam's Highway 15. This road forms part of the 400-km motorbike 'Loop' taking in the impressive karst landscape of the Mahaxai area and a number of impressive caves.

Boats run across the border to Thailand from Thakhek (see box, page 544), but the nearby bridge is now a more common means of making the crossing.

Tip...

Don't miss the 'Loop' if you're a road trip fan, but be sure to hire quality wheels for the journey and give your motorbike a thorough inspection before heading out. Be aware that during the rainy season (September/October) some of the roads may be impassable. Good information about the 'Loop' can be found at **Thakhek Travel Lodge**, see page 420.

Time required

The area could be traversed in a day but it's worth allowing a few extra days for the worthwhile detours. Three to five days to do the 'Loop' by motorbike.

permitted. The beautiful green waters of the lake morph into different shades season to season due to the dissolved calcium from the surrounding limestone outcrops. It is very difficult to get to the lake independently and sometimes the track is completely inaccessible except on foot. The Tourist Information Centre in Thakhek organizes excellent treks to the lake.

Listings Thakhek and around

Tourist information

Tourist Information Centre
Vientiane Rd, in a signposted chalet-like building, T052-212512, Mon-Fri 0800-1130 and 1330-1630, Sat-Sun 0800-1130 and 1400-1700.
Has particularly helpful staff. This is a good stop-off place for advice. Proceeds from the tours go to poor, local communities.

Where to stay

$$$-$$ Hotel Riveria
Setthathirat Rd, T051-250000, www.hotelriveriathakhek.com.
This huge white building is the 1st structure that arrivals from Thailand will see. Situated right on the riverfront, it offers comfort at a price; go for the superior deluxe which is a good size. There's a restaurant, pool and gym and Wi-Fi is available in the lobby. The views of the karst landscape are beautiful from the upper floors.

$$-$ Inthira Hotel
Chao Anou Rd, close to the fountain, T051-251237, www.inthira.com.
A stylish small hotel with some very attractive rooms that are warmly decorated; however, the standard rooms are extremely cramped, so opt for the deluxe. Restaurant and Wi-Fi available.

$ Southida Guesthouse
Chao Anou Rd (a block back from the river), T051-212568.
Very popular guesthouse in the centre of town. Clean comfortable rooms with a/c, TV,

and hot water; cheaper with fan. Very helpful staff; often booked up as this is a solid budget option.

$ Thakhek Travel Lodge
2 km from the centre of town, T030-530 0145, travell@laotel.com.
Popular guesthouse set in a restored old house. Fantastic outdoor seating area and with nightly open fire creating a very social atmosphere and making it a good place to get tips for the 'Loop'. There's also an excellent logbook for those intending to travel independently around the 'Loop' and motorcycle hire can be arranged. The rooms are rather basic, but people only tend to stay here as a quick stop before and after their motorcycle adventure.

Restaurants

Thakhek is not a place to come to for its cuisine, but you will find the usual array of noodle stalls (try the one in the town 'square', which also sells good fruitshakes). Warm baguettes are also sold on the square in the morning. The best place to eat is at one of the riverside restaurants on either side of the square. Otherwise, most of the restaurants are attached to the hotels and guesthouses.

$ Kaysone Restaurant
In the centre of town, T051-212563.
Although from the outside this looks like someone's backyard, inside is a sprawling restaurant compound. *Sindat*, Korean barbecue, and fantastic ice cream. Karaoke on site.

$ Lao-named restaurant
On the corner of Ounkham Rd and the east–west street leading to Wat Nabo.
English menu with Lao and Western dishes, mainly centred on seafood. Popular with local expats.

$ Phoukanna
Vientiane Rd.
Big choice of Western and Lao dishes plus new noisy bar.

$ Sabaidee
1 km towards the river from Travel Lodge (see below), T051-251245. Closed 1500-1700.
Serves great backpacker fare (burgers, salads, sandwiches) plus a range of Lao dishes on cheery red-checked tablecloths. Book exchange and CNN on TV.

$ Sukiyaki
Vientiane Rd, T020-5575 1533.
A pokey but exceptionally friendly restaurant where you can barbecue your own meal on the tables.

$ Thakhek Travel Lodge
See Where to stay.
The food in the lodge's restaurant is not all good but recommended is the Hawaii curry and barbecue (which needs to be ordered in advance). The service, on the other hand, is unacceptably slow and haphazard.

Bars

Boua's Place on the Mekong is great for a sunset drink. There are a lot of drinking holes strung along the front here.

Shopping

Markets
There are 3 markets in Thakhek. The largest, **Talaat Lak Saam**, is at the bus terminal, 4 km east of town and is a good place to pick up odds and ends, with tuk-tuks ferrying market-goers to and fro (10,000 kip). **Talaat Lak Song** is at the eastern end of Kouvoravong Rd, 1.5-2 km from the centre. It is a mixed, mainly dry goods market,

although basketry and handcrafted buffalo bells are also sold. North on Chaoanou Rd is the **Talaat Nabo**. A new night market has opened in the fountain area.

What to do

The tourist office (page 420) is very helpful and organizes the following treks and excursions: 3-day trip to Kong Lor Cave, 770,000 kip per person for 2; to Phou Hin Poun for lakes and caves, 600,000 kip per person for 2; to Buddha Cave, 300,000 kip per person for 2. Also runs Route 12 trips.

Green Climbers Home, *12 km east of Thakek, see website for directions, T020-5966 7532, www.greenclimbershome.com. Oct-May.* An absolute heaven for seasoned climbers and those who want to learn. 10 bungalows and 2 dorm rooms set among some breathtaking karst scenery. Basic 'just climb' half-day courses start at 130,000 kip and 2-day courses on rope work and skills start at 300,000 kip. Climbing routes are 12-40 m long and range from 3+ to 8a+/8b.
Thakhek Travel Lodge, *see Where to stay, T020-2220 5070.* The owner, Mr Ku is a wealth of information about travelling the 'Loop' and has many contacts. Motorbikes can be rented from his lodge daily from 0700-1100 and 1500-1930. He recommends riders take 4 days. He will help out in an emergency and advises on no-go times; for example, in Sep and Oct during the rains.

Transport

Bus/truck
Thakhek's **main bus station** is 4 km northeast of town, T051-251519. It is a large station with a mini-market and is open throughout the night and offers inter-provincial and international buses. Frequent daily connections from 0400-1200 northbound to **Vientiane**, 346 km, 6 hrs; the VIP bus also dashes through town in the morning at around 0900. Frequent scheduled buses to **Paksan**, 0400-1200,

190 km, 4-5 hrs; it is also possible to pick up a bus to Paksan en route to Vientiane. Get off at **Ban Lao** for connections along Route 12.

Southbound buses to **Savannakhet**, from 1030, every 30 mins daily, 139 km, 2½-3 hrs; to **Pakse**, every hour 1030-2400 daily, 6-7 hrs; Pakse VIP bus leaves at 2400; also to **Sekong**, 3 daily; to **Attapeu**, 1500 and 2300 daily; to **Don Khong**, 2300 daily, 15 hrs.

To Vietnam There are buses to **Vinh** daily; to **Dong Hoi**, Mon, Wed, Sat and Sun; to **Hué**, Wed, Thu, Sat and Sun. Also services to **Hanoi**. For the border crossing, see box, page 544.

To Thailand With the opening of the 3rd Friendship bridge 16 km north of Thakek, this is now a very simple and efficient border crossing with a bus taking passengers straight across. There's a customs and immigration office on the Lao side open daily 0800-1730. From Nakhon Phanom, scheduled buses depart for **Udon Thani** and **Bangkok**. Arriving from Thailand, 30-day Lao visas are available at the border.

The **local bus station** is at Talaat Lak Sarm and services towns and villages within the province. From here *songthaew* depart hourly between 0900 and 1300 to **Mahaxai**, 45 km, 2-3 hrs; **Nakai**, 0800-1600, 77 km, 2-4 hrs; **Na Phao** (Vietnam border) 142 km, 6-7 hrs; and **Na Hin**, 45,000 kip. There is also a *songthaew* to **Kong Lor** village.

Motorbike hire
Bikes can be rented from **Thakhek Travel Lodge** and the **Provincial Tourism Office**.

Excursions off Route 12

spectacular karst scenery; a trip to the Buddha Cave is a must

The caves along Route 12 can be visited on day trips from Thakhek, although some are difficult to find without a guide and access may be limited in the wet season. Some sights have no English signposts but locals will be more than happy to point you in the right direction.

Tham Xang (Tham Pha Ban Tham)
9 km northeast of town. Follow Route 12 for about 7 km until you pass the bridge, then turn right (difficulties can arise in the wet season due to flooding).

This is the closest cave to Thakhek. It is considered an important Buddhist shrine and contains a number of Buddhist artefacts, including some statues and a box containing religious scripts. The Buddhist component, however, pales into insignificance compared to the 'elephant head' that has formed from calcium deposits. Locals herald it as a miracle and in the Lao New Year they sprinkle water on it. Visitors will need a torch to find the formation along a small passage at the right-hand corner of the cave, behind the golden Buddha

★ Tham Pha (Buddha Cave)
Ban Na Khangxang, off Route 12, 18 km from Thakhek. Boat 5000 kip and entrance to the cave 2000 kip. Women will need to hire a sinh (sarong) at the entrance, 3000 kip.

A trip out here is highly recommended not just for the cave itself, which is impressive in its own historical right, but for the surrounding villages, pristine waterways and wonderful karst scenery. A farmer hunting for bats accidentally stumbled across Buddha Cave (also knowns as Tham Pa Fa – Turtle Cave) in April 2004. On climbing up to the cave's mouth, he found 229 bronze Buddha statues, believed to be over 450 years old, and ancient palm leaf scripts. The Buddhas were part of the royal collection believed to have been hidden here when the Thais ransacked Vientiane. Since its discovery, the cave has become widely celebrated, attracting pilgrims from as far away as Thailand, particularly around **Pi Mai** (Lao New Year). In the wet season it is possible to bathe in the beautifully clear waters surrounding the cave, though women will need to wear a *sinh* (sarong). A wooden ladder and ugly concrete steps have been built to access the cave but it is still quite difficult to get to, as the road from Thakhek is in poor condition.

Tha Falang (Vang Santiphap – Peace Pool)
To get there, follow Route 12 until Km 13, and then turn north on a track for 2 km. In the wet season it may be necessary to catch a boat from the Xieng Liab Bridge.

This lovely emerald billabong is surrounded by pristine wilderness and breathtaking cliffs. The swimming pool, created by the Nam Don River, was a favourite French picnic spot during the colonial period and it's a nice place to spend the afternoon or break your journey if you're doing the 'Loop' (see page 424). The water is less pleasant in the dry season, when it can become a bit stagnant.

Tham Xiang Liab
Turn off Route 12 at Km 14 (1 km past the turn-off for Tham Xang) and follow the track south to reach the cave.

Tham Xiang Liab was the first cave in the province to be officially opened to tourists. The 200-m-long cave sits at the foot of a 300-m-high limestone cliff, with a small swimming hole (in the dry season) at the far end. It is not easy to access the interior of the cavern on your own; in the wet season it can only be navigated by boat, as it usually floods. This cave, called 'sneaking around cave', derived its name from a legend of an old hermit who used to meditate here with his beautiful daughter. A novice monk fell in love with the hermit's daughter and the two love birds planned sneaky trysts around this cave and Tham Nan Aen (see below). When the hermit found out he flew into a rage and did away with the novice monk; the daughter was banished to the cave for the rest of her life. There are limestone formations on the roof of the cave and experts have suggested that there may be some cave drawings hidden among the shadows.

Tham Sa Pha In
Follow route 12 to Km 17; beyond the narrow pass turn to the left (north) and follow the path for 400 m.

This little-visited cave contains a small lake, reputed to be 75 m long, and a couple of interesting Buddhist shrines. Swimming in the lake is strictly prohibited as the auspicious waters are believed to have magical powers.

Nam Don Resurgence/Khoun Nam Don
Close to Ban Na, off Route 12 at Km 14, 25 km northeast of Thakhek.

This beautiful lagoon is located within a cave and shaded by a sheer 300-m-tall cliff. The lagoon offers about 20 m of swimming then filters off into an underground waterway network, believed to extend for 3 km. In 1998 French surveyors found a rare species of blind cave fish 23 m below the surface here. If you follow the cave wall round, there is another entrance which offers a good vista of the turquoise pool below. A trip to Nam Don Resurgence can be done in conjunction with the 'Loop' but requires a few hours. It is also a bit tricky to find on your own so you might need to ask the locals or recruit a local guide.

During the wet season, access is often only by boat. Thakek tourist office, page 420, runs some good tours which include this sight.

Tham Nan Aen
South of Route 12, at Km 18, a path leads 700 m to the cave entrance.

Tham Nan Aen is the giant of the local caverns at 1.5 km long and over 100 m high. It has multiple chambers and the entrances are illuminated by fluorescent lighting; it also contains a small underground freshwater pool.

Mahaxai
Mahaxai is a beautiful small town 50 km east of Thakhek on Route 12. The sunset here is renowned but even more stunning is the surrounding scenery of exquisite valleys and imposing limestone bluffs. A trip to Mahaxai could be combined with a visit to one or more of the spectacular caves along Route 12 and some river excursions to see the Xe Bang Fai gorges or to run the rapids further downstream.

The 'Loop' → *Colour map 3, A/B 2/3.*
Contact Thakhek Travel Lodge (see What to do, page 421) for excellent information about the 'Loop' route and for motorbike hire.

The impressive karst landscape of the Mahaxai area is visible to the northeast of town and can be explored on a popular motorbike tour from Thakhek, known as the 'Loop'. This is a magnificent trip which runs from Thakhek along Route 12 to Mahaxai, then north to Lak Sao, west along Route 8 to Ban Na Hin and then south back to Thakhek on Route 13, taking in caves and other beautiful scenery along the way. The circuit should take approximately three days but allow four to five, particularly if you want to sidetrack to Tham Kong Lor and the other caves.

Listings Excursions off Route 12

Where to stay

Mahaxai

$ Mahaxai Guesthouse
Just north of town.
These simple bungalows are just the ticket for those on the 'Loop', especially as the attached restaurant serves good food. Each individual bungalow has a small balcony ideal for sipping a cold *Beerlao*.

Restaurants

Mahaxai
Food is generally of a high quality in the local noodle shops and foodstalls.

Transport

Mahaxai
Songthaew leave from the station in the morning.

Savannakhet
Province

Savannakhet Province has the highest provincial population in Laos. It consists of 15 districts, with 826,000 inhabitants dispersed within its boundaries. Like most provinces in the country, it comprises a kaleidoscope of ethnicities, including the Lao, Phouthai, Thaidam, Katang, Chali, Lava, Souai, Pako, Kaleng, Mangkong and Tai. The cultural diversity is even more visible in Savannakhet city, which has large Chinese and Vietnamese populations. Vietnamese and Thai merchants sell their products throughout the city, while the ubiquitous colonial houses and fading shopfronts are an ever-present reminder of its French influence. Due to its proximity to both Thailand and Vietnam, Savannakhet is considered an important economic corridor. The province has several natural attractions, although the majority are a fair hike from the provincial capital.

★Situated on the banks of the Mekong and at the start of the Route 9 to Danang in Vietnam, Savannakhet – or Savan as it is usually known – is an important river port and the gateway to the south. It is also an important trading centre with Thailand.

Sights

Like any town of this size, Savan has quite a number of wats; none are particularly notable but most are quite beautiful. **Wat Sounantha** on Nalao Road has a three-dimensional raised relief on the front of the *sim*, showing the Buddha in the *mudra* of bestowing peace, separating two warring armies. **Wat Sayaphum** on the Mekong is rather more attractive and has several early 20th-century monastery buildings. It is both the largest and oldest monastery in town, although it was only built at the end of the 19th century. Some monks at **Wat Sayamungkhun** speak a bit of English and are pleased to talk about their 50-year-old monastery. There is a large temple school here and, if you arrive during lessons, you may get roped into some impromptu English teaching.

Savan's **colonial architecture** can be seen throughout the central part of town. Perhaps the most attractive area is the square east of the old immigration office between Khanthabouli and Phetsalath roads. Simuang Road, near the Catholic church, is also rewarding in this regard.

Evidence of Savan's diverse population is reflected in the **Chua Dieu Giac**, a Mahayana Buddhist pagoda at the intersection of Soutthanu and Phetsalath roads that serves the town's Vietnamese population. In deference to Theravada tradition, the *chua* has a *that* in the courtyard. There's also a Chinese school close to the Catholic church. The church, which dominates the historic centre, holds Mass at 0800 on Sunday.

Unfortunately, the beautiful French colonial building housing the local museum has closed. The **Provincial Museum** ⓘ *Khanthabouli Rd, Mon-Sat 0800-1200 and 1330-1600, 5000 kip*, now has a purpose-built building. The museum has plenty of propaganda-style displays but little that is terribly enlightening, unless you are interested in the former revolutionary leader Kaysone Phomvihane.

Another attraction is the **Dinosaur Museum** ⓘ *Khanthabouli Rd, south of the stadium, T041-212597, daily 0800-1200 and 1300-1600, 5000 kip*, which houses a collection of four different dinosaur and early mammalian remains, and some fragments of a meteorite that fell to earth

Essential Savannakhet Province

Finding your feet

There is an airport at Savannakhet, which receives flights from Vientiane and Bangkok. By bus, it takes three hours to travel from Vientiane to Savannakhet (125 km) along the main north–south highway, Route 13. Route 9 cuts through the region from east to west and is served by daily buses between Savannakhet and Danang in Vietnam, via the border at Xepon. Just south off Route 9 is the Dong Phou Vieng National Protected Area and Ho Chi Minh Trail, though getting to the latter is not easy and should only be attempted with a 4WD in the dry season (November to March).

Tip...

The **Eco Guide Unit** (see page 430) is a great source of information.

over 100 million years ago. The first fossils in the region were unearthed in 1990 by a team of French and Lao scientists. All exhibits are accompanied by explanations in Lao and French; some staff speak good English and French and are happy to explain their work. A DVD in French explains the discoveries.

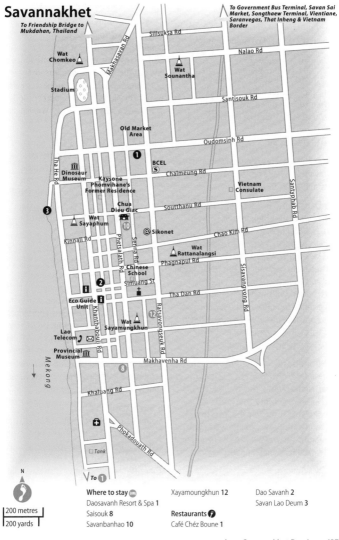

Savannakhet

To Friendship Bridge to
Mukdahan, Thailand

To Government Bus Terminal, Savan Sai Market, Songthaew Terminal, Vientiane, Saranvegas, That Inheng & Vietnam Border

Wat Chomkeo

Siisuksa Rd

Nalao Rd

Kakhaaazan Rd

Wat Sounantha

Stadium

Santisouk Rd

Old Market Area

Oudomsinh Rd

Tha He Rd

Dinosaur Museum

BCEL (S)

Chaimeung Rd

Kaysone Phomvihane's Former Residence

Vietnam Consulate

Santyphab Rd

Chua Dieu Giac

Southhanu Rd

Wat Sayaphum

@ Sikonet

Chao Kim Rd

Kinnali Rd

Phetsalath Rd

Sena Rd

Wat Rattanalangsi

Phagnaput Rd

Sisavangyong Rd

Chinese School

Simuang St

Tha Dan Rd

Eco Guide Unit

Khanthabouli Rd

Wat Sayamungkhun

Ratsavongseuk Rd

Lao Telecom

Provincial Museum

Makhavenha Rd

Mekong

Khatuang Rd

Phokadouath Rd

Tank

N

To

200 metres
200 yards

Where to stay 🛏
Daosavanh Resort & Spa **1**
Saisouk **8**
Savanbanhao **10**

Xayamoungkhun **12**

Restaurants 🍴
Café Chéz Boune **1**

Dao Savanh **2**
Savan Lao Deum **3**

Tourist information

Provincial Tourism Office
Chaleun Meuang Rd, T041-212755.
Mon-Fri 0800-1200 and 1300-1600.
One of the least helpful in the country. Much better is the nearby **Eco Guide Unit** (see page 430). The tourism office has at least produced a series of useful leaflets including a worthwhile self-guided walking tour of the historic quarter, called *Savannakhet Downtown*, distributed at guesthouses, the tourism office and the Eco Guide Unit.

Where to stay

Savannakhet has a good selection of places to stay for US$5 and upwards but rock-bottom budget accommodation is scarce.

$$$ Daosavanh Resort & Spa Hotel
1 km south of the historic centre,
T041-252188, www.daosavanh.com.
A newer resort with attractive rooms (those with Mekong views cost more), super mattresses, rain shower in bathrooms, great pool and Wi-Fi, though bathrooms need much better ventilation. It's a little stuck out of the centre but great for the spa and pool. Let's hope they preserve the lovely French colonial building, the former provincial museum, which is in the grounds.

$$ Phonepasut
Santisouk Rd, 1 km from town centre in quiet street, T041-212158.
Motel-like place with 2 courtyards, restaurant and pool (US$10 for non-residents to use). The rooms are clean, with hot water in the bathrooms, a/c and satellite TV. Friendly and well run with business support services.

$$ Sala Savanh
A block south of the Catholic church, T041-212445, www.salalao.com.
A small hotel (5 spacious rooms) in an historic building that used to be the Thai consulate.

There is original tiling throughout. This is an old building with no soundproofing so you would be wise to opt for the upstairs rooms. Friendly management and excellent location.

$$-$ Hoongthip
Phetsarath Rd, T041-212262,
hoongtip@laotel.com.
Dark rooms with big en suite bathrooms, a/c and satellite TV. The new rooms are large but austere with bathtubs in the en suites. Breakfast included. Other services include sauna, and car hire with driver. Wi-Fi in lobby.

$ Nongsoda
Tha He Rd, T041-212522.
If you're not put off by the oodles of white lace draped everywhere, you'll find clean rooms with a/c and en suite bathrooms with wonderfully hot water. During the low season the hotel drops its room rate. Motorbike hire (80,000 kip) and bike hire (10,000 kip) also available.

$ Saisouk
Makhavenha Rd, T041-212207.
A real gem, this new guesthouse has good-sized twin and double rooms which are immaculately furnished and spotlessly clean, with a/c in some rooms, communal bathrooms and cold water. It's beautifully decorated with interesting *objets d'art* and what look like dinosaur bones. There are plenty of chairs and tables on the large verandas. It is efficiently run by very friendly staff who speak English. Homely.

$ Savanbanhao Hotel
Senna Rd, T041-212202, sbtour@laotel.com.
Centrally located hotel comprising 4 colonial-styles houses set around a quiet but large concrete courtyard, with a range of rooms. There are cheaper rooms in '4th class' (not musty, contrary to appearances). The more expensive rooms have en suite showers and hot water. Some a/c. Large balcony. **Savanbanhao Tourism Co** is attached (see

What to do, below). Good choice for those who want to be in and out of Savannakhet, quickly, with relative ease.

$ Xayamoungkhun
85 Rasavongseuk Rd, T041-212426.
An excellent little guesthouse with 16 rooms in an airy colonial-era villa. Central with a largish compound. Range of very clean rooms available, with hot water, a/c and fridge in the more expensive ones. Friendly owners. Second-hand books available.

Restaurants

Several restaurants on the riverside serve good food and beer. The market also has stalls offering decent fresh food, including excellent Mekong river fish. Phengsy coffee shop at the bottom of the square is a great people-watching spot and serves good coffee too.

$$$ Bungva Lake Restaurant
On Bung Va Lake. Daily 0800-2200.
Stilted restaurant in the lake, with individual dining rooms. Enjoy fresh seafood washed down with *Beerlao*. A lovely way to pass the afternoon.

$$$-$ Dao Savanh
Simuang St, T041-260888. Open 0700-2200.
A newcomer to the restaurant scene, this place occupies a restored French colonial building and provides good but pricey food. It's worth splashing out on a set menu (65,000-95,000 kip). Sit at one of the outdoor tables for views of the central square.

$$-$ Savan Lao Deum
Old ferry pier, T041-252125.
This lovely place has taken over the old ferry pier area. The attractive wooden restaurant juts out onto the river on a floating veranda. It's a particularly good venue for a sunset drink. The food is delicious, too, especially steamed fish and herbs. You might like to try some of the more adventurous options: fried tree ant eggs, grilled buffalo skin and roasted cicadas. The service is exceptional.

$ Café Chéz Boune,
Opposite the old market, T041-215190. Open 0700-2300.
This place provides good travellers' fare in attractive surrounds.

Bars and clubs

There are several large discos/beer gardens in Savannakhet, most of which stage live bands and are open 7 days a week. **Seven** on Ratsavongseuk Rd is especially popular with young Lao.

Entertainment

Savan Vegas Casino, *T041-252200, www. savanvegas.com.* At the city roundabout, dominated by dinosaur statues, a sign reads 'Welcome to Lao Vegas'. If you want to play, it's Thai baht only; if you want to stay, the comfortable rooms overlook the casino hall; there's a spa and pool too.

Festivals

Feb **Than Ing Hang** (movable) similar to the festival at Wat Phou, Champasak (see page 445).

Shopping

One District One Product, *Km 6, T020-5554 0226, not too far from Savan Vegas.* A large warehouse with all sorts of handicrafts and wares on sale.
Talaat Savan Sai (Central Market), *behind the government bus station, north of town. Daily 0700-1700.* The central market has moved from its former location to a new site in the north of town. Though not as convenient for tourists, the spanking new building, built and managed by a Singaporean company, comes complete with parking spaces and one of the few escalators in Laos. You'll find the usual selection of meat, vegetables, fruit, dry goods, clothes, fabrics and baskets, plus an abundance of gold and silversmiths.

There is a branch of **Lao Cotton** on Ratsavongseuk Rd.

What to do

Spa
Champa Savanh Spa, *at the Daosavanh Resort, T041-252188 ext 402, www.daosavan hhtl.com. Open 1300-2200.* This spa offers a broad range of treatments. Go for the kitsch waterfall experience and steam rooms and then make use of the large swimming pool.

See also **Savan Vegas**, under Entertainment, above.

Swimming
Non-guests can use the pool at the **Daosavanh Resort** (see Where to stay) for 50,000 kip. It has an attractive sala in which to lounge after your swim.

Trekking
Savanbanhao Tourism Co, *at the Savanbanhao Hotel (see Where to stay), T041-212944, sbhtravel@yahoo.com. Mon-Sat 0800-1200 and 1330-1630.* Provides trips to most sights in the vicinity as well as bus tickets to Vietnam. Savannakhet Eco Guide Unit, *Rasphanit Rd, T041-214203, www.savannakhet-trekking. com. Mon-Fri 0800-1130 and 1330-1700, Sat-Sun 0800-1130 and 1400-1700.* This unit, run by Oudomsay Thongsavath, operates excellent ecotours and treks to the national parks in the area. There are several keen and enthusiastic English-speaking guides to take tourists out to see the local ethnic culture and sights. Highly worthwhile treks have been established, with proceeds filtering down to local communities.

Note that some treks only operate Nov-Mar. Tours include 1- to 5-day treks (with homestay) to Dong Phou Vieng NPA, Phu Xang Hae NPA, Dong Natad protected area to see the honey collection (Feb-Mar), tree oil extraction, Nom Lom Lake and the ancient ruins of Meuang Kao. Also runs 1-day cycling trips to Dong Natad and Bungva Lake takes in That Ing Hang and village visits; and a 2-day cycling trip takes in a homestay at Ban Phonsim. The minimum price for a 1-day trekking tour for 2-3 people is US$26, including transport, food, water and a guide. Book in advance. The office can also arrange guides and drivers for other trips. Highly recommended.

Transport

Air
Lao Airlines (T041-212140) flies to **Vientiane** and **Bangkok** 3 times a week. A tuk-tuk from the airport is 20,000 kip.

Bus/truck
The government bus terminal is on the northern edge of town, near the Savan Xai market, T041-213920. A tuk-tuk to the centre should cost about 10,000 kip. Just west of the bus station is the *songthaew* terminal, where vehicles depart to provincial destinations.

From the bus station, frequent northbound buses depart daily to **Vientiane** (0600-1130), 457 km on a good road, 9 hrs, 80,000 kip. Most of the Vientiane-bound buses also stop at **Thakhek**, 125 km, 2½-3 hrs, 25,000 kip; **Paksan**, 5-6 hrs, 55,000 kip; and **Pak Kading**, 7-8 hrs, 55,000 kip. There are also specially scheduled morning buses to **Thakhek**.

Southbound buses to **Pakse** depart daily at 0700, 0900, 1030, 1230, 1730, 6-7 hrs, 35,000 kip; buses in transit from Vientiane to Pakse will usually also pick up passengers here. A VIP bus leaves at 2130, 8 hrs, 95,000 kip. To **Don Khong**, 1900 daily, 9-10 hrs, 75,000 kip; to **Salavan**, 1230 daily, 8-10 hrs, 60,000 kip; to **Attapeu**, 0900 and 1900 daily, 9-12 hrs, 70,000 kip. This road is also in pretty good condition.

Eastbound buses depart daily to: **Xepon** at 0700, 0800, 1000, 1100, 1230, 4 hrs, 30,000 kip; and **Lao Bao** (Vietnam border), at 0630, 0900 and 1200 daily, 6 hrs, 40,000 kip.

To Vietnam A bus departs at 2200 daily for destinations within Vietnam, including **Hué**, 13 hrs, 90,000 kip; **Danang**, 508 km,

13 hrs, 110,000 kip; and **Hanoi**, 24 hrs, 200,000 kip on Tue and Sat; there are additional services at 1000 (VIP bus to Hué). Luxury Vietnam-bound buses can be arranged through the **Savanbanhao Hotel** (see Where to stay), 90,000 kip. Although buses claim to be direct, a bus change is required at the border. Buses leave on even days at 0800 and arrive in Hué at 1600. For details of the border crossing between Dansavanh (Laos) and Lao Bao (Vietnam), see box, page 545.

To Thailand Crossing the border to **Mukdahan** via the Friendship Bridge is now straightforward. Buses leave the terminal in Savannakehet throughout the day, last bus 1900. It takes 10 mins. The bus will pick you up on the other side of Lao immigration to take you on to the Thai authorities. There are regular buses to **Ubon Ratchathani** from

Mukdahan, 3 hrs; and also to **Bangkok**. Lao visas (30 days) are available at the border with one passport photo. If you are coming from Thailand and miss the regular connecting bus to Savannakhet, you can hire a songthaew. There are ATMs at both borders.

Car, motorbike and bicycle hire
Cars and drivers can be hired from the **Savanbanhao Hotel** (see Where to stay). Some of the guesthouses rent bicycles for 10,000 kip and motorbikes for 50,000-80,000 kip.

Tuk-tuk and saamlor
Most tuk-tuks charge around 10,000 kip per person for a local journey. There is one traditional old bicycle *saamlor* still operating in town. Track down the old man that runs it for a leisurely jaunt around the colonial core.

Around Savannakhet
flora and fauna, architecture and local culture

That Inheng
12 km northeast of Savannakhet, 0800-1800, 5000 kip.

That Inheng is a holy 16th-century *that* or stupa. It was built during the reign of King Sikhottabong at the same time as That Luang in Vientiane, although local guides may try to convince you it was founded by the Indian emperor Asoka over 2000 years ago. Needless to say, there is no historical evidence to substantiate this claim. The wat is the site of an annual festival at the end of November akin to the one celebrated at Wat Phou, Champasak (see page 445).

The regular tuk-tuks that ferry people between Savannakhet and Xeno will usually take you to That Inheng (100,000 kip return). Otherwise, take a shared *songthaew* to Xeno and ask to hop off at That Inheng. They will usually take you all the way, but if they drop you at the turning it is only a 3-km walk from the road. Alternatively, hire a bicycle in town and cycle out here. Another option is to travel by the **Bungva Lake**, 7 km outside of Savannakhet, and stop for lunch at the lakeside restaurant.

★Dong Phou Vieng National Protected Area
The **Savannakhet Eco Guide Unit** (see page 430) runs excellent treks through the Dong Phou Vieng National Protected Area (NPA), south of Route 9, which is home to wildlife such as Siamese crocodiles, Asian elephants, the endangered Eld's deer, langurs and wild bison (most of which you would be incredibly lucky to see). Located within the NPA is a **Song Sa Kae** (sacred forest and cemetery), revered by the local Katang ethnic group, who are known for their buffalo sacrifices. The well-trained local guides show how traditional natural produce is gathered for medicinal, fuel or other purposes. The tours are exceptionally good value and homestays are included. Most of the tours only run during the dry season.

Southern Laos

Laos' southern provinces offer a varied array of enticements and a different character from the north of the country. Base yourself in the region's unofficial capital, Pakse, to explore the many attractions of Champasak Province, including the romantic, pre-Angkorian ruins of Wat Phou and Ban Kiet Ngong, with its opportunities for elephant trekking.

Inland from Pakse is the Bolaven Plateau, an area that was earmarked by the French for settlement and coffee production. The rivers running off the plateau have created a series of spectacular waterfalls, including towering Tad Fan and stunning Tad Lo.

A highlight of any trip down south is Siphandon, where the Mekong divides into myriad channels and 'Four Thousand Islands'. The idyllic, palm-fringed Don Khone, Don Deth and Don Khong provide perfect places to relax and absorb riverine life, as fisherman cast nets amongst lush green islets and children frolic on the sand bars.

Best for
Beaches ▪ Dolphins ▪ Khmer ruins ▪ Waterfalls

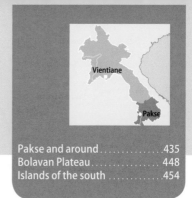

Footprint
picks

★ **Champasak**, page 440

A sleepy riverside town where colonial-era buildings sit alongside traditional Lao wooden houses.

★ **Don Daeng Island**, page 440

Life on this tranquil river island continues much as it has done for centuries.

★ **Wat Phou**, page 443

Laos' own mini-Angkor is worth taking a day to explore.

★ **Xe Pian National Protected Area**, page 446

One of Laos' most important nature reserves, with extensive wetlands home to rare wildlife.

★ **Tad Lo**, page 451

A base for exploring the Bolaven Plateau; take a picnic at the enchanting Tad Yeung falls.

★ **Four Thousand Islands (Siphandon)**, page 454

Best explored by bicycle, these idyllic islands are a traveller haven.

Gulf of Tonkin

VIETNAM

SAVANNAKHET

THAILAND

SALAVAN

SEKONG

CHAMPASAK

ATTAPEU

CAMBODIA

N

20 km
20 miles

Pakse (Pakxe)
& around

Pakse is the largest town in the south and is strategically located at the junction of the Mekong and Xe Don rivers. Pakse is a busy commercial town, built by the French early in the 20th century as an administrative centre for the south. The town has seen better days but the tatty colonial buildings lend an air of old-world charm. Pakse is a major staging post for destinations further afield, such as the old royal capital of Champasak, famed for its pre-Angkor, seventh-century Khmer ruins of Wat Phou. The town's colonial ebb is quickly succumbing to Thai and Vietnamese influences, with whole areas now dominated by Vietnamese shops and businesses.

Close to Pakse are various ecotourism projects where elephant treks, birdwatching and homestays can easily be arranged. *Colour map 3, C3.*

Pakse, by anyone's standards, is not a seething metropolis, which, of course, is much of its charm. But this is starting to change now that infrastructure has improved and Pakse is firmly linked into the Thai economy; it has become a major crossroads between the two countries. A strong Vietnamese influence is also apparent.

There's not that much to see in Pakse, so far as official sights are concerned. However, those who are charmed by slightly dishevelled mid-20th-century architecture will find plenty to photograph here. There is a lot of good food on offer in the form of barbecue meats and beer snacks along the Xe Don River and some excellent Vietnamese options in the Vietnamese area. This is also a great place to observe early morning alms giving in a much more low key way than Luang Prabang. Finally, Pakse is a good place to base yourself to visit destinations further afield, including Tad Lo, Tad Fan and Wat Phou. Facilities such as post office, Telecom office, internet and tourist information are readily available.

Essential Pakse and around

Finding your feet

Pakse is southern Laos' transport hub: from here you can get to anywhere in the southern region, and travel between smaller towns in the region often requires a connection through Pakse. Although it is not on the border with Thailand, Pakse is the largest Lao town close to the border crossing at Chongmek. From the Thai side, *songthaew* continue on to Ubon Ratchathani in Thailand. There is also an airport at Pakse which has domestic connections with Vientiane as well as international flights from Thailand, Vietnam and Cambodia.

Tuk-tuks and *saamlors* are the main means of local transport and can be chartered. The main tuk-tuk 'terminal' is at the Daoheung market, although they can easily be picked up in the guesthouse area. Cars, motorbikes and bicycles are available for hire from hotels and tour companies. Note that the town's roads are numbered as if they were highways: No 1 Road through to No 46 Road.

Best places to stay

The River Resort, Champasak, page 441
Kingfisher Ecolodge, Xe Pian National Protected Area, page 446

Listings Pakse

Tourist information

Champasak Provincial Tourism Office
No 11 Rd, T031-212021. Daily 0800-1130 and 1330-1630.
They have some fantastic ecotours on offer to unique destinations; some are offered in conjunction with local travel agents, such as **Green Discovery** (see page 438). They also have maps, bus times and a wide range of tourist information. Good, English-speaking staff. Well worth a visit.

Where to stay

$$$ Champasak Grand
Near the Japanese Bridge, T031-255111, www.champasakgrand.com.
Gargantuan new business hotel with large rooms, ranging from deluxe to executive suites. Being slightly out of town, the large windows give superb views of the Mekong and the surrounding hills. Also has a good

pool and lays on an impressive buffet breakfast. Good value for money.

$$$-$$ Champasak Palace
No 13 Rd, T031-212263, www.champasak-palace-hotel.com.
This is a massive chocolate box of a hotel with 55 rooms and lit up like a Christmas tree. It was conceived as a palace for a minor prince, complete with bellhops in traditional uniforms. The hotel has lost much of its original character but some classic touches remain: wooden shutters, some art deco furniture and lovely tiles. If you want to kick back for a day or 2, splash out on the King suite for the kitsch factor, jacuzzi and private balcony.

$$$-$$ Pakse Hotel
No 5 Rd, T031-212131, www.paksehotel.com.
The **Pakse Hotel** has a definite charm – a little worn and already feeling like it's from a bygone era, it is nevertheless a firm favourite. The French owner, Mr Jérôme, has integrated local handicraft decorations and rosewood accents. The eco-rooms are good value and the deluxe rooms are a welcome bonus. Breakfast is included and Wi-Fi available. There's also an atmospheric rooftop restaurant with a perfect view over the city.

$ Nang Noi
No 5 Rd, T 030-956 2544, bounthong1978@hotmail.com.
Opened in 2011, **Nang Noi** offers some of Pakse's best budget digs, with kitsch bedcovers covering comfy beds. Some rooms come with peaceful balconies, so ask to see a few first. The family rooms include a/c at extra cost. Run by a very welcoming Lao/Vietnamese husband and wife team who offer a laundry service, tours and bus bookings. Motorcycles can be rented.

$ Phi Dao Hotel
125/13 Rd, T031-215588, phidaohotel@gmail.com.
Vietnamese-owned with very friendly staff. All rooms are decorated in relaxing cream tones with flatscreen TV and fridge, offering good value. Spotless, tiled bathrooms. The big twin rooms at the front have large balconies. Most doubles have a window, but some twins do not, so be sure to check. Also has a decent café-cum-restaurant on the ground floor.

Restaurants

A string of open-air restaurants line the Mekong from the boat landing, many serving sindat and fish dishes. There are also many great river front beer verandas-cum-restaurants along the Xe Don River – some are quiet; others, such as the very popular Topa, get quite raucous later in the evening with a good party atmosphere and live music. Various low-key Vietnamese restaurants can be found by wandering along Rd 46 east of the hospital – expect excellent *pho* noodle soup, *bun thit nuong* (vermicelli with herbs and marinated pork) and good *nem* (spring rolls). For a cheap meal of rice with various toppings look for the *'com'* signs. There are a couple of fantastic *sindat* (barbecue) places near the Da Heung market that are extremely popular with the locals.

$$ Na Dao
Opposite the Champasak Grand Hotel near the bridge.
A cosy French restaurant serving a range of classics and some fusion dishes. Good wine list and a welcoming ambiance.

$$ Pakse Hotel
See Where to stay.
The fantastic rooftop restaurant has atmospheric lighting and offers a range of Lao dishes plus pretty good pizza, delicious chicken curry soup and some delectable cocktails including gin fizz and great mojitos from 1600.

$$-$ Dok Mai
Rd 24, T020-9800 8652.
A real find, this intimate Italian serves a broad range of excellent pasta dishes and some good salads. Try the eggplant with parmesan

dish – it's superb. The house wines are good value. The owner is very welcoming and does a great job of making diners feel right at home. A lovely spot and highly recommended.

$ Delta Coffee
Rd 13, opposite the Champasak Palace Hotel, T020-5534 5895.
This place is a real find if you are craving some Western comfort food. The menu is tremendously varied and offers everything from pizza and lasagne to Thai noodles. The coffee is brilliant too, and staff are exceptionally friendly.

$ Lan Kham
In front of Lan Kham hotel.
Longstanding beef noodle joint serving up a solid rendition of the Vietnamese classic until lunchtime. Pancakes and baguettes can be had from a stall next door. Free Chinese tea. Recommended.

$ Nazim's Restaurant
In a new location on Rd 12, T031-252912.
An excellent Indian restaurant with a fantastic choice of meat dishes. The service is a little slow as dishes are prepared fresh.

$ Xuan Mai
Near Pakse Hotel, T031-213245.
Vietnamese restaurant with outdoor kitchen and eating area. Serves good shakes and fresh spring rolls.

Cafés and bakeries
Crusty baguettes are available across town; they're great for breakfast with wild honey and fresh Bolaven coffee. Low-key coffee shops are found on every street serving coffee strong and on ice.

Café Sinouk
Corner Rd 11, www.sinouk-cafe.com.
This new French-style café is charming and the staff are great. The outside view is a non-event but inside is comfortable seating, framed black-and-white photos, and a range of patisserie and jams, honey and teas to buy in attractive packaging.

What to do

Massage and sauna
There is a small sauna and massage centre at the **Champasak Palace Hotel**, and a good massage place right across the road from the **Pakse Hotel**.

Tour operators
There are a number of tour agencies in town, all of which will arrange tours to local sites like Wat Phou, Phu Asa, Siphandon, Bolaven Plateau and Champasak. Most of the hotels arrange day tours; of these the best is **Wat Phou Travels** at the Pakse Hotel. The **Provincial Tourism Office** (see page 436) also offers a variety of trips including a new 3-day trip to Phou Xieng Thong National Protected Area.

Green Discovery, *T031-252908, www. greendiscoverylaos.com.* Offers a range of adventure tours and ecotourism treks around Champasak province including Ban Kiet Ngong, Bolaven waterfalls, Xe Pian trekking, Siphandon trip, Wat Phou trip and trekking in Dong Hua Sao National Protected Area. Highly recommended.

Sabaidy 2 Guesthouse, *T031-212992, www.sabaidy2tour.com.* Mr Vong and crew offer a wide range of tours around a variety of provincial sites, very good value and recommended for visitors who are only around for 1-2 days. The 1-day Bolaven tour is popular with backpackers. Mr Vong contributes to a school project charity in the province: www.kokphungtai-primaryschool-fund.com.

Vat Phou Mekong Cruises, *www.vatphou. com.* Offers a 3-day/2-night cruise that starts and finishes in Pakse taking in Wat Phou, the Oum Muong ruins at Huei Thamo, 4000 Islands and Pha Pheng waterfall on the Cambodian border.

Xplore Asia, *opposite Jasmine Restaurant, Rd 13, T031-212893, www.xplore-laos.com.* Offers a variety of tours and useful tour services (including a minivan service to Siphandon).

Air

The airport is 2 km northwest of town; cross the bridge over the Xe Don River, next to Wat Luang, and continue straight up No 13 Road; take a tuk-tuk from town. There is a small café and BCEL exchange inside the terminal building. There are domestic flights **Vientiane** several times a week, as well as international flights to **Bangkok**, **Ho Chi Minh City** and **Siem Reap** and **Phnom Penh**. There is a **Lao Airlines** office west of the BCEL by the river in Pakse, open Mon-Fri.

Boat

Public boats to **Champasak** leave from the main pier daily at 0800, 2 hrs. It is also possible to charter a boat, at quite a cost.

Bus/songthaew

You can charter a tuk-tuk to the airport, northern bus station, southern bus station or the VIP station – most guesthouses will help.

Northern terminal Km 7 on Route 13 north, T031-251508, for buses to the north. Hourly departures daily 0730-1630 to **Savannakhet**, 250 km, 5 hrs; **Thakhek**, 7-8 hrs; and **Vientiane**, 16-18 hrs. Local buses can be painfully slow due to the number of stops they make. For those heading to **Vientiane** it makes more sense to pay a couple of extra dollars and get on the much quicker and more comfortable VIP bus at the VIP station.

Southern terminal Km 8 south on Route 13, T031-212981, for buses to the south. There are regular connections with **Champasak**, 1030-1400 (1-2 hrs). If you are travelling to **Wat Phou** (see page 443), take the Champasak bus and ask for 'Ban Lak Sarm Sip' (translates as 'village 30 km'), where there is a signpost and you turn right and

travel 4 km towards **Ban Muang** (2-3 km) on the eastern side of the Mekong. In the village people sell tickets for the ferry (extra charge for motorbikes) across to **Ban Phaphin**, on the western side of the Mekong, 2 km north of Champasak; from here walk or take a tuk-tuk into town. The ferry runs regularly from 0630-2000, or you can charter a ferry direct from Ban Muang to the boat landing in Champasak itself.

Buses travelling through from **Vientiane** provide the main means of transport to other destinations in the south, so can be slightly off kilter.

Songthaew run east to the **Bolaven Plateau**: to **Paksong**, at 0930, 1000, 1230, 3 hrs; **Tad Fan**, 5 morning departures, 1 hr; and **Ban Kiet Ngong**, at 1200, 2 hrs.

Buses/*songthaew* leave for **Siphandon** (**Muang Khong**) in the far south at 0830, 1030, 1130, 1300, 1430 and 1600, 3-4 hrs; for **Ban Nakasang** (the closest port to Don Deth/Don Khone) several departures at 0700, 0800, 0900, 1130, 1200, 1430 and 1400, 3-4 hrs. Several of the buses to Ban Nakasang also stop at **Ban Hat Xai Khoune** (the stop-off for Don Khong). Make sure that you let the bus/*songthaew* driver know that you are going to Ban Nakasang or Ban Hat Xai Khoune rather than saying the name of the islands.

A quicker more comfortable option to Siphandon is to take the minivan service to **Don Deth/Don Khong** offered by Pakse operators, 2-2½ hrs. This is highly recommended and, once you have paid all the fees involved with local transport, it costs about the same.

VIP Khiang Kai/international terminal (with neighbouring **Seangchaolearn terminal**), on the edge of the hotel area, is where you'll most likely arrive if travelling from Vientiane or from across the border. A VIP sleeping bus with comfy beds, duvet, cake and films leaves at 0830 arriving in **Vientiane** at 0600 (stopping en route to **Thakhek**). The beds are double, so unless you book 2 spaces you might end up sleeping next to a stranger. If you are tall ask for a bed towards the back of the bus.

To Vietnam Buses leave for Vietnam via the **Bo Y** border. Guesthouses and agents offer varying schedules. To **Danang**, 0700 and 1900, 18 hrs; to **Hué**, 0700 and 1900, 15½ hrs; to **Dong Ha**, 0700 and 1900, 14 hrs; to **Lao Bao**, 1700, 11 hrs. For details of the border crossing between Yalakhuntum (Laos) and Vietnam (Bo Y), see box, page 545.

To Cambodia Buses run to **Stung Treng** at 0830, 4½ hrs; to **Kratie**, 0800, 6½ hrs; to **Kampong Cham**, 0800, 9½ hrs; to **Phnom Penh**, 0800, 13½ hrs; and to **Seam Reap**, 0800, 17 hrs. For details of the border crossing between Voen Kham (Laos) and Don Kralor (Cambodia), see box, page 544.

To Thailand *Songthaew* for the border at **Vang Tao** (Laos) depart from the Daoheung market in Pakse, daily 0800-1600 every hour, 45 km, 1 hr. The border is open daily 0500-2000 but allow extra time as the *songthaew* is slow. Once you've been dropped off at Vang Tao, walk 250 m to the building where you will receive an exit stamp. Walk another 50 m or so to the Thai border at **Chongme**, where you will be issued with a 30-day Thai visa. Regular buses run to **Ubon Ratchathani** and **Bangkok**. A combination of minibus and sleeper train to **Bangkok** can also be booked from Pakse.

Motorbike and bicycle hire
The **Lankham Hotel**, on Rd 13, rents out bicycles, standard small motorbikes and larger dirt bikes.

Private transport
For out-of-town journeys, hotels such as the **Pakse Hotel** and **Champasak Palace**, and tour companies such as **Xplore-Asia** charter cars and minibuses (with driver). A private *songthaew* from Pakse to **Champasak** (with ferry and tuk-tuk included) can be arranged.

Champasak and around

underrated charming town close to Wat Phou

★The appealing agricultural town of Champasak, which stretches along the west bank of the Mekong for 4 km, is the nearest town to Wat Phou and a good base from which to explore the site and the surrounding area. Although the trip to Wat Phou can be done in a day from Pakse (it is about 40 km south of Pakse), the sleepy town of Champasak is quaint and charming and now offers a couple of quality mid- and upper-end accommodation options.

Sights
Champasak is dotted with stunning colonial buildings. The former residence of Champasak hereditary Prince Boun Oum and former leader of the right-wing opposition, who fled the country in 1975 after the Communist takeover, is quite possibly the most magnificent colonial building in Laos. It is not open to tourists but worth a look from the outside.

Champasak is known for its wooden handicrafts and you'll find vases and other carved ornaments for sale near the jetty. About 15 km southwest of Champasak is **Don Talaat**, which is worth a visit for its weekly market (Saturday and Sunday).

★Don Daeng Island
This idyllic river island sits right across from Champasak and is accessed by a cheap boat ride. It stretches for 8 km and is the perfect place for those wishing to see quintessential village life, with basket weaving, fishing and rice farming, with little hustle and bustle.

There is a path around the island that can be traversed on foot or by bicycle. A crumbling ancient brick stupa, built in the same century as Wat Phou, is in the centre of the island and there are a few ancient remnants from the construction in **Sisak village**. The inhabitants of **Pouylao village** are known for their knife-making prowess.

There is a lovely sandy beach on the Champasak side of the island, perfect for a dip. If you would like to stay overnight, **La Folie Lodge** is a beautiful spot (see Where to stay, below).

Listings Champasak and around

Tourist information

Champasak District Visitor Information Centre
Mon-Fri (daily in high season) 0800-1230 and 1400-1630.
Can arrange boats to Don Daeng, guides to Wat Phou and tours to surrounding sights.

Where to stay

Champasak

$$$ The River Resort
14a Rd, T020-5685 0198, www.theriver resortlaos.com.
A class apart from the neighbouring offerings, this superb US-owned resort comprises 24 rooms across 12 split level modernist villas. Each is decorated in white with blue Lao and Thai ethnic fabrics and bamboo furnishings. All suites include indoor and outdoor showers and the more expensive ones have sweeping Mekong views that are worth every penny. An infinity pool looks over the river next to an open-air restaurant. Private river boat cruises as well as private dining can be arranged. Also has a lovely spa *sala*. Polished service. Highly recommended.

$$ Inthira Champakone Hotel
Diagonally opposite Vong Pasued, T031-511011, www.inthirahotels.com.
This is a lovely hotel with a friendly Lao manager. The spacious twin rooms in the courtyard come with outdoor rain showers and wooden floors. There are also 2-storey duplex suits, each with mezzanine bed area, balcony, shower room and bathroom. The bar is the only place in town with Beerlao on tap.

$ Anouxa Guesthouse
1 km north of the roundabout, T031-213272.
A wide range of accommodation from dingy bamboo structures with cold water to wooden bungalows through to concrete rooms with hot water and either a/c (extra) or fan. The concrete villas are the best, with a serene river vista from the balconies. The restaurant, overlooking the river, is one of the best in town. However, service can be slow and the lower-end rooms are rather poor. Bikes and motorbikes for hire.

Don Daeng Island

$$$$-$$$ La Folie Lodge
T030-5347603, www.lafolie-laos.com.
24 rooms housed in lovely wooden bungalows, each with private balcony overlooking the river. The lodge has a stunning pool surrounded by landscaped tropical gardens. The restaurant serves good wine and a cocktail selection. Bicycle hire and pool use is available to non-guests for a fee. It's a luxurious base from which to explore the island.

$ Homestays are offered in a community lodge and at 17 homes in Ban Hua Don Daeng. The wooden lodge has 2 common rooms, sleeping 5 people with shared bathrooms and dining area. Meals are 20,000 kip. Contact the **Champasak Tourism Office** for details.

Restaurants

Champasak
Most restaurants are in the guesthouses; all are cheap.

$ Anouxa Guesthouse
See Where to stay.
Has a restaurant set over the river, with a small but good menu. The fish dishes are especially good. Also offers a selection of wines. Service can be very slow.

$ Inthira Champakone Hotel
See Where to stay.
The **Inthira** does Western burgers and pizzas as well as Asian dishes in handsome surroundings. The iced coffee is fabulous.
For higher-end dining, head to **The River Resort** (see Where to stay).

What to do

Champasak
Champasak Spa, *T020-5649 9739, www. champasak-spa.com. Daily 1000-1200 and 1300-1900.* This new venture, run by a French couple, is lovely. It aims to be sustainable and they plan to hand it over to local management after training is complete. The massages are simply divine (opt for coconut oil) and the service exceptional. The foot massage is perfect after a morning at the ruins. Booking advised after 1600.

Don Daeng Island
The tourist office in Pakse organizes a 2-day biking and long-tail boat trip around Don Daeng that departs from Pakse and takes in Wat Phou. It is possible to hire bikes from **La Folie Lodge** (see Where to stay) to explore the island.

Transport

Champasak
Transport to Champasak is by minibus, tuk-tuk or boat. The ferry from Ban Muang (on the eastern side of the Mekong) runs regularly to **Ban Phaphin** (on the western side, 2 km north of Champasak). From Ban Phaphin, tuk-tuks run into town. Alternatively, charter a ferry from Ban Muang directly to the boat landing in Champasak.

A more upmarket option from Pakse is to take a cruise which stop at **Wat Phou**, the Oum Muong ruins at **Huei Thamo**, **4000 islands** and **Pha Pheng waterfall** on the Cambodian border.

To get to **Wat Phou**, either take a tuk-tuk or hire a bicycle at one of the guesthouses and cycle the 8 km.

There are buses and *songthaew* to **Pakse**, as well as daily boats (2 hrs), all of which leave in the morning. Ask at your guesthouse for details and arrange your ticket through them. The ferry from **Ban Phaphin** (2 km north of Champasak) to **Ban Muang** runs 0630-2000.

From Champasak, it is also possible to get a *songthaew* to **Siphandon**, which leaves in the morning, and a boat to **Don Daeng**.

★Wat Phou lies at the foot of the Phou Pasak, 8 km southwest of Champasak and is the most significant Khmer archaeological site in Laos. With its teetering, weathered masonry, it conforms exactly to the Western ideal of the lost city. The mountain behind Wat Phou is called **Linga Parvata**, as the Hindu Khmers thought it resembled a lingam – albeit a strangely proportioned one. Although construction of the original Hindu temple complex was begun in the fifth and sixth centuries, much of what remains today is believed to have been built in the 10th to 11th centuries. Wat Phou was a work in progress and was constructed and renovated over a period spanning several hundred years.

Visiting Wat Phou

Wat Phou is best visited as a day trip from Champasak or Pakse. You can get a tuk-tuk from Champasak, though most tourists prefer to cycle the 8 km – bicycles are available at most guesthouses.

The official website is www.vatphou-champassak.com. The site is open daily 0800-1800. Admission is 35,000 kip and goes towards restoration of the wat (entering the site before hours or staying after hours incurs an extra 10,000 kip fee). It is possible to enter at 0600 by paying 40,000 kip at the main gate. A bus service that must rank as the most expensive per metre in Southeast Asia is now available to transport visitors 500 m from the gate to the main site for 15,000 kip.

There is also the Wat Phu Exhibition Centre (closes 1600) at the entrance, a good museum with a fantastic array of artefacts (entrance to the centre is included in admission to the temple). A guide for the museum and the wat area itself costs 100,000 kip per group.

A few times a year a full moon event is held when there is an atmospheric exploration of the site with lights – check the listed website for dates.

Exploring the site

Processional causeway The king and dignitaries would originally have sat on a platform above the 'tanks' or *baray* and presided over official ceremonies or watched aquatic games. In 1959 a palace was built on the platform so the king had somewhere to stay during the annual **Wat Phou Festival** (see page 445). A smaller house had been for the king's entourage. These have now been dismantled. A long avenue leads to the pavilions. The **processional causeway** was probably built by Khmer King Jayavarman VI (1080-1107), and may have been the inspiration for a similar causeway at Angkor Wat. This grand approach to the temple would originally have been flanked by statues of lions and mythical animals, but few traces of these remain.

Pavilions The sandstone pavilions, on either side of the processional causeway, were added after the main temple and are thought to date from the 12th century (in all probability from the reign of Suryavarman II). Although crumbling, with great slabs of laterite and collapsed lintels lying aesthetically around, both pavilions are

> **Tip...**
>
> The site can get busy so try to visit early in the morning or late in the afternoon. It is also cooler during these times and the light is better for photography. There is little shade so take lots of water and a sunhat.

Wat Phou

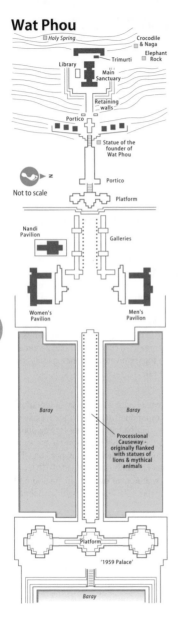

Holy Spring

Crocodile & Naga

Elephant Rock

Trimurti

Library

Main Sanctuary

Retaining walls

Portico

Statue of the founder of Wat Phou

N

Not to scale

Portico

Platform

Nandi Pavilion

Galleries

Women's Pavilion

Men's Pavilion

Baray

Baray

Processional Causeway - originally flanked with statues of lions & mythical animals

Platform

'1959 Palace'

Baray

remarkably intact and, as such, are the most photographed part of the temple complex. The pavilions were probably used for segregated worship by pilgrims, one for women (left) and the other for men (right). The porticoes of the two huge buildings face each other. The roofs were thought originally to have been poorly constructed with thin stone slabs on a wooden beam-frame and later replaced by Khmer tiles.

Only the outer walls of the pavilions now remain but there is enough still standing to fire the imagination: the detailed carving around the window frames and porticoes is well preserved. The laterite used to build the complex was brought from **Um Muang**, also called Tomo Temple, a smaller Khmer temple complex located a few kilometres downriver, but the carving is in sandstone. The interiors were without permanent partitions, although it is thought that rush matting was used to divide areas, and furniture was limited – reliefs depict only low stools and couches. At the rear of the women's pavilion are the remains of a brick construction, which is believed to have been the queen's private quarters. Brick buildings were very costly at that time.

Nandi Pavilion and temple Above the main pavilions is the Nandi Pavilion, a small temple with entrances on two sides. It is dedicated to Nandi, the bull (Siva's vehicle), and is a common feature in Hindu temple complexes. There are three chambers, each of which would originally have contained statues – these have been stolen. As the hill begins to rise above the Nandi temple, the remains of six brick temples follow the contours, with three on each side of the pathway. All six are completely ruined and their function is unclear. Archaeologists and Khmer historians speculate that they may have been Trimurti temples. At the bottom of the steps is a portico and statue of the founder of Wat Phou, Pranga Khommatha. Many of the laterite paving stones and blocks used to build the steps have holes notched down each side; these would have been used to help transport the slabs to the site and drag them into position.

Tip...

Make sure you climb all the way to the top – it's well worth the effort for the wonderful views over the whole site. Wear sturdy shoes as the steps are quite steep in places.

Main sanctuary The main sanctuary, 90 m up the hillside and orientated east–west, was originally dedicated to Siva. The rear section (behind the Buddha statue) is part of the original sixth-century brick building. Sacred spring water was channelled through the hole in the back wall of this section and used to wash the sacred linga. The water was then thrown out, down a chute in the right wall, where it was collected in a receptacle. Pilgrims would then wash in the holy water. The front of the temple was constructed later, probably in the eighth to ninth century, and has some fantastic carvings: apsaras, dancing Vishnu, Indra on a three-headed elephant (the former emblem of the kingdom of Lane Xang) and, above the portico of the left entrance, a carving of Siva, the destroyer, depicted tearing a woman in two.

The Hindu temple was converted into a Buddhist shrine, either in the 13th century during the reign of the Khmer king Jayavarman VII or when the Lao conquered the area in the 14th century. A large Buddha statue now presides over its interior. There is also a modern Buddhist monastery complex on the site.

Listings Wat Phou map p444

Festivals

Late Jan-early Feb **Phu Asa (Ban Kiet Ngong)** The Elephant Festival sees lots of elephants gather from all over the province and *mahouts* dressed in traditional costume. There's a procession to the top of Phu Asa.
Feb **Wat Phou Festival** lasts for 3 days around the full moon of the 3rd lunar month (usually Feb). Pilgrims come from far and wide to leave offerings at the temple. In the evening there are competitions – football, boat racing, bullfighting and cockfighting, Thai boxing, singing contests and the like. There is also some pretty extravagant imbibing of alcohol.

A *Son et Lumière* of sorts has been arranged at each full moon in the dry season with thousands of lamps lighting the archaeological site. For further information before heading to Champasak ask at the tourist office in Pakse or at the **Pakse Hotel.**

★The Xe Pian National Protected Area has a rich variety of birdlife, including large water birds and great hornbills, and is home to sun bears, Asiatic black bears and the yellow-cheeked crested gibbon. The best time for birdwatching is December-February.

Visiting Xe Pian National Protected Area

Ban Kiet Ngong is the base for exploring the area. From Pakse it takes about 1½ hours by motorbike. From Pakse follow Route 13 until you get to the Km 48 junction with Route 18 at Thang Beng village (the Xe Pian National Protected Area office is here). Follow Route 18 east for 7 km, turn right at the signpost for the last 1.5 km to Ban Kiet Ngong. To organize an elephant trek go to the Eco-Guide Unit at the **Champasak Provincial Tourism Office** in Pakse (see page 436), or the **Kingfisher Ecolodge**, if you are staying there (see Where to stay, below).

Sights

North of Xe Pian, the village of **Ban Kiet Ngong** is at the **Kiet Ngong Wetland**, the largest wetland in southern Laos. Here you'll find a community-based project which offers elephant trekking, wetland walks, canoeing trips and homestay accommodation.

The villagers have traditionally been dependent on elephants for agricultural work for centuries, and these days elephants are also used for treks (see What to do, below) to the amazing fortress of **Phu Asa**. Located 2 km from Kiet Ngong at the summit of a small jungle-clad hill, this ancient ruined fortress is an enigmatic site that has left archaeologists puzzled. It consists of 20 stone columns, 2 m high, arranged in a semi-circle – they look a bit like a scaled-down version of Stonehenge.

The **Kiet Ngong Village Elephant Festival** is held annually in late January or early February. It takes place in the village and on the curious archaeological remains at Phu Asa, which provides a fascinating backdrop.

Listings Xe Pian National Protected Area

Where to stay

$$$-$$ Kingfisher Ecolodge
1 km east of Kiet Ngong, T030-534 5016, www.kingfisherecolodge.com.
A bonafide ecolodge facing the wetlands. The set of 6 glass-fronted bungalows are very romantic, complete with 4-poster beds. There are also 4 attractive thatched rooms with nearby shared bathroom. The restaurant, set on the 2nd floor of the lodge, has stunning views over the Pha Pho wetlands. Elephant-related activities can be arranged, as well as massage. The owners are very helpful. Highly recommended.

$ Homestay
Ban Kiet Ngong.
The villagers offer basic homestay accommodation with meals. You can book at the **Kiet Ngong Visitor Centre** or at the tourism office in Pakse (see page 436).

Restaurants

Eating in Ban Kiet Ngong is very basic and, with the exception of nearby Kingfisher Ecolodge, you will have to rely on the local food available – generally *feu* and noodle soup, rustled up on the spot.

$$ Kingfisher Ecolodge
See Where to stay.

This genuine ecolodge includes an excellent restaurant with lovely views. The menu includes a range of Western and Lao dishes. Also stocks wine.

What to do

Elephant treks and birdwatching
There are several 2- to 3-day trekking/homestay trips offered in the area. These include elephant treks across the **Xe Pian** forests, wetlands and rocky outcrops; treks from Kiet Ngong Village to the top of **Phu Asa** (this takes about 2 hrs; the elephant baskets can carry 2 people); and birdwatching trips. There is a 2-day canoe/trekking/homestay trip called the **Ban Ta Ong Trail** with guides trained in wildlife and the medicinal uses of plants. Many tour operators in Pakse can also organize trips to the area. Contact the **Provincial Tourism Office** in Pakse (see page 436) for complete information.

Green Discovery, *see page 438*. Offers a 2-day camping excursion into the protected area, taking visitors deep in to the jungle; and the more challenging 3-day camping **Kiet Ngong-Ta Ong Trail** which includes a homestay and an elephant ride. These tours are designed to ensure that local communities reap the rewards of tourism in a sustainable fashion and are highly recommended.

Kingfisher Ecolodge, *see Where to stay*. One of the best contacts for advanced internet bookings, can arrange 1-day courses for you to train to be a bona fide elephant rider with a traditional *mahout* (elephant keeper).

Transport

Songthaew run to the 4000 Islands or ask a private tourist bus running south to stop at the **Ban Kiet Ngong** junction. **Kingfisher Ecolodge** can arrange transport to the village, but call in advance. The easiest way is to hire a private tuk-tuk or car via an agent.

Bolaven Plateau

The French identified the Bolaven Plateau, in the northeast of Champasak Province, as a prime location for settlement by hardy French farming stock. It is named after the Laven minority group that resides in the area. The soils are rich and the upland position affords some relief from the summer heat of the lowlands. Fortunately, their grand plans came to nought and, although some French families came to live here, they were few in number and all left between the 1950s and 1970s as conditions deteriorated. The area also suffered another setback during the war years, when the major surrounding towns were completely destroyed by US bombing campaigns. Even so, the area was developed as a coffee-, rubber-, tea- and cardamom-growing area. The cool breeze of the plateau, with an average altitude of 600 m, offers much respite from the stifling heat of the surrounding lowlands, particularly in April and May.

Today it is inhabited by a colourful mix of ethnic groups, such as the Laven, Alak, Tahoy and Suay, many of whom were displaced during the war. There are numerous villages dotted between the small settlement of Tha Teng and Salavan. The premier attraction in the area is the number of roaring waterfalls plunging off the plateau. Today, Tad Lo and Tad Fan are popular tourist destinations, while grand Tad Yeung makes a perfect picnic destination. The plateau also affords excellent rafting and kayaking trips. A trip to a coffee or tea plantation also provides an interesting insight into the region.

The main town on the Bolaven Plateau is Paksong, a small market town 50 km east of Pakse. It was originally a French agricultural centre, popular during the colonial era for its cooler temperatures. Paksong was yet another casualty of the war and was virtually destroyed. The area is famous for its fruit and vegetables; even strawberries and raspberries can be cultivated here.

The town occupies a very scenic spot. However, the harsh weather in the rainy season changes rapidly, making it difficult to plan trips around the area. The town consists of little more than a couple of blocks of old shops and a big produce market, which acts as a trading centre for many of the outlying villages of the plateau.

Waterfalls around Paksong

Just 17 km from Paksong are the twin falls of **Tad Mone** and **Tad Meelook**. Once a popular picnic spot for locals, the area is now almost deserted and the swimming holes at the base of the falls are an idyllic place for a dip. To reach the falls take Route 23 northeast of Paksong towards Tha Teng and Salavan, until you reach a signposted turning; follow the road for about 3.5 km to reach the falls.

Not far from Paksong, 1 km off the road to Pakse, is **Tad Fan**, a dramatic 120-m-high waterfall, which is believed to be one of the tallest cascades in the country. The fall splits into two powerful streams roaring over the edge of the cliff and plummeting into the pool below, with mist and vapour shrouding views from above. The fall's name derives from the species of barking deer which formerly surrounded the area and local legends talk of large numbers of the species falling to their death.

Around 2 km from Tad Fan and 1 km from the main road is **Tad Yeung** (pronounced 'Tad N'Yeung'). Set amongst beautiful coffee plantations and sprinkled with wooden picnic huts, these falls are possibly the best on the plateau. Packing a picnic in Pakse and bringing it along for an afternoon trip is recommended. The cascades plummet 50 m to a pool at the bottom, which is possible to swim in, in the dry season. During the wet season the waterways create numerous little channels and islands around the cascades. Behind the main falls sits a cave – however it is best to get someone to guide you here. There is a slippery walkway from the top of the falls to the bottom, where you can swim.

Essential Bolaven Pleateau

Best places to stay

Tad Lo Lodge, Tad Lo, page 452
Palamei Guesthouse, Tad Lo, page 452

Finding your feet

As tourism expands in Laos, so areas like the Bolaven are sure to become more accessible. For the moment, though, the tourist infrastructure is limited. Tour companies, especially in Pakse, 30 km away (see page 438), can organize trips. Alternatively, the best base is Tad Lo (see page 451). Other places near or on the Bolaven are Salavan, Sekong and Attapeu; guesthouses in these towns can also offer assistance and information on exploring the area.

Best restaurants

Chom, Tad Lo, page 452
Tee Na, Tad Lo, page 453

The falls sit on the edge of the **Dong Hua Sao National Protected Area** and access via the falls is one of the only ways to explore the area. Previously, it was inhabited by a number of rare species now dwindling in number. It is believed that a local population of tigers still resides in the protected area but the chances of spotting one are minimal.

Trekking is offered around the waterfall but is quite difficult in the wet season due to slipperiness and leaches, so it's best to hire one of the guides at the **Tad Fan Resort**. If you follow the track to the left off the main road at Ban Lak, Km 38, at the end of the track, a path leads down to a good viewpoint halfway down the horseshoe-shaped gorge. The magnificent falls offer stunning views but if you wish to swim you should trek further along to **Tad Gniang**, 2 km east of Tad Fan. Tad Gniang, named after the wild stags that populate the area, is only recommended for a dip during the dry season (October to the end of March). There is a charge of 2000 kip per person to visit the falls, plus an additional 3000 kip per motorbike. Tours to Tad Fan and Tad Gniang can be organized through most travel agents in Pakse (see page 438).

Thirty-six kilometres northeast of Pakse is **Paseum Waterfall** and **Utayan Bajiang Champasak** ① *T031-251294*, a strange ethnic theme park. The large compound features the small cascades, restaurant, model ethnic village, gardens and plenty of trails in between.

Listings Paksong (Pakxong) and around

Where to stay

$ Borlavan Guesthouse
Route 23, 2 km north of the market, beyond Paksong town.
The new brick and wood building has a cabin feel and is surrounded by coffee trees, corn fields and a flower garden. The simple rooms are clean and bright (with pink floral sheets) with en suite bathrooms but no hot water. The very friendly owner speaks English.

Waterfalls around Paksong

$$ Tad Fan Resort
Opposite Tad Fane falls, T020-5553 1400, www.tadfane.com.
Perched on the opposite side of the ravine from the Tad Fane falls, this resort offers a series of wooden bungalows with nicely decorated rooms and en suite bathrooms, with hot-water showers. The 2nd floor of the excellent open-air restaurant has a distant view of the falls and serves a wide variety of good Lao, Thai and Western food. Great

service. Treks to the top of falls and the Dan-Sin-Xay Plain can be arranged.

Restaurants

There is a small string of barbecue restaurants, past the market away from Route 23. The market also has a large restaurant section and there's a row of Vietnamese restaurants along Route 23 near the bank.

What to do

To organize kayaking and rafting trips to the Bolaven Plateau, contact **Green Discovery**, in Pakse, see page 438.

Transport

Bus
Regular connections to **Pakse**'s southern bus terminal 0830-1530, 1½ hrs. For the onward journey to **Tad Fan** ask the *songthaew* to stop at Km 38 and follow signs. Also buses to **Attapeu**, daily 0830 and 1200, 3½-4½ hrs.

★Tad Lo is a popular, extremely pretty little village on the edge of the Bolaven Plateau, 30 km from Salavan, and nestled alongside three rolling cascades. The Xe Xet (or Houei Set) flows through Tad Lo, crashing over two sets of cascades: Tad Hang, the lower series of waterfalls, is overlooked by the Tad Lo Lodge and (see Where to stay, page 452), while Tad Lo, the upper series, is a short hike away. The Xe Xet is yet another of the area's rivers that has been dammed to produce hydropower for export to Thailand.

There are several places to stay in this idyllic retreat, good hiking, fantastic waterfalls and elephant trekking.In the vicinity of Tad Lo there are also several villages, which can be visited in the company of a local villager. The area has become particularly popular with the backpacker set, many of whom prefer to stay here rather than in Pakse.

Visiting Tad Lo

The turning for Tad Lo is Ban Houei Set on Route 20 between Pakse and Salavan. Catch a bus or *songthaew* from either town; most drivers know Tad Lo and will stop at Ban Houia Set (2½ hours from Pakse and under an hour from Salavan). There is a sign here indicating the way to Tad Lo – a 1.8-km walk along a dirt track and through the village of Ban Saen Wang. Usually you can get a tuk-tuk to Tad Lo for around 10,000 kip.

Trekking

The two-day trek to Phou Tak Mountain involves a stay in an ecolodge near a mixed Katu/ Souay village. The Tad Soung trek is a fairly demanding day out giving awesome views across the plateau. There is also a five-day trek to the Xe Sap National Protected Area, involving sleeping in hammocks and the chance to see deer and many bird species.

All the guesthouses in Tad Lo also arrange guided treks. Elephant treks can be arranged from the Tad Lo Lodge.

Around Tad Lo

There are two Alak villages, Ban Khian and Tad Soung, close to Tad Lo; the latter is approximately 10 km away from the main resort area and has the most panoramic falls in the vicinity.

The Alak are an Austro-Indonesian ethno-linguistic group. Their grass-thatched huts, with rounded roofs, are not at all Lao in style and are distinct from those in neighbouring Lao Theung villages. Most fascinating is the Alak's seeming obsession with death. The head of each household carves coffins out of logs for himself and every member of his family (even babies), then stacks them, ready for use, under their rice storage huts. This tradition serves as a reminder that life expectancy in these remote areas is around 40 and infant mortality around 100 per 1000 live births; the number one killer here is malaria.

Katou villages such as Ban Houei Houne (on the Salavan–Pakse road) are famous for their weaving of a bright cloth used locally as a *pha sinh* (sarong). This village also has an original contraption to pound rice: on the river below the village are several water-wheels which power the rice pounders. The idea originally came from Xam Neua and was brought to this village by a man who had fought with the Pathet Lao.

Tourist information

Tourist Information Centre
Just after the turn onto the main guesthouse road, T020-5445 5907, kouka222@hotmail.com.
Excellent centre managed by Kouka, which runs a variety of treks from 1 to 5 days.

Where to stay

$$ Tad Lo Lodge
By the falls, T034-211889, souriyavincente@yahoo.com.
The hotel reception is on the east side of the falls, with chalet-style accommodation, some built almost on top of the waterfalls, on the opposite side. The accommodation is comfortable, with cane rocking chairs on the balconies overlooking the falls. Rates include breakfast, during which it's possible to watch the elephants being brought down to the water for their morning dip – quite a special experience. The restaurant serves plenty of Lao and Thai food.

$ Fandee
Main guesthouse road, www.fandee-guesthouse.com.
Run by Frenchman Louis since 2013, this is the first place you'll see on the 'main' road of guesthouses. Lovely wooden bungalows, a cool chill-out area with plenty of hammocks and black and white films projected for the tourists and the community to enjoy. Fandee translates as 'good dream' – a very apt name.

$ Green Garden
Just beyond Palamei Guesthouse (clearly signed).
This is a very laid-back spot set among trees. The communal area has fantastic West African-style rosewood chairs. Food is available and don't miss the home-made cookies with freshly ground Arabica coffee. The Czech owner, Martin, is learning the art of coffee-roasting on his wok. The 3 basic rooms are in a building modelled on a Katu spirit house while the lone bungalow is like a home away from home, with a small outdoor kitchen.

$ Palamei Guesthouse
Just past the turning to the falls, T030-962 0192, palamei.guesthouse@gmail.com.
Run by Mr Poh, this family place has absolutely beautiful views over rice paddies from the large bungalows at the rear. Mr Poh has 19 kids, some of whom are adopted, so this is a great place to feel part of a Lao family. Breakfast and lunch are served, and in the evening guests can eat with the whole family and even learn to cook. Free transport to the bus station 2 km away. Also sells bus tickets and organizes guided treks, which Mr Poh himself sometimes runs. A very special spot.

$ Sipaseuth Guesthouse & Restaurant
Right next to the bridge, T020-5430 4380.
Wooden bungalows right on the riverbank are slightly rundown but have fans and en suite bathrooms. The restaurant serves good Lao food with great view. Very friendly owners. Trekking organized; private transport arranged.

Restaurants

$ Chom
Main guesthouse road, T055-667900.
A simple joint with wooden bench-style seating in the open-air. A very solid range of Lao food although during daytime hours it is limited. Also home to one of the country's most laid-back dogs. Recommended.

$ Sabai Sabai
Next to Chom.
Run by a Lao/Spanish couple who like to party, this place offers Spanish classics as well as pizza and some lethal cocktails.

$ Tee Na Restaurant
Opposite Chom, no phone.
Very friendly service and extremely good larb (minced meat salad) and spring rolls (the fresh version, not the fried) in the most basic of surrounds. Also offers a homestay and laundry service. Bungalows set to open. Recommended.

$ Tim Guesthouse
Main guesthouse road.
Once the most popular place in town, this place still does a good range of food but the atmosphere can now be a little lacking.

Festivals

Mar Buffalo ceremony This Ta Oy ceremony takes place in a village near Tad Lo on the first full moon in Mar. It is dedicated to the warrior spirit, who is asked for protection. **Apr** Annually just before Lao New Year there is a **full moon sacrifice** by Nghe and Katu people in villages around Tad Lo. It is important to employ a guide if you wish to visit the festivities in order to ensure local customs are respected.

What to do

Elephant trekking
This is an excellent way to see the area as elephants can go where jeeps cannot. It is also a thrill being on the back of an elephant. **Tad Lo Lodge** (see Where to stay) organizes treks throughout the day; 2 people per elephant.

Trekking
The best place to head for information on tours in the area is the **Tourist Information Centre** (see page, opposite). All the local guesthouses run treks to Ban Khian and Tad Soung, but Mr Poh at **Palamei Guesthouse** (see Where to stay) is particularly recommended.

Transport

Bus
There are buses from Ban Houei Set (1 km north of Tad Lo) to **Pakse**, hourly until 1630, plus a VIP sleeping bus to **Vientiane** or **Thakek**. Buses also run to **Salavan** but times are sporadic. For information and tickets, contact the Tourist Information Centre.

Islands of
the south

★This area, locally known as Siphandon, 'The 4000 Islands', is an idyllic picture-perfect ending to any trip to Laos. The three main islands offer something for all tourists: the larger Don Khong is great for exploring traditional Lao rural life; Don Deth is a backpacker haven and perfect if you want to while away the days with a good book in a hammock; and Don Khone is better for those wanting to take in some tourist sites such as the Li Phi falls or colonial ruins. These are just three of the many islands littered across the Mekong right at the southern tip of Laos near the border with Cambodia. Half of the islands are submerged when the Mekong is in flood. Just before the river enters Cambodia it divides into countless channels. The distance between the most westerly and easterly streams is 14 km – the greatest width of the river in its whole 4200-km course. The river's volume is swelled by the Kong, San Srepok and Krieng tributaries, which join just upstream from here. Pakha, or freshwater dolphins, can sometimes be spotted in this area between December and May, when they come upstream to give birth to their young, but they are increasingly endangered. *Colour map 3, C3.*

Don Khong is the largest of the Mekong islands at 16 km long and 8 km wide. It's a tremendous place to relax or explore by bicycle. Visitors might be surprised by the smooth asphalt roads, electricity and general standard of amenities that exist on the island but two words explain it all – Khamtai Siphandone – Laos' former president, who has a residence on the island. The island was also electrified about five years before the surrounding mainland areas and it is not unusual to see heavily armed personnel cruising around the place.

Muang Khong

Don Khong's 'capital' is Muang Khong, a small former French settlement. 'Muang' means city but, although Muang Khong is the district's main settlement, it feels more like a village than a town, with only a few thousand inhabitants. Pigs and chickens scrabble for food under the houses and just 50 m inland the houses give way to paddy fields.

There are two wats in the town. **Wat Kan Khong**, also known as Wat Phuang Kaew, is visible from the jetty: a large gold Buddha in the *mudra* of subduing Mara garishly overlooks the Mekong. Much more attractive is **Wat Chom Thong** at the upstream extremity of the village, which may date from the early 19th century but which was much extended during the colonial period. The unusual Khmer-influenced *sim* may be gently decaying but it is doing so with style, and the wat compound, with its carefully tended plants and elegant buildings, is a peaceful and relaxing place. The *naga* heads on the roof of the main *sim* are craftily designed to channel water, which issues from their mouths. The old *sim* to the left of the main entrance is also notable, although it is usually kept locked because of its poor condition.

Essential Islands of the south

Finding your feet

The easiest way to get to all three major Siphandon islands (Don Khong, Don Deth and Don Khone) from Pakse is by private minivan, arranged by tour operators in Pakse. The most luxurious way is aboard the **Vat Pho**, www.vatphou.com, a boutique riverborne hotel that does a three-day/two-night cruise from Pakse to Champasak and Wat Phou to Don Khong returning to Pakse.

Using public transport, take a bus or *songthaew* from Pakse to Ban Hat Xai Khoune from where ferries make the short crossing to Don Khong; or further south, at Ban Nakasang, where boats shuffle tourists to Don Deth and Don Khone. Once on the islands, most guesthouses can help arrange private boats for exploring. It's possible to walk between Don Deth and Don Khone across the bridge, for which there is a small charge (also used as a ticket for Li Phi Falls). The islands are small and can be easily navigated by foot on by bicycle.

When to go

The best time to visit the area is during the dry season (November to March), when the waters recede and the islands can be clearly seen. This is also the best time to spot the rare freshwater dolphins as they come up the river to breed.

Time required

The islands are small and the main sights could be seen within a day or two, but it's best to allow a few days to really relax and enjoy the pace of island life.

For early risers the **morning market** in Muang Khong is also worthwhile – if only to see the fish before they are sold to the restaurants here and consigned to the cooking pot. Note that the market only really operates between 0530 and 0730. If you are getting up for the market, it is worth setting the alarm clock even earlier to get onto the banks of the Mekong before 0600, when the sun rises over the hills to the east, picking out the silhouettes of fishermen in their canoes.

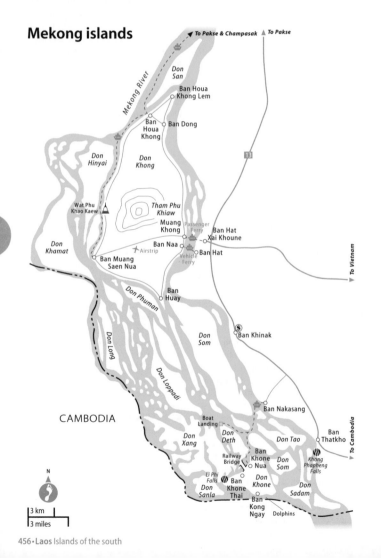

Mekong islands

All of the guesthouses can arrange bicycle hire. Some places hire motorbikes too. There is a **Lao Agriculture Promotion** bank in Muang Khong; hours are erratic. **Pon's Hotel** and **Pon's Arena Khong Hotel** advance cash against Visa and Mastercard for a fee.

Exploring the island

Most people come to Muang Khong as a base for visiting the **Li Phi** and **Khong Phapheng Falls** (see page 461) in the far south of Laos. However, these trips, alongside dolphin-watching trips are much easier to arrange from Don Deth or Don Khone. But the island is a destination in itself, and offers a great insight into Lao rural life without all the hustle and bustle found in more built-up areas. To a certain extent – apart from electricity, a sprinkling of cars and a couple of internet terminals – time stands still in Dong Khong.

The island is worth exploring by bicycle and deserves more time than most visitors give it. The coastal area is flat (though the interior is hilly) and the roads are quiet and the villages and countryside offer a glimpse of traditional Laos. Most people take the southern 'loop' around the island, via **Ban Muang Saen Nua**, a distance of about 25 km (two to three hours by bike). The villages south of Ban Muang Saen Nua are wonderfully picturesque with buffalos grazing in the field and farmers tending to their rice crops. Unlike in other parts of Laos the residents here are fiercely protective of their forests and illegal logging incurs very severe penalties.

About 6 km north of Ban Muang Saen Nua is a hilltop wat which is arguably Don Khong's main claim to national fame. **Wat Phou Khao Kaew** (Glass Hill Monastery) is built on the spot where an entrance leads down to the underground lair of the *nagas*, known as **Muang Nak**. This underground town lies beneath the waters of the Mekong, with several tunnels leading to the surface – another is at That Luang in Vientiane. Lao legend has it that the *nagas* will come to the surface to protect the Lao whenever the country is in danger. Some people believe that the Thais tricked the Lao to build *thats* over the holes to prevent the *nagas* coming to their rescue – the hole at Wat Phou Khao Kaew is covered.

Tham Phou Khiaw is tucked away among the forests of the **Green Mountain** in the centre of the island. It's a small cave, containing earthenware pots. Buddha images and other relics and offerings litter the site. Every Lao New Year (April) townsfolk climb up to the cave to bathe the images. Although it's only 15 minutes' walk from the road, finding the cave is not particularly straightforward except during Lao New Year when it is possible to follow the crowds. Head 1.5 km north from Muang Khong on the road until you come to a banana plantation, with a couple of wooden houses. Take the pathway just before the houses through the banana plantation and at the top; just to the left, is a small gateway through the fence and a fairly well-defined path. Head up and along this path and, after 300 m or so, there is a rocky clearing. The path continues from the top right corner of the clearing for a further 200 m to a rocky mound that rolls up and to the left. Walk across the mound for about 20 m, until it levels out, and then head back to the forest. Keeping the

> **Tip...**
>
> There are no banks on the islands but some guesthouses change money. Mr Phao of **Phao's Riverview** on Don Deth will take you by boat to Ban Khinak, north of Ban Nakasang, where there is a Visa and MasterCard ATM. There are internet cafés on Don Deth and Don Khone and many restaurants and guesthouses have Wi-Fi. If you need to make an international call, it's cheapest to call via the net. Guesthouses may let you call from their mobiles, at US$4 or more a minute.

rock immediately to your right, continue round and after 40 m there are two upturned tree trunks marking the entrance to the cave.

On the northern tip of the island is a sandy beach, though swimming is generally not advised due to parasites in the water and potentially strong currents. Word on the ground is that Lao's former President Siphandone is building a resort here. In nearby **Ban Houa Khong**, approximately 13 km north of Muang Khong, is the former president's modest abode set in traditional Lao style.

Listings Don Khong

Where to stay

Most guesthouses now have Wi-Fi.

$$$-$$ Pon Arena Hotel
40 m north of the main street, T020-221 8166, www.ponarenahotel.com.
There are 2 distinct properties, one on the river and another set in a garden across the road. The less expensive garden rooms may lack the Mekong view, but they are larger and the garden view is pleasant. All rooms are very tastefully decorated with high ceilings. Some rooms have tiny balconies. Wi-Fi throughout. Breakfast served on the upstairs veranda.

$$$-$ Senesothxeune Hotel
100 m to the left of the main ferry point, T030-526 0577, www.ssxhotel.com.
Tastefully designed, modern interpretation of colonial Lao architecture. Beautiful fittings, including carved wooden fish above each entrance and brass chandeliers. Splurge a little for the superior room with private balcony. The restaurant menu is mainly confined to Asian dishes. The hotel is run by a very friendly team. Recommended.

$ Pon's River Guesthouse
T031-214037.
Same owner as **Pon Arena Hotel**. The large, spotless a/c rooms are very good value, with hot showers, mosquito nets and comfortable beds. Mr Pon, who speaks French and English, is very helpful and well-informed. He can arrange motorbike and bike rental, as well as trips to the Cambodian border, to

Don Deth and Don Khon and back to Pakse. The restaurant is still the most popular on the island.

$ Rattana
Next to the boat landing.
While the service here is very slack, the upstairs rooms do represent very good value with the cheapest river views in town. Bathrooms have tiny shower areas, but are otherwise adequate. A good budget option, but for hospitality and advice, head to **Pon's**.

$ Villa Khang Kong
Set back from the main road, near the ferry point, T031-213539.
Fantastic traditional Lao wooden building recently painted in black and white. A great veranda and communal lounging area. Spacious clean rooms, with or without a/c. No river views.

Restaurants

In the low season most restaurants will only be able to fulfil about half of the menu options and some will be devoid of other diners. Local fish with coconut milk cooked in banana leaves, *mok pa*, is truly a divine local speciality and makes a trip to the islands worthwhile in itself – order in advance.

$$ Pon's Arena
See Where to stay.
Serves a broadly similar menu to everywhere else in town but adds a more refined setting, dim lighting and cheesy background music.

$ Souksan Chinese Restaurant
Next to Pon's, on stilts over the river.
Attractive place with a stunning, unobscured view of the river. Good local fish, tasty honeyed chicken and basil pork with chilli.

$ Pon's Hotel and Restaurant
See Where to stay.
Good atmosphere and busy when everywhere else is dead. Excellent food, try the chicken curry or the fish soup. The *mok pa* here is excellent, order 2 hrs in advance. Very popular. Service can be rather haphazard when busy.

Festivals

Dec A 5-day **Boat Racing festival** takes place early in the month, on the river opposite Muang Khong. It coincides with **National Day** on 2 Dec and is accompanied by a great deal of celebration, feasting and drinking.

What to do

All the guesthouses in Don Khong run tours to Don Deth and Don Khone, taking in the Phaphaeng Falls and dolphin watching.

Transport

Boat
Pon's Hotel (reliable and recommended) and others can arrange boats to **Don Deth** or **Don Khone**. There are also several boatmen on the riverfront who are more than happy to take people for the right price.

Bus/truck
Songthaew and buses head to **Pakse** at 0630, 0700, 0800, 0830, 3-4 hrs. Or cross to Ban Hat Xai Khoune and then try for transport south.

The minibus service back to **Pakse** can be organized by Mr Pon, 2 hrs. Drop-off at Ban Muang for **Champasak** possible. Guesthouses also arrange transport to the Cambodian border and beyond to **Siem Reap**, to **Phnom Penh**, **Kratie** and **Stung Treng**.

Motorbike and bicycle
Many of the guesthouses including **Pon's** and **Senesothxene** offer motorbikes and bicycles.

Don Deth, Don Khone and around

beautiful and relaxed backpacker hub

The islands of Don Khone and Don Deth are the pot of gold at the end of the rainbow for most travellers who head to the southern tip of Laos, and it's not hard to see why. After the transport headaches around the Bolaven Plateau and the architectural wonder of Wat Phou, the bamboo huts that stretch along the banks of these two staggeringly beautiful islands are filled with contented travellers in no rush to move on. Don Deth is more of a backpacker haven, while Don Khone has been able to retain a more authentically Lao charm. Travelling by boat in this area is very picturesque: the islands are covered in coconut palms, flame trees, stands of bamboo, kapok trees and hardwoods; the river is riddled with eddies and rapids and it demands a skilled helmsman to negotiate them. In the distance, a few kilometres to the south, are the Khong Hai Mountains, which dominate the skyline and delineate the frontier between Laos and Cambodia.

Ban Nakasang
Ban Nakasang, the jumping-off point for Don Khone and Don Deth, is not the most pleasant of Lao towns. However, it has a thriving market, where most of the islanders stock

up on their goods, so it's worth having a look around before you head off to the islands, particularly if you need to pick up supplies.

Don Deth

This island has really woken up to tourism and the riverbank is peppered with cheap-as-chips bamboo huts and restaurants geared to accommodate the growing wave of backpacker travellers that floods south to stop and recoup in this idyllic setting. A good book, hammock and icy beverage are the orders of the day here, but those with a bit more energy should explore the truly stunning surroundings. It's a great location for watching sunrises and sunsets, for walking through shady palms and frangipani trees and for swimming off the beaches, which attract the hordes in the dry season. Away from the picturesque waterfront, the centre of the island comprises rice paddies and farms; you should take care not to harm crops when exploring the island.

Don Deth & Don Khone

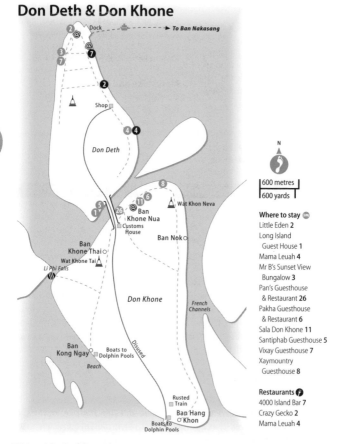

600 metres
600 yards

Where to stay 🛏
Little Eden 2
Long Island
  Guest House 1
Mama Leuah 4
Mr B's Sunset View
  Bungalow 3
Pan's Guesthouse
  & Restaurant 26
Pakha Guesthouse
  & Restaurant 6
Sala Don Khone 11
Santiphab Guesthouse 5
Vixay Guesthouse 7
Xaymountry
  Guesthouse 8

Restaurants 🍴
4000 Island Bar 7
Crazy Gecko 2
Mama Leuah 4

The national tourism authorities have been coordinating with locals to ensure that the beautiful island doesn't become 'Vang Vieng-ified', so you'll find no *Friends* DVDs here, although 'happy' shakes have started to appear. The islands got electricity in 2009 although not everyone has signed up to the 24-hour connection; there are no cars (except for the odd truck and tourist open-sided buses) and few other modern conveniences. Internet has made its way to the island, however, and it's still possible to get mobile phone coverage. Most guesthouses run tours to the falls/dolphins. The dwindling population of dolphins appears between December and May. If you do take a boat out make sure you keep your distance from them.

A few entrepreneurial types are starting to promote adventure tourism here. Kayaking and rafting trips can be organized. Several guesthouses also have tubes for rent. The river's current here is probably the strongest in all of Laos, so it is definitely inadvisable to go tubing in the wet season and probably not a good idea at any other time. It is also inadvisable to go by yourself; there is a huge set of falls at the bottom of Laos. Swimming, visiting the falls and other activities all need to be undertaken with the utmost caution as several tourists have drowned here.

Don Khone and Li Phi Falls

From the railway bridge, follow the southwest path through **Ban Khone Thai** and then wind through the paddy fields for 1.7 km (20 minutes' walk) to **Li Phi Falls** ⓘ *aka Somphamit or Khone Yai falls, 10,000 kip entry fee, paid at the bridge*. These are a succession of raging rapids, crashing through a narrow rocky gorge. In the wet season, when the rice is green, the area is beautiful; in the dry season, it is scorching. From the main vantage point on a jagged, rocky outcrop, the falls aren't that impressive, as a large stretch of them are obscured. 'Phi' means ghost, a reference, it is believed, to the bodies that floated down the river from the north during the war.

It's best to visit Li Phi around June or July, when all the fishermen are putting out their bamboo fish traps. Every year Cambodia's Tonlé Sap lake reverses its flow sending millions of fish up the Mekong into Laos. During this time, each fish trap can catch 1000-2000 kg of fish in a day. In theory, enough fish are caught in these two short months to feed half the population of Laos, although most of the catch is exported to Thailand.

Dolphin spotting

The Mekong, south of Don Khone, is one of the few places in the world where it is possible to see freshwater dolphins. They can be spotted from December to May, from the French pier at the end of the island, not far from the village of **Ban Hang Khon**. The walk across Don Khone from the railway bridge is some 4 km and bicycles can be hired. (A much better bicycle route is to head north round the tip and down to Hang Khon, 45 minutes; the disused railway bridge is not a comfortable ride for bikes as it's rocky.) However the dolphins reside in deep-water pools and catching a glimpse of them is more likely if you're in a boat (from **Ban Kong Ngay** or **Ban Hang Khon**.

Khong Phapheng Falls

Ban Thatko, 10,000 kip entry fee for foreigners. There are a number of food and drinks stalls. Guesthouses on Don Deth and Don Khone organize trips to the falls and will usually be booked in conjunction with a trip to see the dolphins (this will cost extra). Boats can no longer go direct to the falls, so most tours will include a tuk-tuk ride from Ban Nakasang.

About 36 km south of Ban Hat Xai Khoune at Ban Thatko, a road branches off Route 13 towards Khong Phapheng Falls, which roar around the eastern shore of the Mekong for

13 km. One fork of the road leads to a vantage point, where a large wooden structure on stilts has a fantastic head-on view of the falls. When you see the huge volume of white water boiling and surging over the jagged rocks below, it is hard to imagine that there is another 10 km width of river running through the other channels. A perilous path leads down from the viewpoint to the edge of the water. Be careful here. Unsurprisingly, the river is impassable at this juncture, as an 1860s French expedition led by adventurers Doudart de Lagrée and Francis Garnier discovered. Another road leads down to the bank of the Mekong, 200 m away, just above the lip of the falls; at this deceptively tranquil spot, the river is gathering momentum before it plunges over the edge. It was said that a tongue of rock once extended from the lip of the falls, and the noise of Khong Phapheng – literally 'the voice of the Mekong' – crashing over this outcrop could be heard many miles away. The rock apparently broke off during a flood surge but the cascades still make enough noise to justify their name.

Listings Don Deth, Don Khone and around *maps p252 and p256*

Tourist information

The **Provincial Tourism Office** in Pakse (see page 436) is responsible for the islands. While on the islands, you will need to ask your guesthouse owner or one of the travel operators.

Where to stay

Don Deth
Sunset side

$$-$ Little Eden
Hua Det, T020-7773 9045, www.little edenguesthouse-dondet.com.
Very close to the island tip and a small hike from the main drop-off dock, this place offers the best view of the stunning sunsets. Miss Noy and her husband Mathieu offer 16 excellent rooms which are the island's most upmarket lodgings. The restaurant, serving top-notch Asian and European dishes, is in a prime position with awesome views.

$ Mr B's Sunset View Bungalow
Near the northern tip, T020-5418 1171.
The bungalows and grounds themselves are a bit lacklustre, however the views are great and the staff are helpful.

$ Vixay Guest House
A short walk from Mr B's, T020-7645 1331.
The extremely affable Mr Vixay offers small bungalows and a reasonable restaurant with great views. The cheaper riverside options come with squat toilets and cold showers, while the more expensive western en suites are set slightly back from the view. The attached restaurant serves great food. Bike hire. Recommended.

Sunrise side

$ Long Island Guest House
Next to Santiphab, T020-5567 9470.
Run by the friendly Mr Kham, a local English teacher who gives classes on site. 4 simple, clean rattan bungalows with hot water showers line the river. Reached via a quaint path linking it with the paddy fields, lit by hanging bulbs at night. A restaurant is being built, with plans for Lao cooking lessons. Wi-Fi.

$ Mama Leuah
A few properties along from Mr Tho, T020-5907 8792, www.mamaleuah-dondet.com.
Ultra basic bungalows that prove ever popular for 3 key reasons: the wonderful, river front garden setting; the ultra-accommodating hosts, Lutz (German) and Pheng (Lao); and the best kitchen

on the island. All bungalows have squat toilets, some shared, some private. Number 7 at the end is the pick of the bunch. Recommended for those seeking ambience, not creature comforts.

$ Mr Phao's Riverview
On the riverfront, T020-5656 9651.
7 relatively new wooden bungalows with lovely carved furniture offering lodgings a notch above the nearby options. Some rooms have showers. Mr Phao is one of the friendliest folk on the island and super helpful. If he has time he will take guests across to opposite Aan island where there is a wat.

$ Santiphab Guesthouse
Far end of the island next to the bridge, T020-5461 4231, www.santiphab-don-det.com.
Alongside the older rattan bungalows, some newer half-wood bungalows have been added. Idyllic setting, flanked by the Mekong on one side and rice paddies on the other. Good for those who want seclusion but also quick access to Don Khone. Very cheap restaurant serves tasty fare including a good peppery fried vegetables with chicken and great iced coffee. A friendly, timeless place with plenty of cute cats milling around. Small general store next door.

Don Khone

$$$-$$ Sala Don Khone
T030-525 6390, www.salalao.com.
Various options are available here, including rooms in the former French hospital built in 1927, each with beautiful tiling and 4 poster beds. In addition, traditional Luang Prabang-style houses have been built in the grounds, with 8 twin rooms, all with en suite hot shower and toilet. On the river itself a series of rafts provide floating rooms, each with plenty of small touches that make them special. Also has a wonderful deck and a fine pool.

$$-$ Pan's Guesthouse
About 250 m from the bridge, T030-534 6939.
These wooden bungalows are exceptionally good value for money. The 6 riverside bungalows with hot water, fan and comfy mattresses are simple but comfortable and ultra clean. The cushioned seating on the balconies is a real plus. The owner is one of the most helpful hosts in Siphandon. Highly recommended for those on a limited budget. Breakfast included.

$ Pakha Guesthouse
20 m past Auberge, T020-5584 7522.
The main track splits this guesthouse in 2, with half the rooms directly on the river and the remainder facing paddy fields to the rear. River rooms are fan only and are joined by a long, peaceful balcony, meaning this is a better spot for meeting fellow travellers than seeking privacy. The paddy facing rooms are larger and come with a/c. The restaurant does a good papaya salad and roasted fish in salt.

$ Xaymountry Guesthouse
Near the old school, no phone.
This huge, beautiful stilt house is home to a range of budget rooms; those at the rear are rather small, but the recently refurbished front rooms offer good value. The veranda area is a peaceful spot for breakfast and the owner is very welcoming.

Restaurants

Ban Nakasang
2 small thatched beachside restaurants serve good chicken *feu*. In the rainy season they move further up the bank. There are also food and drinks stalls on the right as you get off the boat.

Don Deth
Most people choose to eat at their guesthouses; most of which all have pretty much the same menu, but there are now a few places worth seeking out.

$$-$ Little Eden
See Where to stay.

A large menu with some good Western and Lao dishes thanks to the Belgian/Lao couple who own it. Superb views.

$ 4000 Island Bar
T020-7793 5802, www.4000islandbar.com.

This is a big hit with the backpacker set as much for the views as for the great Indian food. Also serves Western fodder.

$ Crazy Gecko
A few mins past the main strip.

An intimate little over-water eatery with lots of funky decorative touches. Serves a simple menu of Lao and Western dishes. Decent wine by the glass. Recommended.

$ Mama Leuah
See Where to stay.

Perhaps the best kitchen on the island, the chef, Lutz, is rightly proud of his cuisine which draws rave reviews. Lutz learned his trade in Thailand, so expect good green and red curries along with a solid pad Thai. The muesli is also a hit as are his German classics. Vegetarians will be pleased to see a great pumpkin burger on the menu.

Don Khone

$$ Auberge Sala Don Khone
See Where to stay.

There's a beautiful view from the restaurant and some good options on the menu.

$ Pakha Guesthouse
See Where to stay.

Ms Noy's steamed fish makes this a good lunch pit stop. No river views, but she will serve food on one of the river bungalow balconies when they're not too busy.

$ Pan's Restaurant
See Where to stay.

Across from the guesthouse, this is a fantastic, cheap option serving up brilliant home-made meals. The fish here is outstanding.

Shopping

Don Deth
There isn't much to buy here. A small grocery store just down from the port has a few essential items and snacks but is not very well stocked. If you're in desperate need of any items, you are better off making a quick trip to Ban Nakasang to pick up things from the market there. Most guesthouse owners go to Ban Nakasang on an almost daily basis and will usually agree to buy things for you if you pay them 5000 kip or so.

What to do

Don Khone and around
Boat trips

Boats can be hired for day trips to the islands, including one where the rice pots are made. Ask at **Mr Pan's**.

Dolphin watching
It is possible to hire a boat to try and spot the dolphins from Kong Ngay, 90,000 kip, maximum 3 people to a boat. Further south, at Ban Hang Khon, it's slightly less expensive – maximum 3 people. Plenty of outfits offer Phapheng tours and dolphin watching. Costs reduce the larger the group of people.

Fishing and kayaking
Most tour operators are able to arrange a day out fishing – prices start from around 75,000 kip per person (4 people). 2-hr sunset boat tours are also on offer.

Swimming
There is a sandy beach on Don Khone where many travellers like to take a dip. However, in the wet season this can be particularly dangerous as there is a nasty undercurrent and tourists have drowned here, so be careful. The other thing to consider when bathing is the possibility of picking up the parasite called schistosomiasis, also known as bilharzia.

Transport

Ban Nakasang
Boat
To **Don Deth** and **Don Khone**, 15-20 mins.
To **Don Khong**, 2 hrs. Between **Don Khone**
and **Don Deth** a few mins.

Bus/songthaew
Decent buses depart from Ban Nakasang's
market, hourly 0600-1000 daily, northbound
for **Pakse**; some continue onwards to
Vientiane; get off at **Ban Hat Xai Khoune**
for the crossing to **Don Khong**. **Xplore-
Asia**, www.explore-asia.com, runs tourist
buses to **Pakse**; the same minivan will stop
at **Ban Muang** for **Champasak**. Agencies
can also arrange bus tickets for destinations
further afield such as **Ubon Ratchathani**
or **Bangkok**.

   To Cambodia To get to **Don Kralor** (on
the Cambodian border) most guesthouses
can organize the trip in a minivan.

Cambodian visas are available on the
border and Lao visas are now also available.
To **Stung Treng**, the largest town on the
other side of the Cambodian border, 2 hrs.
Tickets can also be bought to more distant
destinations in Cambodia. For details of the
border crossing at Voen Kham (Laos) to Don
Kralor (Cambodia), see box, page 544.

Don Deth, Don Khone and around
Boat
For scheduled boat transport, see page 459.
Almost every guesthouse can arrange tours,
transport and tickets. Tour operators offer
tickets for transport out of Siphandon down to
Cambodia or back up to other parts of Laos.

   To **Ban Nakasang** the 1st boat is the
market boat, leaving at 0630.

   There are 2 ways to get to **Don Khong**
from Ban Nakasang, either by boat, 2 hrs,
or by bus. Although it's slower and more
expensive, the boat trip is one of the loveliest
in Laos.

Background

History of
Vietnam

The earliest record of humans in Vietnam is from an archaeological site on Do Mountain, in the northern Thanh Hoa Province. The remains discovered here have been dated to the Lower Palaeolithic (early Stone Age). So far, all early human remains have been unearthed in North Vietnam, invariably in association with limestone cliff dwellings. Unusually, tools are made of basalt rather than flint, the more common material found at similar sites in other parts of the world.

Archaeological excavations have shown that between 5000 BC and 3000 BC, two important Mesolithic cultures occupied North Vietnam: these are referred to as the **Hoa Binh** and **Bac Son** cultures after the principal excavation sites in Tonkin. Refined stone implements and distinctive hand axes with polished edges (known as Bacsonian axes) are characteristic of the two cultures. These early inhabitants of Vietnam were probably small, dark-skinned and of Melanesian or Austronesian stock.

There are 2000 years of recorded Vietnamese history and another 2000 years of legend. The Vietnamese people trace their origins back to 15 tribal groups known as the **Lac Viet** who settled in what is now North Vietnam at the beginning of the Bronze Age. Here they established an agrarian kingdom known as Van-lang that seems to have vanished during the third century BC.

A problem with early **French archaeological studies** in Vietnam was that most of the scholars were either Sinologists or Indologists. In consequence, they looked to Vietnam as a receptacle of Chinese or Indian cultural influences and spent little time uncovering those aspects of culture, art and life that were indigenous in origin and inspiration.

Pre-colonial history

The beginning of Vietnamese recorded history coincides with the start of **Chinese cultural hegemony** over the north, in the second century BC. The Chinese dominated Vietnam for more than 1000 years until the 10th century AD and the cultural legacy is still very much in evidence, making Vietnam distinctive in Southeast Asia. Even after the 10th century, and despite breaking away from Chinese political domination, Vietnam was still overshadowed and greatly influenced by its illustrious neighbour to the north. Nonetheless, the fact that Vietnam could shrug off 1000 years of Chinese subjugation and emerge with a distinct cultural heritage and language says a lot for Vietnam's strength of national identity.

Ly Dynasty
The Ly Dynasty (1009-1225) was the first independent Vietnamese dynasty. Its capital, Thang Long, was at the site of present day Hanoi and the dynasty based its system of government and social relations closely upon the Chinese Confucianist model.

The first Ly emperor, and one of Vietnam's great kings, was Ly Cong Uan who was born in AD 974. He is usually known by his posthumous title, **Ly Thai To**, and reigned for 19 years from 1009-1028. Ly Cong Uan was raised and educated by monks and acceded to the throne when, as the commander of the palace guard in Hoa Lu (the capital of Vietnam before Thang Long or Hanoi) and with the support of his great patron, the monk Van Hanh, he managed to gain the support of the Buddhist establishment and many local lords. During his reign, he enjoyed a reputation not just as a great soldier, but also as a devout man who paid attention to the interests and wellbeing of his people. He tried to re-establish the harmony between ruler and ruled which had suffered during the previous years and he even sent his son to live outside the walls of the palace so that he could gain a taste of ordinary life and an understanding of ordinary people.

Ly Cong Uan was succeeded by his son, Ly Phat Ma, who is better known as **Ly Thai Tong** (reigned 1028-1054). Ly Phat Ma had been prepared for kingship since birth and he proved to be an excellent ruler during his long reign. It is hard to generalize about this period in Vietnamese history because Ly Phat Ma adapted his pattern of rule no less than six times during his reign. Early on he challenged the establishment, contending for example that good governance was not merely a consequence of following best practice but depended upon good kingship. Later he was more of an establishment figure. Perhaps his greatest military success was the mounting of a campaign to defeat the Cham in 1044 from which he returned with shiploads of plunder. His greatest artistic legacy was the construction of the One Pillar Pagoda or Chua Mot Cot in Hanoi (see page 43).

Ly Phat Ma was succeeded by his son, Ly Nhat Ton, posthumously known as **Ly Thanh Tong** (reigned 1054-1072). History is not as kind about Ly Thanh Tong as it is about his two forebears. Nonetheless he did challenge the might of the Chinese along Vietnam's northern borders – largely successfully – and like his father also mounted a campaign against Champa (see page 470) in 1069. Records indicate that he spent a great deal of time trying to father a son and worked his way through numerous concubines and at last, a son was born to a concubine of common blood in 1066 and named Ly Can Duc.

Ly Can Duc was proclaimed emperor in 1072 when he was only six years old and, surprisingly, remained king until he died in 1127. His death marks the end of the Ly Dynasty for he left no heir and the crown passed to the maternal clan of his nephew. There followed a period of instability and it was not until 1225 that a new dynasty – the Tran Dynasty – managed to subdue the various competing cliques and bring a semblance of order to the country.

Tran Dynasty

Scholars do not know a great deal about the four generations of kings of the Tran Dynasty. It seems that they established the habit of marrying within the clan, and each king took queens who were either their cousins or, in one case, a half-sister. Such a long period of intermarriage, one imagines, would have had some far-reaching genetic consequences, although ironically the collapse of the dynasty seems to have been brought about after one foolish king decided to marry outside the Tran clan. The great achievement of the Tran Dynasty was to resist the expansionist tendencies of the Mongol forces, who conquered China in the 1250s and then set their sights on Vietnam. In 1284 a huge Mongol-Yuan force, consisting of no fewer than four armies, massed on the border to crush the Vietnamese. Fortunately the Tran were blessed with a group of brave and resourceful princes (the most notable of whom was Tran Quoc Tuan, better known – and now immortalized in street names in just about every Vietnamese town – as Tran Hung Dao), and in the end the forces of the Tran Dynasty were victorious.

Le Loi

Despite 1000 years of Chinese domination and centuries of internal dynastic squabbles the Viet retained a strong sense of national identity and were quick to respond to charismatic leadership. As so often in Vietnam's history one man was able to harness nationalistic sentiment and mould the country's discontent into a powerful fighting force: in 1426 it was Le Loi. Together with the brilliant tactician **Nguyen Trai**, Le Loi led a campaign to remove the Chinese from Vietnamese soil. Combining surprise, guerrilla tactics and Nguyen Trai's innovative and famous propaganda, designed to convince defending Ming of the futility of their position, the Viet won a resounding victory which led to the enlightened and artistically distinguished Le period. Le Loi's legendary victory lives on in popular form and is celebrated in the tale of the restored sword in water puppet performances across the country. Following his victory against the Ming he claimed the throne in 1428 and reigned until his death five years later.

Le Thanh Ton

With Le Loi's death the Le Dynasty worked its way through a succession of young kings who seemed to hold the throne barely long enough to warm the cushions before they were murdered. It was not until 1460 that a king of substance was to accede: Le Thanh Ton (reigned 1460-1497). His reign was a period of great scholarship and artistic accomplishment. He established the system of rule that was to guide successive Vietnamese emperors for 500 years. He also mounted a series of military campaigns, some as far as Laos to the west.

Le expansion

The expansion of the Vietnamese state, under the Le, south from its heartland in the Tonkin Delta, followed the decline of the Cham Kingdom at the end of the 15th century. By the early 18th century the Cham were extinct as an identifiable political and military force and the Vietnamese advanced still further south into the Khmer-controlled territories of the Mekong Delta. This geographical over-extension and the sheer logistical impracticability of ruling from distant Hanoi, disseminating edicts and collecting taxes, led to the disintegration of the – ever tenuous – imperial rule. Noble families, locally dominant, challenged the emperor's authority and the Le Dynasty gradually dissolved into internecine strife and regional fiefdoms, namely Trinh in the north and Nguyen in the south, a pattern that was to reassert itself some 300 years later. But although on paper the Vietnamese – now consisting of two dynastic houses, Trinh and Nguyen – appeared powerful, the people were mired in poverty.

There were numerous peasant rebellions in this period, of which the most serious was the **Tay Son rebellion** of 1771. One of the three Tay Son brothers, Nguyen Hue, proclaimed himself **Emperor Quang Trung** in 1788, only to die four years later. His death paved the way for the establishment of the **Nguyen Dynasty** – the last Vietnamese dynasty – in 1802. Despite the fact that this period heralded the arrival of the French – leading to their eventual domination of Vietnam – it is regarded as a golden period in Vietnamese history. During the Nguyen Dynasty, Vietnam was unified as a single state and Hué emerged as the heart of the kingdom.

Any history of Vietnam must include the non-Vietnamese peoples and civilizations. The central and southern parts of Vietnam have only relatively recently been dominated by the Viets. Before that, these lands were in the hands of people of Indian or Khmer origins.

Funan (AD 100-600)

According to Chinese sources, Funan was a Hindu kingdom founded in the first century AD with its capital, Vyadhapura, close to the Mekong River near the border with Cambodia. A local legend records that Kaundinya, a great Indian Brahmin, acting on a dream, sailed to the coast of Vietnam carrying with him a bow and arrow. When he arrived, Kaundinya shot the arrow and where it landed he established the capital of Funan. Following this act, Kaundinya married the princess Soma, daughter of the local King of the Nagas (giant water serpents). The legend symbolizes the union between Indian and local cultural traditions – the naga representing indigenous fertility rites and customs, and the arrow, the potency of the Hindu religion.

Oc-Eo

Funan built its wealth and power on its strategic location on the sea route between China and the islands to the south. Maritime technology at the time forced seafarers travelling between China and island Southeast Asia and India to stop and wait for the winds to change before they could continue on their way. This sometimes meant a stay of up to five months. The large port city of Oc-Eo offered a safe harbour for merchant vessels and the revenues generated enabled the kings of the empire to expand rice cultivation, dominate a host of surrounding vassal states as far away as the Malay coast and South Burma, and build a series of impressive temples, cities and irrigation works.

Funan reached the peak of its powers in the fourth century and went into decline during the fifth century AD when improving maritime technology made Oc-Eo redundant as a haven for sailing vessels. By the mid-sixth century, Funan, having suffered from a drawn-out leadership crisis, was severely weakened. The Cham ultimately conquered. What is interesting about Funan is the degree to which it provided a model for future states in Southeast Asia. Funan's wealth was built on its links with the sea, and with its ability to exploit maritime trade. The later rulers of Champa, Langkasuka (Malaya), Srivijaya (Sumatra), and Malacca (Malaya) repeated this formula.

Champa (AD 200–1720)

In South Vietnam, where the dynastic lords achieved hegemony only in the 18th century, the kingdom of Champa – or Lin-yi as the Chinese called it – was the most significant power. The kingdom evolved in the second century AD and was focused on the narrow ribbon of lowland that runs north–south down the Annamite coast with its various capitals near the present-day city of Danang. Chinese sources record that in AD 192 a local official, Kiu-lien, rejected Chinese authority and established an independent kingdom. From then on, Champa's history was one of conflict with its neighbour; when Imperial China was powerful, Champa was subservient and sent ambassadors and tributes in homage to the Chinese court; when it was weak, the rulers of Champa extended their own influence and ignored the Chinese.

The difficulty for scholars is to decide whether Champa had a single identity or whether it consisted of numerous mini-powers with no dominant centre. The accepted wisdom at the moment is that Champa was more diffuse than previously thought and that only rarely during its history is it possible to talk of Champa in singular terms. The endless shifting of the capital of Champa is taken to reflect the shifting centres of power that characterized this 'kingdom'.

Like Funan, Champa built its power on its position on the maritime trading route through Southeast Asia. During the fourth century, as Champa expanded into formerly Funan-controlled lands, they came under the influence of the Indian cultural traditions of the Funanese. These were enthusiastically embraced by Champa's rulers who tacked the suffix '-varman' onto their names (for example, Bhadravarman) and adopted the Hindu-Buddhist cosmology. Though a powerful trading kingdom, Champa was geographically poorly endowed. The coastal strip between the Annamite highlands to the west, and the sea to the east, is narrow and the potential for extensive rice cultivation limited. This may explain why the Champa Empire was never more than a moderate power: it was unable to produce the agricultural surplus necessary to support an extensive court and army, and therefore could not compete with either the Khmers to the south nor with the Viets to the north. But the Cham were able to carve out a niche for themselves between the two, and to many art historians, their art and architecture represent the finest that Vietnam has ever produced.

For over 1000 years the Cham resisted the Chinese and the Vietnamese. But by the time Marco Polo wrote of the Cham, in 1285, their power and prestige were much reduced. Champa saw a late flowering under King Binasuos who led numerous successful campaigns against the Viet, culminating in the sack of Hanoi in 1371. Subsequently, the treachery of a low-ranking officer led to Binasuos' death in 1390 and the military eclipse of the Cham by the Vietnamese. The demographic and economic superiority of the Viet coupled with their gradual drift south contributed most to the waning of the Cham Kingdom, but finally, in 1471 the Cham suffered a terrible defeat at the hands of the Vietnamese. Some 60,000 of their soldiers were killed and another 36,000 captured and carried into captivity, including the King and 50 members of the royal family. The kingdom shrank to a small territory in the vicinity of Nha Trang that survived until 1720 when surviving members of the royal family and many subjects fled to Cambodia to escape from the advancing Vietnamese.

The colonial period

One of the key motivating factors that encouraged the **French** to undermine the authority of the Vietnamese emperors was their treatment of Roman Catholics. Emperor Minh Mang issued an imperial edict outlawing the dissemination of Christianity as a heterodox creed in 1825. The first European priest to be executed was François Isidore Gagelin who was strangled by six soldiers as he knelt on a scaffold in Hué in 1833. In 1840 Minh Mang actually read the Old Testament in Chinese translation, declaring it to be 'absurd'.

Yet, Christianity continued to spread as Buddhism declined and there was a continual stream of priests willing to risk their lives proselytizing. In addition, the economy was in disarray and natural disasters common. Poor Vietnamese saw Christianity as a way to break the shackles of their feudal existence. Fearing a peasants' revolt, the Emperor ordered the execution of 25 European priests, 300 Vietnamese priests, and 30,000 Vietnamese Catholics between 1848 and 1860. Provoked by these killings, the French attacked and took Saigon in 1859. In 1862 **Emperor Tu Duc** signed a treaty ceding the three southern provinces to the French, thereby creating the colony of **Cochin China**. This treaty of 1862 effectively paved the way for the eventual seizure by the French of the whole kingdom.

In 1883 and 1884, the French forced the Emperor to sign treaties making Vietnam a French protectorate. The Emperor called on China for assistance and demanded that provinces resist French rule; but the imperial bidding proved ineffective, and in 1885 the

Treaty of Tientsin recognized the French protectorates of Tonkin (North Vietnam) and Annam (Central Vietnam), to add to that of Cochin China (South Vietnam).

Resistance to the French: the prelude to revolution

Like other European powers in Southeast Asia, the French managed to achieve military victory with ease, but they failed to stifle Vietnamese nationalism. After 1900, as Chinese translations of the works of Rousseau, Voltaire and social Darwinists such as Herbert Spence began to find their way into the hands of the Vietnamese intelligentsia, so resistance grew. Foremost among these early nationalists were Phan Boi Chau (1867-1940) and Phan Chau Trinh (1871-1926) who wrote tracts calling for the expulsion of the French. But these men and others such as Prince Cuong De (1882-1951) were traditional nationalists, their beliefs rooted in Confucianism rather than revolutionary Marxism. Their efforts and perspectives were essentially in the tradition of the nationalists who had resisted Chinese domination over previous centuries.

Quoc Dan Dang (VNQDD), founded at the end of 1927, was the first nationalist party, while the first significant communist group was the **Indochina Communist Party** (ICP) established by **Ho Chi Minh** in 1930. Both the VNQDD and the ICP organized resistance to the French and there were numerous strikes and uprisings, particularly during the harsh years of the Great Depression. The Japanese 'occupation' from August 1940 (Vichy France permitted the Japanese full access to military facilities in exchange for allowing continued French administrative control) saw the creation of the **Viet Minh** to fight for the liberation of Vietnam from Japanese and French control.

The Vietnam wars

The First Indochina War (1945-1954)

The war started in September 1945 in the south of the country and in 1946 in the north. These years marked the onset of fighting **between the Viet Minh and the French** and the period is usually referred to as the First Indochina War. The communists, who had organized against the Japanese, proclaimed the creation of the **Democratic Republic of Vietnam** (DRV) on 2 September 1945 when Ho Chi Minh read out the Vietnamese **Declaration of Independence** in Hanoi's Ba Dinh Square. Ironically, this document was modelled closely on the American Declaration of Independence. Indeed, the US was favourably disposed towards the Viet Minh and Ho Chi Minh. Operatives of the OSS (the wartime precursor to the CIA) met Ho Chi Minh and supported his efforts during the war and afterwards Roosevelt's inclination was to prevent France claiming their colony back. Only Winston Churchill's persuasion changed his mind.

The French, although they had always insisted that Vietnam be returned to French rule, were in no position to force the issue. Instead, in the south, it was British troops (mainly Gurkhas) who helped the small force of French against the Viet Minh. Incredibly, the British also ordered the Japanese, who had only just capitulated, to help fight the Vietnamese. When 35,000 French reinforcements arrived, the issue in the south – at least superficially – was all but settled, with Ca Mau at the southern extremity of the country falling on 21 October. From that point, the war in the south became an underground battle of attrition, with the north providing support to their southern comrades.

In the north, the Viet Minh had to deal with 180,000 rampaging Nationalist Chinese troops, while preparing for the imminent arrival of a French force. Unable to confront both at the same time, and deciding that the French were probably the lesser of two evils, Ho Chi

Minh decided to negotiate. To make the DRV government more acceptable to the French, Ho Chi Minh proceeded cautiously, only nationalizing a few strategic industries, bringing moderates into the government, and actually dissolving the Indochina Communist Party (at least on paper) in November 1945. But in the same month, he also said: "The French colonialists should know that the Vietnamese people do not wish to spill blood, that it loves peace. But if it must sacrifice millions of combatants, lead a resistance for long years to defend the independence of the country, and preserve its children from slavery, it will do so. It is certain the resistance will win."

Chinese withdrawal In February 1946, the French and Chinese signed a treaty leading to the withdrawal of Chinese forces and shortly afterwards Ho Chi Minh concluded a treaty with French President de Gaulle's special emissary to Vietnam, Jean Sainteny, in which Vietnam was acknowledged as a 'free' (the Vietnamese word *doc lap* being translated as free, but not yet independent) state that was within the French Union and the Indochinese Federation.

It is interesting to note that in negotiating with the French, Ho Chi Minh was going against most of his supporters who argued for confrontation. But Ho Chi Minh, ever a pragmatist, believed at this stage that the Viet Minh were ill-trained and poorly armed and he appreciated the need for time to consolidate their position. The episode that is usually highlighted as the flashpoint that led to the resumption of hostilities was the French government's decision to open a customs house in Haiphong at the end of 1946. The Viet Minh forces resisted and the rest, as they say, is history. It seems that during the course of 1946 Ho Chi Minh changed his view of the best path to independence. Initially he asked: "Why should we sacrifice 50 or 100,000 men when we can achieve independence within five years through negotiation?" although he later came to the conclusion that it was necessary to fight for independence. The customs house episode might, therefore, be viewed as merely an excuse. The French claimed that 5000 Vietnamese were killed in the ensuing bombardment, versus five Frenchmen; the Vietnamese put the toll at 20,000.

In a pattern that was to become characteristic of the entire 25-year conflict, while the French controlled the cities, the Viet Minh were dominant in the countryside. By the end of 1949, with the success of the Chinese Revolution and the establishment of the Democratic People's Republic of Korea (North Korea) in 1948, the US began to offer support to the French in an attempt to stem the 'Red Tide' that seemed to be sweeping across Asia. At this early stage, the odds appeared stacked against the Viet Minh, but Ho Chi Minh was confident that time was on their side. As he remarked to Sainteny "If we have to fight, we will fight. You can kill 10 of my men for every one I kill of yours but even at those odds, I will win and you will lose". It also became increasingly clear that the French were not committed to negotiating a route to independence.

Dien Bien Phu (1954) and the Geneva Agreement The decisive battle of the First Indochina War was at Dien Bien Phu in the hills of the northwest, close to the border with Laos. At the end of 1953 the French, with American support, parachuted 16,000 men into the area in an attempt to protect Laos from Viet Minh incursions and to tempt them into open battle. The French in fact found themselves trapped, surrounded by Viet Minh and overlooked by artillery. There was some suggestion that the US might become involved, and even use tactical nuclear weapons, but this was not to be. In May 1954 the French surrendered – the most humiliating of French colonial defeats – effectively marking the end of the French presence in Indochina. In July 1954, in Geneva, the French and

ON THE ROAD

Ho Chi Minh: 'He who enlightens'

Ho Chi Minh, one of a number of pseudonyms Ho adopted during his life, was born Nguyen Sinh Cung, or possibly Nguyen Van Thanh (Ho did not keep a diary during much of his life, so parts of his life are still a mystery), in Nghe An Province near Vinh on the 19 May 1890, and came from a poor scholar-gentry family. In the village, the family was aristocratic; beyond it they were little more than peasants. His father, though not a revolutionary, was a dissenter and rather than go to Hué to serve the French, he chose to work as a village school teacher. Ho must have been influenced by his father's implacable animosity towards the French, although Ho's early years are obscure. He went to Quoc Hoc College in Hué and then worked for a while as a teacher in Phan Thiet, a fishing village in South Annam.

In 1911, under the name Nguyen Tat Thanh, he travelled to Saigon and left the country as a messboy on the French ship *Amiral Latouche-Tréville*. He is said to have used the name 'Ba' so that he would not shame his family by accepting such lowly work. This marked the beginning of three years of travel during which he visited France, England, America (where the skyscrapers of Manhattan both amazed and appalled him) and North Africa. Seeing the colonialists on their own turf and reading such revolutionary literature as the French Communist Party newspaper *L'Humanité*, he was converted to communism. In Paris he mixed with leftists, wrote pamphlets and attended meetings of the French Socialist Party. He also took odd jobs: for a while he worked at the **Carlton Hotel** in London and became an assistant pastry chef under the legendary French chef Georges Escoffier.

An even more unlikely story emerges from Gavin Young's *A Wavering Grace* In the book he recounts an interview he conducted with Mae West in 1968 shortly after he had returned from reporting the Tet offensive. On hearing of Vietnam, Mae West innocently said that she "used to know someone *very*, very important there ... His name was Ho ... Ho ... Ho something". At the time she was staying at the Carlton while starring in a London show, *Sex*. She confided to Young: "There was this waiter, cook, I don't know what he was. I know he had the slinkiest eyes though. We met in the corridor. We – well ..." Young writes that "Her voice trailed off in a husky sigh..."

Gradually Ho became an even more committed communist, contributing articles to radical newspapers and working his way into the web of communist

---

Vietnamese agreed to divide the country along the 17th parallel, so creating two states – the communists occupying the north and the non-communists occupying the south. The border was kept open for 300 days and over that period about 900,000 – mostly Roman Catholic – Vietnamese travelled south. At the same time nearly 90,000 Viet Minh troops along with 43,000 civilians went north, although many Viet Minh remained in the south to continue the fight there.

The Second Indochina War (1954-1975)

The Vietnam War, but particularly the American part of that war, is probably the most minutely studied, reported, analysed and recorded in history. Yet, as with all wars, there are still large grey areas and continuing disagreement over important episodes.

and leftist groups. At the same time he remained, curiously, a French cultural chauvinist, complaining for example about the intrusion of English words like *le manager* and *le challenger* (referring to boxing contests) into the French language. He even urged the French prime minister to ban foreign words from the French press. In 1923 he left France for Moscow and was trained as a communist activist – effectively a spy. From there, Ho travelled to Canton where he was instrumental in forming the Vietnamese communist movement. This culminated in the creation of the Indochina Communist Party in 1930. His movements during these years are scantily documented: he became a Buddhist monk in Siam (Thailand), was arrested in Hong Kong for subversive activities and received a six month sentence, travelled to China several times, and in 1940 even returned to Vietnam for a short period – his first visit for nearly 30 years. Despite his absence from the country, the French had already recognized the threat that he posed and sentenced him to death in absentia in 1930. He did not adopt the pseudonym by which he is now best known – Ho Chi Minh – until the early 1940s.

Ho was a consummate politician and, despite his revolutionary fervour, a great realist. He was also a charming man, and during his stay in France between June and October 1946 he made a great number of friends. Robert Shaplen in his book *The Lost Revolution* (1965) talks of his "wit, his oriental courtesy, his savoir-faire… above all his seeming sincerity and simplicity". He talked with farmers and fishermen and debated with priests; he impressed people wherever he travelled. He died in Hanoi at his house in the former governor's residence in 1969.

Since the demise of communism in the former Soviet Union, the Vietnamese leadership have been concerned that secrets about Ho's life might be gleaned from old comintern files in Moscow by nosy journalists. To thwart such an eventuality, they have, reportedly, sent a senior historian to scour the archives. To date, Ho's image remains largely untarnished – making him an exception amongst the tawdry league of former communist leaders. But a Moscow-based reporter has unearthed evidence implying Ho was married, challenging the official hagiography that paints Ho as a celibate who committed his entire life to the revolution. It takes a brave Vietnamese to challenge established 'fact'. In 1991, when the popular Vietnamese *Youth* or *Tuoi Tre* newspaper dared to suggest that Ho had married Tang Tuyet Minh in China in 1926, the editor was summarily dismissed from her post.

Ngo Dinh Diem

At the time of the partition of Vietnam along the 17th parallel, the government in the south was chaotic and the communists could be fairly confident that in a short time their sympathizers would be victorious. This situation was to change with the rise of Ngo Dinh Diem. Born in Hué in 1901 to a Roman Catholic Confucian family, Diem wished to become a priest. He graduated at the top of his class from the French School of Administration and at the age of 32 was appointed to the post of minister of the interior at the court of Emperor Bao Dai. Here, according to the political scientist William Turley, "he worked with uncommon industry and integrity" only to resign in exasperation at court intrigues and French interference. He withdrew from political activity during the First Indochina War and in 1946 Ho Chi Minh offered him a post in the DRV government – an offer he declined.

Turley describes him as a man who was a creature of the past: "For Diem, the mandarin, political leadership meant rule by example, precept and paternalism. His Catholic upbringing reinforced rather than replaced the Confucian tendency to base authority on doctrine, morality and hierarchy. Utterly alien to him were the concepts of power-sharing and popular participation. He was the heir to a dying tradition, member of an elite that had been superbly prepared by birth, training, and experience to lead a Vietnam that no longer existed."

In July 1954 Diem returned from his self-imposed exile at the Maryknoll Seminary in New Jersey to become Premier of South Vietnam. It is usually alleged that the US administration was behind his rise to power, although this has yet to be proved. He held two rigged elections (in October 1955, 450,000 registered voters cast 605,025 votes) that gave some legitimacy to his administration in American eyes. He proceeded to suppress all opposition in the country. His brutal brother, Ngo Dinh Nhu, was appointed to head the security forces and terrorized much of Vietnamese society.

During the period of Diem's premiership, opposition to his rule, particularly in the countryside, increased. This was because the military's campaign against the Viet Minh targeted – both directly and indirectly – many innocent peasants. At the same time, the nepotism and corruption that was endemic within the administration also turned many people into Viet Minh sympathizers. That said, Diem's campaign was successful in undermining the strength of the Communist Party in the south. While there were perhaps 50,000-60,000 party members in 1954, this figure had declined through widespread arrests and intimidation to only 5000 by 1959.

The erosion of the Party in the south gradually led, from 1959, to the north changing its strategy towards one of more overt military confrontation. The same year also saw the establishment of Group 559, which was charged with the task of setting up what was to become the Ho Chi Minh Trail, along which supplies and troops were moved from the north to the south. But, even at this stage, the Party's forces in the south were kept from open confrontation and many of its leaders were hoping for victory without having to resort to open warfare. There was no call for a 'People's War' and armed resistance was left largely to guerrillas belonging to the Cao Dai and Hoa Hao (Buddhist millenarian) sects. The establishment of the National Liberation Front of Vietnam in 1960 was an important political and organizational development towards creating a credible alternative to Diem – although it did not hold its first congress until 1962.

The escalation of the armed conflict (1959-1963)

Viet Cong

The armed conflict began to intensify from the beginning of 1961 when all the armed forces under the communists' control were unified under the banner of the **People's Liberation Armed Forces** (**PLAF**). By this time the Americans were already using the term Viet Cong (or VC) to refer to communist troops. They reasoned that the victory at Dien Bien Phu had conferred almost heroic status on the name Viet Minh. American psychological warfare specialists therefore invented the term Viet Cong, an abbreviation of *Viet-nam Cong-san* (or Vietnamese Communists) and persuaded the media in Saigon to begin substituting it for Viet Minh from 1956.

retrospect, he argues that the US should have withdrawn in late 1963, and certainly by late 1967. Massive quantities of US arms and money were preventing the communists from making much headway in urban areas, while American and ARVN forces were ineffective in the countryside – although incessant bombing and ground assaults wreaked massive destruction. A black market of epic proportions developed in Saigon, as millions of dollars of assistance went astray. American journalist Stanley Karnow once remarked to a US official that "we could probably buy off the Vietcong at US$500 a head". The official replied that they had already calculated the costs, but came to "US$2500 a head".

The Tet Offensive, 1968: the beginning of the end

By mid-1967, the communist leadership in the north felt it was time for a further escalation of the war in the south to regain the initiative. They began to lay the groundwork for what was to become known as the Tet (or New Year) Offensive – perhaps the single most important series of battles during the American War in Vietnam. During the early morning of 1 February 1968, shortly after noisy celebrations had welcomed in the New Year, 84,000 communist troops – almost all Viet Cong – simultaneously attacked targets in 105 urban centres. Utterly surprising the US and South Vietnamese, the Tet Offensive had begun.

Preparations for the offensive had been laid over many months. Arms, ammunition and guerrillas were smuggled and infiltrated into urban areas and detailed planning was undertaken. Central to the strategy was a 'sideshow' at Khe Sanh. By mounting an attack on the marine outpost at **Khe Sanh**, the communists successfully convinced the American and Vietnamese commanders that another Dien Bien Phu was underway. General Westmoreland moved 50,000 US troops away from the cities and suburbs to prevent any such humiliating repetition of the French defeat. But Khe Sanh was just a diversion, a feint designed to draw attention away from the cities. In this the communists were successful; for days after the Tet offensive, Westmoreland and the South Vietnamese President Thieu thought Khe Sanh to be the real objective and the attacks in the cities the decoy.

The most interesting aspect of the Tet Offensive was that although it was a strategic victory for the communists, it was also a considerable tactical defeat. They may have occupied the US embassy in Saigon for a few hours but, except in Hué, communist forces were quickly repulsed by US and ARVN troops. The government in the South did not collapse nor did the ARVN. Cripplingly high casualties were inflicted on the communists – cadres at all echelons were killed – morale was undermined and it became clear that the cities would not rise up spontaneously to support the communists. Tet, in effect, put paid to the VC as an effective fighting force. The fight was now increasingly taken up by the North Vietnamese Army (NVA). This was to have profound effects on the government of South Vietnam after reunification in 1975; southern communists and what remained of the political wing of the VC – the government in waiting – were entirely overlooked as northern communists were given all the positions of political power, a process that continues. This caused intense bitterness at the time and also explains the continued mistrust of many southerners for Hanoi. Walt Rostow wrote in 1995 that "Tet was an utter military and political defeat for the communists in Vietnam", but adding "yet a political disaster in the United States". But this was not to matter; Westmoreland's request for more troops was turned down and US public support for the war slumped still further as they heard reported that the US embassy itself had been 'over-run'. Those who for years had been claiming it was only a matter of time before the communists were defeated seemed to be contradicted by the scale and intensity of the offensive. Even President Johnson was stunned by the VC's successes for he too had believed the US propaganda.

As it turned out the VC incursion was by a 20-man unit from Sapper Battalion C-10 who were all killed in the action. Their mission was not to take the embassy but to 'make a psychological gesture'. In that regard at least, the mission must have exceeded the leadership's wildest expectations.

The **Phoenix Programme**, established in the wake of the Tet Offensive, aimed to destroy the communists' political infrastructure in the Mekong Delta. Named after the Vietnamese mythical bird the Phung Hoang, which could fly anywhere, the programme sent CIA-recruited and trained Counter Terror Teams – in effect assassination units – into the countryside. The teams were ordered to try and capture communist cadres; invariably they fired first and asked questions later. By 1971, it was estimated that the programme had led to the capture of 28,000 members of the VCI (Viet Cong Infrastructure), the death of 20,000 and the defection of a further 17,000. By the early 1970s the countryside in the Mekong Delta was more peaceful than it had been for years; towns that were previously strongholds of the Viet Cong had reverted to the control of the local authorities. Critics have questioned what proportion of those killed, captured and sometimes tortured were communist cadres, but even communist documents admit that it seriously undermined their support network in the area. In these terms, the Phoenix Programme was a great success.

The costs

The Tet Offensive concentrated American minds. The costs of the war by that time had been vast. The US budget deficit had risen to 3% of Gross National Product by 1968, inflation was accelerating, and thousands of young men had been killed for a cause that, to many, was becoming less clear by the month. Before the end of the year President Johnson had ended the bombing campaign. Negotiations began in Paris in 1969 to try and secure an honourable settlement for the US. Although the last American combat troops were not to leave until March 1973, the Tet Offensive marked the beginning of the end. It was from that date the Johnson administration began to search seriously for a way out of the conflict. The illegal bombing of Cambodia in 1969 and the resumption of the bombing of the north in 1972 (the most intensive of the entire conflict) were only flurries of action on the way to an inevitable US withdrawal.

The Paris Agreement (1972)

US Secretary of State **Henry Kissinger** records the afternoon of 8 October 1972, a Sunday, as the moment when he realized that the communists were willing to agree a peace treaty. There was a great deal to discuss, particularly whether the treaty would offer the prospect of peaceful reunification, or the continued existence of two states: a communist north, and non-communist south. Both sides tried to force the issue: the US mounted further attacks and at the same time strengthened and expanded the ARVN. They also tried to play the 'Madman Nixon' card, arguing that **President Richard Nixon** was such a vehement anti-communist that he might well resort to the ultimate deterrent, the nuclear bomb. It is true that the PAVN was losing men through desertion and had failed to recover its losses in the Tet Offensive. Bao Ninh in his book *The Sorrow of War* about Kinh, a scout with the PAVN, wrote: "The life of the B3 Infantrymen after the Paris Agreement was a series of long suffering days, followed by months of retreating and months of counter-attacking, withdrawal, then counter-attack. The path of war seemed endless, desperate, and leading nowhere."

But the communist leadership knew well that the Americans were committed to withdrawal – the only question was when, so they felt that time was on their side. By 1972, US troops in the south had declined to 95,000, the bulk of whom were support troops.

The north gambled on a massive attack to defeat the ARVN and moved 200,000 men towards the demilitarized zone that marked the border between north and south. On 30 March the PAVN crossed into the south and quickly overran large sections of Quang Tri province. Simultaneous attacks were mounted in the west highlands, at Tay Ninh and in the Mekong Delta. For a while it looked as if the south would fall altogether. The US responded by mounting a succession of intense bombing raids that eventually forced the PAVN to retreat. The spring offensive may have failed, but like Tet, it was strategically important, for it demonstrated that without US support the ARVN was unlikely to be able to withstand a communist attack.

Both sides, by late 1972, were ready to compromise. Against the wishes of South Vietnam's President Nguyen Van Thieu, the US signed a treaty on 27 January 1973, the ceasefire going into effect on the same day. Before the signing, Nixon ordered the bombing of the north – the so-called Christmas Campaign. It lasted 11 days from 18 December (Christmas Day was a holiday) and was the most intensive of the war. With the ceasefire and President Thieu, however shaky, both in place, the US was finally able to back out of its nightmare and the last combat troops left in March 1973. As J William Fulbright, a highly influential member of the Senate and a strong critic of the US role in Vietnam, observed: "We [the US] have the power to do any damn fool thing we want, and we always seem to do it."

The Final Phase 1973-1975

The Paris Accord settled nothing; it simply provided a means by which the Americans could withdraw from Vietnam. It was never going to resolve the deep-seated differences between the two regimes and with only a brief lull, the war continued, this time without US troops. Thieu's government was probably in terminal decline even before the peace treaty was signed. Though ARVN forces were at their largest ever and, on paper, considerably stronger than the PAVN, many men were weakly committed to the cause of the south. Corruption was endemic, business was in recession, and political dissent was on the increase. The North's Central Committee formally decided to abandon the Paris Accord in October 1973; by the beginning of 1975 they were ready for the final offensive. It took only until April for the communists to achieve total victory. ARVN troops deserted in their thousands, and the only serious resistance was offered at Xuan Loc, less than 100 km from Saigon. President Thieu resigned on 27 April. ARVN generals, along with their men, were attempting to flee as the PAVN advanced on Saigon. The end was quick: at 1045 on 30 April a T-54 tank (number 843) crashed its way through the gates of the Presidential Palace, symbolizing the end of the Second Indochina War. For the US, the aftermath of the war would lead to years of soul searching; for Vietnam, to stagnation and isolation. A senior State Department figure, George Ball, reflected afterwards that the war was "probably the greatest single error made by America in its history".

Legacy of the Vietnam War

The Vietnam War (or 'American War' to the Vietnamese) is such an enduring feature of the West's experience of the country that many visitors look out for legacies of the conflict. There is no shortage of physically disabled Vietnamese. Many men were badly injured during the war, but large numbers also received their injuries while serving in Cambodia (1979-1989). It is tempting to associate deformed children with the enduring effects of the pesticide **Agent Orange** (1.7 million tonnes had been used by 1973), although this has yet to be proven scientifically; American studies claim that there is no significant difference in congenital malformation. One thing is certain: Agent Orange is detectable today only in tiny isolated spots, often near former military bases where chemicals were dumped. No scientific survey has found lingering widespread effects.

Bomb damage

Bomb damage is most obvious from the air: well over five million tonnes of bombs were dropped on the country (north and south) and there are said to be 20 million bomb craters – the sort of statistic people like to recount, but no one can legitimately verify. Many craters have yet to be filled in and paddy fields are still pockmarked. Some farmers have used these holes in the ground to farm fish and to use as small reservoirs to irrigate vegetable plots. War scrap was one of the country's most valuable exports. The cities in the north are surprisingly devoid of obvious signs of the bombing campaigns; Hanoi remains remarkably intact. In Hué the Citadel and the Forbidden Palace were extensively damaged during the Tet offensive in 1968 although much has now been rebuilt.

Psychological effect of the war

Even harder to measure is the effect of the war on the Vietnamese psyche. The Vietnamese Communist Party leadership still seem to be preoccupied by the conflict and school children are routinely shown war museums and Ho Chi Minh memorials. But despite the continuing propaganda offensive, people harbour surprisingly little animosity towards America or the West. Indeed, of all Westerners, it is often Americans who are most warmly welcomed, particularly in the south.

But it must be remembered that about 60% of Vietnam's population has been born since the US left in 1973, so have no memory of the American occupation. Probably the least visible but most lasting of all the effects of the war is in the number of elderly widowed women and the number of middle aged women who never married.

The deeper source of antagonism is the continuing divide between the north and south. It was to be expected that the forces of the north would exact their revenge on their foes in the south and many were relieved that the predicted bloodbath didn't materialize. But few would have thought that this revenge would be so long lasting. The 250,000 southern dead are not mourned or honoured, or even acknowledged. Former soldiers are denied jobs and the government doesn't recognize the need for national reconciliation.

This is the multiple legacy of the War on Vietnam and the Vietnamese. The legacy on the US and Americans is more widely appreciated. The key question that still occupies the minds of many, though, is, was it worth it? Economic historian Walt Rostow, ex-Singaporean prime minister Lee Kuan Yew and others would probably answer 'yes'. If the US had not intervened, communism would have spread farther in Southeast Asia; more dominoes, in their view, would have fallen. In 1973, when the US withdrawal was agreed, Lee Kuan Yew observed that the countries of Southeast Asia were much more resilient and resistant to communism than they had been, say, at the time of the Tet offensive in 1968. The US presence in Vietnam allowed them to reach this state of affairs. Yet Robert McNamara in his book *In Retrospect: the Tragedy and Lessons of Vietnam*, and one of the architects of US policy, wrote:

"Although we sought to do the right thing – and believed we were doing the right thing – in my judgment, hindsight proves us wrong. We both overestimated the effects of South Vietnam's loss on the security of the West and failed to adhere to the fundamental principle that, in the final analysis, if the South Vietnamese were to be saved, they had to win the war themselves."

The Socialist Republic of Vietnam (SRV) was born from the ashes of the Vietnam War on 2 July 1976 when former North and South Vietnam were reunified. Hanoi was proclaimed as the capital of the new country. But few Vietnamese would have guessed that their emergent country would be cast by the US in the mould of a pariah state for almost 18 years. First President George Bush I, and then his successor Bill Clinton, eased the US trade embargo bit by bit in a dance of appeasement and procrastination, as they tried to comfort American business clamouring for a slice of the Vietnamese pie, while also trying to stay on the right side of the vociferous lobby in the US demanding more action on the MIA (missing in action) issue. Appropriately, the embargo, which was first imposed on the former North in May 1964, and then nationwide in 1975, was finally lifted a few days before the celebrations of Tet, Vietnamese New Year, on 4 February 1994.

On the morning of 30 April 1975, just before 1100, a T-54 tank crashed through the gates of the Presidential Palace in Saigon, symbolically marking the end of the Vietnam War. Twenty years later, the same tank – number 843 – became a symbol of the past as parades and celebrations, and a good deal of soul searching, marked the anniversary of the end of the War. To many Vietnamese, in retrospect, 1975 was more a beginning than an end: it was the beginning of a collective struggle to come to terms with the war, to build a nation, to reinvigorate the economy and to excise the ghosts of the past.

Re-education camps
The newly formed Vietnam government ordered thousands of people to report for re-education camps in 1975. Those intended were ARVN members, ex-South Vietnam government members and those that had collaborated with the south regime including priests, artists, teachers and doctors. It was seen as a means of revenge and a way of indoctrinating the 'unbelievers' with communist propaganda. It was reported in the Indochina Newsletter in 1982 that some 80 camps existed with an estimated 100,000 still languishing in them seven years after the war ended. Detainees were initially told that they would be detained for between three days and one month. Those that were sent to the camp were forced to undertake physical labour and survived on very little food and without basic medical facilities.

The boat people
Many Vietnamese also fled, first illegally and then legally through the Orderly Departure Programme.

Invasion of Cambodia
In April 1975, the Khmer Rouge took power in Cambodia. Border clashes with Vietnam erupted just a month after the Phnom Penh regime change but matters came to a head in 1977 when the Khmer Rouge accused Vietnam of seeking to incorporate Kampuchea into an Indochinese Federation. Hanoi's determination to oust Pol Pot only really became apparent on Christmas Day 1978, when 120,000 Vietnamese troops invaded. By 7 January they had installed a puppet government that proclaimed the foundation of the People's Republic of Kampuchea (PRK): Heng Samrin, a former member of the Khmer Rouge, was appointed president. The Vietnamese compared their invasion to the liberation of Uganda from Idi Amin – but for the rest of the world it was an unwelcome Christmas present. The new government was accorded scant recognition abroad, while the toppled government of Democratic Kampuchea retained the country's seat at the United Nations.

But the country's 'liberation' by Vietnam did not end the misery; in 1979 nearly half of Cambodia's population was in transit, either searching for their former homes or fleeing across the Thai border into refugee camps. The country reverted to a state of outright war again, for the Vietnamese were not greatly loved in Cambodia – especially by the Khmer Rouge. American political scientist Wayne Bert wrote: "The Vietnamese had long seen a special role for themselves in uniting and leading a greater Indochina Communist movement and the Cambodian Communists had seen with clarity that such a role for the Vietnamese could only be at the expense of their independence and prestige."

Under the Lon Nol and Khmer Rouge regimes, Vietnamese living in Cambodia were expelled or exterminated. Resentment had built up over the years Hanoi – exacerbated by the apparent ingratitude of the Khmer Rouge for Vietnamese assistance in fighting Lon Nol's US-supported Khmer Republic in the early 1970s. As relations between the Khmer Rouge and the Vietnamese deteriorated, the communist superpowers, China and the Soviet Union, polarised too – the former siding with Khmer Rouge and the latter with Hanoi.

The Vietnamese invasion had the full backing of Moscow, while the Chinese and Americans began their support for the anti-Vietnamese rebels.

Following the Vietnamese invasion, three main anti-Hanoi factions were formed. In June 1982 they banded together in an unholy alliance of convenience to fight the PRK and called themselves the Coalition Government of Democratic Kampuchea (CGDK), which was immediately recognised by the UN. The three factions of the CGDK were: The Communist Khmer Rouge whose field forces had recovered to at least 18,000 by the late 1980s. Supplied with weapons by China, they were concentrated in the Cardamom Mountains in the southwest and were also in control of some of the refugee camps along the Thai border. The National United Front for an Independent Neutral Peaceful and Co-operative Cambodia (Funcinpec) – known by most people as the Armée National Sihanoukiste (ANS). It was headed by Prince Sihanouk – although he spent most of his time exiled in Beijing; the group had fewer than 15,000 well-equipped troops – most of whom took orders from Khmer Rouge commanders. The anti-Communist Khmer People's National Liberation Front (KPNLF), headed by Son Sann, a former prime minister under Sihanouk. Its 5000 troops were reportedly ill-disciplined in comparison with the Khmer Rouge and the ANS.

The three CGDK factions were ranged against the 70,000 troops loyal to the government of President Heng Samrin and Prime Minister Hun Sen (previously a Khmer Rouge cadre.) they were backed by Vietnamese forces until September 1989.

In the late 1980s the Association of Southeast Asian Nations (ASEAN) – for which the Cambodian conflict had almost become its raison d'être – began steps to bring the warring factions together over the negotiating table. ASEAN countries were united in wanting the Vietnamese out of Cambodia. After Mikhail Gorbachev had come to power in the Soviet Union, Moscow's support for the Vietnamese presence in Cambodia gradually evaporated. Gorbachev began leaning on Vietnam as early as 1987, to withdraw its troops. Despite saying their presence in Cambodia was 'irreversible', Vietnam completed its withdrawal in September 1989, ending nearly 11 years of Hanoi's direct military involvement. The withdrawal led to an immediate upsurge in political and military activity, as forces of the exiled CGDK put increased pressure on the now weakened Phnom Penh regime to begin a round of power- sharing negotiations.

Border incursions with China

In February 1979 the Chinese marched into the far north of northern Vietnam justifying the invasion because of Vietnam's invasion of Cambodia, its treatment of Chinese in

Vietnam, the ownership of the Paracel and Spratley Islands in the East Sea also claimed by China and a stand against Soviet expansion into Asia (Hanoi was strongly allied with the then USSR). They withdrew a month later following heavy casualties although both sides have claimed to be victorious. Vietnamese military hardware was far superior to the Chinese and their casualties were estimated to be between 20,000 and 60,000; Vietnamese casualties were around 15,000. In 1987 fighting again erupted on the Sino-Vietnamese border resulting in high casualties.

Modern Vietnam

Politics

The **Vietnamese Communist Party (VCP)** was established in Hong Kong in 1930 by Ho Chi Minh and arguably has been more successful than any other such party in Asia in mobilizing and maintaining support. While others have fallen, the VCP has managed to stay firmly in control. To enable them to get their message to a wider audience, the Communist Party of Vietnam have their own website, www.cpv.org.vn.

Vietnam is a one party state. In addition to the Communist Party the posts of president and prime minister were created when the constitution was revised in 1992. The president is head of state and the prime minister is head of the cabinet of ministries (including three deputies and 26 ministries), all nominated by the National Assembly. The current president is Truong Tan Sang and the current prime minister is Nguyen Tan Dung. Although the National Assembly is the highest instrument of state, it can still be directed by the Communist Party. The vast majority of National Assembly members are also party members. Elections for the National Assembly are held every five years. The Communist Party is run by a politburo of 15 members. The head is the general secretary, currently Nguyen Phu Trong. The politburo meets every five years and sets policy directions of the Party and the government. There is a Central Committee made up of 161 members, who are also elected at the Party Congress.

In 1986, at the Sixth Party Congress, the VCP launched its economic reform programme known as *doi moi*, which was a momentous step in ideological terms (see page 492). However, although the programme has done much to free up the economy, the party has ensured that it retains ultimate political power. Marxism-Leninism and Ho Chi Minh thought are still taught to Vietnamese school children and even so-called 'reformers' in the leadership are not permitted to diverge from the party line. In this sense, while economic reforms have made considerable progress (but see below) – particularly in the south – there is a very definite sense that the limits of political reform have been reached, at least for the time being.

From the late 1990s to the first years of the new millennium there were a number of arrests and trials of dissidents charged with what might appear to be fairly innocuous crimes (see The future of communism in Vietnam, page 490) and, although the economic reforms enacted since the mid-1980s are still in place, the party resolutely rejects any moves towards greater political pluralism.

Despite the reforms, the leadership is still divided over the road ahead. But the fact that debate is continuing, sometimes openly, suggests that there is disagreement over the necessity for political reform and the degree of economic reform that should be encouraged.

In the country as a whole there is virtually no political debate at all, certainly not in the open. There are two reasons for this apparently curious state of affairs. First there is a genuine fear of discussing something that is absolutely taboo. Second, and more importantly, is the booming economy. Since the 1990s, **economic growth** in Vietnam has been unprecedented. In 2006 the growth rate was 8.2% but this dropped to 5.3% in 2009. As every politician knows, the one thing that keeps people happy is rising income. Hence with not much to complain about most Vietnamese people are content with their political status quo.

That said, in 2006, Bloc 8406, a pro-democracy group named after its founding date of 8 April 2006, was set up. Catholic priest Father Nguyen Van Ly, editor of the underground online magazine *Free Speech* and a founding member of Bloc 8406, was sentenced to eight years in jail for **anti-government activity**. Four others were also sentenced with him. In March 2007 Nguyen Van Dai and Le Thi Cong Nhan, two human rights lawyers, were arrested on the grounds of distributing material "dangerous to the State" and were sentenced to four and five years in prison respectively. As well as Bloc 8406, other pro-democracy movements include the US-based Viet Tan Party, www.viettan.org, with offices also in Australia, France, Japan, and the People's Democratic Party, among others.

International relations

In terms of international relations, Vietnam's relationship with the countries of the **Association of Southeast Asian Nations (ASEAN)** have warmed markedly since the dark days of the early and mid-1980s and in mid-1995 Vietnam became the association's seventh – and first communist – member. The delicious irony of Vietnam joining ASEAN was that it was becoming part of an organization established to counteract the threat of communist Vietnam itself – although everyone was too polite to point this out. No longer is there a deep schism between the capitalist and communist countries of the region, either in terms of ideology or management. The main potential flashpoint concerns Vietnam's long-term historical enemy – China. The enmity and suspicion that underlies the relationship between the world's last two real communist powers stretches back over 2000 years. Indeed, one of the great attractions to Vietnam of joining ASEAN was the bulwark that it created against a potentially aggressive and actually economically ascendant China.

China and Vietnam, along with Malaysia, Taiwan, Brunei and the Philippines, all claim part (or all) of the East Sea **Hoang Sa** (formerly **Spratly Islands**). These tiny islands, many no more than coral atolls, would have caused scarcely an international relations ripple were it not for the fact that they are thought to sit above huge oil reserves. Whoever can prove rights to the islands lays claim to this undersea wealth. China has been using its developing blue water navy to project its power southwards. This has led to skirmishes between Vietnamese and Chinese forces, and to diplomatic confrontation between China and just about all the other claimants. Although the parties are committed to settling the dispute without resort to force, most experts see the Spratly Islands as the key potential flashpoint in Southeast Asia – and one in which Vietnam is seen to be a central player. **Truong Sa** (formerly **Paracel Islands**) further north are similarly disputed by Vietnam and China.

Rapprochement with the US One of the keys to a lasting economic recovery was a normalization of relations with the US. From 1975 until early 1994 the US made it largely illegal for any American or American company to have business relations with Vietnam. The US, with the support of Japan and other Western nations, also blackballed attempts by Vietnam to gain membership to the IMF, World Bank and Asian Development Bank, thus cutting off access to the largest source of cheap credit. In the past, it has been the former Soviet Union and the countries of the Eastern Bloc that have filled the gap, providing billions of dollars of aid (US$6 billion 1986-1990), training and technical expertise. But in 1990 the Soviet Union halved its assistance to Vietnam, making it imperative that the government improve relations with the West and particularly the US.

In April 1991 the US opened an official office in Hanoi to assist in the search for Missing in Action (MIAs), the first such move since the end of the war, and in December 1992 allowed US companies to sign contracts to be implemented after the US trade embargo had been lifted. In 1992, both Australia and Japan lifted their embargoes on aid to Vietnam and the US also eased restrictions on humanitarian assistance. Support for a **full normalization of relations** was provided by French President Mitterand during his visit in February 1993, the first by a Western leader since the end of the war. He said that the US veto on IMF and World Bank assistance had "no reason for being there", and applauded Vietnam's economic reforms. He also pointed out to his hosts that respect for human rights was now a universal obligation, which did not go down quite so well. Nonetheless he saw his visit as marking the end of one chapter and the beginning of another.

This inexorable process towards normalization continued with the full lifting of the trade embargo on 4 February 1994 when President Bill Clinton announced the normalization of trade relations. Finally, on 11 July 1995 Bill Clinton declared the full normalization of relations between the two countries and a month later Secretary of State Warren Christopher opened the new American embassy in Hanoi. On 9 May 1997 Douglas 'Pete' Peterson, the first 'post-war' American ambassador to Vietnam and a former POW who spent six years of the war in the infamous 'Hanoi Hilton', took up his post in the capital.

The progress towards normalization was so slow because many Americans still harbour painful memories of the war. With large numbers of ordinary people continuing to believe that servicemen shot down and captured during the war and listed as MIAs were still languishing in jungle jails, presidents Bush and Clinton had to tread exceedingly carefully.

The normalization of trade relations between the two countries was agreed in a meeting between Vietnamese and US officials in July 1999 and marked the culmination of three years' discussions. But conservatives in the politburo prevented the agreement being signed into law worried, apparently, about the social and economic side effects of such reform. This did not happen until 28 November 2001 when Vietnam's National Assembly finally ratified the treaty. It has led to a substantial increase in bilateral trade. In 2003 the USA imported US$4.5 billion worth of Vietnamese goods, roughly four times more than it exported to Vietnam. And not only goods: by 2004 the US Consulate General in Ho Chi Minh City handled more applications for American visas than any other US mission in the world.

Further developments More good news came for Vietnam when it became the 150th member of the World Trade Organization in January 2007. The immediate effect was the lifting of import quotas from foreign countries thereby favouring Vietnamese exporters. Full benefits are expected to be realised when Vietnam hope to gains full market economy status in 2020. In June 2007 President Nguyen Minh Triet became the first president of Vietnam to visit the US. He met with George W Bush in Washington to discuss relations between the two countries; trade between the two former enemies now racks up US$9 billion a year. And, in October 2007, Vietnam was elected to the UN Security Council from 1 January 2008 as a non-permanent member for two years. In 2009, the International Bank for Reconstruction and Development loaned the country US$500 million.

The future of communism in Vietnam

In his book *Vietnam at the Crossroads*, BBC World Service commentator Michael Williams asks the question: "Does communism have a future in Vietnam?" He answers that "the short answer must be no, if one means by communism the classical Leninist doctrines and central planning". Instead some bastard form of communism has been in the process of evolving.

There is certainly **political opposition** and disenchantment in Vietnam. At present this is unfocused and dispersed. Poor people in the countryside, especially in the north, resent the economic gains in the cities, particularly those of the south. But this rump of latent discontent has little in common with those intellectual and middle class Vietnamese itching for more political freedom or those motivated entrepreneurs pressing for accelerated economic reforms or those Buddhist monks and Christians demanding freedom of worship and respect for human rights. Unless and until this loose broth of opposition groups coalesces, it is hard to see a coherent opposition movement evolving.

Nonetheless, each year a small number of brave, foolhardy or committed individuals challenge the authorities. Most are then arrested, tried, and imprisoned for various loosely defined crimes including anti-government activity.

The tensions between reform and control are constantly evident. A **press law** which came into effect in mid-1993 prohibits the publication of works "hostile to the socialist homeland, divulging state or [communist] party secrets, falsifying history or denying the gains of the revolution". Ly Quy Chung, a newspaper editor in Ho Chi Minh City, described the Vietnamese responding to the economic reforms "like animals being let out of their cage". But, he added, alluding to the tight control the VCP maintains over political debate, "Now we are free to graze around, but only inside the fences." The Party's attempts to control debate and the flow of information have extended to the internet. In 1997 a National Internet Control Board was established and all internet and email usage is strictly monitored. The authorities try to firewall topics relating to Vietnam in a hopeless attempt to censor incoming information. The government continues to crack down on blogs and websites it sees critical of the government, according to Human Rights Watch. Facebook has also been periodically blocked and access to the BBC is limited in many places. The Vietnamese cyber police clearly credit the information highway with greater influence than any surfer.

Economy

Partition and socialist reconstruction 1955-1975 When the French left North Vietnam in 1954 they abandoned a country with scarcely any industry. The north remained predominantly an agrarian society and just 1.5% of 'material output' (the Socialist equivalent of GDP) was accounted for by modern industries. These employed a few thousand workers out of a population of about 13 million. The French added to the pitiful state of the industrial sector by dismantling many of the (mostly textile) factories that did exist, shipping the machinery back to France.

With **independence**, the government in the north embraced a socialist strategy of reconstruction and development. In the countryside, agricultural production was collectivized. Adopting Maoist policies, land reform proceeded apace. Revolutionary cadres were trained to spot 'greedy, cruel and imperialist landlords', farmers of above average wealth who might themselves have owned tiny plots. Leaders of land reform brigades applied Chinese-inspired rules through people's tribunals and summary justice. An estimated 10,000 people died; Ho Chi Minh was opposed to the worst excesses and, although he failed to curb the zealots, land reform in Vietnam was a much less bloody affair than it was in China.

In industry, likewise, the means of production were nationalized, co-operati[ve]s formed, and planning was directed from the centre. Although evidence is hard [to come] by, it seems that even as early as the mid-1960s both the agricultural and industrial sectors were experiencing shortages of key inputs and were suffering from poor planning and mismanagement. The various sectors of the economy were inadequately linked, and the need for consumer goods was largely met by imports from China. But it was just at this time that the US bombing campaign 'Rolling Thunder' began in earnest (see page 478), and this served to obscure these economic difficulties. It was not until the late 1970s that the desperate need to introduce reforms became apparent. The bombing campaign also led to massive destruction and caused the government in the north to decentralize activity to the countryside in order to protect what little industry there was from the American attacks.

Reunification and a stab at socialist reconstruction (1975-1979) With the reunification of Vietnam in 1975, it seems that most leaders in the north thought that the re-integration of the two economies, as well as their re-invigoration, would be a fairly straightforward affair. As one of the Party leadership tellingly said during the Sixth Plenum at the end of 1979: "In the euphoria of victory which came so unexpectedly, we … somewhat lost sight of realities; everything seemed possible to achieve, and quickly." This is understandable when it is considered that the north had just defeated the most powerful nation on earth. But the war disguised two economies that were both chronically inefficient and poorly managed, albeit for different reasons and in different ways. The tragedy was that just as this fact was becoming clear, the Vietnamese government embarked on another military adventure; this time the invasion and subsequent occupation of Cambodia in December 1978. Shortly afterwards, Hanoi had to deploy troops again to counter the Chinese 'invasion' in 1979. As a result, the authorities never had the opportunity of diverting resources from the military to the civilian sectors.

Conditions in the south were no better than in the north. The US had been supporting levels of consumption far above those which domestic production could match, the shortfall being met through massive injections of aid. Following the communists' victory, this support was ended – overnight. The Americans left behind an economy and society scarred by the war: three million unemployed, 500,000 prostitutes, 100,000 drug addicts, 400,000 amputees and 800,000 orphans. Nor did many in the south welcome their 'liberation'. The programme of socialist transition that began after 1975 was strongly resisted by large sections of the population and never achieved its aims. As resistance grew, the government became more repressive, thus leading to the exodus of hundreds of thousands of Vietnamese, who became known as the boat people. Even as late as 1978, with the economy close to crisis, sections of the leadership were still maintaining that the problems were due to poor implementation, not to the fact that the policies were flawed. The key problem was bureaucratic centralism: if a factory wished to transport umbrellas from Tay Ninh to Ho Chi Minh city, less than 100 km apart, it was required to go through 17 agencies, obtain 15 seals, sign five contracts and pay numerous taxes.

The roots of economic reform (1979-1986) In a bid to re-invigorate the economy, the Vietnamese government – like others throughout the communist and former communist world – has been introducing economic reforms. These date back to 1979 when a process of administrative decentralization was set in train. Farmers signed contracts with their collectives to deliver produce in return for access to land and inputs like fertilizers and pesticides, thereby returning many aspects of decision making to the farm level. Surplus production could be sold privately. Factories were made self-accounting, and workers' pay was linked to productivity. The reforms of 1979 also accepted a greater role for the private sector in marketing, agriculture and small-scale industry.

Unfortunately these reforms were generally unsuccessful in stimulating Vietnam's moribund economy. Agriculture performed reasonably, but industry continued to decline. Cadres at the regional and local levels often ignored directives from the centre and critical inputs needed to fuel growth were usually unavailable. Both national income and per capita incomes continued to shrink. The reform process is referred to as *doi moi* (renovation), the Vietnamese equivalent of Soviet perestroika, and implementation has not been easy.

Some commentators have argued that the economic reforms of 1979 showed that the Vietnamese government was forward-looking and prescient. However there is also considerable evidence to show that the pressure for reform was coming as much from the bottom as from the top. Farm households and agricultural cooperatives, it seems, were engaged in what became known as 'fence-breaking', bypassing the state planning system. The communist party, to some degree, was forced to follow where peasants had already gone. This raises the questions of how far Vietnam's command economy was truly commanding. Peasants devoted enormous efforts in time and energy to the cultivation of their small private plots and tried to bypass the collective system through what became known as *khóan chui* (sneaky contracts).

Doi moi: the end of central planning Recognizing that the limited reforms of 1979 were failing to have the desired effect, the VCP leadership embraced a further raft of changes following the **Sixth Congress in 1986**. At the time, the Party daily, *Nhan Dan* wrote that never had "morale been so eroded, confidence been so low or justice been so abused". Subsidies on consumer goods were reduced and wages increased partially to compensate. There was also limited monetary reform although prices were still centrally controlled. In late 1987 the central planning system was reformed. The net effect of these changes was to fuel inflation.

Again, appreciating that the reforms were not having the desired effect, and with the advice of the IMF, a third series of changes were introduced in 1988 and 1989. The market mechanism was to be fully employed to determine wages, output and prices for the great majority of goods. The domestic currency, the dong, was further devalued to bring it into line with the black market rate and foreign investment actively encouraged.

But, with each series of reform measures, disquiet in some sections of the Party grew. For example, in 1993 government salary differentials were widened to better reflect responsibilities. Whereas under the old system the differential between the highest and lowest paid workers was only 3.5 to one, the gap under the new system is 13 to one. This may make good sense to World Bank economists, but it is hard to swallow for a party and leadership who have been raised on ideals of equality.

Until the Asian crisis was heralded with the collapse of the Thai baht at the end of the last century, the Vietnamese economy had done well to ride some pretty serious external shocks. With the collapse of communism in Eastern Europe, around 200,000 migrant workers returned to the country and had to be reintegrated. The decline in aid and assistance from the former Soviet Union (which was only partially compensated by aid from Russia) and the corresponding precipitous decline in trade from US$1.8 billion in 1990 to US$85 million in 1991 illustrates the extent to which Vietnam had to re-orientate its economy in the face of global political and economic change. No longer able to rely on the Soviet Union to bail it out (although even before then the Vietnamese would lament that the Soviets were 'Americans without dollars'), the Vietnamese government took the drastic step of banning the import of all luxury consumer goods in October 1991 in an attempt to save valuable foreign exchange.

Economic challenges Let's start with the good news: Vietnam's economy is resilient and growing fast, the population is comparatively well educated and it has good access to world markets. Vietnam currently enjoys the highest rate of growth in one of the most economically dynamic regions in the world. This happy state of affairs is the product of a hard-working, underpaid labour force generating massive profits and of the switch from an agrarian economy to an industrial economy. In other words, 200 years after Britain, Vietnam is now undergoing its industrial revolution. Indeed industry and construction now account for 41% of Vietnam's economy with services accounting for an additional 38% and this figure is rising fast. One of the driving forces behind this growth has been the export of textiles – chiefly to the USA.

Not that it has always been this good. Not only did the Asian crisis put talk of Tiger economies on the back burner, but even before the crisis there were voices of caution. The gloss of the immediate post-*doi moi* years has dulled and people now accept that reforms will need to be both deeper and wider. For a start, many of the reforms apparently in place are not being implemented in the expected manner. Foreign investors, who initially piled into the country thinking there was money to be made, then started shying away, daunted by the red tape, bureaucratic inertia and corruption and since 2001 investment has rapidly increased. The greatest beneficiaries have been Ho Chi Minh City followed by Hanoi, Dong Nai and Binh Duong. By sector it is the service industry proving the overall winner with offices and apartments being the most heavily invested sector followed by hotels and tourism.

But Vietnam's problems do not begin and end with the reform programme. There are also many more rather more familiar challenges.

The population is growing rapidly in a country where there are 900 people for every square kilometre of agricultural land. As the World Bank has pointed out, this means "the country will have to develop on the basis of human resources rather than natural resources". But the human resources themselves need substantial 'upgrading'; despite rapid progress in poverty elimination, poverty in the countryside over large areas of the north and interior uplands remains the norm rather than the exception. Education and health facilities also require massive investment, not to mention the physical infrastructure including roads and power.

The country's export base is also still comparatively narrow: coffee, coal, oil, textiles, rice, footwear and marine products are the country's key exports. But this list grows all the time.

Economic growth has brought its own problems in the same way that has occurred in China. Inequalities, both spatial and personal, are widening. Growth in agriculture is down, while industry is expanding. So, while the economies of Hanoi and Ho Chi Minh City have been growing annually, the countryside is lagging far behind. Over recent years rural incomes have fallen as rice prices and other agricultural commodities have remained depressed. This is drawing people in from the countryside, creating urban problems both socially (for instance, unemployed people living in poor conditions with a lack of educational facilities) and economically (such as strains on the physical infrastructure).

These inequalities will widen further in the short to medium term as the process of industrialization continues apace.

As with industry, the leadership is reluctant to allow rural people to run their own businesses and lives, continually interfering and fine-tuning and without addressing the key shortages which are of credit, training, skills and management. As Bui Quang Toan, senior researcher at the National Institute of Agricultural Planning and Projection, explained to a journalist from the Far Eastern Economic Review: "Cooperatives should be free of politics, free of administrative control … the government must give up the idea that they can use cooperatives as a tool to manage the people." Nevertheless Vietnam has made dramatic strides at reducing poverty, including rural poverty.

History of
Cambodia

Archaeological evidence suggests that the Mekong Delta and the lower reaches of the river – in modern-day Cambodia – have been inhabited since at least 4000 BC. But the wet and humid climate has destroyed most of the physical remains of the early civilizations. Excavated remains of a settlement at Samrong Sen on the Tonlé Sap show that houses were built from bamboo and wood and raised on stilts exactly as they are today. Where these people came from is uncertain but anthropologists have suggested that there were two waves of migration; one from the Malay peninsula and Indonesia and a second from Tibet and China.

Rise of the Lunar and Solar dynasties

For thousands of years Indochina was isolated from the rest of the world and was virtually unaffected by the rise and fall of the early Chinese dynasties. India and China 'discovered' Southeast Asia in the first millennium AD and trade networks were quickly established. The Indian influence was particularly strong in the Mekong basin. The Khmers adopted and adapted Indian script as well as their ideas about astrology, religion (Buddhism and Hinduism) and royalty (the cult of the semi-divine ruler). Today, several other aspects of Cambodian culture are recognizably Indian in origin, including classical literature and dance. Religious architecture also followed Indian models. These Indian cultural influences that took root in Indochina gave rise to a legend to which Cambodia traces its historical origins. An Indian Brahmin called Kaundinya, travelling in the Mekong Delta area, married Soma, daughter of the Naga (the serpent deity), or Lord of the Soil. Their union, which founded the 'Lunar Dynasty' of Funan (a pre-Angkorian Kingdom), symbolized the fertility of the kingdom and occupies a central place in Khmer cosmology. The Naga, Soma's father, helpfully drank the floodwaters of the Mekong, enabling people to cultivate the land.

Funan

The kingdom of Funan – the forerunner of Kambuja – was established on the Mekong by tribal people from South China in the middle of the third century AD and became the earliest Hindu state in Southeast Asia. Funan was known for its elaborate irrigation canals which controlled the Mekong floodwaters, irrigated the paddy fields and prevented the incursion of seawater. By the fifth century Funan had extended its influence over most of present-day Cambodia, as well as Indochina and parts of the Malay peninsula. Leadership was measured by success in battle and the ability to provide protection, and in recognition of this fact, rulers from the Funan period onward incorporated the suffix 'varman' (meaning protection) into their names. Records of a third-century Chinese embassy give an idea of what it was like: "There are walled villages, places and dwellings. The men ... go about naked and barefoot ... Taxes are paid in gold, silver and perfume. There are books and libraries and they can use the alphabet." Excavations conducted in the last 100 years or so suggest a seafaring people engaged in extensive trade with both India and China, and elsewhere.

The 'Solar Dynasty' of Chenla was a vassal kingdom of Funan, probably first based on the Mekong at the junction with the Mun tributary, but it rapidly grew in power, and was centred in the area of present-day southern Laos. It was the immediate predecessor of Kambuja and the great Khmer Empire. According to Khmer legend, the kingdom was the result of the marriage of Kambu, an ascetic, to a celestial nymph named Mera. The people of Chenla – the Kambuja, or the sons of Kambu – lent their name to the country. In AD 540 a Funan prince married a Chenla princess, uniting the Solar and Lunar dynasties. The prince sided with his wife and Funan was swallowed by Chenla. The first capital of this fusion was at **Sambor**. King Ishanavarman (AD 616-635) established a new capital at Sambor Prei Kuk, 30 km from modern Kompong Thom, in the centre of the country (the monuments of which are some of the best preserved of this period). His successor, Jayavarman I, moved the capital to the region of Angkor Borei near Takeo.

Quarrels in the ruling family led to the break-up of the state later in the seventh century: it was divided into 'Land Chenla', a farming culture located north of the Tonlé Sap (maybe centred around Champassak in Laos), and 'Water Chenla', a trading culture based along the Mekong. Towards the end of the eighth century Water Chenla became a vassal of Java's powerful Sailendra Dynasty and members of Chenla's ruling family were taken back to the Sailendra court. This period, from the fall of Funan until the eighth century, is known as the pre-Angkorian period and is a somewhat hazy time in the history of Cambodia. The Khmers remained firmly under Javanese suzerainty until Jayavarman II (AD 802-850) returned to the land of his ancestors around AD 800 to change the course of Cambodian history.

Angkor and the god-kings

Jayavarman II, the Khmer prince who had spent most of his life at the Sailendra court, claimed independence from Java and founded the Angkor Kingdom to the north of the Tonlé Sap in AD 802, at about the same time as Charlemagne became Holy Roman Emperor in Europe. They were men cast in the same mould, for both were empire builders. His far-reaching conquests at Wat Phou (Laos) and Sambhupura (Sambor) won him immediate political popularity on his return and he became king in AD 790. In AD 802 he declared himself a World Emperor and to consolidate and legitimize his position he arranged his coronation by a Brahmin priest, declaring himself the first Khmer devaraja, or god-king, a tradition continued today. From then on, the reigning monarch was identified with Siva, the king of the Hindu gods. In the centuries that followed, successive devaraja strove to outdo their predecessors by building bigger and finer temples to house the royal linga, a phallic symbol which is the symbol of Siva and the devaraja. The god-kings commanded the absolute allegiance of their subjects, giving them control of a vast pool of labour that was used to build an advanced and prosperous agricultural civilization. For many years historians and archaeologists maintained that the key to this agricultural wealth lay in a sophisticated hydraulic – that is irrigated – system of agriculture which allowed the Khmers to produce up to three harvests a year. However, this view of Angkorian agriculture has come under increasing scrutiny in recent years and now there are many who believe that flood-retreat – rather than irrigated – agriculture was the key. Jayavarman II installed himself in successive capitals north of the Tonlé Sap, secure from attack by the Sailendras, and he ruled until AD 850, when he died on the banks of the Great Lake at the original capital, Hariharalaya, in the Roluos area (Angkor).

Jayavarman III (AD 850-877) continued his father's traditions and ruled for the next 27 years. He expanded his father's empire at Hariharalaya and was the original founder of the laterite temple at Bakong. **Indravarman** (AD 877-889), his successor, was the first of the great temple-builders of Angkor and somewhat overshadowed the work of Jayavarman III. His means to succession are somewhat ambiguous but it is generally agreed that he overthrew Jayavarman III violently. Unlike his predecessor, Indravarman was not the son of a king but more than likely the nephew of Jayavarman's II Queen. He expanded and renovated the capital, building Preah Ko Temple and developing Bakong. Indravarman is considered one of the key players in Khmer history. Referred to as the "lion among kings" and "prince endowed with all the merits", his architectural projects established precedents that were emulated by those that followed him. After Indravarman's death his sons fought for the King's title. The victor, at the end of the ninth century was **Yasovarman I** (AD 889-900). The battle is believed to have destroyed the palace, thus spurring a move to Angkor. He called his new capital Yasodharapura and copied the water system his father had devised at Roluos on an even larger scale, using the waters of the Tonlé Sap. After Yasovarman's death in 900 his son **Harshavarman** (AD 900-923) took the throne, until he died 23 years later. Harshavarman was well regarded, one particular inscription saying that he "caused the joy of the universe". Upon his death, his brother **Ishanarvarman II**, assumed the regal status. In AD 928, **Jayavarman IV** set up a rival capital about 65 km from Angkor at Koh Ker and ruled for the next 20 years. After Jayavarman IV's death there was a period of upheaval as **Harsharvarman II** tried unsuccessfully to lead the empire. **Rajendravarman** (AD 944-968), Jayarvarman's nephew, managed to take control of the empire and moved the court back to Angkor, where the Khmer kings remained. He chose to build outside of the former capital Bakheng, opting instead for the region south of the East Baray. Many saw him as the saviour of Angkor with one inscription reading: "He restored the holy city of Yashodharapura, long deserted, and rendered it superb and charming." Rajendravarman orchestrated a campaign of solidarity – bringing together a number of provinces and claiming back territory, previously under Yasovarman I. From the restored capital he led a successful crusade against the Champa in what is now Vietnam. A devout Buddhist, he erected some of the first Buddhist temples in the precinct. Upon Rajendravarman's death, his son **Jayavarman V** (AD 968-1001), still only a child, took the royal reigns. Once again the administrative centre was moved, this time to the west, where Ta Keo was built. The capital was renamed Jayendranagari. Like his father, Jayavarman V was Buddhist but was extremely tolerant of other religions. At the start of his tenure he had a few clashes with local dissidents but things settled down and he enjoyed relative peace during his rule. The next king, **Udayadityavarman I**, lasted a few months before being ousted. For the next few years Suryavarman I and Jayaviravarman battled for the King's title.

The formidable warrior **King Suryavarman I** (1002-1049) won. He was a determined leader and made all of his officials swear a blood oath of allegiance. He undertook a series of military campaigns geared towards claiming Mon territory in central and southern Thailand and victoriously extended the Khmer empire in Lower Menam, as well as into Laos and established a Khmer capital in Louvo (modern day Lopburi in Thailand). Suryavarman holds the record for the greatest territorial expansion ever achieved in the Khmer Empire. The Royal Palace (Angkor Thom), the West Baray and the Phimeanakas pyramid temples were Suryavarman's main contributions to Angkor's architectural heritage. He continued the royal Hindu cult but also tolerated Mahayana Buddhism.

On Suryavarman's death, the Khmer Kingdom began to fragment. His three successors had short, troubled reigns and the Champa kingdom captured, sacked and razed the capital. When the king's son, **Udayadityavarman II** (1050-1066), assumed the throne, havoc ensued as citizens revolted against him and some of his royal appointments.

When Udayadityavarman II died, his younger brother, **Harsharvarman III** (1066-1080), last in the line of the dynasty, stepped in. During his reign, there were reports of discord and further defeat at the hands of the Cham.

In 1080 a new kingdom was founded by a northern provincial governor claiming aristocratic descent. He called himself **Jayavarman VI** (1080-1107) and is believed to have led a revolt against the former king. He never settled at Angkor, living instead in the northern part of the kingdom. He left monuments at Wat Phou in southern Laos and Phimai, in Thailand. There was an intermittent period where Jayavarman's IV brother, **Dharanindravarman** (1107-1112) took the throne but he was overthrown by his grand-nephew **Suryavarman II** (1113-1150), who soon became the greatest leader the Angkor Empire had ever seen. He worked prolifically on a broad range of projects and achieved some of most impressive architectural feats and political manoeuvres seen within the Angkorian period. He resumed diplomatic relations with China, the Middle Kingdom, and was held in the greatest regard by the then Chinese Emperor. He expanded the Khmer Empire as far as Lopburi, Siam, Pagan in Myanmar, parts of Laos and into the Malay peninsula. He attacked the Champa state relentlessly, particularly Dai Vet in Northern Vietnam, eventually defeating them in 1144-1145, and capturing and sacking the royal capital, Vijaya. He left an incredible, monumental legacy behind, being responsible for the construction of Angkor Wat, an architectural masterpiece that represented the height of the Khmer's artistic genius, Phnom Rung temple (Khorat) and Banteay Samre. A network of roads was built to connect regional capitals.

However, his success was not without its costs – his widespread construction put serious pressure on the general running of the kingdom and major reservoirs silted up during this time; there was also an intensified discord in the provinces and his persistent battling fuelled an ongoing duel between the Cham and Khmers that was to continue (and eventually be avenged) long after his death.

Suryavarman II deposed the King of Champa in 1145 but the Cham regained their independence in 1149 and the following year, Suryavarman died after a disastrous attempt to conquer Annam (northern Vietnam). The throne was usurped by **Tribhuvanadityavarman** in 1165, who died in 1177, when the Cham seized their chance of revenge and sacked Angkor in a surprise naval attack. This was the Khmer's worst recorded defeat – the city was completely annihilated. The 50-year-old **Jayavarman VII** – a cousin of Suryavarman – turned out to be their saviour. He battled the Cham for the next four years, driving them out of the Kingdom. In 1181 he was declared king and seriously hit back, attacking the Chams and seizing their capital, Vijaya. He expanded the Khmer Kingdom further than ever before; its suzerainty stretched from the Malay peninsula in the south to the borders of Burma in the west and the Annamite chain to the northeast.

Jayavarman's VII's first task was to plan a strong, spacious new capital – Angkor Thom; but while that work was being undertaken he set up a smaller, temporary seat of government where he and his court could live in the meantime – Preah Khan meaning 'Fortunate City of Victory' (see page 265). He also built 102 hospitals throughout his kingdom, as well as a network of roads, along which he constructed resthouses. But because they were built of wood, none of these secular structures survive; only the foundations of four larger ones have been unearthed at Angkor.

Angkor's decline

As was the case during Suryavarman II's reign, Jayavarman VII's extensive building campaign put a large amount of pressure on the kingdom's resources and rice was in short supply as labour was diverted into construction.

Jayavarman VII died in 1218 and the Kambujan Empire fell into progressive decline over the next two centuries. Territorially, it was eroded by the eastern migration of the Siamese. The Khmers were unable to prevent this gradual incursion but the diversion of labour to the military rice farming helped seal the fate of Angkor. Another reason for the decline was the introduction of Theravada Buddhism in the 13th century, which undermined the prestige of the king and the priests. There is even a view that climatic change disrupted the agricultural system and led to Kambuja's demise. After Jayavarman VII, no king seems to have been able to unify the kingdom by force of arms or personality – internal dissent increased while the king's extravagance continued to place a crippling burden on state funds. With its temples decaying and its once-magnificent agricultural system in ruins, Angkor became virtually uninhabitable. In 1431 the royal capital was finally abandoned to the Siamese, who drove the Khmers out and made Cambodia a vassal of the Thai Sukhothai Kingdom.

Explaining Angkor's decline

Why the Angkorian Empire should have declined has always fascinated scholars in the West – in the same way that the decline and fall of the Roman Empire has done. Numerous explanations have been offered, and still the debate remains unresolved. As Anthony Barnett argued in a paper in the *New Left Review* in 1990, perhaps the question should be "why did Angkor last so long? Inauspiciously sited, it was nonetheless a tropical imperium of 500 years' duration."

There are essentially five lines of argument in the 'Why did Angkor fall?' debate. First, it has been argued that the building programmes became simply so arduous and demanding of ordinary people that they voted with their feet and moved out, depriving Angkor of the population necessary to support a great empire. Second, some scholars present an environmental argument: the great irrigation works silted up, undermining the empire's agricultural wealth. (This line of argument conflicts with recent work that maintains that Angkor's wealth was never based on hydraulic – or irrigated – agriculture.) Third, there are those who say that military defeat was the cause – but this only begs the question: why they were defeated in the first place? Fourth, historians with a rather wider view, have offered the opinion that the centres of economic activity in Southeast Asia moved from land-based to sea-based foci, and that Angkor was poorly located to adapt to this shift in patterns of trade, wealth and, hence, power. Lastly, some scholars argue that the religion that demanded such labour of Angkor's subjects became so corrupt that it ultimately corroded the empire from within.

After Angkor – running scared

The next 500 years or so, until the arrival of the French in 1863, was an undistinguished period in Cambodian history. In 1434 the royal Khmer court under Ponheayat moved to Phnom Penh, where a replica of the cosmic Mount Meru was built. There was a short-lived period of revival in the mid-15th century until the Siamese invaded and sacked the capital again in 1473. One of the sons of the captured King Suryavarman drummed up enough Khmer support to oust the invaders and there were no subsequent invasions during the 16th century. The capital was established at Lovek (between Phnom Penh and Tonlé Sap) and then moved back to the ruins at Angkor. But a Siamese invasion in 1593 sent the royal court fleeing to Laos; finally, in 1603, the Thais released a captured prince to rule over the Cambodian vassal state. There were at least 22 kings between 1603 and 1848.

Politically, the Cambodian court tried to steer a course between its powerful neighbours of Siam and Vietnam, seeking one's protection against the other. King **Chey Chetta II** (1618-1628), for example, declared Cambodia's independence from Siam and in order to back up his actions he asked Vietnam for help. To cement the allegiance he was forced to marry a Vietnamese princess of the Nguyen Dynasty of Annam, and then obliged to pay tribute to Vietnam. His successors – hoping to rid themselves of Vietnamese domination – sought Siamese assistance and were then forced to pay for it by acknowledging Siam's suzerainty. Then in 1642, **King Chan** converted to Islam, and encouraged Malay and Javanese migrants to settle in Cambodia. Considering him guilty of apostasy, his cousins ousted him – with Vietnamese support. But 50 years later, the Cambodian **Ang Eng** was crowned in Bangkok. This see-saw pattern continued for years; only Siam's wars with Burma and Vietnam's internal disputes and long-running conflict with China prevented them from annexing the whole of Cambodia, although both took territorial advantage of the fragmented state.

By the early 1700s the kingdom was centred on Phnom Penh (there were periods when the king resided at Ondong). But when the Khmers lost their control over the Mekong Delta to the Vietnamese in the late 18th century, the capital's access to the sea was blocked. By 1750 the Khmer royal family had split into pro-Siamese and pro-Vietnamese factions. Between 1794-1811 and 1847-1863, Siamese influence was strongest; from 1835-1837 the Vietnamese dominated. In the 1840s, the Siamese and Vietnamese armies fought on Cambodian territory, devastating the country. This provoked French intervention – and cost Cambodia its independence, even if it had been nominal for several centuries anyway. On 17 April 1864 (the same day and month as the Khmer Rouge soldiers entered Phnom Penh in the 20th century) King Norodom agreed to French protection as he believed they would provide military assistance against the Siamese. The king was to be disappointed: France honoured Siam's claim to the western provinces of Battambang, Siem Reap and Sisophon, which Bangkok had captured in the late 1600s. And in 1884, King Norodom was persuaded by the French governor of the colony of Cochin China to sign another treaty that turned Cambodia into a French colony, along with Laos and Vietnam in the Union Indochinoise. The establishment of Cambodia as a French protectorate probably saved the country from being split up between Siam and Vietnam.

French colonial period

The French did little to develop Cambodia, preferring instead to let the territory pay for itself. They only invested income generated from tax revenue to build a communications network and from a Cambodian perspective, the only benefit of colonial rule was that the French forestalled the total disintegration of the country, which would otherwise have been divided up between its warring neighbours. French cartographers also mapped Cambodia's borders for the first time and in so doing forced the Thais to surrender the northwestern provinces of Battambang and Siem Reap.

For nearly a century the French alternately supported two branches of the royal family, the Norodoms and the Sisowaths, crowning the 18-year-old schoolboy **Prince Norodom Sihanouk** in 1941. The previous year, the Nazis had invaded and occupied France and French territories in Indochina were in turn occupied by the Japanese – although Cambodia was still formally governed and administered by the French. It was at this stage that a group of pro-independence Cambodians realized just how weak the French control of their country actually was. In 1942 two monks were arrested and accused of preaching anti-French sermons; within two days this sparked demonstrations by more than 1000 monks in Phnom Penh, marking the beginning of **Cambodian nationalism**. In March 1945 Japanese forces ousted the colonial administration and persuaded King Norodom Sihanouk to proclaim independence. Following the Japanese surrender in August 1945, the French came back in force; Sihanouk tried to negotiate independence from France and they responded by abolishing the absolute monarchy in 1946 – although the king remained titular head of state. A new constitution was introduced allowing political activity and a National Assembly elected.

Independence and neutrality

By the early 1950s the French army had suffered several defeats in the war in Indochina. Sihanouk dissolved the National Assembly in mid-1952, which he was entitled to do under the constitution, and personally took charge of steering Cambodia towards independence from France. To publicize the cause, he travelled to Thailand, Japan and the United States, and said he would not return from self-imposed exile until his country was free. His audacity embarrassed the French into granting Cambodia independence on 9 November 1953 – and Sihanouk returned, triumphant.

The people of Cambodia did not want to return to absolute monarchy, and following his abdication in 1955, Sihanouk became a popular political leader. But political analysts believe that despite the apparent popularity of the former king's administration, different factions began to develop at this time, a process that was the root of the conflict in the years to come. During the 1960s, for example, there was a growing rift between the Khmer majority and other ethnic groups. Even in the countryside, differences became marked between the rice-growing lands and the more remote mountain areas where people practised shifting cultivation, supplementing their diet with lizards, snakes, roots and insects. As these problems intensified in the late 1960s and the economic situation deteriorated, the popular support base for the Khmer Rouge was put into place. With unchecked population growth, land ownership patterns became skewed, landlessness grew more widespread and food prices escalated.

Sihanouk managed to keep Cambodia out of the war that enveloped Laos and Vietnam during the late 1950s and 1960s by following a neutral policy – which helped attract millions of dollars of aid to Cambodia from both the West and the Eastern Bloc. But when a civil war broke out in South Vietnam in the early 1960s, Cambodia's survival – and Sihanouk's own survival – depended on its outcome. Sihanouk believed the rebels, the National Liberation Front (NLF) would win; and he openly courted and backed the NLF. It was an alliance which cost him dear. In 1965-1966 the tide began to turn in South Vietnam, due to US military and economic intervention. This forced NLF troops to take refuge inside Cambodia. When a peasant uprising in northwestern provinces in 1967 showed Sihanouk that he was sailing close to the wind his forces responded by suppressing the rebellion and massacring 10,000 peasants.

Slowly – and inevitably – he became the focus of resentment within Cambodia's political elite. He also incurred American wrath by allowing North Vietnamese forces to use Cambodian territory as an extension of the **Ho Chi Minh Trail**, ferrying arms and men into South Vietnam. This resulted in his former army Commander-in-Chief, **Marshal Lon Nol** masterminding Sihanouk's removal as Head of State while he was in Moscow in 1970.

Lon Nol abolished the monarchy and proclaimed a republic. One of the most auspicious creatures in Khmer mythology is the white crocodile. It is said to appear 'above the surface' at important moments in history and is said to have been sighted near Phnom Penh just before Lon Nol took over.

Third Indochina War and the rise of the Khmer Rouge

On 30 April 1970, following the overthrow of Prince Norodom Sihanouk, US President Richard Nixon officially announced **Washington's military intervention in Cambodia** – although in reality it had been going on for some time. The invasion aimed to deny the Vietnamese Communists the use of Sihanoukville port through which 85% of their heavy arms were reaching South Vietnam. The US Air Force had been secretly bombing Cambodia using B-52s since March 1969. In 1973, facing defeat in Vietnam, the US Air Force B-52s began carpet bombing Communist-controlled areas to enable Lon Nol's inept regime to retain control of the besieged provincial cities.

Historian David P Chandler wrote: "When the campaign was stopped by the US Congress at the end of the year, the B-52s had dropped over half a million tons of bombs on a country with which the United States was not at war – more than twice the tonnage dropped on Japan during the Second World War.

The war in Cambodia was known as 'the sideshow' by journalists covering the war in Vietnam and by American policy-makers in London. Yet the intensity of US bombing in Cambodia was greater than it ever was in Vietnam; about 500,000 soldiers and civilians were killed over the four-year period. It also caused about two million refugees to flee from the countryside to the capital."

As Henry Kamm suggested, by the beginning of 1971 the people of Cambodia had to face the terrifying realisation that nowhere in the country was safe and all hope and confidence in Cambodia's future during the war was lost. A year after the coup d'etat the country was shattered: guerrilla forces had invaded Angkor, Lol Non had suffered a stroke and had relocated to Hawaii for months of treatment, Lol Non's irregularly paid soldiers were pillaging stores at gunpoint, and extreme corruption was endemic.

By the end of the war, the country had become totally dependent on US aid and much of the population survived on American rice rations. Confidence in the Lon Nol government collapsed as taxes rose and children were drafted into combat units. At the same time, the **Khmer Rouge** increased its military strength dramatically and began to make inroads into areas formerly controlled by government troops. Although officially the Khmer Rouge rebels represented the Beijing-based Royal Government of National Union of Cambodia (Grunc), which was headed by the exiled Prince Sihanouk, Grunc's de facto leaders were Pol Pot, Khieu Samphan (who, after Pol Pot's demise, became the public face of the Khmer Rouge), Ieng Sary (later foreign minister) and Son Sen (Chief of General Staff) – all Khmer Rouge men. By the time the American bombing stopped in 1973, the guerrillas dominated about 60% of Cambodian territory, while the government clung tenuously to towns and cities. Over the next two years the Khmer Rouge whittled away Phnom Penh's defence perimeter to the point that Lon Nol's government was sustained only by American airlifts into the capital.

Some commentators have suggested that the persistent heavy bombing of Cambodia, which forced the Communist guerrillas to live in terrible conditions, was partly responsible for the notorious savagery of the Khmer Rouge in later years. Not only were they brutalized by the conflict itself, but they became resentful of the fact that the city-dwellers had no inkling of how unpleasant their experiences really were. This, writes US political scientist Wayne Bert, "created the perception among the Khmer Rouge that the bulk of the population did not take part in the revolution, was therefore not enthusiastic about it and could not be trusted to support it. The final step in this logic was to punish or eliminate all in these categories who showed either real or imagined tendencies toward disloyalty". And that, as anyone who has watched *The Killing Fields* will know, is what happened.

'Pol Pot time': building Year Zero

On 1 April 1975 President Lon Nol fled Cambodia to escape the advancing Khmer Rouge. Just over two weeks later, on 17 April, the victorious Khmer Rouge entered Phnom Penh. The capital's population had been swollen by refugees from 600,000 to over two million. The ragged conquering troops were welcomed as heroes. None in the crowds that lined the streets appreciated the horrors that the victory would also bring. Cambodia was renamed Democratic Kampuchea (DK) and Pol Pot set to work establishing a radical Maoist-style agrarian society. These ideas had been first sketched out by his longstanding colleague Khieu Samphan, whose 1959 doctoral thesis – at the Sorbonne University in Paris – analyzed the effects of Cambodia's colonial and neo-colonial domination. In order to secure true economic and political independence he argued that it was necessary to isolate Cambodia completely and to go back to a self-sufficient agricultural economy.

Within days of the occupation, the revolutionaries had forcibly evacuated many of the inhabitants of Phnom Penh to the countryside, telling citizens that the Americans were about to bomb the capital. A second major displacement was carried out at the end of the year, when hundreds of thousands of people from the area southeast of Phnom Penh were forced to move to the northwest.

Prior to the Khmer Rouge coming to power, the Cambodian word for revolution (*bambahbambor*) had a conventional meaning, 'uprising'. Under Pol Pot's regime, the word *pativattana* was used instead; it meant 'return to the past'. The Khmer Rouge did this by obliterating everything that did not subscribe to their vision of the past glories of ancient Khmer culture. Pol Pot wanted to return the country to '**Year Zero**' – he wanted to begin again. One of the many revolutionary slogans was "we will burn the old grass and new will grow"; money, modern technology, medicine, education and newspapers were outlawed. Khieu Samphan, who became the Khmer Rouge Head of State, following Prince Sihanouk's resignation in 1976, said at the time: "No, we have no machines. We do everything by mainly relying on the strength of our people. We work completely self-sufficiently. This shows the overwhelming heroism of our people. This also shows the great force of our people. Though bare-handed, they can do everything".

The Khmer Rouge, or *Angkar Loeu* ('The Higher Organization') as they touted themselves, maintained a stranglehold on the country by dislocating families, disorientating people and sustaining a persistent fear through violence, torture and death. At the heart of their strategy was a plan to unfurl people's strongest bonds and loyalties: those that existed between family members. The term *kruosaa*, which traditionally means 'family' in Khmer, came to simply mean 'spouse' under the Khmer Rouge. In Angkar, family no longer existed. *Krusosaa niyum*, which loosely translated to 'familyism' (or pining for one's relatives) was a criminal offence punishable by death. Under heinous interrogation procedures people were intensively probed about their family members (sisters, brothers, grandparents and

BACKGROUND

Pol Pot – the idealistic psychopath

Prince Norodom Sihanouk once referred to Pol Pot as "a more fortunate Hitler". Unlike his erstwhile fascist counterpart, the man whose troops were responsible for the deaths of perhaps two million fellow Cambodians has managed to get away with it. He died on 15 April 1998, either of a heart attack or, possibly, at his own hands or somebody else's.

Pol Pot's real name was Saloth Sar – he adopted his nom de guerre when he became Secretary-General of the Cambodian Communist Party in 1963. He was born in 1928 into a peasant family in Kompong Thom, central Cambodia. His services to the Democrat Party won him a scholarship to study electronics in Paris. He became a Communist in France in 1949 and spent more time at meetings of Marxist revolutionary societies than in classes. In his 1986 book *Sideshow*, William Shawcross notes that at that time the French Communist Party, which was known for its dogmatic adherence to orthodox Marxism, "taught hatred of the bourgeoisie and uncritical admiration of Stalinism, including the collectivization of agriculture". Pol Pot finally lost his scholarship in 1953.

Returning to newly independent Cambodia, Pol Pot started working as a school teacher in Phnom Penh and continued his revolutionary activities in the underground Cambodian Communist Party (which, remarkably kept its existence a secret until 1977). In 1963, he fled the capital for the countryside, fearing a crackdown of the left by Sihanouk. There he rose to become Secretary-General of the Central Committee of the Communist Party of Kampuchea. He was trained in guerrilla warfare and he became a leader of the Khmer Rouge forces, advocating armed resistance to Sihanouk and his 'feudal entourage'. In 1975 when the Khmer Rouge marched into Phnom Penh, Pol Pot was forced out of the shadows to take the role of leader, 'Brother Number One'. Although he took the title of prime minister, he ruled as a dictator and set about reshaping Cambodia with his mentor, Khieu Samphan, the head of state. Yet, during the years he was in power, hardly any Cambodians – save those in the top echelons of the Khmer Rouge – had even heard of him.

The Vietnam-backed Hun Sen government, which took over the country after the overthrow of the Khmer Rouge in December 1978, calculated that by demonizing Pol Pot as the mastermind of the genocide, it would avert the possibility of the Khmer Rouge ever making a comeback. Within Cambodia, he has been portrayed simply as a tyrannical bogey-man.

In a review of David Chandler's biography of Pol Pot (*Brother Number One: A Political Biography of Pol Pot*, Westview Press, 1992), Peter Carey – the co-director of the British-based Cambodia Trust – was struck by what he called "the sinister disjunction between the man's evident charisma ... and the monumental suffering wrought by his regime". Carey concludes: "one is left with the image of a man consumed by his own vision, a vision of empowerment and liberation that has little anchorage in Cambodian reality".

in-laws) and encouraged to inform on them. Those people who didn't turn over relatives considered adversaries (teachers, former soldiers, doctors, etc) faced odious consequences, with the fate of the whole family (immediate and extended) in danger.

Memoirs from survivors detailed in the book *Children of Cambodia's Killing Fields* repeatedly refer to the Khmer Rouge dictum "to keep you is no benefit to destroy you is no loss." People were treated as nothing more than machines. Food was scarce under Pol Pot's inefficient system of collective farming and administration was based on fear, torture and summary execution. A veil of secrecy shrouded Cambodia and, until a few desperate refugees began to trickle over the border into Thailand, the outside world was largely ignorant of what was going on. The refugees' stories of atrocities were, at first, disbelieved. Jewish refugees who escaped from Nazi occupied Poland in the 1940s had encountered a similarly disbelieving reception simply because (like the Cambodians) what they had to say was, to most people, unbelievable. Some left-wing academics initially viewed the revolution as an inspired and brave attempt to break the shackles of dependency and neo-colonial domination. Others, such as Noam Chomsky, dismissed the allegations as right wing press propaganda.

It was not until the Vietnamese 'liberation' of Phnom Penh in 1979 that the scale of the Khmer Rouge carnage emerged and the atrocities witnessed by the survivors became known. The stories turned the Khmer Rouge into international pariahs – but only until 1982 when, remarkably, their American and Chinese sympathizers secured them a voice at the United Nations. During the Khmer Rouge's 44-month reign of terror, it had hitherto been generally accepted that around a million people died. This is a horrendous figure when one considers that the population of the country in 1975 was around seven million. What is truly shocking is that the work undertaken by a team from Yale University indicates that this figure is far too low.

Although the Khmer Rouge era in Cambodia may have been a period of unprecedented economic, political and human turmoil, they still managed to keep meticulous records of what they were doing. In this regard the Khmer Rouge were rather like the Chinese during the Cultural Revolution, or the Nazis in Germany. Using Australian satellite data, the team was expecting to uncover around 200 mass graves; instead they found several thousand. The Khmer Rouge themselves have claimed that around 20,000 people died because of their 'mistakes'. The Vietnamese have traditionally put the figure at two to three million, although their estimates have generally been rejected as too high and politically motivated (being a means to justify their invasion of the country in 1978/1979 and subsequent occupation). The Documentation Center of Cambodia, involved in the heavy mapping project, said that 20,492 mass graves were uncovered containing the remains of 1,112,829 victims of execution. In addition, hundreds of thousands more died from famine and disease; frighteningly, the executions are believed to only account for about 30-40% of the total death toll.

How such a large slice of Cambodia's people died in so short a time (1975-1978) beggars belief. Some were shot, strangled or suffocated; many more starved; while others died from disease and overwork. The Khmer Rouge transformed Cambodia into what the British journalist, William Shawcross, described as: "a vast and sombre work camp where toil was unending, where respite and rewards were non-existent, where families were abolished and where murder was used as a tool of social discipline. The manner of execution was often brutal. Babies were torn apart limb from limb, pregnant women were disembowelled. Men and women were buried up to their necks in sand and left to die slowly. A common form of execution was by axe handles to the back of the neck. That saved ammunition".

The Khmer Rouge revolution was primarily a class-based one, fed by years of growing resentment against the privileged elites. The revolution pitted the least-literate, poorest rural peasants (referred to as the 'old' people) against the educated, skilled and foreign-influenced urban population (the 'new' people). The 'new' people provided an endless flow of numbers for the regime's death lists. Through a series of terrible purges, the members of the former governing and mercantile classes were liquidated or sent to work as forced labourers. But Peter Carey, Oxford historian and Chairman of the Cambodia Trust, argues that not all Pol Pot's victims were townspeople and merchants. "Under the terms of the 1948 Genocide Convention, the Khmer Rouge stands accused of genocide," he wrote in a letter to a British newspaper in 1990. "Of 64,000 Buddhist monks, 62,000 perished; of 250,000 Islamic Chams, 100,000; of 200,000 Vietnamese still left in 1975, 100,000; of 20,000 Thai, 12,000; of 1800 Lao, 1000. Of 2000 Kola, not a trace remained." American political scientist Wayne Bert noted that: "The methods and behaviour compare to that of the Nazis and Stalinists, but in the percentage of the population killed by a revolutionary movement, the Khmer Rouge holds an unchallenged record."

It is still unclear the degree to which these 'genocidal' actions were controlled by those at the centre. Many of the killings took place at the discretion of local leaders, but there were some notably cruel leaders in the upper echelons of the Khmer Rouge and none can have been ignorant of what was going on. Ta Mok, who administered the region southwest of Phnom Penh, oversaw many mass executions for example. There is also evidence that the central government was directly involved in the running of the Tuol Sleng detention centre in which at least 20,000 people died. It has now been turned into a memorial to Pol Pot's holocaust (see page 219).

In addition to the legacy left by centres such as Tuol Sleng, there is the impact of the mass killings upon the Cambodian psyche. One of which is – to Western eyes – the startling openness with which Khmer people will, if asked, matter-of-factly relate their family history in detail: this usually involves telling how the Khmer Rouge era meant they lost one or several members of their family. Whereas death is talked about in hushed terms in Western society, Khmers have no such reservations, perhaps because it touched, and still touches, them all.

Vietnamese invasion

The first border clashes over offshore islands between Khmer Rouge forces and the Vietnamese army were reported just a month after the Khmer Rouge came to power. These erupted into a minor war in January 1977 when the Phnom Penh government accused Vietnam of seeking to incorporate Kampuchea into an Indochinese federation. Hanoi's determination to oust Pol Pot only really became apparent however, on Christmas Day 1978 when 120,000 Vietnamese troops invaded. By 7 January (the day of Phnom Penh's liberation) they had installed a puppet government which proclaimed the foundation of the People's Republic of Kampuchea (PRK): Heng Samrin, a former member of the Khmer Rouge, was appointed president. The Vietnamese compared their invasion to the liberation of Uganda from Idi Amin – but for the Western world it was unwelcome. The new government was accorded scant recognition abroad, while the toppled government of Democratic Kampuchea retained the country's seat at the United Nations.

The country's 'liberation' by Vietnam did not end the misery; in 1979 nearly half Cambodia's population was in transit, either searching for their former homes or fleeing across the Thai border into refugee camps. American political scientist Wayne Bert wrote: "The Vietnamese had long seen a special role for themselves in uniting and leading a greater Indochina Communist movement and the Cambodian Communists had seen with clarity that such a role for the Vietnamese could only be at the expense of their independence and prestige."

Under the Lon Nol and Khmer Rouge regimes, Vietnamese living in Cambodia were expelled or exterminated. Resentment had built up over the years in Hanoi – exacerbated by the apparent ingratitude of the Khmer Rouge for Vietnamese assistance in fighting Lon Nol's US-supported Khmer Republic in the early 1970s. As relations between the Khmer Rouge and the Vietnamese deteriorated, the Communist superpowers, China and the Soviet Union, polarized too – the former siding with the Khmer Rouge and the latter with Hanoi. The Vietnamese invasion had the full backing of Moscow, while the Chinese and Americans began their support for the anti-Vietnamese rebels.

Following the Vietnamese invasion, three main anti-Hanoi factions were formed. In June 1982 they banded together in an unholy and unlikely alliance of convenience to fight the PRK and called themselves the Coalition Government of Democratic Kampuchea (CGDK), which was immediately recognized by the United Nations. The Communist **Khmer Rouge**, whose field forces recovered to at least 18,000 by the late 1980s were supplied with weapons by China and were concentrated in the Cardamom Mountains in the southwest and were also in control of some of the refugee camps along the Thai border. The National United Front for an Independent Neutral Peaceful and Co-operative Cambodia (Funcinpec) – known by most people as the **Armée Nationale Sihanoukiste** (ANS) was headed by Prince Sihanouk although he spent most of his time exiled in Beijing. The group had fewer than 15,000 well-equipped troops – most of whom took orders from Khmer Rouge commanders. The anti-Communist **Khmer People's National Liberation Front** (KPNLF), headed by Son Sann, a former prime minister under Sihanouk. Its 5000 troops were reportedly ill-disciplined in comparison with the Khmer Rouge and the ANS.

The three CGDK factions were ranged against the 70,000 troops loyal to the government of President Heng Samrin and Prime Minister Hun Sen (previously a Khmer Rouge cadre). They were backed by Vietnamese forces until September 1989. Within the forces of the Phnom Penh government there were reported to be problems of discipline and desertion. But the rebel guerrilla coalition was itself seriously weakened by rivalries and hatred between the different factions: in reality, the idea of a 'coalition' was fiction. Throughout most of the 1980s the war followed the progress of the seasons: during the dry season the PRK forces with their tanks and heavy arms took the offensive but during the wet season this heavy equipment was ineffective and the guerrilla resistance made advances.

Road towards peace

In the late 1980s the Association of Southeast Asian Nations (ASEAN) – for which the Cambodian conflict had almost become a raison d'être – began steps to bring the warring factions together over the negotiating table. ASEAN countries were united primarily in wanting the Vietnamese out of Cambodia. While publicly deploring the Khmer Rouge record, ASEAN tacitly supported the guerrillas. Thailand, an ASEAN member-state, which has had a centuries-long suspicion of the Vietnamese, co-operated closely with China to ensure that the Khmer Rouge guerrillas over the border were well-supplied with weapons.

After Mikhail Gorbachev had come to power in the Soviet Union, Moscow's support for the Vietnamese presence in Cambodia gradually evaporated. Gorbachev began leaning on Vietnam as early as 1987, to withdraw its troops. Despite saying their presence in Cambodia was 'irreversible', Vietnam completed its withdrawal in September 1989, ending nearly 11 years of Hanoi's direct military involvement. The withdrawal led to an immediate upsurge in political and military activity, as forces of the exiled CGDK put increased pressure on the now weakened Phnom Penh regime to begin power-sharing negotiations.

Modern Cambodia

In September 1989, under pressure at home and abroad, the Vietnamese withdrew from Cambodia. The immediate result of this withdrawal was an escalation of the civil war as the rebel factions tried to take advantage of the supposedly weakened Hun Sen regime in Phnom Penh. The government committed itself to liberalizing the economy and improving the infrastructure in order to undermine the political appeal of the rebels – particularly that of the Khmer Rouge. Peasant farmers were granted life tenancy to their land and collective farms were substituted with agricultural co-operatives. But because nepotism and bribery were rife in Phnom Penh, the popularity of the Hun Sen regime declined. The rebel position was further strengthened as the disparities between living standards in Phnom Penh and those in the rest of the country widened. In the capital, the government became alarmed; in a radio broadcast in 1991 it announced a crackdown on corruption claiming it was causing a "loss of confidence in our superb regime ... which is tantamount to paving the way for the return of the genocidal Pol Pot regime".

With the withdrawal of Vietnamese troops, the continuing civil war followed the familiar pattern of dry season government offensives, and consolidation of guerrilla positions during the monsoon rains. Much of the fighting focused on the potholed highways – particularly Highway 6, which connects the capital with Battambang – with the Khmer Rouge blowing up most of the bridges along the road. Their strategy involved cutting the roads in order to drain the government's limited resources. Other Khmer Rouge offensives were designed to serve their own economic ends – such as their capture of the gem-rich town of Pailin.

The Khmer Rouge ran extortion rackets throughout the country, even along the strategic Highway 4, which ferried military supplies, oil and consumer goods from the port of Kompong Som (Sihanoukville) to Phnom Penh. The State of Cambodia – or the government forces, known as SOC – was pressed to deploy troops to remote areas and allot scarce resources, settling refugees in more secure parts of the country. To add to their problems, Soviet and Eastern Bloc aid began to dry up.

Throughout 1991 the four warring factions were repeatedly brought to the negotiating table in an effort to hammer out a peace deal. Much of the argument centred on the word 'genocide'. The Prime Minister, Hun Sen, insisted that the wording of any agreement should explicitly condemn the former Khmer Rouge regime's 'genocidal acts'. But the Khmer Rouge refused to be party to any power-sharing deal which labelled them in such a way. Fighting intensified as hopes for a settlement increased – all sides wanted to consolidate their territory in advance of any agreement.

Rumours emerged that China was continuing to supply arms – including tanks, reportedly delivered through Thailand – to the Khmer Rouge. There were also accusations that the Phnom Penh government was using Vietnamese combat troops to stem Khmer Rouge advances – the first such reports since their official withdrawal in 1989. But finally, in June 1991, after several attempts, Sihanouk brokered a permanent ceasefire during a meeting of the Supreme National Council (SNC) in Pattaya, South Thailand. The SNC had been proposed by the United Nations Security Council in 1990 and formed in 1991, with an equal number of representatives from the Phnom Penh government and each of the resistance factions, with Sihanouk as its chairman. The following month he was elected chairman of the SNC, and resigned his presidency of the rebel coalition government in exile. Later in the year, the four factions agreed to reduce their armed guerrillas and militias by 70%. The remainder were to be placed under the supervision of the United Nations Transitional Authority in Cambodia (UNTAC), which supervised Cambodia's transition to multi-party democracy. Heng Samrin decided to drop his insistence that reference should be made to the former Khmer Rouge's 'genocidal regime'. It was also agreed that elections should be held in 1993 on the basis of proportional representation. Heng Samrin's Communist Party was promptly renamed the Cambodian People's Party, in an effort to persuade people that it sided with democracy and capitalism.

Paris Peace Accord

On 23 October 1991, the four warring Cambodian factions signed a peace agreement in Paris which officially ended 13 years of civil war and more than two decades of warfare. The accord was co-signed by 15 other members of the International Peace Conference on Cambodia. There was an air of unreality about the whole event, which brought bitter enemies face-to-face after months of protracted negotiations. There was, however, a notable lack of enthusiasm on the part of the four warring factions. Hun Sen said that the treaty was far from perfect because it failed to contain the word 'genocide' to remind Cambodians of the atrocities of the former Khmer Rouge regime and Western powers obviously agreed. But in the knowledge that it was a fragile agreement, everyone remained diplomatically quiet. US Secretary of State James Baker was quoted as saying "I don't think anyone can tell you there will for sure be lasting peace, but there is great hope."

Political analysts ascribed the successful conclusion to the months of negotiations to improved relations between China and Vietnam – there were reports that the two had held secret summits at which the Cambodia situation was discussed. China put pressure on Prince Norodom Sihanouk to take a leading role in the peace process, and Hanoi's new understanding with Beijing prompted Hun Sen's participation. The easing of tensions between China and Moscow – particularly following the Soviet Union's demise – also helped apply pressure on the different factions. Finally, the United States had shifted its position: in July 1990 it had announced that it would not support the presence of the Khmer Rouge at the UN and by September US officials were talking to Hun Sen.

On 14 November 1991, Prince Norodom Sihanouk returned to Phnom Penh to an ecstatic welcome, followed, a few days later, by Son Sen, a Khmer Rouge leader. On 27 November Khieu Samphan, who had represented the Khmer Rouge at all the peace negotiations, arrived on a flight from Bangkok. Within hours mayhem had broken out, and a lynch mob attacked him in his villa. Rumours circulated that Hun Sen had orchestrated the demonstration, and beating an undignified retreat down a ladder into a waiting armoured personnel carrier, the bloodied Khmer Rouge leader headed back to Pochentong Airport. The crowd had sent a clear signal that they, at least, were not happy to see him back. There were fears that this incident might derail the entire peace process – but in the event, the Khmer Rouge won a small public relations coup by playing the whole thing down. When the Supreme National Council (SNC) finally met in Phnom Penh at the end of December 1991, it was unanimously decided to rubberstamp the immediate deployment of UN troops to oversee the peace process in the run-up to a general election.

UN peace-keeping mission

Yasushi Akashi, a senior Japanese official in the United Nations, was assigned the daunting task of overseeing the biggest military and logistical operation in UN history. UNTAC comprised an international team of 22,000 peacekeepers – including 16,000 soldiers from 22 countries; 6000 officials; 3500 police and 1700 civilian employees and electoral volunteers. The first 'blue-beret' UN troops began arriving in November 1991, even before the SNC had agreed to the full complement of peacekeepers. The UN Advance Mission to Cambodia (UNAMIC) was followed four months later by the first of the main peacekeeping battalions. The odds were stacked against them. Shortly after his arrival, Akashi commented: "If one was a masochist one could not wish for more."

UNTAC's task

UNTAC's central mission was to supervise free elections in a country where most of the population had never voted and had little idea of how democracy was meant to work. The UN was also given the task of resettling 360,000 refugees from camps in Thailand and of demobilizing more than a quarter of a million soldiers and militiamen from the four main factions. In addition, it was to ensure that no further arms shipments reached these factions, whose remaining forces were to be confined to cantonments. In the run-up to the elections, UNTAC also took over the administration of the country, taking over the defence, foreign affairs, finance, public security and information portfolios as well as the task of trying to ensure respect for human rights.

Khmer Rouge pulls out

At the beginning of 1993 it became apparent that the Khmer Rouge had no intention of playing ball, despite its claim of a solid rural support base. The DK failed to register for the election before the expiry of the UN deadline and its forces stepped up attacks on UN personnel. In April 1993 Khieu Samphan and his entire entourage at the Khmer Rouge compound in Phnom Penh left the city. It was at this stage that UN officials finally began expressing their exasperation and anxiety over the Khmer Rouge's avowed intention to disrupt the polls. It was well known that the faction had procured fresh supplies of Chinese weapons through Thailand – although there is no evidence that these came from Beijing – as well as large arms caches all over the country.

By the time of the elections, the group was thought to be in control of between 10% and 15% of Cambodian territory. Khmer Rouge guerrillas launched attacks in April and May 1993. Having stoked racial antagonism, they started killing ethnic Vietnamese villagers and settlers, sending up to 20,000 of them fleeing into Vietnam. In one particularly vicious attack, 33 Vietnamese fishermen and their families were killed in a village on the Tonlé Sap. The Khmer Rouge also began ambushing and killing UN soldiers and electoral volunteers.

The UN remained determined that the elections should go ahead despite the Khmer Rouge threats and mounting political intimidation and violence between other factions, notably the Cambodian People's Party and Funcinpec. In the event, however, there were remarkably few violent incidents and the feared coordinated effort to disrupt the voting failed to materialize. Voters took no notice of Khmer Rouge calls to boycott the election and in fact, reports came in of large numbers of Khmer Rouge guerrillas and villagers from areas under their control, turning up at polling stations to cast their ballots.

UN-supervised elections

The days following the election saw a political farce – Cambodian style – which, as Nate Thayer wrote in the *Far Eastern Economic Review* "might have been comic if the implications were not so depressing for the country's future". In just a handful of days, the Phnom Penh-based correspondent went on, Cambodia "witnessed an abortive secession, a failed attempt to establish a provisional government, a royal family feud and the manoeuvres of a prince [Sihanouk] obsessed with avenging his removal from power in a military coup more than 20 years [previously]". The elections gave Funcinpec 45% of the vote, the CPP 38% and the BLDP, 3%. The CPP immediately claimed the results fraudulent, while Prince Norodom Chakrapong – one of Sihanouk's sons – announced the secession of the country's six eastern provinces. Fortunately, both attempts to undermine the election dissolved. The CPP agreed to join Funcinpec in a power-sharing agreement while, remarkably, the Khmer Rouge were able to present themselves as defenders of democracy in the face of the CPP's claims of vote-rigging. The new Cambodian constitution was ratified in September 1993, marking the end of UNTAC's involvement in the country. Under the new constitution, Cambodia was to be a pluralistic liberal-democratic country. Seventy-year-old Sihanouk was crowned King of Cambodia, reclaiming the throne he relinquished in 1955. His son Norodom Ranariddh was appointed First Prime Minister and Hun Sen, Second Prime Minister, a situation intended to promote national unity but which instead lead to internal bickering and dissent.

An uncivil society?

Almost from day one of Cambodia's rebirth as an independent state espousing the principles of democracy and the market, cracks began to appear in the rickety structure that underlay these grand ideals. Rampant corruption, infighting among the coalition partners, political intrigue, murder and intimidation all became features of the political landscape – and have remained so to this day. There are three bright spots in an otherwise pretty dismal political landscape. First of all, the Khmer Rouge – along with Pol Pot – is dead and buried. Second, while there have been coups, attempted coups, murder, torture and intimidation, the country does still have an operating political system with an opposition of sorts. And third, the trajectory of change in recent years has been upwards. But, as the following account shows, politics in Cambodia makes Italy seem a model of stability and common sense.

From the elections of 1993 through to 1998, relations between the two key members of the ruling coalition, the CPP and Funcinpec, went from bad to quite appalling. At the end of 1995 Prince Norodom Sirivudh was arrested for plotting to kill Hun Sen and the prime minister ordered troops and tanks on to the streets of Phnom Penh. For a while the capital had the air of a city under siege. Sirivudh, secretary-general of Funcinpec and King Norodom Sihanouk's half-brother, has been a vocal critic of corruption in the government, and a supporter of Sam Rainsy, the country's most outspoken opposition politician and the bane of Hun Sen's life. The National Assembly voted unanimously to suspend Sirivudh's immunity from prosecution. Few commentators really believed that Sirivudh had plotted to kill Hun Sen. In the end Hun Sen did not go through with a trial and Sirivudh went into self-imposed exile.

In 1996, relations between the CPP and Funcinpec reached another low. First Prime Minister Prince Norodom Ranariddh joined his two exiled brothers – princes Chakkrapong and Sirivudh – along with Sam Rainsy, in France. Hun Sen smelled a rat and when Ranariddh threatened in May to pull out of the coalition his worries seemed to be confirmed. Only pressure from the outside prevented a meltdown. Foreign donors said that continuing aid was contingent on political harmony, and ASEAN sent the Malaysian foreign minister to knock a few heads together. Some months later relations became chillier following the drive-by killing of Hun Sen's brother-in-law as he left a restaurant in Phnom Penh.

Things, it seemed, couldn't get any worse – but they did. In February 1997, fighting between forces loyal to Ranariddh and Hun Sen broke out in Battambang. March saw a grenade attack on a demonstration led by opposition leader Sam Rainsy outside the National Assembly leaving 16 dead and 150 injured – including Rainsy himself who suffered minor injuries. In April, Hun Sen mounted what became known as the 'soft coup'. This followed a complicated series of defections from Ranariddh's Funcinpec party to the CPP which, after much to-ing and fro-ing overturned Funcinpec's small majority in the National Assembly. In May, Hun Sen's motorcade was attacked and a month later, on 16 June, fighting broke out between Hun Sen and Ranariddh's bodyguards leaving three dead. It was this gradual decline in relations between the two leaders and their parties which laid the foundations for the coup of 1997.

In July 1997 the stage was set for Cambodia to join ASEAN. This would have marked Cambodia's international rehabilitation. Then, just a month before the historic day, on 5-6 June, Hun Sen mounted a coup and ousted Norodom Ranariddh and his party, Funcinpec, from government. It took two days for Hun Sen and his forces to gain full control of the capital. Ranariddh escaped to Thailand while the United Nations Centre for Human Rights reported that 41 senior military officers and Ranariddh loyalists were hunted down in the days following the coup, tortured and executed. In August the National Assembly voted to withdraw Ranariddh's immunity from prosecution. Five months later, in January 1998, United Nations High Commissioner for Human Rights Mary Robinson visited Cambodia and pressed for an investigation into the deaths – a request that Hun Sen rejected as unwarranted interference. ASEAN, long used to claiming that the Association has no role interfering in domestic affairs, found it had no choice but to defer Cambodia's accession. The coup was widely condemned and on 17 September the UN decided to keep Cambodia's seat vacant in the General Assembly.

Following the coup of 1997 there was some speculation that Hun Sen would simply ignore the need to hold elections scheduled for 26 July. In addition, opposition parties threatened to boycott the elections even if they did occur, claiming that Hun Sen and his henchmen were intent on intimidation. But despite sporadic violence in the weeks and months leading up to the elections, all parties ended up participating. It seems that intense international pressure got to Hun Sen who appreciated that without the goodwill of foreign aid donors the country would simply collapse. Of the 4.9 million votes cast – constituting an impressive 90% of the electorate – Hun Sen's Cambodian People's Party won the largest share at just over 41%.

Hun Sen offered to bring Funcinpec and the SRP into a coalition government, but his advances were rejected. Instead Rainsy and Ranariddh encouraged a series of demonstrations and vigils outside the National Assembly – which quickly became known as 'Democracy Square', à la Tiananmen Square. At the beginning of September 1998, following a grenade attack on Hun Sen's residence and two weeks of uncharacteristic restraint on the part of the Second Prime Minister, government forces began a crackdown on the demonstrators. A week later the three protagonists – Ranariddh, Sam Rainsy and Hun Sen – agreed to talks presided over by King Sihanouk in Siem Reap. These progressed astonishingly well considering the state of relations between the three men and two days later the 122-seat National Assembly opened at Angkor Wat on 24 September. In mid-November further talks between the CPP and Funcinpec led to the formation of a coalition government. Hun Sen became sole prime minister and Ranariddh chairman of the National Assembly. While the CPP and Funcinpec took control of 12 and 11 ministries respectively, with Defence and Interior shared, the CPP got the lion's share of the key portfolios. **Sam Rainsy** was left on the opposition benches. It was only after the political détente that followed the elections that Cambodia was given permission to occupy its UN seat in December 1998. At a summit meeting in Hanoi around the same time, ASEAN also announced that they had agreed on the admission of Cambodia to the grouping – which finally came through on 30 April 1999.

A return to some kind of normality

The year 1997 was the low point in Cambodia's stuttering return to a semblance of normality. The Asian economic crisis combined with the coup (see above) to rock the country back on its heels. On 3 February 2002 free, fair and only modestly violent local commune elections were held. The CPP won the vote by a landslide and although there is little doubt that Hun Sen's party used a bit of muscle here and there, foreign election observers decided that the result reflected the will of the 90% of the electorate who voted. The CPP, despite its iron grip on power, does recognize that democracy means it has to get out there and make a case. Around one third of the CPP's more unpopular commune chiefs were replaced prior to the election. Funcinpec did badly, unable to shake off the perception that it sold out its principles to join the coalition in 1998. The opposition Sam Rainsy Party did rather better, largely for the same reason: the electorate viewed it as standing up to the might of the CPP, highlighting corruption and abuses of power.

In July 2002 Hun Sen took on the rotating chairmanship of ASEAN and used a round of high-profile meetings to demonstrate to the region, and the wider world, just how far the country has come. Hun Sen, who hardly has an enviable record as a touchy-feely politician, used the chairmanship of ASEAN to polish his own as well as his country's credentials in the arena of international public opinion. But despite the PR some Cambodians are concerned that Hun Sen is becoming a little like Burma's Ne Win. Like Ne Win, Hun Sen seems to be obsessed with numbers. His lucky number is nine; in 2002 he brought the local elections forward by three weeks so that the digits in the date would add up to nine. In 2001 he closed down all Cambodia's karaoke bars. With over 20 years as prime minister there is no one to touch Hun Sen and he seems to revel in his strongman reputation. Judges bow to his superior knowledge of the judicial system; kings and princes acknowledged his unparalleled role in appointing the new king; many journalists are in thrall to his power. If even the most fundamental of rights are negotiable then it would seem that only Cambodia's dependence on foreign largesse constrains his wilder impulses.

Compared to its recent past, the last 10 years has been a period of relative stability for Cambodia. Political violence and infighting between parties continues to be a major problem – by international standards the elections were borderline unacceptable, although most of the major parties were reasonably satisfied with the results which saw Hun Sen's landslide victory. The 2003 election wasn't smooth-sailing either. Prior to the June 2003 election the alleged instructions given by representatives of the CPP to government controlled election monitoring organizations were: "If we win by the law, then we win. If we lose by the law, we still must win." Nonetheless a political deadlock arose, with the CPP winning a majority of votes but not the two-thirds required under the constitution to govern alone. The incumbent CPP-led administration assumed power and took on a caretaker role, pending the creation of a coalition that would satisfy the required number of National Assembly seats to form government. Without a functioning legislature, the course of vital legislation was stalled. After almost a year-long stalemate, the National Assembly approved a controversial addendum to the constitution, which allowed a new government to be formed by vote. The vote took place on July 15 2004, and the National

Assembly approved a new coalition government, an amalgam of the CPP and FUNCINPEC, with Hun Sen at the helm as prime minister and Prince Norodom Ranariddh as president of the national assembly.

The government's democratic principles came under fire once again in February 2005, when opposition leader Sam Rainsy fled the country after losing his parliamentary immunity from prosecution. Rainsy is perceived as something of a threat due to his steadily gaining popularity with young urban dwellers, whose growing disenchantment with the current government he feeds off. On the one hand, his 'keep the bastards honest' style of politics has added a new dimension of accountability to Cambodian politics, but on the other, his nationalist, racist rantings, particularly his anti-Vietnamese sentiments, could be a very bad thing for the country. In May, 2005 Hun Sen said that Sam Rainsy would have to wait until the "next life" before he would guarantee his safety. However, having received a pardon in February 2006, he returned to the political fray soon after.

The lingering death of the Khmer Rouge

What many outsiders found hard to understand was how the Khmer Rouge enjoyed such popular support among Cambodians – even after the massacres and torture.

The Khmer Rouge was not, of course, just a political force. Its political influence was backed up and reinforced by military muscle. And it has been the defeat of the Khmer Rouge as an effective fighting force that seems to have delivered the fatal blow to its political ambitions.

In mid-1994 the National Assembly outlawed the Khmer Rouge, offering a six-month amnesty to rank-and-file guerrillas. By the time the six months was up in January 1995, 7000 Khmer Rouge had reportedly defected to the government, leaving at that time somewhere between 5000 and 6000 hardcore rebels still fighting. A split in this core group can be dated to 8 August 1996 when Khmer Rouge radio announced that former 'brother number two', Ieng Sary, had betrayed the revolution by embezzling money earned from mining and timber contracts, and branded him a traitor.

This was the first evidence available to Western commentators that a significant split in the Khmer Rouge had occurred. In retrospect, it seems that the split had been brewing for some years – ever since the UN-sponsored elections had revealed a division between 'conservatives' and 'moderates'. The latter, apparently, wished to co-operate with the UN, while the former group desired to boycott the elections. In 1996 the moderate faction, headed by Ieng Sary, finally broke away from the conservatives led by Pol Pot and hardman General Ta Mok. Hun Sen announced soon after the radio broadcast in August 1996 that two Khmer Rouge commanders, Ei Chhien and Sok Pheap had defected to the government. At the end of September Ieng Sary held a press conference to declare his defection. On 14 September King Norodom Sihanouk granted Ieng Sary a royal pardon.

The Cambodian government's conciliatory line towards Ieng Sary seemed perplexing given the man's past. Although he cast himself in the mould of 'misguided and ignorant revolutionary', there are few who doubt that he was fully cognisant of what the Khmer Rouge under Pol Pot were doing even if, as Michael Vickery argues, he was not Brother Number Two, just Brother Number Four or Five. Indeed he has admitted as much in the past. Not only is he, as a man, thoroughly unpleasant – or so those who know him have said – but he was also a key figure in the leadership and was sentenced to death in absentia by the Phnom Penh government. Stephen Heder of London's School of Oriental & African Studies was quoted as saying after the September press conference: "It's totally implausible that Ieng Sary was unaware that people were being murdered [by the Khmer Rouge]". The split in the Khmer Rouge and the defection of Ieng Sary deprived the Khmer Rouge of 3000-5000 men – halving its fighting force – and also denied the group important revenues from key gem mining areas around Pailin and many of the richest forest concessions.

The disintegration of the Khmer Rouge continued in 1997 after a complicated deal involving Pol Pot, Khieu Samphan, Son Sen and Ta Mok, as well as members of Funcinpec, collapsed. In early June Khieu Samphan, the nominal leader of the Khmer Rouge, was thought to be on the verge of brokering an agreement with Funcinpec that would give Pol Pot and two of his henchmen immunity from prosecution. This would then provide the means by which Khieu Samphan might enter mainstream Cambodian politics. It seems that Hun Sen, horrified at the idea of an alliance between Khieu Samphan and Funcinpec, mounted the coup of June 1997 to prevent the deal coming to fruition. Pol Pot was also, apparently, less than satisfied with the terms of the agreement and pulled out – killing Son Sen in the process. But before Pol Pot could flee, Ta Mok captured his erstwhile leader on June 19th at the Khmer Rouge stronghold of Anlong Veng.

A little more than a month later the 'Trial of the Century' began in this jungle hideout. It was a show trial – more like a Cultural Revolution lynching. A crowd of a few hundred people were on hand. Pol Pot offered the usual Khmer Rouge defence: the revolution made mistakes, but its leaders were inexperienced. And, in any case, they saved Cambodia from annexation by Vietnam. (There is an argument purveyed by some academics that the Khmer Rouge was essentially involved in a programme of ethnic cleansing aimed at ridding Cambodia of all Vietnamese people and influences.) Show trial or not, few people had any sympathy for Pol Pot as he was sentenced by the Khmer Rouge 'people's' court to life imprisonment for the murder of Son Sen. A Khmer Rouge radio station broadcast that with Pol Pot's arrest and sentencing, a 'dark cloud' had been lifted from the Cambodian people.

Confirmation of this bizarre turn of events emerged in mid-October when journalist Nate Thayer of the *Far Eastern Economic Review* became the first journalist to interview Pol Pot since 1979. He reported that the former Khmer Rouge leader was "very ill and perhaps close to death". Even more incredibly than Ieng Sary's defence, Pol Pot denied that the genocide had ever occurred and told Nate Thayer that his 'conscience was clear'.

In March 1998 reports filtered out of the jungle near the Thai border that the Khmer Rouge was finally disintegrating in mutinous conflict. The end game was at hand. The government's amnesty encouraged the great bulk of the Khmer Rouge's remaining fighters to lay down their arms and in December 1998 the last remnants of the rebel army surrendered to government forces, leaving just a handful of men under hardman 'The Butcher' Ta Mok still at large. But even Ta Mok's days of freedom were numbered. In March 1999 he was captured near the Thai border and taken back to Phnom Penh.

The death of Pol Pot

On 15 April 1998 unconfirmed reports stated that Pol Pot – a man who ranks with Hitler, Stalin and Mao in his ability to kill – had died in a remote jungle hideout in the north of Cambodia. Given that Pol Pot's death had been announced several times before, the natural inclination among journalists and commentators was to treat these reports with scepticism. But it was already known that Pol Pot was weak and frail and his death was confirmed when journalists were invited to view his body the following day. Pol Pot was reported to have died from a heart attack. He was 73.

A new era?

The question of what to do with Ieng Sary was the start of a long debate over how Cambodia – and the international community – should deal with former members of the

Buddhist temple wars and beyond

The stunning temple complex at Preah Vihear, in the remote region of northern Cambodia, has long been a source of contention between Thailand and the Khmers. Since the colonial-era borders were established back in the early 20th century, Thailand has made repeated attempts to annex the area. However, in 1962, the argument was arbitrated by the International Court of Justice in The Hague which ruled that the temple fell within the boundaries of Cambodia. Unfortunately this was proved to be far from the last the international community saw of the dispute and over the years Preah Vihear has been at the centre of tensions between these neighbours.

In the 1990s Thailand suddenly closed access to the site, citing the illegal use of the border. In January 2003 there was further escalation of tensions after the misinterpretation of remarks allegedly made by a Thai actress insinuating that Thailand should regain control of the area. There were riots and the Thai embassy in Phnom Penh was badly damaged along with many Thai-owned businesses. In May 2005 the two countries both deployed troops on the border surrounding Preah Vihear.

Fast forward to 2008 and a long-standing application for Preah Vihear to be placed on the UNESCO World Heritage Site list came to fruition. Initially the Thai government supported the move, even though this meant accepting the contested areas were inside Cambodian territory. The thinking at the time was that the site could now benefit both nations.

Khmer Rouge. The pragmatic, realist line is that if lasting peace is to come to Cambodia, then it may be necessary to allow some people to get away with – well – murder. As one Western diplomat pondered: "Do you owe fealty to the dead for the living?" This would seem to be Hun Sen's preferred position. By late 1998, with the apparent end of the Khmer Rouge as a fighting force, the government seemed happy to welcome back the rank and file into mainstream Cambodian life while putting on trial key characters in the Khmer Rouge like Ta Mok, Khieu Samphan and Nuon Chea. While the government was considering what to do, former leaders of the Khmer Rouge were busy trying to rehabilitate their muddied reputations. After years of living pretty comfortable lives around the country, particularly in and around Pailin, by late 2007 the old guard of the Khmer Rouge were finally being brought to book. This turn of events was finally set in motion in March 2006 with the nomination of seven judges by the then Secretary General of the United Nations, Kofi Annan for the much anticipated Cambodia Tribunal. With Ta Mok dying in prison in early July 2006 the first charges were laid against the notorious head of the Tuol Sleng prison, Khang Khek Ieu, aka 'Comrade Duch'. Indicted on 31 July with crimes against humanity and after spending eight years behind bars, Duch is due to go on trial soon. Yet it was with the arrests in late 2007 of Ieng Sary, Nuon Chea and Khieu Samphan that the tribunal finally began to flex its muscles. Each of these arrests made international news and it seems, almost 30 years after the Vietnam invasion ended the abhorrent Khmer Rouge regime, that Cambodia may finally be coming to terms with its horrific past.

With pressure coming to bear on the then Peoples' Power Party (PPP) goverment from the extreme fascistic nationalists of the Peoples' Alliance for Democracy (PAD), Thailand withdrew its support for UNESCO status and reneged on its promise to finally recognize Cambodia's claims. Nonetheless, UNESCO declared Preah Vihear a World Heritage Site in July 2008. Much sabre rattling ensued, with shots fired and military units mobilized. Thai nationalists were arrested by the Cambodians as they tried to plant a Thai flag in the Preah Vihear's grounds and bizarre black magic rituals were claimed to have been enacted by both sides. With the Thai foreign minister forced to resign and Thailand completely entrenched, a conflict seemed inevitable.

In October 2008 the fighting started in earnest leaving several soldiers on both sides dead or injured. War seemed imminent. Fortunately, after intervention by the international community, both sides saw sense and pulled back from the brink.

Since 2008, the situation has remained tense and there have been occasional skirmishes. In late 2013, the matter appeared to be settled when the International Court of Justice ruled in Cambodia's favour and insisted the Thai trops leave the area. Peace between the two countries still reigns but many governments are still advising against travel to the temple, due mainly to political instability in Thailand. Extremists nationalists linked to the Thai army rejected the ICJ's ruling and future conflict cannot be ruled out entirely.

If you do visit we would recommend, at the very least, you take good advice from locals about the situation at the time of travel and also use the services of a reputable tour operator or guide.

What is obvious is that as the Tribunal progressed, many of the old divisions that have riven Cambodian society for generations where taking hold again. In late 2007 Cambodia was officially and internationally recognised as one of the most corrupt countries in history. Spend five minutes in Phnom Penh and this air of corruption is staring you in the face – Toyota Land Cruisers, giant, black Lexus SUVs and Humvees plough through the streets without regard for anyone or anything. When these vehicles do crush or kill other road users, the driver's well-armed body guards hop out, pistols waving, and soon dissuade any eager witnesses. This kind of event is commonplace and the poorer locals know this. Speak to a moto or tuk-tuk driver and you'll soon sense the resentment, "We hate the corrupt and we'd be happy to see them die", is a frequent comment reminiscent of Cambodia's darker times. The establishment of a rich new elite is not leading to the trickle-down of wealth but the entrenchment of certain groups who have no regard at all for building a new society. Even the aid community is complicit in this – one senior worker made this damning off-therecord comment, "We view corruption as the only stabilizing factor in Cambodian society. It is awful but what else is there?"

The July 2008 general election changed little. Hun Sen was returned with an enlarged majority after a campaign that drew both praise and criticism from EU observers. On the upside the election was seen as being 'technically proficient' and possibly the best-run vote in Cambodia's history. Not that that's saying much; Hun Sen's ruling CPP was seen to have abused its position and not only dominated the media but also disenfranchised tens of thousands of opposition voters. Yet the same EU observers also felt the CPP would have

BACKGROUND
Cambodia Tribunal

In 1997, with the country's interminable civil war set to end, the Cambodian government made an official approach to the UN to establish a court to prosecute senior members of the Khmer Rouge. The thinking at the time was that Cambodia lacked the institutions and know-how to handle such a big trial and that outside expertise would be needed.

At first, things for the prosecution looked promising, with an agreed handing over of Pol Pot (who was holed up in northern Cambodia in Anlong Veng), set to take place in April 1998. But he never made it to court, mysteriously dying the night before his supposed arrest. Some say from a heart attack, others suspect that he took his own life.

In 1999, Kaing Guek Eav aka 'Comrade Duch', the commandant of the infamous Tuol Sleng prison camp in Phnom Penh, surrendered to the Cambodian authorities. In the same year, Ta Mok, another blood-soaked Khmer Rouge leader, was also arrested (he died in custody seven years later in 2006). Initially, however, no power or legal authority existed to try them and it wasn't until 2001 that the Cambodian government agreed to pass a law setting up what came to be known as the 'Extraordinary Chambers in the Courts of Cambodia for the Prosecution of Crimes Committed during the Period of Democratic Kampuchea' or, for short, the Cambodia Tribunal.

Several more years passed, with the sometimes indifferent Cambodians stating that they had no money to finance the trials and the international community unwilling to fund a process in a country where corruption was so rampant. But

won despite any machinations by Hun Sen and the vote was accepted in the international community. At the same time the election was taking place a row began to brew with Thailand over the contested Preah Vihear temple near the Thai/Cambodian border (see box, page 131). In early July the Cambodian-led effort to turn the revered Preah Vihear into a UNESCO World Heritage Site was greeted by huge celebrations in Phnom Penh. For the Cambodians this meant that the long-contested temple was now firmly recognized as being in their territory. By early October 2008 a troop build-up escalated into an exchange of fire that led to a tense two-week stand-off and resulted in several deaths. Eventually, after pressure from the international community, both sides backed down but the dispute is still not settled and, at present, one of the region's most spectacular sites is off-limits.

It wasn't all bad news though as on 17 February 2009, 30 years after the fall of the Khmer Rouge regime, the first trial finally began against one of its former commanders began when Comrade Duch, the infamous commander of the Tuol Sleng death camp. As it progressed on through 2009, Duch's trial attracted a huge amount of international attention, not least for the plea the accused made in November 2009 to be released. While it must be said Duch has been one of the few senior Khmer Rouge leaders to have expressed any regret, this was still a staggering moment. By July 2010 a guilty verdict and a 35-year prison sentence had been handed down to Tuo Sleng's former custodian. By July 2011 several of the other cases of remaining senior Khmer Rouge figures also began and in August 2014 both Nuon Chea and Khieu Samphan were found guilty of crimes against humanity and received life sentences.

despite this, in early 2006, buildings just outside Phnom Penh were requisitioned, the UN nominated its judges and by July of the same year a full panel of 30 Cambodian and UN judges were fully sworn in. A list of five main suspects was drawn up in July 2007 and the first person formally charged was the already incarcerated Comrade Duch on 31 July 2007.

Then, in late 2007, after years of snail-like progress, and with the main protagonists approaching their twilight years, a flurry of dramatic arrests occurred. Former Khmer Rouge ideologue and Foreign Minister Ieng Sary and his wife, the Minister of Social Affairs, Ieng Thirith, former Chief of State and Pol Pot's number two, Khieu Samphan, were all taken into custody and charged with war crimes and crimes against humanity (their trials along with the former 'number two' in Pol Pot's regime, Nuon Chea, began in July 2011).

The first trial of Extraordinary Chambers in the Courts of Cambodia for the Prosecution of Crimes Committed during the Period of Democratic Kampuchea began with Comrade Duch in February 2009. By the end of the same year his trial was over and in July 2010 Duch was found guilty of crimes against humanity, torture, and murder, receiving a 35-year prison sentence which was increased to life in early 2012.

There's no doubt that Duch's public trial marked a turning point for Cambodia. For the first time the Khmer Rouge's crimes were aired in the cold, calculated and unambiguous efficiency of a courtroom. Victims confronted their tormentor with Duch expressing remorse and, more bizarrely, asking to be released by the court. Then, in August 2014, as if to underline the entire process, two of the few remaining Khmer Rouge figures, Khieu Samphan and Nuon Chea, were given life sentences for crimes against humanity. They still face another charge of genocide, which the court is pursuing.

The other main issue that has dominated Cambodia over the last period has been its relations with its neighbour, Thailand. Ostensibly focused on the disputed Preah Vihear temple (see box, page 131), this dispute has already reached the shooting stage on several occasions with soldiers on both sides being killed. There's also little doubt that the appointment of deposed Thai PM Thaksin – who is loathed by the controlling Thai elite and has been defined as a wanted 'criminal' by the Thai state – as an economic adviser by Hun Sen only exacerbated the situation. After Thaksin arrived in Cambodia in late 2009 the Thais withdrew their ambassador, threatened to tear up long-standing trade agreements and demanded that Cambodia, an ASEAN partner, arrest Thaksin and extradite him to Thailand to face a prison cell.

Hun Sen, with some justification, refused, citing that Thaksin's criminal conviction in Thailand was politicized and that Cambodia could choose who it wanted as an economic adviser. After the Thais threw a few more toys out of the pram, things calmed down enough for Hun Sen to visit Thailand for an ASEAN meeting and by mid-2010 it seemed as though the Thaksin element in Thai/Cambodia relations was no longer a defining factor.

Unfortunately, by 2011, the Preah Vihear issue, largely due to the antagonistic approach taken by extreme nationalists in Thailand, did reach a new nadir and for a while full-blown war looked like a possibility although, due mainly to the efforts of the new democratically elected Thai government, the situation was a lot calmer by the end of 2011 (see box, page 131). In late 2013 the matter appeared to be settled when the International Court of

Justice ruled in Cambodia's favour and declared the territory around Preah Vihear to be part of Cambodia.

In mid-2012 Hun Sen also faced voters in local elections in what many saw as a prelude to the parliamentary elections due to be held in 2013. His party, the Cambodian People's Party, won another landslide victory. Despite his enduring popularity Hun Sen certainly has his critics and his government's human rights record has been justifiably criticized in recent years. As Reuters put it in June 2012 – "A shrewd political tactician with an image as a tough-talking strongman, Hun Sen's supporters say he is popular among the millions of rural poor, having overseen unprecedented growth, stability and development since the decades of war that turned the former French colony into a failed state. Critics say Hun Sen is a ruthless leader who has intimidated his opponents into submission or frightened them out of the country."

However, Hun Sen's grip on power took a significant knock when the Sam Rainsy-led opposition made significant gains in the 2013 general election. With claims that Hun Sen's party engaged in voter fraud, the opposition held a number of protests, many of which ended in violence and some deaths. By late 2014 Hun Sen seemed to have negotiated the aftermath of these protests yet many questions remain about how much longer he can cling to power. Moving out of the shadow of Hun Sen will prove the next decisive and necessary step for Cambodia.

History of Laos

Scholars of Lao history, before they even begin, need to decide whether they are writing a history of Laos; a history of the Lao ethnic group; or histories of the various kingdoms and principalities that have, through time, been encompassed by the present boundaries of the Lao People's Democratic Republic. Historians have tended to confront this problem in different ways without, often, acknowledging on what basis their 'history' is built. It is common to see 1365, the date of the foundation of the kingdom of Lane Xang, as marking the beginning of Lao history. But, as Martin Stuart-Fox points out, prior to Lane Xang the principality of Muang Swa, occupying the same geographical space, was headed by a Lao. The following account provides a brief overview of the histories of those peoples who have occupied what is now the territory of the Lao PDR.

Archaeological and historical evidence indicates that most Lao originally migrated south from China. This was followed by an influx of ideas and culture from the Indian subcontinent via Myanmar (Burma), Thailand and Cambodia – something which is reflected in the state religion, Theravada Buddhism.

Being surrounded by large, powerful neighbours, Laos has been repeatedly invaded over the centuries by the Thais (or Siamese) and the Vietnamese – who both thought of Laos as their buffer zone and backyard. They too have both left their mark on Lao culture. In recent history, Laos has been influenced by the French during the colonial era, the Japanese during the Second World War, the Americans during the Indochinese wars and, between 1975 and the early 1990s, by Marxism-Leninism.

It is also worth noting, in introduction, that historians and regimes have axes to grind. The French were anxious to justify their annexation of Laos and so used dubious Vietnamese documents to provide a legal gloss to their actions. Western historians, lumbered with the baggage of Western historiography, ignored indigenous histories. And the Lao People's Revolutionary Party uses history for its own ends too. The official three volume *History of Laos* is being written by Party-approved history hacks. The third volume (chronologically speaking) was published in 1989 and, working back in time, the first and second thereafter. As Martin Stuart-Fox remarks in his *A History of Laos*, "the communist regime is as anxious as was the previous Royal Lao government [pre-1975] to establish that Laos has a long and glorious past and that a continuity exists between the past and the present Lao state". In other words, Laos has not one history, but many. Take your pick.

First kingdom of Laos

Myth, archaeology and history all point to a number of early feudal Lao kingdoms in what is now South China and North Vietnam. External pressures from the Mongols under Kublai Khan and the Han Chinese forced the Tai tribes to migrate south into what had been part of the Khmer Empire. The mountains to the north and east served as a cultural barrier to Vietnam and China, leaving the Lao exposed to influences from India and the West. There are no documentary records of early Lao history (the first date in the Lao chronicles to which historians attach any real veracity is 1271), although it seems probable that parts of present-day Laos were annexed by Lannathai (Chiang Mai) in the 11th century and by the

Khmer Empire during the 12th century. But neither of these states held sway over the entire area of Laos. Xieng Khouang, for example, was probably never under Khmer domination. This was followed by strong Siamese influence over the cities of Luang Prabang and Vientiane under the Siamese Sukhothai Dynasty. Laos (the country) in effect did not exist, although the Laos (the people) certainly did.

The downfall of Sukhothai in 1345 and its submission to the new Siamese Dynasty at Ayutthaya (founded in 1349) was the catalyst for the foundation of what is commonly regarded as the first truly independent Lao Kingdom – although there were semi-independent Lao *muang* (city states, sometimes transliterated as *meuang*) existing prior to that date.

Fa Ngum and Lane Xang

The kingdom of Lane Xang (Lan Chang) emerged in 1353 under Fa Ngum, a Lao prince who had grown up in the Khmer court of Angkor. There is more written about Fa Ngum than about the following two centuries of Lao history. It is also safe to say that his life is more fiction than fact. Fa Ngum was reputedly born with 33 teeth and was banished to Angkor after his father, Prince Yakfah, was convicted of having an incestuous affair with a wife of King Suvarna Kamphong. In 1353 Fa Ngum led an army to Luang Prabang and confronted his grandfather, King Suvarna Kamphong. Unable to defeat his grandson on the battlefield, the aged king is said to have hanged himself and Fa Ngum was invited to take the throne. Three years later, in 1356, Fa Ngum marched on Vientiane – which he took with ease – and then on Vienkam, which proved more of a challenge. He is credited with piecing together Lang Xang – the Land of a Million Elephants – the golden age to which all histories of Laos refer to justify the existence (and greatness) of Laos.

In some accounts Lang Xang is portrayed as stretching from China to Cambodia and from the Khorat Plateau in present-day Northeast Thailand to the Annamite mountains in the east. But it would be entirely wrong to envisage the kingdom controlling all these regions. Lane Xang probably only had total control over a comparatively small area of present-day Laos and parts of Northeast Thailand; the bulk of this grand empire would have been contested with other surrounding kingdoms. In addition, the smaller *muang* and principalities would themselves have played competing powers off, one against another, in an attempt to maximize their own autonomy. It is this 'messiness' that led scholars of Southeast Asian history to suggest that territories as such did not exist, but rather zones of variable control. The historian OW Wolters coined the term *mandala* for "a particular and often unstable political situation in a vaguely defined geographical area without fixed boundaries and where smaller centres tended to look in all directions for security. *Mandalas* would expand and contract in concertina-like fashion. Each one contained several tributary rulers, some of whom would repudiate their vassal status when the opportunity arose and try to build up their own network of vassals".

Legend relates that Fa Ngum was a descendant of Khoum Borom, "a king who came out of the sky from South China". He is said to have succeeded to the throne of Nanchao in 729, aged 31, and died 20 years later, although this historical record is, as they say, exceedingly thin. Khoum Borom is credited with giving birth to the Lao people by slicing open a gourd in Muong Taeng (Dien Bien Phu, Vietnam) and his seven sons established the great Tai kingdoms. He returned to his country with a detachment of Khmer soldiers and united several scattered Lao fiefdoms. In those days, conquered lands were usually razed and the people taken as slaves to build up the population of the conquering group. (This largely explains why today there are far more Lao in northeastern Thailand than in Laos – they were forcibly settled there after King Anou was defeated by King Rama III of Siam in 1827 – see page 419). The kings of Lane Xang were less philistine, demanding only subordination and allegiance as one part of a larger *mandala*.

Luang Prabang became the capital of the kingdom of Lane Xang. The unruly highland tribes of the northeast did not come under the kingdom's control at that time. Fa Ngum made Theravada Buddhism the official religion. He married the Cambodian king's daughter, Princess Keo Kaengkanya, and was given the Pra Bang (a golden statue, the most revered religious symbol of Laos), by the Khmer court.

It is common to read of Lane Xang as the first kingdom of Laos; as encompassing the territory of present-day Laos; and as marking the introduction of Theravada Buddhism to the country. On all counts this portrait is, if not false, then deeply flawed. As noted above, there were Lao states that predated Lane Xang; Lane Xang never controlled Laos as it currently exists; and Buddhism had made an impact on the Lao people before 1365. Fa Ngum did not create a kingdom; rather he brought together various pre-existing *muang* (city states) into a powerful *mandala*. As Martin Stuart-Fox writes, "From this derives [Fa Ngum's] historical claim to hero status as the founder of the Lao Kingdom." But, as Stuart-Fox goes on to explain, there was no central authority and rulers of individual *muang* were permitted considerable autonomy.

After Fa Ngum's wife died in 1368, he became so debauched, it is said, that he was deposed in favour of his son, Samsenthai (1373-1416), who was barely 18 when he acceded the throne. He was named after the 1376 census, which concluded that he ruled over 300,000 Tais living in Laos; *samsen* means, literally, 300,000. He set up a new administrative system based on the existing *muang*, nominating governors to each that lasted until it was abolished by the Communist government in 1975. Samsenthai's death was followed by a period of unrest. Under King Chaiyachakkapat-Phaenphaeo (1441-1478), the kingdom came under increasing threat from the Vietnamese. How the Vietnamese came to be peeved with the Lao is another story which smacks of fable more than fact. King Chaiyachakkapat's eldest son, the Prince of Chienglaw, secured a holy white elephant. The emperor of Vietnam, learning of this momentous discovery, asked to be sent some of the beast's hairs. Disliking the Vietnamese, the Prince dispatched a box of its excrement instead, whereupon the Emperor formed an army of an improbably large 550,000 men. The Prince's army numbered 200,000 and 2000 elephants. The massive Vietnamese army finally prevailed and entered and sacked Luang Prabang. But shortly thereafter they were driven out by Chaiyachakkapat-Phaenphaeo's son, King Suvarna Banlang (1478-1485). Peace was only fully restored under King Visunarat (1500-1520).

Increasing prominence and Burmese incursions

Under King Pothisarath (1520-1548) Vientiane became prominent as a trading and religious centre. He married a Lanna (Chiang Mai) princess, Queen Yotkamtip, and when the Siamese King Ketklao was put to death in 1545, Pothisarath's son claimed the throne at Lanna. He returned to Lane Xang when his father died in 1548. Asserting his right as successor to the throne, he was crowned Setthathirat in 1548 and ruled until 1571 – the last of the great kings of Lane Xang.

At the same time, the Burmese were expanding East and in 1556 Lanna fell into their hands. Setthathirat gave up his claim to that throne, to a Siamese prince, who ruled under Burmese authority. (He also took the **Phra Kaeo** – Thailand's famous 'Emerald' Buddha and its most sacred and revered image – with him to Luang Prabang and then to Vientiane. The Phra Kaeo stayed in Vientiane until 1778 when the Thai general Phya

Chakri 'repatriated' it to Thailand.) In 1563 Setthathirat pronounced Vieng Chan (Vientiane) the principal capital of Lane Xang. Seven years later, the Burmese King Bayinnaung launched an unsuccessful attack on Vieng Chan itself.

Setthathirat is revered as one of the great Lao kings, having protected the country from foreign domination. He built Wat Phra Kaeo (see page 325) in Vientiane, in which he placed the famous Emerald Buddha brought from Lanna. Setthathirat mysteriously disappeared during a campaign in the southern province of Attapeu in 1574, which threw the kingdom into crisis. Vientiane fell to invading Burmese the following year and remained under Burmese control for seven years. Finally the anarchic kingdoms of Luang Prabang and Vientiane were reunified under Nokeo Koumane (1591-1596) and Thammikarath (1596-1622).

Disputed territory

From the time of the formation of the kingdom of Lane Xang to the arrival of the French, the history of Laos was dominated by the struggle to retain the lands it had conquered. Following King Setthathirat's death, a series of kings came to the throne in quick succession. King Souligna Vongsa, crowned in 1633, brought long awaited peace to Laos. The 61 years he was on the throne are regarded as Lane Xang's golden age. Under him, the kingdom's influence spread to Yunnan in South China, the Burmese Shan States, Issan in Northeast Thailand and areas of Vietnam and Cambodia.

Souligna Vongsa was even on friendly terms with the Vietnamese: he married Emperor Le Thanh Ton's daughter and he and the Emperor agreed the borders between the two countries. The frontier was settled in a deterministic – but nonetheless amicable – fashion: those living in houses built on stilts with verandas were considered Lao subjects and those living in houses without piles and verandas owed allegiance to Vietnam.

During his reign foreigners first visited the country, but other than a handful of adventurers, Laos remained on the outer periphery of European concerns and influence.

The three kingdoms

After Souligna Vongsa died in 1694, leaving no heir, dynastic quarrels and feudal rivalries once again erupted, undermining the kingdom's cohesion. In 1700 Lane Xang split into three: Luang Prabang under Souligna's grandson, Vientiane under Souligna's nephew and the new kingdom of Champasak was founded in the south 'panhandle'. This weakened the country and allowed the Siamese and Vietnamese to encroach. *Muang*, which previously owed clear allegiance to Lane Xang, began to look towards Vietnam or Siam. Isan muang in present day Northeast Thailand, for example, paid tribute to Bangkok; while Xieng Khouang did the same to Hanoi and, later, to Hué. The three main kingdoms that emerged with the disintegration of Lane Xang leant in different directions: Luang Prabang had close links with China, Vientiane with Vietnam's Hanoi/Hué and Champassak with Siam.

By the mid-1760s Burmese influence once again held sway in Vientiane and Luang Prabang and before the turn of the decade, they sacked Ayutthaya, the capital of Siam. Somehow the Siamese managed to pull themselves together and only two years later in 1778 successfully rampaged through Vientiane. The two sacred Buddhas, the Phra Bang and the Phra Kaeo (Emerald Buddha), were taken as booty back to Bangkok. The Emerald Buddha was never returned and now sits in Bangkok's Wat Phra Kaeo.

King Anou (an abbreviation of Anurutha), was placed on the Vientiane throne by the Siamese. With the death of King Rama II of Siam, King Anou saw his chance of rebellion, asked Vietnam for assistance, formed an army and marched on Bangkok in 1827. In mounting this brave – some would say foolhardy – assault, Anou was apparently trying to emulate the great Fa Ngum. Unfortunately, he got no further than the Northeast Thai town of Korat where his forces suffered a defeat and were driven back. Nonetheless, Anou's rebellion is considered one of the most daring and ruthless rebellions in Siamese history and he was lauded as a war hero back home.

King Anou's brief stab at regional power was to result in catastrophe for Laos – and tragedy for King Anou. The first US arms shipment to Siam allowed the Siamese to sack Vientiane, a task to which they had grown accustomed over the years. (This marks America's first intervention in Southeast Asia.) Lao artisans were frogmarched to Bangkok and many of the inhabitants were resettled in Northeast Siam. Rama III had Chao Anou locked in a cage where he was taunted and abused by the population of Bangkok. He died soon afterwards, at the age of 62. One of his supporters is said to have taken pity on the king and brought him poison, other explanations simply say that he wished himself dead or that he choked. Whatever the cause, the disconsolate Anou, before he died, put a curse on Siam's monarchy, promising that the next time a Thai king set foot on Lao soil, he would die. To this day no Thai king has crossed the Mekong River. When the agreement for the supply of hydroelectric power was signed with Thailand in the 1970s, the Thai king opened the Nam Ngum Dam from a sandbank in the middle of the Mekong.

Disintegration of the kingdom

Over the next 50 years, Anou's kingdom was destroyed. By the time the French arrived in the late 19th century, the virtually unoccupied city was subsumed into the Siamese sphere of influence. Luang Prabang also became a Siamese vassal state, while Xieng Khouang province was invaded by Chinese rebels – to the chagrin of the Vietnamese, who had always considered the Hmong mountain kingdom (they called it Tran Ninh), to be their exclusive source of slaves. The Chinese had designs on Luang Prabang too and in order to quash their expansionist instincts, Bangkok dispatched an army there in 1885 to pacify the region and ensure the north remained firmly within the Siamese sphere of influence. This period was one of confusion and rapidly shifting allegiances.

The history of Laos during this period becomes, essentially, the history of only a small part of the current territory of the country: namely, the history of Luang Prabang. And because Luang Prabang was a suzerain state of Bangkok, the history of that kingdom is, in turn, sometimes relegated to a mere footnote in the history of Siam.

The French and independence

Following King Anou's death, Laos became the centre of Southeast Asian rivalry between Britain, expanding east from Burma, and France, pushing west through Vietnam. In 1868, following the French annexation of South Vietnam and the formation of a protectorate in Cambodia, an expedition set out to explore the Mekong trade route to China. Once central and north Vietnam had come under the influence of the Quai d fOrsay in Paris, the French became increasingly curious about Vietnamese claims to chunks of Laos. Unlike the Siamese, the French – like the British – were concerned with demarcating borders and establishing explicit areas of sovereignty. This seemed extraordinary to most Southeast Asians at the time, who could not see the point of mapping space when land was so abundant. However, it did not take long for the Siamese king to realize the importance of maintaining his claim to Siamese territories if the French in the east and the British in the south (Malaya) and west (Burma) were not to squeeze Siam to nothing.

However, King Chulalongkorn was not in a position to confront the French militarily and instead he had to play a clever diplomatic game if his kingdom was to survive. The French, for their part, were anxious to continue to press westwards from Vietnam into the Lao lands over which Siam held suzerainty. Martin Stuart-Fox argues that there were four main reasons underlying France's desire to expand West: the lingering hope that the Mekong might still offer a back door into China; the consolidation of Vietnam against attack; the rounding out of their Indochina possessions; and a means of further pressuring Bangkok. In 1886, the French received reluctant Siamese permission to post a vice consul to Luang Prabang and a year later he persuaded the Thais to leave. However, even greater humiliation was to come in 1893 when the French, through crude gunboat diplomacy – the so-called Paknam incident – forced King Chulalongkorn to give up all claim to Laos on the flimsiest of historical pretexts. Despite attempts by Prince Devawongse to manufacture a compromise, the French forced Siam to cede Laos to France and, what's more, to pay compensation. It is said that after this humiliation, King Chulalongkorn retired from public life, broken in spirit and health. So the French colonial era in Laos began.

What is notable about this spat between France and Siam is that Laos – the country over which they were fighting – scarcely figures. As was to happen again in Laos' history, the country was caught between two competing powers who used Laos as a stage on which to fight a wider and to them, more important, conflict.

Union of Indochina

In 1893 France occupied the left bank of the Mekong and forced Thailand to recognize the river as the boundary. The French Union of Indochina denied Laos the area that is now Isan, northeast Thailand, and this was the start of 50 years of colonial rule. Laos became a protectorate with a *résident-superieur* in Vientiane and a vice-consul in Luang Prabang. However, Laos could hardly be construed as a 'country' during the colonial period. "Laos existed again", writes Martin Stuart-Fox, but not yet as a political entity in its own right, for no independent centre of Lao political power existed. Laos was but a territorial entity within French Indochina. The French were not interested in establishing an identifiable Lao state; they saw Laos as a part and a subservient part at that, of Vietnam, serving as a resource-rich appendage. Though they had grand plans for the development of Laos, these were only expressed airily and none of them came to anything. "The French were never sure what to do with Laos", Stuart-Fox writes. Unlike Cambodia to the south, the French did not perceive Laos to have any historical unity or coherence and therefore it could be hacked about and developed or otherwise, according to their whim.

In 1904 the Franco-British convention delimited respective zones of influence. Only a few hundred French civil servants were ever in Vientiane at any one time and their attitude to colonial administration – described as 'benign neglect' – was as relaxed as the people they governed. To the displeasure of the Lao, France brought in Vietnamese to run the civil service (in the way the British used Indian bureaucrats in Burma). But for the most part, the French colonial period was a 50-year siesta for Laos. The king was allowed to stay in Luang Prabang, but had little say in administration. Trade and commerce was left to the omni-present Chinese and the Vietnamese. A small, French-educated Lao élite did grow up and by the 1940s they had become the core of a typically laid-back Lao nationalist movement.

Japanese coup

Towards the end of the Second World War, Japan ousted the French administration in Laos in a coup in March 1945. The eventual surrender of the Japanese in August that year gave impetus to the Lao independence movement. Prince Phetsarath, hereditary viceroy and premier of the Luang Prabang Kingdom, took over the leadership of the Lao Issara, the Free Laos Movement (originally a resistance movement against the Japanese). They prevented the French from seizing power again and declared Lao independence on 1 September 1945. Two weeks later, the north and south provinces were reunified and in October, Phetsarath formed a Lao Issara government headed by Prince Phaya Khammao.

France refused to recognize the new state and crushed the Lao resistance. King Sisavang Vong, unimpressed by Prince Phetsarath's move, sided with the French, who had their colony handed back by British forces. He was crowned the constitutional monarch of the new protectorate in 1946. The rebel government took refuge in Bangkok. Historians believe the Issara movement was aided in their resistance to the French by the Viet Minh – Hanoi's Communists.

Independence

In response to nationalist pressures, France was obliged to grant Laos ever greater self government and, eventually, formal independence within the framework of the newly reconstructed French Union in July 1949. Meanwhile, in Bangkok, the Issara movement had formed a government-in-exile, headed by Phetsarath and his half-brothers: Prince Souvanna Phouma (see box, page 528) and Prince Souphanouvong. Both were refined, French-educated men. The Issara's military wing was led by Souphanouvong who, even at that stage, was known for his Communist sympathies. This was due to a temporary alliance between the Issara and the Viet Minh, who had the common cause of ridding their respective countries of the French. Within just a few months the so-called Red Prince had been ousted by his half-brothers and joined the Viet Minh where he is said to have been the moving force behind the declaration of the Democratic Republic of Laos by the newly formed Lao National Assembly. The Lao People's Democratic Republic emerged – albeit in name only – somewhere inside Vietnam, in August 1949. Soon afterwards, the Pathet Lao (the Lao Nation) was born. The Issara movement quickly folded and Souvanna Phouma went back to Vientiane and joined the newly formed Royal Lao Government.

By 1953, Prince Souphanouvong had managed to move his Pathet Lao headquarters inside Laos and with the French losing their grip on the north provinces, the weary colonizers granted the country full independence. France signed a treaty of friendship and association with the new royalist government and made the country a French protectorate.

The rise of Communism

French defeat

While all this was going on, King Sisavang Vong sat tight in Luang Prabang instead of moving to Vientiane. But within a few months of independence, the ancient royal capital was under threat from the Communist Viet Minh and Pathet Lao. Honouring the terms of the new treaty, French commander General Henri Navarre determined in late 1953 to take the pressure off Luang Prabang by confronting the Viet Minh who controlled the strategic approach to the city at Dien Bien Phu. The French suffered a stunning defeat that presaged their withdrawal from Indochina. The subsequent occupation of two north Lao provinces by the Vietnam-backed Pathet Lao forces, meant the kingdom's days as a Western buffer state were numbered. The Vietnamese, not unlike their previous neighbours, did not respect Laos as a state, but as a extension of their own territory to be utilized for their own strategic purposes during the ensuing war.

ON THE ROAD

Prince Souvanna Phouma

Prince Souvanna Phouma was Laos' greatest statesman: an architect of independence and helmsman of catastrophe. He was prime minister on no less than eight occasions for a total of 20 years between 1951 and 1975. He dominated mainstream politics from independence until the victory of the Pathet Lao in 1975. But he was never able to preserve the integrity of Laos in the face of much stronger external forces. "Souvanna stands as a tragic figure in modern Lao history," Martin Stuart-Fox writes, a "stubborn symbol of an alternative, neutral, 'middle way'."

He was born in 1901 into a branch of the Luang Prabang royal family. Like many of the Lao elite he was educated abroad, in Hanoi, Paris and Grenoble, and when he returned to Laos he married a woman of mixed French-Lao blood. He was urbane, educated and arrogant. He enjoyed fine wines and cigars, spoke French better than he spoke Lao, and was a Francophile – as well as a nationalist – to the end.

In 1950 Souvanna became a co-founder of the Progressive Party and in the elections of 1951 he headed his first government which negotiated and secured full independence from France.

Souvanna made two key errors of judgement during these early years. First, he ignored the need for nation building in Laos. And, second, he under-estimated the threat that the Communists posed to the country. With regard to the first of these misjudgements, he seemed to believe – and it is perhaps no accident that he trained as an engineer and architect – that Laos just needed to be

With the **Geneva Accord** in July 1954, following the fall of Dien Bien Phu in May, Ho Chi Minh's government gained control of all territory north of the 17th parallel in neighbouring Vietnam. The Accord guaranteed Laos freedom and neutrality, but with the Communists on the threshold, the US was not prepared to be a passive spectator: the demise of the French sparked an increasing US involvement. In an operation that was to mirror the much more famous war with Vietnam to the East, Washington soon found itself supplying and paying the salaries of 50,000 royalist troops and their corrupt officers. Clandestine military assistance grew, undercover special forces were mobilized and the CIA began meddling in Lao politics. In 1960 a consignment of weapons was dispatched by the CIA to a major in the Royal Lao Army called Vang Pao – or VP, as he became known – who was destined to become the leader of the Hmong.

US involvement: the domino effect

Laos had become the dreaded first domino, which, using the scheme of US President Dwight D Eisenhower's famous analogy, would trigger the rapid spread of Communism if ever it fell. The time-trapped little kingdom became the focus of superpower brinkmanship. At a press conference in March 1961, President Kennedy is said to have been too abashed to announce to the American people that US forces might soon become embroiled in conflict in a far-away flashpoint that went by the inglorious name of 'Louse'. For three decades administered efficiently to become a modern state. He appeared either to reject, or to ignore the idea that the government first had to try and inculcate a sense of Lao nationhood. The second misjudgement was his long-held belief that the Pathet Lao was a nationalist and not a Communist organization. He let the Pathet Lao grow in strength and this, in turn, brought the US into Lao affairs.

By the time the US began to intervene in Lao affairs in the late 1950s, the country already seemed to be heading for catastrophe. But in his struggle to maintain some semblance of independence for his tiny country, he ignored the degree to which Laos was being sucked into the quagmire of Indochina. As Martin Stuart-Fox writes: "He [Souvanna] knew he was being used, and that he had no power to protect his country from the war that increasingly engulfed it. But he was too proud meekly to submit to US demands – even as Laos was subjected to the heaviest bombing in the history of warfare. At least a form of independence had to be maintained."

When the Pathet Lao entered Vientiane in victory in 1975, Souvanna did not flee into exile. He remained to help in the transfer of power. The Pathet Lao, of course, gave him a title and then ignored him as they pursued their Communist manifesto. Again, Martin Stuart-Fox writes: "Souvanna ended his days beside the Mekong. He was to the end a Lao patriot, refusing to go into exile in France. The leaders of the new regime did consult him on occasions. Friends came to play bridge. Journalists sought him out, although he said little and interviews were taped in the presence of Pathet Lao minions. When he died in January 1984, he was accorded a state funeral."

From Martin Stuart-Fox's *Buddhist Kingdom, Marxist State: the Making of Modern Laos* (White Lotus, 1996).

Americans have unwittingly mispronounced the country's name as Kennedy decided, euphemistically, to label it 'Lay-os' throughout his national television broadcast.

Coalitions, coups and counter-coups

The US-backed Royal Lao Government of independent Laos – even though it was headed by the neutralist, Prince Souvanna Phouma – ruled over a divided country from 1951 to 1954. The US played havoc with Laos' domestic politics, running anti-Communist campaigns, backing the royalist army and lending support to political figures on the right (even if they lacked experience or political qualifications). The Communist Pathet Lao, headed by Prince Souphanouvong and overseen and sponsored by North Vietnam's Lao Dong party since 1949, emerged as the only strong opposition. By the mid-1950s, Kaysone Phomvihane, later prime minister of the Lao PDR, began to make a name for himself in the Indochinese Communist Party. Indeed the close association between Laos and Vietnam went deeper than just ideology. Kaysone's father was Vietnamese, while Prince Souphanouvong and Nouhak Phounsavanh both married Vietnamese women.

Government of National Union

Elections were held in Vientiane in July 1955 but were boycotted by the Pathet Lao. Souvanna Phouma became prime minister in March 1956. He aimed to try to negotiate the integration of his half-brother's Pathet Lao provinces into a unified administration and coax the Communists into a coalition government. In 1957 the disputed provinces were returned to royal government control under the first coalition government. This coalition government, much to US discontent, contained two Pathet Lao ministers including Souphanouvong and Phoumi Vongvichit. This was one of Souvanna Phouma's achievements in trying to combine the two sides to ensure neutrality, although it was only short-lived. In May 1958 elections were held. This time the Communists' Lao Patriotic Front (Neo Lao Hak Xat) clinched 13 of the 21 seats in the Government of National Union. The Red Prince, Souphanouvong and one of his aides were included in the cabinet and former Pathet Lao members were elected deputies of the National Assembly.

Almost immediately problems that had been beneath the surface emerged to plague the government. The rightists and their US supporters were shaken by the result and the much-vaunted coalition lasted just two months. Driven by Cold War prerogatives, the US could not abide by any government that contained Communist members and withdrew their aid, which the country had become much dependent upon. Between 1955 and 1958 the US had given four times more aid to Laos than the French had done in the prior eight years and it had become the backbone of the Lao economy. If Laos was not so dependent on this aid, it is quite plausible that the coalition government may have survived. The National Union fell apart in July 1958 and Souvanna Phouma was forced out of power. Pathet Lao leaders were jailed and the rightwing Phoui Sananikone came to power. With anti-Communists in control, Pathet Lao forces withdrew to the Plain of Jars in Xieng Khouang province. A three-way civil war ensued, between the rightists (backed by the US), the Communists (backed by North Vietnam) and the neutralists (led by Souvanna Phouma, who wanted to maintain independence).

Civil war

CIA-backed strongman General Phoumi Nosavan thought Phoui's politics rather tame and with a nod from Washington he stepped into the breach in January 1959, eventually overthrowing Phoui in a coup in December and placing Prince Boun Oum in power. Pathet Lao leaders were imprisoned without trial.

Within a year, the rightist regime was overthrown by a neutralist *coup d'état* led by General Kong Lae and Prince Souvanna Phouma was recalled from exile in Cambodia to become prime minister of the first National Union. Souvanna Phouma incurred American wrath by inviting a Soviet ambassador to Vientiane in October. With US support, Nosavan staged yet another armed rebellion in December and sparked a new civil war. In the 1960 general elections, provincial authorities were threatened with military action if they did not support the rightwing groups and were rigged to ensure no Pathet Lao cadres could obtain a seat in office. By this stage, the Pathet Lao had consolidated considerable forces in the region surrounding the Plain of Jars and, with support from the Vietnamese, had been able to expand their territorial control in the north. This represented a major crisis to the incoming Kennedy administration that Stuart Martin-Fox describes as "second only to Cuba".

Zurich talks and the Geneva Accord

The new prime minister, the old one and his Marxist half-brother finally sat down to talks in Zurich in June 1961, but any hope of an agreement was overshadowed by escalating tensions between the superpowers. In 1962, an international agreement on Laos was hammered out in Geneva by 14 participating nations and accords were signed, once again guaranteeing Lao neutrality. By implication, the accords denied the Viet Minh access to the **Ho Chi Minh Trail**. But aware of the reality of constant North Vietnamese infiltration through Laos into South Vietnam, the head of the American mission concluded that the agreement was "a good bad deal".

Another coalition government of National Union was formed under the determined neutralist Prince Souvanna Phouma (as prime minister), with Prince Souphanouvong for the Pathet Lao and Prince Boun Oum representing the right. A number of political assassinations derailed the process of reconciliation. Moreover, antagonisms between the left and the right, both backed financially by their respective allies, made it impossible for the unfunded neutralists to balance the two sides into any form of neutrality. It was no surprise when the coalition government collapsed within a few months and fighting resumed. This time the international community just shrugged and watched Laos sink back into civil war. Unbeknown to the outside world, the conflict was rapidly degenerating into a war between the CIA and North Vietnamese jungle guerrillas.

Secret war

The war that wasn't

In the aftermath of the Geneva agreement, the North Vietnamese, rather than reducing their forces in Laos, continued to increase their manpower on the ground. With the Viet Minh denying the existence of the Ho Chi Minh Trail, while at the same time enlarging it, Kennedy dispatched an undercover force of CIA men, green berets and US-trained Thai mercenaries to command 9000 Lao soldiers. By 1963, these American forces had grown to 30,000 men. Historian Roger Warner believes that by 1965 "word spread among a select circle of congressmen and senators about this exotic program run by Lone Star rednecks and Asian hillbillies that was better and cheaper than anything the Pentagon was doing in South Vietnam." To the north, the US also supplied Vang Pao's force of Hmong guerrillas, dubbed 'Mobile Strike Forces'. With the cooperation of Prince Souvanna Phouma, the CIA's commercial airline, Air America, ferried men and equipment into Laos from Thailand (and opium out, it is believed). Caught between Cold War antagonisms it was impossible to maintain a modicum of neutrality as even the most staunch neutralist, Souvanna Phouma, began to become entangled. As Robbins argues, by the early 1960s, Sovanna Phouma – trying to reinforce the middle way – had given permission "for every clandestine manoeuvre the United States made to match the North Vietnamese. In turn Souvanna demanded that his complicity in such arrangements be kept secret, lest his position in the country become untenable." Owing to the clandestine nature of the military intervention in Laos, the rest of the world – believing that the Geneva settlement had solved the foreign interventionist problem – was oblivious as to what was happening on the ground. Right up until 1970, Washington never admitted to any activity in Laos beyond 'armed reconnaissance' flights over northern provinces.

Meanwhile the North Vietnamese were fulfilling their two major strategic priorities in the country: continued use of the Ho Chi Minh trail (by this stage the majority of North Vietnamese munitions and personnel for the Viet Cong was being shuffled along the trail) and ensuring that the Plain of Jars did not fall under the control of the right, where the US could launch attacks on North Vietnam. This latter goal amounted to supporting the Pathet Lao in their aim to hold on to as much territory as possible in the north. The Pathet Lao, in turn, were dependent on the North Vietnamese for supplies – both material and manpower. With both the US bankrolling the Royalist right and the Vietnamese puppeteering the Pathet Lao, within the country any pretence of maintaining a balance in the face of Cold War hostilities was shattered for neutralists like Souvanna Phouma.

Souvanna Phouma appropriately referred to it as 'the forgotten war' and it is often termed now the 'non-attributable war'. The willingness on the part of the Americans to dump millions of tonnes of ordnance on a country which was ostensibly neutral may have been made easier by the fact that some people in the administration did not believe Laos to be a country at all. Bernard Fall wrote that Laos at the time was "neither a geographical nor an ethnic or social entity, but merely a political convenience", while a Rand Corporation report written in 1970 described Laos as "hardly a country except in the legal sense". More colourfully, Secretary of State Dean Rusk described it as a "wart on the hog of Vietnam". Perhaps those in Washington could feel a touch better about bombing the hell out of a country which, in their view, occupied a sort of political Never Never Land – or which they could liken to an unfortunate skin complaint.

Not everyone agrees with this view that Laos never existed until the French wished it into existence. Scholar of Laos Arthur Dommen, for example, traces a true and coherent Lao identity back to Fa Ngum and his creation of the kingdom of Lane Xang in 1353, writing that it was "a state in the true sense of the term, delineated by borders clearly defined and consecrated by treaty" for 350 years. He goes on:

"Lao historians see a positive proof of the existence of a distinct Lao race (*sua sat Lao*), a Lao nation (*sat Lao*), a Lao country (*muong Lao*) and a Lao state (*pathet Lao*). In view of these facts, we may safely reject the notion, fashionable among apologists for a colonial enterprise of a later day, that Laos was a creation of French colonial policy and administration h.

American bombing of the North Vietnamese Army's supply lines through Laos to South Vietnam along the Ho Chi Minh Trail in East Laos started in 1964 and fuelled the conflict between the Royalist Vientiane government and the Pathet Lao. The neutralists had been forced into alliance with the Royalists to avoid defeat in Xieng Kouang province. US bombers crossed Laos on bombing runs to Hanoi from air bases in Thailand and gradually the war in Laos escalated.

America's side of the secret war was conducted from a one-room shack at the US base in Udon Thani, 'across the fence' in Thailand. This was the CIA's Air America operations room and in the same compound was stationed the 4802 Joint Liaison Detachment – or the CIA logistics office. In Vientiane, US pilots supporting Hmong General Vang Pao's rag-tag army, were given a new identity as rangers for the US Agency for International Development; they reported directly to the air attaché at the US embassy. In his book *The Ravens* (1987), Christopher Robbins writes that they "were military men, but flew into battle in civilian clothes – denim cut-offs, T-shirts, cowboy hats and dark glasses. Their job was to fly as the winged artillery of some fearsome warlord, who led an army of stone age mercenaries in the pay of the CIA and they operated out of a secret city hidden in the mountains of a jungle kingdom."

The most notorious of the CIA's unsavoury operatives was Anthony Posepny – known as Tony Poe, on whom the character of Kurtz, the crazy colonel played by Marlon Brando in the film *Apocalypse Now*, was based. Originally, Poe had worked as Vang Pao's case officer; he then moved to North Laos and operated for years, on his own, in Burmese and Chinese border territories, offering his tribal recruits one US dollar for each set of Communist ears they brought back. Many of the spies and pilots of this secret war have re-emerged in recent years in covert and illegal arms-smuggling rackets to Libya, Iran and the Nicaraguan Contras.

By contrast, the Royalist forces were reluctant warriors: despite the fact that civil war was a deeply ingrained tradition in Laos, the Lao themselves would go to great lengths to avoid fighting each other. One foreign journalist, reporting from Luang Prabang in the latter stages of the war, related how Royalist and Pathet Lao troops, encamped on opposite banks of the Nam Ou, agreed an informal ceasefire over Pi Mai (Lao New Year), to jointly celebrate the king's annual visit to the sacred Pak Ou Caves. Most Lao did not want to fight. Correspondents who covered the war noted that without the constant goading of their respective US and North Vietnamese masters, many Lao soldiers would have happily gone home. Prior to the war, one military strategist described the Lao forces as one of the worst armies ever seen, adding that they made the (poorly regarded) "South Vietnamese Army look like Storm Troopers". "The troops lack the basic will to fight. They do not take initiative. A typical characteristic of the Laotian Army is to leave an escape route. US technicians attached to the various training institutions have not been able to overcome Lao apathy". (Ratnam, P, *Laos and the Superpowers*, 1980).

Air Force planes were often used to carry passengers for money – or to smuggle opium out of the **Golden Triangle**. In the field, soldiers of the Royal Lao Army regularly fled when faced with a frontal assault by the Vietnam People's Army (NVA). The officer corps was uncommitted, lazy and corrupt; many ran opium-smuggling rackets and saw the war as a ticket to get rich quick. In the south, the Americans considered Royal Lao Air Force pilots unreliable because they were loath to bomb their own people and cultural heritage.

The air war

The clandestine bombing of the Ho Chi Minh Trail caused many civilian casualties and displaced much of the population in Laos' eastern provinces. By 1973, when the bombing stopped, the US had dropped over two million tonnes of bombs on Laos – equivalent to 700 kg of explosives for every man, woman and child in the country. It is reported that up to 70% of all B-52 strikes in Indochina were targeted at Laos. To pulverize the country to this degree 580,994 bombing sorties were flown. The bombing intensified during the Nixon administration: up to 1969 less than 500,000 tonnes of bombs had been dropped on Laos; from then on nearly that amount was dropped each year. In the 1960s and early 1970s, more bombs rained on Laos than were dropped during the Second World War – the equivalent of a plane load of bombs every eight minutes around the clock for nine years. This campaign cost American taxpayers more than US$2 million a day but the cost to Laos was incalculable. The activist Fred Branfman, quoted by Roger Warner in *Shooting at the Moon*, wrote: "Nine years of bombing, two million tons of bombs, whole rural societies wiped off the map, hundreds of thousands of peasants treated like herds of animals in a Clockwork Orange fantasy of an aerial African Hunting safari."

The war was not restricted to bombing missions – once potential Pathet Lao strongholds had been identified, fighters, using rockets, were sent to attempt to destroy them. Such was the intensity of the bombing campaign that villagers in Pathet Lao-controlled areas are said to have turned to planting and harvesting their rice at night. Few of those living in Xieng Khouang province, the Bolaven Plateau or along the Ho Chi Minh Trail had any idea of who was bombing them or why. The consequences were often tragic, as in the case of Tham Piu Cave.

After the war, the collection and sale of war debris turned into a valuable scrap metal industry for tribes' people in Xieng Khouang province and along the Ho Chi Minh Trail. Bomb casings, aircraft fuel tanks and other bits and pieces that were not sold to Thailand have been put to every conceivable use in rural Laos. They are used as cattle troughs, fence posts, flower pots, stilts for houses, water carriers, temple bells, knives and ploughs.

But the bombing campaign has also left a more deadly legacy of unexploded bombs and anti-personnel mines. Today, over 30 years after the air war, over 500,000 tonnes of deadly **unexploded ordnance** (UXO) is believed to still be scattered throughout nine of Laos' 13 provinces. Most casualties are caused by cluster bombs, or 'bombis' as they have become known. Cluster bombs are carried in large canisters called Cluster Bomb Units (CBUs), which open in mid-air, releasing around 670 tennis ball-sized bomblets. Upon detonation, the bombie propels around 200,000 pieces of shrapnel over an area the size of several football fields. This UXO contamination inhibits long-term development, especially in Xieng Khouang Province, turning Laos' fertile fields, which are critical for agricultural production, into killing zones.

The land war

Within Laos, the war largely focused on the strategic Plain of Jars in Xieng Khouang province and was co-ordinated from the town of Long Tien (the secret city), tucked into the limestone hills to the southwest of the plain. Known as the most secret spot on earth, it was not marked on maps and was populated by the CIA, the Ravens (the air controllers who flew spotter planes and called in air strikes) and the Hmong.

The Pathet Lao were headquartered in caves in Xam Neua province, to the north of the plain. Their base was equipped with a hotel cave (for visiting dignitaries), a hospital cave, embassy caves and even a theatre cave.

The Plain of Jars (colloquially known as the PDJ, after the French Plaine de Jarres), was the scene of some of the heaviest fighting and changed hands countless times, the Royalist and Hmong forces occupying it during the wet season, the Pathet Lao in the dry. During this period in the conflict the town of Long Tien, known as one of the country's 'alternate' bases to keep nosy journalists away (the word 'alternate' was meant to indicate that it was unimportant), grew to such an extent that it became Laos' second city. James Parker in his book *Codename Mule* claims that the air base was so busy that at its peak it was handling more daily flights than Chicago's O'Hare airport. Others claim that it was the busiest airport in the world. There was also fighting around Luang Prabang and the Bolaven Plateau to the south.

The end of the war

Although the origins of the war in Laos were distinct from those that fuelled the conflict in Vietnam, the two wars had effectively merged by the early 1970s and it became inevitable that the fate of the Americans to the east would determine the outcome of the secret war on the other side of the Annamite Range. By 1970 it was no longer possible for the US administration to shroud the war in secrecy: a flood of refugees had arrived in Vientiane in an effort to escape the conflict.

During the dying days of the US-backed regime in Vientiane, CIA agents and Ravens lived in quarters south of the capital, known as KM-6 – because it was 6 km from town. Another compound in downtown Vientiane was known as 'Silver City' and reputedly also sometimes housed CIA agents. On the departure of the Americans and the arrival of the new regime in 1975, the Communists' secret police made Silver City their new home. Today, Lao people still call military intelligence officers 'Silvers' – and from time to time during the early 1990s, as Laos was opening up to tourism, Silvers were assigned as tour guides.

A ceasefire was agreed in February 1973, a month after Washington and Hanoi struck a similar deal in Paris. Power was transferred in April 1974 to yet another coalition government set up in Vientiane under the premiership of the ever-ready Souvanna Phouma. The neutralist prince once again had a Communist deputy and foreign affairs minister. The Red Prince, Souphanouvong, headed the Joint National Political Council. Foreign troops were given two months to leave the country. The North Vietnamese were allowed to remain along the Ho Chi Minh Trail, for although US forces had withdrawn from South Vietnam, the war there was not over.

The Communists' final victories over Saigon (and Phnom Penh) in April 1975 were a catalyst for the Pathet Lao who advanced on the capital. Grant Evans in a *Short History of Laos* says that the most intriguing element of the Communist takeover of Laos was the slow pace in which it was executed. It is widely hailed as the 'bloodless' takeover. Due to the country's mixed loyalties the Pathet Lao government undertook a gradual process of eroding away existing loyalties to the Royalist government. As the end drew near and the Pathet Lao began to advance out of the mountains and towards the more populated areas of the Mekong valley – the heartland of the Royalist government – province after province fell with scarcely a shot being fired. The mere arrival of a small contingent of Pathet Lao soldiers was sufficient to secure victory – even though these soldiers arrived at Wattay Airport on Chinese transport planes to be greeted by representatives of the Royal Lao government. It is possible that they were not even armed.

Administration of Vientiane by the People's Revolutionary Committee was secured on 18 August. The atmosphere was very different from that which accompanied the Communist's occupation of Saigon in Vietnam the same year. In Vientiane peaceful crowds of several hundred thousand turned out to hear speeches by Pathet Lao cadres. The King remained unharmed in his palace and while a coffin representing 'dead American imperialism' was ceremonially burned this was done in a 'carnival' atmosphere. Vientiane was declared 'officially liberated' on 23 August 1975. The coalition government was dismissed and Souvanna Phouma resigned for the last time. All communications with the outside world were cut.

While August 1975 represents a watershed in the history of Laos, scholars are left with something of a problem: explaining why the Pathet Lao prevailed. According to Martin Stuart-Fox, the Lao revolutionary movement "had not mobilized an exploited peasantry with promises of land reform, for most of the country was underpopulated and peasant families generally owned sufficient land for their subsistence needs. The appeal of the Pathet Lao to their lowland Lao compatriots was in terms of nationalism and independence and the preservation of Lao culture from the corrosive American influence; but no urban uprising occurred until the very last minute when effective government had virtually ceased to exist ... The small Lao intelligentsia, though critical of the Royal Lao government, did not desert it entirely and their recruitment to the Pathet Lao was minimal. Neither the monarchy, still less Buddhism, lost legitimacy." He concludes that it was external factors, and in particular the intervention of outside powers, which led to the victory of the Pathet Lao. Without the Vietnamese and Americans, the Pathet Lao would not have won. For the great mass of Laos' population before 1975, Communism meant nothing. This was not a mass uprising but a victory secured by a small ideologically committed elite and forged in the furnace of the war in Indochina.

As the Pathet Lao seized power, rightist ministers, ranking civil servants, doctors, much of the intelligentsia and around 30,000 Hmong escaped into Thailand, fearing they would face persecution from the Pathet Lao. Although the initial exodus was large, the majority of refugees fled in the next few years up until 1980 as the Lao government introduced new reforms aimed at wiping out decadence and reforming the economic system.

The refugee camps

By the late 1980s, a total of 340,000 people – 10% of the population and mostly middle class – had fled the country. At least half of the refugees were Hmong, the US's key allies during the war, who feared reprisals and persecution. From 1988, refugees who had made it across the border began to head back across the Mekong from camps in Thailand and to asylum in the US and France. More than 2000 refugees were also repatriated from Yunnan Province in China. For those prepared to return from exile overseas, the government offered to give them back confiscated property so long as they stayed for at least six months and become Lao citizens once again.

Nonetheless, many lived for years in squalid refugee camps, although the better connected and those with skills to sell secured US, Australian and French passports. For Laos, a large proportion of its human capital drained westwards, creating a vacuum of skilled personnel that would hamper – and still does – efforts at reconstruction and development. But while many people fled across the Mekong, a significant number who had aligned themselves with the Royalists decided to stay and help build a new Laos.

Laos under communism

The People's Democratic Republic of Laos was proclaimed in December 1975 with Prince Souphanouvong as president and Kaysone Phomvihane as secretary-general of the Lao People's Revolutionary Party (a post he had held since its formation in 1955). The king's abdication was accepted and the ancient Lao monarchy was abolished, together with King Samsenthai's 600-year-old system of village autonomy. But instead of executing their vanquished foes, the LPRP installed Souvanna and the ex-king, Savang Vatthana, as 'special advisers' to the politburo. On Souvanna's death in 1984, he was accorded a full state funeral. The king did not fare so well: he later died ignominiously while in detention after his alleged involvement in a counter-revolutionary plot (see below).

Surprisingly, the first actions of the new revolutionary government was not to build a new revolutionary economy and society, but to stamp out unsavoury behaviour. Dress and hairstyles, dancing and singing, even the food that was served at family celebrations, was all subject to rigorous official scrutiny by so-called 'Investigation Cadres'. If the person(s) concerned were found not to match up to the Party's scrupulous standards of good taste they were bundled off to re-education camps.

Relations with Thailand, which in the immediate wake of the revolution remained cordial, deteriorated in late 1976. A military coup in Bangkok led to rumours that the Thai military, backed by the CIA, was supporting Hmong and other right-wing Lao rebels. The regime feared that Thailand would be used as a spring-board for a royalist coup attempt by exiled reactionaries. This prompted the arrest of King Savang Vatthana, together with his family and Crown Prince Vongsavang, who were all dispatched to a Seminar re-education camp in Sam Neua province. They were never heard of again. In December 1989 Kaysone Phomvihane admitted in Paris, for the first time, that the king had died of malaria in 1984 and that the queen had also died "of natural causes" – no mention was made of Vongsavang. The Lao people have still to be officially informed of his demise.

Re-education camps

Between 30,000 and 40,000 reactionaries who had been unable to flee the country were interned in remote, disease-ridden camps for 're-education'. These camps, referred to as *Samanaya*, took their name from the Western word, seminar. The reluctant scholars were forced into slave labour in squalid jungle conditions and subjected to incessant political propaganda for anything from a few months up to 15 years. Historian Grant Evans suggests that many internees were duped into believing that the government wanted complete reconciliation and so went away for re-education willingly. Evans says the purpose of the camps was to "break the will of members of the old regime and instil in them fear of the new regime." Old men, released back into society after more than 15 years of re-education were cowed and subdued, although some were prepared to talk in paranoid whispers about their grim experiences in Xam Neua.

By 1978, the re-education policy was starting to wind down, although, in 1986, Amnesty International released a report on the forgotten inhabitants of the re-education camps, claiming that 6000-7000 were still being held. By that time incarceration behind barbed wire had ended and the internees were 'arbitrarily restricted' rather than imprisoned. They were assigned to road construction teams and other public works projects. Nonetheless, conditions for these victims of the war in Indochina suffered from malnutrition, disease and many died prematurely in captivity. It is unclear how many died, but at least 15,000 have been freed. Officials of the old regime, ex-government ministers and former Royalist air force and army officers, together with thousands of others unlucky enough to have been on the wrong side, were released from the camps, largely during the mid to late 1980s. Most of the surviving political prisoners have now been re-integrated into society. Some work in the tourism industry and one, a former colonel in the Royal Lao Army, jointly owns the **Asian Pavilion Hotel** (formerly the **Vieng Vilai**) on Samsenthai Road in downtown Vientiane. After years of being force-fed Communist propaganda he now enjoys full government support as an ardent capitalist entrepreneur.

The Lao are a gentle people and it is hard not to leave the country without that view being reinforced. Even the Lao People's Revolutionary Party seems quaintly inept and it is hard to equate it with its more brutal sister parties in Vietnam, Cambodia, China or the former Soviet Union. Yet five students who meekly called for greater political freedom in 1999 were whisked off by police and have not been heard of since.

Reflecting on 10 years of 'reconstruction'

Laos' recent political and economic history is covered under Modern Laos (see below). But it is worth ending this account of the country's history by noting the brevity of Laos' experiment with full-blown Communism. Just 10 years after the Pathet Lao took control of Vientiane, the leadership were on the brink of far-reaching economic reforms. By the mid-1980s it was widely acknowledged that Marxism-Leninism had failed the country. The population was still dreadfully poor; the ideology of Communism had failed to entice more than a handful into serious and enthusiastic support for the party and its ways; and graft and nepotism were on the rise.

Modern Laos

Politics

President Kaysone Phomvihane died in November 1992, aged 71. His right-hand man, Prince Souphanouvong – the so-called Red Prince – died just over two years later, on 9 January 1995. As one obituary put it, Kaysone was older than he seemed, both historically and ideologically. He had been chairman of the LPRP since the mid-1950s and had been a protégé and comrade of Ho Chi Minh, who led the Vietnamese struggle for independence from the French. After leading the Lao Resistance Government – or Pathet Lao – from caves in Xam Neua Province in the north, Kaysone assumed the premiership on the abolition of the monarchy in 1975. But under his leadership – and following the example of his mentors in Hanoi – Kaysone became the driving force behind the market-orientated reforms. The year before he died, he gave up the post of prime minister for that of president.

His death didn't change much, as other members of the old guard stepped into the breach. Nouhak Phounsavanh – a sprightly 78-year-old former truck driver and hardline Communist – succeeded him as president, but in February 1998 was replaced by 75-year-old General Khamtai Siphandon – the outgoing prime minister and head of the LPRP. Khamtai represents the last of the revolutionary Pathet Lao leaders who fought the Royalists and the Americans. In April 2006, Siphandon, the last of the old guard from the caves in Vieng Xai, was replaced as president by Choummaly Sayasone.

Recent years

With the introduction of the New Economic Mechanism in 1986 there were hopes that economic liberalization would be matched by political *glasnost*. So far, however, the monolithic Party shows few signs of equating capitalism with democracy. While the Lao brand of Communism has always been seen as relatively tame, it remains a far cry from political pluralism. Laos' first constitution since the Communists came to power in 1975 was approved in 1991. The country's political system is referred to as a popular democracy, yet it has rejected any significant moves towards multi-party reforms.

Take the elections to the 108-seat National Assembly on 24 February 2002. All of the candidates standing for election had been approved by the LPRP's mass organization, the Lao Front for National Construction. While it is not necessary for a candidate to be a member of the LPRP to stand, they are closely vetted and have to demonstrate that they have a 'sufficient level of knowledge of party policy'. As with the previous elections to the National Assembly at the end of 1997, only one of the 108 deputies elected was not a member of the Lao People's Revolutionary Party. This pattern of party cadres maintaining political seats was repeated in the National Assembly elections held in April 2006, where LPRP members won 114 out of 115 parliamentary seats.

On the dreamy streets of Vientiane, the chances of a Tiananmen-style uprising are remote. But the events of the late 1980s and early 1990s in Eastern Europe and Moscow did alarm hardliners – just as they did in Beijing and Hanoi. They can be reasonably confident, however, that in their impoverished nation, most people are more worried about where their next meal is going to come from than they are about the allure of multi-party democracy. Day-to-day politics aren't on the radar of most Lao citizens and many would find it hard to name the president and prime minister.

The greatest concern for the Lao leadership is what effect westernization is having upon the population. The economic reforms, or so the authorities would seem to believe, have brought not only foreign investment and new consumer goods, but also greed, corruption, consumerism and various social ills from drugs to prostitution.

Today, the politburo still largely controlled the country and, for now, sweeping changes are unlikely. Most of the country's leaders are well into their 60s and were educated in communist countries like Russia and Vietnam. However, the younger Lao people (particularly those that have studied abroad in Japan, Australia, UK or the US) are starting to embrace new political and economic ideas. The government takes inspiration from Vietnam's success and is more likely to follow the lead of its neighbour rather than adopting any Western model of government.

Practicalities

Getting there

Gateway cities

Bangkok **Suvarnabhumi International Airport** (pronounced su-wan-na-poom) ⓘ *www. suvarnabhumiairport.com*, is around 25 km southeast of the city. All facilities at the airport are 24 hours, so you'll have no problem exchanging money, getting something to eat or taking a taxi or other transport into the city at any time.

Kuala Lumpur **Kuala Lumpur International Airport (KLIA)** ⓘ *Sepang, 72 km south, T+60 (0)3-8776 2000, www.klia.com.my*, provides a slick point of entry. Glitzy and high-tech, it has all the usual facilities including restaurants, shops and banks. The Tourism Malaysia desk has pamphlets and a useful map.

The **Low Cost Carrier Terminal (LCCT)** ⓘ *20 km south of KLIA, www.lcct-klia.com*, is used by most budget airlines. Shuttle buses connect KLIA and the LCCT (20 minutes) for RM1.40. Always check your ticket to confirm which terminal you're flying from. The LCCT terminal is dominated by the hugely successful **Air Asia** ⓘ *www.airasia.com*, which is the region's main low-cost carrier, with flights as far afield as China, Australia and the UK. Internet bookings provide the best deals. Tickets booked well in advance are the cheapest.

Singapore **Changi Airport** ⓘ *on the eastern tip of the island, 20 km from downtown, www.changiairport.com*, is Southeast Asia's busiest airport and most long-haul airlines fly here. It is also a hub for budget Asian airlines. Changi is regularly voted the world's leading airport: it takes only 20 minutes from touchdown to baggage claim. Facilities include free Wi-Fi, boutique shops and a rooftop swimming pool. There is an Arrivals lounge in Terminal 3 for those who arrive too early to check into a hotel. The lounge offers showers and peace. Car hire desks, open 0700-2300, are in the Arrivals halls of the three terminals. Useful airlines for onward connections from Changi include: **AirAsia** ⓘ *www.airasia.com*; **Jetstar Asia** ⓘ *www.jetstar.com*, and **Tiger Airways** ⓘ *www.tigerairways.com*. Many of the cheapest fares are available exclusively on the internet. If you want to work out connections with specific cities, the Changi website has a useful flight-planning facility.

Air

The easiest and cheapest way to access the region is via the gateway cities of Bangkok, Kuala Lumpur or Singapore. However, **Vietnam Airlines** runs several direct flights from Europe, North America and Australasia to Vietnam. Cambodia and Laos are only accessible from within Asia.

Vietnam There are two main international airports in Vietnam: **Tan Son Nhat Airport** (SGN) in Ho Chi Minh City, see page 185, and **Noi Bai Airport** (HAN) in Hanoi, see page 60. **Danang** (DAD), see page 118, also has some international flights.

Cambodia The most important entry point for Cambodia remains **Phnom Penh** (PNH), which has direct flights from Bangkok, Singapore, Kuala Lumpur, Ho Chi Minh City, Vientiane, Taipei, Hong kong, Shanghai, Guangzhou and Incheon. There are also an increasing number of flights to **Siem Reap** (REP) from the main regional hubs as well as Hanoi, Ho Chi Minh City and Luang Prabang.

Laos There are international flights to **Vientiane** (VTE) from the following countries: Cambodia (Phnom Penh and Siem Reap), China (including Kunming and Nanning), Thailand (including Bangkok and Chiang Mai) and Vietnam (Hanoi and Ho Chi Minh City) and Malaysia (Kuala Lumpur). Most people visiting Laos from outside Southeast Asia travel via Bangkok.

There are also flights from Hanoi, Bangkok and Chiang Mai to **Luang Prabang** (LPQ). A cheaper option for getting to Laos from Bangkok is to fly to Udon Thani in Thailand, about 50 km south of the border, and travel overland from there, crossing at the Friendship Bridge (see page 340).

An alternative route is to fly from Bangkok to Chiang Rai in Thailand, before overlanding to Chiang Khong and crossing into northern Laos at Houei Xai. From Houei Xai there are flights to Vientiane and boats to Luang Prabang via Pakbeng.

Flights from Europe
In Western Europe, there are direct flights to Vietnam from London, Paris and Frankfurt with **Vietnam Airlines/Air France**. These code-shared flights last 12 hours. There are also direct **Vietnam Airlines** flights from Moscow.

Flights from other European hubs go via Bangkok, Singapore, Kuala Lumpur, Hong Kong or UAE states. Airlines include **Air France**, **Cathay Pacific**, **Emirates**, **Thai Airways**, **Singapore Airlines**, **Malaysia Airlines**, **Lufthansa** and **Qatar**. It is possible to fly into Hanoi and depart from Ho Chi Minh City although this does seem to rack up the return fare. Check details with flight agents and tour operators.

Flights from the US and Canada
By far the best option is to fly via **Bangkok**, **Taipei**, **Tokyo** or **Hong Kong** and from there to Vietnam, Cambodia and Laos. The approximate flight time from Los Angeles to **Bangkok** is 21 hours. **United** flies from LA and Chicago via Tokyo and from San Francisco via Seoul to Vietnam. **Thai Airways**, **Delta**, **United** and **Air Canada** fly to Bangkok from a number of US and Canadian cities.

Flights from Australia and New Zealand
There are direct flights from Adelaide, Melbourne, Sydney, Perth, Auckland and Wellington with **Cathay Pacific**, **Malaysia Airlines**, **Singapore Airlines** and **Thai Airways**. **Qantas** flies from Sydney, Adelaide and Melbourne to Ho Chi Minh City. Air Asia has cheap flights via KL.

From Sydney the flights to Vietnam are eight hours 45 minutes direct. There is also the option of flying into Hanoi and out of Ho Chi Minh City, or vice versa.

Getting around

Vietnam

If time is limited, by far the best option is to get an open-jaw flight where you fly into one city, say Hanoi, and out of Ho Chi Minh City (HCMC), although generally it is cheaper overall to fly into HCMC return and get an internal flight back to HCMC.

Remember that distances are huge and one or two internal flights may be needed. **Vietnam Airlines** has an excellent domestic network and services are good while **VietJetAir** is a budget carrier with an expanding network. Hiring a self-drive car in Vietnam is not possible and trains (although a great way to travel) and public buses are very slow. Alternatives to the domestic air network include the tourist Open Tour Bus transport, taxis and tour operators for tours and transfers.

Air

Vietnam Airlines is the national carrier and flies to multiple domestic destinations. VietJetAir is the low-cost alternative and offers a good service. Remember that during holiday periods flights get extremely busy.

Rail

Train travel is exciting and overnight journeys are a good way of covering long distances. The Vietnamese rail network extends from Hanoi to Ho Chi Minh City. **Vietnam Railways** ⓘ *www.vr.com.vn*, runs the 2600-km rail network down the coast. With overnight stays at hotels along the way to see the sights, a rail sightseeing tour from Hanoi to Ho Chi Minh City should take a minimum of 10 days but you would need to buy tickets for each separate section of the journey.

The difference in price between first and second class is small and it is worth paying the extra. There are three seating classes and four sleeping classes including hard and soft seats and hard and soft sleepers; some are air-conditioned, others are not. The prices vary according to the class of cabin and the berth chosen; the bottom berth is more expensive than the top berth. All sleepers should be booked three days in advance. The kitchen on the Hanoi to Ho Chi Minh City service serves soups and simple, but adequate, rice dishes (it is a good idea to take additional food and drink on long journeys). The express trains (**Reunification Express**) take between an advertised 29½ to 34 hours.

Most ticket offices have some staff who speak English. Queues can be long and some offices keep unusual hours. If you are short of time and short on patience it may well pay to get a tour operator to book your ticket for a small commission or visit the Ho Chi Minh City railway office in Pham Ngu Lao or the Hanoi agency in the Old Quarter.

There are also rail routes from Hanoi to Haiphong, to Lang Son and to Lao Cai. The **Victoria** hotel chain runs a luxury carriage on the latter route.

River

The **Victoria** ⓘ *www.victoriahotels-asia.com*, hotel chain runs a Mekong Delta service for its guests. Ferries operate between Ho Chi Minh City and Vung Tau; Rach Gia and Phu Quoc; Ha Tien and Phu Quoc; Haiphong and Cat Ba Island; and Halong City and Cat Ba and Mong Cai. There are also services from Chau Doc to Phnom Penh (see border box, page 544).

Official border crossings

Bavet (Cambodia)–Moc Bai (Vietnam)

This crossing on Highway 1 connects Phnom Penh with Ho Chi Minh City via Tay Ninh Province.

Kaam Samnor (Cambodia)–Vinh Xuong (Vietnam)

Further south, there is a crossing at Kaam Samnor to Vinh Xuong via Chau Doc in the Mekong Delta by boat. Capitol and Narin guesthouses organize buses to the Neak Luong ferry crossing on the Mekong from where a fast boat transports passengers to the Vietnamese border. After the border crossing there is a boat to Chau Doc. Departs 0800, arrives Chau Doc 1400, US$12.

Phnom Den (Cambodia)–Tinh Bien (Vietnam)

Further south, this road crossing is approximately 22 km south of Chau Doc.

Kep (Cambodia)–Ha Tien (Vietnam)

Right at the very south of the country there is a scenic border crossing at Ha Tien. Fares are roughly US$5 for a moto and US$10 for a tuk-tuk.

Don Kralor (Cambodia)–Voem Kham (Laos)

The official border crossing is at Don Kralor, an hour north of Stung Treng. Visas for both countries are available at the border. For Cambodia, the usual entry requirements apply: two passport photos and US$20. For Laos, fees vary (US$20-42) depending on nationality. You will need a passport photo as well. The border is officially open 0800-1600. On both sides of the border, officials will charge a small fee to stamp your passport.

Most travellers pass directly through the border on bus services as the crossing point is at a remote location and few facilities are available there. All buses wait for travellers to acquire visas. At present the company Sorya, www.ppsorya transport.com, runs the best direct service from Phnom Penh to Siphandon (4000 Islands) and Pakse, in Laos. This bus also stops in Stung Treng where you can hop on if there are any seats left. Heading the other way, most tour operators can arrange buses from Don Khong, Don Deth and Done Khone to the border and onwards to Stung Treng, Phnom Penh and Kampong Cham.

Sop Hun (Laos)–Tay Trang (Vietnam)

The border linking Vietnam's Dien Bien Phu with this part of Laos is now daily 0800-1700. A Laos visa can be obtained on arrival, but Vietnamese visas cannot. There is limited transport on the Laos side to Muang Khua. There is a direct bus from Muang Khua to Dien Bien Phu, which lets you off for border formalities. It leaves from the opposite side of the river bank to Muang Khua at 0600, so it is necessary to get to the river bank in good time to make the crossing – take a torch as it may be quite dark this early. Most guesthouses in Muang Khua can help with information.

Na Maew (Laos)–Nam Xoi (Vietnam)

Route 6A heads east from Xam Neua to this border crossing. You'll need to get your Laos or Vietnam visa in advance. The border is open 0730-1130 and 1330-1700. It may be necessary to pay a processing or overtime fee.

The trip to the border is two hours from Vieng Xai. Songthaew leave Vieng Xai at 0640 from the main Xam Neua–Na Maew road, 1 km from the centre of Vieng Xai, 20,000 kip. It is also possible to take a songthaew from Xam Neua station at 0630-0715 (three or four hours), 30,000 kip, or to charter one to the border from Xam Neua for about US$50.

Beware of unethical tourism operators on the Vietnamese side of this border charging a fortune for transport. A motorbike taxi to Quan Son should cost around US$10. If you get stuck on the Vietnam side contact Mr Pham Xuan Hop in Na Maew, T0084-9923 7425, who may be able to organize minivan rental (US$42-50 to Quan Son).

There are two guesthouses in Na Maew (Phucloc Nha Tru and Minhchien); they both offer rudimentary facilities for US$3-5 per night).

A bus runs from Na Maew to Thanh Hoa Tuesday, Thursday and Saturday at 1130, US$8; check all transport details in Xam Neua, at the bus station or tourism office.

Nam Phao (Laos)–Cau Treo (Vietnam)

The border is 30 km east of Lak Xao. There are buses to the border from Vientiane (via Paksan, see page 415). Songthaew leave Lak Xao market every hour and take about 50 minutes. The border is open 0800-1800. Be prepared for an overtime fee at weekends. You need to organize Vietnamese visas in advance (ideally in Vientiane) as they aren't issued at the border. Once in Vietnam transport can be caught to Vinh from where buses service all the major cities. Arriving from Vietnam, 30-day Laos visas are issued at the border.

Dansavanh (Laos)–Lao Bao (Vietnam)

The Vietnam border is 236 km east of Savannakhet (45 km from Xepon). Buses leave Savannakhhet for the border throughout the morning and take four or five hours. There are buses that run from Savannakhet to Dong Ha, Hué and Danang, but for some you will need to change buses at the border.

The Lao border post is at Dansavanh, from where it is about 500 m to the Vietnamese immigration post and a further 3 km to Lao Bao, the first settlement across the border; motorbike taxis are available. We have received reports of long delays at this border. The problem is at the Vietnamese end but those with a Vietnamese visa (required) should be OK. The closest Vietnamese consulate is in Savannakhet. Lao immigration can also issue 30-day tourist visas. Expect to pay 'overtime fees' on the Lao side if you come through on a weekend.

Yalakhuntum (Laos)–Bo Y (Vietnam)

This crossing on Route 18B (113 km from Attapeu) is open daily 0800-1600. Lao 30-day visas are issued at the border; Vietnamese visas are not, and must be obtained in advance. Buses leave Attapeu for Vietnam daily.

Road

If travelling to Vietnam by road, ensure that your visa is appropriately stamped with the correct entry point or you will be turned back at the border. Don't forget visas for Vietnam are not available at the border.

Roads in Vietnam are notoriously dangerous. As American humourist PJ O'Rourke wrote: "In Japan people drive on the left. In China people drive on the right. In Vietnam it doesn't matter." Since Highway 1 is so dangerous and public transport buses are poor and slow, most travellers opt for the cheap and regular **Open Tour Bus** (private minibus or coach) that covers the length of the country. Almost every Vietnamese tour operator/travellers' café listed in this guide will have an agent. The buses run daily from their own offices and include the following stops: Ho Chi Minh City, Mui Ne, Nha Trang, Dalat, Hoi An, Hué, Ninh Binh and Hanoi. They will also stop off at tourist destinations along the way such as Lang Co, Hai Van Pass, Marble Mountains and Po Klong Garai for quick visits. You may join at any leg of the journey, paying for one trip or several as you go.

If you do opt for **public buses** note that most bus stations are on the outskirts of town; in bigger centres there may be several stations. Long-distance buses invariably leave very early in the morning (0400-0500). Buses are the cheapest form of transport, although sometimes foreigners find they are being asked for two to three times the correct price. Prices are normally prominently displayed at bus stations. Less comfortable but quicker are the minibus services, which ply the more popular routes.

Car hire Self-drive car hire is not available in Vietnam. It is, however, possible to hire cars with drivers and this is a good way of getting to more remote areas with a group of people. Car hire prices increase by 50% or more during Tet.

Motorbike and bicycle hire Most towns are small enough to get around by bicycle, and this can also be a pleasant way to explore the surrounding countryside. However, if covering large areas (touring around the Central Highlands, for example) then a motorbike will mean you can see more and get further off the beaten track.

Motorbikes and bicycles can be hired by the day in the cities, often from hotels and travellers' cafés. You do not need a driver's licence or proof of motorbike training to hire a motorbike in Vietnam, however, it is compulsory to wear a helmet. Also, lack of a license will no doubt invalidate your travel insurance.

Motorbike taxi and cyclo Motorcycle taxis, known as *xe om* (*ôm* means to cuddle) are ubiquitous and cheap. You will find them on most street corners, outside hotels or in the street. If they see you before you see them, they will whistle to get your attention.

Cyclos are bicycle trishaws. Cyclo drivers charge double or more that of a *xe om*. A number of streets in the centres of Ho Chi Minh City and Hanoi are one-way or out of bounds to cyclos, necessitating lengthy detours which add to the time and cost. It is a wonderful way to get around the Old Quarter of Hanoi.

Taxi Taxis ply the streets of Hanoi and Ho Chi Minh City and other large towns and cities. They are cheap, around 12,000d per km. Always use the better-known taxi companies to avoid any issues. Mai Linh is one of the most widely found reliable firms.

Cambodia

Air

At the moment the only domestic route within Cambodia that operates safely and with any frequency is between Phnom Penh and Siem Reap. National carrier, **Cambodia Angkor Air**, flies this route but its website, www.cambodiaangkorair.com, doesn't allow bookings; their office in Phnom Penh is at 1-2/294 Mao Tse Tung, T023-666 6786. All departure taxes are now included in your fare.

River

All the Mekong towns and settlements around the Tonlé Sap are accessible by boat. It is a very quick and relatively comfortable way to travel and much cheaper than flying. The route between Siem Reap and Phnom Penh is very popular, while the route between Siem Reap and Battambang is one of the most scenic. With the new road opening, boats are no longer used as a main form of transport along the Mekong and in the northeast.

Road

Over the last few years the road system in Cambodia has dramatically improved. A trunk route of international standards, apart from a few bumpy stretches, from Stung Treng to Koh Kong is due for completion in the near future. Much of the rest of the network is pretty basic and journeys can sometimes be long and laborious. Also, to some parts, such as Ratanakiri, the road is a graded laterite track, unpaved and potholed. In the rainy season expect to be slowed down on many roads to a slithering muddy crawl. The Khmer-American Friendship Highway (Route 4), which runs from Phnom Penh to Sihanoukville, is entirely paved, as is the National Highway 6 between Siem Reap and Phnom Penh. The infamous National Highway 6 between Poipet and Phnom Penh via Siem Reap has also had extensive work, as has National Highway 1. The Japanese in particular have put considerable resources into road and bridge building.

Bus and shared taxi There are buses and shared taxis to most parts of the country. Shared taxis are not as common as they used to be. The taxi operators charge a premium for better seats and you can buy yourself more space. It is not uncommon for a taxi to fit 10 people in it, including two sitting on the driver's seat. Fares for riding in the back of the truck are half that for riding in the cab. The Sihanoukville run has an excellent and cheap air-conditioned bus service.

Car hire and taxi A few travel agents and hotels may be able to organize self-drive car hire and most hotels have cars for hire with a driver (US$30-50 per day). There is a limited taxi service in Phnom Penh.

Moto and tuk-tuk The most popular and sensible options are the motorbike taxi, known as 'moto', and the tuk-tuk. They costs around the same as renting your own machine and with luck you will get a driver who speaks a bit of English and who knows where he's going. Once you have found a good driver stick with him. Outside Phnom Penh and Siem Reap, do not expect much English from your moto/tuk-tuk driver.

Motorbike and bicycle hire Motorbikes can be rented from between US$5 and US$8 per day and around US$1 for a bicycle. If riding either a motorbike or a bicycle be aware that the accident fatality rate is very high. This is partly because of the poor condition of many of the vehicles on the road; partly because of the poor roads; and partly because of the horrendously poor driving. If you do rent a motorbike ensure it has a working horn (imperative) and buy some rear-view mirrors so you can keep an eye on the traffic. Wear a helmet (even if using a motodop).

Laos

Air

Lao Airlines runs domestic flights from Vientiane to Luang Prabang, Phonsavanh (Xieng Khouang), Pakse, Houei Xai, Udomxai, Luang Namtha and Savannakhet.

River

It is possible to take river boats up and down the Mekong and its main tributaries. Boats stop at Luang Prabang, Pakbeng and Houei Xai in the northwest; Nong Khiaw and Phongsali on the Nam Ou River in the north; and around Don Deth and Don Khong in the south. Luxury services operate between Houei Xai and Luang Prabang and between Pakse and Wat Phou in Champasak Province. Aside from the route down from Houei Xai to Luang Prabang, often there are no scheduled services, and departures may be limited in the dry season. Take food and drink and expect crowded conditions on the Houei Xai–Luang Prabang route. Speedboats cover some routes, but are dangerous and uncomfortable.

Road

Roads have greatly improved in recent years, making journeys much faster. Quite a few bus, truck, tuk-tuk, *songthaew* (see below) and taxi drivers understand basic English, French or Thai, although it is helpful to have the name of the place you are trying to get to written out in Lao. Many people will not know road names, but will know all the sights of interest.

Bus/truck/minivan It is possible to travel to most areas by bus, truck or songthaew (converted pickup truck) in the dry season, although road travel in the rainy season can be tricky if not impossible in some areas. VIP buses are comfortable night buses, usually allowing you to sleep – but watch out for karaoke on board (earplugs may be useful). In the south, an overnight bus plies the route from Pakse to Vientiane. Book a double bed if you don't want to sleep next to a stranger. Robberies have been reported on the night buses so keep your valuables secure.

A decent network of minivans transport foreigners from one main tourist destination to another; for example, Luang Prabang to Vang Vieng. Pick-ups from guesthouses are usually part of the service.

Car hire Car hire is possible both with and without a driver. Insurance is generally included (you will need an international driver's permit). Check **Avis** ⓘ *www.avis.la*, for current rates.

Motorbike and bicycle hire There are an increasing number of motorcycles available to hire from guesthouses and shops in major towns. 110cc bikes cost around US$10 per day. Bicycles are a cheap way to see the sights. Many guesthouses have bikes for rent at around US$2 per day. Mountain bikes can be rented from specialist outlets.

Tuk-tuk The motorized three-wheelers known as 'jumbos' or tuk-tuks are large motorbike taxis with two bench seats in the back. You'll find them in most cities and metropolitan areas. They can be hired by the hour or the day to reach destinations out of town.

In city centres make sure you have the correct money for your tuk-tuk as drivers are often conveniently short of change.

Essentials A-Z

Contact the relevant emergency service and your embassy. Make sure you obtain police/medical records in order to file insurance claims. If you need to report a crime visit your local police station and take a local with you who speaks English.

Vietnam Ambulance T115, **Fire** T114, **Police** T113.

Cambodia Ambulance T119 /724891, **Fire** T118, **Police** T117/112/012-999999.

Laos Ambulance T195, **Fire** T190, **Police** T191.

Children

The region is not particularly geared up for visiting children but there are activities that will appeal to both adults and children. Children are often excellent passports into a local culture and you will also receive the best service and help from officials and members of the public if you have kids with you. Fruit can be bought cheaply: papaya and banana are excellent sources of nutrition, and can be self-peeled, ensuring cleanliness. Powdered milk is available in provincial centres, although most brands have added sugar. Avoid letting your child drink tap water as it may carry parasites. Bottled water is sold widely.

Some attractions in **Vietnam** offer a child's concession. The railways allow children under 5 to travel free and charge 50% of the adult fare for those aged 5-10. The Open Tour Bus tickets and tours are likewise free for children under 2 but those aged 2-5 pay 75% of the adult price. Baby products are found in major supermarkets in the main cities. In the remoter regions, such as the north and the Central Highlands and smaller towns, take everything with you.

In **Cambodia** be aware that expensive hotels as well as market stalls may have squalid cooking conditions and try to ensure that children do not drink any water (especially important when bathing). Baby food can also be bought in some towns – the quality may not be the same as equivalent foods bought in the West, but it is perfectly adequate for short periods. Disposable nappies can be bought in Phnom Penh, but are often expensive.

In **Laos**, disposable nappies can be bought in Vientiane and other larger provincial capitals, but are often expensive. Public transport may be a problem; long bus journeys are restrictive and uncomfortable. Chartering a car is the most convenient way to travel overland but rear seatbelts are scarce and child seats even rarer. Lao people love children and it is not uncommon for waiters and waitresses to spend the whole evening looking after your child.

Customs and duty free

Vietnam

Duty-free allowance is 400 cigarettes, 50 cigars or 100 g of tobacco, 1.5 litres of spirits, plus items for personal use. Export of wood products or antiques is banned. You can't import pornography, anti-government literature, photographs or movies, nor culturally unsuitable children's toys.

Cambodia

Roughly 200 cigarettes or the equivalent quantity of tobacco, 1 bottle of liquor and perfume for personal use can be taken out of the country without incurring customs duty. Taking any Angkorian-era images out of the country is strictly forbidden.

Laos

The duty free allowance is 500 cigarettes, 2 bottles of wine and a bottle of liquor.

Laos has a strictly enforced ban on the export of antiquities and all Buddha images.

Disabled travellers

Considering the proportion of the region's population that are seriously disabled (Cambodia has the world's highest incidence of one-legged and no-legged people due to landmine injuries), foreigners might expect better facilities for the immobile. However, some of the more upmarket hotels do have a few designated rooms for the physically disabled. For those with walking difficulties many of the better hotels have lifts. Wheelchair access is improving with more shopping centres, hotels and restaurants providing ramps for easy access. While there are scores of hurdles that disabled people will have to negotiate, local people are likely to go out of their way to be helpful.

People sensitive to noise will find **Vietnam**, for example, at times, almost intolerable. The general situation in **Cambodia** is no better. The Angkor Complex can be a real struggle for disabled or frail persons. The stairs are very steep and semi-restoration of areas means that visitors will sometimes need to climb over piles of bricks. Hiring an aide to help you climb stairs and generally get around is a very good idea and costs around US$5-10 a day. In **Laos** pavements are often uneven, there are potholes and missing drain covers galore, pedestrian crossings are ignored, ramps are unheard of, lifts are few and far between and escalators are seen only in magazines and high-end hotels and a sprinkling of shopping complexes.

Disability Rights UK, www.disabilityrights uk.org.
RADAR, 12 City Forum, 250 City Rd, London, EC1V 8AF, T0207-250 3222, www.radar.org.uk.
SATH, 347 Fifth Avenue, Suite 605, New York City, NY 10016, T0212-447 7284, www.sath.org.

Drugs

Vietnam

In the south you may be offered weed, but rarely anything else, although ecstasy is becoming more popular among the younger generation. Attitudes to traffickers are harsh, although the death penalty (now by lethal injection and not firing squad) is usually reserved for Vietnamese and other Asians whose governments are less likely to kick up a fuss.

Cambodia

Drug use is illegal in Cambodia but drugs are a widespread problem. Many places use marijuana in their cooking and the police seem to be quite ambivalent to dope smokers (unless they need to supplement their income with bribe money, in which case – watch out). The backpacker areas near the lake in Phnom Penh and Sihanoukville are particularly notorious for heavy drug usage by Westerners. One of the biggest dangers for travellers who take drugs in Cambodia today is dying of an overdose. The frequency of overdoses is largely attributed to the fact that the people buying drugs aren't getting what they thought they were. Note that cocaine and ecstasy do not really exist in Cambodia, despite what you may be told; it is in fact heroin. Avoid yaa baa, a particularly insidious amphetamine. It has serious side effects and can be lethal. In a nutshell: don't buy illicit drugs in Cambodia, it is dangerous.

Laos

Drug use is illegal and there are harsh penalties ranging from fines through to imprisonment or worse. Police have been known to levy heavy fines on people in Vang Vieng for eating so-called 'happy' foods, or for being caught in possession of drugs. Though opium has in theory been eradicated, it is still for sale in northern areas and people have died from overdosing. *Yaa baa* (a methamphetamine and caffeine tablet) is also available here and should be avoided at all costs.

Electricity

Vietnam Voltage 110-240. Sockets are round 2-pin. Sometimes they are 2 flat pin. A number of top hotels now use UK 3 square-pin sockets.
Cambodia Voltage 220. Sockets are usually round 2-pin.
Laos Voltage 220, 50 cycles in the main towns. 110 volts in the country; 2-pin sockets are common. Blackouts used to be frequent outside Vientiane as many smaller towns are not connected to the national grid and only have power during the evening. Nowadays even remote areas are being wired up.

Embassies and consulates

For a list of embassies and consulates in Vietnam, Cambodia and Laos see http://embassy.goabroad.com.

Festivals and public holidays

Vietnam
Late Jan-Mar (movable, 1st-7th day of the new lunar year): **Tet** is the traditional new year. The big celebration of the year, the word Tet is the shortened version of *tet nguyen dan* ('first morning of the new period'). Tet is the time to forgive and forget and to pay off debts. It is also everyone's birthday – everyone adds one year to their age at Tet. Enormous quantities of food are consumed and new clothes are bought. It is believed that before Tet the spirit of the hearth, Ong Tao, leaves on a journey to visit the palace of the Jade Emperor where he must report on family affairs. To ensure that Ong Tao sets off in good cheer, a ceremony is held before Tet, Le Tao Quan, and during his absence a shrine is constructed (Cay Neu) to keep evil spirits at bay until his return. On the afternoon before Tet, Tat Nien, a sacrifice is offered at the family altar to dead relatives who are invited back to join in the festivities.

Great attention is paid to preparations for Tet, because it is believed that the 1st week of the new year dictates the fortunes for the rest of the year. The first visitor to the house on New Year's morning should be an influential, lucky and happy person, so families take care to arrange a suitable caller.
Apr (movable, 5th or 6th of the 3rd lunar month): **Thanh Minh (New Year of the Dead or Feast of the Pure Light)**. The Vietnamese walk outdoors to evoke the spirit of the dead and family shrines and tombs are cleaned and decorated.
Aug (movable, 15th day of the 7th lunar month): **Trung Nguyen (Wandering Souls Day)**. During this time, prayers can absolve the sins of the dead who leave hell and return, hungry and naked, to their relatives. The Wandering Souls are those with no homes to go to. There are celebrations in Buddhist temples and homes, food is placed out on tables and money is burnt.
Sep (movable, 15th day of the 8th lunar month): **Tet Trung Thi (Mid-Autumn Festival)**. This festival is particularly celebrated by children. It is based on legend. In the evening families prepare food including sticky rice, fruit and chicken to be placed on the ancestral altars. Moon cakes (egg, green bean and lotus seed) are baked, lanterns are made and painted, and children parade through town with music.

Public holidays
1 Jan **New Year's Day**.
3 Feb **Founding anniversary of the Communist Party of Vietnam**.
30 Apr **Liberation Day of South Vietnam and HCMC**.
1 May **International Labour Day**.
19 May **Anniversary of the Birth of Ho Chi Minh** (this is a government holiday). The majority of state institutions will be shut but businesses in the private sector carry on regardless.
2 Sep **National Day**.
3 Sep **President Ho Chi Minh's Anniversary**.

Cambodia

Apr (13-15) Bonn Chaul Chhnam (Cambodian New Year). A 3-day celebration to mark the turn of the year when predictions are made for the forthcoming year. The celebration is to show gratitude to the departing demi-god, filled with offerings of food and drink. Homes are spring cleaned. Householders visit temples and traditional games like *angkunh* and *chhoal chhoung* are played and festivities are performed.

Apr/May Visak Bauchea (dates vary with the full moon), the most important Buddhist festival; a triple anniversary commemorating Buddha's birth, enlightenment and his *Paranirvana* (state of final bliss).

Oct/Nov (movable) Bon Om Tuk (Water Festival or Festival of the Reversing Current). Celebrates the movement of the waters out of the Tonlé Sap with boat races in Phnom Penh. Boat races extend over 3 days with more than 200 competitors but the highlight is the evening gala in Phnom Penh when a fleet of boats, studded with lights, row out under the full moon. Under the Cambodian monarchy, the king would command the waters to retreat. In 2010 several 100 people died during a stampede at the festival and visitors are reminded to be aware of their safety if they decide to attend this event.

Public holidays

1 Jan National Day and Victory over Pol Pot.
7 Jan Celebration of the fall of the Khmer Rouge in 1979.
8 Mar Women's Day. Processions, floats and banners in main towns.
17 Apr Independence Day.
1 May Labour Day.
9 May Genocide Day.
1 Jun International Children's Day.
18 Jun Her Majesty Preah Akkaek Mohesey Norodom Monineath Sihanouk's Birthday.
Sep (movable) End of Buddhist 'lent'.
24 Sep Constitution Day.
23 Oct Paris Peace Accord.
30 Oct-1 Nov King's Birthday.

9 Nov Independence Day (1953).
10 Dec Human Rights Day.

Laos

Jan/Feb (movable) Chinese New Year. Celebrated by Chinese and Vietnamese communities. Many businesses shut down for 3 days.

Apr (13-15) Pi Mai (Lao New Year). The 1st month of the Lao new Year is actually Dec but it is celebrated in Apr when days are longer than nights. One of the most important annual festivals, particularly in Luang Prabang. Statues of Buddha (in the 'calling for rain' posture) are ceremonially doused in water, which is poured along an intricately decorated trench (*hang song nam pha*). The small stupas of sand, decorated with streamers, in wat compounds are symbolic requests for health and happiness over the next year. It is celebrated with traditional Lao folksinging (*mor lam*) and the circle dance (*ramwong*). There is usually a 3-day holiday. 'Sok Dee Pi Mai' (good luck for the New Year) is usually said to one another during this period.

May (movable) Boun Bang Fai. The rocket festival is a Buddhist rain-making festival. Large bamboo rockets are built and decorated by monks and carried in procession before being blasted skywards. The higher a rocket goes, the bigger its builder's ego gets. Designers of failed rockets are thrown in the mud. The festival lasts 2 days.

Sep/Oct (movable) Boun Ok Phansa. The end of the Buddhist Lent when the faithful take offerings to the temple. It is the '9th month' in Luang Prabang and the '11th month' in Vientiane, and marks the end of the rainy season. Boat races take place on the Mekong River with crews of 50 or more men and women. On the night before the race small decorated rafts are set afloat on the river.

Oct Lai Heua Fai (Fireboat Festival). See Luang Prabang, page 372.

Nov (movable) Boun That Luang. Celebrated in all Laos' *thats*, most enthusiastically and colourfully in Vientiane (see page 335).

Public holidays

1 Jan **New Year's Day.**
6 Jan **Pathet Lao Day.**
20 Jan **Army Day.**
8 Mar **Women's Day.**
22 Mar **People's Party Day.**
1 May **Labour Day.**
1 Jun **Children's Day.**
2 Dec **Independence Day.**

GLBT

Vietnam

The Vietnamese are broadly tolerant of homosexuality although legal marriage unions remain impossible. There are no legal restraints for 2 people of the same sex co-habitating in the same room whether they Vietnamese or non-Vietnamese. There are several gay/gay friendly bars in central HCMC and Hanoi.

Cambodia

Gay and lesbian travellers will have no problems in Cambodia. Men often hold other men's hands as do women, so this kind of affection is commonplace. Any kind of passionate kissing or sexually orientated affection in public, however, is taboo – both for straight and gay people. The gay scene is just starting to develop in Cambodia but there is definitely a scene in the making. Linga Bar in Siem Reap and the Salt Lounge in Phnom Penh are both gay bars and are excellent choices for a night out.

Laos

Gay and lesbian travellers should have no problems in Laos. Openly sexual behaviour, whether straight or gay, is contrary to local culture and custom. Officially, it is illegal for any foreigner to have a sexual relationship with a Lao person they aren't married to.

Health

See your doctor or travel clinic at least 6 weeks before your departure for general advice on travel risks, malaria

and vaccinations (see also below). Make sure you have travel insurance, get a dental check-up (especially if you are going to be away for more than a month), know your own blood group and if you suffer a long-term condition such as diabetes or epilepsy make sure someone knows or that you have a **Medic Alert** bracelet/necklace with this information on it (www.medicalert.co.uk).

It is risky to buy medicine, and in particular antimalarials, in developing countries, as they may be substandard or part of a trade in counterfeit drugs.

Vaccinations

It is advisable to vaccinate against polio, tetanus, typhoid, hepatitis A, and rabies if going to more remote areas. Japanese encephalitis may be advised for some areas, depending on the duration of the trip and proximity to rice-growing and pig-farming areas. Yellow fever does not exist in Vietnam, Cambodia or Laos, however, the authorities may wish to see a certificate if you have recently arrived from an endemic area in Africa or South America.

Health risks

The most common cause of travellers' **diarrhoea** is from eating contaminated food. Drinking water is rarely the culprit in the region, although it's best to be cautious (see below). Swimming in sea or river water that has been contaminated by sewage can also be a cause; ask locally if it is safe. Diarrhoea may be also caused by viruses, bacteria (such as E-coli), protozoal (such as giardia), salmonella and cholera. It may be accompanied by vomiting or by severe abdominal pain. Any kind of diarrhoea responds well to the replacement of water and salts. Sachets of rehydration salts can be bought in most chemists and can be dissolved in boiled water. If the symptoms persist, consult a doctor. Tap water in the major cities is in theory safe to drink but it may be advisable to err on the side of caution and drink only bottled or boiled water. Avoid having ice in drinks unless you trust that it is from a reliable source.

Mosquitoes are more of a nuisance than a serious hazard but some, of course, are carriers of serious diseases such as **malaria**. This exists in rural areas in Vietnam. However, there is no risk in the Red River Delta and the coastal plains north of Nha Trang. Neither is there a risk in Hanoi, Ho Chi Minh City, Danang and Nha Trang. Malaria exists in most of Cambodia, except the capital Phnom Penh. Malaria is prevalent in Laos and remains a serious disease; about a third of the population contracts malaria at some stage in their lives. The choice of malaria prophylaxis will need to be something other than chloroquine for most people, since there is such a high level of resistance to it. Always check with your doctor or travel clinic for the most up-to-date advice. In addition to taking prophylaxis, try and avoid being bitten as much as possible by sleeping off the ground and using a mosquito net and some kind of insecticide. Mosquito coils release insecticide as they burn and are available in many shops, as are tablets of insecticide, which are placed on a heated mat plugged into a wall socket.

The most serious viral disease is **dengue fever**, which is hard to protect against as the mosquitos bite throughout the day as well as at night.

Each year there is the possibility that **avian flu** or **swine flu** might rear their ugly heads. Check the news reports. If there is a problem in an area you are due to visit you may be advised to have an ordinary flu shot or to seek expert advice.

There are high rates of **HIV** in the region, especially among sex workers. **Rabies** and **schistosomiasis** (bilharzia, a water-borne parasite) may be a problem in Laos.

If you get sick

Contact your embassy or consulate for a list of doctors and dentists who speak your language, or at least some English. Doctors and health facilities in major cities are also listed in the Directory sections of this book. Make sure you have adequate insurance (see below).

Vietnam

Western hospitals staffed by foreign and Vietnamese medics exist in Hanoi and HCMC. **Columbia Asia** (Saigon International Clinic), 8 Alexander de Rhodes St, HCMC, T08-3823 8888, www.columbiaasia.com. International doctors offering a full range of services. **International SOS**, Central Building, 51 Xuan Dieu, Tay Ho, Hanoi, T04-3934 0666, and 167A Nam Ky Khoi Nghia St, Q3, T08-3829 8424, www.internationalsos.com/countries/vietnam. Open 24 hrs for emergencies, routine and medical evacuation. It provides dental service too.

Cambodia

Contact your embassy or consulate for a list of doctors and dentists who speak your language, or at least some English. Make sure you have adequate insurance (see below). Ask at your hotel for a good local doctor. Hospitals are not recommended anywhere in Cambodia (even at some of the clinics that profess to be 'international'). If you fall ill or are injured your best bet is to get yourself quickly to either **Bumrungrad Hospital** or **Bangkok Nursing Home**, both in Bangkok. Both hospitals are of an exceptional standard, even in international terms.

Laos

Hospitals are few and far between and medical facilities are poor in Laos. Emergency treatment is available at the **Mahosot Hospital** and **Clinique Setthathirath** in Vientiane. The Australian embassy also has a clinic for Commonwealth citizens with minor ailments. There are also hospitals in Pakse, Phonsavanh and Savannakhet. Better facilities are available in Thailand and emergency evacuation to Nong Khai or Udon Thani (Thailand) can usually be arranged at short notice. In cases of emergency where a medical evacuation is required, contact **Lao West Coast Helicopter**, Hangar 703, Wattay

International Airport, T021-512023, www.laowestcoast.com. Contact your embassy or consulate for a list of doctors and dentists who speak your language, or at least some English. Healthcare can be expensive, especially hospitalization. Make sure you have adequate insurance (see below).

Thailand

Aek Udon Hospital, Udon Thani, Thailand T+66-42-342555, www.aekudon.com. A 2½-hr trip from Vientiane.
Bumrungrad Hospital, 33 Sukhumvit 3, Bangkok, T+66-2-667 1000, www.bumrungrad.com. The best option: a world-class hospital with brilliant medical facilities.
Wattana Hospital Group www.wattanahospital.net, is at Udon Thani, T+66 42-325999, and Nong Khai, T+66 42-465201; the latter in particular is a better alternative to the hospitals in Vientiane and only a 40-min trip from the capital.

Useful websites

www.btha.org British Travel Health Association (UK). This is the official website of an organization of travel health professionals.
www.cdc.gov US government site that gives excellent advice on travel health and details of disease outbreaks.
www.fco.gov.uk British Foreign and Commonwealth Office travel site has useful information on each country, people, climate and a list of UK embassies/consulates.
www.fitfortravel.scot.nhs.uk A-Z of vaccine/health advice for each country.
www.numberonehealth.co.uk Travel screening services, vaccine and travel health advice, email/SMS text vaccine reminders and screens returned travellers for tropical diseases.
www.who.int The WHO *Blue Book* lists the diseases of the world.

Insurance

Always take out travel insurance before you set off and read the small print carefully.

Check that the policy covers the activities you intend or may end up doing. Check exactly what your medical cover includes, eg ambulance, helicopter rescue or emergency flights back home. Also check the payment protocol. You may have to cough up first before the insurance company reimburses you. It is always best to dig out all the receipts for expensive personal effects like jewellery or cameras. Take photos of these items and note down all serial numbers.

You are advised to shop around. Please also note your nation's ongoing travel warnings – if you travel to areas or places that are not recommended for travel your insurance may be invalid.

Internet

Vietnam

Although emailing is easy and Wi-Fi is widespread, access to the web is slightly restricted, for example BBC and Facebook are periodically blocked.

Cambodia

Wi-Fi is available pretty much everywhere in Cambodia, including cafés and restaurants, and internet shops have now almost closed down.

Laos

Wi-Fi can now be found in cafés, hotel and bars in all major tourist centres. These places will also have some dedicated internet/gaming cafés.

Language

Vietnam

You are likely to find some English spoken wherever there are tourist services but outside tourist centres communication can be a problem for those who have no knowledge of Vietnamese. Furthermore, the Vietnamese language is not easy to learn. For example, pronunciation presents enormous difficulties as it is tonal. On the plus side, Vietnamese is written in a Roman alphabet making life much easier; place and street names are instantly recognizable. French is still spoken and often very well by the more elderly and educated Vietnamese and older German speakers are common in the north too.

Cambodia

In Cambodia the national language is Khmer (pronounced 'Khmei'). It is not tonal and the script is derived from the southern Indian alphabet. French is spoken by the older generation who survived the Khmer Rouge era. English is the language of the younger generations. Away from Phnom Penh, Siem Reap and Sihanoukville it can be difficult to communicate with the local population unless you speak Khmer.

Laos

Lao is the national language but there are many local dialects, not to mention the languages of the minority groups. Lao is closely related to Thai and, in a sense, is becoming more so as the years pass. Though there are important differences between the languages, they are mutually intelligible – just about. French is spoken, though only by government officials, hotel staff and educated people over 40. However, most government officials and many shopkeepers have some command of English.

Media

Vietnam

The English-language daily *Việt Nam News* is widely available. Inside the back page is a 'What's on' section. *The Word* (www. wordhcmc.com and www.wordhanoi.com), a tourism and culture magazine, is available throughout the country. *The Guide*, a monthly magazine on leisure and tourism produced by the *Vietnam Economic Times*, can be found in tourist centres. *Asia Life*, Vietnam Traveller and *Time Out* all carry features. Online check out www.saigoneer.com for information on the south and www.hanoigrapevine.com for the north. There is news in English on VTV4 and

a wide range of international channels is now widely available, especially at the better hotels.

Cambodia

Cambodia has a vigorous English-language press that fights bravely for editorial independence and freedom to criticize politicians. The principal English-language newspapers are the fortnightly *Phnom Penh Post*, which many regard as the best, and the *Cambodia Daily*, published 5 times a week. There are also tourist magazine guides.

Laos

The *Vientiane Times*, www.vientianetimes. org.la, is published 5 days a week and provides quirky pieces of information and some interesting cultural and tourist-based features, as well as eye-catching stories translated from the local press and wire service. The national TV station broadcasts in Lao. In Vientiane **CNN**, **BBC**, **ABC** and a range of other channels are broadcast. Thailand's **Channel 5** gives English subtitles to news. The **Lao National Radio** broadcasts news in English. The **BBC World Service** can be picked up on shortwave.

Money

Vietnam → *US$1 = 21,277đ, £1 = 33,033đ, €1 = 24171đ (Apr 2015).*
The unit of currency is the Vietnamese **dong** (VND). Under law, shops should only accept dong but in practice this is not enforced and dollars in some places. ATMs are plentiful in HCMC and Hanoi and are now pretty ubiquitous in all but the smallest of town, but it is a good idea to travel with US dollars cash as a back-up. Try to avoid tatty notes.

Banks in the main centres will change other major currencies including UK sterling, Hong Kong dollars, Thai baht, Swiss francs, euros, Australian dollars, Singapore dollars and Canadian dollars. Credit cards are increasingly accepted, particularly Visa, MasterCard, Amex and JCB. Large hotels, expensive restaurants and medical centres invariably take them but beware a surcharge of between 2.5% and 4.5%. Most hotels will not add a surcharge onto your bill if paying by credit card. Prepaid currency cards allow you to preload money from your bank account, fixed at the day's exchange rate, and are accepted anywhere that you can use debit or credit cards. They are issued by specialist money changing companies, such as **Travelex**, **Caxton FX** and the post office. You can top up and check your balance by phone, online and sometimes by text.

Cambodia → *US$1 = 4035 riels, £1 = 6268 riels, €1 = 4586 riels (Apr 2015).*

The **riel** (KHR) is the official currency though US dollars are widely accepted and easily exchanged. In Phnom Penh and other towns most goods and services are priced in dollars and there is little need to buy riel. In remote rural areas prices are quoted in riel (except accommodation). Money can be exchanged in banks and hotels. US$ traveller's cheques are easiest to exchange – commission ranges from 1% to 3%. Cash advances on credit cards are available. Credit card facilities are limited but some banks, hotels and restaurants do accept them, mostly in the tourist centres. **ANZ Royal Bank** has opened a number of ATMs throughout Phnom Penh, as well as several in provincial Cambodia. Most machines give US$ only.

Laos → *US$1 = 8091 kip, £1 = 12,564 kip, €1 = 9193 kip (Apr 2015).*

The **kip** (LAK) is the official currency. The lowest commonly used note is the 500 kip. US dollars and sometimes Thai baht (B) can be used as cash in some tourist shops, restaurants and hotels, and the Chinese Yuan (¥) is starting to be more widely accepted in northern parts of Laos, close to the Chinese border. A certain amount of cash (in US$ or Thai baht) can also be useful in an emergency.

Banks include the **Lao Development Bank** and **Le Banque pour Commerce Exterieur**

Lao (BCEL). ATMs are now widely available in all but the smallest of towns.

Payment by credit card is becoming steadily easier – although beyond the more upmarket hotels and restaurants in Vientiane and Luang Prabang, you should not expect to be able to get by on plastic in Laos.

Cost of travelling

Vietnam is better overall value than Cambodia and Laos as it has a better established tourism infrastructure and more competitive services. On a budget expect to pay around US$6-15 per night for accommodation and about US$6-12 for food. A good mid-range hotel will cost US$15-35. There are comfort and cost levels anywhere from here up to more than US$200 per night. For travelling, many use the **Open Tour Buses** as they are inexpensive and, by Vietnamese standards, 'safe'. Slightly more expensive are trains followed by planes.

The budget traveller will find that a little goes a long way in **Cambodia**. Numerous guesthouses offer accommodation at around US$3-7 a night. Food-wise, the seriously strapped can easily manage to survive healthily on US$4-5 per day, so an overall daily budget (not allowing for excursions) of US$7-9 should be enough or the really cost-conscious. For the less frugally minded, a daily allowance of US$30 should see you relatively well-housed and fed, while at the upper end of the scale, there are, in Phnom Penh and Siem Reap, plenty of restaurants and hotels for those looking for Cambodian levels of luxury. A mid-range hotel (attached bathroom, hot water and a/c) will normally cost around US$25 per night and a good meal at a restaurant around US$5-10.

An increase in domestic flights means that the bruised bottoms, dust-soaked clothes and stiff limbs that go hand-in-hand with some of the longer bus/boat rides can be avoided by those with thicker wallets in **Laos**. However, as roads gradually improve and journey times diminish, buses and minivans have emerged above both planes and boats as the preferred (not to mention most reasonably priced) transportation option. Long overnight bus journeys cost from around 200,000 kip. Budget accommodation costs US$3-10; a mid-range hotel costs US$20-30. Local food is very cheap and it is possible to eat well for under US$2 a meal. It's possible to splurge in upmarket restaurants in Luang Prabang and Vientiane.

Opening hours

Vietnam
Banks Mon-Fri 0800-1600. Many close 1100-1300 or 1130-1330.
Offices Mon-Fri 0730-1130, 1330-1630.
Restaurants, cafés and bars Daily from 0700 or 0800 although some open earlier. Bars are generally closed by midnight, but some stay open much later, particularly in HCMC.
Shops Daily 0800-2000. Some stay open longer, especially in tourist centres.

Cambodia
Banks Mon-Fri 0800-1600. Some close 1100-1300. Some major branches are open until 1100 on Sat.
Offices Mon-Fri 0730-1130, 1330-1630.
Restaurants, cafés and bars Daily from 0700-0800 although some open earlier. By law bars close by 2400.
Shops Daily from 0800-2000. Some, however, stay open for a further 1-2 hrs, especially in tourist centres. Most markets open daily between 0530/0600-1700.

Laos
Banks Mon-Fri 0830-1600 (some close at 1500).
Bars/restaurants Usually close around 2200-2300 depending on how strictly the curfew is being reinforced. In smaller towns, most restaurants and bars close by 2200.
Businesses Mon-Fri 0900-1700; those that deal with tourists open a bit later and also

over the weekend. Government offices close at 1600 and take a 1- to 2-hr lunch break.
Post offices In general, post offices open 0800-1200 and 1300-1600.
Shops Most keep regular business hours but those catering to tourists stay open longer into the evening.

Photography

Sensitivity pays when taking photographs. Be very wary in areas that have (or could have) military importance, such as airports, where photography is prohibited. Also exercise caution when photographing official functions and parades. Always ask permission before taking photographs in a monastery and before photographing groups of people or individuals.

Police and the law

Vietnam
If you are robbed in Vietnam, report the incident to the police (for your insurance claim). If you are arrested, ask for consular assistance and English-speaking staff.

Involvement in politics, possession of political material, business activities that have not been licensed by appropriate authorities, or non-sanctioned religious activities (including proselytizing) can result in detention. Sponsors of small, informal religious gatherings such as bible-study groups in hotel rooms, as well as distributors of religious materials, have been detained, fined and expelled (source: US State Department). The army are extremely sensitive about all their military buildings and become exceptionally irate if you take a photo. Indeed there are signs to this effect outside all military installations.

Cambodia
A vast array of offences are punishable in Cambodia, from minor traffic violations through to possession of drugs (see above). If you are arrested or are having

difficulty with the police contact your embassy immediately.

Corruption is a problem and contact with the police should be avoided, unless absolutely necessary. Most services, including the provision of police reports, will require the payment of bribes. Law enforcement is very haphazard, at times completely subjective and justice can be hard to find. Some smaller crimes receive large penalties while perpetrators of greater crimes often get off scot-free.

Laos

If you are robbed, your insurer will need you to obtain a police report. You may find the police will try to solicit a bribe for this service. Although not ideal, you will probably have to pay this fee to obtain your report. Laws aren't strictly enforced but when the authorities do prosecute people the penalties can be harsh, ranging from deportation through to prison sentences. If you are arrested, seek embassy and consular support as soon as possible. If you are arrested or encounter police, try to remain calm and friendly. Although drugs are available throughout the country, the police levy hefty fines and punishments if caught.

Post

Vietnam

Postal services are pretty good. Post offices open daily 0700-2100; smaller ones close for lunch. Outgoing packages are opened and checked by the censor.

Cambodia

International service is unpredictable but it is reasonably priced and fairly reliable (at least from Phnom Penh). Only send mail from the GPO in any given town rather than sub POs or mail boxes. **Fedex** and **DHL** also offer services.

Laos

The postal service is inexpensive and reliable but delays are common. As the National Tourism Authority assures: in Laos the stamps will stay on the envelope. Contents of outgoing parcels must be examined by an official before being sealed. Incoming mail should use the official title, Lao PDR. There is no mail to home addresses or guesthouses, so mail must be addressed to a PO Box. The post office in Vientiane has a Poste restante service. EMS (Express Mail Service) is available from main post offices in larger towns. In general, post offices open 0800-1200 and 1300-1600. In provincial areas, **Lao Telecom** is usually attached to the post office. **DHL, Fedex** and **TNT** have offices in Vientiane.

Safety

The US State Department's travel advisory: **Travel Warnings & Consular Information Sheets**, www.travel.state.gov; and the **UK Foreign and Commonwealth Office**'s travel warning section, www.fco.gov.uk, are useful for up-to-date information.

Vietnam

Do not take any valuables on to the streets of HCMC as bag and jewellery snatching is a problem. The situation in other cities is not so bad but take care in Nha Trang and Hanoi, as you would in any city. Always use major taxi firms and avoid those with blacked-out windows.

Lone women travellers generally have fewer problems than in many other Asian countries. The most common form of harassment usually consists of comic and harmless displays of macho behaviour.

Unexploded ordnance is still a threat in some areas. It is best not to stray too far from the beaten track especially in Central Vietnam.

In HCMC around Pham Ngu Lau Western men may be targeted by prostitutes on street corners, in tourist bars and those cruising on motorbikes.

Cambodia

Cambodia is not as dangerous as some would have us believe. The country has really moved forward in protecting tourists and violent crime towards visitors is comparatively low. As Phnom Penh has a limited taxi service, travel after dark poses a problem. Stick to moto drivers you know. Women are particularly targeted by bag snatchers. Khmer New Year is known locally as the 'robbery season'. Theft is endemic at this time of year so be on red alert. A common trick around New Year is for robbers to throw water and talcum powder in the eyes of their victim and rob them. Leave your valuables in the hotel safe or hidden in your room.

Outside Phnom Penh safety is not as much of a problem. Visitors should be very cautious when walking in the countryside, however, as landmines and other unexploded ordnance is a ubiquitous hazard. Stick to well-worn paths, especially around Siem Reap and when visiting remote temples. There is currently unrest on the border with Thailand around the Preah Vihear temple; check the situation before travelling.

Laos

Crime rates are very low but it is advisable to take the usual precautions. Most areas of the country are now safe – a very different state of affairs from just over a decade ago when foreign embassies advised tourists not to travel along certain roads and in certain areas (in particular Route 13 between Vientiane and Luang Prabang; and Route 7 between Phonsavanh and Route 13). Today these risks have effectively disappeared.

If riding on a motorbike or bicycle, don't carry your bag strap over your shoulder – if someone goes to snatch your bag you could get pulled off the bike and end up seriously hurt. In the Siphandon and Vang Vieng areas, theft seems to be more common. It's advisable to use a hotel security box if available.

Road accidents are on the increase. The hiring of motorbikes is becoming more

popular and consequently there are more tourist injuries. Wear a helmet.

Be careful around waterways, as drowning is one of the primary causes of tourist deaths. Be particularly careful during the rainy season (May-Sep) as rivers have a tendency to flood and can have extremely strong currents. Make sure if you are kayaking, tubing, canoeing, travelling by fast-boat, etc, that proper safety gear, such as life jackets, is provided. 'Fast-boat' river travel can be dangerous due to excessive speed and the risk of hitting something in the river and capsizing.

Xieng Khouang Province, the Bolaven Plateau, Xam Neua and areas along the Ho Chi Minh Trail are littered with bombies (small anti-personnel mines and bomblets from cluster bomb units). There are also numerous, large, unexploded bombs; in many villages they have been left lying around. Only walk on clearly marked or newly trodden paths. Consult the Mines Advisory Group (www.maginternational.org), which works in Laos.

Student travellers

There are discounts available on the train in **Vietnam**. Discount travel is provided to those under 22 and over 60. There are no specific student discounts in **Cambodia** or **Laos**. Anyone in full-time education is entitled to an **International Student Identity Card** (www.isic.org). These are issued by student travel offices and travel agencies and offer special rates on all forms of transport and other concessions and services. They sometimes permit free admission to museums and sights, at other times a discount on the admission.

Telephone

Vietnam → *Country code +84.*
The IDD code (for dialling out of Vietnam) is 00. Directory enquiries: 1080. Operator-assisted domestic long-distance calls: 103.

International directory enquiries: 143.
Yellow pages: 1081.

To make a domestic call dial 0 + area code + phone number. Note that all numbers in this guide include the area code. All post offices provide international telephone services. Pay-as-you-go SIM cards are available from a number of operators including **Mobiphone** and **Vinaphone**. These are cheap and so are calls and data.

Cambodia → *Country code +855.*
The IDD code (for dialling out of Cambodia) depends on which company you are using: 001 - Telecom Cambodia; 007 - Royal Telecom; 008 – VoIP.

Landline linkages are so poor in Cambodia that many people and businesses prefer to use mobile phones instead. If you have an unlocked phone and intend to be in the country for a while, it is relatively easy to buy a SIM card. This can save you money if you wish to use your phone regularly. International and domestic Cambodian call charges are relatively cheap. There is an excellent mobile network throughout Cambodia. Most mobile phone numbers begin with 01 or 09. The 3-digit prefix included in a 9-digit landline telephone number is the area (province) code. If dialling within a province, dial only the 6-digit number.

International calls can be made from most guesthouses, hotels and phone booths but don't anticipate being able to make them outside Phnom Penh, Siem Reap and Sihanoukville. Use public MPTC or Camintel card phone boxes dotted around Phnom Penh to make international calls (cards are usually sold at shops near the booth). International calls are expensive, starting at US$4 per min in Phnom Penh, and more in the provinces. Internet calls are without a doubt the cheapest way to call overseas.

Laos → *Country code +856.*
The IDD code (for dialling out of Laos) is 00. International operator: T170. Directory enquiries: T16 (national); T171 (international).

Public phones are available in Vientiane and other major cities. You can also go to **Lao Telecom** offices to call overseas. Phone cards are widely available in most convenience stores. Mobile telephone coverage is now good across the country. Pay-as-you-go SIM cards are available cheaply and 3G service is good.

Time

Vietnam, Cambodia and Laos are 7 hrs ahead of Greenwich Mean Time.

Tipping

Vietnamese do not normally tip if eating in small family restaurants but may tip extravagantly in expensive bars. Foreigners normally leave the small change. Big hotels and some restaurants add 5-10% service charge and the government tax of 10% to the bill. Taxis are rounded up to the nearest 5000d, hotel porters 20,000d. Tipping is rare but appreciated in Cambodia. Neither is it common practice in Laos, even in hotels. However, it is a kind gesture to tip guides and some more expensive restaurants. Salaries in restaurants and hotels are low and many staff hope to make up the difference in tips. As with everywhere else, good service should be rewarded. If someone offers you a lift, it is a courtesy to give them some money for fuel.

Tour operators

Numerous operators offer organized trips to this region, ranging from a whistle-stop tour of the highlights to specialist trips that focus on a specific destination or activity. The advantage of travelling with a reputable operator is that your transport, accommodation and activities are all arranged for you in advance, which is particularly valuable if you only have limited time. By travelling independently, however, you can be more flexible and spontaneous about where you go and what you do. You will be able to explore less-visited areas and you will save money, if you budget carefully. On arrival in Vietnam, many travellers hire operators to take them on day and week-long trips. These tours cater for all budgets and you will benefit from an English-speaking guide and safe vehicles. Some of the most popular trips include week-long tours around the northwest or into the Mekong Delta.

For regional tour operators, such as **Asian Trails** (www.asiantrails.travel), refer to the What to do listings throughout this guide.

In the UK

Adventure Company, 15 Turk St, Alton, Hampshire GU34 1AG, T0870-794 1009, www.adventurecompany.co.uk.
Audley Travel, New Mill, New Mill Lane, Witney, Oxfordshire OX29 9SX, T01993-838000, www.audleytravel.com.

Buffalo Tours UK, The Old Church, 89B Quicks Rd, Wimbledon, London SW19 1EX, T020-8545 2830, www.buffalotours.com.
Intrepid Travel, 1 Cross and Pillory Lane, Alton GU34 1HL, T01420 595020, www.intrepidtravel.com.
Magic of the Orient, 14 Frederick Pl, Clifton, Bristol BS8 1AS, T0117-311 6050, www.magicoftheorient.com. Tailor-made holidays to the Far East.
Regent Holidays, 15 John St, Bristol BS1 2HR, T0117-921 1711, www.regent-holidays.co.uk.
See Asia Differently, T020-8150 5150, www.seeasiadifferently.com. A UK/Asian-based tour company specializing in customized Southeast Asian tours.
Silk Steps, Deep Meadow, Edington, Bridgwater, Somerset TA7 9JH, T01278-722460, www.silksteps.co.uk.
Steppes Travel, 51 Castle St, Cirencester, Glos GL7 1QD, T01285-880980,

www.steppestravel.co.uk. Specialists in tailor-made holidays and small group tours.
Symbiosis Expedition Planning, 3B Wilmot Pl, London NW1 9JS, T0845-123 2844, www.symbiosis-travel.com.

Trans Indus, Northumberland House, 11 The Pavement, Popes Lane, London W5 4NG, T020-8566 2729, www.transindus.co.uk.
Travelmood, 214 Edgware Rd, London W2 1DH, T0870-001002, www.travelmood.com.
Visit Vietnam (Tennyson Travel), 30-32 Fulham High St, London SW6 3LQ, T020-7736 4347, www.visitvietnam.co.uk. Also deals with Cambodia, www.visitasia.co.uk.

In North America
Adventure Center, 1311 63rd St, Suite 200, Emeryville, CA, T+1-800 228 8747, www.adventurecenter.com.
Global Spectrum, 3907 Laro Court, Fairfax, VA 22031, T+1-800 419 4446, www.globalspectrumtravel.com.
Hidden Treasure Tours, 509 Lincoln Boulevard, Long Beach, NY 11561, T877-761 7276 (USA toll free), www.hiddentreasuretours.com.
Journeys, 107 April Drive, Suite 3, Ann Arbor, MI 48103-1903, T734-665 4407, www.journeys.travel/.
Myths & Mountains, 976 Tree Court, Incline Village, Nevada 89451, T+1-800 670-MYTH, www.mythsandmountains.com.
Nine Dragons Travel & Tours, PO Box 24105, Indianapolis, IN 46224, T1-317-329 0350, T1-800 909 9050 (USA toll free), www.nine-dragons.com.

In Australia and New Zealand
Buffalo Tours, L9/69 Reservoir St, Surry Hills, Sydney, Australia 2010, T61-2-8218 2198, www.buffalotours.com.
Intrepid Travel, 360 Bourke St, Melbourne, Victoria 3000, T+61-03-8602 0500, www.intrepidtravel.com.au.
Travel Indochina, Level 10, HCF House, 403 George St, Sydney, NSW 2000, T1300-138755 (toll free), www.travelindochina.com.au.

In Southeast Asia
Asian Trails, 9th floor, SG Tower, 161/1 Soi Mahadlek Luang 3, Lumpini, Pathumwan, Bangkok 10330, T66-2-626 2000, www.asiantrails.travel. Southeast Asia Specialist. Also has offices in Ho Chi Minh City, Phnom Penh and Vientiane.
Asia Pacific Travel, 127 Ban Co St, District Q3, T+84 (0)91322 4473, www.asiapacifictravel.vn. Arranges tours throughout Vietnam, Cambodia and Laos.
Buffalo Tours, L10, Vietbank Building, 70-72 Ba Trieu, Hoan Kiem District, Hanoi, T+84 4 3828 0702; or No 102/5 Kaysone Phomvihane Rd, Luang Prabang, Laos, T071-254395; www.buffalotours.com.
Discovery Indochina, 63A Cua Bac St, Hanoi, Vietnam, T+84 (0)43 716 4132, www.discoveryindochina.com.Private and customized tours covering Cambodia, Vietnam and Laos.
Exotissimo, 80-82 Phan Xich Long St, Phu Nhuan District, Ho Chi Minh City, T+84 8-3995 9898; 4666 - 06/044 Pangkham St, Vientiane, Laos, T021-241861; 44/3 Ban Vat Nong, Khemkong Rd, Luang Prabang, Laos, T071-252879; www.exotissimo.com.
Indochina Travelland, 10 Hang Mam, T+84 984 999 386, www.indochinatravelland.com.
Luxury Travel, 5 Nguyen Truong To St, Ba Dinh District, Hanoi, T+84 (0)4 3927 4120, www.luxurytravelvietnam.com. Luxury tours to Vietnam, Cambodia and Laos, as well as Myanmar and Thailand. Tailor-made itineraries, including golf, family holidays, beach holidays and honeymoons.

Tourist information

Contact details for tourist offices and other information resources are given in the relevant 'Arriving in' sections throughout the book.

Vietnam
Contact details for tourist offices and other resources are given in the listings sections throughout the text.

The national tourist office is **Vietnam National Administration of Tourism** (www.vietnamtourism.com), whose role is to promote Vietnam as a tourist destination rather than to provide tourist information. Visitors to its offices can get some information and maps but they are more likely to be offered tours. Good tourist information is available from tour operators in the main tourist centres.

Cambodia

Government tourism services are minimal at best. The **Ministry of Tourism**, 3 Monivong Blvd, T023-426876, is not able to provide any useful information or services. The tourism office in Siem Reap is marginally better but will only provide services, such as guides, maps, etc, for a nominal fee. You are better off going through a private operator for information and price.

Laos

Contact details for tourist offices and other information resources are given at the start of listings in the relevant town. Many provincial tourist offices now have an Eco Guide Unit attached or operating from a separate office. The best in the country is the one in Savannakhet.

The **Laos National Tourism Authority**, Lane Xang, Vientiane, T021-212248, www.tourismlaos.org, provides a range of maps and brochures.

Some provincial tourist offices are excellent and staffed with helpful, knowledgeable and willing people. There are particularly good tourism offices in Thakhek, Vieng Xai, Xam Neua, Udomxai and Phongsali. The tourism authority has teamed up with local tour operators to provide a number of ecotourism opportunities, such as trekking and village homestays.

Useful websites

www.asean-tourism.com
www.cambodia.org
www.ecotourismlaos.com
www.embassyofcambodia.org
www.gocambodia.com
www.khmer440.com
www.stdplaos.com
www.mekongtourism.org
www.tourismcambodia.com
www.travelfish.org
www.travel.state.gov
www.visit-mekong.com

Visas and immigration

30-day tourist visas are granted on arrival in Bangkok. Visitors from UK, USA, Canada, Australia, New Zealand and most European countries are able to enter Malaysia and Singapore without a visa for a short period of time.

Vietnam

Visitors have 2 options for visas. The first is to apply for a visa at a Vietnamese embassy in your home country. The price for this changes regularly so it is best to contact the embassy direct. You must send the application form, fee and photos together with your passport. The second option avoids this hassle and involves applying for an invitation letter, from a company such as **Indochina Travelland** (see Tour operators, above), and then paying for your visa on arrival at the airport. Those travelling in the region can obtain visas at Vietnamese consulates.

Visa extensions can be arranged within Vietnam from immigration offices in Hanoi: 40A Hang Bai St, T4-3826 6200; and Ho Chi Minh City: 254 Nguyen Trai St, T08-3832 2300. These offices can change the visa to specify overland exit via Moc Bai if travelling to Cambodia, or for overland travel to Laos or China.

Cambodia
E-visas

It is now possible to get an e-visa for entry to Cambodia which can be bought, online, before arrival. At present, it is only usable at certain entry and exit points but is likely to be rolled out everywhere in the future. The best thing about this visa is being able to avoid any visa scams etc when arriving at Cambodia's notorious land crossings – at least at those where it can be used.

To apply for an e-visa visit www.evisa.gov.kh. The fee is US$30 plus a US$7 handling fee; it takes 3 working days to process and is valid for 3 months but only for 30 days in Cambodia. There is a list on the website of the entry and exit points where the visa is valid. It can also be extended for 30 days at National Police Immigration Department, Ministry of Interior, 332 Russian Blvd, opposite **Phnom Penh International Airport**, Phnom Penh, Cambodia. T012-581558, www.immigration.gov.khwww.immigration.gov.kh.

Visas on arrival

Visas for a 30-day stay are available on arrival at Phnom Penh and Siem Reap airport. Tourist visas cost US$30 and your passport must be valid for at least 6 months from the date of entry. You will need a passport photo.

Officially, visas are not available on the Lao border. Many people have reported successfully obtaining visas here but don't rely on it. Travellers using the Lao border should try to arrange visa paperwork in advance in either Phnom Penh, Bangkok or Vientiane.

The **Cambodian Embassy in Bangkok**, 185 Rajdamri Rd, T+66-254 6630, issues visas in 1 day if you apply in the morning, as does the **Consulate General in HCMC**, Vietnam, 41 Phung Khac Khoan, T+84-8829 2751, and in **Hanoi** at 71 Tran Hung Dao St, T+84-4942 4788. In both Vietnam and Thailand, travel agencies are normally willing to obtain visas for a small fee. Cambodia has a few missions overseas from which visas can be obtained.

Note Travellers leaving by land must ensure that their Vietnam visa specifies Moc Bai or Chau Doc as points of entry otherwise they could be turned back. You can apply for a Cambodian visa in HCMC and collect in Hanoi and vice versa.

Visa extensions

Extensions can be obtained at the Department for Foreigners on the road to the airport, T023-581558 (passport photo required). Most travel agents arrange visa extensions for around US$40 for 30 days. Those overstaying their visas are fined US$5 per day; officials at land crossings often try to squeeze out more.

Laos

A 30-day **tourist visa** can be obtained at most (but not all) borders. See Official border crossings, page 544. Visa prices are based on reciprocity with countries. 'Overtime fees' are often charged if you enter after 1600 or on a weekend. To get a visa you need a passport photograph and the name of a hotel you plan on staying in.

The Lao government also issues **business visas** that are available for 30 days with the possibility of extending. This is a more complicated process and usually requires a note from an employer or hefty fees from a visa broker. These visas are best organized from your home country and can take a long time to process.

Tourist visa extensions can be obtained from the **Lao Immigration Office** in the Ministry of the Interior opposite the Morning Market in Vientiane, on Phai Nam Rd, T021-212529. Travel agencies in Vientiane and other major centres can also handle this service for you for a fee.

Index → Entries in bold refer to maps

Advertisers' index

Acknowledgements

For help on the road in Vietnam, my thanks go to: Ashley Carruthers, Allan Goodman, Ben Mitchell, Caroline Mills, Cyril Boucher, Deb and Howard Limbert, Etienne Bossot, Kon Sa Nay Luet, Khiem Vu, Linh Phan, Luke H Ford, Nguyen Tuan Dung, Nguyen Thanh Truc, Binh, Bamboo and all the other guides at Oxalis, Ryan Deboodt, Sophie Hughes, Soeren Pinstrup, Tran Nhat Quang and Van Phan Trang.

In Laos I would like to thank: Mr Somphone Khantivong for the elementary Lao lessons and unrivalled knowledge of the country's roads; Khamkeo, Parn, Vieng Thong and Paul Eshoo of the Nam Nern Night Safari in the Nam Et-Phou Louey NPA; in Vieng Xai, Mr Neng; in Luang Prabang, Jenn of the Friends Visitor Centre, the ever-helpful Elizabeth Vongsaravanh of Icon Klub, Rachna Sachasinh, and Brandon Sousa; at Buffalo Tours Mr Thongxay (Kay) and Mr Touy; in Nong Khiaw, Mr Boun of NK Adventure and Thom of Green Discovery; in Luang Prabang, Kaz Freiberg; in Tad Lo Mr Poh of Palamei Guesthouse, Louis and Mr Kouka.

I am also indebted to Claire Boobbyer, previous author of this book. Finally, my thanks go to my wife, Beck, for once again putting up with my nomadic ways.

Notes

Credits

Footprint credits
Editor: Nicola Gibbs
Production and layout: Emma Bryers
Maps: Kevin Feeney
Colour section: Angus Dawson

Publisher: Patrick Dawson
Managing Editor: Felicity Laughton
Administration: Elizabeth Taylor
Advertising sales and marketing:
John Sadler, Kirsty Holmes

Photography credits
Front cover: Chingyunsong/
Dreamstime.com
Back cover: Top: Em7/Shutterstock.com.
Bottom: danhvc/shutterstock.com

Colour section
Inside front cover: shutterstock: trong do,
Bule Sky Studio. **Page 1**: shutterstock: MJ
Prototype. **Page 2**: shutterstock: Carey Nguyen.
Page 4: shutterstock: ThangCao. **Page 5**:
shutterstock: Piter HaSon, Pablo Rogat, Truong
Cong Hiep, Jimmy Tran. **Page 6**: David W Lloyd/
David W Lloyd; shutterstock: xuanhuongho,
Bule Sky Studio, KieuKieu, chkin Alexey/
Shutterstock.com. **Page 7**: shutterstock:
PlusONE, karinkamon. **Page 10**: shutterstock:
Denis Rozan. **Page 11**: shutterstock: Alexander
Mazurkevich, VanderWolf Images. **Page 12**:
superstock: Cubo Images/Cubo Images, age
fotostock/age fotostock; shutterstock: Galyna
Andrushko. **Page 13**: shutterstock: Phong.Tran,
Hoang Cong Thanh, Ozerov Alexander. **Page
14**: shutterstock: TheLightPainter. **Page 15**:
shutterstock: Tonkin image; superstock: Stuart
Pearce/age fotostock. **Page 16**: shutterstock:
R.M. Nunes.

Black and white spreads
Vietnam: shutterstock: Piter HaSon.
Cambodia: shutterstock: GuoZhongHua.
Laos: shutterstock: iceink.

Printed in Spain by GraphyCems

Publishing information
Footprint Vietnam, Cambodia & Laos
5th edition
© Footprint Handbooks Ltd
May 2015

ISBN: 978 1 910120 33 0
CIP DATA: A catalogue record for this book
is available from the British Library

® Footprint Handbooks and the Footprint
mark are a registered trademark of Footprint
Handbooks Ltd

Published by Footprint
6 Riverside Court
Lower Bristol Road
Bath BA2 3DZ, UK
T +44 (0)1225 469141
F +44 (0)1225 469461
footprinttravelguides.com

Distributed in the USA by National Book
Network, Inc.

Every effort has been made to ensure that
the facts in this guidebook are accurate.
However, travellers should still obtain advice
from consulates, airlines, etc about travel
and visa requirements before travelling. The
authors and publishers cannot
accept responsibility for any loss, injury
or inconvenience however caused.

Map 2

CHINA

Ha Giang

Lung Khau Nin
Can Cau
Muong Khuong
Coc Ly
Bac Ha
Lao Cai
Viet Quang
Ta Phin
Cam Duong
Sapa
Pho Lu
Sin Chai
Cat Cat
Lau Chai
Vinh Tuy
Ta Van
LAU CHAI
Thac Ba Lake
Hoang Lien Son Mountain
Con Voi Mountain Range
Red
YEN BAI
Yen Binh
Yen Bai

Pa So
Muong Hum
Sin Ho
Lai Chau
Tam Duong
Fan Si Pan (3143m)

Phu Si Lung (3076m)
Muong Te

LAI CHAU

Muong Lay

Da

Phu Luong (2985m)

Tuan Giao
Ban Co
Thuan Chau
Son La
Na San

Dien Bien Phu
Co Pia (1817m)

TayTrang
SON LA
Song Da Lake

Sop Hun
Muong Mai
Pak Ban
Muang Khua
Xieng Kho
Moc Chau
Pak Nam Noi
Pak Luong
Muang Et
Chieng Yen
Sop Kine
Pha Nang
Muang Khao
Sop Y
Sop Bau
Lac
Muang La
Muang Ngoi Neua
Nong Khiaw & Ban Saphoun
Muang Son
Het
Namo Tai
Na Houang
Udomxai
Pak Mong
Nam Bak
Se
Muang Muoi
Xam Neua
Vieng Xai
Poun Song
Hua Hin
Nam Nga
Houei Van
Muang Ham
Nam Xoi
Pathet Lao Caves
Muang Poun
MXAI
Muang Beng
Coc Nang
Sop Tiek
LUANG PRABANG
HUA PHAN
Hua Muong
Hoeui Sam
Muang Inga
Pak Ou Caves
Sao Hintang
Muang Kan
Lat Hane
Phou Lao
Nam Nouan
Xam Tai
Hat Teu
Luang Prabang
Khan
Muang Na
Tao
Xeung Bo
Sam Thong
Neun
Kwang Si Falls
Tran Ninh Highlands
Muang Kham
Mat
Kiou Kacham
Muang Sui
Xang
Khien
Nam Khan
ha Deua
Muang Nan
Muang Phou Khoun
Sen Kom
Phonsavanh
NGHE AN
Khoum
Sayaboury
Pha Sung
Plain of Jars
Muang Khoune
Annamite Range
Truong Son Mountain Range
Kasi
Phon
Sen Luang
XIENG KHOUANG
Thieng
Pha Tang
Na Vang
Nam Ngum
Phu Bia (2819m)
Ca
VIENTIANE
Tam
Vang Vieng
Tam Kalong
Muang Cha
Ta Viang
Khone Xa Na
Say He
Muang Mok
Ban Houay (North Port)
Muang Sam
XAYSOMBOUN
Nam Cap
Ban Thala
North Town
Na Pho
Hat Kham
BOLIKHAMXAI
Phonhong
South Port
Thulakhom
Muang Hom
Ban Hat
Khai
Tad Leuk
Vangxang
Ban Keun
Thabok
Kouei
Paksan
Phou Khao
Ban Na

Lan Toui
Khang
Ngot Ou
Ou
Muang Va
Ngay Neua
Boua Neua
Hat Xa
Nam Pung
Phongsali
PHONGSALI
Boun Tai
ui

① ② ③

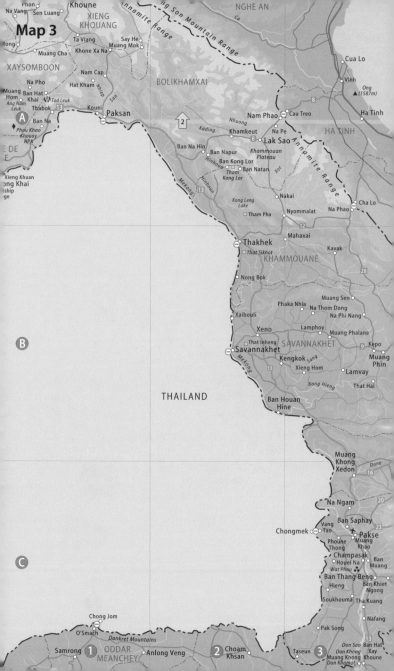

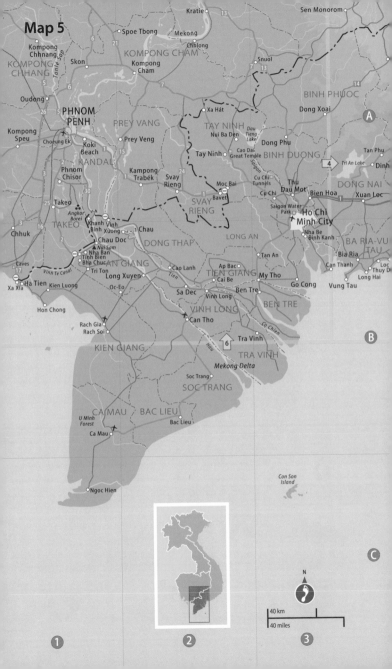

Map 5

Kratie

Sen Monorom

Spoe Tbong

Mekong

Chlong

KOMPONG
CHHNANG

Kompong
Chhnang

Skon

KOMPONG CHAM

Snuol

BINH PHUOC

Kompong
Cham

Oudong

Xa Hát

Dong Xoai

Tonle Sap

PHNOM
PENH

PREY VANG

TAY NINH

Kompong
Speu

Choeung Ek

Koki
Beach

Prey Veng

Nui Ba Den

Dau
Tieng
Lake

Tan Phu

BINH DUONG

KANDAL

Phnom
Chisor

Kampong
Trabék

Svay
Rieng

Tay Ninh

Cao Dai
Great Temple

Dong Phu

Tri An Lake

DONG NAI

Dinh

Takeo

24

Moc Bai

Cu Chi
Tunnels

Thu
Dau Mot

Bien Hoa

Xuan Loc

Xa Hát

Bavet

SVAY
RIENG

Cu Chi

Saigon Water
Park

Ho Chi
Minh City

Chhuk

Angkor
Borei

TAKEO

Khanh
Vinh

Binh
Xuong

Chau

DONG THAP

LONG AN

Nha Be
Dinh Kanh

BA RIA-VU
TAU

Caves

Chau Doc

Nui Sam
Nha Ban
Tinh Bien
Bha Chuc

Cao Lanh

Ap Bac

Tan An

Bia Ria

Can Thanh

Loc
Thuy D

Xa Xia

Ha Tien

Kien Luong

Tri Ton

Long Xuyen

AN GIANG

Tien

Oc-Eo

Cai Be

TIEN GIANG

My Tho

Go Cong

Long Hai

Vung Tau

Hon Chong

Sa Dec

Ben Tre

Rach Gia
Rach Soi

Can Tho

VINH LONG

Vinh Long

BEN TRE

KIEN GIANG

Hau

6

Tra Vinh

Co Chien

TRA VINH

Mekong Delta

Con Son
Island

SOC TRANG

Soc Trang

CA MAU

BAC LIEU

U Minh
Forest

Bac Lieu

Ca Mau

Ngoc Hien

N

40 km

40 miles

1   **2**   **3**

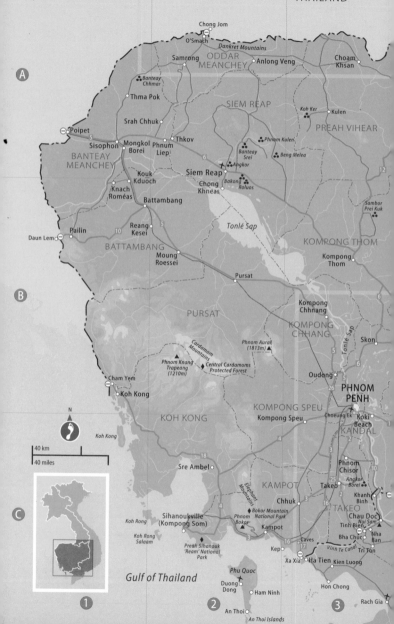

David W Lloyd

David W Lloyd is a photographer and writer. He has been based in Hanoi since 2011. His photography and feature writing has appeared in a wide variety of publications including the *New York Times*, *Wanderlust* and *Travel + Leisure*. He is also the author and photographer for *Footprint Laos* and co-author of *Footprint Vietnam, Cambodia & Laos*. Alongside this, David undertakes commercial and wedding photography assignments and offers bespoke photography tours in Vietnam. To find out more, visit www.davidwlloydphotography.com.

Andrew Spooner

Andrew Spooner has been travelling and writing about Southeast Asia's culture and politics for over 20 years. After a reasonably successful career working as freelance feature writer for *The Guardian* and *Independent on Sunday*, amongst many others, Andrew now lives in Southwest London with his partner and cat and works as a freelance consultant for private clients on a range of issues. Follow him on twitter – @andrewspoooner. Andrew is also the author of Footprint's *Thailand*, and *Thailand's islands & beaches*.

Price codes

Where to stay

$$$$ over US$100

$$$ US$46-100

$$ US$20-45

$ under US$20

Price codes refer to the cost of two people sharing a double room in the high season

Restaurants

$$$ over US$12

$$ US$6-12

$ under US$6

Price codes refer to the cost of a two-course meal for one person excluding drinks or service charge.